Deeply Private, Incredibly Public

Readings on the Sociology of Human Reproduction

Revised First Edition

Edited by Catherine Marrone

Bassim Hamadeh, CEO and Publisher
Michael Simpson, Vice President of Acquisitions and Sales
Jamie Giganti, Senior Managing Editor
Jess Busch, Senior Graphic Designer
John Remington, Senior Field Acquisitions Editor
Natalie Lakosil, Licensing Manager
Kate McKellar, Interior Designer

Copyright © 2016 by Cognella, Inc. All rights reserved. No part of this publication may be reprinted, reproduced, transmitted, or utilized in any form or by any electronic, mechanical, or other means, now known or hereafter invented, including photocopying, microfilming, and recording, or in any information retrieval system without the written permission of Cognella, Inc.

First published in the United States of America in 2016 by Cognella, Inc.

Trademark Notice: Product or corporate names may be trademarks or registered trademarks, and are used only for identification and explanation without intent to infringe.

Printed in the United States of America

ISBN: 978-1-5165-0048-2 (pbk) / 978-1-5165-0049-9 (br)

www.cognella.com   800-200-3908

Contents

Preface — ix
    Catherine Marrone

1 The Start of Reproduction

Introduction — 3
    Catherine Marrone

A Strange Stirring — 5
    Stephanie Coontz

The Family and Household Transition — 15
    John R. Weeks

The Medicalization of Birth — 38
    Nancy Schrom Dye

The Birth of a Doula: From Curiosity to Advocacy — 51
    Misty Curreli

Maternity Care in Crisis: Where are the Doctors? — 53
    Marsden Wagner

Male and Female Farming Systems   60
   Ester Boserup

Family Planning and Abortion: 72
Cultural Norms Versus Actual Practices in Nigeria
   Funmi Togonu-Bickersteth

Challenges and Opportunities: 77
The Population of the Middle East and North Africa
   Farzaneh Roudi-Fahimi and Mary Mederios Kent

Revolution, War, and Modernization: 100
Population Policy and Fertility Change in Iran
   Mohammad Jalai Abassi, et al

2   Autonomy, Patriarchy, and Reproductive Control

Introduction   115
   Cathy Marrone

Patriarchal Structure and Demographic Change   117
   Mead T. Cain

Social Structural Determinants of Fertility   129
   Asoka Bandarage

AIDS, Pregnancy, and Poverty Trap Ever More African Girls   150
   Sharon LaFraniere

No More Little Girls   153
   Elisabeth Bumiller

Excerpts from **Burned Alive**: *A Victim of the Law of Men*   165
   Souad and Marie-Therese Cuny

Motherhood and Morality in America   173
   Kristin Luker

Abortion in American Medicine: 186
A Recent History
    Lori R. Freedman

Pro-Life Nation 195
    Jack Hitt

Excerpts from **Men and Abortion**: 205
Losses, Lessons and Love
    Arthur B. Shostak, Gary McLouth, and Lynn Seng

Enlisting Men in Support of Reproductive Freedom 229
    Alexander Sanger

Excerpts from **This Common Secret**: 237
My Journey as an Abortion Doctor
    Alan Kesselheim and Susan Wicklund

The Male Partner Involved in Legal Abortion 254
    A. Kero, A. Lalos, U. Högberg, and L. Jacobsson

The Fertility Doctor Meets the Pill 264
    Margaret Marsh and Wanda Ronner

Go Forth and Multiply: *Faith and Family Planning* 271
    George D. Moffett

High Dowry Demands Causing Issues in Society, 287
Islamic Scholar Says
    Ayesha Al Khoori

3 What Are We Really Creating?

Introduction
    Cathy Marrone 291

The Right to Control Fertility: *Sterilization and Contraception* 293
    Robert Blank and Janna C. Merrick

Women and the Dilemmas of Modern Motherhood   304
    Liza Mundy

Who Doesn't Have Children?   324
    Susan L. Lang

Dropping Sperm Counts   330
    Cynthia Daniels

In re: Baby M   349
    Case 537 A.2d 1227, New Jersey Supreme Court

The Curious Lives of Surrogates   354
    Lorraine Ali and Raina Kelley

Breaking the Silence   360
    Ann Fessler

The Give and Take of Adoption   369
    Barbara Katz Rothman

Excerpt from **Adoption Nation**   376
    Adam Pertman

The Post-Nazi Era   383
    Masha Gessen

All You Need Is Life   389
    Dominic Lawson

Inconceivable   393
    Carolyn and Sean Savage

Genomics and Its Impact on Science and Society   401
    U.S. Department of Energy Office of Science

Excerpts from **Motherhood, Rescheduled**: 408
*The New Frontier of Egg Freezing and the
Women Who Tried It*
    Sarah Elizabeth Richards

Excerpts from **Medical Apartheid**: 411
*The Black Stork: The Eugenic Control of
African American Reproduction*
    Harriet Washington

4 Appendices

Appendix A: Points for Further Discussion   417

Appendix B: Film Resources   419

Preface

By Cathy Marrone

When I was first asked to teach this course, some twelve years ago, not only had I not taken a class of its like, but my focus at the time was on constructing a course on the Sociology of Medicine. I had been trained as a Medical Sociologist and had just completed a post-doctoral fellowship at a school of Epidemiology and Public Health. However, a departing faculty member at Stony Brook, one whom I had great admiration for, intended to transfer her "Sociology of Human Reproduction" course to me. We met in her office as she was packing boxes and discussed her experience with the content for the course she had designed—and enjoyed teaching—and how she had created a unique set of bound readings tailor-made for her vision of the course and its place in the department [and curriculum] of Sociology. I thought her work masterful, and wound up using most of her readings in those early semesters. Today, a small few still remain part of my reading list.

Over time and with the modifications I had made, I came to regard this course, and in fact its material, as in some ways, essential curriculum for the Undergraduate Student, particularly those majoring in Sociology and Women's Studies. The countless students in my classes from the Natural Sciences and the Arts and beyond have consistently reminded me of the importance of this course to a broad and well-rounded education. And it has been the young and older men in my classes, more in number in my classrooms than ever before, who have become important barometers to me, convincing me of the utter relevance of Reproduction—its "history," its political bearings—to all things social and, more critically, to both genders.

I have come to believe there are countless ways to design a course on Reproduction and am aware that many other wonderful faculty members have done so on a good number of campuses and within different curricula. I have allowed culture, time constraints and the interests of my students to help shape the way I both arrange my course and design my readings schedule. My students want to know more about the incredibly fast dress—and stage—changes taking place within Reproductive Medicine and Technology. They want to know more about the meaning of reproductive power for women and men around the world. And quite endearing really, they want to know what reproduction and "a family" might mean for them someday, even if they don't just now quite know how to imagine it. This Reader, with all of its *material* insights, I hope offers us all a bit, or more, of what we want. May this course on Reproduction inspire in you, as it does for me, the sense of wonder surrounding this area of study that is at once both exceptionally private and incredibly public.

Section 1

The Start of Reproduction

Introduction

The Start of Reproduction

By Cathy Marrone

The "imperatives" for reproduction are myriad and complex. Students well understand those evolutionary principles they bring with them to class at the start of the term. Later, they seem to be drawn to the anthropological and sociological explanations for how reproduction both maintains and shapes the culture. So it seems rather essential to me to start our class on human reproduction with discussions on how we wind up mating as we do and how the selection (or lack of) matters to our culture. Perhaps more to the point of the course, we will explore just how and why it is we come to rear and "value" our children as we do. Interestingly enough, from there we will proceed backwards to investigate how the experience of birth itself has changed over time, particularly, in the United States. It is in our country where we see the height of the medicalization movement, present and well-entrenched in norms of reproduction.

From here, we begin to examine in what ways the economic and social worth and therefore, the value, of women impact global and local demographics, and how this sets the stage for control over reproduction, an act that is both political and powerful. It is indeed in this name of "control" that this course and its intentions are best expressed and clearly revealed. How hard we have tried, throughout the world, to manage—often quite forcefully—how reproduction, especially socially, ought to function. And often what follows is nothing less than the utter loss of control, and the serious repercussions for whole groups that may have never understood they ever had control. The "control" over human reproduction then, in more than just political or economic terms, severely restricts the ability of reproduction to be what it must be first—a human experience.

Before this first section comes to a close to prepare the students for the next one, we will read about the small but growing voices among women and men, particularly in the US, to make childbirth something different, "less medical" if you will and less controlled. Many of us are beginning to seek such change because of the realization that the experience of birth to a woman (and often to her partner as well) is identity-shaping and life-changing, and more importantly, is an experience to be shared. Therein lies perhaps the truest of imperatives for human reproduction: it is social, so very social.

A Strange Stirring

The Contradictions of Womanhood in the 1950s

By Stephanie Coontz

Friedan painted the 1950s as a time of political conformity, cultural conservatism, social repressiveness, and female passivity. Although this was true for many Americans, revolutionary changes were occurring below the surface in women's behaviors and options. One puzzling question is why these changes, which were well under way by the mid-1950s, did not undercut the media definition of women as home-makers long before the 1963 publication of The Feminine Mystique, and why so many of Friedan's readers found her defense of women's right and need to work a revelation.

Although women's employment had fallen dramatically in the immediate aftermath of World War II, by 1947 it was growing again. And by 1955 a higher percentage or women worked for wages than ever had during the war. In fact, their employment rate grew four times faster than men's during the 1950s. The employment of wives tripled and the employment of mothers increased fourfold.

The social acceptability of women working also increased during the 1950s. In the era's romantic comedies and popular love stories, it was often the girl who worked at a fun job, not the "girl next door," who got her man. Once she got him, she usually quit work. But polls showed enthusiastic approval of an engaged woman taking a job so the couple could marry sooner.

There was even growing acceptance of wives earning extra money for the family, as long as the husband did not object and the wife did not go back to work before her children were in school. Many opinion-shapers even encouraged women to take jobs once their children were grown, arguing that with the age of marriage and childbirth continuing to fall, most women were still healthy and active in their empty-nest years and should do something useful rather than fritter away their time in bridge parties and other idle pursuits.

In the 1930s, laws and policies had prohibited employers from hiring married women if their husbands were employed by the same company or government agency. By 1941, almost 90 percent of the nation's local school districts refused to hire married women, and 70 percent required female teachers to quit work when they married. Married women were welcomed into the workforce during the war, but as soon as the war ended they were urged to go home and tend to their husbands' needs. The government even reformed the tax law to give a special bonus to male-breadwinner families. Framers of the new provisions explicitly argued that this would encourage women to turn "to the pursuit of homemaking."

But as the demand for service and retail workers soared in the postwar boom, politicians and business leaders began to see women as an untapped resource for filling labor shortages and making America more competitive with the rival Soviet Union. In the 1950s, the National Manpower Council exhorted employers to hire women

Stephanie Coontz, "The Contradictions of Womanhood in the 1950s," *A Strange Stirring: The Feminine Mystique and American Women at the Dawn of the 1960s*. Copyright © 2011 by Stephanie Coontz. Reprinted with permission by Basic Books, a Member of The Perseus Books Group.

and urged women to seek paying jobs, although it tended to favor policies that encouraged wives to withdraw from work after childbearing and reenter when the children were older.

In 1956, President Dwight Eisenhower asked Congress to pass a bill requiring equal pay for equal work, something women's lobbyists had long urged. The bill, which made no provision for equal access to jobs, didn't pass. But Eisenhower's approach represented a change from the attitude of President Truman, who in 1948 had labeled any talk of women's rights in the public arena as "a lot of hooey."

Women also made substantial gains in education during the 1950s. More girls completed high school in that decade than in any previous era, and a higher percentage of them went on to college. One study of young white women found that they were twice as likely to go to college as their mothers had been.

And yet even as ever more women joined the labor force, there was a concerted effort to define the limits of what was acceptable. Marynia Farnham and Ferdinand Lundberg, authors of the virulently antifeminist 1947 work Modern Woman: The Lost Sex, had conceded that there was some work women could do without violating their natures. But they insisted that pursuing a "career," which they defined as work plus prestige, was antifeminine to its core and an assault on men's self-respect. This theme, stripped of its antifeminist vitriol and sugarcoated as concern for women's true happiness, became increasingly prominent in the 1950s.

Movies, Broadway plays, and popular literature depicted women who had prestigious or high-paying careers as ready to quit them the instant they landed a man. In All About Eve (1950), Bette Davis plays a successful, award-winning Broadway actress. But once she marries the man who has long loved her, she gives up an acting part she always coveted because "I've finally got a life to live" and something "to do with my nights." In The Tender Trap (1955), Debbie Reynolds's character gets picked for her first part on Broadway. But when Frank Sinatra asks her if she is excited, she responds halfheartedly that it's "all right." "A career is just fine," she explains, "but it's no substitute for marriage."

It was acceptable for a woman to keep her job after marriage if her husband didn't object and she didn't like her work too much. It was not acceptable for a woman to want a job that would be satisfying enough to compete with her identity as wife or impinge on her husband's sense that he was the primary breadwinner.

This point was made over and over in advice columns. In the March 1954 issue of Coronet, one expert held up the example of "Jacqueline M." as a model for working women. Jacqueline had been earning more money than her husband when she married him, but she promptly "gave up her job, and took one that paid less, because she knew how important it was for her husband to feel he was unquestionably supporting her." In Lena Levine's 1957 advice book, The Modern Book of Marriage, Levine told women that they could work for pay and still have a happy marriage only "if they remember one important thing": A woman must "let her husband know that her job is secondary, that her first interest is always the home."

Popular culture encouraged wives and mothers who worked for pay in the 1950s to lead what film critic Brandon French has called a "double life" rather than a "full" one. They were urged to completely "dissociate their identities from their jobs ... defining themselves entirely through their roles as wives, mothers, and homemakers, regardless of what else they did." To the extent women were willing to do this, society was happy to have them fill the lower rungs of the occupational ladder, freeing up men for more important and remunerative jobs. The October 16, 1956, issue of Look magazine assured its readers that working women "gracefully conceded" the upper levels of the work world to men. A March 17, 1962, editorial in the Saturday Evening Post opined that society could welcome women into the workforce now that "they have finally outgrown their childlike need to compete with men."

Even as more opportunities opened for men to move into middle-class or upper-middle-class professions and unionized blue-collar workers saw dramatic increases in their earnings power, women's employment gains were mostly in the lower-echelon, nonunionized segments of the workforce. Between 1947 and 1966, the inflation-adjusted hourly wages of men increased by 50 percent, with men in their twenties making the greatest gains of all. Reflecting these income gains, home ownership rates of men in their thirties more than doubled between 1940 and 1960.

But the wages of young women remained relatively low and flat. Accordingly, historians Jordan Stanger-Ross, Christina Collins, and Mark Stern note, women's "best opportunity to share in the wealth of their young male counterparts was to marry."

From 1951 to 1955, female full-time workers earned 63.9 percent of what male full-time workers earned. By 1963, women's pay had fallen to less than 59 percent of men's. Meanwhile, the proportion of women in high-prestige jobs declined: Fewer than 6 percent of working women held executive jobs in the 1950s.

The experience of Sandra Day O'Connor illustrates the obstacles faced by women who aspired to a challenging career. In 1981, a decade after the women's movement had begun to open up unprecedented opportunities to talented women, O'Connor became the first woman to sit on the U.S. Supreme Court. But when she entered the job market in 1952, having graduated second in her class at Stanford Law School and served on the prestigious Stanford Law Review, she got only one job offer from all the major California firms to which she submitted a resume. This firm explained that it did not employ women as attorneys but would be happy to hire her as a legal secretary.

For the typical single woman, such discriminatory attitudes and narrow opportunities made marriage look especially attractive. Polls conducted by the Survey Research Center at The University of Michigan found that in 1957, single women were much more likely than their married counterparts to hold positive views about marriage and to regard it as their best option for self-fulfillment and happiness. Twenty years later, when single women had many more educational and occupational opportunities, their view of the benefits of marriage had dropped sharply.

The idea that marriage was the best possible investment in a woman's future was heartily endorsed by parents. While many mothers and fathers did not think it worthwhile to invest heavily in their daughter's education, by the end of the 1950s, the typical expenditure on a daughter's wedding represented 66 percent, or two-thirds, of an average family's yearly income—a higher proportion than in 2000, when the average wedding cost only 53 percent of median family income and the bride and groom often shared the cost with their parents.

Still, with almost a third of married women working for pay by the late 1950s, why didn't their existence challenge society's definition of women exclusively as wives and mothers? One reason was the demographic characteristics of the married women who entered the workforce. Most of the wives and mothers who got jobs did so when they were in their late thirties or older and their children were well along in school. One recent estimate suggests that no more than 250,000 women with small children were in the paid labor force, although this probably undercounts the numbers of African-American, Chicana, and Latina mothers working for pay. And the majority of working wives worked only part-time or seasonally.

Cultural perceptions were also skewed by the tendency of the press, then as now, to devote more attention to what was happening in new segments of the population than to the average experience. The explosive growth of suburbia preoccupied the media then, and people tended to move to the suburbs to start their families. The suburbs had not existed long enough to have many empty-nest families or opportunities for part-time employment. As a result, less than 10 percent of suburban wives worked for pay.

Finally, there is much truth in the common perception that the 1950s were the height of the male-breadwinner family. The total female labor force participation was growing, but the number of families where the wife did unpaid work on a farm or in a small business was falling and the number of families who relied on the labor of children and teens was sharply down. Add to that the falling age of marriage, the rising birthrate, and the expansion of male earning power, and it's fair to say that never before had there been so many families where young children were being raised by full-time homemakers supported by their husband's earnings rather than by a wider family labor force.

For all these reasons, most Americans believed that the "normal" life for a modern mother was to become a homemaker in a male-breadwinner family and live according to the cultural stereotypes about womanhood that Friedan described as the feminine mystique. If a woman with younger children did have to work, it was often at a job that was unsatisfying and poorly paid, with a husband unwilling to help her with the housework when she got home. So it is not surprising that many such women aspired to become full-time homemakers. And even though married women were more likely to express negative views of marriage than single women—or than their own husbands—most believed that they ought to be happy homemakers and that almost every other woman in the nation was.

Those assumptions and aspirations were reinforced by the mass media and advertising industries. Today the media makes a point of niche marketing, targeting diverse segments of the audience and trying to cater to their perceived needs and fantasies. But the opposite was true in the 1950s and early 1960s, when older local sources of knowledge, values, and even entertainment were displaced by a homogenized national culture that literally whited out America's diversity.

The astounding growth of television was one potent disseminator of this national, homogeneous culture. In 1948, 500,000 homes had televisions. By 1952, the number was 19 million. By 1960, 87 percent of all households had a television, including 80 percent of rural households. Unlike radio, which featured some ethnic, regional, and class diversity in its programming, television portrayed an idealized white middle-class male-breadwinner family as the norm.

Another important influence in shaping women's understanding of "normality" were women's magazines, which reached a much higher percentage of female readers than they do today and accounted for a much larger segment of what women read. In 1964, McCall's, which had invented the "togetherness" slogan of 1950s domesticity ten years earlier, had 21 million readers, mostly between the ages of eighteen and forty- nine, in a population of about 37 million women that age. The Ladies' Home journal and Good Housekeeping each had almost 15 million readers.

In The Feminine Mystique, Betty Friedan claimed that during the 1950s these influential women's magazines "printed virtually no articles except those that serviced women as housewives, or described women as housewives, or permitted a purely feminine identification like the Duchess of Windsor or Princess Margaret." She reported that in 1958 and 1959 she "went through issue after issue of the three major women's magazines … without finding a single heroine who had a career, a commitment to any work, art, profession, or mission in the world, other than 'Occupation: housewife.'"

Friedan exaggerated the ubiquity of the happy housewife. In a survey of monthly magazines from 1946 to 1958, historian Joanne Meyerowitz found that the mass-circulation magazines of the postwar era frequently profiled women who combined marriage with careers or public service outside the home. Although the sharp critiques of Freudian antifeminism found in magazines of the late 1940s had faded by the early 1950s, leftist journalist Eve Merriam wrote witty dissections of the cult of the happy housewife in the pages of The Nation. In 1953, sociologist Mirra Komarovsky, whose work Friedan relied on more than she acknowledged, wrote a well-reviewed book decrying society's failure to understand the importance of work and education in women's lives. And sociologists Alva Myrdal and Viola Klein, anticipating many of Friedan's points, argued in their 1956 book, Women's Two Roles: Home and Work, that the "glorification" of homemaking and motherhood substituted flattery for respect. They noted that this exaltation of homemaking constituted "the cheapest method at society's disposal of keeping women quiet without seriously considering their grievances or improving their position."

But most of this discussion was confined to the pages of "highbrow" journals, such as Harper's and Atlantic Monthly, and the academic press, both of which were suspect in the atmosphere of McCarthyism and the Cold War. Liberals and leftists had largely been driven out of the mass media by anticommunist blacklists, such as the 1950 publication Red Channels: The Report of Communist Influence in Radio and Television, which listed 151 composers, writers, announcers, singers, and actors whose support for liberal or left-wing causes, or even for the work of the United Nations, made them "potential subversives." Allies of Senator Joseph McCarthy sat on the Federal Communications Commission, keeping their eyes peeled for shows that did not abide by such ever-widening blacklists.

In the political realm, the Civil Service Commission fired almost 3,000 people as "security risks" and reported that more than 4,000 others had resigned under the pressure of investigations into their political associations and beliefs. Feminists, and educated women in general, were particularly suspect. The House Un-American Activities Committee warned that "girls' schools and women's colleges contain some of the most loyal disciples of Russia. Teachers there are often frustrated females."

In this atmosphere, most women who continued to focus on women's rights during this period tended to do so behind the scenes. They were, in historian Linda Eisenmann's words, "quieter, less demanding, and more accommodating than women's advocates before 1920 and after 1965."

Friedan may have overstated her case, but considerable evidence supports her contention that women's magazines became more traditionalist on marriage and gender roles during the 1950s. Sociologist Francesca Cancian surveyed articles on marriage from high-circulation magazines such as the Ladies' Home Journal, McCall's, and The Readers' Digest tor each decade from 1900–1909 through 1970–1979 and found that during the 1950s there were fewer articles endorsing flexible gender roles than in the 1920s, 1930s, or 1940s. She also found that advocacy of egalitarian marital values, such as communicating openly with one's husband or expressing one's own individuality, became less frequent, while there was more emphasis on women's sacrifice of aspirations beyond the home. Another detailed examination of magazine articles, TV scripts, and child-rearing manuals of the 1950s found a marked reassertion of traditional gender roles and male dominance in manage during the latter part of the decade.

A similar trend occurred in popular entertainment, according to historian James Gilbert's analysis of scripts for The Adventures of Ozzie and Harriet, which began on the radio in the 1940s and then moved to television. In the years immediately after World War II, episodes often mocked Ozzie's illusion that women were incapable of doing "men's" tasks and found humor in setting up occasions for gender role switching. During the 1950s, however, the show abandoned these themes. In addition, the visual portrayal of Harriet in the TV series, where she was constantly holding a tray of cookies or running a vacuum cleaner, overshadowed the verbal give-and-take that had characterized the radio broadcasts.

In movies as well, the images of acceptable female behavior narrowed, especially when it came to portraying women and work. Friedan's claim that during the late 1940s and the 1950s the career woman replaced the seductress as the femme fatale who must he punished for her sins is supported by film critic Peter Biskind, who argues that the "Scarlet Letter A," symbol of the ultimate female transgression, increasingly stood for "ambition" rather than "adultery."

Friedan was also correct in contending that the media paid less attention to women's rights during the 1950s than in earlier decades. A study of how newspapers and popular magazines covered such issues between 1905 and 1970 found that coverage was highest during the suffrage struggle, between 1905 and 1920. It reached its lowest point between 1950 and the early 1960s and did not rise again until the late 1960s. Coverage by the New York Times was fairly high at the beginning of the 1950s but then declined steadily to a low point in 1960 before beginning a gradual recovery.

What the media did cover incessantly during the 1950s—along with the refrain that smothering homemakers created homosexuality, narcissism, and neurosis—was the drumbeat of claims from politicians, psychiatrists, social workers, and judges that working mothers were the cause of all other childhood ills, including delinquency, insanity, and all forms of criminality. Lynn Parker recalls that her mother "had been a career woman before she married my father" but then became a stay-at-home wife. Parker's mother went back to work when Parker was in high school, and she noticed that this improved her mother's depression. "I could see that it was very good for her to be working and I admired her for going to work, she recalls. But Parker had also absorbed the tremendous social disapproval of working mothers, so she chose to "lie on school forms that asked for mother's occupation. I continued to check the housewife box, because I feared my teacher would judge her poorly."

Friedan blamed these conservative cultural trends on the growing influence of Freudianism. In the 1920s, she noted, Freud's emphasis on freedom from sexual repression made his theories appear to support women's emancipation. But from the 1940s on, Freudian ideas "became the ideological bulwark of the sexual counter-revolution in America." Psychiatrists increasingly focused on Freud's notion of "penis envy," which, they declared, led many women to reject the passivity that women needed to reach true sexual fulfillment, thus dooming themselves and their families to maladjustment and misery. "Narcissism," dependence, and even "masochism," traits seen as pathological in men, were considered normal or healthy in women.

The most vicious psychoanalytical attacks on women began in the 1940s rather than the 1950s, with books such as Philip Wylie's Generation of Vipers, Marynia Farnham and Ferdinand Lundberg's Modem Woman: The Lost Sex, and Edward Strecker's Their Mothers' Sons. But during the 1950s Wylie and others continued to heap invective both on "castrating" career women and on overly controlling stay-at-home mothers. By 1955, Generation of Vipers had gone through twenty printings. In the early 1960s, Wylie was still finding a wide audience for his attacks on "The Womanization of America," brought about, in his view, by an unholy alliance of career women and housewives who had established a "she-tyranny" over American men.

Perhaps even more damaging to women's sense of self were the gentler, and hence more insidious, versions of these ideas that were endlessly recycled in the media during the 1950s. Studies of postwar culture show that Freudian notions of sexual difference permeated popular culture, becoming a major explanatory device for human behavior in movies, magazines, and news stories. As Friedan put it, Freudian antifeminism settled over the American landscape "like fine volcanic ash."

In 1953, Collier's ran an article whose banner headline asked: "Does Your Family Have a Neurosis?" If the family was "mother-fixated." The answer was definitely yes, but even happy and devoted families could be neurotic, the article said. By the mid-1950s, it was scarcely possible to find a magazine that did not talk knowingly about one or another form of neurosis, usually caused by women's failure to conform to their feminine "instincts."

The assignment of women to a passive, secondary role in social life, which had once been ascribed to duty, social custom, God's will, or innate differences in ability, was now declared to be a woman's only route to personal fulfillment. Psychiatrist Helene Deutsch declared that the modern woman renounced "originality" and personal aspiration not out of coercion but "out of her own needs," which were best met by identifying with her husband's achievements. A normal woman found complete satisfaction in her role as homemaker, mother, and sexual companion to her husband. Any woman who did not find such complete fulfillment, psychiatrists explained in circular reasoning disguised as the latest scientific thinking, was clearly not normal.

Sociologists argued that unless society encouraged a clear differentiation of the sexes, everything from the nuclear family to the economy itself could disintegrate. The renowned Harvard sociologist Talcott Parsons and his collaborator Robert Bales claimed that the most functional form of family for modern industrial society was one where the husband played the "instrumental" role, earning the family living, and the wife played the "expressive" role, providing emotional support to the wage earner and nurturing the children. From this it followed that boys must be reared to accept the masculine identity that would prepare them to be family decision-makers and breadwinners, and girls should be channeled into activities that would prepare them for homemaking and motherhood.

Farnham put it succinctly in a 1952 article in Parents magazine: Boys could not develop into successful men nor girls into fulfilled women if society made the mistake of regarding its citizens "not primarily as male and female, but as people." Clearly the title of Friedan's 1960 article, "Women Are People too," was not as self-evident as it now sounds.

In 1947, LIFE magazine's June issue on the dilemmas facing women in the postwar world had taken a relatively neutral view about the choices women made concerning work and family. Revisiting the topic in December 1956, the magazine took a stronger stand against combining work with motherhood. The introduction to the issue, by "Mrs. Peter Marshall," praised feminism for making women healthier and "more attractive than ever before" and for increasing the infant survival rate. But, she warned, feminism often led women to lose sight of their real source of fulfillment, and that was when "their troubles begin. "A normal woman's most satisfying moments in life, Mrs. Marshall declared, occurred not when she got her first job or proved her intellectual abilities, but when she wore her first formal gown, was taken into the arms of the man she loved, or held her baby in her arms.

The same issue did feature one article by a husband who took the controversial stand that his wife's full-time job was "good for her, good for him, good for their children—and good for the budget." But his opinion could hardly compete with Robert Coughlin's interviews with five psychiatrists, all of whom agreed that the primary cause of marital unhappiness, divorce, and disturbed children was "wives who are not feminine enough and husbands [who are] not truly male."

In 1947, LIFE's editors had balanced the antifeminist views of Farnham and Lundberg with acerbic criticisms of Freudian pronouncements by several well-known female authors, but in 1956, not one rebuttal of Coughlin's experts was to be heard. Several of the psychiatrists conceded that some women had no choice but to work, but they were unanimous in telling Coughlin that those who wanted to work—especially at a full-time job—were "rejecting the role of wife and mother." A woman who made this choice, as Coughlin summed up the consensus, "may find many satisfactions in her job, but the chances are that she, her husband and her children will suffer psychological damage, and that she will be basically an unhappy woman."

Freudian ideas about gender difference even seeped into women's colleges, the one arena where women had traditionally been encouraged to aspire to a life of the mind. Some educators used Freudian precepts to argue that traditional subjects such as physics, philosophy, and calculus were not relevant to women's role in society and were causing "discontent and restlessness." Friedan quoted Lynn White, president of Mills College from 1943 to 1958, who suggested in 1950 that colleges should educate women to be housewives rather than train them in skills they would never use. "Why not study the theory and preparation of a Basque paella, of a well-marinated shish-kebob, lamb kidneys sauteed in sherry, an authoritative curry?" asked White.

Not all educators took the ideas of "sex-directed education" as far as White, but in March 1962, psychiatrist Edna Rostow, writing in the Yale Review, chastised those who failed to put into practice what modern researchers now knew about the needs of "femininity." It is a psychological fact, she contended, "that many young women—if not the majority—seem to be incapable of dealing with future long-range intellectual interests until they have proceeded through the more basic phases of their own healthy growth as women"—marriage, childbearing, and child rearing. Or as Grayson Kirk, president of Columbia University from 1953 to 1968 put it, "It would be preposterously naive to suggest that a B.A. can be made as attractive to girls as a marriage license."

"Ideally," Rostow wrote, a woman's life in the prime years of family building "should contain no elements of competition with men in the world of work." Instead, "it should reflect her full emotional acceptance of the role she is living: receptive, bearing, nurturing." Encouraging a young woman to embrace any other goal "can adversely affect the development of her full identity." Only after she has fulfilled her natural destiny as wife and mother should she consider what other occupations and identities she might wish to assume. Rostow recommended that women not even begin training for any profession until they were between the age of thirty and forty (about ten to twenty years after most women in the era had their first child). That was "the natural starting point for serious professional study in the rhythmic pattern of modern woman's life."

All this did not mean, as Friedan claimed at one point in her book, that for more than fifteen years, "there was no word ... in the million of words written about women to challenge the myth of the happy housewife." In fact, as Friedan acknowledged elsewhere in the book, the one women's issue that regularly did make it into the mass media, right alongside the celebration of domesticity, was the puzzling question of why many women seemed unhappy or dissatisfied with their lives. Young mothers felt exhausted and "trapped," magazines lamented; older housewives were bored. As early as 1949, LIFE reported that "suddenly and for no plain reason" American women had been "seized with an eerie restlessness." Under a "mask of placidity" and an outwardly feminine appearance, one physician wrote in 1953, some housewives were "seething" with resentment and anxiety. Long before Friedan labeled their discontent "the problem with no name," doctors were puzzling over the mysterious "housewife syndrome."

But until Friedan attributed women's unhappiness to the contradictions between women's needs and the precepts of the feminine mystique, there was no widely publicized alternative to the psychiatric explanation of female discontent as an individual problem of sexual or gender malcontent. When women described being trapped in their homes, dominated by their husbands, or resentful of their economic dependence, this was taken as a symptom rather than a potential cause of their disturbance, something to be treated by analysis, medication, and even electroshock therapy. As sociologist Carol Warren notes in Madwives, a study of women hospitalized for schizophrenia in the 1950s, there was at that time, unlike today, "no legitimizing cultural vocabulary" for housewives who felt isolated in their homes, unhappy in their marriages, or damaged in their sense of self.

So the prescribed treatment for "the housewife syndrome" was not to figure out how a discontented woman could change her life to gain a stronger sense of self, but how she could change her feelings to reconcile herself to her role in the family. In 1963, psychiatrist Herbert Modlin described his success in dispensing such treatment to five "paranoid" women. Their "distorted perceptions" about male persecution disappeared, he reported, once he and his colleagues helped them learn to value their "feminine social role."

The patients Warren studied were pronounced cured only when they admitted that their discontent had been unjustified. One woman reported in her discharge interview that she had been advised to enter the hospital in the first place because "I felt ashamed that I was dominated." Since then, "I've had a chance to think things out." Another wife described how her treatment had helped her: "I feel like baking cookies ... and that's because made up my mind to be a homemaker instead of always worrying about a career."

Less extreme than commitment to a mental hospital but much more widespread was medication. When tranquilizers became readily available in the second half of the 1950s, they were initially prescribed for high-charging businessmen such as those portrayed in the TV series Mad Men. Yet by the second half of the 1960s, women were twice as likely as men to use tranquilizers, and most consumers of "mother's little helper" were white and better educated than average.

Not everyone in America considered it crazy for wives and mothers to have interests outside the home before they reached middle age. Many educators persisted in believing that women should be taught to use their minds and imaginations for something besides cooking. And the same popular magazines that disparaged "the career woman" as an ideal or goal often commended individual women who had successful careers. In many of the magazines she surveyed, historian Meyerowitz writes, "domestic ideals coexisted in an ongoing tension with an ethos of individual achievement." She found many articles that celebrated both domestic devotion and public success—"sometimes in the same sentence."

A 1953 Coronet article about the female mayor of Portland, Oregon, was titled "The Lady Who Licked Crime in Portland." The mayor was described as "an ethereally pale housewife" who tipped "the scales at 110 pounds." But she was also labeled a feminist, intensely concerned "with the status of women." And no one suggested that she needed to be institutionalized or medicated.

So there were more mixed messages, exceptions, and contradictions in the media's depictions of the ideal feminine life than Friedan admitted in her book. In the long run, these mixed messages, combined with the trends toward increased workplace participation and education for women, helped pave the way for a new women's movement that would have happened with or without Betty Friedan. Indeed, by the time Friedan's book appeared in 1963, many young women were already rejecting "the feminine mystique" without ever having heard it called that.

But many women never heard the exceptions and caveats to the feminine mystique that historians now recognize in retrospect. And the few who did hear them seem to have found them all the more confusing. "It would have been easier if everyone had been as negative as Philip Wylie," Joan C. told me. "Then you could have gotten indignant. But it was like being enveloped in a big cloud of cotton candy, sweet and sticky. You couldn't punch your way out."

Anne Parsons, the daughter of sociologist Talcott Parsons, wrote to Friedan describing her sense of isolation and marginalization as an intelligent woman trying to build a research career in the 1950s. "I began to wish that someone would call me names or throw stones or threaten to send me to a concentration camp so that at least I would know for certain that the world was against me."

A strong-minded woman determined to pursue a career could have cobbled together enough supportive quotes and celebrated role models to justify her resolve, and many did. But the individuals praised in women's magazines for successfully reconciling family life with a career were painted in such heroic, larger-than-life terms that they could not possibly serve as role models for most women. The descriptions of how these women pulled off their successes underscored Dorothy Thompson's 1939 warning that only one in a thousand could manage such a thing. Articles on successful women would invariably marvel at their "ceaseless activity," "amazing" energy, and ability to "get along without sleep." Many readers admired these women, and perhaps even envied them, but few could imagine emulating them.

Today women often resent the psychological pressures created by the pressure to "have it all." But in the 1950s, women were firmly told that they could "have it or" meaning they could be anything they wanted to be in the public world, or they could be happy.

You are free to choose, the prevailing ideology said. You can do anything you want and society will no longer try to stop you. But modern science has proven that if you do not first devote yourself to being a homemaker, you will probably end up desperately unhappy, and your choice may be a sign that you already suffer from a deep illness.

Prior to the 1940s and 1950s, a woman was condemned if she did not do what was expected of her. In the 1950s, she was pitied if she did not want what was expected of her.

For most of American history, a woman's role as wife and mother had been seen as a sometimes painful duty. People talked about a woman's lot, not a woman's choice. And a woman's lot involved self-sacrifice, not self-realization. But in the world of 1950s advertising, all that changed. One of the marketing research books Friedan accessed informed its clients that "the modern bride is deeply convinced of the unique value of married love, of the possibilities of finding real happiness in marriage and of fulfilling her personal destiny in it and through it." She "seeks as a conscious goal that which in many cases her grandmother saw as a blind fate and her mother as slavery"—to "belong to a man ... to choose among all possible careers the career of wife-mother-homemaker."

Postwar ideology was particularly disorienting for many women because it often came in the guise of a forward-thinking rejection of "traditional" ideas about gender and sexuality. The new ideology of marriage promised women satisfaction in their home life that their mothers and grandmothers would never have dreamed possible. The modern woman would find joy and creativity in the housework that had been pure drudgery for her grandmother. She would experience sexual pleasures unimaginable to her repressed Victorian foremothers. And she would reach new heights of egalitarian intimacy with her husband, who would come home each evening eager to participate in the joys of togetherness.

In the long run, such heightened expectations about marriage helped make many women more assertive in their relationships and gave some women the courage to end empty and unsatisfying marriages. But in the short run, these expectations often added to a woman's guilt and confusion, because they were not yet attached to any new expectations about men's behavior. Women were encouraged to expect more than ever from marriage, but they were told that when a marriage fell short, it was almost invariably because they were not good enough wives. If a husband's bad behavior threatened the marriage, it was up to the wife to figure out what she had done to trigger this behavior and how she must change to bring out her husband's better side.

Studying the advice of marital experts in this era, historian Rebecca Davis found a widespread consensus that the path to marital happiness lay in the wife adjusting her own wishes to her husband's needs, whims, and even neuroses. After four counseling sessions at Ohio State University's marriage clinic, for example, a twenty-year-old pregnant wife dutifully concluded that her husband's infidelities were probably due to her failure to take enough care with her own appearance and that of her home. She therefore resolved to be "better groomed, cleaner." If such rededication to domesticity did not create the bliss that a true woman ought to find in marriage, "resignation," one social worker remarked, could offer "protection from excessive frustration."

Other mixed messages abounded. A woman was told that she should put nothing above her devotion to her children, her love for her husband, and her delight in her home, but she was sternly warned against devoting so much attention to her family that she smothered her children and emasculated her husband. In the nineteenth century it would have been unthinkable to call a woman too devoted a wife or mother. But by the 1950s, the woman who focused too intensely on being a housewife and mother was deemed as big a menace to society—and to men—as the woman who rejected domesticity in favor of a paid career. The pursuit of domestic bliss—the one outlet for a woman's dreams and aspirations—turned out to damage the men on whom women were supposed to rely.

And in the hierarchy of cultural concerns during that era, the dilemmas facing American women paled in comparison to the "crisis" facing American men. Pundits bemoaned the eclipse of the risk-taking entrepreneur by "the organization man." They worried that men were losing their hard edge because they increasingly worked in impersonal bureaucracies where "feminine" characteristics such as teamwork, compromise, and concern for others' opinions were more important than individual initiative and aggressiveness. Men, said sociologist David Riesman, were becoming "other-directed instead of "inner-directed."

The material comforts that were promised as the reward of a successful family were simultaneously feared as a threat to the nation's moral fiber. Some commentators fretted that modern affluence had created a culture of leisure that was undermining the work ethic of yore. Others worried that "status-seeking" men were working too hard to amass material goods. But however contradictory the problems described, almost everyone agreed that they were the fault of women.

If a woman left home to get a job, she was threatening the last bastions of masculinity. But if she devoted all her attention to making her home a place of comfort and fulfillment, she was either overdomesticating her husband or putting too much pressure on him to keep up with the Joneses. If she left a child with a babysitter to take a part-time job, she was neglecting the next generation. But if she lavished too much attention on her children, she might produce a whole generation of homosexuals.

Even the mutually satisfying sex life that was supposed to be one of the rewards of conforming to the 1950s model of masculinity and femininity contributed to the sense of masculine crisis. Sociologist Riesman warned that as women became avid consumers of sexual and romantic advice, "the anxiety of men lest they fail to satisfy the woman also grows."

One of the quickest routes to a best-selling book in the 1950s was to explain how women's behavior—whether as wives, mothers, or career women—was to blame for the "crisis of masculinity" that supposedly characterized the era. An issue of Look magazine titled "The Decline of the American Male," reprinted as a book in 1958, squarely laid the blame for men's problems on that same domesticity that was elsewhere being celebrated as women's best hope for happiness and society's best hope for stability.

The book described a litany of problems facing American men, all of them stemming from the power their wives supposedly exerted. "Women's new rank in the family has encouraged her to make extraordinary and often frustrating economic demands on her husband." Women were making new sexual demands as well, so that the poor man could no longer "concentrate on his own pleasure, he must concern himself primarily with satisfying his wife." The upshot? "Men overwork themselves to supply their wives with material possessions" and then exhaust themselves trying to satisfy them sexually. Adding insult to injury, the "fad of togetherness" had led wives to ask husbands to do "things around the house that their fathers didn't even know had to be done."

Even critics of suburban domesticity in the 1950s, liberal as well as conservative, directed their anger not toward the system that kept women trapped in the mystique of housewifery and consumerism, but toward the wives themselves. In 1956, The Crack in the Picture Window gathered widespread attention for its searing indictment of suburbia. The author, John Keats, combined sociology and satirical fiction to chronicle the lives of two hapless suburban dwellers, Mr. and Mrs. John Drone, Keats quoted Dr. Harold Mendelsohn of American University's Bureau of Social Research about the "terrifying monotony" of suburbia and the loneliness of wives whose husbands could at least escape during the day. But in the next breath he argued that suburbia was producing a "matriarchal society" that turned the average woman into a "nagging slob" and her husband into "a woman-bossed, inadequate, money-terrified neuter."

Keats's prescription for Mr. Drone was to throw off his domination by women and reject his wife's attempts to domesticate him. But he advised Mrs. Drone to isolate herself even further in the lonely job of homemaking, becoming someone who "baked her own bread, painted her own pictures, and had as little to do with her neighbors as was humanly possible."

The Family and Household Transition

John R. Weeks

Households used to be created by marriage and dissolved by death—in between there were children. Throughout the world this pattern has been transformed by what some have called the "second demographic transition," which I will discuss as the "family and household transition" in the context of the broader demographic transition. "The demographic transition is in essence a transition in family strategies: the reactive, largely biological family-building decision rules appropriate to highly uncertain environments come eventually to be supplanted by more deliberate and forward-looking strategies that require longer time horizons" (Cohen and Montgomery 1998:6); that is, the transition from "family building by fate" to "family building by design" (Lloyd and Ivanov 1988:141) that I mentioned ... as being key to the fertility transition.

In general terms, we can describe this as the shift in family and household structure occasioned by people living longer with fewer children born, increasingly in urban settings, and subject to higher standards of living, all as part of the demographic transition. Households no longer depend on marriage for their creation, nor, do they depend on death to dissolve them, and children are encountered in a wide array of household and living arrangements. "The family is in crisis, as witnessed by increasing instability of unions, fluidity of the 'marital' home and the economic stress, experienced by women and children of disrupted marriages" (Makinwa-Adebusoye 1994:48). Although that certainly sounds like the subject matter of books and tailed shows in the United States, the author of that quote is referring to sub-Saharan Africa. "Marriage is becoming rarer and the age at first marriage is increasing; the number of couples who cohabit before and without marrying is rapidly increasing, and so as a consequence, are births out of wedlock" (Blossfeld and de Rose 1992:73). That, too, could be a description of the United States, but in this instance the authors are talking about Italy.

All over the world changes in household formation and living arrangements are being discussed and discoursed, and in the United States it has been suggested that "one of the most widely debated issues in contemporary sociology has been how to interpret patterns of family change ..." (Brooks 2002:191). Curiously, however, these debates rarely include a review of the underlying demographic changes that helped spawn this massive social shift, and so my purpose in this chapter is to rectify that deficiency for you. The changes we see occurring all over the world are the inevitable result of powerful social forces unleashed by the demographic transition. I am not going to go so far as to suggest that we can predict exactly which changes will take place at a given time in a given society, but I will suggest to you that no social system could remain unchanged in the face of massive declines in mortality, followed by massive declines in fertility, and accompanied by massive migration and dramatic change in the age structure—all of the changes we have discussed in the previous chapters.

John R. Weeks, "The Family and Household Transition," *Population: An Introduction to Concepts and Issues*, pp. 402–429. Copyright © 2008 by Cengage Learning, Inc. Reprinted with permission.

I begin the chapter with a discussion of exactly how the structure of households and living arrangements have, in fact, changed over time—how big is this transition in the United States and elsewhere? Particularly noteworthy is the change in the status of women. I have referred to that repeatedly in previous chapters, but we need to keep reminding ourselves that gender equity is central to the well-being of any society. Then I turn to the specific demographic changes that have contributed to the increasing diversity in household structure. A critical element is the changing set of life chances that people are experiencing in the United States and all over the world—changes in the population (or demographic) characteristics that influence how your life will turn out. These include especially education, labor force participation, occupation, and income, which in turn affect gender roles (the social roles considered appropriate for males or females) and marital status. All of these things have influenced the changing family and household structure, although differently for some cultural groups than others. Indeed, race and ethnicity, along with religion mediate the impact of life chances in every human society. The intersection of your population characteristics and family and household structure is a crucial determinant of what life will be like for you. Similarly, at the societal level, the distribution of the population by different characteristics and by family and household structure will be influenced by where a society is in the demographic transition, so we are in a position to say something about the future by fitting all of these pieces together.

Defining Family Demography and Life Chances

In virtually every human society ever studied, people have organized their lives around a family unit. In a general sense, a family is any group of people who are related to one another by marriage, birth, or adoption. The nature of the family, then, is that it is a kinship unit (Ryder 1987). But it is also like a minisociety, a micro-population that experiences births, deaths, and migration, as well as changing age structures, as it goes through its own life course. The changes that occur in the broader population—the subject of this book in general—mainly occur within the context of the family unit, and so the study of population necessitates that we study the family (see, for example, Goldscheider 1995). Implicit in the definition of a family is that its members share a sense of social bonding: the mutual acceptance of reciprocal rights and obligations, and of responsibility for each other's well-being. We usually make a distinction between the nuclear family (at least one parent and their/his/her children) and the extended family, which can extend to other generations (add in grandparents and maybe even great-grandparents) and can also extend laterally to other people within each generation (aunts and uncles, cousins, and so forth).

The next question of interest to us is: Where do these people live? People live in a housing unit, which is the physical space used as separate living quarters for people. It may be a house, an apartment, a mobile home or trailer, or even a single room or group of rooms. People who share a housing unit are said to have formed a household. The household is thus a residential unit and so you can see that a family household is a housing or residential unit occupied by people who are all related to one another. More specifically, we can say that a family household is a household in which the householder (defined by the U.S. Census Bureau as the person in whose name the house is owned or rented) is living with one or more persons related to her or him by birth, marriage, or adoption. On the other hand, a nonfamily household is a housing unit that includes only a person who lives alone, or consists of people living with nonfamily coresidents, such as friends living together, a single householder who rents out rooms, or cohabiting couples. Especially important to the concept of the family household is that the family part of it makes it a kinship unit, as noted above, while the household part of it makes it a consumption unit (Wall, Robin, and Laslett 1983). Part of the responsibility that family members have when they live in the same household is to produce goods and services that are shared by, and for the mutual benefit of, the family members who live together. So, family members do not necessarily share a household, and household members are not necessarily family members. But when family members share a housing unit we have the most powerful kinship and consumer unit that we are likely to find in any society.

Family demography is concerned largely with the study and analysis of family households: their formation, their change over time, and their dissolution. Families represent the fusion of people from other families and long before a family household dissolves, it is likely to have fissured into other families, as children born into the family grow up and leave the family household of their parents to create (fuse) their own households. All humans grow up in, and typically live for all of their lives, in social groups that represent some sort of family, so our lives are shaped and bounded by our membership in the group. We cannot understand the changes taking place elsewhere in society unless we connect those changes to what is happening to the family.

We can describe a family in terms of its geographic location because where you are in the world will influence the kinds of social, cultural, economic, and physical resources that will be available to the family. We can also describe a family in terms of its social location (where it is positioned in the local social system) because that will influence the family's access to whatever local resources exist on which the family can draw. And we can describe the family in terms of its own social structure, which refers to the number of people within the family, their age and gender, and their relationship to each other. Each of these characteristics of the family will influence the life chances of family members. Your own life chances refer, for example, to your probability of having a particular set of demographic characteristics, such as having a high-prestige job, lots of money, a stable marriage or not marrying at all, and a small family or no family at all. These differences in life chances, of course, are not necessarily a reflection of your worth as an individual, but they are reflections of the social and economic makeup of society—indicators of the demographic characteristics that help to define what a society and its members are like.

We are born with certain ascribed characteristics, such as sex or gender and race and ethnicity, over which we have essentially no control (except in extreme cases). These characteristics affect life chances in very important ways because virtually every society uses such identifiable human attributes to the advantage of some people and the disadvantage of others. Religion is not exactly an ascribed characteristic, but worldwide it is typically a function of race or ethnicity and, as with as ascribed characteristics, it is often a focal point for prejudice and discrimination, which influence life chances.

Life chances are also directly related to achieved characteristics or your personal human capital, those sociodemographic characteristics, such as education, occupation, labor force participation, income, and marital status, over which you do exercise some degree of control. For example, the better educated you are, the higher your occupational status is apt to be, and thus the higher your level of income will likely be. Indeed, income is a crass, but widely accepted, index of how your life is turning out. Ascribed characteristics affect your life chances primarily by affecting your access to achieved characteristics, which then become major ingredients of social status—education, occupation and income. Population characteristics affect your own demographic behavior, especially family formation and fertility, although they also influence mortality and migration …

The demographics of your family, in turn, affect life chances through the possession or acquisition of social capital—the ability to facilitate or retard your access to opportunities for higher education, a higher-status occupation, or a better-paying job. All of these aspects of population characteristics and their influence on life chances converge to affect the kind of family we choose to create and the type of household we form.

The Family and Household Transition

The "traditional" family household of a married couple and their children is no longer the statistical norm in North America and in many other parts of the world, even if it remains the ideal type of household in the minds of many people. Families headed by females, especially with no husband present, are increasingly common, as are "nontraditional" households inhabited by unmarried people (including never-married, divorced, widowed, and cohabiting couples), by older adults raising their grandchildren, or by married couples with no children. You are almost certainly aware of these societal shifts through personal experience or the mass media. What may be less obvious is that these changes are closely linked to demographic trends. The variability from place to place may be culturally and societally specific, but the basic reasons for change are distinctly demographic in nature. Let us look first at the changes that are taking place, focusing especially on the United States.

Household Composition and Family Structure

The total number of households in the United States increased from 63 million in 1970 to 106 million in 2000, but within that increase was a dramatic change in the composition of the American household, as Figure 1.2.1 illustrates. In 1970, the classic "married with children" households accounted for 40 percent of all households in the United States. Married couples without children (either before building a family or after the kids were grown) accounted for another 30 percent. The "other" families include male- and, disproportionately, female-headed households in which other family members (usually children) are living with the householder. In Figure 1.2.1, you can see that the light shading represents all family households (a household in which the householder is living with one or more persons related to her or him by birth or marriage). In 1970, they comprised 81 percent of all households—a drop from 90 percent in 1940, when the Census Bureau first began to compile these data (Fields 2001). By 2000, it had dropped even further to 68 percent, and by then less than one in four households included a married couple with children.

As married couples with children have become less common, they have been replaced most often by female-headed, mother-only families, and by nonfamily households, including people who live alone, and nonfamily coresidents (friends living together, a single householder who rents out rooms, cohabiting couples, etc.). The phrase that best describes the changes in household composition as shown in Figure 1.2.1 is increased diversity or "pluralization" (meaning that no single category captures a majority of households). Although I focus here on the United States, Canada and most European nations have also experienced a decline in the relating importance of households composed of a married couple with children, along with an increase in female-headed households with children present (McLanahan and Casper 1995), although the rise in the latter is more pronounced in the U.S. than in Europe (Kuijsten 1999). Indeed, in Italy almost all children are born to a married mother and there is very little

Figure 1.2.1 U.S. Households Have Become Increasingly Diverse

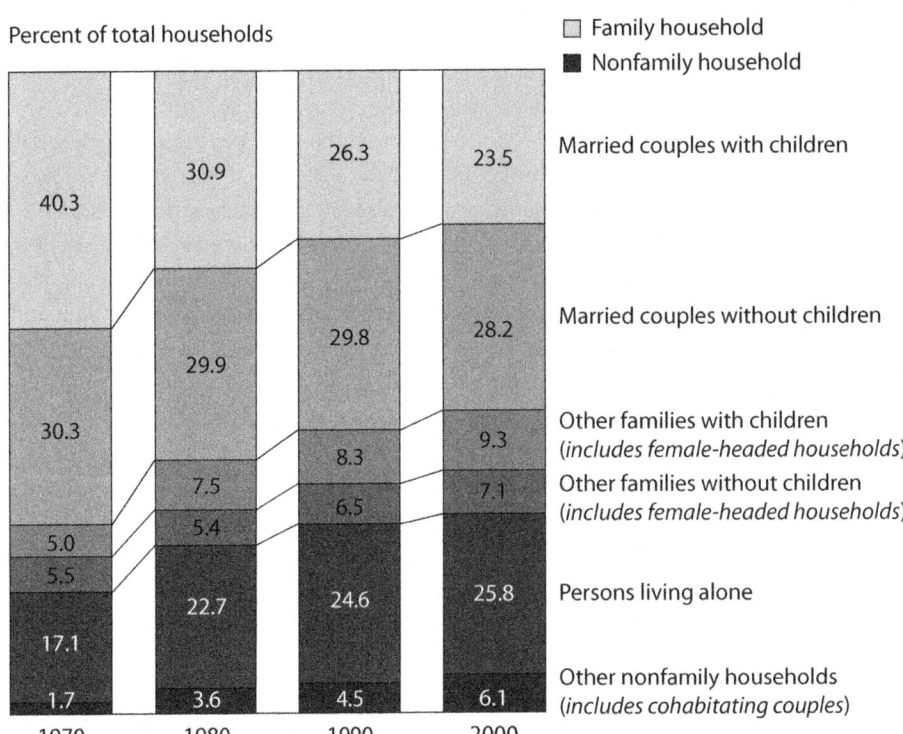

Sources: Data for 1970 through 1990 are from Jason Fields, 2001, "America's Families and Living Arrangements: 2000." Current Population Reports P20–537, Figure 1; data for 2000 are from U.S. Census Bureau, 2001h, Census 2000, Table DP-1, Profile of General Demographic Characteristics, 2000.

Figure 1.2.2 U.S. Racial/Ethnic Differences in Percentage of Households with Children that Are Mother-Only Families

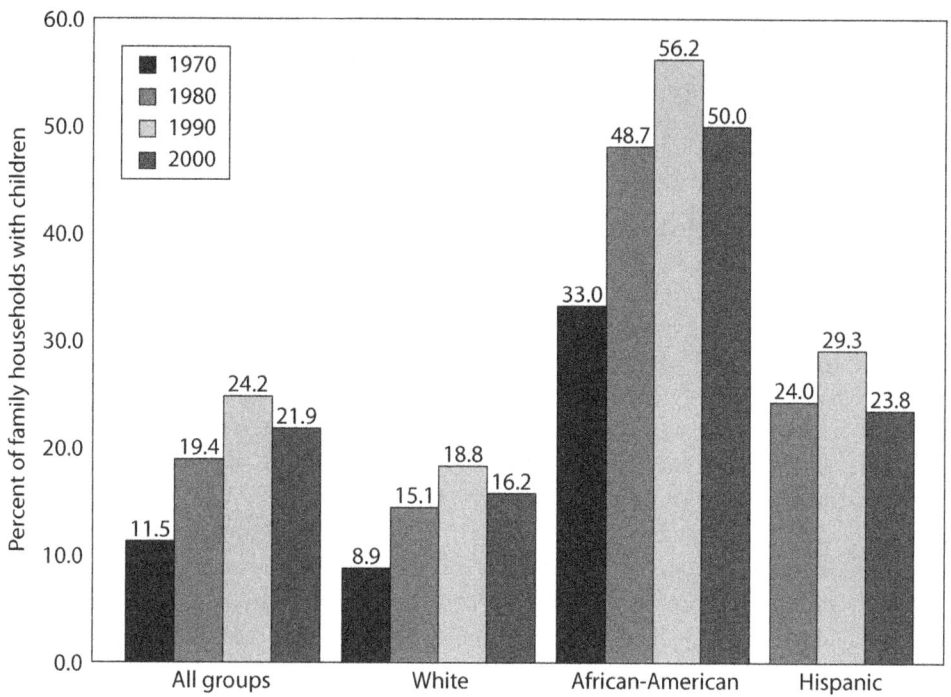

Sources: Data for 1970 through 1990 are from S. Rawlings, 1994, "Household and Family Characteristics: March 1993," Current Population Reports P20–477, Table F; data for 2000 are from Jason Fields, 2001, "America's Families and Living Arrangements: 2000." Current Population Reports, P20–537, Table F.

divorce among parents with children in the home (Anderson 2002). At the same time, Italy has one of the world's highest rates of delayed marriage and lowest rates of fertility, so there is undoubtedly a connection here.

Increasing diversity is a result of the several elements of the demographic transition. The demographic transition promotes a diversity of family types and household types because (1) people are living longer and this means that they are likely to be widowed, more likely to tire of the current spouse and divorce, and less likely to feel pressure to marry early and begin childbearing; (2) the latter pressure is relieved by the decline in fertility, which means that women, in particular do not need to begin childbearing at such a young age, and both men and women have many years of life after the children are grown; and (3) an increasingly urban population is presented with many acceptable lifestyle options besides marriage and family-building. I will discuss these in more detail later in the chapter.

The rise in female-headed households is not a necessary component of the changes that occur during the demographic transition, but, as I will discuss below, it is tied at least transitionally to the rise in the status of women. Between 1970 and 2000, the number of female-headed families with children (mother-only families) went up from 2.8 million to 7.6 million in the United States, whereas the number of married-couple-with-children families went down from 25.5 million to 24.8 million. In 1970, female-headed households accounted for 10 percent of families with children, but by 2000 that had jumped to 22 percent (see Figure 1.2.2). Even those numbers hide the true scope of the transformation, because a married-couple family in 2000 was more likely than in 1970 to be a recombined family, involving previously married spouses and children from other unions. At the end of this chapter I discuss the social impact of these transformations, but my goal at present is to describe the changes. One obvious point to make is that female-headed households represented a smaller fraction of all family households with children in 2000 than had been true in 1990.

Widely discussed in public debate is the fact that substantial racial/ethnic differences exist with respect to female-headed households, especially among families with children as shown in Figure 1.2.2. Although the rise in mother-only families has been experienced by all groups in American society, in 1970, African-American families were already more apt to be headed by a female than were white or Hispanic households at any time between 1970 and 2000. Ruggles (1994a) has found that, since at least 1880, African-American children have been far more likely to reside with only their mothers (or with neither parent) than white children. Nonetheless, the data in Figure 1.2.3 show that the percentage of African-American mother-only families has increased considerably just in the past few decades, although it too declined a bit between 1990 and 2000.

In 2000, nearly three out of 10 households in the United States were non-family households, as you can see looking back at Figure 1.2.2. This is part of the trend away from what is often thought of as the traditional family, enshrined by old TV sitcoms—a family in which a married couple live together with their children and the husband works full-time while the wife cares for the children and attends to domestic chores (Hernandez 1993). In fact, this type of "Leave It to Beaver" family is a relatively new phenomenon historically—a product of the demographic transition. High mortality alone (but especially when combined with high fertility and an agrarian economic environment) prevented this type of household from being the norm for most of human history. Let me explain.

Human beings are by nature social animals. We prefer to live with others and nearly all human economic activities are based on cooperation and collaboration with other humans. Our identity as individuals paradoxically depends on our interaction with other people. We only know who we are by measuring the reaction of other people to us, and we depend on others to teach us how to behave and how to negotiate the physical and social worlds. Furthermore, humans are completely dependent creatures at birth, and every known society has organized itself into social units (households/families) to ensure the survival of children and the reproduction of society. In high-mortality societies, the rules about who can and should be part of that social unit must be a bit flexible because death can take a mother, father, or other important household member at almost any time.

I referred [earlier] to the Nuatl-speaking Mexican families in Morelos in the sixteenth century, who lived in a "demographic hell," where high mortality produced high rates of orphan- and widowhood. In response to these "vagaries of severe mortality," they developed a complex household structure that was "extremely fluid and in constant flux. Headship and household composition shifted rapidly because marriages and death occurred at what must have been a dizzying pace" (McCaa 1994:10). Zhao (1994) has used genealogies from China from the thirteenth through the nineteenth centuries to show that high mortality kept most Chinese from actually living in a multigenerational family at any particular time, although, as in Mexico, the high death rate produced a complex form of the family because of shifting membership.

The bottom line here is that what we think of as the "traditional" family is, in fact, not very traditional at all. It depends on low mortality, which is a historically recent phenomenon, in combination with a fairly young structure, characterized by young adults with their children. This combination of demographic processes is found largely in the middle phase of the demographic transition, when mortality has dropped, but fertility is still above replacement level. Over time, as mortality remains low and fertility drops to low levels, the population ages, ... older married couples are left without children any longer in the household, and then women are left without husbands in the household. But, at younger ages, people are still marrying and having children, marrying and not having children, not marrying but having children, and neither marrying nor having children. All of those things are possible in a low-mortality, low-fertility society with a barrel-shaped age structure.

Given the fact that societies have historically changed in response to demographic conditions, it should be no surprise to you that since the end of World War II, with demographic conditions undergoing tremendous change all over the globe, the status of women is one of the facets of social organization undergoing a significant transition.

Gender Equity and the Empowerment of Women

The demographic transition does not inherently produce gender equity and the empowerment of women, but it creates the conditions under which they are much more likely to happen. The combination of longer life and lower fertility, even if achieved in an environment in which women are still oppressed, opens the eyes of society—including women themselves—to the fact that women are in a position to contribute to society in the same way that men do when not burdened by full-time parenting responsibility. And, as I have already mentioned, the fact that this combination of low mortality and low fertility typically occurs in an urban setting means that women have many more opportunities than would exist in rural areas to achieve the same kind of economic and social independence that has been largely the province of men for much of human history.

Let me suggest to you that at no time in human history has there been a good justification for the domination of women by men, but the demographic conditions that prevailed for most of human history did at least facilitate that domination. Demographic conditions no longer provide that prop and in most of the world, the impediment to full social, economic, and political empowerment of women is simply the attitude of men, often aided by women who have grown up as "codependents" in the system of male domination. At the beginning of the twentieth century, it would have been unthinkable for a woman in America to go out to dinner without being accompanied by a man, and equally unthinkable for her to drive one of the cars that were making their first appearance at that time. At the beginning of the twenty-first century, those things are still unthinkable to most women in Saudi Arabia, but just as demographic changes were occurring in the United States 100 years ago, so they are occurring in Saudi Arabia today.... The changes under way mean that the life chances for women are beginning to equal those of men, and thus women are in a position to voluntarily head their own household if they want to, or to do so successfully even if forced into that position. It is certainly no coincidence that those countries still in the earlier stages of the demographic transition are also those where the rights of women are most trampled. In Kenya and Tanzania, as in much of sub-Saharan Africa and South Asia, women's access to economic resources is restricted by severe limitations on their ability to inherit property and own land (World Bank 1999). In India, women's access to the formal labor market is restricted, and so women wind up in the informal sector, where they are far more likely to be economically exploited (Dunlop and Velkoff 1999).

Countries at the later stages of the demographic transition have generally discovered the benefits of unleashing the resources of the half of the population that had previously been excluded from full societal participation. Since 1979, the United Nations has been encouraging all countries to sign on to the Convention on the Elimination of All Forms of Discrimination Against Women (CEDAW) and as of 2004, 175 countries had ratified it, although the United States was not one of them at the time of this writing (United Nations Division for the Advancement of Women 2004). The empowerment of women contributes to further change in society by expanding women's life chances, which can expand economic opportunity and enrich society and households. All of these transformations contribute to the diversity of family and household structure. Let us now examine some of the direct proximate causes of the household structure transformation societies have been experiencing.

Proximate Determinants of Family and Household Changes

The increasing diversity in household structure is a result of several interdependent trends taking place in society (see, for example, United Nations Population Division 2003b). This is especially due to a delay in marriage, accompanied by young people leaving their parents' home (which in most more-developed nations has increased the incidence of cohabitation), and an increase in divorce (which also contributes to cohabitation); whereas at the older ages, the greater survivability of women over men has increased the incidence of widowhood, which has an obvious impact on family and household structure. In between the younger and older ages, the smaller number of children in each family means that a much shorter period of time in each parent's life is devoted to activities directly related to childbearing. The life course of the family has thus been revolutionized.

Delayed Marriage Accompanied by Leaving the Parental Nest

One of the most important mechanisms preventing women from achieving equality with men is early marriage. When a girl is encouraged or even forced to marry young age, she is likely to be immediately drawn into a life of

Table 1.2.1 Average Difference in Age of Brides and Grooms Declines as Percent of Women Married at Ages 15–19 Goes Down

% of women married at ages 15–19	Average difference in age between bride and groom	Number of countries
40 or higher	6.5	15
30–39	5.8	11
20–29	4.2	21
10–19	3.3	53
Less than 10	2.7	93
Total	4.5	193

Source: Calculated from data in United Nations Population Division, 2000, World Marriage Patterns, 2000 (New York: United Nations).

childbearing and family-building that makes it very difficult, if not impossible, for her to contemplate other options in life. This is one of the principal reasons why high fertility is so closely associated with low status for women. … You will not be surprised to notice that the highest percentage married at young ages occurs in those countries where fertility is highest and where the status of women is known to be low. By contrast, it is no coincidence that in the low-fertility regions of North America, Europe, Oceania, and Eastern Asia, the percentage of women who marry at young ages is very low and the status of women is higher than in other places in the world.

Even though women typically marry at young ages in high-fertility societies, men tend to be under less constraint on that score. This means that in those places where women are young when they marry, the chance is good that their husband is several years older. This further contributes to the ability of a man to dominate his spouse. "A girl with minimal education, raised to be submissive and subservient, married to an older man, has little ability to negotiate sexual activity, the number of children she will bear or how she spends her time" (Gupta 1998:22). The flip side of this is that a rising age at marriage in sub-Saharan Africa since the 1970s has had the beneficial side-effect of reducing the rate of polygynous marriages, which normally involve a young woman marrying an older man as his second or third wife—a situation that typically will diminish a woman's life chances (Chojnacka 2000).

Table 1.2.1 shows that as the percentage of women who are married at ages 15–19 goes up, the difference in age between husband and wife also increases. Thus, in those countries where less than 10 percent of women are married at ages 15–19, a man is on average 2.7 years older than the woman he marries. At the other end of the continuum, in those countries where 40 percent or more of women are married at ages 15–19, the average difference between bride and groom is 6.5 years. Although husbands tend to be older than their wives in the United States, data for the year 2000 show that 32 percent of married couples are within one year of each other, and in 12 percent of couples, the wife is older than the husband by at least two years (Fields 2001). An increasing body of evidence from Demographic and Health Surveys indicates that the age at marriage is on the rise in many developing countries, signaling a potential change in fertility, female empowerment, and family change in those parts of the world (Westoff 2003).

In the United States, as in many northern and western European countries, the early decline in fertility more than 100 years ago was accomplished especially by a delay in marriage. It is thus not too surprising that it was in these countries that some of the early feminist movements were able to take root. At a time when very few effective contraceptives were available, and when it was extremely difficult to get a divorce, postponement of marriage was the principal route by which women were able to increase their options in life. In 1890, more than one-third of all women aged 14 and older (34 percent) and close to one-half of all men (44 percent) were single in the United States. Between 1890 and 1960, being single became progressively less common as women, and especially men, married at earlier ages. Only since the 1960s has there been a resurgence of delayed marriage. By 2000, the

How Does the Age Transition Promote a Delay in Marriage?

In this chapter, I point out that the rise in the status of women in the United States and other industrialized nations has been aided by a series of long-term demographic events, but that a catalytic force such as the women's movement was necessary to unleash the power built into demographic forces. Ironically, many analysts (for example, Davis and van den Oever 1982; Heer and Grossbard-Schechtman 1981) have argued that the women's movement itself was triggered by one of the major demographic phenomena of the baby boom—the marriage squeeze. The marriage squeeze is "an evocative though imprecise term used to describe the effects of an imbalance between the number of males and females in the prime marriage ages" (Schoen 1983:61). It is a by-product of the combination of different-sized cohorts and the fact that women do not usually marry men their own age. The former is, of course, built into the age transition; whereas the latter is a remnant of tradition in most societies that doesn't serve any practical purpose.

... Although more boy babies are born than girl babies, higher male mortality evens the sex ratio by early adulthood. Thus a young woman expecting to marry someone her own age would have virtually a 100 percent chance of finding someone. However, in nearly every human society, women typically marry someone older than themselves. Now, if there are fewer older males, due to the facts that the number of births was lower prior to the woman's year of birth or the death rate was declining and each year there are more survivors per birth cohort than in the previous year, then her probability drops of finding someone of the usual marriageable age. Since men her own age may not be expecting to marry for another few years, she too may be forced to postpone marriage.

American and Canadian women, on average, marry a man who is two years older, and over time the vast majority of American women have preferred marriage (at least at some point in life) to remaining single. Assuming that people will continue to want to marry, the imbalance in the number of males or females can lead to a delay in marriage for the sex with excess numbers. This is exactly what has happened to women of the baby boom. In 1950, there were 98 men aged 22–26 for every 100 women two years younger (aged 20–24). Thus, there was near equality in the number of males and females of typical marriageable ages at that time. If we assume that women preferred men three years older than themselves (the age gap in 1950 was three years, which has since dropped to two), the ratio was even closer to equity. There were 99 men aged 23–27 in 1950 per 100 women aged 20–24. But that ratio dropped precipitously through the years as the pre-baby boom and baby boom cohorts reached marriage age, because in nearly every year from 1937–1957, there were more people born in the United States than in the previous year. Women looking at the age group two to three years older kept seeing fewer men than women of their own age. In 1960, there were only 84–86 men per women of the usual marriageable age, and in 1970 the ratio was in the 85–87 range. The result was that many women were forced to postpone marriage, a phenomenon I discussed in this chapter that has also been well documented for Canada (Foot 1996).

By 1980, relative equity had been achieved again in the sex ratio at the usual marriage ages, but by that time some remarkable changes had already taken place in American gender roles. "The Women's Liberation Movement may be interpreted, on the one hand, as a collective means by which women helped themselves to reorient each other to the new lower compensation for the traditional female role and, on the other, as the means by which the increasing number of women outside of the traditional wife-mother role sought to combat the discrimination meted out to women in the job world" (Heer and Grossbard-Schechtman 1981:49). Either interpretation can be viewed as women's responses to demographic forces at work in the marriage market (Grossbard-Schechtman 1985; 1993). In the late 1980s and early 1990s, North American males were experiencing a marriage squeeze as the declining number of births through the 1960s and early 1970s produced a dearth of women of the usual marriage age. This led to a better bargaining position for women in the marriage market, and almost certainly helped in some measure to improve gender equality.

Guttentag and Secord (1983) used the concept of sex ratio to develop a theory of gender relations, based on Becker's new household economics theory. In general, their hypothesis was that a shortage of women relative to men encourages domesticity, marital stability, and a maintenance of male dominance over women. Conversely, a low sex ratio (more women than men) encourages women to find alternatives to traditional role models, since there are too few men of marriageable age. Guttentag and Secord used nineteenth-century America as an example. On the frontier, the sex ratio was high and female roles were typically very traditional, with an emphasis on family building and family life. At the same time, the New England states had a much lower sex ratio and it was in that part of the country, perhaps not coincidentally, that the suffrage movement began.

African-Americans have for several decades had a sex ratio lower than that of whites because of higher male mortality from birth on. The sex ratio has been further lowered because of the higher proportion of black than white males in prison. Guttentag and Secord argued that this low sex ratio led to greater independence among black women and to lower marital stability as well, because a relative surplus of women allows men to be choosier and thus more assertive.

It is probably dangerous to be too deterministic with respect to demography, but there can be little question that as long as age differences in marriage exist between men and women, then the changing size of cohorts in the context of the age transition will upset the previous ratios and force changes in behavior. Bhrolchain (2001) has noted quite correctly that most marriage squeezes could be readily alleviated by greater flexibility in the ages at which people marry. In the main, this would mean that the age of wives and husbands would converge, which has been the pattern in North America and the United States. To do that, however, requires that men be willing to give up some of the marital power that seems to accrue to the older partner in a relationship, and that in itself would be clear evidence of a move toward greater gender equality.

In the 1980s, Schoen (1983) noted that a number of developing countries were increasingly beginning to experience marriage squeezes resulting from the declines in infant mortality since the end of World War II that have produced a demographic effect very similar to the American baby boom. The relative scarcity of husbands for women, produced by the age transition, is almost certainly one of the reasons for delays in marriage in almost every less-developed nation. In societies that allow polygamous marriages, such a situation could have been dealt with in the past by forcing a woman to become the second or higher-order wife of an already married man. However, other changes taking place in the world, especially including international efforts to improve the status of women, are helping change the way women are likely to perceive the marriage situation. Part of the international message is that a delay in marriage is crucial for women to avoid the oppression of early motherhood, as well as male domination.

In India, where the status of women remains low by international standards, a marriage squeeze as described by Schoen has been implicated as a factor that forces families to use ever more of their limited resources for a dowry in order to marry their daughters in an increasingly competitive marriage market (Rao 1993). Goodkind (1997) has even discovered what he calls a "double marriage squeeze" for the Vietnamese. In Vietnam, the combination of population change, war, and excess male migration produced a shortage of men and thus a marriage squeeze for females, leading to a rise in the age at marriage and a decrease in the marriage rate. At the same time, the male migrants who left the country faced an overseas marriage squeeze because there are not enough overseas Vietnamese women to go around, so the men, too, have had to delay or forego marriage.

Overall, then, the lesson is one that I have repeated throughout the book, which is that almost everything of consequence in the social world has an important demographic component, and that to understand how the world is really working we must comprehend the demographic forces that quietly, but impressively, shape our lives.

average (median) age at marriage for females had risen to 25.1, the highest level in U.S. history, while for males it had increased to 26.8, also higher than the level of 1890 (Fields 2001). In fact, in 2000, 39 percent of all American women aged 25–29 were still single, compared with only 11 percent in 1970, and 52 percent of all men of that age had not yet married, a huge increase from only 19 percent in 1970. Changes in the popularity of early marriage have been roughly similar for both African-Americans and whites, although African-Americans have been more likely than whites to delay marriage or remain single (McLanahan and Casper 1995).

Since the 1960s, the slowdown of economic growth, accompanied by stiff competition for jobs brought about by baby boom children growing up, has made it more advantageous for couples to postpone marriage to take maximum advantage of educational and career opportunities. And, very importantly, the contraceptive revolution, especially the birth control pill, has allowed people to disconnect marriage from sexual intercourse. People have known about and used birth control methods for a long time. However, the failure rate of all of those prepill methods was significantly higher than that of the pill, and a couple engaging in intercourse ran a clear risk of an unintended pregnancy. Prior to 1973 and the legalization of abortion in the United States, an American woman could end an unintended pregnancy only by flying to a country such as Sweden, where abortion was legal, or by seeking an illegal (and often dangerous) abortion.

In more traditional societies (including the United States and Canada until the 1960s), an unintended pregnancy was most apt to lead to marriage, although a woman might also bear the child quietly and give it up for adoption. Illegitimacy was widely stigmatized and having a child out of wedlock was the course of last resort. Marriage was the only genuinely acceptable route to regular sexual activity, and only married couples were routinely granted access to available methods of birth control. That situation still prevails in most of the world's predominantly Muslim nations.

In the late nineteenth century, the older age at marriage already alluded to in North America and Europe had been accomplished by a delay in the onset of regular sexual activity—the Malthusian approach to life. Intercourse was delayed until marriage, and in this way nuptiality was the main determinant of the birth rate: Early marriage meant a higher birth rate, and delayed marriage meant a lower one (Wrigley and Schofield 1981). A variety of social and economic conditions might discourage an early marriage. The societal expectation that a man should be able to provide economic support for his wife and children tended to delay marriage for men until those expectations could be met. Under conditions of rising material expectations, as was the case in the late nineteenth century, marriage had to be delayed even a bit longer than in previous generations because the bar had been raised higher than before. Delayed marriage typically meant that young people stayed with their parents in order to save enough money to get ahead financially and thus be able to afford marriage. Staying with parents also minimized the opportunities for younger people to be able to engage in premarital sexual intercourse, which might lead to an unintended pregnancy and destroy plans for the future. Thus, prior to the latter half of the twentieth century, delayed marriage did not typically lead younger people to leave home and set up their own independent household prior to marriage.

In the early post-World War II period, economic robustness allowed a young person to leave the parental home at an earlier age without an economic penalty and, since the risk of pregnancy meant that intercourse was still tied closely to marriage, the age at marriage reached historic lows in the United States and Europe. In discussing the situation in Germany, Blossfeld and de Rose (1992) have argued that "until the late 1960s, the opportunity for children to leave their parental home had increased remarkably because of the improvement of economic conditions. But the social norm that they had to be married if they wanted to live together with a partner of the opposite sex was still valid, so that age at entry into marriage was decreasing until the end of the 1960s." Similar arguments could be made for the United States and for other European countries, with the exceptions of Italy and Spain, where out-of-wedlock births still tend to be socially unacceptable, so a delay in marriage has meant lower fertility than in other European countries because women are not compensating for delaying marriage by having children outside of marriage. In southern Europe, women may also be reluctant to marry and have children because employment opportunities are more fragile than in other parts of Europe and once they leave the labor force to have a child they find it difficult to return (Adsera 2004).

Modern contraception has allowed sex to be disconnected from marriage and this has been accompanied by a dramatic rise in the fraction of young people who leave their parental home before marriage, even while delaying marriage. In 1940, 82 percent of unmarried males and females aged 18–24 lived with their parents (Goldscheider and Goldscheider 1993); by 2000, that had declined to only 42 percent for women and 56 percent for men (Fields 2001). "By the 1980s, leaving home before marriage had evidently become institutionalized in the United States" (Goldscheider and Goldscheider 1993:34). Goldscheider and Goldscheider (1994) analyzed data from the National Survey of Families and Households to show that until the early 1960s, the majority of women who left home after age 18 were doing so to get married. That pattern changed in the 1960s, and by the late 1980s, only one-third of women were leaving home to marry. Men, however, have been leaving home for reasons other than marriage for a long time. So, the recent delay in marriage and nest-leaving behavior has been more significant as a force of change for women than for men.

You may have asked yourself how the data on increasing independence of young people can square with the wide array of stories about these same people returning home to live with their parents. The answer is that as the fraction of young people who leave home to live independently increases, the absolute volume of people available to move back in with parents increases. Children graduating from college and those returning from the military are especially likely to return home for a short while, whereas those who left home to marry are the least likely to return home (Goldscheider and Goldscheider 1999), Nonetheless, because children do not necessarily return for very long, a snapshot photo of society (such as the census or a survey) does not capture many young people who have returned home, even though a fairly high percentage may do so at some time or another. Data from Canada show that from 1981 to 1996 the percentage of young people remaining in their parents' home increased (Boyd and Norris 2000), but even this is consistent with the fact that delayed marriage increases the options available to young people and allows both an increase in leaving home for reasons other than marriage and an increase in staying in or returning to their parental home.

Cohabitation

The delay in marriage has not necessarily meant that young people have been avoiding a familylike situation, nor that they have necessarily avoided having children out of wedlock. When leaving the parental home, young people may set up an independent household either by living alone or sharing a household with nonfamily members, or they may move into nonhousehold group quarters such as a college dormitory. From these vantage points, many then proceed to *cohabitation*, which can be defined as the sharing of a household by unmarried persons who have a sexual relationship (Cherlin 1999). As this trend was unfolding in the 1970s, the Census Bureau created estimates of its extent from data on household composition. The resulting measure was "partners of the opposite sex sharing living quarters," which became widely known as POSSLQ (pronounced "PA-sul-cue"). As the measure has been refined based on more direct questions about unmarried partners, researchers have found that this was, in fact, a pretty good measure, although it probably underestimated cohabiting couples with children (Casper and Cohen 2000).

In 1970, when the average age at marriage for women was 20.3, there were about 500,000 cohabiting couples in the United States, and the ratio of cohabiting to married couples was 1 to 100. By 2000, when the average age at marriage for women had climbed to 25.1, the number of cohabiting couples had increased to 3.8 million and the ratio of cohabiting to married couples also had jumped to 6 per 100 (Fields 2001). That number almost certainly underestimated the importance of cohabitation, however, because it has become a widely accepted part of the life course in many low-fertility societies. Rather than being an alternative to marriage (a "poor person's marriage"), it has become a stepping-stone to marriage for many, as well as a step back from marriage after a divorce for others. Although only a small fraction of couples are cohabiting at any one time, the data for the United States suggest that nearly half of all people under age 35 have cohabited at least once, usually for a fairly short period of time (Graefe and Lichter 1999). Survey data from France suggest that in 1965 only 8 percent of couples cohabited before marriage, but by 1995 that figure had jumped to 90 percent (Toulemon 1997).

The desire to have children may determine the timing of formal marriage for cohabiting couples, although in many instances the birth of the child may precede the marriage. Bumpass and Lu (2000) have estimated that half of the out-of-wedlock births in the United States are born to cohabiting couples. Nonetheless, cohabiting couples seem to have lower levels of fertility than married couples and, once married, couples who had cohabited prior to marriage appear to follow essentially the same pattern of family building as couples who had not cohabited (Manning 1995).

Out-of-Wedlock Births

Given the delay in marriage, which has been accompanied by high rates of premarital sexual activity (aided by the fact that young people have been getting out of the parental home before marriage), it should not be surprising that the United States and some of the other low-fertility nations have been experiencing an increase in the proportion of out-of-wedlock births. This is an event, of course, that immediately transforms a woman living alone, or an unmarried couple living together, from a nonfamily to a family household. In France, the percentage of births outside marriage increased from 6 percent in 1965 to 40 percent in 1998 (Munoz-Perez and Prioux 2000). Between 1970 and 2002, the proportion of babies in the United States who were born out-of-wedlock increased from 11 percent to 34 percent, according to data from live birth records (Martin et al. 2003; National Center for Health Statistics 1994).

Data from the Current Population Survey provide a broader portrait of the women who are bearing a child out-of-wedlock, as shown in Figure 1.2.3. You can see that 89 percent of births to women aged 15–19 in 2002 were born out-of-wedlock, and the fraction drops rapidly with increasing age. To be sure, when you get above the average age at marriage, almost all births are to married women. Among younger women, the nonuse of contraception and lack of local access to abortion may push up the likelihood of young women getting pregnant and bearing a child. The United States is more restrictive than most low-fertility societies are in providing teenagers with easy and inexpensive access to methods of fertility limitation. Prior to the 1970s, most young women conceiving out-of-wedlock would have married prior to the baby's birth (Bachu 1999), and so the illegitimacy ratio (the

Figure 1.2.3 Profile of Women Bearing Children Out-of-Wedlock in U.S.

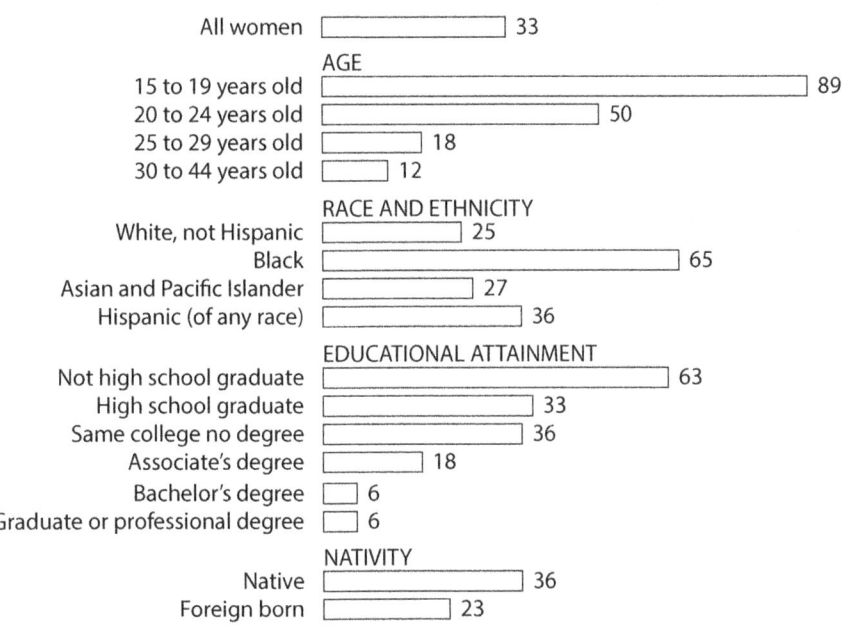

Source: Barbara Downs, "Fertility of American Women: June 2002," Current Population Reports, P20–548: Figure 1.

ratio of out-of-wedlock births to all births) would have been much lower, even with the same level of premarital conceptions. Of course, the odds were also very high that the marriage would have ended in divorce after only a few years, so neither scenario is particularly rosy for the mother and her baby.

A disproportionate share of younger women bearing children out-of-wedlock are African American. Since birth rates overall are nearly as low for blacks as they are for whites in the United States, the proportion of out-of-wedlock births represents a different pattern of parenting, not a different overall level of childbearing. The pattern is to have children at a younger age than the rest of the population, and then to stop having them at a younger age as well. Thus, in 2002, the age-specific birth rates for black women were quite a bit higher than for whites at ages younger than 25, but then lower than for whites at ages 25 and higher (Martin et al. 2003). It is not clear why this pattern exists, but even in the 1930s, when only 6 percent of white women in the United States were having a baby out-of-wedlock, the percentage among blacks was 31 (Bachu 1999).

Regardless of the reasons, the data suggest that only 15 percent of black mothers raise their children in an intact two-parent family, compared with 60 percent of non-Hispanic white mothers (Rendell 2000). Furthermore, it is not just that the children are born outside of marriage; the fact that 22 percent of black children are born to teenage mothers (compared to 11 percent of whites) negatively affects their life chances. Even in Sweden, childbearing in adolescence disadvantages both the mother and child in later life (Olausson et al. 2001).

These data have fueled enormous public debate about the social cost of out-of-wedlock births (measured monetarily by welfare benefits and socioculturally by the deprivations suffered by fatherless children) and they have been interpreted as signs of imminent cultural decay. But, as McLanahan and Casper (1995) point out, the situation is not quite what it seems:

> The increase in the illegitimacy ratio between 1960 and 1975 was due to two factors: the decline in the fertility of married women and the delaying of marriage. But not to an increasing birth rate among unmarried women. Beginning in the mid-1970s, marital fertility rates stopped declining, nonmarital fertility rates began to rise, and the age at first marriage continued to rise. After 1975, the rise in the illegitimacy ratio was due to increases in nonmarital fertility as well as to increases in the number of women at risk of having a nonmarital birth.

Although in the past few years the probability has increased that an unmarried woman will bear a child, part of the rise in the illegitimacy ratio was actually because married women were having fewer or no children, thus tilting the ratio of births in the direction of those born out-of-wedlock.

Childlessness

About 10 percent of couples may remain childless because of impaired fecundity.... In the 1970s, data from the Current Population Survey suggested that, in fact, this percentage of women (10 percent) was reaching ages 40–44 without having had a child. Since then, however, the percentage has slowly but steadily increased to 18 percent by 2002 (Downs 2003). Many of these women have decided that they did not want to have any children Some fraction of them probably "drifted" toward childlessness by continually postponing the first child, since we know that most reproductive decisions, in both high- and low-fertility societies, are made sequentially from one birth to the next (Morgan 1996). This also means that some women who start out in life thinking that they do not want to have children wind up later changing their mind.

An important consequence of gender equality is that there is less pressure on a woman to have children, even if she is married, particularly if she has a rewarding career that she doesn't want to interrupt or, as certainly happens in some cases, she and her husband simply prefer a life without children. Childlessness increases household diversity by increasing the percentage of households represented either by someone living alone, or a married couple with no children of their own, or a cohabiting couple with no children, or a multiple-person nonfamily household.

Divorce

Not only has marriage been increasingly pushed to a later age, but once accomplished, marriages are also more likely to end in divorce than at any previous time in history (Schoen and Weinick 1993). This trend reflects many things. An obvious reason is that changes in divorce laws since the 1970s have made it easier for either partner to end the marriage at any time for any reason (Waite 2000). Friedberg (1998) concluded that divorce laws alone can explain about 17 percent of divorces in the United States. For the other 83 percent of the explanation, we can start by asking ourselves why legislators were motivated to make those changes; for answers, we can look to the loosening hold of men over women and the longer lives we are leading, both of which may produce greater conflict within marriage. In 1857 in the United States, there was only a 27 percent chance that a husband aged 25 and a wife aged 22 would both still be alive when the wife reached 65, but for couples marrying in the early twenty-first century, the chances have rocketed to 60 percent. Conversely, only about 5 percent of marriages contracted in 1867 ended in divorce (Ruggles 1997), whereas it has been estimated that about half of the marriages contracted since the 1970s will end in divorce (Kreider and Fields 2002; Raley and Bumpass 2003).

The United States is certainly not unique in experiencing an increase in divorce probabilities. Goode (1993) compiled data showing that throughout Europe the percentage of marriages ending in divorce virtually doubled between 1970 and the mid-1980s. For example, in Germany in 1970, it was estimated that 16 percent of marriages would end in divorce, increasing to 30 percent in 1985. In France, the increase went from 12 percent to 31 percent during that same time period. Australia has experienced similar trends (Bracher et al. 1993).

Cherlin (1999) summarizes the major risk factors for divorce as including low income for the couple (which causes stresses and tension), early age at marriage (which often means a poorer job of choosing a spouse), spouse's similarity (known as *homogamy*, referring to the fact that people who are more similar to one another are more likely to get along with each other or, conversely, those who are less similar will be more likely to divorce), parental divorce (the "copy-cat" phenomenon, in which people whose parents divorced are more likely themselves to divorce), and cohabitation. Given the previous discussion of cohabitation, it is of some interest to note that, contrary to popular belief in the value of "trial" marriage, cohabitation before marriage appears to be one of the factors that increases the odds of a marriage ending in divorce, at least in North America. Several studies have suggested that cohabitation is selective of people who are mistrustful of marriage, probably because of their own "social inheritance of divorce" (Diekmann and Englehardt 1999). If cohabitation leads to marriage among these people, they may thus be more prone to end that marriage by divorce (Axinn and Thornton 1992; Hall and Zhao 1995).

Many marriages that in earlier days would have been dissolved by death are now dissolved by divorce. This seems apparent from the fact that the annual combined rate of marital dissolution from both the death of one spouse and divorce remained remarkably constant for more than a century. The overall rate of marital dissolution was essentially unchanged between 1860 and 1970 (Davis 1972a). As widowhood declined, divorce rose proportionately. Only with the rapid increase in divorce during the 1970s did that pattern begin to diverge. So dramatic was the rise in divorce in the 1970s that in the mid-1960s the elimination of divorce would have added an additional 6.7 years to the average marriage, whereas by the mid-1970s its elimination would have added 17.2 years (Goldman 1984).

Widowhood

As death has receded to older ages, the incidence of widowhood has steadily been pushed to older years as well. Divorce is a more important cause of not being married than is widowhood up to age 65, beyond which widowhood increases geometrically because of the higher death rate of men, undoubtedly compounded by the tendency of divorced women to change their status to widow upon the death of a former husband. As is true with so many social facts in the United States, African-American women are disadvantaged compared to whites in terms of marital status. At every age, blacks are more likely to be either divorced or widowed.

The Combination of These Determinants

As the demographic transition unfolds, then, we are finding that people are waiting longer to marry and when they do marry, their marriage is more likely to end in divorce than in widowhood. Schoen and Weinick (1993) used life table methodology to try to quantify the relative importance of these changes in family demography. Their results showed, for example, that between 1970 and 1988, the proportion of women surviving to age 15 who could expect ever to marry declined from 96 percent to 88 percent. At the same time, the average age at marriage was increasing, the percentage of marriages ending in divorce was increasing, and the percentage of marriages ending in widowhood was declining. Furthermore, as life expectancy increases while the average duration of a marriage shortens, and the percentage of divorced people remarrying goes down, the percentage of a person's life spent being married declines, thus adding to the individual diversity of household types in which a person might live during an entire lifetime.

Having described the principal features of the transformation of families and households in industrialized societies, let us see how they have been influenced by changing life chances and how, in turn, life chances interact with family formation and household structure.

Changing Life Chances

The leading explanations for the shift in household structure in Western nations combine elements of the demographic transition perspective with the life course perspective. The demographic transition perspective relates changing demographic conditions (especially declining mortality, declining fertility, and urbanization) to the rise in women's status. This was aided especially by increasing age at marriage, which encouraged higher levels of educational attainment. In turn, this has increased a woman's ability to enter the labor force and earn sufficient income to have the economic and social freedom to choose her own pattern of living. As these changes have unfolded, women's differing life chances have contributed to the transformation of families and households. Again, I emphasize that these demographic conditions are probably necessary, but not sufficient, to initiate the current rise in the status of women in industrialized societies. What is also required is some change in circumstance to act as a catalyst for the underlying demographic factors. This is where the life course perspective is drawn on, because women who have grown up in a different demographic and social milieu, and thus see the world differently than did earlier generations of women, have the potential to generate change in society. It is easy to know where to begin the discussion of changes in life chances, because nothing is more important than education.

Education

Becoming educated is probably the most dramatic and significant change you can introduce into your life. It is the locomotive that drives much of the world's economic development and it is a vehicle for personal success used by generation after generation of people in the highly developed nations of the world. Still, the relative recency with which advanced education has taken root in American society can be seen in Table 1.2.2. In 1940, less than one in four Americans aged 25 or older had graduated from high school, although women were more likely than men to have done so. Slightly more than 5 percent of men and less than 4 percent of women were college graduates. You can see that the median number of years of education was 8.6 for men and 8.7 for women. A historically short six decades later, in 2000, 84 percent of both men and women were high school graduates and about one in four Americans had graduated from college—with men still being more likely than women to be in that category.

If we look at the youngest ages, we can get a better sense of the most recent trends. Among people aged 25–34 in 2000, 89 percent of women were high school graduates compared to 87 percent of men, and 30 percent of women were college graduates, compared to 29 percent of men. In Canada in 1996, among people aged 20–44,

Table 1.2.2 U.S. Educational Attainment Has Increased Significantly Over Time

	Male			Female		
Year	% High School Graduate Or More	% College Graduate	Median Years of Education	% High School Graduate Or More	% College Graduate	Median Years of Education
2000	84.2	27.8	13.2	84.0	23.6	13.0
1990	77.7	24.4	12.8	77.5	18.4	12.7
1980	69.2	20.9	12.6	68.1	13.6	12.4
1970	55.0	14.1	12.2	55.4	8.2	12.1
1960	39.4	9.6	10.3	42.5	5.8	10.9
1950	31.5	7.1	9.0	35.1	5.0	9.6
1940	22.3	5.4	8.6	25.9	3.7	8.7

Sources: Data for 1940 to 1990 are from U.S. Census Bureau, 2000, Educational Attainment Historical Table A-1 (http://www.census.gov, accessed 2001); data for 2000 are from U.S. Census Bureau, 2000, Educational Attainment of the Population 15 Years and Over, by Marital Status, Age, Sex, Race, and Hispanic Origin; March 2000, Table 3. Median year calculations for 2000 are by the author.

76 percent of men and 79 percent of women were high school graduates, while 19 percent of men and 20 percent of women were college graduates. Thus, gender equality exists in education in Canada as in the U.S., although educational levels are not quite as high in Canada. From the 2000 census in Mexico, we have data on the median number of years of school completed and the data show an average of 7.8 for men and 7.3 for women—levels below those that prevailed in the U.S. in 1940.

The world as a whole has been experiencing an increasing equalization of education among males and females—an important component in raising the global status of women. The ratio of females per males attending secondary school has been steadily increasing worldwide from since at least the 1970s, according to World Bank estimates. In some areas of the world, such as North America and Europe, women have already achieved parity with men, or are even more likely than men to be enrolled in secondary school (the pattern in central and eastern Europe). In sub-Saharan Africa and south Asia, as well as in northern Africa and western Asia, where the status of women has been notably low and where education for girls continues to lag behind that of boys, there have nonetheless been notable improvements in the ratio of girls to boys attending school. These trends will affect the world early in the twenty-first century as the gender gap is closed in education, Fargues (1995) has noted that in the middle of the twentieth century, most of the countries of northern Africa and western Asia had gender equity with respect to education in the sense that most people—males and females alike—were illiterate. Education was extended first to young men, creating for a while both a gender and a generation gap in education. Now, by the beginning of this century, as more generations of children have been educated, and as education has been offered to girls as well as boys, both of those gaps are closing and this could help accelerate the process of social and economic development.

The comments about closing the gap should not be taken to mean that we have arrived at gender equity in education everywhere on the planet. Table 1.2.3 lists the 30 countries in the world (representing 29 percent of the world's population) in which illiteracy among young women (aged 15–24) was at least 10 percentage points higher than for males that age as of 2001. Thus, in Yemen, a western Asian nation (just south of Saudi Arabia) of 20 million people, 16 percent of men aged 15–24 are unable to read or write, compared to 51 percent of women that age, for a difference of 35 percentage points. Yemen is tied with Benin, a western African nation of nearly seven million

Table 1.2.3 World Educational "Hot Spots": Countries Where Illiteracy Rate Among Young (Aged 15–24) Women is at Least 10 Percentage Points Higher Than for Young Men, 2001

Country	Region	Population	Youth (15–24 illiteracy) 2001 Boys	Girls	Excess Illiteracy of Girls
Yemen	Western Asia	20,010	16	51	35
Benin	Western Africa	6,736	28	63	35
Nepal	South Central Asia	25,164	23	56	33
Liberia	Western Africa	3,367	14	46	32
Iraq	Western Asia	25,175	40	70	30
Pakistan	South Central Asia	153,578	28	57	29
Guinea-Bissau	Western Africa	1,493	26	54	28
Mozambique	Eastern Africa	18,863	24	52	28
Togo	Western Africa	4,909	12	35	23
Burkina Faso	Western Africa	13,002	53	75	22
Mali	Western Africa	13,007	52	74	22
Eritrea	Eastern Africa	4,141	19	39	20
Niger	Western Africa	11,972	67	86	19
Malawi	Eastern Africa	12,105	19	38	19
Côte d'Ivoire	Western Africa	16,631	29	46	17
Senegal	Western Africa	10,095	40	57	17
Bangladesh	South Central Asia	146,736	43	60	17
Morocco	Northern Africa	30,566	23	40	17
Georgia	Western Asia	5,126	33	49	16
Syrian Arab Republic	Western Asia	17,800	4	20	16
Mauritania	Western Africa	2,893	43	59	16
Central African Republic	Middle Africa	3,865	23	39	16
India	South Central Asia	1,065,462	20	34	14
Lao People's Democratic Republic	Southeastern Asia	5,657	15	28	13
Egypt	Northern Africa	71,931	23	36	13
Chad	Middle Africa	8,598	25	38	13
Uganda	Eastern Africa	25,827	14	27	13
Guatemala	Central America	12,347	14	27	13
Ethiopia	Eastern Africa	70,678	38	50	12
Sudan	Northern Africa	33,610	17	27	10

Source: World Bank, *World Development Indicators 2003* (Washington, DC: World Bank Group).

people, for this "honor" of lowest level of gender equity with respect to literacy. Twenty of the 30 countries are on the African continent, nine are in Asia, and one (Guatemala) is in Central America.

Our interest in education lies especially in the fact that by altering your world view, education tends to influence nearly every aspect of your demographic behavior and outcomes. ... Data from censuses and from sources such as the Demographic and Health Surveys show that nearly anywhere you go in the world, the more educated a woman is, the fewer children she will have. Not that education is inherently antinatalist; rather, it opens, up new vistas—new opportunities and alternative approaches to life, other than simply building a family—and in so doing, it delays the onset of childbearing, which is a crucial factor in setting the tone for subsequent fertility (Marini 1984; Rindfuss, Morgan, and Offutt 1996). So, education tends to lower fertility, or to keep it lower than it might otherwise be, and this contributes to the variety of household and family structures we will see.

The fact that education alters the way you view the world also has implications for the marriage market in the United States. For much of American history, a major concern in choosing a marriage partner was to pick someone who shared your religious background (social scientists call this "religious homogamy"). Over time, however, the salience of religion has given way to "educational homogamy" people want to marry someone with similar amounts of education, and so education has been replacing religion as an important factor in spouse selection (Kalmijr 1991; Mare 1991; Smits, Ultee, and Lammers 1998).

The greater proportion of people going to college has altered the lifestyles of many young Americans. It has been accompanied by delayed marriage, delayed and a diminished amount of childbearing, and, consequently, higher per-person income among young adult householders. Young people today have more personal disposable income than any previous generation. In 2002, women consistently earned less than men, but for both men and women, the data in Table 1.2.4 show that those with a postgraduate degree were earning more than twice as much per year as those who were only high school graduates. This has become known as the "college premium," and its existence has almost certainly contributed to increased education (investment in human capital) and increased economic productivity. However, for the investment in education to pay off for people, households, and society more generally, it must lead to higher levels of labor force participation and more productive occupations. Let us examine these aspects of your life chances.

Table 1.2.4 Better-Educated Workers Have Higher Incomes

Year-Round Full-Time Workers Aged 25+		Males	Females	Ratio of Female Income to Male income
Total		$41,616	$31,356	0.75
High School	Not high school graduate	$24,364	$18,096	0.74
	Graduate	$34,723	$25,302	0.73
College	Some college, no degree	$41,045	$30,418	0.74
	Associate's degree	$42,776	$32,152	0.75
	Bachelor's degree	$55,929	$40,994	0.73
	Master's degree	$70,898	$50,668	0.71
	Professional degree	$100,000	$61,747	0.62
	Doctorate degree	$86,965	$62,122	0.71

Source: Adapted from U.S. Census Bureau, 2003, "Educational Attainment in the United States, March 2002, Detailed Tables," Table 8.

Labor Force Participation

As education increases, so does the chance of being in the labor force. Among both males and females in the United States in 2000, the higher the level of education attainment among people aged 25 and older, the higher the percentage of people who were currently in the labor force. Women are less likely than men to be in the labor force at any given level of education, but it is nonetheless true that the pattern over time has been for women to be working more, and men to be working less. Prior to the 1970s, for example, women who worked typically did so only before they married or became pregnant. Thus, the labor force participation rates by age peaked in the early 20s and declined after that. That is still a common pattern in many less-developed countries, but it no longer characterizes women in the more-developed nations; labor force participation rates by age are now very similar for males and females.

Keep in mind as we talk about labor force participation rates that most countries include unemployed persons as being in the labor force. Thus, if you are looking for work, even though you are not actually working or even if you have never before held a job, you are considered to be in the labor force. Unemployment rates are strongly related to age—the older the age, the lower the rate. At younger ages, considerable numbers of people are looking for work even if they haven't found it yet, whereas at older ages, people are more likely to give up on employment and seek a retirement pension as soon as it is available if they experience difficulty finding a job. Women also tend to have lower unemployment rates than men.

By far the biggest gain in employment over the past few decades has been the movement of baby boom women, especially married women, into the labor market. They literally burst their way into the workforce in the 1970s, and by 2000, 78 percent of women aged 35–54 (the baby boomers) had a job. In 1960, just before the baby boomers came of age, labor force participation rates among married women in the United States were well below those for single women at every age from 20 through 64. By 1970, as the first wave of baby boomers had reached adulthood, the rates for married women were clearly on the rise, and by 2000 they had nearly reached those of single women.

Female Labor Force Participation and Fertility

Working, as I have mentioned before, cuts down on fertility under normal circumstances. It is certainly no coincidence that the birth rate in the United States began to drop at about the same time that labor force participation rates for married women began to rise. Even in 2002, when fertility was generally very low, it was still true that those who were in the labor force had slightly fewer children than those who were not (Downs 2003). Some of that difference is due to the fact that working women, even those currently married, are more likely to be childless than women who are not in the labor force. Overall, the highest levels of fertility in the United States are found among poor women who do not work, whereas the lowest levels of fertility are among those who do work and are well paid.

The ability of married women to work helps bring fertility down and maintain it at low levels, but … it can also help keep fertility from dropping to below-replacement levels. When women are able to combine having a family, even if small, and a career, they are more likely to choose both. But, in European countries such as Italy and Spain, where family values discourage that combination, women seem to choose in favor of career over family, contributing to very low levels of fertility. The pattern that has emerged in more-developed countries is that a high proportion of women work before marriage, remain working after marriage, and adjust their fertility downward to accommodate their working. How far down they adjust may depend on how much familial and societal support they receive in making that accommodation. If child care is readily available and if husbands share domestic chores, we may well expect that fertility will be slightly higher than if a woman is expected to shoulder all of those burdens.

In Mexico, an increase in labor force participation has accompanied a decline in fertility, as we would expect. In 1979, when the total fertility rate in Mexico was 5.0, only 21.5 percent of women were in the labor force; by the mid-1990s, total fertility had dropped to 3.4 and female labor force participation had climbed to 31.4 percent (Fleck and Sorrentino 1994). It is unlikely that one directly caused the other; rather, each change helped stimulate the other. An initial decline in fertility, for example, may lead to a small increase in the percentage of women in the labor force, which may encourage other women to limit fertility, which may promote other opportunities in the labor force. Each event cumulatively causes the other, and when two things occur together, it is difficult to sort out cause and effect.

In a similar vein, a study of two seemingly different villages in India revealed that in the village where women were employed rolling cigarettes for a local contractor, the employment gave women, very serendipitously, substantial autonomy and increased their use of contraception. In another village without employment opportunities, the researchers expected to find that contraceptive use had remained low. Yet, in that village, the time spent not working had been spent instead on additional education for women and that, it seems, had increased contraceptive use (Dharmalingam and Morgan 1996). There are multiple and cumulative paths to low fertility and to improved social situations for women.

We have already discussed the new household economics as an approach to explaining why fertility is kept low in developed societies and why households might encourage family members to migrate. Now, we can call on it again to explain why the rise in the status of women and increased female labor force participation might generate the household transformations we have been reviewing in this chapter. The basic idea is that "the rises in women's employment opportunities and earning power have reduced the benefits of marriage and made divorce and single life more attractive. While marriage still offers women the benefits associated with sharing income and household costs with spouses, for some women these benefits do not outweigh other costs, whatever these may be" (McLanahan and Casper 1995:33).

Female Labor Force Participation and Empowerment

In most social systems, people who can take care of themselves and have enough money to be self-reliant have higher status and greater freedom than those who depend economically on others. Further, a pecking order tends to exist among those who are economically independent, with higher incomes being associated with higher status than are low incomes. Being independent, though, is definitely the starting point, and an increasing number of women in the world are arriving at that point. However much you might take for granted the fact that in a rich nation women are as readily employable in the paid labor force as men, it is actually a rather recent phenomenon.

Although mortality and fertility have been declining since the nineteenth century in the United States and urbanization has been occurring throughout that time, it was during World War II that the particular combination of demographic and economic circumstances arose to provide the leading edge of a shift toward labor force equality of males and females. The demand for armaments and other goods of war in the early 1940s came at the same time that men were moving out of civilian jobs into the military, and there was an increasing demand for civilian labor of almost every type. Earlier in American history, the demand for labor would have been met by foreign workers migrating into the country, but the immigration Act passed in the 1920s had set up national quotas that severely limited immigration. The only quotas large enough to have made a difference were those for immigrants from countries also involved in the war and thus not a potential source of labor.

With neither males nor immigrants to meet the labor demand, women were called into the labor force, indeed, not just women per se, but more significantly, married women, and even more specifically, married women with children. Single women had been consistently employable and employed since at least the beginning of the century, as each year 45–50 percent of them had been economically active, as I pointed out earlier. But in the early 1940s, there were not enough young single women to meet labor needs, partly because the improved economy was also making it easier for young couples to get married and start a family. It was older women, past their childbearing years, who were particularly responsive to making up the deficit in the labor force (Oppenheimer 1967; Oppenheimer 1994).

These were the women who broke new ground in female employment in America, with the biggest increase in labor force participation between 1940 and 1950 coming from women aged 45 to 54, and because more than 92 percent of those women were married, this obviously represented a break with the past. Who were these women? They were the mothers of the Depression, mothers who had sacrificed the larger families they wanted to scrape by during one of America's worst economic crises. They were women who had smaller families than their mothers and thus were more easily able to participate in the labor force. However, the ideal family size remained more than three children, and the improved economy permitted the low fertility of the 1930s to give way to higher levels in the 1940s and 1950s. Women with small families from the Depression actually opened the door to employment for married women, but younger women were not ready to respond to those opportunities in the 1940s and 1950s. Indeed, between 1940 and 1950 the labor force activity rates of women aged 25 to 34 actually declined.

Things changed, as you know, and so between 1950 and 2000, there was a substantial increase in the number and proportion of American women who were in the labor force and earning independent incomes. In 1950, for example, there were 29 female, year-round, full-time workers for every 100 males in that category; by 2000, there were 70 females working full-time, year-round per 100 male workers. This increase in labor force activity was accomplished initially by younger women; the younger the cohort, the more rapidly did labor force involvement increase, especially beyond ages 25 to 34, when children tend to be in school.

Getting a job is one thing, of course, but the kind of job you get—your occupation—depends heavily on education, and is also influenced by factors such as gender and race/ethnicity.

Occupation

Occupation is without question one of the most defining aspects of a person's social identity in an industrialized society. It is a clue to education, income, and residence—in general, a clue to lifestyle and an indicator of social status, pointing to a person's position in the social hierarchy. From a social point of view, occupation is so important that it is often the first (and occasionally the only) question a stranger may ask about you. It provides information about what kind of behavior can be expected from you, as well as how others will be expected to behave toward you. Although such a comment may offend you if you believe that "people are people," it is nonetheless true that there is no society in which all people are actually treated equally.

Since there are literally thousands of different occupations in every country, we need a way of fitting occupations into a few slots. Organizations like the ILS, Census Bureau and the International Labour Organization have devised classification schemes to divide occupations into several mutually exclusive categories. ... The occupational categories changed a bit over time, but you can still see that the distribution of occupations for women looked more like that for men in 2002 than it had back in 1970. Indeed, the index of dissimilarity (sometimes also known as the Gini coefficient) was .43 in 1970 and had been reduced to .32 in 2002. We would interpret that to mean that in 2002, you would have to have moved 32 percent of women into other occupational categories to have exactly the same distribution as for men. That does not yet signal equality, but it was a clear improvement over the situation in 1970. In both years, there was a clear tendency for women to be disproportionately in clerical occupations, while men were disproportionately in laborer occupations.

There is a global tendency for women to be stuck in less desirable jobs than men, and there are three important issues that the International Labour Organization sees as still needing considerable improvement in order to achieve gender equality in the workplace: (1) the "glass ceiling" (women being less likely than men to make it to top management), (2) the gender pay gap (worldwide, women earn an average of about two-thirds what men earn), and (3) the "sticky floor" (women tend to get stuck in the lowest-paid jobs) (International Labour Organization 2003).

People holding the higher-status occupations are more likely to think of themselves as having a career as opposed to just a job, and they are apt to derive more intrinsic satisfaction from their work. They are also less likely to be working in what Kalleberg and his associates (Kalleberg, Reskin, and Hudson 2000) have labeled as "bad jobs"—those with low pay and no health or pension benefits. Nearly one in seven jobs in the United States fits this categorization, and they are the types of jobs more likely to be held by women than by men, especially if the woman is not a college graduate (McCall 2000). The kind of job you have, and the income you earn from it, will be your key to economic and social independence.

Income

The average CEO (chief executive officer) at the 200 biggest companies in the United States made $11.4 million in 2001, including salary, bonuses, and stock gains (Lowenstein 2001). This works out to more than $40,000 a day, so if we assume a normal work day, this average CEO has already made $10,000 by the time the doughnuts arrive for his (yes, "his") morning coffee break. The CEO's average daily salary, by the way, was nearly equivalent to the entire annual income for the average American household ($43,052 in 2002). There is a good deal of controversy about whether the average CEO is worth that kind of money, but for the rest of us, income is at least partially a consequence of the way in which we have parlayed a good education into a good job.

The Medicalization of Birth

By Nancy Schrom Dye

Giving birth has always fascinated us. No other experience involves the intersection of biology and culture and the union of nature and art that birth entails. At once a biological process and a cultural event, childbirth has been shaped and defined by attitudes toward women, toward medical knowledge and authority, and toward nature itself. We live in a society in which giving birth is defined as a medical event, requiring the supervision and expertise of a physician. But birth has not always been so defined. Indeed, the central question of childbirth history in America has become: How did the management of birth, for centuries indisputably the province of women, become a medical event, controlled and managed by physicians?

Scholars (Leavitt, 1983; Wertz and Wertz, 1977) have identified three distinct periods in the history of American childbirth. The years from the early seventeenth century through the mid-eighteenth centuries marked an era characterized by what Dorothy and Richard Wertz have aptly called "social childbirth," during which all women had community responsibilities for attending friends and neighbors in birth. The second era in American childbirth history began in the mid-eighteenth century, as a generation of American physicians became aware of the revolution in obstetrical knowledge and practice taking place in Britain and France. This period, spanning from the 1750s through most of the nineteenth century, was a transitional stage, during which physicians staked their claim to the management of birth. The third era covered the years from the 1870s to the 1940s. These decades witnessed the consolidation of medical authority over birth.

In each of these three periods, developments in the professionalization of medicine, the state of knowledge concerning parturition, technology, and cultural attitudes toward birth help explain how and why birth ultimately became the medical experience it now is in contemporary America.

Childbirth in Early America

This morning was very Cloudy. Not only abroad as to the weather but in the house with respect to my wife who for about Three hours was in great Extremity. I thought I had not been earnest enough with God yet.... Then again Engaged in a Short but fervent Devotion and Ten Minutes past Eight my wife was delivered of a Daughter. I cryed unto God most high, unto God who is a very present Help in time

Nancy Schrom Dye, "The Medicalization of Birth," *The American Way of Birth*, ed. Pamela Eakins, pp. 21–46. Copyright © 1986 by Temple University Press. Reprinted with permission.

of Trouble … and He brought Salvation. He put joy and gladness into our Hearts; and O that we may never forget his Benefits!—"The Diary of Ebenezer Parkman," September 14, 1725.

A great number of unpleasant and stormy Sabbaths have happened this winter and have prevented my attending meeting for a long time—and now *my situation* incapacitates me for it—how long it may be before I again visit the Courts of my God I know not—my hour of Difficulty and danger is not far distant—'tis a dreaded event—and nothing but a firm reliance of the supporting aid of my Maker and Sovereign could make the expectation supportable—O may I be prepared for whatever awaits me—may I be resigned to life or Death. —Diary of Elizabeth Cranch Norton, January 27, 1799.

For early Americans, death—particularly the death of infants and young children—was an everyday reality. Throughout the seventeenth and eighteenth centuries, Americans perceived birth as a time of sickness and danger and often described birthing as a terrible ordeal. Although American women probably died less frequently in childbirth than did their English counterparts (Wertz and Wertz, 1977:19–20), virtually every woman in the small communities that constituted colonial America must have known friends and relatives who died or were invalided in birth. Whatever the statistical probabilities, death in childbirth seemed close at hand, and birth itself was viewed as an unpredictable and potentially calamitous event, very much part of the daily precariousness of human existence.

Diaries testify to the frequency with which birth and death were closely related experiences in colonial America. Mary Vial Holyoke, of Salem, Massachusetts, bore twelve children between 1760 and 1782; eight died in infancy or early childhood. Like many colonial diaries, hers is a sparely written chronicle of birth and infant death. From September through December of 1767, for instance, Mary Holyoke (Dow, 1911:67) recorded the following:

- September 5. I was brought to bed about 2 o'Clock A.M. of a daughter.
- September 6. The Child Baptized Mary.
- September 7. The Baby very well till ten o'Clock in the evening and then taken with fits.
- September 8. The Baby remained very ill all day.
- September 9. It Died about 8 o'Clock in the morning.
- September 10. Was buried.
- September 11. Mrs. Woodbridge brought to bed.
- September 17. Mrs. Van and Mrs. Cranch brought to bed.
- October 2. Mrs. Mackay's baby Buried.
- October 8. Mrs. Van's baby Buried.
- October 11. I first got to meeting. Mrs. Oliver brought to bed. Child named Peter.
- November 13. Mrs. Walter brought to bed.
- November 15. Mr. Walter's Child Christen'd Lynd.
- December 15. Mrs. Webster brought to bed.

It is in this context of frequent birth and frequent death that early American childbirth must be placed. Colonial Americans dealt with the omnipresent possibility of death by committing their welfare to an omnipotent divine Providence. God, and God alone, could control the outcome of pregnancy. When the eighteenth-century Massachusetts clergyman Ebenezer Parkman attributed his wife's difficult labor to his not being "earnest enough with God," he was giving voice to the sentiments typically held in the first centuries of American history.

Colonial Americans surrounded birth with well-defined rituals and traditions, perhaps in an attempt to lend some order and security to a process that seemed beyond human control. Parkman's diary provides a particularly revealing picture of the social context of birth. Parkman married his second wife, Hannah, in 1737. In the first three years of their marriage, Hannah Parkman experienced three pregnancies. Her first child, born late in 1738, lived sixteen days. Almost exactly a year after her first labor, Hannah Parkman delivered a premature stillborn son. And late in 1740, after suffering from eclampsia, she gave birth to a daughter.

Hannah Parkman's births, like those of all colonial women, were community events. When she began labor, her husband rode through the countryside to summon his wife's friends and relatives to her side:

> My Wife had been Somewhat ill all night but in the morning was so full of Pain that I rode away to fetch Granny Forbush [a midwife] to her. The Snow which fell last night added to the former … made it extraordinarily difficult passing. I was overmatch'd with it at old Mr. Maynards. Ebenezer Maynard and Neighbor Pratt took their horses and rode before me, by which means I succeeded. Brother Hicks carry'd up his wife, and fetch'd Mrs. How and Ensign Forbush's wife. Ensign Maynard brought his wife and fetch'd Mrs. Whipple. Mr. Williams also brought over his (Parkman, December 27, 1740).

As various historians have noted (Wertz and Wertz, 1977:2–10; Scholten, 1977:429–434; Leavitt, 1984), this "gathering together of women" served several social functions: the presence of friends and relatives at birth ensured women that they would have support during labor and the first weeks of mothering. But the particular ways in which Parkman and other diarists described this custom suggest that the tradition met psychological needs as well. Like other colonial husbands, Parkman made extraordinary efforts to ensure that his wife was surrounded by friends when she gave birth; they, in turn, made extraordinary efforts to be present. Parkman made careful note of each woman who attended his wife, and how long she stayed. Women's attendance at birth seems to have been an important responsibility, as Parkman had occasion to learn in 1747: "Mrs. Chamberlin (wife of John) here," he noted. "Had talk with her about her being disgusted at my desiring my wife might be excused from being at her last groaning—it being sabbath Day, and when I was not very well" (Walett, 1963:59).

Until the 1760s, midwives were the only practitioners to attend women in labor. Although a physician attended Hannah Parkman in each of her first three pregnancies, bleeding her in an attempt to control her eclamptic convulsions, and prescribing blistering and various anodynes for the phlegmasia alba dolens she suffered after her first pregnancy, he did not attend her in childbirth. Labor and delivery were clearly the midwife's province.

Unfortunately we know very little about the identity or practices of colonial midwives. Most seem to have lacked formal training. Many probably practiced medicine or "physic," for the line between midwifery and "doctoring" was not firmly drawn in a society in which medical knowledge was neither monopolized nor mystified. The journal of an eighteenth-century Maine midwife, Martha Ballard (Nash, 1904), the most complete account we have of early American midwifery practice, indicates that in addition to attending some thirty to forty births each year, she gathered medicinal plants; prescribed salves, elixirs, and syrups; applied poultices and plasters; cut the tongues of "tongue-tied" infants; and treated burns, fevers, injuries, and all manner of diseases. When remedies failed, she washed and laid out the dead.

Only a few colonies regulated midwifery, and at best such regulation was sporadic. Nevertheless, community standards did exist. Competent midwives enjoyed respect and high status (Wertz and Wertz, 1977:10–15; Thoms, 1933:1–20). Those whose competence was questioned, could find themselves in serious trouble. In 1648, a Boston midwife named Elizabeth Tilley stood accused of "the miscarrying of many women and children under her hand," of treating her patients cruelly by "using threatening words," and of interfering too much in the birth process. Mrs. Tilley was arrested and jailed pending trial, and her case generated considerable controversy. In all, Bostonians submitted six petitions to the governor and the magistrates. One, signed by six women and three men, reiterated the charges against her. Five others, signed by more than 100 women, testified to her "ability and kindness" (Tilley, 1648).

Because birth was viewed as a perilous event, women midwives and attendants managed birth but did not believe that they exercised significant control over the experience. Indeed, birth, for early Americans, was out of the realm of human control altogether.

The Revolution in Obstetrical Knowledge, 1762–1870

> In our present highly artificial state there are numerous causes at work, and numerous difficulties experienced, unknown to more primitive times and conditions, and we therefore require greater skill and more extensive resources. Females have in fact become more in want of help and less able to assist. Many new discoveries have been made lately, which enable us to facilitate delivery and ease its pains, so that it is now robbed of many of its former terrors and dangers. —Frederick Hollick, *The Matron's Manual of Midwifery and the Diseases of Women During Pregnancy and Childbed,* 1848.

> I was amused by a doctor telling me, lately, some women refused to take ether for extracting teeth or anything, thinking it wicked so to evade the discipline of life of which physical pain is a part. As if, with all the etherial relief, there is not suffering enough left in the world, not to speak of the kind no gas can reach. —Fanny Appleton Longfellow to a friend, July 11, 1847.

In 1758 William Shippen, Jr., like a growing number of affluent young gentlemen interested in a medical career, left for Europe to round off his medical education in Britain and France. His most important training took place in London. There he studied under the anatomist William Hunter from whom he learned the anatomy and physiology of pregnancy. He also sat in on the lectures offered by William Smellie, the most famous of English "men-midwives," who instructed him in practical midwifery, including how and when to use the still-novel obstetrical forceps. Shippen returned to America in 1762 with a full set of Hunter's anatomical engravings and a conviction that midwifery was a proper branch of medical science, to be investigated, taught, and practiced. By 1765 he was offering instruction to physicians and those midwives "who have the virtue enough to own their own ignorance" Donegan, 1978:115–120).

As Shippen's educational biography suggests, the eighteenth century witnessed the laying of the foundation of modern obstetrical knowledge and practice. One cornerstone was new knowledge of the anatomy and physiology of gestation. The anatomical dissections and painstaking engravings of Hunter and others enabled physicians to visualize the pregnant uterus and how the fetus positioned itself in the womb. At the same time, French physicians charted the mechanical processes of labor and pioneered the science of pelvic measurements, thus establishing a basis for predicting whether labors would be normal or difficult (Wertz and Wertz, 1977:29–76).

The second cornerstone of modern obstetrics consisted of developments in birth technology, most importantly the obstetrical forceps. The forceps revolutionized obstetrical practice because they gave practitioners an alternative to the mutilating operations of craniotomy and embryotomy that killed infants and often mothers as well. In fact, forceps were invented early in the seventeenth century by one Peter Chamberlen the Elder, but, because four generations of Chamberlen physicians managed to keep the reason for their astounding success with difficult labors a family secret, a published description of the forceps and their use did not appear until 1734. Thereafter, however, knowledge of the instruments and their use became widespread (Donegan, 1978; 38–83; Radcliffe, 1947:5–37).

By the time of the Revolution, American physicians were well aware of these obstetrical advances. Some, like Shippen, studied abroad. Others circulated copies of William Smellie's *Treatise on the Theory and Practice of Midwifery* and other English works. New medical schools established professorships of midwifery, and physicians began to present papers on obstetrical cases to fledgling medical societies. Once Americans began to publish their own medical journals early in the nineteenth century, obstetrics was the subject of numerous articles.

Physicians who served as accoucheurs found much demand for their services. As Catherine Scholten (1977: 430–436) has documented, affluent women in coastal cities readily turned to physicians for care in childbirth. Although midwives continued to practice throughout the nineteenth century in the countryside and among the urban poor, by the early 1900s physician attendance had become the norm for urban women of means.

Why did many American women turn so readily to physicians? How were doctors successful in establishing themselves as childbirth attendants? Why did midwives, so long preeminent in the management of birth, virtually disappear during the first half of the nineteenth century?

The alacrity with which women turned to doctors indicates that they believed that medical practitioners could make birth safer and easier. Then, too, as Scholten (1977: 430–432) has argued, doctors' newfound interest in obstetrics indicated their belief in the power of human agency. By the early nineteenth century, both women and their doctors shared a growing faith in the power of human beings to master the natural world. Although many nineteenth-century women continued to dread childbirth, they had come to believe that pain and death were not necessarily God-given outcomes.

The new faith in human agency was particularly evident in the history of obstetrical anesthesia. Although social conservatives opposed its use, arguing that God intended women to suffer in childbirth, many physicians and their patients eagerly adopted ether and chloroform when they were introduced in the 1840s (Duffy, 1964: 32–44; Leavitt, 1983). Fanny Longfellow, the first American woman to experience an etherized birth, was ecstatic, concluding that the anesthesia was "certainly the greatest blessing of the age" (July 1847). The success of physicians in gaining acceptance as accoucheurs was the result not only of innovations in birth technology but also, equally important, of their access to knowledge. Throughout the late eighteenth and nineteenth centuries, physicians developed ways to transmit clinical findings and medical discoveries. The widespread availability of medical books (including English translations of continental writers), the new medical societies and schools, and the appearance of medical journals all provided a growing network for medical communication.

The obstetrical history of ergot is an excellent example of the early nineteenth-century communication revolution in medicine. Traditional histories credit John Stearns, an early nineteenth-century New York physician, with the discovery that ergot induces powerful uterine contractions. But Stearns, who published his *Observations on the Secale Cornutum, or Ergot, With Directions for Its Use in Parturition* in 1822, candidly acknowledged that he had learned about ergot from "an ignorant Scotch woman" (quoted in Thoms, 1933:40). Midwives like Stearns's "ignorant Scotch woman" may well have known of ergot's uses for centuries. Unlike doctors, however, they had no effective way to communicate their findings and experiences. Given the fact that a significant percentage of American women was illiterate in 1800, it is quite probable that even personal correspondence was not an option for many (Lockridge, 1974).

The lack of a communications network for midwives helps explain their rapid decline. Doctors criticized midwives but seem to have made little concerted effort to curtail their practice. Indeed, as Dorothy and Richard Wertz have suggested (1977:44), American physicians apparently envisioned an alliance between themselves and educated midwives. The acrimonious midwife debate that raged among English practitioners had no counterpart in the United States. Denied access to the new knowledge and technology of birth, however, midwives faded into obscurity. Their closest nineteenth-century counterpart in middle-class America was the "monthly Nurse"—a woman hired to assist at birth and with the first weeks of baby care. The monthly nurse, unlike the traditional midwife, was a servant and clearly subordinate to the physician.

Nevertheless, physicians were not without their critics in the first half of the nineteenth century. Social conservatives condemned the presence of men in the lying-in chamber as indecent and called for either a return to midwives or for the training of female physicians (e.g., Gregory, 1848; Skinner, 1850; Donegan, 1978:164–228). Sectarian practitioners such as botanics and homeopaths also criticized regular practitioners" management of birth, arguing that birth was a process that could be more easily understood and managed by intelligent women themselves. Giving birth, they maintained, was a natural physiological process that rarely, if ever, warranted the heroic measures they accused physicians of being all too willing to employ: bloodlettings, ergot, opium, and the use of instruments (e.g., Hersey, 1836:xii-xiii, 136–148; Skinner, 1850:3–5).

Nineteenth-century physicians agreed that childbirth was fundamentally a natural and healthy process. As a group, they may not have been as prone to intervene in the birthing process as their critics suggested. One young practitioner described his management of an 1828 case in the following manner: "Encouraged my patient with assurances of her safe delivery, and telling her that nature should never be meddled with, when she has the power to accomplish her purposes alone, I lay down" (Metcalf, February 21, 1828).

Yet, if doctors believed that childbirth was fundamentally a normal, healthy process, how did they justify their presence at birth? Many argued that modern urban life was in itself unnatural and rendered women unfit to give birth without medical assistance. As Harvard professor Walter Channing explained, labor ordinarily terminated with but little agency on the part of the practitioner, and it was obviously intended that labor should always be thus easily terminated. The circumstances, however, in which women have been placed in the progress of civilization have tended so far to interfere with the original design as to render delivery almost always a painful, frequently a formidable, and sometimes even a dangerous process.

Nineteenth-century obstetrical literature is full of references to the supposed ease with which Native American and black women gave birth. These women, doctors argued, were less "civilized," and therefore closer to nature, than the middle-class urban women who made up their practices.

Doctors also based their claim to childbirth attendance on their superior knowledge of anatomy and physiology. As E. Augustus Holyoke, a late eighteenth-century physician, concluded after describing a disastrous midwife-managed delivery that ended in the complete inversion of the patient's uterus, "what better can be expected from an Operator utterly destitute of all knowledge of the figure, situation, and anatomy of the parts" (1783). More than fifty years later, Maria Meservey, a physician practicing in Delaware, agreed that lay practitioners' ignorance caused untold amounts of mischief. As she wrote to a friend, "The old midwife has her patients go through a strange sort of gymnastics and in every case there is an inverted or a prolapsed uterus (the result of her haste in removing the afterbirth). … I do not believe there is any need of a woman being left so broken down—I always intend to have my patients get up as well and strong as before marriage" (February 19, 1867).

As early as the 1820s, obstetrical practitioners began to insist that a medical education be a requirement for managing birth. "No one can thoroughly understand the nature and treatment of labour who does not understand thoroughly the profession of medicine as a whole," insisted John Ware (1820:7), and Channing concurred. Midwifery, he stressed, could not be understood without a thorough study of physiology and anatomy.

By the mid-nineteenth century, doctors had become American's primary birth attendants. In many respects, the transition from social childbirth to medically managed childbirth was remarkably smooth. But it is easy to overestimate the authority of doctors at the time. Their control of birth was limited in good part by the relatively low status and divided nature of the medical profession. When J. Marion Sims's father reacted to his decision to study medicine by declaring, "to think that my son should be going around from house to house through this county, with a box of pills in one hand and a squirt in the other, to ameliorate human suffering, is a thought I never supposed I should have to contemplate" (Sims, 1884:116), he probably reflected the sentiments of many Americans. And although nineteenth-century doctors did not face serious competition from midwives, "regular" practitioners did contend with sectarians, who challenged their legitimacy.

Although doctors made much of their knowledge, the obstetrical learning of even the most conscientious of physicians was sadly deficient. Nowhere were such limitations more evident than in the confusion over the etiology and prevention of puerperal fever, the main cause of maternal death throughout the nineteenth century. Puerperal fever was so widespread that some degree of postpartum infection seems to have been commonplace, even expected. Theories purporting to explain this bewildering affliction that affected only parturient women abounded; the disease was caused by miasma, by climatic conditions, or by infected women themselves. That scrupulous cleanliness could dramatically reduce the incidence of puerperal fever had been documented since the 1770s (White, 1773; Gordon, 1795). And in the 1840s, Oliver Wendell Holmes, in Boston, and Ignaz Semmelweis, in Vienna, independently came to the conclusion that doctors themselves spread the disease from woman to woman by carrying infectious matter on their persons, especially on their hands (Holmes, 1843, 1855). Holmes's essay "The Contagiousness of Puerperal Fever" was widely read and discussed, and many physicians put into practice his recommendation that practitioners with a patient who developed puerperal fever stop attending midwifery cases for a considerable length of time. But at a time when doctors were unaware of the existence of bacteria, and unimpressed with statistics, Holmes's explanation seemed to many no more convincing than others. Moreover, without a technique for effective antisepsis, no practitioner, however careful, could protect his patients.

Equally important, as Leavitt (1983:294–296) has documented, was the fact that women themselves limited doctors' authority. Although childbirth lost the public aspects that had characterized birth in early America, women continued to give birth at home with friends as well as a doctor in attendance. Nineteenth-century standards of decorum circumscribed physicians' practices (Donegan, 1978:141–157). For example, obtaining permission to conduct a vaginal examination during labor involved delicate negotiations between the physician and an intermediary—a friend or nurse—who would convey the request to the patient. Finally, nineteenth-century women knew a great deal about birth. Giving birth and attending birth remained frequent and familiar experiences throughout the century. Because knowledge of the birthing process was not yet the exclusive property of physicians, patients and their friends felt free to challenge or contradict their doctors' authority. Doctors often deferred to the wishes and sensibilities of their patients. One doctor recorded that a case he had just attended involved a "very severe labor without the aid of forceps. I urged the use of instruments but she objected so strongly that I yielded to her wishes" (Snow, 1865). Then, too, women maintained folk beliefs that conflicted with medical knowledge. One practitioner reported his patient's reaction when he informed her that her baby had been born with a caul. "The woman was sorry I had destroyed it," he wrote, "as it would tell when the child was going to be sick, [I] told her I was sorry but could not help it, as I was ignorant of its use." (Metcalf) In day-to-day practice, then, obstetrics was not based entirely on the systematic application of anatomical and physiological knowledge. Instead, obstetrics was often haphazard, determined in good part by the clinical experience of the doctor and by the social values and customs of his patient (Leavitt, 1983:294–295).

The Medicalization of Birth, 1870–1940

The old idea that childbirth is limited to a process of expulsion or extraction of a child from a uterus in a woman's abdomen by way of the narrow tortuous canal of the human pelvis; by the forces of nature alone, or with the aid of man stretching or tearing or cutting the soft parts or even severing the pelvis itself, has passed away in the light of aseptic abdominal surgery. Today no man is a competent obstetrical specialist who is not a trained abdominal surgeon as well as a qualified pelvic operator. ... Normal women come to us demanding a cesarean delivery to avoid the agonies of childbirth. While none would grant this request, it is well to remember that what is a fantasy today may be a fact tomorrow. A cesarean section is the easiest way for any primaparous woman to have her baby, and it is the surest way of having a live baby. It is the only painless childbirth that occurs today. —O. Paul Humpstone, "Cesarean Section versus Spontaneous Delivery," *American Journal of Obstetrics and Gynecology* 1 (June 1921).

We cannot sit back and say, "One woman in 150 dies in childbirth. It is a chance all women have to take. Let nature take its course." All women should not have to take that chance. —R. F. Wadsworth, "Mothers in Danger," *Collier's* 86 (July 5, 1930).

In the early twentieth century, childbirth came to be defined entirely in medical terms. Several developments hastened the full medicalization of birth. The professionalization of medicine in the years around the turn of the century was accompanied by the specific efforts by obstetricians to win prestige and recognition for their own specialty. This they did by upgrading standards of training and practice, by eliminating midwifery as a feasible alternative in maternity care, and by linking forces with the surgical specialty of gynecology. The development of antiseptic and aseptic techniques made possible another development essential to the medicalization of birth: the move from home to hospital as the primary birthplace. Finally, the early twentieth-century maternal and child welfare movement, fueled by new, urgent concern about the high death rates of American mothers and babies, encouraged women to think of childbirth as a medical process that demanded specialized care.

Late nineteenth-century obstetricians were uncomfortably aware of their field's limitations. Obstetrics, so exciting and full of promise a century earlier, had become a medical backwater that attracted too few talented young practitioners. The key to improving obstetrics, doctors came to believe, lay in better instruction (Williams, 1912; Kobrin,

1966). Most students' training consisted solely of entirely didactic lectures, with no opportunities for observing, let alone managing, actual labor. Poor training encouraged careless, incompetent practice and a lack of respect toward obstetrics. But how could clinical training be improved? Given nineteenth-century standards of modesty and decorum, a practitioner could hardly parade students into his patients' bedchambers to view their labors. Obstetricians, in short, lacked clinical material.

Ambitious, scientifically oriented practitioners made their way to the *Frauenkliniks* of Austria and Germany, the centers of late nineteenth-century research and practice. In European teaching hospitals, where destitute women served as clinical material in exchange for free medical care, doctors worked without the cultural constraints imposed on physicians in America (Morton, 1937:50–70), When American practitioners came home, they too began to look to poor women for instructional purposes. As Virginia Drachman (1979:80) has suggested, "in .the post Civil War period, doctors evolved a working agreement with the growing population of poor urban women.... They gave them medical attention and, in return, used them as a resource for clinical instruction." Poor and working-class women were thus essential to the medicalization of birth (Dye, 1983).

To reach working-class women, doctors established out-patient obstetrical clinics in impoverished urban neighborhoods. They also took a new interest in lying-in hospitals. Founded early in the nineteenth century, lying-ins existed primarily as charitable institutions for the refuge of homeless women and the reclamation of "fallen" women with illegitimate children. For decades, physicians had little to do with the lying-ins. Late in the century, however, many doctors took on hospital practices to take advantage of the opportunities for clinical observation and experimentation (Vogel, 1980).

Doctors enjoyed far more authority and autonomy in the lying-ins than they did in private practice. In the hospital, a doctor did not have to worry about pleasing the patient and her family by accommodating himself to cultural standards of decorum or popular birthing customs. Instead, hospitals and dispensaries enabled practitioners to restructure the doctor-patient relationship along new lines. In hospital birth, there was no room for negotiation between doctor and patient: the physician expected to be acknowledged as the expert and to control the management of labor. Doctors came to expect patients to be passive and to accept their medical authority. The full medicalization of birth rested in no small part on this restructuring of the social relationship between doctors and their patients (Dye, 1983:2–3).

Nevertheless, very few women used hospitals. In 1900 only 5 percent of American women gave birth in them, for hospitals were associated with depravity and were exceedingly dangerous. It was, of course, the high incidence of puerperal sepsis that rendered hospital birth so perilous. From 1872 to 1873, for example, 56 percent of the patients at the New England Hospital for Women and Children showed evidence of sepsis, and fully 9 percent suffered severe systemic infections (Call, 1908:396–397).

As doctors gradually became convinced that puerperal fever was a bacterial infection and not a specific disease, they adapted surgical antiseptic technique to obstetrics. The popularization of obstetrical antisepsis in the early 1880s was the result in good part of the work of Henry Garrigues, the attending obstetrician at New York's Charity Hospital. One of the first physicians to insist that hospital birth could be made safe, Garrigues introduced stringent standards of cleanliness in the obstetrical wards, kept maternity patients in isolation, and made liberal use of bichloride of mercury to disinfect women before, during, and after labor. By 1883 Garrigues could demonstrate that his methods had dramatically reduced sepsis (Garrigues, 1877:592–643; 1886:19–31). Other hospitals adopted antisepsis with similar results. In the 1890s, asepsis supplemented antisepsis, as hospitals began to sterilize instruments and dressings. Puerperal fever rates again dropped dramatically. By 1907, for instance, more than 92 percent of New England Hospital patients remained free from infection (Call, 1908:392–404).

Antisepsis, though far from perfect in its application in late nineteenth-century hospitals, ushered in a new era of operative obstetrics, as lower sepsis rates gave doctors more confidence about performing surgical procedures. From the 1890s through the 1920s, the incidence of Cesarean section, internal version, forceps deliveries, and labor induction, or accouchement force, rose dramatically. New operations such as pubiotomy and symptiysiotomy, both of which involved fracturing and separating pelvic bones to widen the birth passage, also found acceptance. By the early twentieth century, many physicians employed forceps in more than 20 percent of their hospital cases (Danforth, 1922:610–611). The career of Irving Potter, an early twentieth-century obstetrician in Buffalo, New York, illustrates the extent to which the new operative obstetrics could reach. Potter attended more than 1,100 births a year. The great majority he delivered by podalic version, a technique that involved reaching into the uterus, turning the infant to a feet-first position, and pulling on the baby's feet to effect rapid delivery, thus eliminating the second stage of labor (Potter, 1918:215–220), The technique of podalic version had been used for centuries in complicated labors, but never before had it been advocated as a routine procedure. Many obstetricians denounced such trends in no uncertain terms, and the differences between radicals and conservatives became an ongoing theme in obstetrical literature from the 1890s through the 1930s (e.g., Bedford, 1888:897–903; Smith, 1898:785–791; Williams, 1912:493–499; Anspach, 1923:566–574). This new emphasis on operative treatment, however, linked obstetrics closely with gynecology, and professional organizations began to formalize this connection. Obstetrics thus became defined as a surgical specialty.

In their efforts to improve the status of obstetrics, doctors also moved to eliminate rival practitioners. Chief among these, of course, was the midwife. By 1900 far more midwives were practicing in the United States than there had been in 1850, largely because of the great influx of European immigrants. Urban midwives, most of them new immigrants, and "granny" midwives in the rural South attended between 40 and 50 percent of American births in 1900 (Kobrin, 1966:351; Litoff, 1978), Although midwives did not pose an economic threat to obstetricians (their clienteles rarely overlapped), obstetricians insisted on eliminating these midwives for two reasons. First, as Frances Kobrin (1966:354–357) has argued, midwives served poor immigrant urban women—precisely the women doctors wanted as clinical material in lying-in hospitals." Second, obstetrics could hardly command prestige and attract talented young practitioners if midwives continued to practice. As Joseph DeLee explained, "If an uneducated woman of the lowest classes may practice obstetrics ... it certainly must require very little knowledge and skill—surely it cannot belong to the science and art of medicine" (1916: 407–408). By the 1920s, through a combination of regulatory and licensing requirements in some states, outright prohibition of midwifery practice in others, and the expansion of free hospital care for the urban poor, midwives had once again been rendered insignificant as birth attendants in all but the most rural areas of the United States (Litoff, 1978).

Obstetricians received help in their campaign against midwifery from early-twentieth-century social reformers concerned about maternal and child welfare. A coalition of clubwomen, settlement residents, public health officials, and social workers founded such organizations as the American Association for the Study and Prevention of Infant Mortality and lobbied successfully for the establishment of the federal Children's Bureau in 1912—the first federal agency empowered to investigate the causes of maternal and infant mortality. These social reformers did much to collect and publicize statistics concerning maternal and infant mortality in the United States and emphasized that the American mortality rates were among the highest in the Western world. In 1915, for example, out of every 10,000 births, 60 mothers died. Only tuberculosis killed more women of childbearing age. In the same year, about one in ten babies born did not live until their first birthdays. The majority of those deaths were in the first month of life (Meigs, 1917; Adair, 1985:389). Although some reformers defended midwives, pointing out that the mortality rates with general practitioners were often higher (Williams, 1912:1–5; Levy, 1923:88–95), most argued that the death rates were so high because many women did not have access to skilled medical care. Persuade women to go to obstetrical dispensaries and hospitals for birth, reformers believed, and the death rates would drop (Women's Municipal League of Boston).

Social reformers introduced prenatal care. As instituted by such organizations as the Women's Municipal League of Boston, prenatal care programs had both medical and educational purposes. Nurses monitored the general health of their impoverished patients to watch for toxemia and other complications. Prenatal workers also served as educators, providing women with information about nutrition, stressing the importance of breast-feeding, and insisting on the necessity of medical attendance at birth, preferably in a hospital. In time, prenatal programs developed formal ties with lying-in hospitals, thus serving outreach and referral functions (Women's Municipal League of Boston). In short, the maternal and infant welfare movement of the early twentieth century linked the concerns of the lay public with those of the medical profession. It was through the efforts of reformers that the medical profession developed serious concern for the poor mortality rates in America. At the same time, reformers worked to medicalize birth in America by adopting medical approaches to childbirth and by communicating the importance of skilled medical attention and hospitalization to women.

Finally, the medicalization of birth depended on redefining the nature of the birth process. Throughout much of the nineteenth century, as we have seen, most physicians defined parturition as fundamentally natural. But many early twentieth-century obstetricians were not content with the largely passive role of "watchful expectancy" that their predecessors had advocated. Chief among those who worked to redefine birth as a pathologic process that demanded active management was Joseph DeLee, a Chicago obstetrician. A perfectionist in his own work, DeLee made no secret of his impatience with what he believed to be the generally low standards of obstetrical practice and with those who believed that childbirth was a simple physiologic process. By no means the most radical of obstetricians in terms of the techniques he advocated (indeed, he regarded himself as conservative compared with doctors like Irving Potter, the advocate of routine podalic version), he nonetheless emphasized the essential pathologic character of labor. "Labor has been called, and still is believed by many to be a normal function" he stated in 1920:

> Everything, of course, depends on what we define as normal. If a woman falls on a pitchfork and drives the handle through her perineum, we call that pathologic—abnormal, but if a large baby is driven through the pelvic floor, we say that is natural, and therefore normal. If a baby were to have his head caught in a door very lightly, but enough to cause a cerebral hemorrhage, we would say that is decidedly pathogenic, but were a baby's head crushed against a tight pelvic floor, and a hemorrhage in the brain kills it, we call this normal, at least we say that the function is natural, not pathogenic. In fact only a small minority of women escape damage, during labor, while 4 percent of the babies are killed and a large indeterminable number are more or less injured by the direct action of the natural process itself. So frequent are these bad effects that I have often wondered whether Nature did not deliberately intend women should be used up in the process of reproduction, in a manner analogous to that of the salmon, which dies after spawning?

DeLee proposed his "prophylactic forceps operation" as a way to minimize birth's natural dangers. By reducing the pain of the first stage of labor with narcotics and scopalomine, DeLee reasoned that he lessened psychic trauma and physical exhaustion. By performing routine episiotomy, he argued that he preserved the perineum from injury. By eliminating the second stage of labor with the routine use of low forceps, DeLee stressed that he spared both mother and child from injury. And by administering pituitrin and manually extracting the placenta, DeLee stated that he reduced hemorrhage and infection. In all, the new technique, down to the last detail, was carefully planned to maximize human control of labor.

Although DeLee's prophylactic forceps operation met with strenuous opposition when he presented the technique to the American Society of Gynecologists in 1920, many of his techniques and attitudes soon became the norm in American obstetrics. In particular, his approach embodied a new view of nature. Whereas nineteenth-century physicians had generally seen nature as a fundamentally benign force that sometimes went awry or that was perverted by the artificial habits and fashions of modern urban civilization, DeLee saw nature itself as much too capricious and cruel to be left to its own devices. Then too he reflected the growing concern in the early twentieth century for the well-being of the child as well as the mother. Throughout the history of obstetrics, the mother had been the sole focus of all obstetrical measures. DeLee's emphasis on the destructive aspects of normal labor for the infant provided an additional rationale for interventionist obstetrics—while a mother might be expected to survive a difficult labor without permanent damage, the dangers to infants were far graver and more difficult to predict. Hence, DeLee and others reasoned, it was better to rely on carefully managed and predictable surgical intervention to counteract what was in essence a destructive natural process.

DeLee's new definition of childbirth as inherently pathologic found ready adherents not only among obstetricians but also among middle-class women. The highly publicized American maternal and infant death rates created new and urgent concern over how to ensure safety in childbirth. Throughout the first decades of the twentieth century, popular periodicals and women's magazines reflected women's fears and urged them to "abandon the moth-eaten tradition that bringing little children into the world is a 'natural process' and therefore in the hands of God" (Richardson, 1915:24). In particular, child-birth reformers cautioned women to "avoid the smiling family practitioner of old who says that there is nothing to worry about—that childbirth is merely a physiological function" (Boyd, 1931:293–295).

One consequence of the heightened anxiety and the new attitudes toward birth was the fact that middle-class women began to enter hospitals to have their babies. Before the 1920s, few doctors and even fewer middle-class women looked to the hospital for private maternity care. By the mid-1920s, however, about 50 percent of births in large cities took place in hospitals. On the eve of World War II, more than 75 percent of urban births were hospitalized. And by 1960, nearly 100 percent of all births—urban and rural—took place in hospital maternity wards (Devitt, 1977:48–49).

In the nineteenth century, hospitals had symbolized disease and poverty; by the 1920s, they had come to symbolize absolute cleanliness and safety.

Tragically, hospitalization and operative intervention did not make childbirth safer in the 1920s and 1930s. Maternal mortality remained high throughout these decades, and sepsis remained the major cause of maternal death (Adair, 1935:384–394; Antler and Fox, 1976:581). The maternal death rate in that period never dropped below the 1915 level of 60 maternal deaths per 10,000 live births. In 1932 the national maternal death rate stood at 63 maternal deaths per 10,000 births, and the urban rate, where hospital birth had become common, was considerably higher: 74 maternal deaths per 10,000 live births (Adair, 1935:389). Maternal mortality did not decline significantly until the late 1930s. Its decline then had nothing to do with hospitalization or surgical intervention. Rather, it was the result primarily of new, more stringent efforts on the part of obstetricians to oversee obstetrical practice (Antler and Fox, 1976) and, perhaps more important, the introduction in the late 1930s and 1940s of sulfa and antibiotics to treat puerperal sepsis.

With the virtually universal hospitalization of birth, the medicalization of childbirth was complete. Hospital birth, as various scholars have emphasized, was by definition physician controlled birth (Leavitt, 1983:297–304; Wertz and Wertz, 1977:132–177). The birth rituals specific to the hospital, many of them originating in the late nineteenth-century regimens to control sepsis, were strikingly different from the rituals and traditions that had surrounded birth at home. Equally important was the fact that once birth took place in institutions, it was isolated from society as a whole. As a result, by the middle of the twentieth century, women knew very little about the process of birth and had no alternative but to accept physicians' authority. Women throughout American history may well have dreaded parturition, but childbirth was a frequent, familiar event about which women knew a great deal. Indeed, as we have seen, nineteenth-century women frequently regarded their own knowledge of birth as equal or even superior to that of physicians. Once birth routinely took place in hospitals, however, few women had the opportunity to participate in births other than their own, and, given the widespread adoption of general anesthesia, often did not experience even their own births. As knowledge of birth became monopolized, birth itself became mystified.

Several factors, then, help explain how birth became a medical event in the United States. Women's fear of pain and death in childbirth, coupled with a new faith in the human power to understand and master nature, help explain why Americans turned to physicians in the late eighteenth century. Technological developments—forceps, anesthesia, antisepsis—help explain Americans' growing willingness to put their faith in doctors to make birth safer and less painful. The extraordinarily successful efforts to professionalize medicine in the late nineteenth and early twentieth centuries, coupled with the relative political weakness and disorganization of alternative practitioners such as midwives, help explain how physicians achieved an unprecedented degree of social and scientific authority in the United States (Starr, 1982:3–29). Technological and professional developments in and of themselves, however, are not sufficient to explain the medicalization of childbirth. Doctors' access to and ultimate control of knowledge concerning birth are, in the final analysis, the most potent factors in explaining why birth became a medical event. In the nineteenth century, as we have seen, doctors developed an extensive and effective communications network—a network from which women were largely excluded. Nevertheless, doctors' ideas about birth and its management competed with those of other practitioners and with the experiential knowledge and traditions of women. As alternative practitioners were eliminated and alternative models of birth management discredited, however, and as birth moved out of the home and into the hospital, American women came to depend on medicine as the only source of knowledge about a central female experience.

References

Adair, Fred L. "Maternal, Fetal, and Neonatal Morbidity and Mortality." *American Journal of Obstetrics and Gynecology* 29(1935); 384–394.

Anspach, Brooke M. "The Trend of Modern Obstetrics—What Is the Danger? How Can It Be Changed?" *American Journal of Obstetrics and Gynecology* 6(1923):566–574.

Antler, Joyce, and Fox, Daniel M. "The Movement Toward a Safe Maternity: Physician Accountability in New York City, 1915–1940." *Bulletin of the History of Medicine* 50(1976):569–595.

Bedford, Henry. "The So-Called Physiological Argument in Obstetrics." *American Journal of Obstetrics and the Diseases of Women and Children* 21(1888):897–903.

Boyd, Mary. "Why Mothers Die." *The Nation* 132(1931);293–295.

Call, Emma. "The Evolution of Modern Maternity Technic." *American Journal of Obstetrics and the Diseases of Women and Children* 58(1908):392–404.

Channing, Walter. Lecture notes. *Walter Channing Papers.* Boston: Massachusetts Historical Society, 1822.

Danforth, W. C. "Is Conservative Obstetrics to Be Abandoned?" *American Journal of Obstetrics and Gynecology* 3(1922):609–616,

DeLee, Joseph B. "Progress Toward Heal Obstetrics." *American Journal of Obstetrics and Gynecology* 73(1916):407–415.

——— "The Prophylactic Forceps Operation," *American Journal of Obstetrics and Gynecology* l(1920):34–44.

Devitt, Neal. "The Transition from Home to Hospital Birth in the United States, 1930–1960." *Birth and the Family Journal* 4(1977): 47–58.

Donegan, Jane. *Women and Men Midwives: Medicine, Morality; and Misogyny in Early America.* Westport, Conn,; Greenwood Press, 1978.

Dow, George Francis, ed. "Diary of Mary Vial Holyoke" In *The Holyoke Diaries, 1709–1866.* Salem, Massachusetts, 1911.

Drachman, Virginia. "The Loomis Trial: Social Mores and Obstetrics in the Mid-Nineteenth Century." In *Health Care in America: Essays in the Social History of Medicine,* edited by Susan Reverby and David Rosner. Philadelphia: Temple University Press, 1979.

Duffy, John. "Anglo-American Reaction to Obstetrical Anesthesia." *Bulletin of the History of Medicine* 38(1964):32–44.

Dye, Nancy Schrom. "Scientific Obstetrics and Working-Class Women: The New York Midwifery Dispensary." Paper presented at meeting of American Historical Association, San Francisco, December 1983.

Garrigues, Henry J. "On Lying-in Institutions, Especially Those in New York." *Transactions of the American Gynecological Society* 2(1877):592–643.

———*Practical Guide in Antiseptic Midwifery in Hospitals and Private Practice,* Detroit: George D. Davis, 1886.

Gordon, Alexander. *Treatise on the Epidemic Puerperal Fervor of Aberdeen.* London, 1795.

Gregory, Samuel. *Man-Midwifery Exposed and Corrected; or, The Employment of Men to Attend Women in Childbirth, and in Other Delicate Circumstances Shown to Be a Modern Innovation.* Boston: G. Gregory, 1848.

Hersey, Thomas. *The Midwife's Practical Directory.; or, Woman's Confidential Friend … The Whole Designed for the Special Use of the Botanic Friends in the United States.* Baltimore: privately printed, 1836.

Hollock, Frederick. *The Matron's Manual of Midwifery and the Diseases of Women During Pregnancy and Childbirth.* New York: T. W. Strong, 1848.

Holmes, Oliver Wendell "The Contagiousness of Puerperal Fever." *U.S. Quarterly Journal of Medicine and Surgery* 1(1843):503.

——— *Puerperal Fever as a Private Pestilence.* Boston, 1855.

Holyoke, E. Augustus. "On Uterine Inversion." *Proceedings of the Massachusetts Medical Society.* Boston: Harvard University, Countway Library of Medicine, 1783.

Humpstone, O. Paul. "Cesarean Section versus Spontaneous Delivery," *American Journal of Obstetrics and Gynecoiogy.* 1(1921): 987–989.

Kobrin, Frances. "The American Midwife Controversy: A Crisis in Professionalization." *Bulletin of the History of Medicine* 40(1966): 350–363.

Leavitt, Judith. "'Science' Enters the Birthing Room: Obstetrics in America since the Eighteenth Century." *Journal of American History* 70(1983):281–304.

——— "Shadow of Maternity: Childbirth and Death Fears." Paper presented at the Sixth Berkshire Conference on the History of Women, June 3, 1984.

Levy, Julius. "Maternal Mortality and Morbidity in the First Month of life in Relation to Attendant at Birth," *American Journal of Public Health* 13(1923):88–95.

Litoff, Judy Barrett. *American Midwives: 1860 to the Present.* Westport, Conn.: Greenwood Press, 1978.

Lockridge, Kenneth A. *Literacy in Colonial New England. An Inquiry into the Social Context of Literacy in the Early Modern West.* New York: W. W. Norton, 1974.

Longfellow, Fanny Appleton. Manuscript Collection, Cambridge, Massachusetts: Longfellow Historical Site, 1847.

Meigs, Grace L. *Maternal Mortality—From All Conditions Connected with Childbirth in the United States and Certain Other Countries.* U.S. Children's Bureau Bulletin #19, Washington: Government Printing Office, 1917.

Meservey, Maria. Correspondence, Shaw-Webb Papers. Worcester, Mass.: American Antiquarian Society, 1867.

Metcalf, John George. *Obstetrical Notebook, 1824–1832.* Boston: Harvard University, Countway Library of Medicine.

Morton, Rosalie Slaughter. *A Woman Surgeon; The Life and Work of Rosalie Slaughter Morton.* New York: Frederick A. Stokes, 1937.

Nash, Charles Elventon, ed. *The History of Augusta; First Settlements and Early Days as a Town, Including the Diary of Mrs. & Martha Moore Ballard (1785 to 1812).* Augusta, Maine; Charles F. Nash and Son, 1904.

Norton,, Elizabeth Cranch. *Diary of Elizabeth Cranch Norton,* Boston: Massachusetts Historical Society, 1799.

Potter, Irving W. "Version, with a Report of Two Hundred Additional Cases Since September, 1916." *American Journal of Obstetrics and the Diseases of Women and Children* 77(1918):215–220.

Radcliffe, Walter. *The Secret Instrument (The Birth of the Midwifery Forceps).* London: William Heinemann, 1947.

Richardson, Anna Steese. "Safety First for Mother." *McClure's* 45(1915):24.

Scholten, Catherine. "'On the Importance of the Obstetrick Art': Changing Customs of Childbirth in America, 1760 to 1825." *William and Mary Quarterly* 34(1977):428–445.

Sims, J. Marion. *The Story of My Life.* New York: D. Appleton, 1884.

Skinner, George W. *Nature Defended, and the Abuses of Custom Exposed: Being an Argument Advocating the Claims of Female Midwifery.* Newburyport, Mass., 1850.

Smith, Thomas C. "What Have You To Offer That Is Better? A Question for Critics," *American Journal of Obstetrics and the Diseases of Women and Children* 38(1898):785–791.

Snow, George. *Obstetrical Casebook, 1865–1875.* Boston: Harvard University, Countway Library of Medicine.

Starr, Paul, *The Social Transformation of American Medicine,* New York: Basic Books, 1982,

Thoms, Herbert. *Chapters in American Obstetrics,* Springfield, Ill.: Charles C. Thomas, 1933.

Tilley, Elizabeth. Petitions in the Case of Elizabeth Tilley. Boston: Massachusetts Historical Society, 1648.

Vogel, Morris. *The Invention of the Modern Hospital, Boston, 1870–1930.* Chicago: University of Chicago Press, 1980.

Wadsworth, R. F. "Mothers in Danger." *Collier's* 86 (July 5, 1930).

Walett, Francis G., ed "The Diary of Ebenezer Parkman, 1719–1747." *Proceedings of the American Antiquarian Society,* 71–76. Worcester, Mass.: American Antiquarian Society.

Ware, John. *Remarks on the Employment of Females as Practitioners in Midwifery. By a Physician.* Boston: Cummings and Hilliard, 1820.

Wertz, Richard W, and Wertz, Dorothy C. *Lying-In: A History of Childbirth in America.* New York: The Free Press, 1977.

White, Charles C. *A Treatise on the Management of Pregnant an Lying-in Women,* London, 1773.

Williams, J. Whitridge. "Medical Education and the Midwife Problem in the United States." *The Journal of the American Medical Association* 58(1912):1–7.

Women's Municipal League of Boston. *Bulletin of the Women's Municipal League of Boston,* 1910–1920.

The Birth of a Doula

From Curiosity to Advocacy

By Misty Curreli

When I signed up for the Doulas of North America (DONA) training, my intent was mostly academic. I was a doctoral student in Sociology and had been studying and teaching about the sociology of human reproduction for a few years. Attending a doula training session seemed like a great opportunity to expand my understanding of the field: What is the state of reproductive care in the United States? What is this doula phenomenon? And another part of me was driven by a personal curiosity. What is childbirth *really* like? Am *I* capable of giving birth?

During this comprehensive training, I learned about the physiology of birth and the statistics about maternity care in the U.S. and in other countries. I also learned about tools for providing continuous physical and emotional support to laboring women and their families, including copious amounts of reassurance, various coping techniques for pain, and resources for anything from care providers to evidence-based research on medical procedures to baby products. Finally, I learned that doula-ing is an old tradition with a long, rich world history, that women experienced in birth have been providing support to their sisters, neighbors, and friends for millennia. Doulas as paid professionals today have taken over the tradition as birth has moved away from homes and into hospitals, where there are restrictions that constrain the historic model of social childbirth.

Perhaps most importantly, my doula training was a call to action. Clearly, there are troubling trends that obtain in medical care today, including: increased inductions of labor, surgical interventions, and maternal mortality. And clearly, expectant mothers are looking for support. In my own small network, the demand was evident. It seems to me that many women feel a bit lost or without a voice in our culture's medicalized, one-size-fits-all approach to reproductive health, and are staking some claim to deliver their children on their own terms. With the training complete, the role of the doula now appeared to me as far more than an academic pursuit or a part-time job. Doing what I could to improve women's experiences of birth suddenly seemed altruistic as well as essential. I felt proud to join the cause as a birth professional who could possibly, if only in small ways, turn the tide on our country's maternity-care crisis.

Before birthing, I help my clients to gather information and to explore options pertaining to birth settings, labor strategies, and their "birth plans." Starting at two weeks before an expectant mother's estimated due date, I am on-call and ready to be by her side at the onset of labor. Once labor starts, I join the expectant parents at their home and do what I can to make mom as content as possible. I suggest various comfort measures (e.g. breathing, positioning, relaxation & massaging techniques) and act as a sounding board for any concerns, fears, and questions that arise. In this way, mom (and her partner) can be empowered to make informed choices. If my clients have decided to give birth at a hospital, I transfer with them and continue with their care, modifying my strategies as labor progresses and the baby is born. Soon after delivery, I facilitate mother-baby bonding with initial lactation consulting and continue with this assistance during the post-partum period. Of course, each experience is different because every mother is different–different bodies, different histories and traumas, different belief structures, different cultural upbringings, different educational backgrounds, different psychologies, and different ideas about the meaning of birth. Whether I'm working with a mother for 4 hours or 34 hours, in the hospital or at her home, with a midwife or an OBGYN, for natural childbirth or a birth with medical intervention, ultimately I seek to support moms to enjoy the birth experience they envision.

To date, 14 randomized controlled studies have identified the benefits of using continuous labor support. By reducing maternal stress, the presence of doulas typically decreases the length of labor and the need for medical interventions (such as cesarean section, forceps, or medicated deliveries), thereby improving outcomes for mom and baby too (Hodnett et al, 2003). In addition, women who use doulas during labor are more likely to have better mother-baby interactions scores (Laundry et al, 1998), reduced rates of depression (Scott et al, 1999) and they report more positive birth experiences (Hodnett et al, 2003).

Although my journey into "doula-dom" was not necessarily purposeful, I am today honored to take part in an ancient tradition that supports and empowers women. Each of the 10 births that I've attended in the past year has been an amazing and unforgettable experience, and I will never cease to be in awe of mothers (including my own) for their strength and courage. As for me and my reproductive future, I am comforted in knowing that I too can benefit from a doula's support when I decide to go down that road.

Works Cited

Hodnett, E.D.; S, Gates; G. J. Hofmeyr; C. Sakala. 2003. "Continuous support for women during childbirth." *The Cochrane Database of Systematic Reviews* Issue 3. Art. No.: CD003766.

Landry, Susan H.; Susan McGrath; John H Kennell, Scott Martin and Laura Steelman. 1998. "The Effect of Doula Support During Labor on Mother-Infant Interaction at 2 Months." *Pediatric Research* Vol. 43: 13–13.

Scott, Kathryn D.; Phyllis H. Klaus, and Marshall H. Klaus. 1999. "The Obstetrical and Postpartum Benefits of Continuous Support during Childbirth." *Journal of Women's Health & Gender-Based Medicine* Vol 8, No. 10: 1257-1264.

Maternity Care in Crisis

Where are the Doctors?

By Marsden Wagner

"We do not see childbirth in many obstetric units now. What we see resembles childbirth as much as artificial insemination resembles sexual intercourse."

Ronald Laing, Psychiatrist

Scene: A large hospital in Oregon. (This is a real-life story, as are the other stories in this book.)

Grabbing the telephone from the maternity ward secretary, the nurse blurts out, "Doctor, I have tried and tried to find the baby's heart beat and then I got my charge nurse who tried and tried. We can't get a fetal heart tone at all. We need you. Please come quick!"

The obstetrician replies, "Right. I'm leaving home now. I'll be there in fifteen minutes, depending on traffic." Click.

"But doctor, what should we do in the meantime?! Oh damn, he's gone."

The nurse rushes back to the labor room, where a woman lies moaning in pain, her face pale and sweaty, classic signs of shock. The nurse throws yet another blanket on and turns up the flow of oxygen in the mask over the woman's face. Sadly, the nurse never consults another doctor, even though there is another obstetrician in the doctor's lounge just down the hall, perhaps because, in general, nurses are discouraged from consulting another doctor if it is a private patient.

The woman's obstetrician arrives twelve minutes later and quickly determines that there are indeed no fetal heart tones, and the woman is in shock. He realizes this is almost certainly a case of uterine rupture, a situation where the woman's uterus, after an especially hard contraction, blows out like a tire. Uterine rupture is a known risk of Cytotec, the drug he has used to induce the woman's labor. Now it is his face that turns pale as he finds himself confronted with the most feared of all birth catastrophes—one that could kill the woman and the baby. "Set up for emergency C-section," he shouts.

It takes twenty minutes to prepare the operating room for an emergency cesarean section, enlist the obstetrician in the lounge to assist, find the anesthesiologist, and get scrubbed. By the time the laboring woman's belly is finally cut open, the baby is floating free in the abdominal cavity, having escaped from the uterus through a large rip in the uterine wall.

Handing the deep blue, flaccid baby to the waiting neonatologist, the obstetrician orders, "Now let's cut out the damaged uterus,"

Marsden Wagner, "Maternity Care in Crisis: Where Are the Doctors?" *Born in the USA: How a Broken Maternity System Must Be Fixed to Put Women and Children First*, pp. 1–12. Copyright © 2008 by the Regents of the University of California. Reprinted with permission by University of California Press.

The assisting obstetrician objects: "But we can repair it."

"No, it's quicker and easier to just remove it."

"But the husband is just outside the operating room door," replies the assisting obstetrician. "We should at least discuss it with him. Removing the uterus means they can't have another baby."

Perhaps because he doesn't want to face the husband, the obstetrician stops all discussion by turning back to the operating table and starting the removal of the damaged uterus.

Meanwhile, the neonatologist has determined that the baby is brain-dead, after nearly one hour without sufficient oxygen, due to the damaged uterus. The baby is rushed to the nearest neonatal intensive care unit, but dies twenty-four hours later. The mother is hemorrhaging from the ruptured uterus and receives a blood transfusion.

The outcomes of this story were tragic. A woman nearly died and a family was left with a dead baby and no possibility of having another baby in the future. Most tragic of all, it need never have happened.

We doctors have a fancy word for the appalling outcomes in a case like this: they are *iatrogenic,* or caused by the doctor. Cytotec is a popular drug among obstetricians who use it to induce labor, even though it has not been approved by the drug manufacturer, or by the FDA, for that purpose, and to date there is no scientific evidence showing that it is safe for that purpose. On the contrary, in 1999, two years after this incident took place, studies proved conclusively that, while the risk of uterine rupture is higher than normal when Cytotec is given to "ripen the cervix" and induce labor, the risk of rupture is significantly greater still when it is given to a pregnant woman (like the woman in Oregon) who has had a cesarean section in the past and already has a weakness in the wall of her uterus at the scar.

Here is another story. This one is about a recent "normal" birth in Northern California.

Ms. C chose Dr. E, an obstetrician, to care for her during her pregnancy and birth. She wanted to have a natural birth and his printed flyers advertised that he "believes pregnancy is not an illness," "works toward making pregnancy a happy experience," and "provides natural delivery methods."

A week before Ms. C's due date, Dr. E proposed that he induce labor with the powerful intravenous drug Pitocin. "Come to the hospital Friday at 7 A.M., and you'll have a baby by dinnertime," he said. What Dr. E did not add was "and I'll be home for dinner."

Inducing labor is medically indicated in rare cases, such as when the patient shows signs of preeclampsia (persistent, severe high blood pressure, edema or swelling due to an accumulation of fluid in the ankles, and protein in the urine)—or when the pregnancy is more than two weeks overdue and there are definite signs of fetal distress. In Ms. C's case, there were no medical indications for inducing labor. Ms. C and her husband refused Dr. E's offer and repeated their desire to let nature take its course.

A week later, Ms. C went into spontaneous labor and was admitted to the hospital at 11 P.M. Dr. E was informed by phone, but perhaps because it was 11 P.M. he did not come in to examine her. Over the phone he ordered the nurse to start Pitocin in the morning to "augment" or speed up the labor, though there was no medical reason to do so, as Ms. C's labor had not slowed or stopped.

The next day, at 8:30 A.M., Dr. E visited Ms. C in the hospital for the first time, nine and a half hours after her admission and two hours after a nurse had started her on a Pitocin intravenous drip. During that time, no other doctor had seen Ms. C, and she was not told she was being given Pitocin.

At 8:40 A.M., and again at 8:43 A.M., there were signs of distress on the electronic fetal heart monitor. Ms. C's chart indicates that her nurses were aware of these signs, but there is no indication that a doctor was called.

When drugs such as Pitocin are used to induce or augment labor, the pain of labor typically becomes much worse than normal. At 8:50 A.M., an anesthesiologist gave Ms. C an epidural block to relieve her pain. Administering an epidural block is a delicate procedure that involves putting a needle into the spinal cord just far enough for the tip to be in the spinal fluid and injecting an anesthetic. An epidural blocks all sensations below the injection site, leaving the lower half of the body without feeling.

Nurses notes indicate that at 8:55 A.M., Ms. C was completely dilated—a sign that it was time for her to push the baby out. However, Ms. C was not told that birth was imminent. A nurse called Dr. E, and on the phone he gave the order, "tell her don't push." But the urge to push is spontaneous and out of the woman's control—like trying not to vomit when the urge to vomit comes. For the next hour and forty-four minutes, the nurses tried to keep the baby from being born before the doctor arrived by urging Ms. C not to push and by pushing on the baby's head to hold it back. Nurses' notes indicate that Dr. E was called several times during this period and urged to come quickly. Nurses also gave Ms. C oxygen while she waited and told her it was for the baby, so we can assume that they were aware that holding the baby back was putting the baby at risk.

Ms. C had made it clear to Dr. E before she went into labor that she and her husband wanted a natural birth without surgical interventions, such as an episiotomy (the practice of cutting the vagina open supposedly to create more room for the baby). During her labor, Ms. C reinforced this point. She repeatedly told a nurse, "I do not want an episiotomy." Dr. E rushed in at 10:39 A.M., more than two hours since his last visit, and gave her an episiotomy, for no apparent reason and without telling her what he was doing. Since she was numb from the waist down, she did not know he was cutting her. When she reminded him that she did not want an episiotomy, he said, "too late." Dr. E then used a vacuum extractor to pull the baby out—again, for no apparent reason. (Dr. E claimed the reason was "fetal distress," but there were no signs of fetal distress on the electronic monitor just before the birth.)

These two birth stories—one with a disastrous outcome, one not at all unusual—illustrate many of the egregious errors that go on in maternity care in the United States. The fundamental flaw: in America, we have highly trained surgeons called obstetricians regularly "attending" normal, or low-risk, births.

The United States and Canada are the only highly industrialized Western countries in the world where this is true. And Canada is rapidly converting to the system used in all other industrialized Western countries, including Australia, the Netherlands, Great Britain, all Scandinavian countries, Germany, and Ireland, and in many other countries, where more than 75 percent of all births are assisted by trained midwives. It is a midwife who provides prenatal care, a midwife who admits a woman to the hospital when labor begins (or goes to her home), a midwife who attends the labor, a midwife who assists at the birth, and a midwife who discharges the woman from the hospital. In these countries, obstetricians serve as specialists. They are essential members of the maternity care team, but they play a role only in the 10 to 15 percent of cases where there are serious complications. Most women have babies without ever setting eyes on a doctor.

In the United States, the numbers are reversed. Obstetricians "attend" 90 percent of births and have a great deal of control, essentially a monopoly, over the maternity care system. Obstetricians are taught to view birth in a medical framework rather than to understand it as a natural process. In a medical model, pregnancy and birth are an illness that requires diagnosis and treatment. It is an obstetrician's job to figure out what's wrong (diagnosis) and do something about it (treatment)—even though, with childbirth, the right thing in most cases is to do nothing. To put it another way, having an obstetrical surgeon manage a normal birth is like having a pediatric surgeon babysit a normal two-year-old. Both will find medical solutions to normal situations—drugs to stimulate normal labor and narcotics for a fussy toddler. It's a paradigm that doesn't work.

This book will show that by embracing a medical model of birth and allowing obstetricians control of our maternity care, we Americans have accepted health care for women and babies that is not only below standard for wealthy countries but often amounts to neglect and abuse.

Let's take a look at the stories above.

The birth certificate says that the obstetrician in Oregon "attended" the birth, but this is obviously a misstatement. It is a well-known fact among health care providers that in U.S. hospitals, "attending" obstetricians are almost never in attendance during a woman's labor, except for occasional drop-in visits, and are often not even in the hospital building. An episode of the award-winning TV series ER showed a woman in labor having convulsions. The emergency room doctor asks the nurse where the woman's obstetrician is. The answer: "Across town in his office seeing patients." If a pregnant woman in America signs on with an obstetrician thinking she will have him around during her labor, she is almost certainly in for a rude awakening.

Doctors are not inclined to discuss the consequences of their absence, but a recent study shows a 12 percent increase in neonatal mortality in babies born between 7 P.M. and midnight and a 16 percent increase in neonatal mortality for babies born between 1 A.M. and 6 A.M. Researchers believe the increased deaths may be attributed to "the availability and quality of physicians, nurses and support personnel, as well as the accessibility of diagnostic tests and procedures."

A review of litigation cases in obstetrics and gynecology, commissioned by the prestigious Institute of Medicine in Washington, D.C., reported that nearly two-thirds of labor and delivery injuries were caused by problems in medical management—that is, failure to adequately supervise or properly monitor. In the Oregon story, the obstetrician's "failure to adequately supervise and monitor" meant that treatment was delayed during a crisis—a crisis that was brought on by the use of Cytotec, a drug that has not been sufficiently studied to have been proven safe. Does that amount to neglect? I think it *is* neglect on at least two levels. To begin with, the physician ignored the most basic principle of medical practice: *First, do no harm.* Second, the woman was given a powerful drug, then left to go through the second stage of labor (when the risk of developing complications increases) without a doctor's continuous attendance but in the care of a nurse who was responsible for several women in labor and could check in only from time to time, as is usual in hospital maternity care.

It is no surprise that patients are neglected in a system where an obstetrician tries to be all things to all women. An American ob/gyn must be a primary care provider assisting normal, healthy pregnancies and births, a specialist in complications of pregnancy and birth, a counselor and family planning provider, a specialist in gynecological diseases, and a highly skilled surgeon. No other specialist anywhere in health care tries to maintain competence in so many areas. It is not humanly possible. Can an obstetrician do a major gynecological surgical procedure—such as a six-hour "pelvic clean-out" on a woman with extensive cancer—and then rush to his office and do a good job of quietly and patiently counseling a healthy pregnant woman about her sex life? Not likely.

In America, obstetricians' plates are full to overflowing. There is no way they can do it all. And of all the things they try to do, the most difficult thing to fit into their busy schedules is normal childbirth, which lasts twelve hours (on average) and, as we all know, can happen night or day, seven days a week. As in these stories, the actual attendant for the majority of births in the United States is a labor and delivery (L&D) nurse with a telephone.

On average, L&D nurses receive only six weeks of on-the-job training in L&D nursing after completing their basic nursing training. They have no autonomy, and so if problems develop they can do nothing without a doctor's orders. At the same time, L&D nurses are held responsible for accurately judging the moment of birth. If a nurse calls the doctor too soon, she may be accused of wasting the doctor's time. If she calls the doctor too late and the doctor misses the birth, the doctor is equally unhappy. It is no wonder that the thirty thousand L&D nurses working in American hospitals are frustrated and exhausted.

In most hospitals, L&D nurses are asked to closely monitor several women in labor simultaneously. Some level of neglect is inevitable in this situation. When you consider the fact that nurses work eight-hour shifts, the chance that a woman in labor will receive continuous, one-on-one care in the hospital is reduced to zero. This is distressing, since many studies have shown that one-on-one, continuous care by the same person throughout labor means a shorter labor, less pain, fewer complications, and better safety for mother and baby. Hospitals and health maintenance organizations (HMOs) say they don't have the money to provide continuous care to women giving birth. Yet somehow they *do* have the money to purchase and maintain expensive electronic fetal monitors and use them on all women—even those having low-risk births, without drugs to induce labor—despite the fact that there is no scientific evidence that routine electronic fetal monitoring improves birth outcomes. Most hospitals believe in machines, not bodies and not human contact, and that is where the money goes.

Now let's look at Dr. E's management of Ms. C's birth in the second story. There are many reasons it is justified to call it abusive. First, Ms. C was given Pitocin for no apparent reason other than the doctor's convenience. Speeding up labor with Pitocin induction has been shown to carry the risk of overly rapid uterine contractions, which can mean insufficient oxygen for the baby and brain damage as well as another serious risk, uterine rupture, which can be fatal for the woman and the baby. Because the risks are severe, women receiving Pitocin must be closely monitored by the doctor. Dr. E ordered the drug without even examining Ms. C and didn't see her until after she'd been on it for two hours. Furthermore, it is likely that it was the Pitocin that caused Ms. Cs labor pains to increase to a level where she needed an epidural, which carries its own risks—such as a sudden fall in blood pressure (depriving the baby of oxygen) as well as the risk to the woman of paralysis or death resulting from the anesthesia. The epidural also meant that Ms. C was robbed of the opportunity to feel the birth of her baby.

A second reason Dr. E's treatment of Ms. C must be considered abusive is that she was given an unnecessary episiotomy. Though it is a common procedure in the United States, episiotomy is actually called for only in rare cases, such as when the baby's head has come out but the shoulders are stuck. There are numerous scientific studies on the risks of episiotomy. One of the proven risks is long-term painful sexual intercourse, a condition which Ms. C has suffered from since this birth.

Pulling the baby out with a vacuum extractor meant even more unnecessary risks, such as an increased risk of permanent urinary and fecal incontinence for Ms. C and an increased risk of brain hemorrhage for her baby. It is ironic that Dr. E said he used an extractor out of concern for the baby, when any difficulties the baby was having almost surely resulted from Dr. E's delaying the birth; if Dr. E had honored Ms. C's body, the birth would have happened an hour and a half earlier. With no other explanation available, it is fair to assume that the birth was delayed on Dr. E's orders, so he could rush in, catch the baby, and take the credit. Delaying birth for convenience is abusive. I first saw this happen as a medical student, and it is still common today, decades later. Based on his behavior, we can speculate that Dr. E was having a busy day (which explains why it took him so long to come when Ms. C was ready to give birth) and, though Ms. C and her baby waited for him, when he finally arrived he was in a hurry to get the birth over with.

Dr. E's management of the case is also abusive on a deeper level. When Dr. E gave Ms. C a drug without her knowledge, he violated her fundamental human right to be fully informed and to consent to any medical intervention prior to it being used on her body. Beyond not giving consent, Ms. C and her husband had made it clear to Dr. E that they did not want Pitocin when he offered it a week earlier. Beyond not giving consent to an episiotomy, Ms. C explicitly said she did not want one. Ms. C was not informed of the risks of using a vacuum extractor nor was she asked for her consent. However, given that she had made her desire for a natural birth very clear, it is safe to assume that if she had been asked she would have refused.

Dr. E blatantly rejected his patient's wish for a natural childbirth, and instead applied a surgical routine that by every standard was unnecessarily aggressive and interventionist. He turned what could have been a happy family event into a miserable surgical event. After the birth, Ms. C tried repeatedly—and unsuccessfully—to get information from Dr. E about why so many interventions were used. After her attempts to get information failed, Ms. C felt so betrayed and abused by Dr. E that she and her husband looked for a lawyer who could help them get some degree of closure. However, because the baby was apparently okay, and Ms. C suffered "only" from sexual problems and mental anguish, no lawyer was willing to take the case. Dr. E's damaging style of practice in this case must be called dishonest and unethical—and, sadly, as this book will show, it is quite common in the American maternity care system.

In a country where consumer rights are taken seriously and legally protected it's hard to accept that a doctor like Dr. E can practice outrageous "false advertising" and expect to get away with it. But as we will see in the next chapter, obstetricians in the United States have great lobbying power, and they have fought hard to prevent regulations and laws that would hold them accountable for their actions. In forty-eight of the fifty states, doctors and hospitals are under no obligation to disclose maternity care statistics (rates for cesarean section, labor induction, episiotomy, and so on) to the public, which makes it very difficult for a woman to find out in advance how she is likely to be treated. When something goes wrong with her treatment, it is all but impossible to find out what happened or who is to blame—without filing a lawsuit. A severe lack of information is one of several reasons that in the United States obstetricians are sued more than any other medical specialist.

The maternity care problems discussed in this book have profound costs for our society. Organized obstetrics groups such as the American College of Obstetricians and Gynecologists tell us that we have the "Cadillac" of maternity care. This is certainly true in one respect, since we pay much more per capita for maternity services than any other country in the world does. There are also good data showing that when obstetricians attend normal births, maternity services are far more expensive than when midwives attend normal births.

But are we getting more bang for all those bucks? Are we number one in providing high-quality care? Hardly. Twenty-eight countries have lower maternal mortality rates (women dying around the time of birth) than we do, and for more than twenty-five years, the number of women dying around the time of birth in the United States has been increasing. Every year, at least one thousand women—that is, three jumbo jets full of our sisters, daughters, and mothers—die around the time of childbirth, and at least half of those deaths could have been prevented. Forty-one countries have lower infant mortality rates (babies dying before their first birthday).

... Our lousy track record is not caused by poor training. Obstetricians in the United States receive high-caliber education and training, and most also have good intentions. The problem lies not with individual doctors but with a system in which stretched-thin doctors have an unjustified monopoly and women and babies are left to pay the price.

It is important to note that in every country that has a lower maternal mortality rate than the United States—or a lower infant mortality rate—it is midwives, not obstetricians, who manage normal pregnancies and births. In some of these countries a significant percentage of births take place in homes and out-of-hospital birthing centers. Studies that allow us to compare low-risk births attended by obstetricians and low-risk births attended by midwives show midwives to be safer, less expensive, and more likely to facilitate a satisfying experience for the mother and family. In the United States, however, most obstetricians are vehemently opposed to midwives and have gone to great lengths to drive them out of business. Far beyond a mere territorial battle between two groups of health care professionals, the persecution of midwives in this country has taken on the fervor of an old-fashioned witch hunt. The result is fewer options for women. In many regions of the United States, a pregnant woman who wants the care of a midwife can't get it unless she's willing to go outside mainstream health care channels, and, in some areas, even risk being persecuted and/or prosecuted herself.

Obstetricians have been telling women for decades that doctors are the only people who can provide them with a safe birth. Fortunately, as Abraham Lincoln said, you can't fool all of the people all of the time. More and more women are finding the courage not to believe everything obstetricians say. The percentage of births attended by midwives in the United States is increasing. Today, the number is 9 percent up from 5 percent just ten years ago.

There are other encouraging developments as well. Health care in the United States is driven by the bottom line, and more and more HMOs are coming to realize that having midwives attend low-risk births saves money. Not only are midwives paid less than half what obstetricians are paid, but the number of risky, expensive, *unnecessary* interventions is cut in half as well.

Another hopeful sign: in 1999, a new edition of *Danforth's Obstetrics*, a popular textbook, devoted the entire first chapter to the value of practicing "evidence-based obstetrics and gynecology," that is, practicing medicine that comes as close as possible to what scientific studies show to be most beneficial and least risky for patients. The next year, a new edition of *Williams Obstetrics*, perhaps the most widely read obstetric textbook in the United States, followed suit. This emphasis on science was continued in the 2005 edition of *Williams*, leaving no doubt that obstetrics standard-bearers see it as the right direction for the field. ... Today's actual obstetrics practices have a long way to go to meet the new standard, but a commitment in theory from the obstetrics establishment is certainly an important move in a positive direction.

Perhaps most promising of all, more women in the United States are coming to see the crisis in maternity care as a women's issue. It's about a woman's rights to control what happens to her body and to have access to the best health care options available. For some time women have lobbied for the right to prevent—or end—an unwanted pregnancy, but a woman's right to control a wanted pregnancy and birth has received less attention. Now women's groups are taking on a wide range of issues related to maternity care, such as the need for transparency and accountability.

One example: after considerable struggle, women's groups in New York State got legislation passed requiring hospitals to report to the public on their maternity care practices, including the percentage of births by cesarean section. Several years after the law was passed, it became clear that few hospitals (if any) were complying with the law. An advocacy group called Choices in Childbirth brought the situation to light, which resulted in a public investigation. In their findings, New York City investigators expressed outrage at the high birth intervention rates in city hospitals and recommended that the law be amended to make failure to disclose required information a finable offense.

Of course, it is also important to remember that maternity care is not just a women's issue—the level of interest and commitment of fathers to the birth of their children, generally, could not be higher. I am frequently reminded of the importance of childbirth to the father when I hear once again that one of those most macho of men, a professional sports star, missed an important game because he rushed home to be with his wife during the birth of their child. It's just about the only excuse coaches and teams accept for an athlete's absence, and I have never once heard of a complaint.

In every country in the world where I have seen real progress in maternity care, it has been women's groups working together with midwives, nurses, doctors, doulas, scientists, journalists, lawyers, and politicians that made the difference. In the United States, the movement for demedicalizing and humanizing birth is gaining momentum. The Coalition for Improving Maternity Services (CIMS) has taken the lead and now has more than fifty member organizations and more than ninety thousand individual members. Their mission: "to promote a wellness model of maternity care that will improve birth outcomes and substantially reduce costs." These are the principles underlying this model:

- Normalcy: treat birth as a natural, healthy process.
- Empowerment: provide the birthing woman and her family with supportive, sensitive, and respectful care.
- Autonomy: enable women to make decisions based on accurate information and provide access to the full range of options for care.
- First, do no harm: avoid the routine use of tests, procedures, drugs, and restrictions.
- Responsibility: give evidence-based care solely for the needs and in the interests of mothers and infants.

It's hard to find fault with these simple but profound concepts, yet they stand in sharp contrast with the reality millions of American women experience each year. If these principles were in place, neither of the real-life stories recounted in this chapter would have happened; women would not be faced with rates of cesarean section and drug induction of labor that are twice as high as science tells us are appropriate, using evidence-based care; and women and families would be free to have the childbirth of their choice.

This book is designed to further an understanding of problems in the maternity care system in the United States, In order to make changes, however, we need to begin envisioning solutions as well. I believe we can learn a lot by studying successful strategies developed in other countries and by looking at regions of the United States, such as New Mexico and Oregon, where important advances have been made.

Male and Female Farming Systems

By Ester Boserup

A main characteristic of economic development is the progress towards an increasingly intricate pattern of labour specialization. In communities at the earliest stages of development, practically all goods and services are produced and consumed within the family group, but with economic development more and more people become specialized in particular tasks and the economic autarky of the family group is superseded by the exchange of goods and services.

But even at the most primitive stages of family autarky there is some division of labour within the family, the main criteria for the division being that of age and sex. Some particularly light tasks, such as guarding domestic animals or scaring away wild animals from the crops, are usually left to children or old persons; certain other tasks are performed only by women, while some tasks are the exclusive responsibility of adult men.

Both in primitive and in more developed communities, the traditional division of labour within the farm family is usually considered "natural" in the sense of being obviously and originally imposed by the sex difference itself. But while the members of any given community may think that their particular division of labour between the sexes is the "natural" one, because it has undergone little or no change for generations, other communities may have completely different ways of dividing the burden of work among the sexes, and they too may find their ways just as "natural."

Many social anthropologists and other scientific observers of human communities have emphasized the similarities in the sex roles in various communities. One very distinguished anthropologist, Margaret Mead, in her book *Male and Female*, gives this summary description of the sex roles: "The home shared by a man or men and female partners, into which men bring the food and women prepare it, is the basic common picture the world over. But this picture can be modified, and the modifications provide proof that the pattern itself is not something deeply biological."

It is surprising that Margaret Mead, with her extensive and intensive personal experience of primitive communities throughout the world, should venture upon such a dubious generalization. She is right in describing the preparation of food as a monopoly for women in nearly all communities, but the surmise that the provision of food is a man's prerogative is unwarranted. In fact, an important distinction can be made between two kinds or patterns of subsistence agriculture: one in which food production is taken care of by women, with little help from men, and one where food is produced by the men with relatively little help from women. As a convenient terminology I propose to denote these two systems as the male and the female systems of farming.

Ester Boserup, "Male and Female Farming Systems," *Woman's Role in Economic Development*, pp. 15–35. Copyright © 2007 by Institute of Environment and Development. Reprinted with permission.

The position of women differs in many basic features in these two community groups. Therefore a study of the role of women in economic development may conveniently begin with an examination of women's tasks in agricultural production in various parts of the underdeveloped regions of the world.

The Division of Labor Within African Agriculture

Africa is the region of female farming *par excellence*. In many African tribes, nearly all the tasks connected with food production continue to be left to women. In most of these tribal communities, the agricultural system is that of shifting cultivation: small pieces of land are cultivated for a few years only, until the natural fertility of the soil diminishes. When that happens, i.e. when crop yields decline, the field is abandoned and another plot is taken under cultivation. In this type of agriculture it is necessary to prepare some new plots every year for cultivation by felling trees or removing bush or grass cover. Tree felling is nearly always done by men, most often by young boys of 15 to 18 years, but to women fall all the subsequent operations: the removal and burning of the felled trees; the sowing or planting in the ashes; the weeding of the crop; the harvesting and carrying in the crop for storing or immediate consumption.

Of course, there are exceptions to this general rule. In some African communities with shifting cultivation, the women have some help from the men beyond the felling of trees. For instance, men may hoe the land or take part in the preparatory hoeing before the crops are planted, but even with such help the bulk of the work with the food crops is done by women. In some other tribes, most of the field work is done by the men. Thus, we may identify three main systems of subsistence farming in Africa according to whether the field work is done almost exclusively by women, predominantly by women, and predominantly by men.

The relative importance in the African setting of these three patterns can be gauged from Figure 1.7.1. This map was prepared forty years ago by H. Baumann, a German expert on African subsistence farming. It appears that forty years ago female farming with no male help except for the felling of trees predominated in the whole of the Congo region, in large parts of South East and East Africa and in parts of West Africa. Female farming was far more

Figure 1.7.1 Areas of Female and Male Farming in Africa, Around 1930

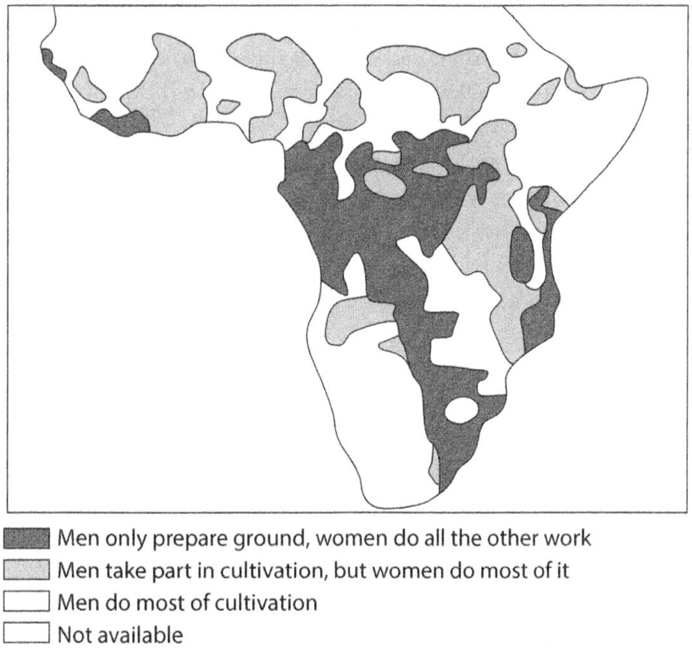

■ Men only prepare ground, women do all the other work
▨ Men take part in cultivation, but women do most of it
☐ Men do most of cultivation
☐ Not available

widespread than systems of male farming and it also seems to have been more widespread than systems of predominantly female farming with some help from males in cultivation; this latter type of farming was characteristic of the region immediately south of the Sahara.

Farming systems which are not based on scientific methods and with no modern industrial input are usually described as "traditional." It is widely but mistakenly assumed that such "traditional" systems are necessarily passed on from one generation to the next without ever undergoing changes either in techniques or in the division of labour between the sexes. In historic times, tribes with female farming systems have been known to change over to male systems, and—less frequently—tribes with male farming systems have been known to adopt a female system of farming.

Changes in the division of labour between men and women seem usually to have been related to changes in population density and in farming techniques. For one reason or other, the tribe may have migrated to another region, or local conditions for agriculture may have changed in the region where the tribe used to live. It might be, for instance, that the forest cover was disappearing as the density of population increased, so that the land had to be cultivated more intensively, with shorter periods of rest.

With the gradual disappearance of the tree cover, the men's tasks of felling must decline, as must the opportunities for hunting—another decidedly male form of work. On the other hand, with increasing population density new forest areas become scarce. As the fertility of the old ones diminishes, so will the soil need more careful preparation before it is planted, to offset less frequent periods of lying fallow. In such cases it may be necessary for men to help with the hoeing, or even to take over this operation completely from the women; a predominantly female farming system can thus change to one where the two sexes share more equally the burden of field work. Sometimes, the increasing population pressure may induce the men to emigrate from the region in search of wage labour elsewhere. In this case of male depletion the women may have to take over some operations previously performed by men. Many such changes have taken place in various parts of Africa during the rapid growth of population in recent times.

Before the European conquest of Africa, felling, hunting and warfare were the chief occupations of men in the regions of female farming. Gradually, as felling and hunting became less important and inter-tribal warfare was prevented by European domination, little remained for the men to do. The Europeans, accustomed to the male farming systems of their home countries, looked with little sympathy on this unfamiliar distribution of the work load between the sexes and understandably, the concept of the "lazy African men" was firmly fixed in the minds of settlers and administrators. European extension agents in many parts of Africa tried to induce the under-employed male villagers to cultivate commercial crops for export to Europe, and the system of colonial taxation by poll tax on the households was used as a means to force the Africans to produce cash crops. These were at least partly cultivated by the men, and the sex distribution of agricultural work was thus to some extent modified on the lines encouraged by the Europeans. In many other cases, however, European penetration in Africa resulted in women enlarging their part in agricultural work in the villages, because both colonial officers and white settlers recruited unmarried males for work, voluntary or forced, in road building or other heavy constructional work, in mines and on plantations.

As a result of all these changes, the present pattern of sex roles in African agriculture is more diversified than the one which gave rise to the European concept of the lazy African men. Therefore, the picture presented by Baumann's map of the sex distribution of work for food production must be broadened and brought up to date to take into account the introduction of cash crops and the changes in the sex proportions in African villages brought about by male migrations.

The available data, although insufficient for drawing up a picture for the whole of Africa, gives very useful information about male and female work input in African farming in a number of local case studies. Sometimes these cover some hundred families selected by accepted sampling methods and representative for the district where they live. In other cases, intensive studies have been made of a small number of families, but these studies, while richer in detail, cannot claim to be representative even for the village in question.*

---

* It must be remembered that even a study of a few families is an extremely time-consuming operation if it is based upon observations of the work of each family member in the fields, day by day for a whole year or more. In larger samples, the

Male and Female Farming Systems

Table 1.7.1 Work Input by Women and Men in African Agriculture

Country in which sample villages are located		Percentage of women in family labour force in agriculture	Average hours worked per week on own farm:			Percentage of work in farm performed by:		
			By active female family members	By active male family members	Female hours as percent of male hours	Active female family members	Active male family members	Hired labour of both sexes
Senegal		53	8	15	53	29	66	
Gambia[a]	A	51	19	11	168	64	36	
	B	52	20	9	213	70	30	
Dahomey			2	24	8			
Nigeria		57	3	21	15	9	49	42
Cameroon		62	13	16	81	56	44	
Central African Republic[b]	A	55	15	15	99	55	45	
	B	58	20	13	150	68	32	
	C	61	10	12	85	57	43	
Congo (Brazzaville)		57	24	15	160	68	32	
Uganda[c]	A	67	28	15	193	79	21	
	B	61	20	15	136	68	32	5
	C	53	18	4	450	45	9	15
	D	54	13	13	100	45	37	7
	E	53	13	8	163	56	29	1
	F	61	16	14	114	53	29	4
	G	50	13	15	87	39	52	
Kenya			23					

[a] The two samples refer to be same village in the years 1949 and 1962 respectively.
[b] The A sample refers to a village where traditional methods were applied, the B sample to a village where improved techniques were used.
[c] In the C–G samples respectively 31, 11, 14, 14, 9 per cent of the work was done by children who were not classified by sex.
Note: Some of the sources from which the information was collected failed to specify the length of the work day, or the type of activities classified as agricultural (for instance, it was sometimes not clear whether threshing and transport to and from the field were included). In cases where workdays per year were given without specification of their length, the total number of hours worked per year was calculated on the assumption of a six-hour day, and this figure was then divided by 52 to give average number of hours worked per week. The assumption of a six-hour day may well be on the high side, since shorter hours were recorded in many of the samples, and days of more than six hours were recorded only in a few cases and then in the busiest seasons only. For these reasons, the figures in the table can convey only a broad picture of the input of work in African farming, and it must not be assumed that the table gives a satisfactory picture of differences in work input among the localities mentioned.

The main results of these various studies of work input by men and women from cultivator families, and of the use of hired labour, are brought together in Table 1.7.1. The first thing to note is that in virtually all the studies the number of women in cultivator families taking part in agricultural work was found to be higher than that of the men. A variety of circumstances can help to explain why a relatively small number of men take part in agricultural work. Older men can often stop working by leaving it to their usually younger wives or to their children, while many old women are widows who must fend for themselves. More boys than girls go to school and more young men than young women are away from the villages, working for wages in towns or plantations or attending schools. Since in African villages virtually all the women and many girls even very young ones, take part in the work, the agricultural labour force tends to become predominantly female.

---

technique is often to visit the family at regular intervals and question them about their work input of the previous day or week, but, obviously, this procedure is much less reliable than the regular observation of the workers over a long period.

Secondly, the table gives information on the amount of agricultural work performed by those men and women who take any part at all in the work. While women in some cases work shorter hour than men, much more frequently they work longer hours or more days per year in agriculture than do the men. Typically, the annual average of work hours per week seems to be between 15 and 20 for women and around 15 for men, but in some cases women work much less and in other cases men's work in agriculture is very limited. In some Gambia and Uganda samples, men were found to work less than 10 hours per week in agriculture. By contrast, in some samples from the Congo (Brazzaville), Uganda and Kenya women were found to do agricultural work for around 25 hours per week.

The joint result of women's high rate of participation in agricultural work and their generally long working hours was that women, in nearly all the cases recorded, were found to do more than half of the agricultural work; in some cases, they were found to do around 70 per cent and in one case nearly 80 per cent of the total. Thus, the available quantitative information about work input by sex seems to indicate that even today village production in Africa south of the Sahara continues to be predominantly female farming. This is all the more remarkable since none of the districts shown in the table is characterized by an agriculture devoted exclusively to subsistence production. All the producers have some cash crops in addition to the food crops cultivated for family consumption, and, as already mentioned, men play a more active part in the production of cash crops than in the production of food crops.

Now it may be asked whether the work done by women tends perhaps to be much lighter than that done by men. The available information does not warrant a hard and fast answer to this question, and only a few suggestions can be offered. Light tasks, such as the guarding of crops against animals and birds, appear to be done mainly by the very young or the very old of both sexes, and able-bodied women are not spared from hard work. One of the sample studies from the Central African Republic mentions that the women generally do the most exhausting and boring tasks, while the performance of the men is sometimes limited simply to being present in the fields to supervise the work of the women.

The samples from Gambia are from a survey and a re-survey of the same village after an interval of ten years during which the number of inhabitants increased and the cultivation of the labour intensive paddy crop expanded. As a result, the women who had been found in the first survey to be already working much longer hours in the fields than the men, were found at the re-survey to be working still longer hours, while the average work input of men had even diminished. In this case, the farming system was thus becoming even more 'female' than it had previously been.

A similar process seems to be under way in the Central African Republic. No re-surveys were done in that country, but two simultaneous surveys were carried out in two different villages, selected for the explicit purpose of identifying the effect of improved and more intensive farming methods. The village of Poyumba (the first line in Table 1.7.1 for the Central African Republic) was selected as a specimen of the old-fashioned village, while the village Madomale (the second line), upon advice from the extension service, had introduced intensive methods for the cultivation of cotton, their main cash crop. The figures show that women were doing more work in the "modernized" village than in the old-fashioned one, while the men were doing less. The reason for this was that women had to do most of the new types of work, while the men had reacted to the higher yields from the new methods by reducing the area of land prepared for cultivation per family below the amount usual in the old-fashioned village with lower crop yields.

The table includes a few cases of "male farming." In the sample, for Dahomey, and in the sample from Nigeria (which refers to a cocoa producing region inhabited by members of the Yoruba tribe), men's average working hours in agriculture were ten times longer than those of women. Nevertheless, average hours of work for men, at least in the case of Nigeria, were not much longer than is typical for African villages generally. This was possible because the absence of any considerable female contribution to agricultural work was compensated by the use of hired workers for more than 40 per cent of agricultural work. These were immigrant seasonal workers from the Northern regions of Nigeria coming in to help with the cocoa crops, and whom the farmers could afford to use

Table 1.7.2 Work Input by Women and Men in Agriculture in Some Asian Countries

Country in which sample villages are located		Percentage of women in family labour force in agriculture	Average hours worked per week on own farm:			Percentage of work in farm performed by:		
			By active female family members	By active male family members	Female hours as percent of male hours	Active female family members	Active male family members	Hired labour of both sexes
Western India	A					17	50	33
	B	32	16	33	48	14	57	29
	C	39	19	35	54	20	56	24
Central India	A	21	18	27	64	6	21	73
	B	27	15	29	52	7	20	74
Southern India		40	20	30	67	25	37	38
Delhi Territory			31					
Malaya[a]	A		7	17	45			
	B		9	14	68			
Philippines		21	30	43	70	13	69	18
China[b], average		30			50	13	72	15
Northern China		27			41	9	75	16
Southern China		31			58	16	69	15
Of which: subregion with multicropping of paddy		42			76	30	62	9

[a] The A sample refers to a village with one annual crop of paddy; the B sample refers to three villages with multi-cropping of paddy. The farm families were smallholders and both men and women had much wage-labour in addition to their work in own farm.
[b] The figures refer to the period 1929–33.

because cocoa production was highly profitable at the time (during the Korean boom) when the sample study was made.[†]

The preceding analysis dealt mainly with Black Africa. This is where female farming systems are most widespread today, but they are by no means unknown in other parts of the world. For instance, in Latin America we find both Indian and Negro communities where agricultural work is entirely in female hands. In Asia, too, many examples of female farming systems are known. They are widespread among tribal peoples in India, where districts are found with women working more hours in farming than men. These Indian tribal farming systems are similar to the types of shifting agriculture in use among African tribes with female farming.[‡]

In all the countries of South East Asia many tribal peoples subsist by shifting cultivation with female farming, and here, as in India, complaints about "lazy men" are heard from Europeans as well as from local peoples belonging to communities with male farming systems. Thus, the Vietnamese find that the Laotians, with shifting cultivation and female farming, are lazy farmers, and the Indians have a similar opinion of the tribes of Manipur (in North-East India) which likewise practise shifting cultivation and female farming. They are said to "take it for granted that women should work and it is quite usual to hear that men while away their time doing nothing very much."

---

† The amount of hired labour used in agriculture is specified in a few cases only, but for most of the studies where the amount of hired labour was not recorded, it is known that little or no hired labour was used.
‡ In some places, however, the forest protection policy of the Indian Forest Department, through the prohibition of shifting cultivation, has succeeded in modifying the farming system.

Table 1.7.3 Labour Force in Agriculture by Sex and Status

Country	Female family labour	Male family labour	Agricultural workers of both sexes
	as percentage of total agricultural labour force as recorded in the most recent population census		
Africa South of the Sahara:			
Sierra Leone	42	57	1
Liberia	42	49	9
Ghana	36	55	9
Union of South Africa	5	29	66
Mauritius	2	13	85
Region of Arab influence:			
Sudan	9	78	13
Morocco	9	72	19
Algeria	37	40	23
Tunisia	38	42	20
Libya	2	79	19
United Arab Republic	2	61	37
Turkey	49	47	4
Jordan	3	70	27
Syria	5	56	39
Iraq	1	74	25
Iran	4	68	28
Pakistan	13	73	14
South and East Asia:			
India	24	48	28
Ceylon	3	43	54
Thailand	50	47	3
Cambodia	75	53	2
Malaya	16	41	43
Singapore	24	49	28
Philippines	13	76	11
Taiwan	19	71	10
Hong Kong	34	46	20
Korea (South)	45	52	3
Latin America:			
Mexico	2	44	54
Honduras	1	73	27
El Salvador		36	64
Nicaragua	3	50	47
Costa Rica		46	54
Panama	3	83	14
Columbia	3	54	43
Ecuador	3	57	40
Chile	2	29	69
Brazil	8	67	25
Venezuela	2	65	33
Cuba		37	63
Jamaica	9	50	41
Dominican Republic	1	74	25
Puerto Rico	1	18	81

Table 1.7.3 contd.

Country	Year	Agricultural labour force (millions)		Percentage of women in agricultural labour force	Agricultural labour force as percentage of total labour force in all occupations
		Women	Men		
Union of South Africa	1936	1.7	1.7	49	64
	1946	0.7	1.7	28	47
	1960	0.2	1.5	12	30
United Arab Republic	1927	0.5	3.0	15	60
	1947	6.9	3.7	51	54
	1960	0.1	3.5	4	53
Philippines	1903	0.2	1.4	13	47
	1948	2.0	2.8	42	66
	1960	0.8	4.4	15	61
	1965	1.3	4.7	21	57
Columbia	1938	1.6	1.8	47	72
	1951	0.1	1.9	4	53
	1964	0.1	2.4	4	41

Note: For many of the countries listed in the table, the number of women from farm families participating in agricultural work is understated, either (a) because the census records only those women who receive a remuneration for their work, while women who help in the family farm without remuneration are classified as housewives or (b) because women who work only in the peak season are classified as housewives. It appears from the figures below for countries which have changed their classification system for rural women that the margin of error for the figures in the Table is very wide indeed.

Because of the wide differences in the system of classification for rural women, a comparison of the female role in economic activities cannot be based upon over-all rates of work participation. For the same reason, the percentage of population engaged in agriculture is not a reliable measure of the stage of development reached by a given country. It appears from the last column in the table above that the statistical elimination of most of the women from the agricultural labour force contributed to reduce the apparent share of population engaged in agriculture in South Africa from 64 to 30 per cent of the active population in a period of twenty-four years while, conversely, the inclusion of more women in the agricultural labour force in the Philippines made the proportion of the agricultural sector appear to have risen from 47 in 1903 to 66 in 1948.

Owing to these differences in the classification of rural women, international comparisons of the proportion of population engaged in agriculture are often based upon figures for male labour only. This, however, is not a valid solution to the problem since women perform a much larger part of agricultural work in some countries than in others. To avoid these difficulties, the criterion for stage of economic development used in this study is not the proportion of active population engaged in agriculture, but the proportion of all adults occupied in 'modern occupations', i.e. employees in industry and trade and all personnel in professional, clerical and administrative occupations. This is thought to minimize the margin of error arising from differences in the classification of women (and men) who work part-time or without remuneration since the numbers of such women (and men) are negligible in the 'modern' occupations.

The Plough, the Veil, and the Labourer

The pattern of female farming described above is found mainly in regions of shifting agriculture where the plough is not used. In the regions of plough cultivation, agricultural work is distributed between the two sexes in a very different way. The main farming instrument in those regions, the plough, is used by men helped by draught animals, and only the hand operations—or some of them—are left for women to perform. Table 1.7.2 shows the distribution of work between men and women in some regions of Asia where plough cultivation is predominant.

The table is arranged in a similar way to Table 1.7.1 which covers African villages with shifting cultivation. A comparison of the two tables gives an impression of women's different roles in these two agricultural systems. The first thing to note is the striking difference in the numbers of women taking part in field work in African villages and in the Asian regions shown in Table 1.7.2. As we have seen, virtually all rural women in Africa take part in farm work, and the agricultural labour force is predominantly female. By contrast, the samples from regions of plough cultivation in Asia show a predominantly male family labour force, because a large proportion of women in the cultivator families are completely exempted from work in the fields. The land is prepared for sowing by men using draught animals, and this thorough land preparation leaves little need for weeding the crop, which is usually the women's task. Therefore women contribute mainly to harvest work and to the care of domestic animals. Because village women work less in agriculture, a considerable proportion of them are completely freed from farm work. Sometimes such women perform only purely domestic duties, living in seclusion within their own homes, and appearing in the village street only under the protection of the veil, a phenomenon associated with plough culture, and seemingly unknown in regions of shifting cultivation where women do most of the agricultural toil.

In regions of plough culture, even those women who do take part in agricultural work are less active than the men. In all the Asian sample areas shown in Table 1.7.2 women work fewer hours than men in agriculture, while the opposite is usually true in African villages, as seen in Table 1.7.1. It is important to note, however, that in the Asian villages covered by Table 1.7.2, those women who did play any part in agricultural work were not generally working shorter hours than those which seem usual for African women. The difference arises from the fact that in Asian agriculture men work 25 to 30 hours per week or even more, while in Africa they usually work around 15 hours per week, or less. Hence, the real difference between the use of the African and Asian agricultural labour force, as revealed by a comparison of the two tables, is that Asian men—the operators of the plough—must work longer hours than African men, while many of the wives of Asian men are free from field work.

But there is an additional and very important difference between the distribution of work in African shifting cultivation and in Asian plough cultivation. The plough is used in regions with private ownership of land and with a comparatively numerous class of landless families in the rural population. Therefore, in many regions of plough cultivation, the farm family gets more help from hired labourers than is usual in regions of shifting cultivation. The percentage of agricultural work done by hired labour varies from 15 per cent to over 70 per cent in the samples from Asia, while very few of the cultivator families in the African samples used significant amounts of hired labour.

Owing to the differences in the use of hired labour and in the technical nature of farming operations under plough cultivation and shifting cultivation, female family labour accounts for a much smaller part of the total agricultural work in the Asian than in the African village. In nearly all cases recorded in Table 1.7.1, the female African family members did more than half of the work in agriculture; the comparable figure for Asian cultivator families was less than one-fifth, as seen in Table 1.7.2.

Figure 1.7.2 Use of Female Family Labour and Hired Labour in Agriculture

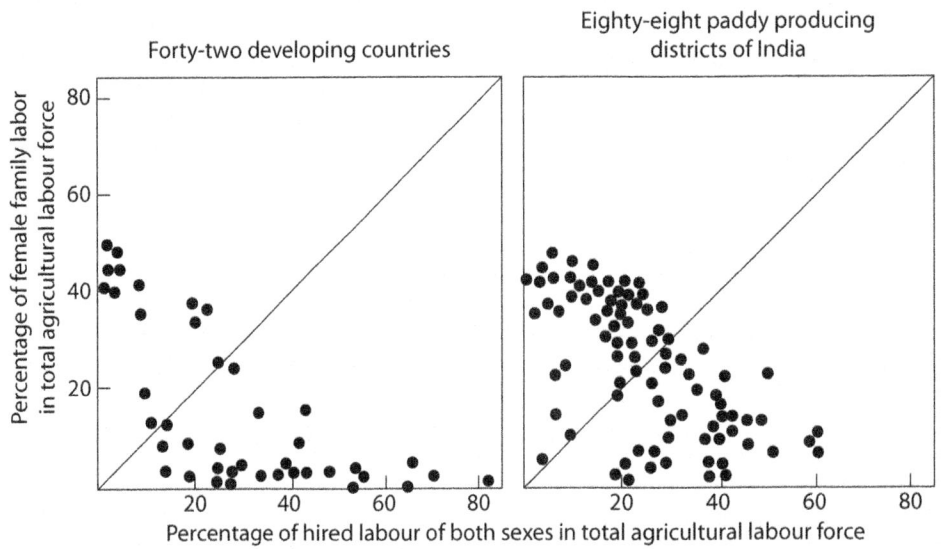

Note: *All percentages are based upon number of persons, without regard to hours of work. See Note to Table 1.7.3.*

Table 1.7.4 Average Hours Worked Per Week by Family Members:

	With crops		With animals		Total in family farm	
	Women	Men	Women	Men	Women	Men
Western India						
Sample B	13	18	3	15	16	33
Sample C	16	23	3	12	19	35
Central India	14	14	2	14	16	28
Southern India	9	16	11	14	20	20
Delhi Territory	9		22		31	

To sum up, there seems to be two basic factors which explain the striking contrast between female farmers in regions of shifting cultivation and secluded, domestic women in most other parts of the developing world: one factor is the difference in agricultural systems; the other is the difference in the pattern of social hierarchy between regions of tribal organization and regions of settled farmers with individual ownership of land. Among the latter, a large proportion of the women are able to devote themselves largely or wholly to work within the confines of the home, leaving work in the fields to male family members and to hired workers.

The great advantage of the type of sample studies we have been examining above is that they give information about the actual input of work, measured in hours or days. By the same token, however, most of these surveys are strictly local, covering only a few villages or districts. Far more comprehensive information can of course be had from population censuses if we decide to be content with information on the numbers of hired labourers and of men and women from farm families who take part, more or less extensively, in agricultural work.

Such information is brought together in Table 1.7.3. There appears to be two clearly identifiable patterns of labour participation in agriculture. Most African and some South East Asian countries (Thailand, Cambodia) have a high percentage of female participation in agriculture and very few agricultural wage labourers; in contrast many Arab and Latin American countries have a small female participation and agricultural wage labourers form a large part of the agricultural labour force. Where there is a low female participation in farm work, extensive plough cultivation is the rule, and there is little need for female labour except in the harvest season.

Table 1.7. 3 (and Figure 1.7.2, left-hand side) are based upon average figures for whole countries although many of them contain regions with strikingly different types of farming and social organization. Therefore, a more correct picture may emerge if we compare the composition of the agricultural labour force in various districts within the countries. In Figure 1.7.2 (right-hand side) such a comparison is made for India. It shows that in rice-producing districts female work participation is high in the farm families where hired labour is little used, but much lower where hired labour accounts for a large part of the labour force.

Thus, it seems to be a general rule, valid for all parts of the developing world, that it is the female members of the farm families who benefit most from the availability of landless families working for wages. As hired labourers are called in, so are the women of cultivator families released from agricultural work. On the other hand, women always seem to bear a large part of the work burden in the more egalitarian communities.

Population Pressure and Sex Roles in Farming

We have seen that male members of farm families work much longer hours in Asian than in African agriculture. To a large extent, differences in animal husbandry and draught power can explain why farmers in Asia are more busy than farmers in Africa.

The shifting cultivator in Africa has no draught animals; he drinks little milk and his consumption of meat is met in some places by hunting and in other places by animals which are kept mostly unguarded and untended in natural grazings far away from the crops and the village. By contrast, the Asian farmer must look after his draught and other domestic animals, which is no small part of his total agricultural effort. The figures above suggest that nearly half the labour input by either male or female family members in Indian farming is accounted for by the labour requirements of draught animals and animal husbandry.

African cultivators can avoid the heavy burden of keeping and feeding animals because with such a thinly populated continent shifting cultivation can be pursued. It may seem surprising, in view of the primitive tools used in shifting cultivation, that families can produce their food and some cash cops with so small an input of labour as that of the African cultivator families in the villages covered by Table 1.7.1. The explanation is that in regions with a favourable land/man ratio, the system of shifting cultivation requires less input of labour per unit of output than primitive systems of permanent cultivation. As long as population densities remain relatively low, labour-intensive systems of land improvement and fertilization need not be applied and it is possible to avoid cultivating land with a low yield due to soil exhaustion after frequent or permanent cultivation without the use of fertilizers.

In other words, the input of labour per family in African subsistence farming can be kept at lower levels than, for instance, in the more densely populated regions of Asia, because the generally much lower population densities in Africa make it possible to stick to an agricultural system with less labour input per unit of agricultural output it is precisely because such labour-extensive farming systems can be used in most of Africa that it is possible for African villagers to leave most of the farming work to women, while the men work very short hours in agriculture, in comparison to male farmers in densely populated regions of subsistence agriculture.

Female farming systems seem most often to disappear when farming systems with ploughing of permanent fields are introduced in lieu of shifting cultivation. In a typical case this change is the result of increasing population density which makes it impossible to continue with a system necessitating long fallow periods when the land must be left uncultivated. When a population increase induces the transition to a system where the same fields are used with no or only short fallow periods, this change often goes hand in hand with the transition from hoeing to ploughing; when the land has to be used continuously, it becomes worthwhile, and indeed necessary, to undertake a large initial investment—the removal of tree stumps and bushes and land levelling—which must precede plough cultivation.§

In recent decades, the rapid population increase in developing countries has prompted a change to plough cultivation in many regions of shifting cultivation with a predominantly female pattern of work. And the advent of the plough usually entails a radical shift in sex roles in agriculture; men take over the ploughing even in regions where the hoeing had formerly been women's work. At the same time, the amount of weeding to be done by the women may decline on land ploughed before sowing and planting, and either men or women may get a new job of collecting feed for the animals and feeding them.

It is not an invariable rule that men operate the plough right from the moment it is introduced. Among some Bantu peoples in South Africa, women steer the plough although it was introduced some time ago. Similarly, in India 2 per cent of the ploughing done for farmers by agricultural labourers is done by women. These women probably belong to tribes with female fanning traditions, and such examples are no more than sporadic exceptions to the general rule that ploughs are operated by men.

Obviously, the adoption of a farming system where the main farming equipment is operated only by men entails a tremendous change in the economic and social relationship between the sexes. It is understandable that social anthropologists regard the distinction between shifting cultivation and plough cultivation as a fundamental criterion for the identification of different social and cultural patterns, and in later chapters we shall hear much about the more general consequences of this shift. But the male members of tribes who are faced with the problem of changing from shifting cultivation to plough cultivation are not concerned with these long-term effects of their

---

§ In a district of Nigeria where the change to plough cultivation was contemplated, it was found that, while 20 man-days of work were needed for the preparation of an acre of virgin savannah land and bush for cultivation by the usual method, an investment of 100 man-days was needed to clear similar land before tractor ploughs could operate on it.

choice. They naturally think mainly in terms of the additional work burden which the ploughing and the care of the draught animals may give them.

Understandably, villagers usually show little enthusiasm for plough cultivation as long as they have land enough to apply shifting cultivation and can cover their protein supply from hunting and fishing or from cattle kept in grazings far from the villages and the crops. And the more the work of hoeing is done by women, the less likely will men be willing to change from hoeing to ploughing. Extension agents may eagerly explain to the fanners how much they can increase their production by ploughing all the land at their disposal and cultivating it permanently with animal manuring instead of having only a part of it hoed and cultivated by their wives. But the husband, measuring his own present work input in agriculture against the prospect of much greater demands for manual work, will be disinclined to change. Many well-meant attempts to foster intensification in African agriculture have been frustrated by this simple mechanism.

In short, the difference in sex distribution of agricultural work in villages of shifting cultivations and in those where the plough is used, is one of the main reasons why shifting cultivators lack enthusiasm for taking to the plough. They seem to agree with the old Arab saying, ascribed to the Prophet himself, that a plough never enters into a farm without servitude entering too.

We saw that when growing population density induces cultivator families to change from shifting cultivation to plough cultivation, men's burden of work usually increases while that of the women diminishes. As long as population density remains low enough to allow extensive plough cultivation without irrigation, there may be little need for weeding, and the animals may need to be hand-fed for only a short period every year, if at all. In such cases, women may have little agricultural work to do.

However, this advantage for the women does not last if the pressure of population increases to the point where it is necessary to use very labour-intensive techniques and to plant very labour-intensive crops in order to maintain the customary income from a smaller area of land. With irrigation, weeding may become a heavy burden for the women, and so may the transplanting of paddy, But men also get more work to do under irrigated farming than under plough cultivation of dry crops, for the digging of irrigation ditches in the fields, the lifting of water from wells and canals, and the repair of terraces and bunds are usually men's work.

Examples of a high degree of work participation by women in densely populated areas are found in Egypt and in China. In the latter, where mostly male farming predominates, women do a large part of the work in the very densely populated regions where agriculture is based upon the double cropping of rice (Table 1.7.2).

To sum up, the sex roles in farming can be briefly described as follows: in very sparsely populated regions where shifting cultivation is used, men do little farm work, the women doing most. In somewhat more densely populated regions, where the agricultural system is that of extensive plough cultivation, women do little farm work and men do much more. Finally, in regions of intensive cultivation of irrigated land, both men and women must put hard work into agriculture in order to earn enough to support a family on a small piece of land.

In the last few decades population in developing countries has been increasing at unprecedented rates. The increased population density in rural areas calls for a change of agricultural system towards higher intensity. Unavoidably, this change must affect the balance of work between the sexes and it must often be necessary for one of the sexes to take over some tasks which were normally done by the other sex within that particular community. The authors of some of the studies quoted above complain that agricultural change is being held back because men—or women—refuse to do more work than is customary, or to do work which according to prevailing custom should be done by persons of the other sex.

Family Planning and Abortion

Cultural Norms Versus Actual Practices in Nigeria

By Funmi Togonu-Bickersteth

With a population of 122 million in 1998, Nigeria was the world's tenth largest country. By the year 2025, Nigeria is expected to be the world's fifth largest country, with an estimated population of 339 million. Nigeria is also a culturally complex country. There are said to be more than 400 ethnic nations and more than 300 dialects spoken in the country. It is therefore not possible to speak of a "Nigerian tradition" in the sense in which one can speak of a "Protestant tradition." The focus of this chapter will, however, be on the Yoruba tradition. This narrows the scope somewhat. When we speak of a Yoruba tradition, we are speaking of a confederation of cultural traditions, many aspects of which can be called religious. Yoruba is not monolithic. The question can be raised, "Whose Yoruba tradition?" Is it that of the Egbas, the Ijebus, the Oyos, the Ondos, or the Ekiti? For these are all Yoruba subethnic groups with their own unique traditions, depending on which of the various deities they lean on for their interpretation of the essence of human existence and the place of humans in the cosmic setup. This chapter will focus on presenting available information on the attitudes of specific ethnic groups in Nigeria and Africa toward fertility, family size, and abortion. The chapter will also examine some of the sayings, proverbs, and societal practices to aid our understanding of the general cultural beliefs about what constitutes appropriate family size and the actual practices extant in the country.

Demographically, Nigeria is one of the rapidly growing nations of the world. Its population in 1970 was 55.1 million, in 1995, 117.1 million, and in the year 2015 it is estimated that the population will be 190.0 million. However, Nigeria has also been witnessing a very gradual decline in its total fertility rate. The fertility rate in 1960 was 6.5; in 1990, 6.0; and in 1998, 5.1. The average rate of reduction in fertility rate was 0.3 percent between 1960 and 1998.[1] However, compared with other countries, the fertility rate for Nigeria, though declining, is still high. There are also regional differences in fertility rates within the country. The fertility rate in the North is said to be higher than those for the south. What sociocultural factors appear to be supportive of this high fertility in Nigeria and indeed in most parts of sub-Saharan Africa?

In many societies in sub-Saharan African countries, women generally attribute to God the number of children they have. As John Mbiti has written, marriage and having children is viewed as a religious duty. To be unmarried and childless is regarded "as stopping the flow of life ... and hence the diminishing of mankind upon earth."[2] In fact, one of the most sensitive questions to ask in any survey is, "How many children do you have?" Among the rural-dwelling Yoruba such questions cannot be asked directly because of the common saying "*A ki ka omo fun olomo*" ("You must not count someone else's children"). Demographers working in the field are familiar with the occurrence of nonnumeric responses to the question, "How many children do you wish to

Funmi Togonu-Bickersteth, "Family Planning and Abortion: Cultural Norms Versus Actual Practices in Nigeria," *Sacred Rights: The Case for Contraception and Abortion in World Religions*, pp. 167–174. Copyright © 2003 by Oxford University Press. Reprinted with permission.

have?" God is perceived as the only one who can answer such a fundamental question. Among the Edos of Nigeria, for example, God is referred to as "bringer of children"[3] and the Yoruba regard children as God's gift or blessing from heaven that cannot be refused. Jacob Olupona writes that in 1992, "Nigeria decided to produce a population blueprint to guide policy on birth control and fertility." Within a week, there was such a popular uproar led by religious leaders from the indigenous religions and also Christians and Muslims that the state had to back off. The policy was seen as an infringement on the people's private religious prerogatives.[4] The Rwandans place such a high premium on the task and privilege of transmitting life that they believe that the number of offspring should not be limited but should be accepted as God-given. The possible fecundity of a would-be bride is an important consideration in approving and forging marriage ties among the Yoruba of Nigeria. Infertility is regarded as justifiable excuse for a husband to seek additional wives.[5] The idea that the infertile partner may be the male usually receives little or no attention. This high desire to prove fertility is also linked with the desire to demonstrate it in a large number of children. The Yorubas expect the new bride to become a mother within the first year of marriage. A typical prayer at wedding ceremonies is, "by this time next year, we will all gather together again to welcome your child."

Olupona observes that he was struck when he read that Princess Diana, when she was pregnant with Prince William, said that she felt that all of Britain was carrying the child with her. Says Olupona: "In African communities this is not just the privilege of royals; the pregnancy of any village woman has special significance for the community."[6] If the whole village feels it is pregnant with your prospective child, your reproductive freedom is limited.

This stress on fecundity is woven into much of African culture. In the popular novel *Things Fall Apart,* by Chinua Achebe, the hero's Uncle Mbata has this advice for him: "We do not ask for wealth because he that has health and children will have wealth. We do not pray to have more money but to have more kinsmen."[7]

A number of factors fuel the ideal of a large family size. Among these factors is what can be called an insurance strategy.[8] This is the practice of having more than the desired number of children because of the fear of infant and child mortality, to ensure survivorship of sons to continue the lineage. In times past the infant mortality rates for most parts of Africa were quite high.[9] Among the Yoruba, the infant mortality rate was so high that the concept of "Abiku" (children who are born, only to die shortly thereafter) was quite widely accepted. Various rituals were performed on those children at death to mark them or to discourage them from returning to the same family. Similarly, many rituals and practices, including scarring of the face and body of the baby, are performed to prevent a currently living baby from supposedly associating with his/her unseen friends in the spirit realm who may take him/her away. Therefore, because a woman was never really sure which of her living children would survive, it made good sense to have as many as she could possibly have. However, because of the general improvement in sanitation and the active immunization drive in the country, infant mortality seems to be on the decline. A particularly useful index is the under-five mortality rate. This is the probability of dying between birth and exactly five years of age, expressed per 1,000 live births. For Nigeria in 1960, the under-five mortality rate was 207, and in 1998, 187. Though gradually decreasing, the rate of decrease is still far from satisfactory, particularly when it is observed that in 1994, the under-five rate for Kenya was already 74.

A second factor most probably associated with large family size is the economic contribution of child labor to the household economy. The larger a man's household, the larger his potential pool of workers. The larger the number of children, the larger the acreage that could be farmed. With modernization, the introduction of Western education, wage employment, and the rural-urban migration, young children who cannot yet hold full formal employment of who have no opportunity to migrate to the urban centers still assist their parents on the farm. However, an increasing proportion of children now assist with enlarging the pool of the family's income by engaging in such activities as street hawking, serving as domestic servants to elite families in the urban centers, and other economic activities. Regrettably, children (under 15 years of age) engage in these activities which are often deleterious to their physical and emotional health, and which deprive them of the opportunity to enroll or remain in schools. Thus, not having gained any additional educational or vocational skills, they have little chance for futures better than those of their parents. Hence, the cycle of poverty continues into the next generation, with an enduring and predictable impact on population increases.

A third factor most probably responsible for the large number of children is the expectation of assistance from adult children during old age. There is no formal public assistance for those elders who worked in the informal sector of the economy. Therefore, in old age, with its diminished economic activity, there is usually a total reliance on support from adult children. Under this situation, ideally, the greater the number of adult children a person has, the greater the degree of assistance he/she can expect in old age.[10]

A related factor in understanding the persistence of high fertility rates is the role of women in reproductive decision making. Among the Yoruba generally, with very few exceptions, the role of the woman in reproductive decision making is constricted by societal expectations and cultural norms. Before marriage, she is under the authority of her parents in matters of her sexuality, as well as other matters. At marriage, these rights are transferred to her husband, whom she publicly declares during the ceremony to be "her friend, her older brother, and her father." In Nigeria it used to be that an unmarried girl had to bring her parents to get family planning services and a married woman had to show she had the husband's consent. A woman who refuses to bear more children, when able to, is likely to incur the displeasure of her husband and her in-laws. The latter might give all encouragement to the husband of the "stubborn" woman to acquire additional younger wives who will gladly oblige him. Given this high price placed on children, it is encouraging to report that there are positive attitudes also toward family planning in Nigeria.

Among the Yoruba, postpartum abstinence and the operation of sex taboos associated with breastfeeding are some of the cultural devices that make it possible for children to be spaced. It is reported that the average space is about 2 to 2 ½ years.[11] This practice works best when the family is an economic unit and the family structure polygamous so that the husband's sexual desires can be met by other wives. The demands of breastfeeding also assumes that the child is kept within the reach of the mother almost all of the time. With the participation of the women in the formal labor force and the introduction of baby formula and creches at the urban centers, this cultural device of birth spacing is becoming unworkable for the urban, educated women living in monogamous family settings. There is therefore a recourse to the newer methods. Studies conducted in Southwestern Nigeria report that a substantial proportion of women approve family planning in principle. Studies further reveal that acquisition of some formal education and skills are vital in gaining family planning information either directly from the mass media or through the public health institutions. The younger and urban based-women have higher approval rates of family planning. Among the reasons given for approving family planning are the mother's health, ability to care for the child, and ability to provide for the child later. There is still, however, the broad opinion that methods of birth control are risky. It is to be noted that there are indigenous methods of birth control that have not been adequately studied.[12]

Regarding the attitude toward family planning, mention must also be made of what has been known as the "male factor" in family planning in sub-Saharan Africa. It has been found in Ghana, Nigeria, and Sudan, for example, that the male partner plays an important role in decision making regarding contraception use, timing, and the number of a couple's children. The tradition of polygamy is also a complicating factor in Africa. Traditionally, polygamy symbolized prestige and affluence, and was an indication of wealth.[13] Polygamy is also associated with men's reproductive preferences. Men may either have more than one wife because they want more children or want more children because they have more wives. For instance, a government proclamation in Nigeria during the reign of President Babangida that recommended four children per woman was generally interpreted to mean that a man who had four wives could then have sixteen children! The fertility preferences of wives in polygamous unions are often not very clear. Wives in such unions may want more children in order to compete favorably with cowives in terms of child-bearing and status in the household. On the other hand, this desire may be curtailed by the fact that women in polygamous unions tend to shoulder greater responsibilities in rearing their children than those in monogamous marriages. In general, what can be concluded is that most people (women in particular) hold two sets of opposing ideas when it comes to contraceptives and family planning: belief that children are a blessing from God and should be accepted and also the belief that family planning is desirable to ensure the health of the mother and the proper upbringing of the children. The pronatalist forces are such that it limits success in the family planning area. For example, contraceptive prevalence for Nigeria for 1990–99 was only 6 percent as compared with a 59 percent for Morocco and 82 percent for the United

Kingdom, This may not take account of indigenous methods, the prevalence of which is not known with any precision.

Abortion

Concerning abortion, the picture is clearer. There is government legislation against abortion in Nigeria, and the general view is that only unmarried people have abortions. The Yoruba disapprove of pregnancy in young girls but they also disapprove of "grandmother pregnancy." To avoid the likelihood of the latter, most Yoruba women abstain from sexual intercourse once their children are married and they become grandmothers. Women consider the occasion of grandmother pregnancy serious enough to call for abortion. Aside from this, abortion is generally perceived as dangerous, immoral, and shameful, but there is strong evidence that it is still resorted to. Despite the seeming public condemnation of abortion in Africa, available evidence suggests that the practice is prevalent. In Nigeria in particular, the most recent information on the issue reveals that at least 610,000 pregnancy terminations occur in Nigeria yearly and 60 percent of the abortions are performed by "nonphysician providers." Included in these nonphysician providers could be fake doctors or herbal doctors, most of whom have knowledge of traditional abortifacients.

The criminalization of abortion has led to an increase in the health risks associated with having illegal abortions and the economic costs of having a proper abortion. Adolescent pregnancy is perceived as a shame not only for the girl but also for the family. It disrupts the girl's education and stigmatizes her. The only one possible option is abortion, a choice society has made unsafe by driving it underground. Estimates on the relationship of maternal deaths to abortion vary from 20 to 30 percent, and, obviously, data is not easy to confirm.

Gaps between the normative prescriptions concerning family reproductive matters and the actual experiences in Nigeria today are revealed in popular sayings and current practices on the social scene. Among the commonest Yoruba idiomatic expressions concerning reasonable family size is: "*Omo beere oosi beere*" ("Many children, many afflictions"). The Yoruba appear to believe that having too many children leads to poverty in the family. Another popular saying is "*Bi a bi okan oga, o ya ju egberun obun omo lo*" ("Better to have just one successful child than to have a thousand useless ones").

The Kikuyu people of Kenya have a saying that many births mean many burials.[14] There is also a general belief among the Yoruba that the larger the family size, the greater the possibility of having abnormal children. It is therefore expected that among children of kings and important personalities who have large families, there will be one or two with deformity or aberrant behavior. Thus, within the same cultural group where children are highly valued, we find in existence elements cautioning against excessive large family size or at least acknowledging the potential problems of having a large family.

Another indicator on the social scene suggests that the cultural stance of zero tolerance for abortion is leading to the practice of abandonment, especially by young mothers, a practice very common in Christian medieval Europe. Traditionally, if any child was abandoned, it was a child with a gross deformity believed to be brought upon the family by malevolent spiritual forces. A few of such children were abandoned. But nowadays, the neonates abandoned are healthy ones. The society has no long-term plans for these abandoned neonates.

Secondly, because of the changes in the socioeconomic conditions and the effects of globalization, both the direct and indirect costs of raising children have increased tremendously. The instrumental values of children to parents appears to be diminishing over time. The economic benefits they provide as extra labor hands, old age support, and risk insurance have declined over time. Current gerontological studies in Nigeria suggest that the expectation of old-age support from adult children may no longer be realistic, as there is already an increase in the visibility of destitute elderly beggars in the major urban centers. Furthermore, transnational migration by an increasing number of youths may mean decreased availability of younger people to care for the aged.

A third factor, which needs to be part of the campaign for a just, humane, and reasonable reproductive health stance, is the AIDS scourge in much of Africa. It has been said that more people have died from AIDS in Africa than have died from the various wars fought on the continent. Furthermore, for developing countries, unsafe sex comes second only to malnutrition among the risk factors associated with percentage of disability-adjusted life years.

Thus, the previously prevailing socioeconomic conditions that provide justification for the pronatalist orientation to reproductive health are no longer salient although they have not quite disappeared either. New health risk factors—for example, AIDS—with potentially devastating and confounding effects on population dynamics have also emerged on the scene. Within this rather fluid context, therefore, an individual's practice with respect to family planning and abortion will depend upon their location in the socioeconomic scale and more especially on their appraisal of the incentives for a reduced family size. Among the poor, rural dwellers where there is always the need to marshal all resources including those of children to meet the basic economic needs of the family, small family size may still be undesired. But among the educated, westernized, urban population, family planning has wider acceptance because the existential living conditions in the urban centers may make large family size a burden rather than a help. Thus, although cultural norms in general extol the desirability of large family size, compliance with that and other norms concerning reproductive decisions depends on the extent to which the norms facilitate the individual's pursuit of his/her existential needs. Hence, as norms shape practice, existential conditions seem also to be shaping the norms in reproductive matters. It is a fluid situation.

NOTES

1. For references to African fertility rates, see *The State of the World's Children,* an annual publication of UNICEF, The United Nations, New York.
2. John Mbiti, *Introduction to African Religion* (New York: Heinemann, 1991), p. 98.
3. Ibid.
4. Jacob Olupona, "African Religions and Global Issues," in *Visions of a New Earth; Religious Perspectives on Population, Consumption, and Ecology* (Albany: State University of New York Press, 2000), pp. 181–82.
5. For discussion of polygamy in African cultures, see N. A. Fadipe, *The Sociology of the Yoruba* (Ibadan: Ibadan University Press, 1970).
6. Olupona, *Visions of a New Earth,* p. 194.
7. Chinua Achebe, *Things Fall Apart* (London: Heinemann, 1958), p. 146.
8. C. B. Lloyd, "The Effects of Improved Child Survival on Family Planning, Practice, and Fertility," *Studies in Family Planning* 19, 1988, pp. 141–61.
9. J. F. May, M. Mukarnanzi, and M. Vekemans, "Family Planning in Rwanda," *Studies in Family Planning,* 21, 1990, pp. 20–31.
10. Funmi Togonu-Bickersteth, "Gender Differences in Expressed Satisfaction with Care from Adult Children Among Older Rural Yoruba," *Southern African Journal of Gerontology,* 6, 1997, pp. 3–6; F. Togonu-Bickersteth, E. O. Akinnawo, O. S. Akinyele, and E. Ayeni, "Public Alms Solicitation Among the Yoruba Elderly in Nigeria," *Southern African Journal of Gerontology,* 6, 1997, pp. 26–31.
11. E. T. Dow, "Breastfeeding and Abstinence Among the Yoruba," *Studies in Family Planning,* 21, 1981, pp. 272–77.
12. See Olupona, *Visions of a New Earth,* p. 195
13. Ibid.
14. G. Barra, *Kikuyu Proverbs* (Nairobi, Kenya: Kenya Literature Bureau, 1939),

Challenges and Opportunities

The Population of the Middle East and North Africa

By Farzaneh Roudi-Fahimi and Mary Mederios Kent

The countries of the Middle East and North Africa (MENA) continue to fascinate and concern the rest of the world. With two-thirds of the world's known petroleum reserves, the region's economic and political importance far outweighs its population size. It has the world's second-fastest growing population, after sub-Saharan Africa. Its demographic trends—especially the rapidly growing youth population—are complicating the region's capacity to adapt to social change, economic strains, and sometimes wrenching political transformations.

The people of the Middle East and North Africa have long played an integral, if sometimes volatile, role in the history of human civilization. Three of the world's major religions originated in the region—Judaism, Christianity, and Islam. MENA contains some of the world's oldest cities; universities existed here long before they emerged in Europe. Today, the population is overwhelmingly Islamic, yet includes substantial Jewish and Christian minorities. And, while Arabic is the predominant language, two of the region's largest countries—Iran and Turkey—and Israel, are not Arabic-speaking.

Thanks to rapidly declining death rates and slowly declining fertility rates, MENA's population size quadrupled in the last half of the 20th century. It stands at about 430 million in 2007. Despite recent fertility declines, MENA's population is projected to surpass 700 million by 2050.

One consequence of the region's recent demographic trends is an increasingly notable youth bulge. One in every three people living in the region is between ages 10 and 24. This young population provides momentum for continued population growth in the region, despite declining fertility.

This large crop of young people also needs jobs and training—in a region currently plagued by high unemployment. While the youth bulge offers a potential demographic dividend—a temporary surge in the proportion of working-age adults in the population that can boost economic growth—there are many obstacles to reaping this windfall. High unemployment, a mismatch of jobs and skill levels, extensive government entitlements, and political instability are among the factors that have made it difficult for the young MENA population to spur economic growth. In addition, citizens must compete with foreigners for jobs in some Persian Gulf countries where one-half or more of the labor force consists of foreign workers.

Whether this large group of young people become healthy and productive members of their societies will depend on how well governments and civil societies invest in social, economic, and political institutions that meet their needs. The fastest growth in the youth population will be in places that are the least prepared economically: Iraq, the Palestinian Territory, and Yemen.

Farzaneh Roudi-Fahimi and Mary Mederios Kent, "Challenges and Opportunities: The Population of the Middle East and North Africa," *Population Bulletin*, vol. 62, no. 2, pp. 3–19. Copyright © 2007 by Population Reference Bureau. Reprinted with permission.

Population growth has also exacerbated natural resource constraints in the region. Most MENA countries already are designated as water scarce because they fall below the international threshold of 1,000 cubic meters of freshwater per capita per year. Environmental factors threaten the region's continued economic development and the well-being of the population. Water scarcity can potentially lead to conflicts both among countries and among population groups within a country, adding to the political instability of the region.

What Defines the Middle East and North Africa?

There is no standard definition of the Middle East.[1] The term was used by the British in the late 19th century to refer to the Persian Gulf region. By 1950, the Middle East included not only Iran, Israel, and the Arab states of Western Asia, but also Cyprus, Egypt, and Turkey. The boundaries are sometimes stretched eastward to take in Afghanistan and westward as far as Morocco.

The area covered in this *Population Bulletin* includes 20 countries in Western Asia and North Africa (see Figure 1.10.1). The boundaries are defined by geography rather than religion, ethnicity, or other socioeconomic characteristics. Thus, the Middle East and North Africa (MENA) includes the non-Arab countries of Iran, Israel, and Turkey. MENA countries fall into three general subregions: North Africa, Western Asia, and the Arabian Peninsula. These subregions do not correspond exactly to the United Nations (UN) regions with the same names.

The majority of the region's population lives in the MENA Western Asian countries, particularly Iran, Iraq, Syria, and Turkey (see Table 1.10.1). The Western Asian countries are highly culturally and religiously diverse.

While Arabs are overwhelmingly Muslim in most of the region, there are exceptions. About one-fourth of Lebanon's population is made up of Arab Christians. Sunni Muslims are the majority in the region, with Shia Muslims a majority in Iran and Iraq. About 20 percent of Israel's population is Arab, and they are overwhelmingly Muslim.

The countries on the Arabian Peninsula have small populations, which nevertheless grew rapidly between the 1950s and 2007, and are projected to continue to grow rapidly over the next 50 years. These countries included about 59 million people in 2007, with 80 percent living in Saudi Arabia and Yemen. All the Arabian Peninsula countries except Yemen border on the Persian Gulf.

Figure 1.10.1
Population in the Middle East and North Africa, 2007

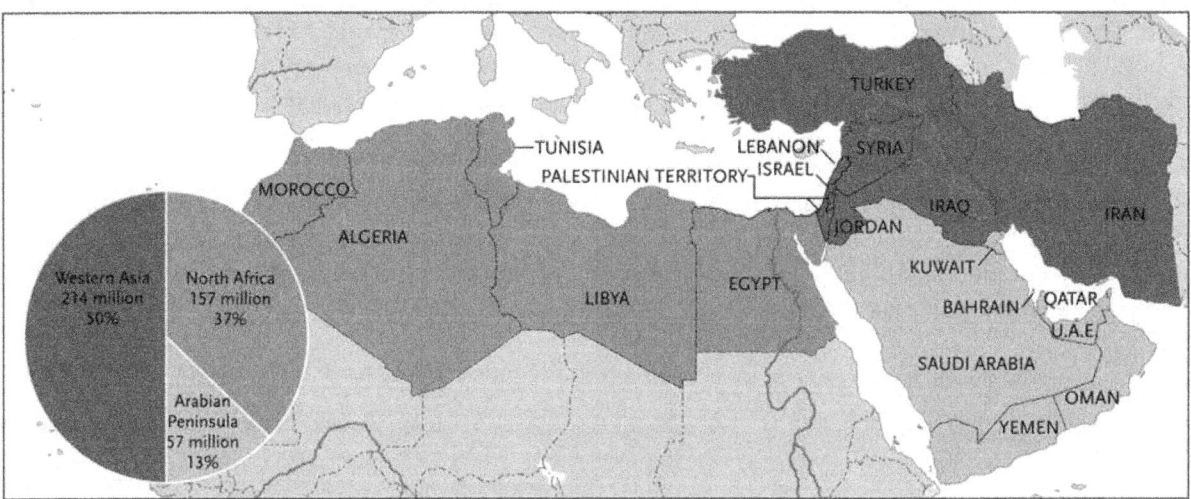

Some of the country boundaries shown are undetermined or in dispute.

Source: UN Population Division, *World Population Prospects: The 2006 Revision* (2007; http://esa.un.org, accessed April 7, 2007).

North Africa is also predominately Arab and Islamic and is dominated demographically by the region's largest country, Egypt. Indeed, one of every four Arabs lives in Egypt.

Establishing National Boundaries

Political and religious movements, as well as natural resources, have shaped the modern Middle East. Much of the region was part of the Roman and then Byzantine Empires until the 7th century, when Islam was introduced. Islam eventually forged a common cultural and religious bond throughout the region. The Islamic, but non-Arab, Turks ruled much of the area between the 13th century until the early 20th century.

The boundaries of most modern MENA nations date from the collapse of the Ottoman Empire after World War I. Former Ottoman territories were carved into many small states, with sometimes arbitrary national boundaries and often under the hegemony of western nations. In 1920, the League of Nations awarded France control of Lebanon and Syria, and the United Kingdom control of Iraq and Palestine. Jordan was created from the slice of Palestine east of the Jordan River. The northern African countries were under largely French or Italian control in the early 20th century, and only became independent nations in the 1950s or 1960s.

Bitter boundary disputes have plagued the region for most of the past century. The most virulent and far-reaching began in the 1940s when the Jewish state of Israel was created within the former British protectorate of Palestine. Many neighboring countries have never recognized Israel, and the discord has sparked several wars and ongoing civil conflicts. In North Africa, Algeria endured a protracted war before it gained independence from France in 1962. In contrast, the union of the Yemen Arab Republic and the Democratic Republic of Yemen in 1990

Table 1.10.1 Population Size and Growth in the Countries of the Middle East and North Africa: 1950, 2007, and 2050

Country and region	Population in thousands			Ratio of population	
	1950	2007	2050*	2007/1950	2050/2007
Middle East and North Africa (MENA)	103,886	431,587	692,299	4.2	1.6
MENA–Western Asia	51,452	215,976	332,081	4.2	1.5
Iran	16,913	71,208	100,174	4.2	1.4
Iraq	5,340	28,993	61,942	5.4	2.1
Israel	1,258	6,928	10,527	5.5	1.5
Jordan	472	5,924	10,121	12.5	1.7
Lebanon	1,443	4,099	5,221	2.8	1.3
Palestinian Territory	1,005	4,017	10,265	4.0	2.6
Syria	3,536	19,929	34,887	5.6	1.8
Turkey	21,484	74,877	98,946	3.5	1.3
Arabian Peninsula	8,336	58,544	123,946	7.0	2.1
Bahrain	116	753	1,173	6.5	1.6
Kuwait	152	2,851	5,240	18.7	1.8
Oman	456	2,595	4,639	5.7	1.8
Qatar	25	841	1,333	33.6	1.6
Saudi Arabia	3,201	24,735	45,030	7.7	1.8
United Arab Emirates	70	4,380	8,521	62.9	1.9
Yemen	4,316	22,389	58,009	5.2	2.6
Northern Africa	44,099	157,068	236,272	3.6	1.5
Algeria	8,753	33,858	49,610	3.9	1.5
Egypt	21,834	75,498	121,219	3.5	1.6
Morocco	8,953	31,224	42,583	3.5	1.4
Libya	1,029	6,160	9,683	6.0	1.6
Tunisia	3,530	10,327	13,178	2.9	1.3

* *Projected*
Source: UN Population Division, World Population Prospects: The 2006 Revision (2007; http://esa.un.org/, accessed April 10, 2007): table A.2.

went remarkably smoothly after the collapse of the Soviet Union, but civil strife and violence continue to take lives and disrupt the economies in parts of the region.

Population Growth and Change

Much of the Middle East and North Africa was sparsely populated for hundreds of years, with population totals fluctuating because of spikes in mortality caused by plagues, droughts, or other disasters. As in much of the world, the 20th century brought accelerating population growth to MENA. The population total reached 104 million by 1950—and then quadrupled, to more than 400 million, by 2000. In 2007, the total stood at 432 million. The latest population projections for the region show the total reaching nearly 700 million by 2050 (see Figure 1.10.2).

Improvements in human survival, particularly during the second half of the 20th century, sparked the rapid population growth in MENA and other less developed regions. The introduction of modern medical services and public health interventions, such as antibiotics, immunization, and sanitation, caused death rates to plummet in the developing world after 1950. The MENA region's fertility remained relatively high, producing high rates of natural increase (the surplus of births over deaths). Spurred by high fertility and declining mortality, MENA's annual population growth peaked at 3 percent around 1980, more than a decade after the world's population growth rate reached its high points at 2 percent annually.[2]

The "demographic transition" from high mortality and fertility to low mortality and fertility tends to occur in stages: declining mortality followed by declining fertility and, finally, relatively stable birth and death rates at low levels. This transition is well underway throughout the region, but it has proceeded at very different rates in different countries.[3]

Immigration has also played an important role in population change in some parts of the region over the last half-century. Economic expansion following the jump in oil revenues in the 1970s attracted millions of foreign workers, especially to the Arabian Peninsula. Millions have also moved from "labor-rich," non-oil-producing countries to seek jobs in the oil-rich countries within the region. A stream of migration out of the region—especially from North Africa and Turkey to Europe—is also creating large Arab and Muslim communities in some developed countries.

Figure 1.10.2
Population Growth in the MENA Regions: 1950, 2007, and 2050

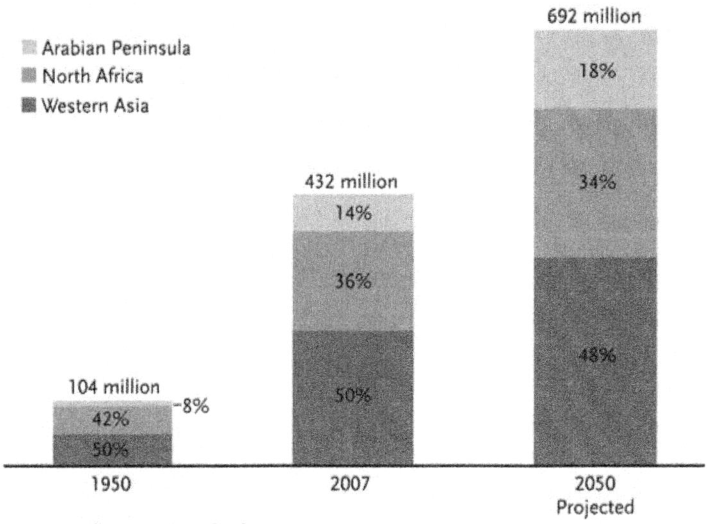

Region	1950 (104 million)	2007 (432 million)	2050 Projected (692 million)
Arabian Peninsula	8%	14%	18%
North Africa	42%	36%	34%
Western Asia	50%	50%	48%

MENA: Middle East and North Africa

Source: UN Population Division, *World Population Prospects: The 2006 Revision* (2007; http://esa.un.org, accessed April 7, 2007).

Mortality Decline Continues

The declines in mortality that occurred in the past 50 years in the developing world especially benefited infants and young children. In MENA, infant mortality (infants dying before their first birthdays) dropped from close to 200 deaths per 1,000 live births in the early 1950s to around 30 deaths per 1,000 live births in the early 21st century. Countries throughout the region saw great improvement n infant mortality, but the decline was especially steep In some, such as Yemen and Turkey (see Figure 1.10.3).

But the regional average remains above that of Latin America and East Asia, and the wide range in national rates signals disparities in health services and living standards within the region. Large differences in maternal mortality and life expectancy at birth among the MENA countries add evidence of unequal access to basic health education and services.

In recent years, infant mortality rates in some oil-rich Persian Gulf states have been quite low—less than 10 infant deaths per 1,000 births around 2005—but the rates ranged up to 40 in Morocco and 75 in Yemen. Likewise, maternal mortality ratios are extremely high—above 200 maternal deaths per 100,000 births—in Morocco and Yemen, but they were less than 8 In Kuwait and Qatar (see Table 1.10.2). The average for industrialized countries in 2000 was 17.[4]

Both infant and maternal mortality drop quickly when mothers have access to medical care and emergency obstetric services during childbirth. The public health system developed in Iran provides an example of how governments can engage the community and improve health services even in rural areas (see Box 1.10.1).

Life expectancy at birth also varies throughout the region, although the regional averages exceeded the world average of 67 years in 2006. The more developed and wealthier MENA countries enjoy average life expectancy equal to that in many developed countries. Around 2005, Israelis lived 80 years on average, and Kuwaitis and Emiratis lived 77 years—about the same as the averages for the United States (78) and Denmark (80). On the lower end, life expectancy was 60 years in Yemen. As infant and child mortality decline, average life expectancies are expected to rise.

While maternal mortality rates remain high by international standards, many countries have made considerable progress. Egypt, for example, dramatically lowered a woman's lifetime risk of dying from pregnancy or childbirth

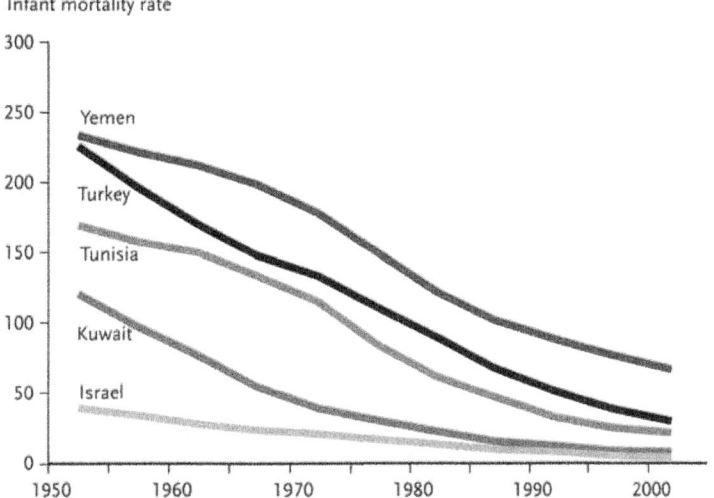

Figure 1.10.3
Patterns of Decline in Infant Mortality, Selected Countries in the Middle East and North Africa, 1950–2005

Note: The infant mortality rate is the number of deaths of infants under age 1 per 1,000 live births.

Source: UN Population Division, *World Population Prospects: The 2006 Revision* (2007: http://esa.un.org/, accessed April 10, 2007).

Table 1.10.2 Mortality Indicators in the Countries of the Middle East and North Africa, Around 2005

Country and region	Infant mortality rate	Maternal mortality ratio	Life expectancy at birth (years)
Middle East and North Africa	31	207	71
MENA–Western Asia	27	104	71
Iran	32	76	70
Iraq	34	250	—
Israel	4	17	80
Jordan	24	41	72
Lebanon	17	150	72
Palestinian Territory	21	100	72
Syria	18	160	73
Turkey	25	70	71
Arabian Peninsula	40	236	68
Bahrain	10	28	74
Kuwait	10	5	77
Oman	10	87	74
Qatar	9	7	73
Saudi Arabia	23	23	72
United Arab Emirates	9	54	77
Yemen	75	570	60
North Africa	33	126	71
Algeria	30	140	75
Egypt	33	84	70
Libya	26	97	76
Morocco	40	220	70
Tunisia	21	120	73

— Not available.
Infant mortality rate: The number of deaths of infants under age 1 per 1,000 live births. Maternal mortality ratio: The number of women dying as a result of pregnancy or childbirth per 100,000 live births. The most recent estimates are for 2000.
Sources: C. Haub, 2006 World Population Data Sheet (www.prb.org, accessed May 1, 2007); UNICEF, UN Population Fund, and World Health Organization, Maternal Mortality 2000 (2003; www.who.int, accessed May 14, 2007); and UNICEF, Statistics: Multiple Indicator Cluster Survey 3, Survey Reports: Iraq (www.childinfo.org, accessed May 15, 2007).

from one in 120 to one in 250 during the 1990s. Now considered a successful model for the region, Egypt achieved this improvement through a comprehensive and coordinated approach to improving the health of expectant mothers. The health ministry, along with national and international health groups, analyzed the specific factors contributing to poor maternal health in Egyptian communities and took definitive steps to address those causes.[5]

Egypt's government is also seeking to increase the use of contraception to help bolster child and maternal health, as well as to lower fertility and slow population growth.[6] A wealth of research shows that mothers who wait until their 20s to have children, space their pregnancies at least two or three years apart, and avoid pregnancies after age 35 have healthier children and enjoy better individual health.[7] The increased use of family planning, better maternal and child health, and lower fertility tend to go hand-in-hand.

Declining Fertility

The burst of population growth in MENA in the late 20th century was dampened as fertility began to decline in more countries in the region. MENA's total fertility rate (TFR), or average number of children born per woman given current birth rates, declined from about seven children in 1960 to three in 2006.[8] MENA countries followed very different paths to lower fertility. The decline started first in Lebanon, then in a few other countries including

Table 1.10.3 Fertility and Contraceptive Use in the Middle East and North Africa, Around 2005

Country and region	Total fertility rate	Percent of married women using contraception	
		Any method	Modern method
Middle East and North Africa (MENA)	3.0	58	45
MENA-Western Asia	2.7	66	45
Iran	2.0	74	56
Iraq	4.8	50	33
Israel	2.8	—	—
Jordan	3.7	56	41
Lebanon	1.9	58	34
Palestinian Territory	4.6	50	39
Syria	3.5	47	35
Turkey	2.2	71	43
Arabian Peninsula	4.8	29	22
Bahrain	2.6	65	—
Kuwait	2.4	52	39
Oman	3.4	24	18
Qatar	2.8	43	32
Saudi Arabia	4.5	32	29
United Arab Emirates	2.2	28	24
Yemen	6.2	23	13
Northern Africa	2.8	59	54
Algeria	2.4	57	52
Egypt	3.1	59	57
Libya	3.4	49	26
Morocco	2.5	63	55
Tunisia	2.0	63	53

—Not available.
Note: The total fertility rate is the total number of births a woman would have given current birth rates. The contraceptive use percentages refer to married women of childbearing age (ages 15-49).
Numbers in italics refer to estimates prior to 2000.
Sources: C. Haub, *2006 World Population Data Sheet* (www.prb.org, accessed May 1, 2007); UNICEF, *Statistics: Multiple Indicator Cluster Survey 3, Survey Reports: OPT and Iraq* (www.childinfo.org, accessed May 15, 2007); and League of Arab States, *PAPFAM Version 3.0* (CD-ROM, 2007).

Egypt, Iran, and Tunisia. These last three countries were among the first to adopt policies to lower fertility to a way to slow population growth.[9]

By the early 2000s, the TFR was below 4.0 in all but four of the 20 countries in the region: Iraq, Saudi Arabia, the Palestinian Territory, and Yemen (see Table 1.10.3).

In Iran, Lebanon, Tunisia, and Turkey, fertility was at or below the replacement level of about 2.1 children per woman. Yemen's TFR has edged downward, but remains the region's highest at 6.2 in 2005. Israel's TFR was the region's lowest in the 1950s, but has not declined as far as in many other countries (see Figure 1.10.4).

Importance of Families

Strong cultural values attached to the family and traditional marriage and childbearing practices delayed the transition to lower fertility in MENA. The family is the center of life in MENA's culture. Families provide social security for the elderly, sick, or disabled, and an economic refuge for financially dependent relatives.[10]

Accordingly, universal marriage and large families were highly valued in MENA. Muslim migrants from MENA countries often bring these family norms to their new homes. Muslims in France and Germany have somewhat higher fertility rates than non-Muslim French and Germans.[11] Within Israel, Muslim women had 4.0 children on average in 2005, compared with 2.7 for Jewish women, and 2.2 for Christian women.[12]

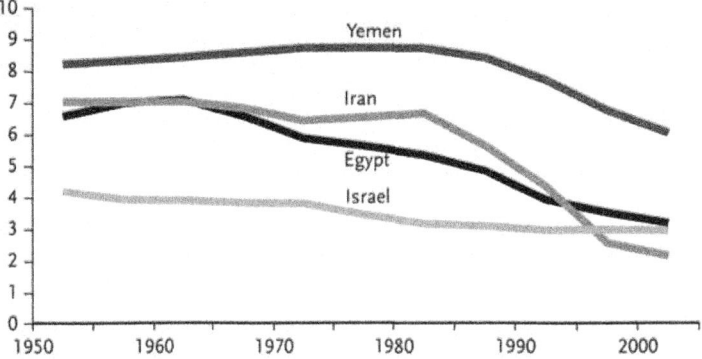

Figure 1.10.4
Patterns of Fertility Decline in Selected Countries in the Middle East and North Africa, 1950–2005

Note: The total fertility rate refers to the average number of children born per woman given current birth rates.

Source: UN Population Division, *World Population Prospects: The 2006 Revision* (2007; http://esa.un.org/, accessed April 10, 2007).

These cultural factors helped delay the transition to lower fertility in MENA, even as the region was developing economically. But several changes in recent decades hastened the decline in fertility: delayed marriage, wider acceptance of and access to family planning services, and increased education of girls and young women. In some countries, the laws that have restricted women's rights and participation in the wider society are being relaxed (see Box 1.10.2). Some observers have noted that these fundamental changes demonstrate that Islam is not itself a barrier to fertility decline or improved status of women as many had assumed, but that the high fertility that persisted in the region for so long reflected a constellation of social and economic as well as religious factors.[13]

Waiting Longer to Marry

Marriage is an important turning point in a young woman's life in MENA. Marriage and childbearing define life for nearly all women in the MENA region. Until the last few decades, women throughout the region typically married while still in their teens or early 20s (see Box 1.10.3). The universal value placed on marriage, compounded by religious and social condemnation of premarital and extramarital sexual relationships, encouraged girls to marry young and to bear children soon thereafter. Only rarely did women remain single and childless.

MENA's fertility decline is linked to a transformation in these marriage patterns: Women are waiting until they are older to marry and are marrying men closer to their own age. And, couples want fewer children.

The age at marriage in the region is rapidly changing. While the average age at first marriage for women was between 18 and 21 in most countries in the 1970s, it was between 22 and 25 by the late 1990s. North African countries saw an especially steep increase in marriage age. In Libya, the average rose from age 19 to age 29 between the mid-1970s and late 1990s. The average marriage was above age 25 in all the North African countries except for Egypt, where it was just 22 in 1998. In high-fertility Yemen, the average age at marriage was about 21 in 1998.[14]

Another remarkable shift in marriage patterns is the increase in number of women who are not married by the time they reach their late 30s, many of whom will never marry. Lebanon stands out, with one-fifth of women ages 35 to 39 still unmarried. The proportion of women remaining single into their late 30s was also high—between one-sixth and one-seventh in the North African countries, except for Egypt. In Egypt, just three out of 100 women were still unmarried by ages 35 to 39. Likewise, less than 5 percent of women stayed single into their late 30s in most of the Arabian Peninsula countries.[15]

The delay in marriage also reflects rising economic aspirations for young people, including a trend toward more couples living on their own. The costs of getting married have been increasing in some countries. But the marriage

> **Box 1.10.1 Iran's Rural Health Care Network**
>
> Iran's rural health care network is the cornerstone of the country's health care system. The network evolved from a series of pilot projects conducted in the early 1970s to find the best system for expanding medical and health services for Iran's widely dispersed rural population. These projects led to the establishment of rural "health houses," based on the idea that vaccine-preventable diseases, acute respiratory infections, and diarrheal diseases can be addressed by making simple technology and information available to even minimally trained personnel. Mobile clinics bring health services to people living in remote areas.
>
> There are now more than 16,000 health houses in Iran, covering around 95 percent of the rural population. Each health house serves around 1,500 people, usually including people from the central village where the health house is located and satellite villages within an hour's walk. Each health house generally has two health providers (in principle, one man and one woman), known as *behvarz*, who receive two years of training. The female *behvarz* is in charge of maternal and child health care and the male is responsible for issues related to environmental health, such as water and food safety. A *behvarz* must be a local resident, which is particularly important for a female *behvarz* because she can continue to live in her home village.
>
> One of the first tasks of a *behvarz* team is to take a population census of the villages to be served by their health house. The census is repeated at the beginning of each Iranian calendar year (March 21), and the age and sex profiles of each village are put in charts. Monthly summary tables of these data are posted on the wall of each health house. The charts can show the number of children who have been born since the beginning of the year, the proportion who have been vaccinated, and the number who died, by cause of death. The data also show the number of married women of reproductive age and their contraceptive prevalence rate by method. A *behvarz* is proactive—comfortable knocking on people's doors to talk about families' health care needs, including family planning, and to schedule appointments to visit the health house.
>
> Reference
>
> Farzaneh Roudi-Fahimi, *Iran's Family Planning Program: Responding to a Nation's Needs* (Washington, DC: Population Reference Bureau, 2002): 4.

delay also marks a broader shift in women's role in MENA society. Women who marry while still in their teens typically are more socially isolated, know less about family planning and reproductive health services, and often lack the power to make decisions about their own health, especially if their husbands are much older. Early marriage is associated with high fertility because—in addition to lower family planning use—a young bride is at risk of pregnancy for more years than women marrying at an older age.[16] The rising marriage age, then, has helped lower fertility in the region, along with other changes in the status of women.

Women's Educational Gains

In conjunction with the rising marriage age, girls in MENA are completing more years of school. They enroll in primary school at about the same rate as boys, and an increasing number of young women are entering universities, in some countries even outnumbering male students.

Girls who are illiterate or have little schooling generally come from poor communities and tend to marry and begin childbearing at a young age. Early marriage cuts short girls' formal education and often traps them in a vicious cycle of low education, high fertility, and poverty.

Programs that keep disadvantaged girls in school, or promote their return to school, and teach them literacy and life skills are important for reducing girls' social isolation and promoting broader social and economic development. Community-based strategies are needed to engage local authorities, religious leaders, and families to help remove barriers to girls' education and participation in community activities. A small number of such pilot projects with successful results have been developed in MENA countries with large rural populations.[17]

Box 1.10.2 Improving Women's Rights: Morocco's New Family Code

A strong body of research shows that the Middle East/North Africa region will not fully develop economically unless women play a larger role in the economy and society. Despite their impressive gains in education and health, women in MENA still face gender discrimination that prevents them from reaching their potential. To varying degrees across MENA countries, discrimination against women is built into the culture, government policies, and legal frameworks. In particular, the region's family laws codify discrimination against women and girls, placing them in a subordinate position to men within the family, a position that is then replicated in the economy and society.

Except for Tunisia and Turkey, family laws in Muslim MENA countries are drawn from *Sharia*, or Islamic law. The traditional reading of Islamic law essentially places women under the guardianship of their fathers, husbands, or another male relative. Young women need their guardians' consent to marry, and women have limited rights regarding divorce, child custody, and inheritance. But a growing number of male and female Islamic scholars have been studying religious teachings to justify equal treatment for men and women, and fight discrimination. Inspired by international human rights conventions, MENA women activists and their supporters are now looking to the *Qur'an* and the *Sunnah* (the sayings and deeds of the Prophet Mohammad and his Companions) to develop new interpretations of family law. These activists believe that Islam is at heart egalitarian, and that parts of the *Sharia* codified in family laws were interpretations by men whose views were rooted in the patriarchal traditions of former times.

This movement is expanding, as women's organizations in more countries work to improve women's rights and opportunities. One success story comes from Morocco, where reform of the family code, or *mudawana*, was endorsed by King Muhammad VI as consistent with the spirit of the *Sharia*, and passed by the Parliament in 2004. The new code—the result of a decade of effort—has been heralded as not only a giant leap in women's rights, but also a huge advance in children's rights. The reforms reflect a new path between traditionalists and women's rights activists, and the political commitment of political leaders.

Some features of the new Moroccan family law include:

- Husband and wife share joint responsibility for the family.

- The wife is no longer legally obliged to obey her husband.

- The adult woman is entitled to self-guardianship and may exercise it freely and independently.

- The right to divorce is a prerogative of both men and women, exercised under judicial supervision.

- The principle of divorce by mutual consent is established.

- The woman has the right to impose a condition in the marriage contract requiring that her husband refrain from taking other wives.

- Polygamy is subject to a judge's authorization and to stringent legal conditions (full disclosure about current wives and no objection from the first wife) that make the practice nearly impossible.

- A divorced mother is given the possibility of retaining custody of her children even upon remarrying or moving out of the area where her ex-husband lives.

- The child's right to acknowledgment of paternity is protected in cases in which the marriage has not been officially registered.

- The minimum legal age for marriage is 18 for both men and women.

Reference

Valentine M. Moghadam and Farzaneh Roudi-Fahimi, *Reforming Family Laws to Promote Progress in the Middle East and North Africa* (Washington, DC: Population Reference Bureau, 2005).

> ### Box 1.10.3 Kin Marriages and Polygamy
>
> The MENA region is undergoing what some demographers have called a "marriage revolution." Just a few decades ago, young women married while in their teenage years. They now wait until their 20s—even their late 20s—to get married. They marry men closer to their own age than in past generations. But many young people in MENA countries are clinging to the tradition of marrying a relative—especially a cousin.[1] The tradition likely arose as a way to help extended families consolidate and protect land and other assets. It also reflects the family's influence in a young woman's choice of a spouse.
>
> In recent years, one-quarter to one-third of marriages within most MENA countries were between first cousins or other relatives. In 2003, 27 percent of Moroccan women ages 15 to 49 were married to blood relatives, with the percentage higher in rural than in urban areas. A 2001 survey in Syria revealed that 40 percent of ever-married women in this age group were married to a close relative; 47 percent of women in rural areas.[2]
>
> Polygamy—although much less common—also persists in the region. Under Islamic law and custom, a man is allowed to take up to four wives, assuming that he can provide for and treat them equally. It is legal in the region except in Turkey (since 1926) and Tunisia (since 1956).[3] Less than 5 percent of women in most countries were reportedly in polygamous unions in the late 1990s and early 2000s, with higher percentages in some Arabian Peninsula countries. About 6 percent of ever-married women in Yemen (ages 15 to 49) reported they were in polygamous unions in 2003, 5 percent in Syria in 2001, and just 2 percent of women Lebanon in 2004.
>
> This mix of traditional practices with fertility decline, delayed marriage, and greater educational gains for women are among the paradoxes of the MENA region in the early 2000s.
>
> References
>
> 1. Dominique Tabutin and Bruno Schoumaker, "The Demography of the Arab World and the Middle East From the 1950s to the 2000s," Population-E 60, nos. 5-6 (2005): 528-29; and Hoda Rashad, Magued Osman, and Farzaneh Roudi-Fahimi, *Marriage in the Arab World* (Washington, DC: Population Reference Bureau 2005): 3, accessed online at www.prb.org, on April 7, 2007.
>
> 2. League of Arab States, *Pan-Arab Project for Family Health (PAPFAM)* (CDROM, Version 3.0, 2007).
>
> 3. Tabutin and Schoumaker, "The Demography of the Arab World and the Middle East" 527.

Increasing Use of Contraception

Rising educational levels and expanding family planning services have contributed to increased use of contraceptive methods in the MENA region. Although Islam does not prohibit family planning, young brides traditionally want or are pressured to produce a child soon after marrying; they are unlikely to use a contraceptive method until they have at least one child.

In the four North African countries, plus Iran and Turkey, at least one-quarter of the wives of reproductive age used a contraceptive method by the late 1980s. In most other countries in the region, this percentage ranged between 4 percent and 10 percent. The rates were exceptionally low in Yemen (1 percent in 1979) and Oman (8 percent in 1988).[18]

The 1990s saw a veritable contraceptive revolution in North Africa and Iran, as contraceptive use rose rapidly. More than one-half of the married women of reproductive age now use modern contraceptives in these countries.

The percentage of married women using modern family planning is lowest in several countries on the Arabian Peninsula (see Table 1.10.3), where less than one-fourth of women of reproductive age used a modern contraceptive method according to the most recent data. Outside the peninsula, rates have also remained low in Iraq and Libya.

Increased use among rural women is a key reason for the fertility decline in some MENA countries. In Egypt, which has a large rural population, the percentage of rural women using a method of family planning increased

> **Box 1.10.4 Family Planning and Islam**
>
> The topic of family planning and contraceptive use has been studied extensively by Islamic scholars, and a majority of jurists believe that family planning is permissible within the teachings of the religion. They have generally argued that Islam is a religion of moderation. In fact, everything is lawful unless explicitly designated otherwise in the *Qur'an* or in the Prophet's tradition. The *Qur'an* does not prohibit birth control or the spacing of pregnancies. The silence on the topic of contraception is not an omission by God, these jurists argue, because God is "all knowing," and Islam is understood to be timeless. Also, coitus interruptus, or withdrawal, was an acknowledged method during the time of Islam's founder, the Prophet Muhammad. The majority of theologians from almost all of the various schools of Islamic jurisprudence agree that withdrawal is permissible with a wife's consent.
>
> The late Arab scholar Abdel Omran argued that Islam is sympathetic to family planning if it promotes the health and well-being of the family. Islam considers the family to be the basic unit of society. Husbands and wives, united through marriage, are the center of family life and promote the important goal of tranquility within the family. While procreation is expected in marriage, sexual relations within marriage need not be only for the purpose of producing children. From the Islamic point of view, procreation should support the family's tranquility and not disrupt it. This teaching appears to endorse the concept of limiting and delaying pregnancies, and therefore the use of contraception within marriage.
>
> Dr. Omran also found Islamic jurisprudence justifies family planning for avoiding the transmission of disease to offspring and for conserving the family's financial resources to benefit those already born.
>
> References
>
> Farzaneh Roudi-Fahimi, *Islam and Family Planning* (Washington, DC: Population Reference Bureau, 2004); and Abdel R. Omran, *Family Planning in the Legacy of Islam* (London: Routledge, 1992).

from 25 percent to 57 percent between 1988 and 2005; use among urban women rose from 52 percent to 63 percent over the same period. As family planning use rose, Egypt's rural TFR dropped from 5.4 children to 3.4 children, while the urban TFR slipped from 3.5 to 2.7.[19]

Accordingly, Morocco's overall TFR has fallen from 5.6 children per woman in 1979–1980, when less than 20 percent of women of reproductive age used a contraceptive method, to 2.5 children per woman in 2003. Contraceptive use has been increasing faster in rural than in urban areas within the country in recent years, rising from 52 percent to 60 percent among rural women of reproductive age between 1997 and 2003. Contraceptive use among urban women—66 percent in 2003—changed little over the period.[20]

Iran has shown the most impressive expansion in the access and use of contraceptives in rural areas through "health houses." More than one-half of rural Iranian women use modern contraceptives (see Box 1.10.1).

Family planning is acceptable under Islamic laws (see Box 1.10.4) and is likely to continue to rise in the region as access to reproductive health services expands and the idea of delaying and limiting births gains wider acceptance.

Migration in MENA: Moving In, Out, and Within

The second half of the 20th century brought large movements of people within, out of, and into the Middle East and North Africa. The most dramatic of these movements were prompted by political change, including the creation of Israel. But the bulk of migration has involved people seeking jobs and the largest of these was prompted by the development of oil fields in the Persian Gulf in the 1950s. Another stream of migrants leads out of MENA for jobs in Europe, beginning with the post-World War II reconstruction.

Table 1.10.4 Share of Foreign-Born in the Countries of the Middle East and North Africa, 2005

Country	Percent of population
Qatar	78
United Arab Emirates	71
Kuwait	62
Palestinian Territory	45
Israel	40
Jordan	39
Saudi Arabia	26
Oman	24
Lebanon	18
Libya	11
Syria	5
Iran	3
Turkey	2
Yemen	1
Algeria	1
Iraq	z
Egypt	z
Morocco	z
Tunisia	z

z— less than 0.5 percent
Note: The estimates of the foreign-born population, or foreign stock, generally refer to residents who were born in another country, but the definitions vary by country.
Source: UN, Trends in Total Migrant Stock: The 2005 Revision (2006; http://esa.un.org accessed April 5, 2007).

Figure 1.10.5
Foreigners' and Nationals' Share of the Labor Force in Saudi Arabia, Bahrain, and Kuwait, 2002 and 2004

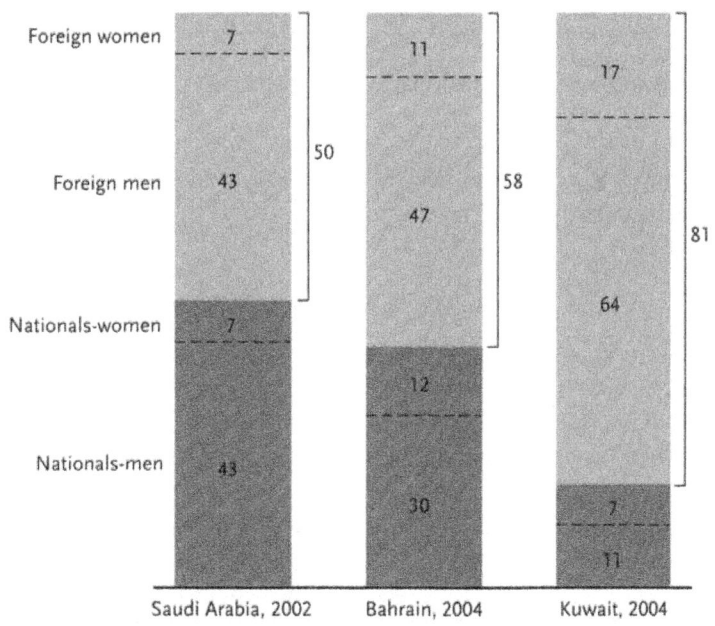

Source: Cooperative Council for the Arab States of the Gulf, *Statistical Bulletin 2006*, Vol. 15 (www.gcc-sg.org, accessed April 6, 2007): table 4.

Table 1.10.5 Major Refugee Populations in the Middle East and North Africa, by Country of Residence in 2005

Country of asylum/Leading countries of origin	Number of refugees	Country of asylum/Leading countries of origin	Number of refugees
MENA-Western Asia		*North Africa*	
Iran	994,000	Algeria	94,500
Afghanistan	940,000	Morocco	90,000
Iraq	54,000	Former Palestine	4,000
Iraq	63,400	Egypt	86,700
Former Palestine	34,000	Former Palestine	57,000
Iran	14,300	Sudan	23,600
Turkey	13,600	Somalia	4,200
Jordan	609,500	Libya	12,000
Iraq	450,000	Former Palestine	8,700
Former Palestine	58,200	Somalia	2,900
Palestinian Territory	1,685,800	Morocco	2,300
Gaza Strip	986,000		
West Bank	699,800	*Countries outside MENA*	
Lebanon	296,800	Germany	
Former Palestine	256,800	Turkey	7,200
Iraq	9,200	Iraq	4,900
Sudan	8,300	Iran	4,400
Syria	866,300	Greece	
Former Palestine	512,100	Iraq	2,100
Iraq	351,000	Mauritania	
Turkey	7,300	Morocco	26,700
Iran	3,600	United States	
Iraq	2,300	Iran	2,800
Arabian Peninsula			
Kuwait	14,300		
Former Palestine	13,500		
Saudi Arabia	240,800		
Former Palestine	240,000		
Yemen	82,700		
Somalia	78,600		

MENA: Middle East and North Africa
Source: U.S. Committee for Refugees and Immigrants, World Refugee Survey 2006 (2006): table 3.

In recent decades, immigrants have sent home billions of dollars in remittances that support their families and add significantly to their country's national income.

Moving For Economic Opportunity

Migration theory holds that people will move the shortest distance possible to attain their desired goal, whether to improve their economic opportunities or to escape political persecution and unrest. It is no surprise, then that considerable migration takes place within the MENA region, especially given the common language of the Arab countries. In particular, migrants from Yemen and Egypt seek jobs in the oil-producing countries of the Gulf states.[21]

When the international price of crude oil jumped from around US$2 a barrel in 1970 to nearly US$40 a barrel in 1980, the oil-rich countries In the Gulf enjoyed an enormous boost in incomes. Many invested these revenues in major projects to create a basic infrastructure and develop modern services. Their own labor forces lacked the numbers, skills, and desire to fill the new jobs. The need for labor in the Gulf was so immediate and so great in the 1970s that these countries recruited workers from outside the region. The number of foreign workers in the six

Gulf states that make up Gulf Cooperative Council (GCC) rose from 1.1 million in 1970 to more than 5.2 million in 1990. Another 2 million Egyptians were working in Iraq in 1990.[22]

The bulk of foreign workers in the Gulf states were from India, Bangladesh, Indonesia, Pakistan, and the Philippines. Natives in the Gulf countries came to depend on these foreigners to fill a wide array of domestic service jobs, as well as more skilled jobs in the private sector. So many workers arrived from South Asia and other MENA countries that they outnumbered the native populations in some Gulf states. Foreigners filled more than 90 percent of private-sector jobs in Kuwait and Qatar in the early 2000s.

But the oil revenues have fluctuated in the GCC, and because petroleum has remained the main source of income, economic growth has also fluctuated. In recent years, concern about the foreign majority and increasing unemployment among the burgeoning youth population have prompted the Gulf countries to enact policies to discourage the hiring of additional foreign workers.[23] Policies include fining employers who do not hire a minimum percentage of nationals and taxing the hiring of foreigners.

But breaking the dependence on foreigners has been difficult for the Gulf countries. Nationals of the wealthy MENA countries initially shunned the manual labor jobs usually performed by foreigners. Private employers often preferred foreign contract workers, who demanded fewer benefits and often were more eager to perform well. Nationals opted for public-sector jobs with more security, higher salaries, and better benefits. There is some evidence that attitudes are changing and natives are more willing to seek lower-status, private-sector jobs such as drivers, caregivers, butchers, or retail workers.[24]

Foreigners' jobs in the region are not only vulnerable to economic ups and downs, but also to political instability and conflicts. Millions of foreign workers were displaced by the 1990 Persian Gulf crisis precipitated by Iraq's invasion of Kuwait. Hundreds of thousands of Palestinians and other non-Kuwaitis were expelled from Kuwait. Close to 1 million Yemeni workers were expelled from Saudi Arabia. This was initially viewed as an opportunity for employers to shift to native workers, but more than 15 years later, the dependence on foreigners continues. In Saudi Arabia, foreigners accounted for one-half of the labor force in 2002 (see Figure 1.10.5). The foreign share of the labor force is much greater in the smaller Gulf states: 58 percent in Bahrain and 81 percent in Kuwait in 2004.

Except in Yemen—a country of emigration—the non-nationals' share of the total population on the Arabian Peninsula ranged from 24 percent in Oman to 78 percent in Qatar (see Table 1.10.4). The social and economic position of foreigners varies by country, as does the definition of "foreign." In about one-half of the MENA countries, foreign-born residents make up less than 10 percent of the national population. In North Africa, which is a region of emigration, foreigners account for less than 1 percent of population.

Money From Immigrants Helps Countries of Origin

Remittances sent home by foreign workers are often vital for their family's well-being and are an important source of national income for the labor-sending countries. Indeed, some countries encourage emigration as a development strategy to cope with high unemployment. Saudi Arabia alone was the source of US$13.6 billion in remittances in 2004. Bangladesh—a major source of foreign workers—received US$3.8 billion in remittances in 2004–2005; 70 percent was sent from Persian Gulf countries. An estimated 13 percent of the Philippines' US$10.7 billion in remittances in 2004 originated from Gulf countries.[25] Egyptians working within the Middle East and elsewhere sent home US$3.3 billion. Foreign remittances accounted for 21 percent of the GDP in Lebanon and 20 percent in the Palestinian Territory.[26]

Foreigners in most MENA countries, and particularly in the Gulf, often work long hours and have limited recourse if employers fail to deliver the pay and other benefits promised.[27] Pressured by international human rights activists, the Gulf countries are increasingly adopting policies to prevent abuses of foreign workers and to ensure workers receive benefits due. But foreigners continue to flock to MENA because they earn more there than they would in their home countries.

Refugees

Another Important group of migrants in MENA is refugees and asylum-seekers, many from neighboring countries. MENA is home to at least 5 million refugees, arguably the largest refugee population in the world.[28] The numbers fluctuate, but Iran has had the largest number of refugees in recent years: nearly 1 million in 2005, mostly from Afghanistan.

The residents of the former Palestine and their descendants are among the oldest and largest refugee groups. Hundreds of thousands of Palestinians became refugees as a result of Arab-Israeli conflicts over the last half century. Many settled in refugee camps that still exist today.

The UN High Commissioner for Refugees refers to Palestinians as "warehoused" populations, and a special UN agency, the UN Relief and Works Agency for Palestinian Refugees in the Middle East (UNRWA) oversees their welfare. Most Palestinian refugees live In neighboring countries: Jordan, Lebanon and Syria (see Table 1.10.5). In addition, 1.7 million Palestinians living in the Palestinian territories of Gaza and the West Bank have refugee status from UNRWA: They account for about 40 percent of the territories' population. Refugee status grants residents certain financial, health, and educational benefits from UNRWA, which is a valued commodity in an economically depressed area.

Moving Out of the Region

Large communities of people from the Middle East and North Africa have grown up outside the region, particularly in France, Germany, and other European countries. Some of this migration resulted from previous colonial ties to a European country, such as Algerians in France, while others, such as the Turkish population in Germany, resulted from recruitment of workers in the 1960s. More recent migration out of MENA has been fueled by people seeking economic opportunities or escaping violence and political instability in their home countries.

In 2004, about one-third of France's 3.3 million foreigners were from one of four MENA countries: Morocco, Algeria, Turkey, and Tunisia. In 2006, Germany reported more than 2 million residents from MENA countries and nearly 1.8 million of them were ethnic Turks. Residents from MENA countries accounted for about one-third of Germany's 6.9 million foreign population. Migration from Morocco to southern Europe has been increasing in recent years, especially to Spain and Italy.[29]

Except for a relatively small share of highly skilled professionals and academics, European residents from the Middle East and North Africa tend to occupy a lower socioeconomic status. Many have been excluded from gaining citizenship or from full participation in public life. The discrimination and high unemployment among immigrant communities has generated frustration that occasionally erupts in violence, as evidenced by street riots in immigrant communities of France in 2005.[30]

With more jobs and advancement opportunities in Europe than in MENA, the stream of immigrants has continued, despite European efforts to slow it down.[31] And the money MENA emigrants earn helps their families back home. Moroccans abroad sent home $4.2 billion in 2004, accounting for 8.5 percent of the national GDP.

Shifting Age Structure

In most countries, the transition from higher to lower mortality and fertility has determined the population age structure. High fertility and rapid growth mean that each birth cohort is larger than the last: A graph of the population by age and sex produces a steep pyramid, such as that shown for Yemen in Figure 1.10.6. This is the classic shape for a population in the early stages of the demographic transition. Recent fertility decline, as in Egypt, is reflected in the shortened bars in lower part of the pyramid, a sign that population growth is slowing. A relatively sudden and dramatic drop in fertility, illustrated by Iran's graph in Figure 1.10.6, causes smaller birth cohorts each year.

Migration is an important demographic wildcard in MENA. It affects the age and sex structure of populations as well as the size. The MENA countries are more affected by migration than most other regions. The influx of foreign

Figure 1.10.6
Age and Sex Structure of Selected Countries in the Middle East and North Africa, 2005

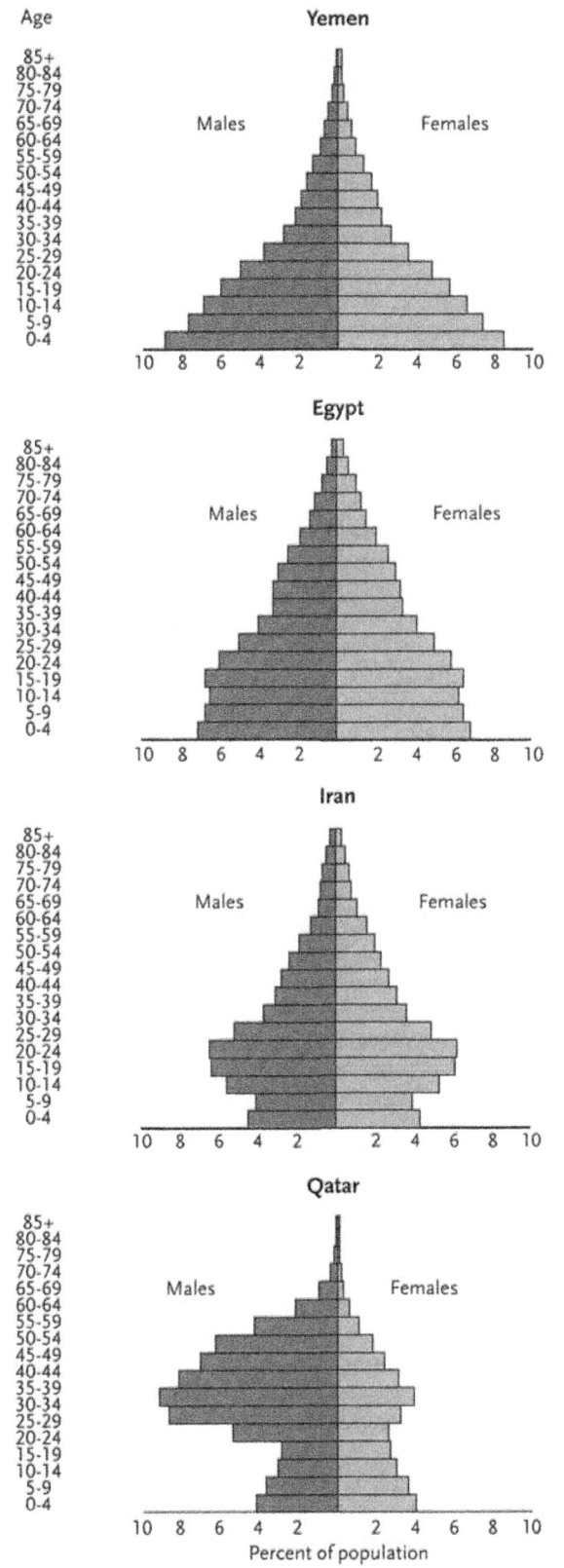

Source: UN Population Division, *World Population Prospects: The 2006 Revision* (2007; http://esa.un.org, accessed April 7, 2007).

Deeply Private, Incredibly Public

men to work in petroleum-rich Persian Gulf countries means there is an unusually high proportion of working-age men in the population, illustrated by Qatar in Figure 1.10.6. Overall, there are nearly three men for every woman between the ages of 20 and 64. In contrast the male side of Yemen's population pyramid shows a slight deficit in the working ages—most likely men who moved to a more wealthy country on the Arabian Peninsula to work

These graphs show that the demographic transition from higher to lower mortality and fertility is occurring at a different pace in different countries. But in general, the population in MENA countries is young, well below the world average of 28 (see Figure 1.10.7). The median is just 17 years in Yemen and the Palestinian Territory, and ranges up to 31 in Qatar. The median is much higher in the Gulf countries that have a significant foreign population, because roost are in their working ages, and often do not have children living with them.

Youth Bulge

The average age of population will increase as fertility declines and children make up a shrinking share of the population. But at the same time, another consequence of MENA's recent demographic history is becoming more noticeable and more important: the youth bulge.

The significant decline in child mortality and the relatively slow decline in fertility led first to an increase in the child population in the 1980s, followed by a rather sudden slowdown in births as fertility declined in the 1990s. The children born in the 1980s and early 1990s—now 15 to 24—emerged as a "youth bulge," because they were followed by smaller birth cohorts. This bulge is most notable in countries such as Iran, where fertility declined sharply in the 1990s. In 2005, 25 percent of Iran's population was between the ages of 15 and 24. The youth population share is 20 percent or higher in much of the region, compared with about 15 percent in the United States.[32]

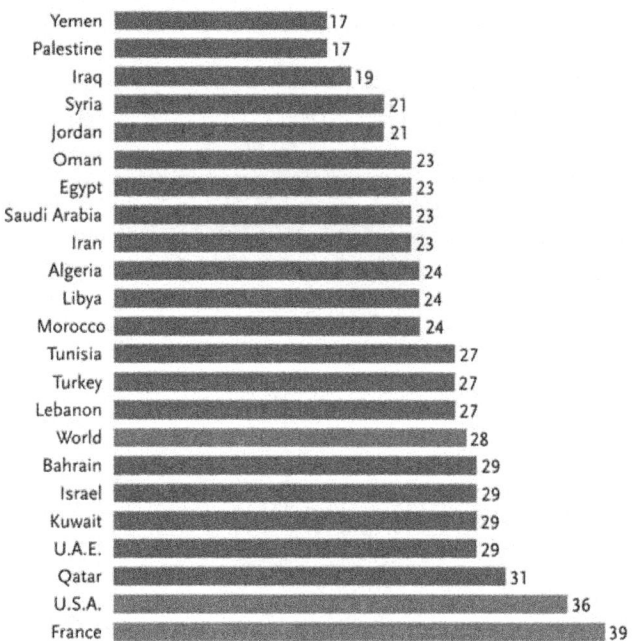

Figure 1.10.7
Median Age of the Populations of MENA Countries, the World, the United States, and France, 2005

MENA: The Middle East and North Africa

U.A.E.: United Arab Emirates

Source: UN Population Division, *World Population Prospects: The 2006 Revision* (2007; http://esa.un.org, accessed April 4, 2007).

Because MENA countries are at different stages of fertility decline, the youth bulge will reach its maximum size in some countries as it is declining in others. Over the next two decades, for example, the youth populations of high-fertility Iraq, Yemen, and the Palestinian Territory will see the fastest growth. In 2007, at least 40 percent of these countries' populations are under age 15. Even considering some fertility decline, 15-to-24-year-olds are projected to make up about one-fourth of the countries' populations in 2025. The number of Iraqi youth is projected to grow by nearly 3 million by 2025, reaching 8.6 million. The number of Palestinian youth will increase 80 percent, to 1.3 million, and Yemeni youth by 70 percent, to total 7.6 million.[33]

In contrast, countries already well into the transition to lower fertility—including Lebanon, Iran, Morocco, and Turkey—will see their youth share decline between 2005 and 2025. The confluence of these trends in higher and lower fertility countries will cause the youth population to peak in 2035 at about 100 million. This phenomenon presents both a challenge for governments to prepare these young people for meaningful participation in society and an opportunity for economic growth fueled by a young and relatively large labor force.

The Potential Demographic Dividend

This youth bulge—concentrated in the young working ages—offers a limited opportunity for a surge in economic growth, a phenomenon credited with helping create an economic boom in East Asia.[34] The increasing participation of women compounds the effect of the youth bulge on labor force growth in MENA. The percentage of women in

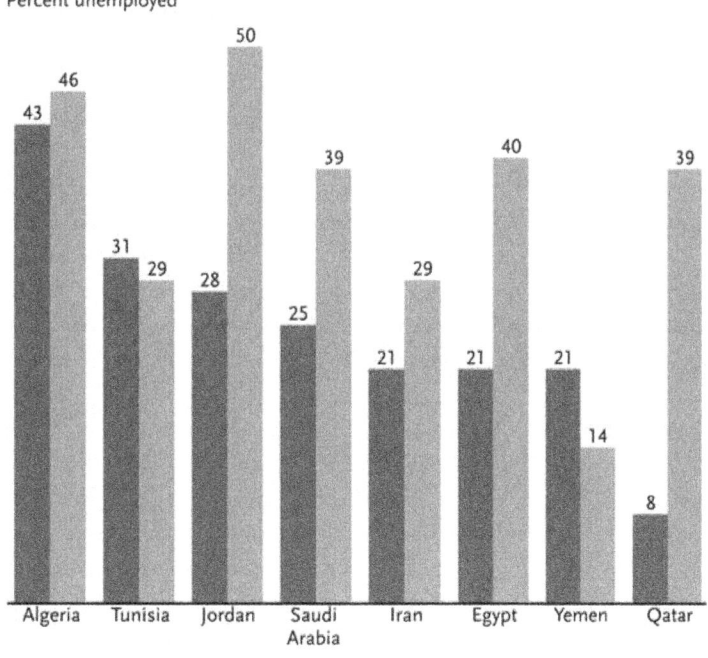

Figure 1.10.8
Unemployment Rates For Young Men and Women in Selected MENA Countries, 2005

MENA: The Middle East and North Africa

Note: The unemployment rate refers to the percent unemployed of those ages 15 to 24 who are in the labor force, that is, currently working or seeking employment.

Source: R. Assaad and F. Roudi-Fahimi, *Youth in the Middle East and North Africa: Demographic Opportunity or Challenge?* (2007; www.prb.org, accessed April 30, 2007).

paid employment increased from about 25 percent in 1980 to about 30 percent in 2006. If women's participation continues to increase closer to the world average of 52 percent, women will constitute a huge potential pool of workers in MENA.[35]

But to reap the benefits of this demographic "bonus" or "dividend," MENA countries will need to adapt their economic, social, and political institutions to capitalize on the growing pool of potential workers. Educational systems, labor markets, housing supply, and health systems will need to expand and adapt to meet the needs of young people and the countries' economies. A demographic bonus can only occur when a large young population is healthy, educated, trained, and ready to be absorbed into a market economy.

MENA countries have several obstacles to overcome if they are to reap this demographic dividend from the working-age bulge. Governments will need to develop institutions to help industry expand the jobs available and revamp inadequate and sometimes obsolete educational systems. They also need to find ways to integrate more women into the labor force. Cultural preferences and limited job opportunities have kept many women out of the labor force in MENA countries. While paid employment for women is gaining acceptance in the region, it will take time for new attitudes to spread throughout the society.

In addition to creating sufficient jobs and preparing a skilled labor force, reaping the demographic dividend will require meeting escalating demands for education, housing, and health care as these young adults start their own families.

Improving Education

The MENA countries have made remarkable progress in reducing illiteracy and increasing education over the past 30 years. Unfortunately, illiteracy and school dropout rates remain unacceptably high in pockets in some MENA countries. The largest numbers of illiterate young people are in Egypt, Iraq, and Yemen. Together, these three countries account for about three-quarters of the 10 million illiterate youth in the region in 2005. About two-thirds of the illiterate youth are girls and young women.

In Egypt, the share of the population age 15 years and older who could read and write shot from 40 percent to 83 percent between 1980 and 2004, thanks to educational expansion at the primary level.[36] Morocco also saw welcome improvements in literacy—from 29 percent to 52 percent. However population growth driven by higher fertility among the less educated population meant that the number of people who were illiterate grew from 8 million in 1980 to 10 million in 2004.

A growing problem in the region is a mismatch between the formal education system and the skill needs of the job market. The educational systems in some counties are largely geared toward public-sector employment, while future job growth will likely be in the private sector. New technologies and a growing integration into world economies have made much of the current educational curricula obsolete. In traditional education, students learn through rote repetition, while the modern economy calls for people with problem-solving skills and familiarity with emerging technologies. Entrepreneurs in the region regularly cite a lack of general job readiness and specific skills in job applicants.[37]

At the same time, the creation of jobs for highly skilled professionals is lagging behind the graduation rate.[38] Accordingly many MENA countries are likely to see additional "brain drain," as many of the most promising youth leave the region to pursue university education and better job opportunities in Europe and North America.

In some countries, recent fertility declines will relieve the pressure for creating more spaces in schools. While the primary school-age population is still growing each year in some countries, fertility declines have caused the numbers to decline in other countries. The number of primary-school-age children in Iran declined by nearly 2 million between 1999 and 2004, At the same time, this population increased in Turkey and the Arab countries.

Expanding Job Opportunities

The MENA countries are not creating jobs fast enough to match the increase in the working-age population. Absorbing the youth bulge will be a challenge, especially with MENA's unemployment rate already the world's highest. In 2006, about 17 percent of the women In the labor force were unemployed, compared with 10 percent of men. In contrast, average unemployment rates globally were 7 percent for women and 6 percent for men, as estimated by the International Labor Organization (ILO).[39]

The unemployment rates for youth just entering the work force—especially for young women—are extremely high. While less than 15 percent of young men and women were unemployed worldwide, the ILO estimated that just over 20 percent of young men and just over 30 percent of young women in MENA were unemployed in 2005.

The situation is particularly dire for members of MENA's youth bulge in some countries. More than 40 percent of Algeria's young men and women were unemployed in 2005, which may be why so many Algerians are emigrating to Europe and elsewhere in search of jobs. Between 21 percent and 31 percent of young men were unemployed in Tunisia, Jordan, Saudi Arabia, and several other MENA countries, along with between 29 percent and 50 percent of young women. Qatar, with a labor force dominated by foreign male workers, has relatively low unemployment for young men, but high unemployment for young women (see Figure 1.10.8).

The high unemployment for young women reflects the rapid increase in women in the labor market, along with fewer government jobs and persistent barriers for women working in the private sector. Private-sector employers have been reluctant to hire women because, among other reasons, the labor market is highly segregated by sex; female employees are potentially more expensive because they may need maternity leave and child care; and women have limited geographic mobility. In addition, the labor-intensive, export-oriented types of industries that might hire women are not expanding in the current economies.

If MENA countries are to benefit from the demographic dividend they will need to reform the generous social benefits and services offered to citizens, especially in the oil-rich Arabian Peninsula countries. Citizens in the Gulf countries have been guaranteed government jobs and are protected by labor laws. But the combination of slower job growth and the drive to replace foreign workers with native-born employees in private-sector jobs has produced a mismatch between the skills of the young people seeking work and the jobs available. Even some of the oil-rich countries in the Gulf, such as Saudi Arabia, which have traditionally had full employment, are faced with high youth unemployment.

Turning MENA's population challenges into demographic dividends will require good governance, engaging civil society, integration into global markets, managing oil resources to create more jobs, and reforming educational systems to match skills needed for the 21st century.[40]

Beyond the Youth Bulge

While the youth bulge and concomitant demands on the labor force, education, housing, health, and other public services are garnering most attention now, other demographic trends will continue to affect the region. As the youth bulge reaches prime family formation age in each country, the number of births is likely to increase, fueling considerable future population growth. The region's population is slated to reach nearly 700 million by 2050, a 60 percent increase over the 2007 total. The population on the Arabian Peninsula is projected to double to reach 124 million by 2050. In Western Asia, Iraq and the Palestinian Territories will more than double in size. Iran and Turkey are slated to have about 100 million people each. In North Africa, Egypt will continue to dominate demographically, with a population exceeding 120 million.

As MENA's total population increases, so will its elderly population. This, in turn, will create new demands for health care and financial security. The elderly will remain a small share of the total population, especially compared with Europe, where one-third of the population will be age 60 or older by 2050, according to recent UN projections. But the numbers entering the older ages in MENA will continue to expand. Between 2000 and 2050, Egypt's population 60 years and older is expected to grow from 4.6 million to 23.7 million: The elderly will account for nearly 20 percent of the total population compared with 7 percent in 2000. Saudi Arabia's elderly population is expected to grow from fewer than 1 million to 8.1 million over the same period, with the percent ages 60 or older rising from 4 percent to 18 percent.

Regardless of the level of economic development or national income, the prospect of larger populations means that governments are increasingly challenged to provide the basic needs for growing numbers of citizens—adequate housing, sanitation, health care, education, and jobs. These same challenges face many of the world's countries, but they are compounded in a region that is politically volatile and where water is scarce. Yet wise investments in today's youth, particularly in girls, can yield potentially large payoffs for MENA's future development.

References

1. Abdel R. Omran and Farzaneh Roudi, "The Middle East Population Puzzle," *Population Bulletin* 48, no. 1 (1993); and United Nations (UN) Population Division, *World Population Prospects: The 2006 Revision* (2007), detailed data accessed online at http://esa.un.org, on April 10, 2007.
2. UN Population Division, *World Population Prospects: The 2006 Revision*.
3. Dominique Tabutin and Bruno Schoumaker, "The Demography of the Arab World and the Middle East From the 1950s to the 2000s," *Population-E* 60, nos. 5–6 (2005): 505–616; and Omran and Roudi, "The Middle East Population Puzzle."
4. World Health Organization (WHO), UNICEF, and the UN Population Fund (UNFPA), *Maternal Mortality 2000* (2004): appendix table J, accessed online at www.who.ints on May 16, 2007.
5. Karima Khalil and Farzaneh Roudi-Fahimi, *Making Motherhood Safer in Egypt* (Washington, DC: Population Reference Bureau, 2004).
6. UN and Egypt Ministry of Planning, *Millennium Development Goals: Second Country Report—Egypt 2004,* accessed online at www.undp.org.eg, on April 13, 2007.
7. Joselyn DeJong et al., *Young People's Sexual and Reproductive Health in the Middle East and North Africa* (Washington, DC: Population Reference Bureau, 2007), accessed online at www.prb.org, on April 30, 2007; Vidya Setty-Venugopal and Ushma D. Upadhyay, "Birth Spacing: Three to Five Saves Lives," *Population Reports,* Series L, No. 13 (Baltimore: Johns Hopkins Bloomberg School of Public Health, Population Information Program, 2002); and the Alan Guttmacher Institute (AGI) and UNFPA, *Adding It Up: The Benefits of Investing in Sexual and Reproductive Health Care* (New York: AGI and UNFPA, 2003): 18.
8. Carl Haub, *2006 World Population Data Sheet* (Washington, DC: Population Reference Bureau, 2006); and UN Population Division, *World Population Prospects: The 2006 Revision*.
9. Carla Makhlouf Obermeyer, "Reproductive Choice in Islam: Gender and State in Iran and Tunisia," *Studies in Family Planning* 25, no. 1 (1994): 41–51; and Saad Eddin Ibrahim and Barbara Lethem Ibrahim, "Egypt's Population Policy: The Long March of State and Civil Society," in *Do Population Policies Matter?* ed. Anrudh Jain (New York: Population Council, 1998): 19–52.
10. Hoda Rashad, Magued Osman, and Farzaneh Roudi-Fahimi, *Marriage in the Arab World* (Washington, DC: Population Reference Bureau, 2005), accessed online at www.prb.org, on April 7, 2007.
11. Omran and Roudi, "The Middle East Population Puzzle"; and Justin Vaisse, "Unrest In France, November 2005: Immigration, Islam and the Challenge Of Integration," presentation to U.S. Congressional staff at the Brookings Institution, Washington, DC Jan. 10 and 12, 2006.
12. Central Bureau of Statistics, *Statistical Abstract of Israel, 2006* (2005): table 3.12, accessed online at www.cbs.il, on April 22, 2007.
13. Tabutin and Schoumaker, "The Demography of the Arab World and the Middle East": 588–90.
14. Tabutin and Schoumaker, "The Demography of the Arab World and the Middle East": table A-4; and Rashad, Osman, and Roudi-Fahimi *Marriage in the Arab World*.
15. Rashad, Osman, and Roudi-Fahimi, *Marriage in the Arab World:* table 1.
16. DeJong et al., *Young People's Sexual and Reproductive Health in the Middle East and North Africa*.
17. Ragui Assaad and Farzaneh Roudi-Fahimi, *Youth in the Middle East and North Africa: Demographic Opportunity or Challenge?* MENA Policy Brief (Washington, DC: Population Reference Bureau, 2007): 4, accessed online at www.prb.org, on April 30, 2007.
18. UN, *Levels and Trends of Contraceptive Use as Assessed in 2002* (New York: UN, 2004): table A. 1.

19. Fatma EJ-Zanaty and Ann Way, *Egypt Demographic and Health Survey 2005* (Cairo: Ministry of Health and Population, National Population Council, El-Zanaty and Assoc., and ORC Macro, 2006): table 4.3.
20. Ministry of Health (Morocco), ORC Macro, and the League of Arab States, *Enquête sur la Population et la Santé Familiare 2003–2004* (Calverton, MD: Ministry of Health and ORC Macro, 2005): 48 and 64.
21. Philippe Farques, "International Migration in the Arab Region," paper presented to the UN Expert Group Meeting on International Migration and Development in the Arab Region: Challenges and Opportunities, Beirut, May 10, 2006, accessed online at www.un.org, on April 10, 2007.
22. UN, *World Population Monitoring Report 1991, Population Studies* no. 126 (New York: UN, 1992); and UNESCWA (Economic and Social Commission for Western Asia), "Arab Labor Migration," paper presented at the Arab Population Conference in Amman, Jordan, April 4–8, 1993.
23. "Middle East: Israel, Jordan, GCC," *Migration News* 13, no. 4 (2006), accessed online at http://migration.ucdavis.edu, on April 26, 2007.
24. Nasra M. Shah, "Restrictive Labour Immigration Policies in the Oil-Rich Gulf: Effectiveness and Implications for Sending Asian Countries," paper presented at the UN Expert Group Meeting on International Migration and Development in the Arab Region: Challenges and Opportunities, Beirut, May 15–17, 2006, accessed online at www.un.org, on May 3, 2007.
25. UN Population Division, "International Migration In the Arab Region"; and Shah, "Restrictive Labour Immigration Policies in the Oil-Rich Gulf."
26. UN Population Division, "International Migration in the Arab Region."
27. UN Population Division, "International Migration in the Arab Region": 21–22.
28. U.S. Committee for Refugees and Immigrants, *World Refugee Regions 2006* (2006), accessed online at www.refugees.org, on April 12, 2007.
29. Organisation for Economic Cooperation and Development (OECD), *International Migration Outlook: SOPEMI 2006 ed.* (Paris: OECD, 2006); and Federal Statistical Office of Germany, *Population: Foreign Population by Country of Origin 2006*, accessed online at www.destatis.de, on April 26, 2007.
30. "France," *Migration News* 14, no. 2 (2007), accessed online at http://migration.ucdavis.edu, on May 17, 2007; and Molly Moore, "France Beefs Up Response to Riots," *The Washington Post,* Nov. 8, 2005.
31. Ayman Zohry, "Migration Without Borders: North Africa as a Reserve of Cheap Labor For Europe," article prepared for the *UNESCO Migration Without Borders Series* (2005), accessed online at http://unesdoc.unesco.org, on April 26, 2007.
32. Assaad and Roudi-Fahimi, *Youth in the Middle East and North Africa.*
33. Assaad and Roudi-Fahimi, *Youth in the Middle East and North Africa.*
34. David E. Bloom, David Canning, and Jaypee Sevilla, *The Demographic Dividend: A New Perspective on the Economic Consequences of Population Change* (Santa Monica, CA: RAND, 2003).
35. International Labour Organisation (ILO), *Global Employment Trends for Women 2007* (2007): table 2, accessed online at www.ilo.org, on May 6, 2007.
36. UNESCO Institute for Statistics, *Adult (15+) Literacy Rates and Illiterate Population by Country and by Gender,* accessed online at http://stats.uis.unesco.org, on May 12, 2007.
37. Assaad and Roudi-Fahimi, *Youth in the Middle East and North Africa.*
38. See Islamic Development Bank, "Brain Drain in IDB Member Countries: Trends and Development Impact, *IDB Occasional Paper* No. 12 (2006), accessed online at www.islamic development.org, on May 13, 2007.
39. ILO, *Global Employment Trends for Women 2007:* table 3.
40. World Bank, *Unlocking the Employment Potential in the Middle East and North Africa: Toward a New Social Contract* (Washington, DC: World Bank, 2004).

Revolution, War, and Modernization

Population Policy and Fertility Change in Iran*

By Mohammad Jalai Abassi, et al

Introduction

The key periods of demographic change in Iran in recent times have been the onset of modest fertility decline, mainly in urban areas, in the early 1970s, a resurgence in fertility rates from 1976 to 1986, and the renewed onset of fertility decline since 1988 (Aghajanian and Mehryar 1999; Abbasi-Shavazi 2000b). These changes coincide rather neatly with three political periods: the later stages of the Shah's regime; the Islamic Revolution and the war against Iraq; and a subsequent period of renewed modernization and pragmatism. There appears, then, to be a relationship between the dramatic political events and fertility trends. The obvious linkage would be the shifts in population policy that took place over the period: antinatalism and a government-sponsored family planning program in the later stages of the Shah's regime; denunciation of family planning and encouragement of early marriage in the post-Revolutionary period; and a pragmatic return to antinatalism in the post-1988 period.

Fertility has declined dramatically since the adoption of a new population policy in 1988. This rapid decline was greeted with incredulity for some time by many overseas observers. The reason was that much of the world was unaware that in the period following the Islamic Revolution, social change consisted not only of a retreat into traditionalism and anti-Western feeling, as symbolized by the enforced adoption of the *chador* by women, but also of widened educational opportunities for girls, improved public health services, increased urbanization and other trends much more favorable to lowered fertility (Hoodfar and Assadpour 2000). This article aims to present as interpretation of Iran's recent demographic history, setting it in the context of the country's turbulent political history.

Historical Background

Until the late 1940s, Iran's population had grown at a very low rate. This was despite the fact that Iran's traditionally pronatalist culture (which emphasized early and universal marriage as a social and religious value) as well as prevailing health and social conditions (high infant mortality and dependence of parents on children as the main source of

---

* An earlier version of this paper was presented at the Demography Program, ANU, and benefited from comments and suggestions made by colleagues. Valuable comments received from Geoffrey McNicoll and Chris Wilson are gratefully acknowledged.

Mohammad Jalal Abbasi, Amir Mehryar, Gavin Jones and Peter McDonald, "Revolution, War, and Modernization: Population Policy and Fertility Change in Iran," *Journal of Population Research*, vol. 19, no. 1, pp. 1–20. Copyright © 2002 by Springer Science+Business Media. Reprinted with permission.

old-age support) provided a favorable environment for high fertility. In this period, mortality was high enough to offset the high fertility and keep the rate of population growth at a very low level.

The first national census of population and housing conducted in 1956 revealed a population of 18.9 million (as compared with an estimated figure of about 10 million in 1900) with an estimated TFR of 7.3 births per woman and an average annual growth rate of 1.74 per cent (Amani 1968; Maroufi Bozorgi 1967). Ten years later, according to the 1966 Census, the size of the Iranian population had risen to about 25.8 million which implied an estimated TFR of 7.7 and an average intercensal growth rate of 3.1 per cent per year (Bulatao and Richardson 1994). Partly in response to this heightened growth rate, the government of Iran adopted a population policy with explicit health and demographic targets. A national family planning program was officially inaugurated in 1967 and the Ministry of Health was given the responsibility for controlling the birth rate.

The impact of this policy change was partly reflected in the results of the third national census taken in 1976 which revealed a population size of 33.7 million and an average annual intercensal growth rate of 2.7 per cent. The TFR estimates derived from the 1976 Census vary from as high as 6.8 (PBO 1993) to 5.5 (Zanjani 1992). A carefully designed Population Growth Estimation study conducted a few years earlier (1973–1976) had revealed a TFR of 6.3 which had not changed by the time the Iran Fertility Survey was conducted in 1977 (Aghajanian 1991).

Population policy shifts after the revolution

Adoption of Pronatalist Ideology and Suspension of the Family Planning Program

Shortly after the Islamic Revolution in early 1979, the family planning program was suspended. In contrast to the previous regime, high fertility and rapid population growth were looked upon favorably. Religious leaders emphasized marriage and family formation as basic Islamic virtues, and the government was urged to adopt economic policies that would facilitate and encourage early and universal marriage.

Simultaneously, grassroots charitable foundations that had emerged in the wake of the Revolution offered tangible economic rewards, in the form of relatively generous wedding gifts or dowries, for early marriage and family formation. Despite this drastic change in emphasis, the Ministry of Health kept the family planning program alive by obtaining *fatwas* regarding the permissibility of contraceptive use from Imam Khomeini and several other leading Ayatollahs (Mehryar, forthcoming).

With the start of the eight-year war with Iraq in September 1980, high fertility and population growth acquired new significance. Population size immediately began to be considered as a matter of comparative advantage. The creation of a popular "Twenty Million Man Army" was adopted as a national slogan early in the war. On a more personal levels the rising casualties of the war encouraged many middle-aged couples to produce more children to replace those whose loss they were anticipating. The universal rationing system that was introduced as a means of ensuring equal access to basic necessities provided farther impetus for high fertility. The rationing system included not only basic food items but also locally produced or imported modern consumer goods like television sets, refrigerators, carpets and even cars. These were distributed on a per capita basis and larger families were entitled to a better share of both the basic commodities and highly prized modern consumer items. Thus, newborn babies were automatically entitled to a separate book of ration coupons which, in the case of ordinary families, was far above the costs involved in raising a child. As the issue of coupons was conditional on having a birth registration certificate, this led to a sudden increase in the coverage and timeliness of birth registration. The reverse may have happened with registration of deaths.

The demographic consequences of this pronatalist policy did not take long to become evident. The first general census of population and housing conducted by the IRI in 1986 indicated that the population of Iran had grown at an average annual rate of 3.9 per cent per year between 1976–1986. Even taking into account the effect of the immigration of Afghan and Iraqi refugees during this period, the natural growth rate was no less than 3.2 per cent The 1986 Census indicated a TFR of 7.1–5.9 in urban and 9.0 in rural areas (SCI 1998). Other TFR estimates derived from the same census vary from as low as 6.4 (PBO 1989: 2–6) to 7.7 (Agha, 1989; Bulatao & Richardson 1994). The unexpectedly large population size (49.3 million) revealed by the 1986 Census was at first hailed as a "God-sent" gift by the Prime Minister and other leaders of the IRI.

Return to an Antinatal Position and Gradual Revival of the Family Planning Program

Publication of the 1986 Census results focussed attention on the long-term economic and social implications of the high rate of fertility and population growth, and behind the scene discussions on the need for a population control policy were initiated. Two government departments are known to have played a major role in the initiation of this debate: the Ministry of Health (MOH) and the Plan and Budget Organization (PBO). The first had been responsible for the family planning program before the Revolution. Indeed, the first Minister of Health of the Islamic Republic of Iran (IRI) discussed the need for family planning with Imam Khomeini a few months after the Revolution and reportedly had secured his oral endorsement of contraceptive use by couples who did not want to have more children. As a result, the MOH had been allowed to continue with the provision of family planning services (including the free distribution of the three modern methods of contraception) to couples visiting its MCH clinics throughout the period when there was no official program. The Plan and Budget Organization, as the national agency responsible for the monitoring and allocation of the government's financial resources, was in a unique position to know the critical state of the war-shattered economy and its fast-dwindling ability to support a large and rapidly increasing population.

To raise public support for the idea of population control and family planning, a three-day "Population and Development" seminar jointly organized by the MOH and PBO was held in the city of Mashad in September 1988. The recommendations of this seminar explicitly called for the adoption of a national population policy aimed at birth control. At the end of the Mashad seminar, the Minister of Health and Medical Education, in a press conferences reiterated Imam Khomeini's *fatwa* regarding the legitimacy of contraceptive use by consenting couples, and announced that a family planning program would soon be established. Almost simultaneously, the prime minister declared that "birth control" was a "destiny factor" for Iran and invited Iranian women to present unwanted pregnancies by seeking help from publicly run clinics and rural health houses. To overcome any misconception regarding the legality of birth control, the head of the judiciary system publicly declared that the use of contraceptive methods for preventing unwanted pregnancies was not against Islamic criminal law.

Following the Mashad seminar, family planning was considered by a group of eminent clergy and religiously minded physicians attending a seminar on "Islamic Perspectives in Medicine" organized by the Mashad University of Medical Sciences in February 1989. This was followed by another seminar explicitly dealing with "Islam and Population Policy" which was held in Esfaban in April 1989, and brought together a large number of eminent theologians and politically influential clergy. Most of the recommendations of the Mashad seminar were taken into consideration in the preparation of the First Five Year Development Plan (FFYDP). Thus, the idea and objectives of population control and family planning were given formal legislative endorsement when the FFYDP bill was approved by the Islamic Legislative Assembly *(Majlis)* in 1989. This was four years before the eventual enactment of the Family Planning Law of the IRl in 1993. The FFYDP had also set some relatively modest demographic targets for the newly established family planning program. These included reduction of the total fertility rate of Iranian women from 6.4 in 1986 to 4.0 by the year 2011 and decrease of the natural rate of growth of the population from 3.2 per cent to 3.05 per cent by the end of the Plan (1993) and to 2.3 per cent by the year 2011. To reach these goals, the coverage of public family planning services was to be extended to 24 per cent of eligible couples by the end of the FFYPD (PBO 1989: 2–6).

In line with the above mentioned goals, the Ministry of Health and Medical Education (MOHME) was given the mandate and the resources to provide free family planning services to all married couples, to promote small family size norms and to help individual couples keep their family size at a reasonably low level (2 to 3 children). Several other Ministries as well as the Islamic Republic of Iran Broadcasting Organization were required to closely cooperate with the Ministry of Health in promoting these objectives. A separate Population and Family Planning

Directorate was set up within the MOHME in 1991 under the overall supervision of the Deputy Minister for Public Health whose office was also in charge of the primary health care and MCH services.

To further ensure the intersectoral cooperation needed, an interdepartmental Family Limitation Commission was set up by a cabinet decree passed in September 1990. Headed by the Minister of Health, the Commission was to include the Ministers of Health, Education, Higher Education, Labor and Social Affairs, National Guidance, and Plan and Budget as well as the head of the Civil Registration Organization of the Ministry of Interior. The main functions of the Commission were to "monitor, supervise and coordinate all government policies and activities bearing on the control of the population growth rate, to report on steps taken by member agencies, to make recommendations on the formation of a High Council on Family Planning and its functions and membership, and to review proposals made for changing laws and regulations that may encourage or inhibit population growth." A remarkable feature of this decree is the attention it gave to such "beyond-family-planning" measures as the reduction of infant mortality, facilitation of women's education and employment, and extension of social security and retirement benefits to all parents so that they would not be motivated to produce a large number of children as a source of old-age security and support.

Most of these points were also incorporated into the Family Planning Law that had been prepared in 1989 but was finally ratified by the Parliament in May 1993. This law not only removed almost all economic incentives for high fertility and large families, but also provided the necessary statutory basis for the population control policy and family planning program envisaged as part of the First Five-Year Plan of Development initiated in 1989. The Parliamentary Bill concerning the Second Five-Year Development Plan of the IRI (SFYPD) passed in 1994 also reiterated the IRI government's commitment to population control and family planning.

Immediate Signs of a Rise in Contraceptive Use

Contrary to the pessimistic stance taken by the authors of the FFYDP (1989) and most oilier experts regarding the short-term effect of the new policy, almost immediately after the revival of the family planning program, there were signs of its effectiveness in both acceptability and Its possible Impact on fertility levels. A KAP survey carried out by the MOHME in 1989, that is, just after the program had commenced, revealed that almost half of married women aged 15–49 years were already using some form of contraception. Most of these (56 per cent) used such modem methods as the pill, condom, and IUD. A larger survey carried out in 1992 showed that contraceptive prevalence rates had risen to almost two-thirds of all married women, 69 per cent of whom used a modem method. These figures indicate a surprisingly high demand for and acceptance of family planning services when compared with the contraceptive prevalence rate (about 37 per cent) that had been achieved by the pre-Revolutionary family planning program by 1977, ten years after its formal introduction (Aghajanian 1991; Aghajanian & Mehryar 1999).

Converging Evidence of Fertility Decline

With regard to actual fertility behavior, some evidence of a gradual decline in fertility rates had already been revealed by a 12-round household survey conducted by the SCI between 1987 and 1989 (Mehryar & Gholipour 1995). This trend was supported by the findings of the combined census/survey carried out in 1991 which showed that the Iranian population had risen to only 55.8 million since 1986. This figure implied an annual growth rate of 2.5 per cent for the period 1986–1991, a 64 per cent decline in comparison with the growth rate of 3.9 per cent revealed by the 1986 Census. Further analysis of the 1991 data indicated that the total fertility rate bad declined from 7.1 to 4.9 during the preceding five years (SCI 1998: Table 1.11.1), although other estimates of TFR implied by the 1991 census/survey range from 4.8 to 6.3 (Bulatao & Richardson 1994: Table 3). Judging by this evidence, the revived family planning program reached all of the demographic targets set for it in the FFYPD before the Plan had in fact been implemented.

Because of the unexpectedly sharp decline in the growth rate indicated by the 1991 census/survey and presumed anomalies in the age structure of the population enumerated, most demographers both within and outside Iran received these results with some skepticism. Even PBO (1993), the parent organization of the SCI, refused to

Figure 1.11.1. Own-children estimates of total fertility rates during 1972–1996, the Islamic Republic of Iran, by rural and suburban areas

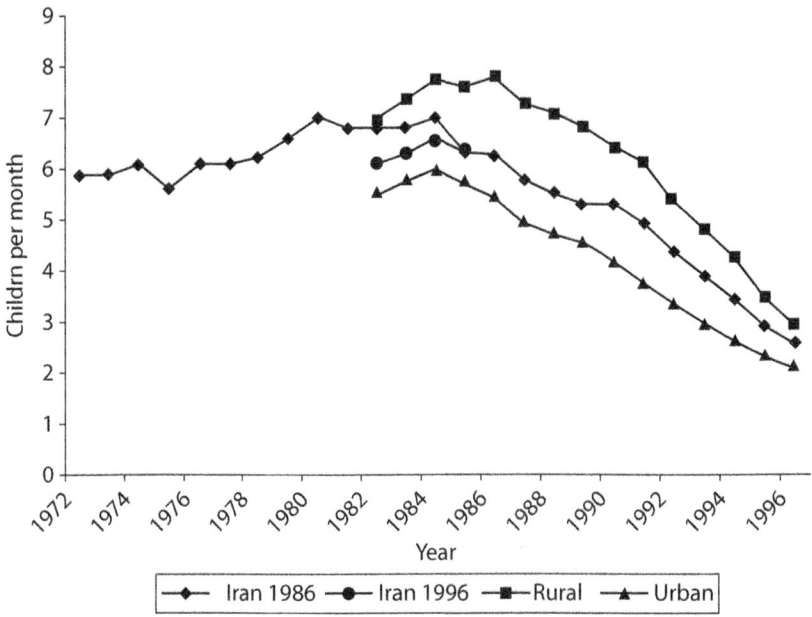

Note: Figures estimated from the own-children data from the 1986 and 1996 censuses obtained from the Statistical Centre of Iran. Source: Abbasi-Shavazi (2000a)

accept the results of the 1991 census/survey as a basis for the projection of population trends during the period of the second plan (1993–1998).[1] However, large-scale annual population surveys conducted by SCI in 1992 and 1993 indicated a continuation of the downward trend revealed by the 1991 census/survey. These were supported by smaller scale, but nationally representative, surveys undertaken by the MOHME as well as a new set of panel surveys on the socioeconomic conditions of Iranian households conducted by the SCI between 1991 and 1995.

All these were received with more than the usual measure of caution, if not disbelief, by demographers outside the MOHME and the SCI. At the same time, evidence of an accelerating fall in the number of births registered by the CRO was not taken seriously even by the demographers working for that organization, presumably because of their known under-coverage. Using the number of officially registered births, Ladier-Fouladi (1996) has noted a marked drop (from 43.4 to 30.4 per thousand) in the crude birth rate of Iran between 1986 and 1991. The corresponding decline in total fertility estimates was from 6.2 to 4.2.

In view of the persistent doubts regarding the coverage and quality of the 1991 census/survey and later surveys conducted by the SCI and MOHME, the 1996 Census had been anxiously awaited. The results of this census indicated an even more precipitous decline in fertility than the 1991 census/survey. Comparing fee population enumerated in 1996 (just over 60 million) with the counts in 1986 and 1991 showed that the total population of Iran had grown at a rate of 2.46 per cent between 1986 and 1996 and at a rate of only 1.47 per cent since 1991. It became obvious that the drop in population growth rate between 1986 and 1996 was due to a sharp drop in fertility. This inference was clearly supported by the marked decline in the number of children aged 0–4 in the 1996 Census (6,163,024) compared with the size of the same age group enumerated in 1991 (8,141,285) and 1986 (9,044,823). The fertility indices officially calculated on the basis of the 1996 Census (TFR=2.96, CBR=20.5) are also indicative of a sharp decline. The TFR (2.96) for 1996 was only 42 per cent of that for 1986 (7.1) and 60 per cent of that for 1991 (4.9). The TFR revealed by the 1996 Censes was only slightly higher than the TFR (2.6) revealed by the large-scale KAP survey conducted by the MOHME in 1996. The level of fertility was also very much in line with the high contraceptive prevalence rate indicated by this survey.

Applying the own-children method to the 1986 and 1996 Censuses, Abbasi-Shavazi (2000a) has analyzed the single-year fluctuation of fertility trends over the period 1972–1996 (Figure 1.11.1). From 1972–1979, the fertility rate rose from 5.8 to 6.5. There was little evidence in this period of any impact on fertility of the family planning program implemented by the Shah's regime. Following the Revolution TFR was very high and fairly constant during the period from 1980 to 1984. As mentioned earlier, government policies of the IRI emphasized early marriage for young adults. The revolutionary slogans were also supportive of the poor, aid people had a rather positive attitude towards the new government subsidies on family expenditure, particularly those on electricity, water, telephone, education and health. Consequently, Iranian couples had every reason to many early and have more children while married.

In the period from 1985 to 1989, the high fertility regime created by the Revolution faltered and fertility started to decline. TFR declined from its peak in 1984 to 6.2 in 1986 and further to around 5.3 in 1989. The decline was, however, slow until 1989 before it accelerated during the 1990s. It is worth noting that the fertility decline in urban areas started in 1985, while rural fertility began to decline two years later, in 1987. Finally, in the period from 1990 onwards, the transition accelerated TFR fell sharply after 1989 dropping from 5.32 in 1990 and further to 2.69 in 1996, a 50 per cent decline in six years. This spectacular decline occurred in both rural and urban areas. In rural areas of Iran, TFR dropped from 7.7 in 1986 to 2.9 in 1996. TFRs for urban areas declined from 5.4 to 2.0 in the same period.

At the provincial level, the majority of provinces experienced a moderate rise in fertility during the period 1976–1986 (Abbasi-Shavazi 2000a). However, all provinces followed the national trend and experienced tremendous declines in the period 1986 to 1996. Generally speaking, TFR fell most significantly in those provinces where fertility was very high during the previous decade. These provinces had had lower socio-economic characteristics compared to the country as a whole and other provinces. On the other hand, the absolute decline In TFR was lower in the more developed provinces such as Tehran and Gilan.

In sum, the dramatic decline in fertility in Iran from 1986 to 1996 was common to both urban and rural areas and to all provinces of Iran irrespective of their level of development.

Changes in Iran's age specific fertility rates are shown in Figure 1.11.2. Between 1972 and the peak of fertility in 1984, fertility rates rose by roughly equal proportions in every age group (except 15–19). Then, between 1984 and 1996, the rates fell substantially so every age group. Conventionally, during fertility transitions, fertility falls mainly at the younger or the older ages or both. The very substantial falls in fertility in the middle, peak ages of childbearing provide the explanation of why the fall in fertility in Iran from 1984 to 1996 was faster than any other recorded case. The sleep fertility decline in all age groups suggests that later starting, increased spacing and earlier slopping of childbearing all occurred at the same time. This cross-sectional effect may have been a compensation for the very high fertility at all ages before 1986.

Figure 1.11.2. ASFRs for Iranian women in 1972, 1984 and 1996

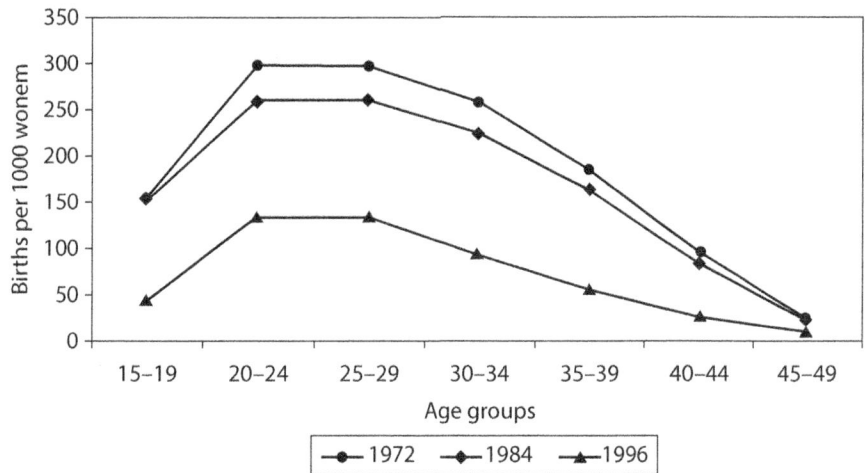

Source: Figures estimated from the own-children data from the 1986 and 1996 censuses obtained from the Statistical Centre of Iran (Abbasi-Shavazi 2000a)

TABLE 1.11.1. Female singulate mean age at marriage (SMAM) and age-specific

Year	SMAM	15–19	20–24	25–29
1976	19.52	0.343	0.786	0.932
1986	19.73	0.335	0.796	0.906
1996	22.09	0.186	0.607	0.852

Sources: Calculated from published data from the 1976, 1986 and 1996 Censuses, Statistical Centre of Iran.

The influence of changes in nuptiality and family planning usage

Nuptiality Change

Fertility transition in developing countries is often associated with an increase in age at marriage for women. This section describes changes in nuptiality in Iran in the period under consideration. Since 1979, the government of the IRI has consistently encouraged early marriage. The legal minimum age at marriage for girls was reduced from sixteen to nine years after the 1979 Islamic revolution. During the following decade, young couples received many incentives for early marriage. However, despite this wholehearted campaign for early marriage, age at first marriage increased slightly during this period (Table 1.11.1). After 1986, there was a profound change in marriage pattern. The singulate mean age at marriage increased from 19.7 to 22.1 years between 1986 and 1996.

The shift to much later marriage during the period 1986–1996 took place in both rural and urban areas. In rural areas, female singulate mean age at first marriage increased from 19.7 in 1986 to 22.1 in 1996, whereas in the urban areas the figure rose from 20.1 to 22.0 (Abbasi-Shavazi 2000b).

Despite the increase in mean age at marriage, universality remains one of the major characteristics of the Iranian marriage pattern. Marriage is strongly supported by both religion and tradition in Iranian society. To get married is not only a matter of personal interest, but also a duty of the young to their families and to society. As a result, the majority of women marry before age 30, and almost all women marry by their early 40s. Although the proportion of ever-married women is slightly higher for rural women, the rural-urban difference is negligible.

The change in marriage pattern is consistent with other socioeconomic changes in the IRI over the last two decades. Economic pressure has been a major factor in the postponement of marriage. It is asserted that age at marriage is late where the direct costs of marriage (both ceremonial and transfer costs) are high (Smith 1983: 496). Iran has been experiencing economic hardship since the revolution, particularly in the decade after the war. The cost of living has risen dramatically in recent years. In order to be able to afford the high living costs, young people tend to delay their marriage until they get a job.

Fertility Control Through Family Planning

The other major factor influencing fertility during a transition is the use of contraception. The total contraceptive prevalence rates of rural and urban segments of the population shown by two national surveys earned out since 1990 are summarized in Table 1.11.2. The table also includes the contraceptive prevalence rates for 1977 and 1989. These provide a good basis for comparing the impact of the family planning program three years after its inauguration with the contraceptive use rates that prevailed during the last years of the pre-Revolutionary period (1977, when there was an active family planning program) and shortly before the revival of the family planning program in 1989.

By 1992, almost two-thirds of married women aged 15–49 were practicing some form of contraception. The overall contraceptive prevalence level revealed by the 1992 survey (65 per cent) is almost twice the level of coverage

TABLE 1.11.2. Contraceptive prevalence rates revealed by national KAP surveys conducted in Iran between 1976 and 1997

Year/Method	1976 Method Type			1989 Method Type			1992 Method Type			1997 Method Type		
Area	M	T	All	M	T	All	M	T	All	M	T	All
Urban	34	21	54	33	31	64	47	27	74	55	23	78
Rural	15	5	20	21	10	31	41	10	51	57	9	66
Total	24	13	37	30	19	49	45	20	65	55	18	73

Notes Method type: M = Modern Methods; T = Traditional Method (Withdrawal)
Source: Aghajanian 1994 (for 1977 survey): Ministry of Health & Medical Education (1989, 1996, 1997) for 1989 and later surveys.

(37 per cent) shown by the Iran Fertility Survey in 1977 which was ten years after the initiation of the earlier family planning program by the old regime of Iran. Five years later, according to the 1997 KAP survey, the contraceptive prevalence rate had risen to almost 75 per cent. The rate for urban women in 1977 (53.8 percent) was almost two and half times that of rural women (19.9 percent). In contrast, the rural-urban difference in contraceptive prevalence in 1992 was only 23 percentage points. Five year later, the urban-rural gap had shrunk to 12 percentage points. This small advantage was mainly due to the fact that a much larger proportion of urban couples (23 per cent) compared with rural (9 per cent) reported using the traditional method of withdrawal which is not encouraged by the program.

The 1989 data, obtained before the program had been officially inaugurated, indicate that almost 50 percent of eligible couples had been using some form of contraception. A series of independent surveys carried out by a joint team of Iranian and French researchers in the Shiraz county of Fars province in 1996–1998 (Agha et al. 1997) revealed similarly high contraceptive prevalence rates in both urban and rural areas.

Although the prevalence of the traditional method of *azl* (withdrawal) had gone up considerably (from 13 to 20 per cent) between 1977 and 1992, the overwhelming majority of current contraceptive users seem to be relying on the modern methods of pill, IUD, and condom. Iran is also one of the few Muslim countries where male and female sterilization are not only permitted but are also actively promoted by the national program. The most commonly used modern methods in 1997 were pill (20.9 per cent), IUD (8.3 per cent), condom (5.4 per cent), injectable (2.9 percent), and Norplant (0.5 per cent). In addition, over 15.5 per cent of women and 1.9 per cent of men had undergone sterilization.

The mix of modern methods seems to be largely determined by the MOHME policy and shows some interesting variations across urban and rural areas and over time. It appears that between 1992 and 1997, the shares of pill and condom users have declined noticeably among both urban and rural users of modern methods. In this period, the share of sterilization has risen in both urban and rural areas. Thus, the proportionate share of women undergoing tubectomy has risen steadily among both urban (16.3 to 27.5 per cent) and rural women (from 18.0 to 29.1 per cent). A similar upward trend is also noticeable for male sterilization in both urban (2.7 per cent to 4.3 per cent) and rural (1.0 to 1.8 per cent) areas.

There are interesting provincial differences in both the overall contraceptive prevalence rate and its modern/traditional mix. The data for 1997 clearly demonstrate these differences. In rural areas, total contraceptive prevalence rates vary from over 80 per cent (Yazd, 85.3 per cent; Semnan, 84.6 per cent; Isfahan, 81.8 per cent) to below 50 per cent (Hormuzgan, 42.5 per cent). Other provinces with relatively low contraceptive prevalence rates in rural areas are Kohgiluyeh-Boyerahmad (54.2 per cent), Sistan-Baluchistan (55.8 per cent), Khuzistan (57.8 per cent), and Bushehr (59.1 per cent). Total contraceptive use rates for urban areas vary within the much narrower range of 87.2 per cent (In Yazd) to 68.2 per cent (in Sistan-Baluchistan). In fact in 12 of the 26 provinces, the CPR of urban couples is above 80 per cent and in only one province (Sistan-Baluchistan) does it fall below 70 per cent. Even in the latter case, over two-thirds of couples are found to be using contraception. As expected, in all provinces urban women have higher overall contraceptive use rates than rural women. This is, however, mainly due to the higher prevalence of the traditional method (withdrawal) among the urban couples.

Relative Impacts on Fertility Decline of Nuptiality and Marital Fertility

Abbasi-Sliavazi (2000b) has decomposed the changes in total fertility rate from 1976 to 1996 into the components of changes in nuptiality and marital fertility for Iran by province as well as for rural and urban areas. He found that total fertility increased from 6.09 in 1976 to 624 in 1986, a difference of 0.14. This increase was due to the increase in marital fertility (0.22), but was offset by nuptiality change (-0.07). The total fertility rate fell substantially by 3.71 (births per woman) from 1986 to 1996. Most of the fall was due to the decline in marital fertility (3.11) with 0.6 being due to nuptiality change. In other words 86 percent of the fertility decline was due to the change in marital fertility and only 14 percent to nuptiality change. The decomposition of the change in TFR for both rural and urban areas is identical to that of the total population.

The Social Context of Contraceptive Use and Fertility Decline

Neither the early repression nor the later revival of the family planning program took place in a social vacuum. They occurred as part of a long, complicated and often rapidly evolving series of historical events involving many players with diverse agendas. A number of major social and political groups with diametrically opposed aims and agendas were involved in the Revolution. The two main uniting themes were a shared opposition to the Shah and the political organization created by him and a rather simplistic belief that Iran had all the natural and human resources for rapid socioeconomic development, modernization, and free access to modem amenities and services enjoyed by people in the West. Few of the revolutionaries could be regarded as being against development and modernization in the sense of raising the level of education of all citizens, improving their health status, ensuring the proper satisfaction of their basic needs as well as providing them with the modem amenities and consumer goods that had flooded Iranian markets after the oil glut of the early 1970s. That even the fundamentalist *ulama* who quickly filled the power vacuum left by the sudden disintegration of the old regime were not against these popular ideals is clearly reflected in several of the speeches made by Imam Khomeini on his return to Iran as well as public pronouncements and promises made by many of his close advisors. In fact, some of the latter promised that the new regime would not only provide all social services free of charge but also abolish all existing taxes and arrange for the regular disbursement of oil revenues among the populace. An announcement by the cleric in charge of the Islamic Housing Foundation created shortly after the revolution, that all people living in Tehran would be given free land and interest-free loans to build a house, is believed to be one of the reasons behind the tremendous increase in migration to Tehran that happened during the first year after the Revolution.

Most of the above-mentioned populist promises were taken into consideration in the preparation of the Constitution of the IRI, drafted hastily and put to public referendum less than a year after the Revolution. The Constitution of the Islamic Republic of Iran clearly envisages a welfare state anticipating many of the ideals currently advocated by the United Nations as part of its new paradigm of Sustainable Human Development (Mehryar 1997). The results of investment in social development are reflected in various indicators of development (Table 1.11.3).

Because of the eight-year war and its enormous costs, the government of the IRI was restricted in the resources it could devote to the social development programs and priorities enshrined in the Constitution. Nevertheless, a recent study of the share of basic social services (primarily education and health) in the government budget and the GDP revealed that, even at the height of the war period, investment in the basic social services accounted for a sizable proportion of the annual budget. Expenditure of 20 per cent of the annual budget on basic social services as proposed by UNDP's 20/20 compact has consistently been exceeded (Mehryar *et al.* 1999). Moreover, a deliberate effort has been made to target the traditionally neglected rural and lower class segments of the population.

As a result of this investment in social services, the past two decades have witnessed significant changes in modernization and in the living standards of the population (Tables 1.11.3 and .4). There have been substantial falls in both infant and maternal mortality rates and rises in expectation of life. Adult literacy has risen greatly and the enrolment ratio for children of secondary school age is above 80 per cent. Urbanization has continued but, at the same time, the urban-rural gap in access to health, education and modem amenities has been considerably narrowed. Almost all rural households have electricity and almost 80 per cent have piped water. Ownership of consumer durables such as refrigerators, gas cookers, radio and television has increased significantly, especially in rural areas.

Progress has also been made in the area of public education. Here not only did the literacy rate rise markedly for both men (from 59 per cent to 85 per cent) and women (from 37 per cent to 74 per cent) between 1976 and 1996, but the level of educational attainment also rose significantly. As a result, by 1996, the number of the non-student population with a secondary school diploma had risen to 4.6 million (compared with 1.28 million in 1976); the number of the non-student population with tertiary education had risen to 1.15 million (compared with 0.28 million in 1976). More important for fertility decline, women's share of the educated population has increased considerably:

1. The share of girls in the primary-level student population has risen to 90 per 100 boys (as compared with 66 per 100 boys in 1976);
2. The share of girls in the secondary-level student population has risen to 81 per 100 boys (as compared with 59 per 100 In 1976);
3. The share of females in the higher education student population has risen to 68 per 100 males (as compared with 47 per 100 in 1976);
4. While the total number of students in 1996 (19.3 million) was over twice that in 1976 (7.5 million), the number of students at senior secondary (3.3 million) was more than three times that in 1976 (0.89 million) and there were six times as many university students in 1996 (976,000) as in 1976 (150,000).
5. The number of non-student women with a secondary school diploma had risen to 2.1 million in 1996 (compared with 447,000 in 1976);
6. The number of non-student women with tertiary education had risen to 495,000 (compared with 75,000 in 1976).

TABLE 1.11.3 Selected socioeconomic and demographic indicators for Iran for 1976, 1986 and 1996

Indicators	Period		
	1976	1989	1996
Infant Mortality Rate			
Male	129	54.4	48.0
Female	142	59.7	52.6
Maternal Mortality[a]	277	140	37
Life expectancy:			
Male	58.7	65.9	67.0
Female	57.8	65.6	66.8
Adult Literacy Rate (%):			
Male	58.5	70.7	84.7
Female	35.3	51.9	74.0
Net enrolment ratio in secondary school	50[b]		81
Urbanization (%)	47.0	54.6	61.3

Notes: a Per 100,000 births, b *The figure is for 1980.*
Sources: Metiryar and Tajdini (1998); World Bank Development Indicators, 2000.

TABLE 1.11.4. Access to electricity and other amenities by rural and urban areas of Iran, 1977 and 1997

Amenities	1977		1997	
	Urban	Rural	Urban	Rural
Household access to:				
Electricity	91	15	99	92
Piped water	80	12	98	78
Telephone	16	1	53	12
Radio	78	52	78	60
TV	52	2.4	93	69
Ownership of:				
Refrigerator	81	15	96	77
Gas cooker	75	29	96	69
Indoor Bathroom	40	3	83	35

Sources: Mehryar and Tajdini (1998).

These gains in women's education have not, however, been associated with any rise in their labor force participation rates. There was in fact a noticeable decline (from 12.9 per cent to 8.2 per cent) In the labor force participation rate of women between 1976 and 1986 and only a slight increase to 1996 (9.1 per cent). The discrepancy in the educational attainment and the labor force participation rate of Iranian women is mainly due to cultural factors which preclude women's employment in such areas as construction, sales, and even food preparation and the hotel industry (Mehryar and Farjadi 2000).

That most of these developments are due to sustained government investment in social services, particularly education and health, is confirmed by the fact that the share of educational expenses in total household expenditure remained under 1 per cent for the period 1979–1989 for both, urban and rural households. It rose above 1 per cent of the total expenses of urban households in 1990 and continued to rise until 1995 when it accounted for about 2.3 percent of total household expenses. In the case of rural households too, there has been a steady rise in the share of educational expenses in total household expenses since 1990. It has accounted for about 1.3 percent of household expenses since 1994. Similarly, the share of health expenses in total household expenditure has fluctuated between 4 and 5 per cent of the total expenses of both urban and rural households for most of the period under review. In recent years, health expenditure has risen just above 5 per cent in urban areas since 1994 and rural areas since 1996 (Tabibian *et al.* 2000).

Thus, there is no convincing evidence that a sharp rise in the costs of children caused the drastic fertility decline observed since the late 1980s. On the other hand, there is evidence that the per capita income of the majority of Iranian families has fallen below its pre-Revolutionary purchasing power while the consumer tastes developed during the oil glut period just preceding the Revolution continue unabated. Because of this, although by objective evidence the poverty level of the Iranian population has not gone up noticeably since the mid-1970s (Mekyar *et al.* 1999), a large proportion of families seem to be suffering from economic hardship.

The comparative perspective of fertility transition in North Africa and West Asia

The Iranian fertility decline can be considered in the context of fertility changes in other predominantly-Islamic countries in North Africa and West Asia (Figure 1.11.3). As a whole, this region was characterized in the past as being bound by a culture founded in Islamic approaches to women that supported the persistence of very high and unchanging fertility (Omran; 1980: Caldwell 1986). In 1992, Obermeyer (1992: 56) concluded that high fertility would persist in this region in the absence of a redefinition of gender roles and the structure of the family. Recent falls in fertility rates in countries from Morocco to Iran have led to a reassessment of this alleged cultural hegemony. Rashad (2000) argues that cultures in North Africa and West Asia, as much as cultures in other parts of the world, have been sensitive to

FIGURE 1.11.3. Trends of TFRs for North Africa, West Asia and Iran, 1950–55 to 1995–00

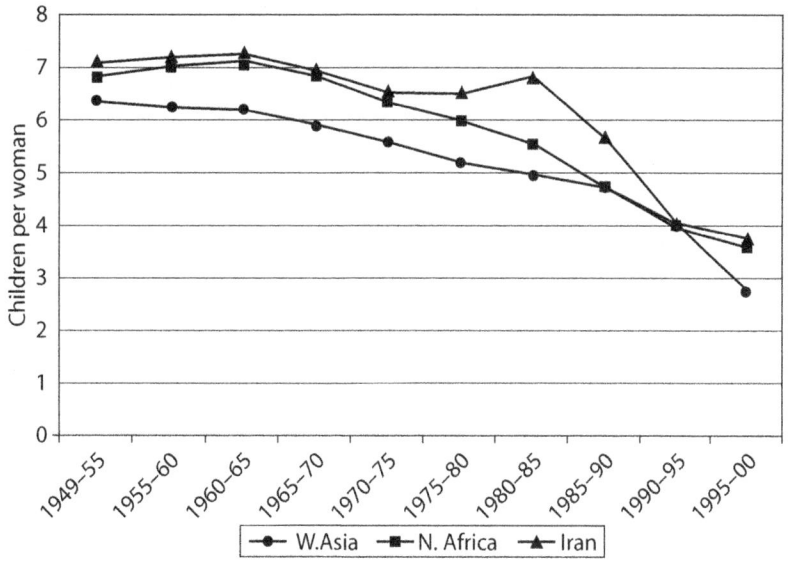

Source: United Nations, 1999.

the needs and aspirations of the people that live in these countries. She shows that fertility decline was slow to start in this region but, once under way, has proceeded at a rapid rate. Her explanation is that the fertility transitions, in North Africa and West Asia are much like other fertility transitions being influenced broadly by modernization factors such as education and changing aspirations.

However, cross-sectional factors, especially the state of the economy, war and political upheaval, have changed the timing and the pace of change in the North African and West Asian countries. In broad terms, Rashad argues that where fertility still remains high in this region, largely in the Gulf countries, it is because these countries have remained very wealthy, so that rising aspirations could be met with a continuance of high fertility. Costs of children in the Gulf countries are highly subsidized by the state. In other countries of the region, however, economic circumstances have been much more difficult and the rising aspirations of families brought on by modernization and education could only be met through later marriage and lower family size. Rashad suggests that later marriage has played a much more prominent role in the fertility transition in this region than fertility control within marriage, despite the fact that new roles for unmarried women in the paid labor force remain very restricted.

In Rashad's view, "Islamic culture" did not stand as an immutable force in opposition to lower fertility in all of North Africa and West Asia. Indeed, Rashad argues that, despite the similarities already described, each country in this region has had its own transition and the evidence in this article shows that this is especially true of Iran, Of all of the countries spread from Morocco to Iran, the changes in fertility in Iran are by far the most spectacular.

Rashad's arguments about the cross-sectional effects of war, political upheaval and economic hardship seem to be particularly apposite to the Iran case. Political upheaval and war not only stalled the fall in fertility in Iran from the late 1970s, they also appear to have led to a sizable increase in cross-sectional fertility rates. This cross-sectional serge in births to women of all ages probably partly precipitated the cross-sectional fall at all ages that began in the mid-1980s because most high-fertility aspirations had been satisfied. However, again consistent with the argument made by Rashad, there is a strong case that economic hardship relative to material aspirations accelerated the fall in fertility in Iran from the mid-1980s. On the other hand, in contrast to the other countries in the region, changes in nuptiality have played only a minor role in the Iran transition which has been dominated by widespread control of fertility within marriage. Here an explanation may be that the prior existence of a well-developed health system that had been extended to all parts of Iran offered the opportunity for the successful and rapid implementation of a national family planning program. Knowledge of the ready availability of contraception within marriage may be supporting the earlier marriage in Iran compared to countries in North Africa and Western Asia where fertility has declined. As in these countries, paid employment opportunities remain restricted for single women in Iran.

Section 2

Autonomy, Patriarchy, and Reproductive Control

Introduction

Autonomy, Patriarchy, and Reproductive Control

By Catherine Marrone

Every semester just after we have finished our first exam and move on to this next set of readings, I tell my students we are about to take a real turn, a darker, but requisite turn. This is because it is through this next set of readings that we begin to draw the incredibly powerful links that bind human reproduction to patriarchal control. For students from outside the world of Women's Studies or Gender Perspectives, this work is at once heady, new, and wholly disturbing. The very idea of women engaging in female infanticide and further, the sense that they do so as some pragmatic and practical response to "Patriarchal Risk," requires us to spend some time grappling with the terms "female autonomy" and "agency." Both terms are extremely limited in meaning in those places where women suffer under the most extreme social restrictions concerning reproduction. I often recommend to students a wonderful book by Karin Evans, *The Lost Daughters of China*, which I find to be perfectly in keeping with this part of the course and theme.

Later in these readings, just when students are feeling rather fortunate to be educated in the United States, we begin to address the issue of Abortion, one that for many (both women and men) might be regarded as the flagship of women's autonomy. But we need to understand that this right to "choice" is certainly not politically impenetrable, nor is it so universally received; never should we assume that all women (or all men) agree on the importance of maintaining its place among constitutional protections. The "dark side" of reproduction reveals itself in the present and past and comes to us in a number of forms and places. Most importantly, this topic and this section of the readings challenge students to understand that religion and politics and gender—never to be removed from our understanding of human reproduction—can combine to create incredibly divisive belief systems and practices and further, often lead to life-altering, world-changing, and all too sadly, caustic ends.

Patriarchal Structure and Demographic Change

By Mead T. Cain

The effect of women's status (variously defined) on fertility is typically described as operating either through the opportunity costs of children or through women's autonomy in decisions relating to reproduction. In both cases, improvements in women's status are thought to have a negative influence on fertility. I will argue that these hypotheses largely misstate the effects of women's status on fertility in contemporary Third World societies; that, while these channels of influence may, indeed, operate in such settings, they are overshadowed by less direct, but more profound, effects. I argue that the principal means by which women's status—defined in terms of the extent of women's economic dependence on men—affects fertility is through preference for the sex of children. I take as given that children are highly valued as sources of economic security by parents in the great majority of contemporary less developed countries and that reproductive goals are strongly influenced by perceived security needs. In societies in which women are highly dependent on men (i.e. where women's status is low), security goals will, of necessity, be defined in terms of surviving sons, Where women are relatively independent economically, it is more likely that children of either sex can serve security needs. Given similar security needs, and other things being equal, fertility will be considerably higher in settings where there is a strong preference for sons than in settings where son-preference is weak.

A Safety-First Model of Fertility

My interpretation of the relationship between women's status and fertility is based on a more general understanding of the determinants of fertility. I have proposed a "safety-first" (LSF) model of fertility elsewhere. The model posits a lexicographic decision process based on the criteria of safety-first. Originally developed to study innovation-adoption behaviour of farmers, the assumption in the LSF model is that farmers, in making production decisions, are motivated not only by a desire to maximize net returns, but also by the condition that net returns should not fall beneath some specified "disaster level."[1] In the case of agricultural production, disaster is crop failure, and the choice variable is crop variety (or some other input decision). In our case, the disaster is income insufficiency in old age (and/or other contingencies), and the choice variable is fertility. It is assumed that parents wish to maximize utility subject to the chance constraint that the probability of inadequate support and quality of life in old age is less than or equal to some target probability. Here, the first priority is to make adequate provision for the future with reasonable certainty. Only

Mead T. Cain, "Patriarchal Structure and Demographic Change," *Women's Position and Demographic Change*, ed. Nora Federici, Karen O. Mason and Solvi Sogner, pp. 43–60. Copyright © 1993 by Oxford University Press. Reprinted with permission.

after this constraint is fulfilled do parents concern themselves with the fertility implications of the more familiar time and commodity costs and benefits of children.

This model suggests that parents define minimum requirements for old age security in terms of a certain number of surviving children. Suppose, for example, that this minimum is one healthy and loyal surviving child. The fertility level that is consistent with this goal will depend primarily on the probability of child survival and the probability of child default. The higher the level of child mortality, the greater the fertility necessary to achieve the goal. Similarly, concern over child default should induce higher fertility than if there were no such concern. Mortality and default risks may cause the operational "rule of thumb" to be revised upward, so that the survival of two children through infancy becomes the goal in particular less developed societies the way in which; targets are defined, and thus their implications for fertility strategies, will depend on several factors. These include the harshness of the risk environment, and the availability and adequacy of alternative sources of insurance.

The Role of Women's Status

Women's status is relevant to the safety-first model in two ways. The first relates to whether or not the sex of offspring is a factor in framing security targets. In societies in which women are relatively independent economically, and where they share relative equality with men with respect to economic opportunity and control of property, parents will be relatively indifferent about the sex of offspring as regards insurance and security, in societies in which women are more dependent on men, and where they are excluded from mainstream economic activities, parents will place a greater premium on sons. Other things being equal, the fertility level associated with a need for sons will be considerably higher than that implied by a security target that can be satisfied by children of either sex.

The second way in which women's status enters the model is as a distinct source of risk for which additional insurance may be needed. Economic dependence on men can entail special risks for women—risks that are independent of other sources, such us natural disasters or the process of ageing, to which both men and women are exposed. Widowhood, divorce separation, or incapacitating illness of the husband are threatening events in societies in which women are excluded from mainstream sources of income and are thus prevented from providing for themselves through their own labour and enterprise. An important source of insurance against the risk of losing the economic support of a husband is sons, The-greater the economic dependence of women on men, the greater the salience of this source of risk.

Both son-preference and "patriarchal risk" stem from the same cause: the economic dependence of women. They do not however, have the same consequences for fertility. Of the two, son-preference may be viewed as the more significant, because it affects security target-setting irrespective of source of risk. If there is a need to have sons in order to achieve security goals, this requirement will hold for old-age security and other contingencies as much as for insurance against patriarchal risk. With respect to the risks that dependent women face, it could well be that the fertility level consistent with the target set for old-age security is sufficiently high to satisfy the demand for insurance created by such risks, in which case the presence of patriarchal risk may only serve to reinforce reproductive goals and make them more resistant to change.

Family Structure: Boundaries of the Corporate Group

Too often, analyses that focus on women's status abstract from the corporate context of the family, and therefore overlook the fact that, regardless of tangible indications of inequality between men and women, women's welfare and interests are often closely aligned with the corporate interests of the family as a whole.[2] It is also important to note, however, that the boundary of the corporate family group is not the same in all developing societies. In Asia, this boundary typically encompasses the nuclear family unit—husband, wife, and children. Although the system of family formation that characterizes this region is aptly labeled "joint"[3] and while most nuclear family units experience periods of extension in their developmental cycles, the majority of households at any given time will, nevertheless, be nuclear in structure. The relatively high degree of corporateness that is typical of the conjugal unit in Asia is, however, not characteristic of sub-Saharan African or Caribbean (and some Latin American) societies.

In the "Caribbean" family system the conjugal bond is relatively weak: formal marriage is the exception rather than the norm, a substantial part of reproduction occurs outside marriage or stable unions, women often experience a series of unions with different men during the course of their reproductive lives, and the biological father often bears little or no financial responsibility for his children.[4] In much of sub-Saharan Africa, the conjugal bond also tends to be weak. There, however, the locus of reproductive decisions, and the appropriate referent when considering the costs and benefits of children, is the larger kin-group, rather than one or another parent as in the case of the Caribbean family system, or the conjugal unit as in Asian family systems.[5]

In both sub-Saharan Africa and the Caribbean, women possess considerable economic autonomy. However, while these regions would tend to be relatively free of the fertility incentives associated with a high degree of women's dependence, aspects of their family systems may introduce other pronatalist forces. In the case of the Caribbean, the fact that a father may share in the benefits of reproduction while avoiding the costs creates the possibility of a "free-rider" situation. In sub-Saharan Africa, it is the dominance of lineage over the conjugal pair and the associated diffusion of the costs (and benefits) of particular children that is of most significance.

A Structural Perspective on Women's Economic Status

Obviously, it is important to locate the analysis of women's status and fertility at the appropriate level of aggregation. It makes little sense to propose or conduct household- or individual-level analyses of a variable that is properly measured al a higher level of aggregation. One can think of many individual-level measures of women's economic dependence on men; however, the factors that condition an individual's experience—the sexual division of labour, labour-market segmentation, inheritance rules, religious norms of behaviour, rules of marriage and family formation—are located in a society's institutional structure. While there may exist, substantial variation in the individual experience of women in a particular society, the distribution of such experience will be constrained by institutionally, determined bounds. In important respects, therefore, women's status—the extent to which they are economically dependent on men—should be viewed as a structural phenomenon.

Situations in which women are highly dependent on men involve structured inequality: systems of stratification that give advantage to men over women. Corporate households notwithstanding, men benefit from their dominant positions in such systems and, just as with élites more generally, they have a vested interest in protecting their rank and the system that elevates them to positions of power and control. These interests represent a potentially powerful source of resistance to change, over and above the "dead hand of tradition."

Patriarchal structure, by which I mean the sum of institutional mechanisms that serve to limit women's economic autonomy relative to men's,[6] may thus possess considerable inertia. When considering the prospects for change in any one element of patriarchal structure women's age at marriage, for example—one must reckon with the weight of the entire structure. For our purposes, knowing why different institutional arrangements have evolved in different regions of the developing world is less important than recognition that particular patriarchal structures have deep historical roots, and that the pattern of variation in patriarchal structure which can be observed today in the developing world is essentially the same as the pattern that existed three and four decades ago, when mortality began its precipitous decline.

Direct Effects of Patriarchal Structure

The direct causal relationships that link patriarchal structure, women's status, and fertility are illustrated in Fig. 2.1.1. Elements of patriarchal control combine to produce a particular degree of women's economic dependence

Fig. 2.1.1 Patriarchal Structure. Women's Status and Fertility

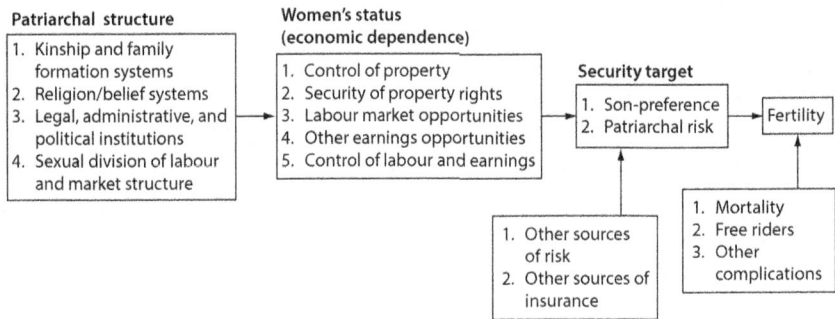

on men, which, in turn, affects security target-setting in two ways. First, and most important, for a given level of risk (and availability of alternative sources of insurance), the dependence of women determines the relevance of sex of children in figuring security needs. Secondly, economic dependence may increase the demand for children as security assets over and above what it would otherwise be, because it introduces an additional source of risk. The security target—expressed in terms of desired number of surviving sons or children—in turn has "implications for the level of fertility;" the level consistent with a particular security target depends on levels of mortality and natural fertility. Other things being equal, the greater the chances of child survival, the lower the fertility necessary for achieving security goals. However, if the security target is high, improvements in mortality may simply facilitate the achievement of a security goal which had previously been out of reach. Where conjugal ties are weak and the nuclear family unit lacks cohesiveness, the free-rider problem may "short-circuit" the connection drawn between the security target and fertility.

Among the "other complications" referred to in Fig. 2.1.1 are infertility, child-fostering, and the possibility of child default. Both extraordinary levels of infertility, and the institution of child-fostering are characteristic of sub-Saharan Africa. High levels of infertility introduce additional uncertainty concerning the achievement of reproductive goals into an environment where uncertainty about child survival is, in general, already great. The tenuous control-over reproduction implied by the combination of a high incidence of infertility and high levels of mortality is antithetical to the notion of deliberate fertility limitation. While the incidence of fertility is by no means uniform throughout sub-Saharan Africa, it is high on average, and, at the upper end of the range, produces rates of childlessness among older women in excess of 30 percent.[7] Child-fostering, as practiced in much of sub-Saharan Africa, provides a means of diffusing and redistributing the costs of reproduction, and also of acquiring child services when reproduction fails. The significance of this institution in relation to reproductive behavior, however, lies less with narrow cost and benefit considerations, than as a reflection of a social organization in which the conjugal bond is relatively weak, the primary corporate group is the lineage rather than the conjugal unit, and costs and benefits of reproduction must be evaluated from the perspective 'of this larger corporate group, rather than that of parents.

Indirect Effects of Patriarchal Structure

The indirect links between patriarchal structure and fertility are depicted in Fig. 2.1.2. The principal indirect effect operates through women's age at marriage, which is viewed as responding to both educational and employment opportunities, given a permissive patriarchal structure. In a similar way, and under similar conditions, infant and child mortality may respond to improvements in women's education, and, in turn, induce a response in fertility. Patriarchal structure thus operates as a covariate: the structure itself is assumed to remain relatively unchanged, but different structures either enable or inhibit other types of change. According to this view, evidence of marked improvements in secondary school enrolment of girls is less an indication of transformation in patriarchal structure than a reflection of the existence of a "favourable" structure.

Fig. 2.1.2. Indirect Effects of Patriarchal Structure on Fertility

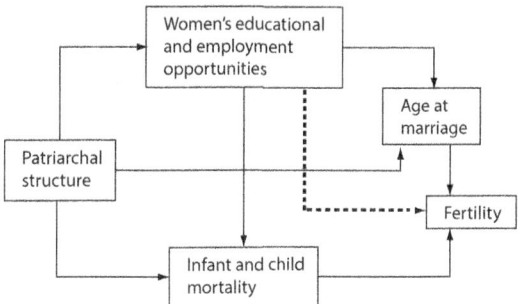

The arrow which connects educational and employment opportunities with fertility in Fig. 2.1.2 is broken, in order to indicate ambiguity of effect and subservience to the causal mechanism described in Fig. 2.1.1. Improvements in women's employment and education may initially serve to increase fertility, by disrupting traditional breast-feeding practices and thus reducing the period of post-partum amenorrhoea.[8] On the other hand, increased women's employment and education may raise the opportunity costs of children, and thus exert a negative influence on fertility. Education arguably has a number of other effects that combine to produce a negative influence on fertility. It may, for example reduce the psychic and real costs of fertility regulation. However, security considerations are expected to take precedence and the potential negative effects of women's employment and education should be evaluated in this context. Thus, an increase in opportunity costs will make children a more expensive form of insurance but, in the absence of change that affects the need for insurance or the availability of alternative forms of insurance; is unlikely to induce a fertility response. Similarly, while reduction In the costs of fertility regulation may well facilitate the achievement of fertility levels that are consistent with security targets, it will not override the determinant influence of these targets.

Empirical Application

The preceding discussion emphasized the theoretical importance of distinguishing the concept of women's economic status from the causally antecedent concept of patriarchal structure. Here we propose to use median age difference between once-married spouses as an indicator of patriarchal structure in a cross-national analysis of fertility.

The age difference between spouses (or partners in unions) has several attractive features as an indicator of patriarchal structure. In most cases, a large difference between the ages of spouses (men older than women) is associated with patrilineal kinship structure and patrilocal residence, while a small difference indicates bilateral kinship and greater flexibility in the residence pattern of newly married couples. A large difference represents a potentially powerful source of control by men over women, and may further reflect the kind of control that derives from the interaction of sex and age hierarchies. Moreover, the larger the age difference between spouses, the greater the probability of widowhood. Widowhood is a critical juncture in a woman's life, and, in societies where women's economic independence is curtailed, is the focal point of patriarchal risk.

Table 2.1.1 shows the median age difference between partners (excess of the man's age over that of the woman) by time elapsed since union for twenty-eight countries grouped by continent.[9] From the first column (time elapsed since union less than ten years), note that median age differences range from a low of 2.5 years in the Philippines to a high of 9.8 in Mauritania, The next three columns show the median age differences for successively shorter periods of time since first union, and thus provide a measure of change in age difference over the fifteen years that precede the date of the survey (in most cases the late 1970s), While some change is indicated, usually towards a narrowing of the age differences, the overall stability of median age differences through time is quite striking. For the most part, the rank order of countries is maintained in Columns 2–4 of Table 2.1.1, and inter-country variance in median age

Table 2.1.1. Median Age Difference Between Partners, by Time Elapsed Since Union, Women in One Union Only (Years)

Country	Less than 10	10–14	5–9	0–4
Africa				
Ghana	7.6	9.5	8.2	7.2
Kenya★	7.1	8.0	6.9	7.3
Lesotho★	5.6	6.5	5.7	5.5
Sudan★	8.4	9.4	8.6	8.2
Nigeria†	9.7	-	-	-
Benin†	6.9	-	-	-
Mauritania†	9.8	-	-	-
Morocco†	6.5	-	-	-
Egypt†	6.2	-	-	-
Asia				
Syria★	6.1	6.8	6.2	6.0
Bangladesh★	9.1	10.1	9.3	9.0
Nepal★	3.8	4.6	4.1	3.6
Pakistan★	6.5	5.9	6.4	6.6
Sri Lanka★	4.8	6.1	5.3	4.3
Indonesia	4.9	5.3	5.2	4.7
Korea, S.	4.0	3.7	4.0	3.9
Malaysia: Malay	4.8	5.1	5.0	4.6
Malaysia: Chinese	3.9	3.6	6.9	3.9
Philippines	2.5	2.7	2.5	2.5
Thailand★	3.3	3.5	3.4	3.2
Yemen†	5.4	-	-	-
Americas				
Colombia	4.6	5.1	5.6	4.6
Paraguay	4.0	4.4	4.1	4.0
Peru	3.8	4.3	3.9	3.8
Costa Rica	3.0	3.7	3.6	2.4
Mexico★	3.0	3.5	3.2	2.9
Haiti	4.1	4.9	4.0	4.2
Jamaica★	4.1	3.3	3.8	4.9
Venezuela†	4.6	-	-	-

★ Data relate only to women currently in union.
† Age difference by duration not reported.
Sources: Casterline and McDonald, and (') Casterline, Williams, and McDonald, both op. cit. in n. 10.

Table 2.1.2. Regression Analysis of Total Fertility

	(1)	(2)	(3)	(4)	(5)
Age difference (0/1)	2.4	2.0	2.1	2.0	1.6
	(0.4)	(0.4)	(0.4)	(0.4)	(0.4)
Infant mortality rate		0.01			
Log. GNP per head			-0.38		
			(0.22)		
Age at marriage				-0.16	
				(0.09)	
Girls' enrolment					-0.03
					(0.07)
Constant	3.9	3.2	6.5	7.3	5.0
R^2	0.65	0.69	0.69	0.69	0.76
F	49.1	28.2	27.8	27.9	40.1

* *Numbers in parentheses are standard errors.*

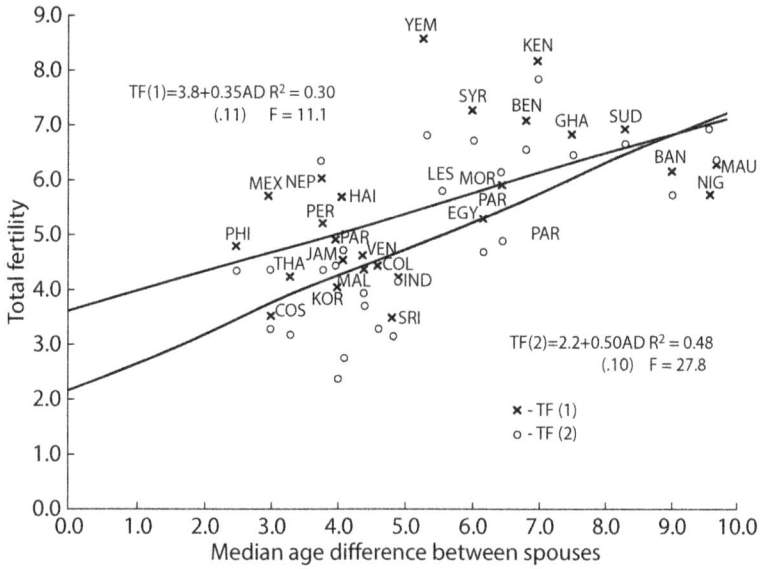

Fig. 2.1.3. Relationship Between Total Fertility and Age Difference Between Spouses

difference dominates inter-temporal variance. Median age differences between spouses are also remarkably invariant between socio-economic groups within countries. For example, contrary to what might be expected, median age differences within the great majority of countries shown in Table 2.1.1 do not vary systematically with wife's years of schooling, husband's occupation, or wife's place of childhood residence (city, town, or village). With respect to its merits as an indicator of patriarchal structure, this invariance is reassuring.

In Fig. 2.1.3 total fertility (TF) is plotted against median age difference between spouses for the countries listed in Table 2.1. Two indices of total fertility are used; the first, designated by X, is that yielded by the World Fertility Survey (WFS) (referred to here as TF(1)), aid the second, designated by O, is the estimate reported in the World Bank's 1987 *World Development Report* (referred to as TF(2)). Fig. 2.1.3 shows a positive relationship between median

Table 2.1.3. Regression Analysis of Total Fertility

	Median Age Difference							
	Less than 5 years (N = 15)				5 years or more (N = 13)			
	(1)	(2)	(3)	(4)	(5)	(6)	(7)	(8)
Infant mortality rate	0.025				−0.01			
	(0.005)*				(0.01)			
Log. GNP per head		−0.51				−0.03		
		(0.26)				(0.43)		
Age at marriage			−0.22				−0.03	
			(0.11)				(0.16)	
Girls" enrolment				−0.035				−0.028
				(0.011)				(0.022)
Constant	2.1	7.4	8.7	5.1	7.2	6.4	6.9	6.6
R^2	0.65	0.23	0.23	0.45	0.10	0	0	0.13
F	24.1	3.9	3.9	10.2	1.2	0	0	1.6

* *Numbers in parentheses are standard errors.*

Table 2.1.4. Ratio of Boy/Girl Responses to Questions About Sex Preference

Strong son-preference		Moderate son-preference		Equal-preference		Daughter-preference	
Pakistan	4.9	Lesotho	1.5	Kenya	1.1	Venezuela	0.8
Mauritius*	4.5	Sri Lanka	1.5	Indonesia	1.1	Jamaica	0.7
Nepal	4.0	Sudan	1.5	Peru	1.1		
Bangladesh	3.3	Morocco*	1.4	Guyana	1.1		
Korea	3.3	Thailand	1.4	Trinidad and Tobago	1.1		
Syria	2.3	Fiji	1.3				
Yemen*	2.3	Malaysia	1.2	Colombia	1.0		
Egypt *	2.0	Dominican Republic	1.2	Paraguay	1.0		
Jordan	1.9			Costa Rica	1.0		
		Mexico	1.2	Panama	1.0		
				Philippines	0.9		
				Haiti	0.9		

* *Ratios for these countries were computed from the final WFS country reports.*

age difference and fertility. The slope of the regression line for TF(2), which reflects recent declines in fertility, is slightly steeper and the line fits better.

It is clear from Fig. 2.1.3 that the strong positive correlation between median age difference and fertility derives from the position of two clusters of countries on the plot: the cluster in the lower left, which contains primarily south-east Asian and Latin American countries, with both relatively low age differences and low fertility; and the cluster in the upper right, made up of African, south Asian (Muslim), and west Asian countries, with large age differences and high fertility. Within each cluster, however, no clear relationship between median age difference and

Fig. 2.1.4 Relationship Between Median Age Difference Between Spouses and Preference for Sex of Children (ratio B/G)

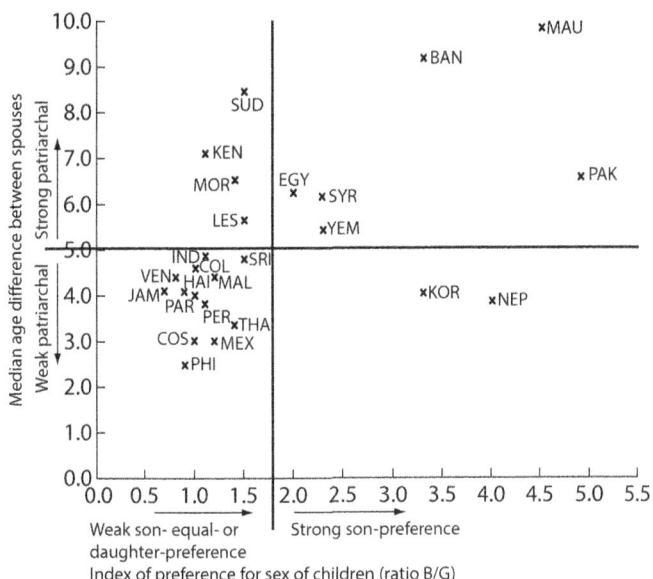

fertility can be discerned. Therefore the indicator of patriarchal structure appears to be able to distinguish, at best, two distinct regimes, one "weak" and one "strong."

One measure of the effect of patriarchal structure on fertility can be obtained by regressing total fertility on median age difference between spouses, controlling for possible confounding variables. The results of these regressions are presented in Table 2.1.2. To facilitate interpretation, median age difference is transformed into a dichotomous variable, set equal to zero when the median age difference is less than five years, and equal to one when it is five years or more. These regression models incorporate successively as controls: infant mortality rate, logarithm of GNP per head, singulate mean age at first marriage (women), and girls secondary school enrolment ratios.[10] The coefficients for mean age difference (the first row in Table 2.1.2) imply that a strong patriarchal regime is responsible for adding approximately two live births to total fertility. In Table 2.1.2 the more recent TF(2) is used as the dependent variable; the results when TF(1) is used are equally consistent, although the estimated coefficients for age difference are slightly smaller.

Another measure of the effect of patriarchal structure focuses on its role as a covariate. Where patriarchal structure is strong, mortality decline may simply facilitate the achievement of security targets that were out of reach previously, in which case one would not necessarily expect fertility to decline in response. In weak patriarchal regimes, however, where intrinsic security targets are already low, one would expect fertility to decline (perhaps with some lag) in response to a decline in mortality, Similarly, in weak patriarchal regimes there is greater inherent flexibility in women's age at marriage education, and employment. These should prove more responsive to change in the course of economic development, and, through the channels described earlier, have an impact on fertility.

To test for the presence of interaction, the regression models of Table 2.1.2 were estimated separately for countries in which median age difference between spouses is less than five years (weak patriarchal regimes) and for those in which it is five years or greater (strong patriarchal regimes). The results are shown in Table 2.1.3 and are quite striking. In strong patriarchal regimes there is no measurable relationship between variations in GNP per head, infant mortality, median age at first marriage, or secondary school enrolment of girls, and fertility levels. In weak patriarchal regimes, on the other hand, the four predictor variables behave very much as expected fertility is positively and significantly related to the infant mortality rate and negatively related to GNP, age at marriage, and girls' school enrolment ratios.

Preference for Sons

Societies in which women have little economic independence should generate a strong preference for sons because of women's need for security particularly in old age. Quite apart from any other potential channel of influence, women's status should have fundamental implications for fertility by determining the extent to which the sex of children is relevant to planning for future security needs.

A recent analysis of preferences for the sex of children, in which WF data were used, was focused on responses to the question "Would you prefer your next (first) child to be a boy or a girl?" asked of all pregnant women and all currently married non-pregnant women who wanted at least one more child and considered themselves capable of having another.[11] As a summary indicator of preferences, the countries were ranked according to the ratio of "boy" responses to "girl" responses, after apportioning the occasionally large group of undecided women equally between the numerator (boys) and the denominator (girls). Four groups of countries were identified on this basis, ranging from "strong son-preference" to "daughter preference" (see Table 2.1.4).

Middle-eastern and south Asian countries dominate the strong-son-preference group; south-east Asian and sub-Saharan African countries are distributed between the moderate-son-preference and equal-preference group; while Latin American and Caribbean countries generally display equal preference. A more detailed analysis of preferences by parity (limited to parities 2–4) and existing sex composition of children shows that, within the strong-son-preference group, a net preference for girls occurs only among women who have no daughters. In the three other categories, preferences reveal a desire for a balanced sex composition. The desire to correct an imbalance is evident in both the moderate-son-preference and equal-preference groups; however, where a balance already exists, the moderate-son-preference group expresses a net preference for sons, while the equal-preference group exhibits no marked preference for either sex.

In Fig. 2.1.4, the sex-preference ratios are plotted against median age difference between spouses for the sample of countries for which both types of data are available. With several notable exceptions, it is possible to distinguish a rough correspondence between the measure of patriarchal structure and the degree of son-preference. Latin American, Caribbean, and south-east Asian countries are clustered in the quadrant lo the lower left, with equal or weak son-preference and a relatively small age difference between spouses, and Muslim south Asian, middle eastern, and north African countries are located in the-upper-right-hand quadrant. The tattered appearance of this plot is due largely to the small sample of countries from the latter region. The misfits in the figure are Korea and

Fig. 2.1.5 Relationship Between Total Fertility and Preference for Sex of Children

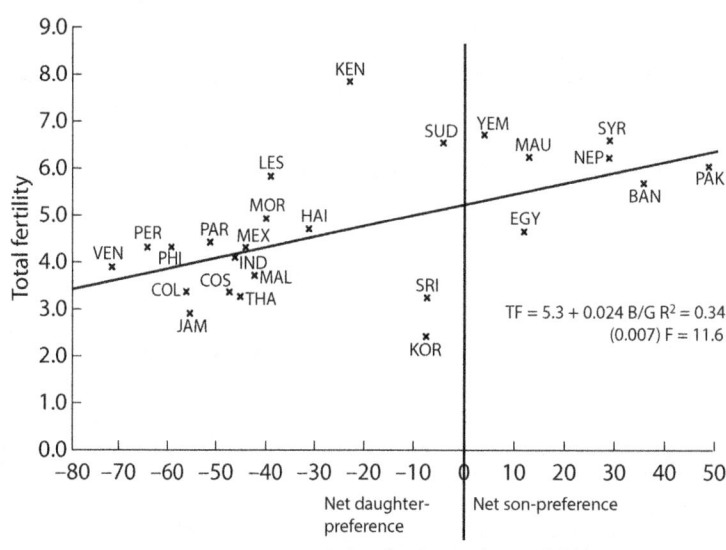

Nepal (low age differences between spouses, strong son-preference) and the African countries (large age differences between spouses, weak son-preference or indifference).

In Africa, the continuing importance of corporate kin groups and the institutions of bride-price and polygyny suggest that large age differences between spouses are more a reflection of lineage (and generational) control than of the economic subordination of women by men. Weak son-preference, or a preference for balanced sex composition, is consistent with this interpretation.

In Korea, it is likely that the material basis for son-preference has been substantially eroded by economic development and the consequent amelioration of risks, development of financial and insurance markets, and growth of social security and employee benefits.[12] This is not to say that the link between material security (particularly in old age) and reproduction has been completely eliminated. The very strong son-preference that persists in Korea is, however, placed in a better perspective by noting that, of currently married, fecund, and non-pregnant women with one son and one daughter, 72 per cent indicated that they did not want any more children, and of women with two sons and one daughter, 97 percent said they wanted no more children.[13]

Although the population of Nepal is very heterogeneous, it contains two major cultural groups: Hindis Indo-Aryan and Tibeto-Burman (primarily Buddhist).[14] In kinship and women's economic status, the former, which is the numerically dominant cultural group (approximately 80 percent of the total population), is akin to the strong patriarchal, "north Indian" pattern. There is no ready explanation why the median age difference between spouses is low in Nepal, however, given women's relatively low economic status in the dominant group, it would seem that, in the aggregate, the country belongs with other strong patriarchal societies, as is suggested by the marked preference for sons.

In Fig. 2.1.5, total fertility is plotted against another measure of child sex preference: the difference between the percentage of women who want a son and the percentage of women who want a daughter among currently married fecund women who already have two living sons and one daughter, and who want more children.[15] For countries in the negative range, there is a net preference for daughters, and for those in the positive range, a net preference for sons. Because these women already have two living sons and because the current sex composition of their children is unbalanced, this index represents a "strong" test of son-preference. The sample of countries includes all those for which data on preference for the sex of children are available. With the exception of Korea, in countries with a marked preference for sons fertility is also high and relatively unyielding. Similarly, in all countries that tend towards a preference for balanced child sex composition (with the exception of sub-Saharan Africa) there has been a substantial fertility decline. As in the case of median age difference between spouses, the sex preference index of Fig. 2.1.5 is capable of distinguishing two distinct regimes: the cluster to the lower left, in which a strong preference for a balanced sex composition is evident, and the cluster to the upper right, where a net preference for sons persists.

Conclusion

The scope-for cross-national quantitative analysis of fertility is sharply constrained by the meagre data that are available. The important conceptual distinction between women's economic status, on the one hand, and its structural determinants, on the other, and the need for independent indicators of both, greatly increase the demands on data. Indicators of women's economic status, even if they are well measured, cannot be used as indicators of underlying patriarchal structure. Incorrect functional form of statistical models is another important potential source of specification error and bias. A recent review of thirty-three cross-national studies of fertility in developing countries conducted between 1962 and 1981[16] showed that in all of them additive models instead of the required interactive form were used.

What is needed more than such cross-national analysis is research that can elaborate the elements of patriarchal structure in different settings, focused on the circumstances of women's economic vulnerability, and the role and importance of sons and daughters as sources of security. High priority should be given to intensive field-based work that can provide comment simultaneously on the economic relationships between parents and children and between men and women, on family and kinship dynamic, and on the locus and criteria of reproductive decisions.

With respect to policy, the analysis here suggests that the task of fertility reduction in societies with strong patriarchal regimes is enormously more difficult than in those with weak ones. For example, in the weak patriarchal regime, the government can act to expand the educational sector and create educational opportunities with a reasonable expectation that such a policy will induce a fertility response, as age at marriage rises and various other channels of influence are activated. In the strong patriarchal regime, the government can expect resistance to school enrolment of girls, because it conflicts with the logic and inertia of patriarchal structure, and to the extent that women's education is promoted, a weaker fertility response.

Recognition that the problem lies at the structural level, while a necessary step towards informed policy, does not make the problem less formidable or more amenable to policy intervention. Among societies with strong patriarchal regimes there are, as yet, no clear demographic success stories from which policy lessons might be drawn; nor are there many example among these societies of concerted policy attacks on the institutional bases of women's economic dependence.

Notes

1. J.A. Roumassel, J. Boussard, and I. Singh (eds.), *Risk, Uncertainty and Agricultural Development* (New York, 1979).
2. M. Cain, 'Perspectives on Family and Fertility in Developing' Countries *Population Studies.*. 36 (1982), pp. 159–76.
3. J. Hajnal, 'Two Kinds of Preindustrial Household Formation Systems *Populations and Development Review*, 8 (1982), pp. 449–94.
4. G.W. Roberts. 'Family Unions in the West Indies and Some of their Implications'. In L.T. Ruzicka (ed.), *Nuptiality and Fertility* (Liège, 1982), pp. 243–69.
5. C. Oppong (ed.), *Female and Male in West Africa* (London, 1983).
6. M. Cain. S. R. Khanam, and S. Nahar. 'Class Patriarchy and Women's Work in Bangladesh' *Population and Development Review*, 5 (1979) pp, 405–38
7. O. Frank. Infertility in sub-Saharan Africa: Estimates and Implications, *Population and Development Review*, 9 (1983), pp. 137—44.
8. M. Nag, 'The Impact of Sociocultural Factors on Breastfeeding and Sexual Behavior', in R Bulatao and R. D. Lee (eds.). *Determinants of Fertility in Developing Countries* (New York, 1983), pp. 134–62.
9. J.B. Casterline and P.F. McDonald, 'The Age Difference between Union Partners, World Fertility Survey, WFS/TECH 2070.20; J.B. Casterline, L. Williams, and P. F. McDonald, 'The Age Difference between Spouses; Variations among Developing Countries', *Population Studies* (1986), pp. 353–74.
10. Sources for infant mortality rate are S. O. Rutstein, *Infant and Child Mortality; Levels, Trends, and Demographic Differentials* (WFS Comparative Studies, 25; London, 1983), and J. Cleland and J. N, Hobcraft *Reproductive Change in Developing Countries* (Oxford, 1985); for GNP per head, *World Development Report* (1983), Table 1; for singulate mean age at marriage, UN, *Fertility Behaviour in the Context of Development: Evidence from the World Fertility Survey* (New York, 1987); for girls' secondary-school enrolment ratios, UNESCO.
11. J. Cleland, J. Verrall, and M. Vaessen, *Preference for the Sex of Children and Their Influence on Reproductive Behaviour*. (WFS Comparative Studies no. 27, Voorburg, 1983).
12. R. Repeito, T. H. Kwon, S.V. Kim, and D.T. Kim, *Economic Development, Population Policy and Demographic Transition in the Republic of Korea* (Cambridge, Mass., 1981).
13. Cleland, Verrall and Vaessen, op. cit. in n. 13.
14. G. L. Harris *et al. Area Handbook for Nepal, Bhutan and Sikkim* (Washington, 1983).
15. Cleland Verral and Vaessen, op. cit. in n. 13.
16. P. Culright, 'Statistical Models of Interrelations between Socioeconomic Development and Fertility in Less Developed Areas', paper prepared for the Fertility & Determinants Project. Indiana University, Bloomington, 1983.

Social Structural Determinants of Fertility

By Asoka Bandarage

Despite falling fertility rates everywhere, significant differences in birth rates still prevail across regions and social groups. To understand divergent fertility rates, we need to look at the varying needs and desires of social classes as well as the sexes and cultural groups. In this chapter, we explore the social conditions that contribute to high fertility as well as to fertility decline by focusing on the dialectics of social class, and gender relations in the contemporary period.

Social Class and Fertility

Affluence and Low Fertility

Among middle and upper social classes in the North today, children are economic liabilities not economic assets. In a context where familial kin and community networks are weak and where the provision of practically all goods and services is commoditized, the cost of raising a child from infancy to adulthood at upper middle-class consumption levels is staggering. Currently, annual tuition and board alone cost over $25,000 in many private colleges-and-universities In the US. Where each child adds a huge economic burden and where children are not expected to provide future support, adults opt for few or no children at all. Parents do not generally expect economic returns from their children; after children complete their education, they leave home to work, marry and start their own families. In this context, childbearing constitutes a consumptive, not an investment, activity. Historically with the shift from large extended families to nuclear families wealth flows from children to parent declined. As demographer John Caldwell has pointed out, in families where the net intergenerational wealth flow is from parents to children, fertility tends to be low.[1]

Such factors as high pressure on women to compete in the paid labor force and high divorce rates make it rational for couples and single women to delay childbearing and to have fewer children. This is reflected in declining birth rates in most industrialized countries in the North. The lack of social support systems makes it extremely difficult to raise large families. The individualism of capitalist culture and the excessively materialist and rationalist attitude towards children have resulted in a devaluation of motherhood. While women are compelled to take up paid employment outside the home, even while raising small children, men are not necessarily sharing in

Asoka Bandarage, "Social Structural Determinants of Fertility," *Women, Population and Global Crisis: A Political-Economic Analysis*, pp. 157–185. Copyright © 1997 by Zed Books. Reprinted with permission.

the domestic work. Parenting is not a rewarded occupation; everywhere, the burdens of raising children are borne overwhelmingly by women.

To succeed in the competitive, professional world, people have to develop the qualities of mobility, impatience, firmness, efficiency and total commitment to self. But these are often antithetical to qualities such as stability, patience, gentleness, a tolerance for chaos and commitment to others needed to succeed as a parent.[2] As both men and women are forced to value professional rationality and paid work outside the home before the work of childrearing, the emotional foundation of the entire society weakens. Children are frequently put out of the home in their infancy into "day care" centers which tend to regiment them within the mechanical clock and the bureaucratic life-style from a tender age.

For middle and upper classes everywhere, childrearing is increasingly an expensive undertaking. Since the beginning of colonialism, privileged classes in the colonies have emulated the values, consumption patterns and lifestyles of the West. In the Third World, as in Europe, privileged social classes that benefited from capitalism achieved the transition to low fertility first. The globalization of middle-class consumerism along with women's education and the necessity of their paid employment to meet rising aspirations have been decisive factors in the decrease in family size across the world. The expansion of education and employment and the availability of "servants" have given some middle and upper class women in the South greater choices in their social and reproductive lives.[3]

Is childbearing a form of "false consciousness" a relic, of patriarchal tradition? Would liberated career women simply give up childbearing or hire younger, poorer women for the task? This seems to be the picture emerging in the brave new world of artificial reproduction and surrogate mothering. Even so, why do some educated career women in the North seek desperately to bear children late in their childbearing years when they expect no economic rewards from them? Is it because of the internalized social pressure, lack of fulfillment by careers or a biological urge guiding women to continue the chain of life?

Indeed, the fact that adults derive sensuality and joy from children, that children are intrinsically valuable and that women have borne children as a natural part of life to satisfy emotional and biological needs throughout history is rarely mentioned in Malthusian explanations of population growth. While the existential question of why women have children cannot be taken up here, we can seek answers to the more limited question of why relatively high fertility persists among poor women.

Poverty and High Fertility

In many regions, a woman's social status is still linked almost entirely to her reproductive role; for many women, children are the only source of power. Failure to bear children, especially sons, is the cause of "ostracism, divorce and even brutality in areas of Africa and southern Asia."[4] Women in patriarchal agricultural societies who derive their only social status and self-esteem from their roles as mothers and mothers-in-law may be reluctant to give them up where better alternatives are not on the horizon. In this regard, one must be careful not to extend middle-class, western rationality and motivations to women living in all-cultures and economic systems. As Germaine Greer reminds feminists in *Sex and Destiny*:

> … Because motherhood is virtually meaningless in our society is no ground for supposing that the fact that women are still defined by their mothering function in other societies is simply an index of their oppression. We have at lease to consider the possibility that a successful matriarch might well pity Western feminists for having being duped into futile competition with men in exchange for the companionship and love of children and other women.[5]

Children are often the only source of happiness and hope for poor people. But this is rarely understood by western experts or their Third World middle-class counterparts viewing the world from the basis of their own experiences. Consider the reaction of a middle-class woman in India to her maid's reluctance to accept family planning: "I have tried to persuade my servant to try it, but she replied, 'It [having children] is the only pleasure we have.' I felt so sad there should be such ignorance in a citizen in India" (emphasis in original).[6]

A field survey of migrant households in Uttar Pradesh and Tamil Nadu in India conducted by demographic researcher Alaka Basu also revealed that in both regions and in all age categories the percentages of women who expressed happiness with life increased with the number of children, Basu found that although happiness is an "amorphous concept," the "consistent relationship between numbers of living children and general contentment with life" could not be dismissed.[7] In the light of Malthusian depictions of children as simply a drain on adults and the planet, such findings need greater consideration.

The links between poverty and population are varied and complicated. For most poor people in the Third World, children are not only a means of pleasure and hope, they are also a means of survival Even by official accounts, which tend to underestimate the extent and value of child labor, in the "developing world," anywhere from 4 to 20% of children in the 10–14 age group are currently working. According to ILO estimates, globally 250 million 5- to 14-year-olds are employed, 50% of them full-time.[8] To understand the conditions under which households voluntarily opt for large families, we must look at the social relations of production and reproduction, with particular attention to such factors as the economic value of children and the persistence of high levels of infant mortality.

Children as Economic Assets

Contrary to the assumptions of Malthusianism, higher fertility among the poor is not the result of ignorance, apathy, irrationality or lack of access to contraceptives. It is not the result of mere persistence of traditional reproductive patterns either. For most poor people, children are economic assets not liabilities. Caldwell's fertility transition theory shows that where wealth flows from children to the parents, fertility tends to be high.[9] The 1984 World Bank *World Development Report* observed that 80–90% of people surveyed in Indonesia, South Korea, Thailand and Turkey expected to rely on their children for support in their old age.[10]

A familiar story told in Brazil captures the rationality of high fertility for the poor particularly well. When asked why he has had nine children, a man replies, "Because three die when they are little; three migrate to São Paulo, Rio de Janeiro, or Brasilia; and three stay here to take care of us when we get old."[11] Indeed, for many poor families in the Third World, having a large family is a rational economic calculation: children are poor people's source of power.[12]

Unlike in the middle classes, each additional child adds only a small marginal cost; in many cases, the economic returns they bring are far higher than the meagre expenses they incur to the parents. By his 15th birthday, a Javanese boy repays the entire investment his family has made in him through his labor. In Bangladesh, a son provides labor and/or income for the family by the age of 6 and by age 12 at the latest he contributes more than he consumes.[13] Caldwell also found that "the economic well-being of the Nigerian family does not change very much with family size and hence the social advantages of eight children outweigh those of four or completely eclipse the horrors of no-, one-, or two-child families."[14]

Since the emergence of settled agricultural societies, children have been an important and often exploited source of labor for adults. For women burdened with the tasks of domestic work and subsistence productions children's, especially girls', labor, is an indispensable and consistent source of support[15] In many parts of the world, starting as early as 5, girls start helping with typically "female tasks" such as caring for younger siblings, carrying water and food production, and preparation.[16] Not only is almost all of this labor unrecognized and unpaid, but also, as Handwerker argues, where parents' well-being is "heavily dependent" on children's labor, "the relationships between parents and children tend to be marked by clear hierarchy, exploitation and coercion even in agricultural societies that otherwise exhibit marked egalitarian characteristics."[17]

Political economist Asok Mitra has pointed out with particular reference to India that as long as the bulk of economic activity in the country depends on the extraction of economic surplus by the heads of households from the "pool of unrecompensed family labour," "the one- or two-child family will remain a far cry."[18] It is also for this reason that China's one-child family law has faced most resistance from peasant households needing family labor for agricultural production.[19]

Differential Reproductive Rationality

The rationality of reproduction and fertility patterns varies significantly by social class, mode of production and time period. In a study of a birth reduction program in a village in Punjab—Manupur—that experienced the modernization of agriculture associated with the Green Revolution in the 1960s, population researcher Mahmood Mamdani discovered that the receptivity to birth control differed according to the labor needs of social classes. Landless agricultural laborers and small farmers with little access to either mechanization or hired labor opted for large families. Based on his conversations with a farmer, Gurdev Singh, the owner of medium-sized holdings, Mamdani reports:

> As he explained, if he had more sons, his labor costs would be significantly reduced and his household maintenance costs only marginally increased. Labor costs are the only variable part of a farmer's production costs, and they can be significantly lowered only by having a large family. Every farmer knows that the cost of having each child declines the more children he has. The benefits, on the other hand, increase. Gurdev Singh expressed the hope that his second son would be married and that his two daughters-in-law would bear him many grandsons so that in the near future they could accumulate enough savings to buy more land.[20]

In contrast, the smaller percentage of farmers with large landholdings in Manupur who could afford to buy tractors and hire laborers opted for smaller families, Similarly, non-agricultural middle-class employees such as school teachers also opted for smaller families. Children were not a source of livelihood for the latter; besides, their higher standards of living required education and other expenses for both male and female children.[21]

There is evidence from other regional contexts and time periods that wage laborers also opt for small families when the value of children as an employable economic asset declines. In the Indian state of Kerala, for example, the availability of universal primary education, the enforcement of minimum wage and child labor laws, better medical facilities and the likelihood of children surviving to adulthood have all contributed to reducing the economic advantages of large families. As anthropologist Joan Mencher has shown, under such circumstances, even poor agricultural labourers become "amenable to family planning."[22] We shall return to the Kerala case later in this chapter.

There is also evidence that for some urban wage laboring classes the economic advantages of children may be diminishing in ways that lead to fertility reductions. Thomas Merrick has argued that fertility declines in Mexico, Colombia and Brazil came in the wake of declining real wages in the 1980s. When faced with an economic squeeze, some families limited births in order to maintain their living standards despite those standards being already very low. Merrick also shows that the spread of education among women and their increased labor force participation were decisive factors in bringing down fertility in families pressured by inflation and rising consumer expectations.[23]

However, as social analysts Frances Moore Lappe and Rachel Schurman have emphasized, "before children can become a net drain on their wage-earning parents, those parents must have jobs."[24] In the burgeoning Third World cities, vast numbers of urban people are unable to find regular wage employment. For many who are forced to survive in the so-called informal sector, children are still assets. Many urban slum communities are supported largely by "street children." In São Paulo and Bangkok, child prostitutes are often the sole supporters of families. Prostitution among young girls often leads lo early childbearing, poverty and other problems such as the spread of AIDS. Still, for many thousands of poor young women in Third World cities, prostitution seems to be the only viable economic option. In a paper discussing the social class relations of human reproduction, Mamdani points out that:

> The marginal employment available to the appropriated masses is daily casual labor: in construction, in hawking, as restaurant waiters or cleaners—in what are euphemistically called the "service industries." But, most important, this employment is skewed in favor of child labor. Children shine shoes, open car doors or clean cars, and most of all they beg. In fact, begging becomes a regular occupation it is

organized. ... Once they grow up, these children may desert their families, but as long as they are young and physically unable to leave, these "innocent ones" in fact support the adults.[25]

Many poor countries, like Bangladesh are using child labor more and more in export production in order to compete globally and achieve economic growths, for example in the garment sector. Poor children everywhere start working at an early age both within and outside the household. But this limits their educational achievements, making "the Intergenerational propagation of class positions a fact of life despite an occasional rise by some members up the economic ladder."[26] The relationship between population growth and poverty is not unidirectional, as postulated in the traditional Malthusian thesis. This relationship is one of reciprocal causality, as has been demonstrated by many analysts in relation to different communities in the world.

Poverty-Fertility Cycle

In a study of population growth and capitalist development in a county of the state of Veracruz in Mexico, economist Nancy Folbre has demonstrated that many poor people see large families as serving their interests. However, she points out that these decisions do not imply the absence of ill effects. Population growth contributes to land fragmentation, the speed-up of the process of decomposition and proletarianization of the peasantry, the creation of a large reserve army of labor and downward pressure on wages.[27]

Benjamin White also found that in Java poor parents were aware that, although high fertility brought benefits to themselves in terms of labor and income the consequences of high fertility for "the welfare of their children are disastrous." Despite their anxiety for their children's economic future, however, many of these poor parents were powerless to break out of the cycle of poverty.[28]

Similarly, Helen Safa found that in conditions of extreme income inequality during the period of Brazil's "economic miracle" in the 1970s the industrial working classes increased their fertility in order to have additional wage-earners in their families. However, Safa also observed that although high fertility levels appeared to be "functional from the perspective of the individual working-class family which has only its labor to sell," in the long run, it had "contradictory" effects on the working class as a whole by increasing competition for jobs both among men and between men and women keeping wages down.[29]

Poverty breeds anxiety, conflict and family violence. Yet without mutual support and without each other, the poor could not survive. The existence of non-monetary supports such as exchange of food and services often provides more security and satisfaction to people than meagre wages or state aid, but in the Third World and in the West, extended kin networks are essential, for the survival of the poor.[30]

Poverty and Fertility in the North

In contrast to the assumptions of many upper-class people, meagre social welfare payments received from the state do not make children economic assets for poor parents in the US. Evidence does not support the common belief that state welfare is an incentive for high fertility.[31] Most welfare recipients have to rely on relatives and other sources of income to make ends meet. Why, then, do early childbearing, large families and extended households consisting of several generations persist among the poor, despite their lack of economic utility? What, in particular, explains the phenomenon of teenage pregnancy among poor, especially Black, communities?

About 33% of births outside of marriage in the US and 29% in the UK are to teenagers.[32] Malthusian analyses and policy makers usually attribute high birth rates among poor teenagers in the US to ignorance and lack of access to contraception, sexual promiscuity, male manipulation of females, and so on. In the period from 1993 to 2010, live births among 15- to 19-year-olds in the US are expected to increase from 60.5 to 62.4 (per 1,000 women).[33] Restrictions on state Medicaid funding for abortion, "gag rules" against abortion counseling, parental notification laws, and so on, have no doubt contributed to rising births among poor teenagers. But lack of access to abortion or contraception is not the only or the primary reason for teenage childbearing.

Table 2.2.1 Physical quality of life and fertility, 1990–1995

Region	Life expectancy	Infant mortality (per 1,000 births)	Adult literacy rate[†] (male/female)	Fertility rate (per woman)
World Total	65	62		3.3
More developed regions	75	12	96.0/93.0	1.9
Less developed regions	62	69		3.6
Africa	53	95	60.9/42.0	6.0
Eastern Africa	49	108	66.7/47.5	6.8
Middle Africa	51	96	63.4/38.4	6.5
Northern Africa	61	69	64.3/39.3	4.7
Southern Africa	63	55	62.8/59.8	4.2
Western Africa	51	102	47.2/25.1	6.5
Asia	65	62	77.6/60.5	3.2
Eastern Asia [§]	72	26	94.2/83.6	2.1
South-Eastern Asia	63	55	82.9/67.6	3.4
Southern Asia	59	90	55.9/32.0	4.3
Western Asia [**]	66	54	77.3/58.6	4.7
Europe	75	10	96.5[•]	1.7
Eastern Europe	71	16	99.8/97.4	2.0
Northern Europe	76	7	99.1[•]	1.9
Southern Europe	76	12	93.2/85.2	1.5
Western Europe	76	7	99.0[•]	1.6
Latin America	68	47	05.1/81.1	3.1
Caribbean	69	47	87.5/84.2	2.8
Central America	69	39	77.6/73.0	3.5
South America	6.7	51	90.2/86.2	2.9
North America	76	8	97.0[•]	2.0
Oceania	73	22	90.8[•]	2.5
Australia—New Zealand	77	7	83.5[•]	1.9
USSR (former)	77	21	98.0[•]	2.3

[†] 1990 figure; all other columns are for the period 1990–1995.
[•] Total population literacy rates.
[§] Mongolia not included in the calculations of the adult literacy rates.
[**] Oman not included in the adult literacy rate for the region.
[:] Melanesia not included in the adult literacy rate for the region.

Source: UNFPA, *The States of World Population 1994*, New York, 1994, pp. 55–65; Central Intelligence Agency, *The World Factbook 1995*. United Nations, *The World's Women 1995: Trends and Statistics, Social Statistics and Indicators*, Series K, No. 12, New York, 1995.

As many scholars and journalists have found, the causes of high teenage pregnancy in poor neighborhoods are social structural. In urban Black communities where poverty is the "dominant factor" in the lives of teenagers, many young Black women and men consciously choose to bear children as a way of expressing their adult status in a harsh and racist world that denies their sense of being.[34] Given blocked economic opportunities, a young "ghetto male" must affirm his manhood through peer-group interaction. He becomes a man when he is able to demonstrate that he has had casual sex with many women and has made one or more of them "have his baby."[35] Likewise, a girl becomes a woman by having a baby.

As Constance Willard Williams, author of a study on Black teenage mothers, has stated, in a world defined by declining neighborhoods and lack of economic opportunities, teenagers do not have-strong reasons to delay "having a baby."[36] William Julius Wilson has also argued that unemployment, imprisonment and high mortality among Black men have reduced the numbers of marriageable Black men, thereby providing no incentives for young Black women to delay childbearing.[37] In the experience of the teenage girls interviewed by Williams for her study, the most secure emotional bonds are made between mothers and children, the ties between children and their fathers and women and the men who father their children not being very dependable.[38]

Despite poverty and the burdens of childbearing, many teenage Black as well as Hispanic mothers say that they are happy to have had babies and that they love them dearly.[39] As Williams points out, these teenage mothers exist in a sub-culture that places a high value on childbearing "without requiring that it occur only after marriage or when one can 'afford' to have children."[40] In fact, many teenage mothers are themselves the daughters of women who were teenage mothers and are female heads of households. As Leon Dash observed in his study of teenage childbearing in a Black community in Washington, DC, "The best predictor of a teenage mother's age at first birth is her adolescent mother's age at first birth."[41] But, as in the Third World, early childbearing and the burdens of child-rearing prevent these young people from furthering their education and improving their lives. It reinforces the culture of poverty and the continuation of the mutually reinforcing cycle of poverty and fertility.

The above observations of intergenerational transmission of poverty in the South and the North should not be taken to mean that population reduction alone will reduce poverty. … In poor countries like Bangladesh and India, reduction of population growth rates has not led to poverty alleviation. In the US, too, family planning, including sterilization and the introduction of Depo-Provera, Norplant and other modern contraceptives among the poor, has not alleviated the social and psychological structures of poverty.

Poor people tend to have relatively large families despite the dismal prospects for the children's future because they are forced to think in terms of immediate survival. High infant and child mortality rates among the poor contribute to short-term rationality and higher birth rates.

Infant Mortality and High Fertility

Although significant decreases in global mortality and infant mortality have taken place in recent decades, great disparities in mortality still persist between regions and social groups. Higher infant mortality and fertility rates can be observed in the poorer countries and poorer classes and racial groups across the world. The current infant mortality rate is 12 per 1,000 live births and the total fertility rate is 1.9 children per woman in the "more developed regions." In contrast, in the "less developed regions," the infant mortality rate is 69 per 1,000 births and the fertility rate is 3.6 per woman. In regions such as Africa, infant mortality and-fertility rates are much higher than in the rest of the South (Table 2.2.1).

Infant mortality rates account only for numbers of children who die in the first year of birth. But many more children die during their early years due to lack of health care, nutrition and other factors associated with poverty (Table 2.2.2). High levels of child mortality necessitate that women give birth to several children. Then at least a few will survive into adulthood, ensuring security for parents in their old age. For example, in India, out of the six or seven children that women gave birth to on the average, in the early 1980s only four were expected to survive into adulthood.[42]

Table 2.2.2 High rates of infant and child mortality: selected countries (per 1,000 live births), 1960 and 1991

Country	Infant mortality rate (under 1)		Under-5 mortality rate	
	1960	1991	1960	1991
Angola	208	170	345	292
Mozambique	190	170	331	292
Afghanistan	215	165	360	257
Sierra Leone	219	146	385	253
Guinea-Bissau	200	143	336	242
Guinea	203	138	337	234
Malawi	206	144	365	228
Mali	200	108	400	225
Niger	191	127	321	218
Chad	195	125	325	213
Ethiopia	175	125	294	212
Somalia	175	125	294	211
Mauritania	191	120	321	209
Burkina Faso	205	120	363	206
Bhutan	203	133	324	205
Zambia	135	132	220	200
Liberia	184	131	310	200
Uganda	133	110	223	190
Rwanda	150	112	255	189
Nigeria	108	86	212	188
Cambodia	146	120	217	188
Senegal	172	82	299	182
Yemen	214	110	378	182
Burundi	153	108	260	181
Zaire	174	117	300	180
Central African Republic	174	106	294	180
Tanzania	147	112	249	178
Madagascar	219	113	364	173
Sudan	170	102	292	169
Gabon	171	97	287	161
Benin	184	89	310	149
Lao, PDR	155	101	233	146
Nepal	186	102	298	147
Togo	182	88	305	144
Iraq	117	111	171	143

Source: UNICEF, State of the World's Children 1993, New York: Oxford University Press 1993, p. 68.

Lactation has been a primary method of birth spacing and fertility reduction throughout history. In Africa, babies are still typically breast-fed for two or more years. But where infant mortality is high, breast-feeding periods are decreased, thereby contributing to more frequent births and high fertility.[43] The marketing of infant formula by transnational corporations in areas without sanitation and clean water harms infants health and undermines breast-feeding, which is safer and more nutritious for infants. Despite the global campaign launched against the Nestle Company and its unethical infant formula promotion in the Third World some years ago, cultural and market pressures to give up breast-feeding continue. As a result, breast-feeding rates are declining in the Third World and women are being deprived of their natural ability to nurture infants and of a natural means of fertility regulation (one that is not entirely reliable, however).[44]

When population control programs are introduced into contexts where child mortality is very high and AIDS and other diseases are wiping out entire populations, the charge of genocide does not seem entirely false. The explanation for high fertility in Sudan given by a woman doctor in that country in 1985 still has applicability in Sudan and many other regions in Africa and the South:

> In a country like ours where the infant mortality rate is 140 per 1,000 births, where infectious diseases kill so many children, where malnutrition affects about. 30–50 percent of the people, where measles is a killer disease although it could be stopped by immunization, how can you tell us to stop having children? When a mother has twelve children, only three or four may live.[45]

High infant and maternal mortality, disease and malnutrition are reflections of the poverty in countries like Sudan. However, as we shall discuss later in this chapter, there are many examples from the South which show that in countries where poverty and infant mortality have been alleviated fertility has declined.

In the North, too, significant disparities in life expectancy and infant mortality can be observed across the races and social classes. For example, life expectancy at birth in 1991 for white males, white females, Black males and Black females was as follows: 72.7; 79.4; 64.5; 73.6 (violence is a major reason why life expectancy for Black males in the US is closer to the Third World rather-than the US norm).[46] A 1995 study by the Center for Disease Control and Prevention in Atlanta revealed that while the infant mortality rate during the first year for women, living above the poverty line was 8.3 (per 1,000), it was 13.5 among those below the line, that is, a 60% increase.[47] As we discuss in the next chapter much larger percentages of Blacks and Hispanics live below the poverty line than whites. These socio-economic differences underlie the currently higher fertility rates among Black and other "non-white" groups relative to whites.

As Handwerker has put it, the neo-Malthusian assumption that the absence of modern contraception is the main reason for high fertility rates "is one of the great myths of our time."[48] In a recent paper, demographer Lant Pritchett has also demonstrated that family planning is only of "marginal relevance" to demographic change.[49] Contraceptive acceptance is not an independent variable; it is dependent on human needs and desires as conditioned by culture and socio-economic relations. The level of fertility in a society is especially dependent on such factors as women's nutrition and workloads, marriage arrangement, land tenure and inheritance patterns, and increasingly women's education.[50]

To understand the poverty-fertility nexus, then, women's roles in economic production and reproduction must be explored. … In the next section of this chapter we shall look at some aspects of women's socio-economic subordination that have a direct bearing on their reproductive rationality and fertility.

Gender and Fertility

Next to the African countries, Western Asia, constituting the prosperous oil-rich Middle East (Northern Africa and Western Asia), had the highest fertility rates, in the world In the 1990–1995 period (Table 2.2.1). The persistence of relatively high fertility rates in this region is commonly attributed to Islam. As Carla Makhlouf Obermeyer suggests, however, the "Islamic" explanation is not adequate for understanding high fertility in that region.[51] The benefits of prosperity and socio-economic development have not been, adequately extended to women. Throughout the Middle East, the enrollment of girls in schools is less than boys; women's labor force participation is negligible, and preference seems to be given to boys' health over girls. Obermeyer's conclusion that "demographic processes are less the direct product of religious rules ... and more the result of strategies and decisions reflecting the structure of power in society" is applicable to all regions across the world.[52]

As sociologist Kathryn Ward, has argued, lowered access to resources, conditions conducive to infant mortality and income inequality and other problems located within the world economic system, as well as the persistence of the high social and economic value of children, underlie the close relationship between women's poverty and high fertility.[53] Health researcher Jodi Jacobson, too, has pointed out that insufficient access to productive-resources and family income and increased pressure on time and labor make women depend on children for social esteem and economic security.[54] Lacking alternative routes to survival some women also have children to legitimate claims on income from men.[55] All these conditions contribute to the perpetuation of the "cycle of low social status, poverty and high fertility of women."

When women cannot increase their own labor any more, they tend to rely more "on the labor of their children, particularly girls. In many areas, women are increasingly keeping girls out of school to help with their work." As Phoebe Asiyo of the United Nations Development Fund for Women states, in Africa, "More and more girls are dropping out of both primary and secondary school or just, missing school altogether due to increasing poverty."[56] This will contribute to continued illiteracy, poverty and high fertility in the future generation of women.

... In many Third World countries living standards have worsened during the 1980s and 1990s due to the debt crisis and structural adjustment policies (SAPs) imposed by the World Bank and the IMF. Many countries in the South which have Fund/Bank Adjustment programs, especially in Africa, have experienced a reversal of social improvements achieved in earlier decades. The result is increasing rates of infant and child mortality, deterioration of female nutrition and healthy and falling rates of primary school enrollment, particularly for girls. By inducing declines in female schooling and health as well as by increasing infant mortality, SAPs have in many places helped maintain conditions of high fertility. As Ingrid Palmer has stated in an ILO working paper for the World Employment Programme:

> What can be stated at once is that all the signs point to a pronatalist impact of structural adjustment policies in the short term. On every count—the value of children's assistance, the threat to women's personal income and the reduction in public expenditure on health-giving facilities—the outcome for fertility is forbidding. More will be expected of (the household labour supply with its gender and age allocation.[57]

Evidence from different regions in the world that experience frequent famines also shows that in the long term famines do not lead to reduction of population growth rates; instead, the insecurity created by famines and the lack of other survival options induce the poor to maintain high levels of fertility.[58] There is also growing evidence, however, that absolute impoverishment may now be leading to crisis-led fertility declines in some parts of the Third World. We shall turn to this issue later in this chapter.

Externally imposed political and economic forces place contradictory pressures oil women's fertility behavior. By increasing women's economic vulnerability, imperialist policies increase women's need for more children while at the same time making it difficult for women to take care of those children. Moreover, family planning programs demand that women reduce their fertility without providing any assurance whatsoever that the children who are born will be able to survive into adulthood.

Nevertheless, women's reproductive behavior cannot be attributed simply to poverty induced by the global economy. Material production and human reproduction in the world today are defined by the social and psychological structures of patriarchy as well as capitalism and racism. The subordination of women is a historical phenomenon that predates capitalism and imperialism. Neither women's poverty nor their fertility can be understood outside of patriarchy and the psychological and physical violence directed habitually against them.

Patriarchy and High Fertility

Even in contexts where poor women may not necessarily perceive children to be economic assets and where their support for traditional fertility norms may be weak, they are often unable to make fertility decisions on their own. Fertility behavior is likely to reflect dominant social class, male and global interests.[59]

Many countries and international organizations are now beginning to recognize the existence of 'significant' forms of violence against women both within and outside the family, for example incest, rape, sexual harassment, battery, genital mutilation (removal of the clitoris or its parts in some Muslim societies). But what is not addressed by population control enthusiasts is the extent to which sexual violence and coerced sex results in pregnancy and childbirth around the world. For example, today, Rwanda is estimated to have between 2,000 and 5,000 children born through rape during the recent civil war.[60] Many women, especially young girls, including many teenagers in the North are coerced or simply cajoled into having unprotected sex. As Martha Ward has noted in her study of adolescent pregnancy in the state of Louisiana, rape or incest may be a systematic factor in 11-year-old girls conceiving.[61] While the compulsory implantation of Norplant may stop such girls from conceiving, it will not stop men from raping those girls. In fact, Norplant implantation could allow men, in the North or the South, to coerce or cajole young women into sexual intercourse without having to face the consequences of pregnancy and fatherhood.

A particular aspect of patriarchal thinking that has a direct bearing on fertility and mortality outcomes is the preference for sons, an issue raised earlier in relation to our discussion of declining female sex ratios. While son preference is a deep-rooted mentality that has its origin in agricultural societies, it continues to exercise a determining influence on reproductive behaviour in the contemporary era.

Preference for Sons

Although women are increasingly active in the public sphere and are often the primary breadwinners of families, the ideology of female dependence continues to be strong. The persistence of such traditions as dowry, that is, the giving of wealth by the bride's family to the groom and his family at marriage in South Asia; the patrilocal custom of women living with the husbands' families after marriage; sons' "roles at parents" during funerals and in ancestor worship, make boys economic and social assets and girls liabilities. Sort preference often contributes to high fertility since families continue to have children until they have enough sons, or at least one son.

In patriarchal societies where women receive social status only as the bearers of children, especially sons, women themselves may uphold high fertility norms. Although women bear children, they do not often make fertility decisions. These are usually made by the husbands and are enforced with psychological and sexual control and violence against women.[62] Surveys have found that even in the state of Kerala, where women have high social status and autonomy relative to other states in India, husbands' disapproval is a common reason for not using contraceptives on the part of women not wanting another child.[63]

Fertility decisions are made not only by the reproductive generation. Where extended family and kin relations continue to be strong, the older generation may encourage beliefs and customs hostile to fertility control and generally favorable to males.[64] A belief like one prevalent in Africa that the dead survive as spirits "only in so far as descendants remember them" contributes to the desire to have many descendants and large families.[65]

However, extreme preference for sons also leads to population reduction where female infanticide is widely practiced. As noted earlier in our discussion of population dynamics in foraging and agricultural societies, female infanticide has long been a population regulation mechanism. Even today in many villages of India and China it is fairly common. Ironically, it is the women, the mothers themselves, who often initiate "putting a child to sleep," the euphemism for infanticide. Many believe that it is better to save a girl from a "lifetime of suffering." One woman in the Salem District of Tamil Nadu in India, where female infanticide and feticide are widely practiced, told Viji Srinivasan, who conducted a detailed study of the area:

> I had one daughter. I "kept" her. I killed the second daughter. Now I am pregnant. I will kill this child if I have a girl. Why bring up girl children? How to prevent husbands from beating her up, from demanding

10 sovereigns and 20 sovereigns of gold? Erukkampal (the milk of the calotropis plant) is an easy killer. Sleeping tablets also. Otherwise the baby is suffocated with a wet towel and put upside down.[66]

As feminist activists point out, the issue of female infanticide is not an isolated one; it is an extreme expression of male supremacy and violence against women. In India, 999 registered cases of dowry deaths—the killing of brides by husbands' families over inadequate wealth transfers—were reported for 1985; 1,319 for 1986; and 1,786 for 1987.[67] Of course, the number of unreported cases is much greater.

Besides such outright killing of women, there are other more routine practices based on inequality and neglect that contribute to the lowering of the female population in countries, such as India.... The disparity in the sex ratio could further widen in countries like China and India due to increased use of sex-selective abortions and other practices directed against female fetuses and baby girls.

There is evidence from around the world that after conception women tend to live longer where both sexes receive similar nutritional attention and health care.[68] However, in many Third World countries, owing to the reduced food and health care received by female, far more girls than boys die during the critical period from infancy until age 5.[69] In South Asia, for example "females receive less care, fewer warm clothes, less medical attention (and that given belatedly) and, in spite of the drain of pregnancy and lactation, less food. They are also subjected to more food restrictions."[70] As John and Pat Caldwell argue, health beliefs and social customs favoring better health amid nutritional care for boys must be seen in relation to "underlying material facts," such as men's greater incomes-earning capacity, girls' dowry costs and marrying out. Women themselves enforce food and health deprivations on their daughters. Women frequently justify their "own misogyny with the claim that boys are inherently weaker than girls and need more food and attention than their sisters."[71]

These disparities are clearly reflected in differences in infant and child mortality rates between the sexes. In both "developed" and "developing" countries, females have a lower mortality ratio than males during the first year of life, with China being the exception for reasons such as female infanticide discussed in Chapter 2. However, for a number of "developing countries" for which UN data are available, within the 1–4 age group, female-child mortality is higher than male child mortality. Especially high female mortality rates exist in countries such as Egypt (1.4) and in Pakistan (1.6) (Table 2.2.3).[72] As noted above, unequal treatment of girls and boys in the areas of health and nutrition underlie the worsening death ratios of girls.

Table 2.2.3 Female/male ratios, infant and child mortality rates selected countries, 1986/1993

Region	Female/Male ratio	
	Infant mortality	Child mortality
Developed Regions (30 countries)	0.8	0.8
Developing regions		
(Northern Africa and Western Asia)		
Egypt	0.9	1.4
Jordan, Morocco, Tunisia, Yemen	0.9	1.1
Sub-Saharan Africa (17 countries)	0.8	1.0
Latin America and Caribbean	0.8	1.0
Asia		
China	1.2	1.0
Pakistan	0.8	1.6
Indonesia, Philippines, Sri Lanka, Thailand	0.8	1.0

Source: United Nations, The World's Women, 1995: Trends and Statistics, Social Statistics and Indicators, Series K, No. 12, New York, 1995, p. 69.

Economist Amartya Sen points out, "economic development is quite often accompanied by a relative worsening in the rate of survey of women (even as life expectancy improves in absolute terms for both men and women)."[73] Indeed, the phenomenon known as "missing women" in Asia needs to be approached from within this broad social context of violence against women. Discrimination in health and nutrition, population control pressure, female infanticide, sex-selective abortions, dowry deaths in India, all contribute in different ways to this phenomenon.

As concluded by Patricia Jeffery, Roger Jeffery and Andrew Lyon, who conducted a case study of women and childbearing in a village in Northern India, the improvement of the position of women calls for "dramatic change in patterns of landholding and employment, in women's work and access to property, in evaluations of their worth, and in the systems of kinship, residence and marriage which constrain them", in other words, changes in "the very basis of rural society." But these authors lament that there is "little on the local horizon chat harbingers a better future" for the village women.[74]

In much of the Third World today, including villages, such as the one studied by Jeffery and colleagues, Malthusian programs are being substituted for fundamental changes in the social relations of production and reproduction. The focus on women within such programs does not extend to alleviation of the structural roots of women's economic and social subordination. At best, they infuse family planning into income generation projects or public health services, which themselves are highly inadequate for improving the lives of women and their communities.

Many WID and GOBI (Growth monitoring, Oral rehydration therapy, Breast-feeding and improved weaning practices and Immunization) programs have often increased demands on women's time and resources and extended their traditional roles as mothers. WID programs, especially the WID Programme of the World Bank, which sets the ground rules for gender policy in much of the Third World, seek to integrate women more tightly into commodity production and to bring them under greater scientific and managerial control of external political-economic and cultural forces. However, this bureaucratic and market approach to gender fails .to address the questions of land distribution, pricing and credit policies and other mechanisms that "reproduce and intensify inequalities within the agrarian sector."[75]

Fertility declines require alleviation of poverty and improvements in the living conditions of the poor, especially women. Where children's labor is not essential for family survival, where women and children have food and nutrition, education, health care and gainful employment, they are more likely to accept birth control and voluntarily lower their fertility. Across the world, a consistent correlation can be observed between female literacy/schooling and reduced child mortality and fertility (Table 2.2.1). Education leads women to increase labor force participation, delay marriage and bear fewer children. In Thailand and Costa Rica, for example, improved health and educational resources for women were decisive factors in significant reductions in fertility during the 1960–1985 period.[76]

Where there are extreme social inequalities and concentration of resources and power in the hands of a small minority, poverty alleviation is not possible. Societies with highly unequal income distribution generally have high fertility whereas those with more equality have lower fertility.[77] There are many examples of countries and regions in the South where fertility has declined significantly due to the combined effects of income distribution, poverty alleviation and improvements in women's lives. These cases require greater attention than they have received within the neo-Malthusian literature. It is to some of those positive examples that we turn next.

Social Justice and Fertility

Studies show that the biggest reductions in fertility occur when the inequalities between economic sectors are reduced and particularly when the income of the poorest groups is increased.[78] A World Bank Staff Report of 1974 based on a study of 64 countries admitted that 50% of income accruing to the richest 15% of households is not as important in influencing overall population growth as the 50% of income received by the poorer 85% of households. This study also showed that when the proportion of income of the poorest group (that is, the bottom 40% of the population in terms of income) increased by just 1%, the overall fertility rate of the country dropped approximately 3%. The same study demonstrated that when literacy rate and life expectancy rates are added to the income analysis these three factors account for 80% of the variation in fertility in the countries surveyed.[79] The 1984 World Bank World Development Report argued that above the poverty threshold, increases in income tend to be correlated with lower fertility levels.[80]

According to economist Robert Repetto, fertility decline in South Korea between 1960 and 1974, one of the fastest fertility declines in any nation in history, was due essentially to "improvement in the living standards and opportunities of the poor majority, and the absence of wide socio-economic disparities, rather than a particular political orientation of the government."[81] Land and educational reforms were important in the achievement of a high degree of social equality. When greater choices were made available, Korean households chose investments in land and their children's education over large families. In Taiwan too the demographic transition cannot be attributed only to public health measures and export-led industrialization. Agricultural reform, expansion of education, and so on, provided the social foundation for the eventual success of the country's family planning program.[82]

Frances Moore Lappe and Rachel Schurman have observed that by the 1980–1985 period, among the more than 70 poor countries in the world, only six had managed to cut their total fertility rates by a third or more since

Table 2.2.4 Socio-demographic indicators: India, Kerala, and Sri Lanka, early 1990s

Indicator	India	Kerala	Sri Lanka
Infant mortality (per 1,000 live births)	72	17	15
Under-5 mortality			
Male	104	-	24
Female	108	-	19
Life expectancy at birth (years)			
Male	62.6	70	70.9
Female	62.9	72	75.4
Literacy			
Male	64	94.4	93
Female	39	86.3	84
Female Age at 1st marriage	18.7**	22	24.4**
Sex ratio (females per 1.000 males)	929	1040	-
GDP per capita ($US c. 1992)	274	298	563
% below poverty line	40	27	-
Births per 1000 population	27.78	19	18.13
Deaths per 1000 population	10.07	5.9	5.78
Total fertility rate	3.56	1.8	2.39
Population growth rate (1995–2000)	1.8	1.3†	1.2
Population (millions)	936.5	29	18.4

Note: All data for early 1090 unless otherwise indicated.
† *1981–1991 figure.* ** *1980–1990 figure.*
Sources. UNDP, *Human Development Report 1994*, New York Oxford University Press, 1994, pp. 144–145; UNFPA, *State of World Population 1995*, New York, 1995, pp. 64–70; Central Intelligence Agency, *The World Factbook 1995*, pp. 196–198; World Hunger Education Service, *Hunger Notes*, Vol. 18, Nos. 9–4, Winter/Spring 1993, p. 5 Washington, DC; B.A. Prakash, ed., *Kerala's Economy: Performance, Problems, Prospects*, New Delhi: Sage publications 1994, pp. 45, 47; also communications to author from William M. Alexander, *Future of the Earth: Resources and People*, San Luis Obispo, CA April 3, 1996.

1960 and reduce their population growth rates to less than 2%. These countries were China, Sri Lanka, Colombia, Chile, Burma arid Cuba. Although not a country, Lappe and Schurman also include the Indian state of Kerala in this group because of its reductions in fertility and population growth rates.[83]

The experience of these countries and Kerala defies the conventional demographic transition theory in many ways. Unlike the European countries or the East Asian "success" economies, these seven did not have very high levels of economic growth, per capita incomes, industrialization or urbanization. They also defy the neo-Malthusian population control theory in that they did not have strong family planning programs in common. What they did have in common were guarantees of basic necessities especially access to a basic diet for all. Four of the seven—China, Kerala, Sri Lanka and Cuba—provided more extensive food guarantee systems than other Third World countries (few reliable data exist on Burma).[84]

Evidence also shows that in these six countries and Kerala fertility reduction was related not merely to improvements in general population, but also to improvements in the position of women. Patriarchy is far from being uprooted in these locations and family planning programs in many of them tend to use sterilization and high-tech contraceptives used elsewhere. However, increased healthy education and economic opportunities for women have significantly improved women's lives in these countries.[85]

Sri Lanka is now in the third phase of the demographic transition, namely, declining fertility. The fertility rate of 2.39 children per woman in 1995 is expected to drop still further, reaching replacement-level fertility by the year 2000. The decline in fertility in Sri Lanka began before the country's family planning program had had much effect. Moreover, as Sri Lankan demographer Indralal de Silva has observed, a third of contraceptive users in Sri Lanka still rely on traditional methods of fertility control.[86] It is social development, more than the modern "contraceptive revolution," that underlies Sri Lanka's demographic transition.

In Sri Lanka, advances made in women's health and education have been crucial factors in increasing women's life expectancy and age at marriage and decreasing infant mortality races. These achievements in turn have contributed to fertility rates and population growth rates far lower than most Third World countries and the rest of South Asia, In Sri Lanka, despite low economic growth rates and per capita incomes during the 1960s and 1970s, benefits provided by the social welfare state such as universal education and health care and food subsidies helped improve the physical quality of life and lower mortality and birth rates. Women's literacy of 84%, average age at marriage of 24.4 (recent estimates even higher) and fertility per woman of 2.4 are unusual for a poor country (Table 2.2.4).[87] The demographic transition in Kerala is even more instructive because it stands in sharp contrast to the rest of India, which has not achieved the same despite "massive and longstanding conventional western approaches" to family planning. Despite over forty years of population control efforts, the population growth rate did not decline significantly. Annual population growth has averaged 2.1% throughout this period. Although the tiny Indian state of Goa has also experienced a demographic transition similar to Kerala, the Goan case remains largely unexplored.[88]

Demographic Transition in Kerala

While Kerala's population density is three times the average of India, and for many decades Kerala had been among the so-called 'lowliest' and most 'overpopulated' of Indian states, within a relatively short span its population growth rate has sharply declined. Mortality declines have been "more rapid and substantial" in Kerala than other states in India (Table 2.2.4). According to social analysts, the size of the fertility decline in Kerala had not been previously seen in a state or nation at similar levels of income and economic growth. The Kerala birth rate declined from 80.5 per 1,000 in the 1971–73 period to 20.7 in the 1987–89 period, thus making it the lowest birth rate in India next to Goa's rate of 17.5.

The demographic transition of Kerala was not the achievement of Malthusian population control strategies. Nor was it simply a "poverty-induced fertility transition," stemming from the inability of Kerala's wage-dependent poor, to continue supporting several children, as argued by demographer Alaka Basu. Rather, the increased receptivity to family planning even among some of the poorest landless laborers must be seen in the context of declining value of children as economic assets across the social classes. The declining economic value of children was associated to a large degree with state-sponsored social reforms.

As John Radcliffe and many other analysts have pointed out, the demographic transition in Kerala was the result of structural reforms that reduced social and economic disparities. Transfer of resources to the poorest groups through a grain distribution system, pension funds, abolition of tenancy through land reform, enforcement of child-labor and minimum-wage laws, widespread health facilities, universal education, public work programs and expansion of agricultural labor unions have all contributed to the Kerala demographic transition. These reforms led to an overall improvements in the Physical Quality of Life Index—infant mortality, life expectancy, literacy—as well as reduction in mortality and birth rates (Table 2.2.4).

The fertility declines in Kerala have to be seen in relation to women's status. Until recently, a large portion of the Kerala population followed matrilineal kinship in which women did not move to husbands' residences upon marriage and property descended along the female line. Although the matrilineal system has weakened, it has given Kerala women a higher social status compared to their counterparts in other, states of India, This is visible in the Kerala sex ratio, which, unlike in other Indian states, is favorable to women over men (Table 2.2.4).

The social reforms in Kerala increased access to health, education and labor force participation for women. These have been the most critical factors in Kerala's birth rate decline. Increased educational levels have led to higher age at marriage for women, making the Kerala female age at marriage at 22 the highest in India (Table 2.2.4). Fewer women in Kerala marry, a full 22% never do so, apparently "because of the attractive alternatives to marriage available to educated females." For India as a whole the comparable figure was only 7% in the mid- to late 1970s. It is in context of these social realities that higher "contraceptive practice" in Kerala relative to the rest of India must be viewed.

The social improvements in Kerala were the outcome of a confluence of historical developments unique in India. Kerala was home to an early educational movement launched by noted Hindu philosopher Sankaracarya between AD 788 and 820; it has long-established international trading and political contacts abroad; and has experienced extensive missionary activity in schooling (20% of the population is now Christian) during more recent centuries. But, as Amartya Sen points out, state-sponsored expansion of basic education, begun almost two centuries ago by the native rulers of the kingdoms of Travancore and Cochin (two kingdoms that defied annexation by the British), may have been the decisive factor in consolidating state efforts in education in recent years. In 1817, the young queen of Travancore, Gouri Parvathi Bai, expressed explicit support for state-funded education:

> The state should defray the entire cost of education of its people in order that there might be no backwardness in the spread of enlightenment among them, that by diffusion of education they might be better subjects and public servants and that the reputation of the State might be advanced thereby.

It was this tradition of state-funded education that has been carried on by leftist governments in recent decades. The Communist Party of India-Marxist (CPI-M), which initiated many of the social reforms, has not been in power throughout. But, as Ratcliffe argues, even when it was out of power, as, for example, after it was "removed from power" in 1959 (due to pressure from Kerala's large landholders), the CPI-M was able to influence the continuation of the social welfare policies due to its popularity with the poor. Peasant organization, strongest among all Indian states, put pressure on the state to enforce minimum wage and child labor laws and other progressive legislation and to carry out land reform, however imperfectly. Unlike in other Indian states, peasant organizations and labor unions in Kerala have ensured that progressive laws are implemented rather than ignored.

The Kerala success, then, is not simply the result of top-down action from a benevolent state; without grass-roots organization and continued vigilance the achievements in Kerala could not have been sustained. In Sri Lanka, too, the welfare state was the product of very high levels of popular participation in electoral politics, as well as the historical strength of the Marxist parties.

The welfare state is not a panacea for all social problems or women's concerns. Certainly, the Kerala and Sri Lankan models have not been perfect. The lessons of these cases, however, is that if reduction of population growth rates is a priority, then social structural changes are essential. As Ratcliffe has pointed out, social equity concerns must take priority over aggregate growth concerns and human needs must: come before the "needs" of externally imposed family planning and other institutional structures. Similarly, as T.N. Krishnan, who has studied the Kerala case extensively, argues that increased education and employment opportunities for women must be made a "potent weapon for breaking the linkages between population growth and poverty."

Analysts like Lappe and Repetto who have examined the poverty-fertility nexus in other Third World contexts have suggested national and international redistribution of wealth and income as the most effective response to the problems of poverty and rapid population increase. National and international women's groups and networks such as the Committee on Women, Population and the Environment are calling specifically for an end to the feminization of poverty and a broader feminist social justice approach to population and development (Appendix 1).

The language and rhetoric of "human development," reproductive health and women's rights have now been incorporated within institutions such as the World Bank. However, as these institutions represent the interests of transnational capital, they block policies towards social justice and economic democracy. Third World governments pay lip service to justice but their interests also lie in control of populations rather than redressing inequality and poverty.

Worsening Inequality and Fertility

North-South, class, gender and ethnic disparities are increasing and global crises of poverty, environmental destruction, and repression are worsening. There is no guarantee that even a region like Kerala could withstand the penetration of international capital and policies of economic restructuring and hold on to its hard-won social, improvements in the, years ahead.

In Sri Lanka, for example, state expenditures on education, health and food subsidies have been slashed due to the confluence of economic liberalization, IMF/World Bank policies, dismantling of the welfare state and militarism. Income disparities have widened and hunger and malnutrition among the "bottom" 20% of the Sri Lankan population have increased. According to 1995 United Nations estimates, 21% of Sri Lankan women were unemployed. The long-term effects of these developments could be increasing class and gender Inequalities and a reversal of earlier achievements in the quality of life of the people.

As already noted, some of the World Bank's earlier studies have shown a close correlation between increases in income of the poorer groups and reductions in fertility. Notwithstanding those findings, the World Bank has continued to oppose income distribution. For example, the World Bank *World Development Report 1984* contradicts itself when it says:

> Raising the incomes of the rich (be it of rich countries or of rich groups within countries) reduces fertility less than does raising the incomes of the poor. There is, however, no good evidence that the distribution of income has an independent effect on fertility; it is influential only to the extent that poor households usually have higher absolute incomes if their share of the total is higher.

Traditional demographic transition theory focuses on the decline of fertility and population growth rates resulting from socio-economic development and voluntary acceptance of contraception. However, in earlier chapters we discussed the growing interest of population control organizations such as the World Bank in bringing down fertility levels through intensified family planning efforts even in the absence of socio-economic development and poverty alleviation. There is now increasing evidence from the Third World of poverty-induced fertility declines as anticipated by the World Bank.

Poverty-Led Fertility Decline

Extreme impoverishment in conjunction with aggressive family planning promotion may be leading to crisis- and poverty-led fertility declines among the so-called "bottom billion" of the world's population.

A new study by anthropologists Patricia and Roger Jeffery based on extensive field work in Uttar Pradesh in India shows that desired family size is declining among many poor peasants, especially women. However, this change does not seem, to be associated with any significant improvement in standards of living or the position of women. Rather, with increasing land pressure, inflation, unemployment and so on, poverty, especially women's poverty, has increased.

There is also evidence of poverty-induced fertility declines in a number of Latin American countries. ... Sterilization has reached extremely high levels among the poorest women in Brazil, especially Black women in the northeastern region, who have been worst affected by the debt crisis and cutbacks in public services and social programs. In a study of the impact of recession and structural adjustment policies on women in Ecuador, Caroline Moser also found that 42% of women surveyed were sterilized. Given the history of sterilization abuse worldwide and the poverty of these women, it is likely that many of them did not have genuine choice in accepting sterilization.

There is evidence that in many regions in Africa fertility may also be declining because of rising costs of childrearing and declining employment opportunities associated with the ongoing socio-economic and ecological crisis. In social climates where people are fearful of future survival and where state policy increasingly promotes family planning over social development, many people are compelled to delay or stop childbearing altogether. As sociologist Ron Lesthaeghe has argued, although historically economic crises have only led to temporary fertility declines as opposed to sustained fertility transitions, the current situation in Africa may prove to be the exception.

... A number of countries in the Third World worst affected by structural adjustment poverty, the AIDS epidemic and wars are experiencing significant mortality increases. Where crisis-led mortality increases are combined with crisis-led fertility decreases, as is potentially the case in a number of the poorest countries in Sub-Saharan Africa, population collapses could be the long-term result. This scenario does not seem entirely far-fetched when we consider how quickly the Third World and especially the African region have moved from depopulation and "underpopulation" to "overpopulation" and then to fertility declines due largely to imperialist policies during the course of global capitalist expansion. Indeed, the contemporary Third World population "explosion" is a temporary phenomenon. It is important, then, to avoid alarmist fears and to approach changing demographic dynamics in a sober and humane way. Poverty-induced fertility decline is not a cause for celebration, as assumed in discussions of the "Bangladesh success" or cost-effectiveness of the "contraceptive revolution." Unlike the earlier European demographic transition, the contemporary Third World demographic transition involving crisis-led fertility declines is built not on democracy and choice, but on inequality and coercion. Similarly, the currently declining teenage pregnancy rate in the US may be a product of worsening poverty and stringent population control efforts rather than improvement in women's lives.

To move the world towards a path of social justice and democracy, it is necessary to examine the social structural causes of the global crisis. To do so, we need to move beyond the Malthusian obsession with fertility and population growth reduction to examine the global political-economic forces which are widening economic inequality and exacerbating poverty, including the feminization of poverty. It is to these issues that we turn in the next chapter.

Notes

1. John Caldwell, *Theory of Fertility Decline,* New York, Academic Press, 1982
2. Penelope Leach, *Children First: What Society Must Do - and Is Not Doing for Children Today,* New York: Vintage Books, 1994.
3. Hanna Papanek, "Class and Gender in Education-Employment Linkages", *Comparative Education Review,* Vol. 29 No. 3, 1985, p. 236. *Social Structural Determinants of Fertility* 183
4. United Nations, *The World's Women 1970–1990: Trends and Statistics,* Social Statistics and Indicators, Series K, No. 8 New York, 1991, p. 7

5. Germaine Greer, *Sex and Destiny: The Politics of Human Fertility,* New York: Harper and Row, 1984, p. 29.
6. Quoted in Patricia Caplan, *Class and Gender in India: Women and their Organizations in a South Indian City,* New York: Methuen, 1986, pp. 202–203.
7. Alaka Malwade Basu, *Culture: The Status of Women and Demographic Behaviour: Illustrated with the Case of India,* Oxford: Clarendon Press, 1992, p. 240.
8. United Nations, *The World's Women 1995: Trends and Statistics,* Social Statistics and Indicators, Series K, No. 12, New York, 1995, p. 117; "U.N. Sharply Increases Estimate of Youngsters at Work Full Time", *The New York Times,* November 12, 1996, p. 6.
9. Caldwell, *Theory of Fertility Decline, passim.*
10. World Bank, *World Development Report 1984,* p. 52.
11. "Poverty Dooms the Planet: Now is the Time to Act", *World Press Review,* June 1992, p. 14.
12. Lappe and Schurman, "The Missing Piece", p. 27.
13. "Ibid., p. 21;.see also White, "The Economic Importance of Javanese Children", *passim.*
14. Caldwell, *Theory of Fertility Decline,* p. 26.
15. Handwerker, "Policies and Reproduction", p. 10.
16. United Nations, *The World's Women 1995,* p. 117.
17. Handwerker, "Politics and Reproduction", p. 11.
18. Asok Mitra, cited in Mazumdar, "Fertility Policy in India", p. 265
19. Elisabeth J. Croll, "Production versus Reproduction: A Threat to China's Development Strategy", *World Development,* Vol. 11, No. 6, 1983, pp. 467–481.
20. Mamdani, *The Myth of Population Control; p.* 85.
21. Ibid., Chap; 5.
22. Joan Mencher, 'The Lessons and Non-Lessons of Kerala: Agricultural Labourers and Poverty", *Economic and Political Weekly,* Special Number, October 1980, p. 1787; see also Alaka Malwade Basu, "Birth Control by Asset less Workers in Kerala: The Possibility of a Poverty Induced Fertility Transition", *Development and Change,* Vol. 17, 1986, pp. 265–282.
23. Thomas W. Merrick, "Recent Fertility Declines in Brazil, Colombia and Mexico", World Bank Staff Working Paper No. 692, Washington, DC, Population and Development Series, No. 1, 1985, pp. 34–35.
24. Lappe and Schurman, "The Missing Piece", p. 24
25. Mahmood Mamdani, "The Ideology of Population Control" in Michaelson, ed, *And the Poor,* p. 48.
26. Patterson and Shrestha, "Population Growth and Development", p. 23.
27. Nancy Folbre, "Population Growth and Capitalist Development in Zongolica, Veracruz", *Latin American Perspective's,* Issue 15, Special issue on Population and Imperialism, Vol. IV No. 4, Fall 1977: p. 50.
28. White, "The Economic Importance of Javanese Children", p. 145.
29. Helen I. Safa, "Women, Production and Reproduction in Industrial Capitalism: A Comparison of Brazilian and U.S. Factory Workers", New York: Women's International Resource Exchange Service, 1978, p. 10.
30. Oscar Lewis, *Five Families: Mexican Case Studies in the Culture of Poverty,* New York: New American Library, 1959; Carol B. Stack, *All Our Kin: Strategies for Survival in a Black Community,.* New York: Harper and Row 1974.
31. "Baby Boom Among Unwed", Newsday (New York), cited in *Daily Hampshire Gazette,* July 14, 1993, p. 1; see also Williams, *Black Teenage Mothers, p. 25.*
32. United Nations, *The World's Women 1970–1990,* p. 16.
33. US Bureau of the Census, *Statistical Abstract of the United States: 1995,* p. 76.
34. Dash, *When Children Want Children* p. 31; see also, Katherine F. Darabi, Joy Dryfoos and Dana Schwartz, 'The Fertility Related Attitudes and Behavior of Hispanic Adolescents in the U.S.", Center for Population and Family Health, Working Paper No. 9, July 1985, Columbia University, New York.
35. Elijah Anderson, "Sex Codes and Family Life among Poor Inner-City Youths", *The Annals of the American Academy of Political & Social Science,* Vol. 50l January 1989; see also William Julius Wilson, "The Underclass: Issues, Perspectives, and Public Policy", ibid., p. 186.
36. Williams, *Black Teenage Mothers,* passim.

37. Ibid., p. 129; see also William Julius Wilson, The Truly Disadvantaged; The Innercity, the Underclass and Public Policy, Chicago: University of Chicago Press, 1987, Chap. 3.
38. Williams, *Black Teenage Mothers*, p. 131.
39. Newsday, "Baby Boom' p.1.
40. Williams, *Black Teenage Mothers*, p. 26
41. Dash, *When Children Want Children*, p. 26.
42. Lappe and Schurmann, "The Missing Piece", p. 24.
43. Ibid., p. 25.
44. Evelyn Hong, "Women as Consumers and Producers in the World Market", *Third World Resurgence,* Nos 61–62, 1995, p. 49; Hartmann, *Reproductive Rights and Wrongs,* p. 11.
45. Cited in Lappe and Schurnan, "The Missing Piece", p. 25.
46. US Bureau of the Census, *Statistical Abstract of the United States 1995,* p. 87.
47. "Infant Deaths Tied to Poverty, Study Confirms", *The New York Times,* December 15, 1995, p. A32.
48. Handwerker, "Politics and Reproduction", pp. 20, 26.
49. Pritchett, "Desired Fertility", p. 40; see also Paul Demeney, as cited in Donaldson, *Nature Against Us,* p. 56.
50. Handwerker, "Politics and Reproduction", p. 20.
51. Carla Makhlouf Obermeyer, "Women, Islam and Population: Is the Triangle Fateful?", Working Paper Series No. 6, Harvard School of Public Health, Harvard Center for Population and Development Studies, July 1991, *passim*.
52. Ibid., p. 12.
53. Kathryn B. Ward. "Toward a New Model of Fertility: The Effects of the World Economic System and the Status of Women on Fertility Behavior", Working Paper No. 20 in Women in International Development, Michigan State University, March 1983.
54. Jodi L. Jacobson, "Women's Health: The Price of, Poverty" in Marge Koblinsky, Judith Timyan and Jill Gay, eds, *The Health of Women: A Global Perspective,* Boulder, CO: Westview Press, 1993; see also Jodi L. Jacobson, "Closing the Gender Gap in Development", in *State of the World,* New York: W.W. Norton, 1993.
55. Handwerker, "Politics and Reproduction", p. 29.
56. Cited in Jacobson, "Women's Health", p. 11; see also *Engendering Adjustment for the 1990s,* Report of a Commonwealth Expert Group on Women and Structural Adjustment, London: Commonwealth Secretariat, 1989; United Nations, *The World's Women 1995,* p. 82.
57. Ingrid Palmer, "Gender Issues in Structural Adjustment of Sub-Saharan African Agriculture and Some Demographic Reflections", Working Paper No. 166, World Employment Programme, ILO, November 1988, cited in Jeanne Vickers, ed. *Women and the World Economic Crisis,* London; Zed Books, 1991, p. 22; see also Ingrid Palmer, *Gender and Population in the Adjustment of African Economies: Planning for Change,* Geneva: ILO, 1991, p. 146.
58. John Bongaarts and Mead Cain, "Demographic Responses to Famine: in Kevin M. Cahill, MD, ed., *Famine,* New York: Obis Books, 1982.
59. Naila Kabeer, "Do Women Gain from High Fertility?", In Haleh Afshar ed., *Women, Work and-Ideology in the Third World*, New York: Methuen, 1986, p. 104; see also Perdita Huston, *Message from the Village,* New York: Epoch B, Foundation, 1978.
60. United Nations, *The World's Women 1970–1990,* p. 19: Royte, "The Outcasts", pp. 37–38 Cited in Handwerker, "Politics and Reproduction", p. 14; see also Matha C. Ward.
61. "The Politics of Adolescent Pregnancy: Turf and Teens in Louisiana", in Handwerker: ed., *Births and Power,* pp. 147–164.
62. Kabeer, "Do Women Gain from High Fertility?" *passim*; Caldwell, *Theory of Fertility Decline,* p. 26.
63. K.C. Zachariah, "The Anomaly of the Fertility Decline in India's Kerala State", World Bank Staff Working Paper, No. 700, Washington, DC, World Bank, 1984, p. 93.
64. Caldwell, *Theory of Fertility Decline,* p. 335.
65. Ibid., p. 26.
66. Srinivasan, "Death to the Female"; and Bumiller *May You be,* p. 108.
67. United Nations, The *World's Women 1970–1990, p.* 19.
68. Amartya Sen, "More than 100 Million Women", p. 61.

69. United Nations, *The World's Woman 1970–1990*, p. 60; also John G. Caldwell and Pat Caldwell, "Gender Implications for Survival in South Asia", Health Transition Working Paper, No. 7, 1990, The Australian National University, Canberra
70. Caldwell and Galdwell, "Gender Implications", p. 17.
71. Ibid., p. 19. '
72. United Nations, *The World's Women 1995*, pp. 67, 69.
73. Sen, "More Than 100 Million Women" p. 61; see also Lisa Leghorn and Mary Roodkowsky, *Who Really, Starves? Women and World Hunger*, New York: Friendship Press, 1977.
74. Jeffery et al. *Labour Pains and Labour Power*, p. 224.
75. Michel Choussudovsky, "The World Bank Derogates Women's Rights", *Third World Resurgence*, Nos 61–62, 1995, p. 47.
76. Lappe and Schurman, "The Missing Piece", p. 64; Robert A. Levine, Sarah E. Levine, Amy Richman, F. Medardo, Tapia Uribe and Clara Sonderland Correa, "Schooling and Survival: The Impact of Maternal Education on Health & Reproduction in the Third World", Working Paper Series, No. 3, May 1991, Harvard School of Public Health, Harvard Center for Population and Development Studies.
77. Lappe and Schurman, "The Missing Piece", p. 65.
78. Sally K. Gallagher, "Economic Disarticulation and Fertility in the Periphery", paper presented at American Sociological Association Meetings, Atlanta, GA, 1988; Scott Menard, "Inequality and Fertility", *Studies in Comparative International Development*, Spring 1985, p. 89; Lappe and Schurman, "The Missing Piece", *passim*; Patterson and Shrestha, "Population Growth and Development", p. 13; Robert Repetto, *Economic Equality and Fertility in Developing Countries*, Baltimore: Johns Hopkins University Press 1979, *passim*.
79. Timothy King (coordinating author), *Population Policies and Economic Development, A World Bank Staff Report*, Baltimore: Johns Hopkins University Press, 1974, Appendix A, pp. 141, 147.
80. World Bank, *World Development Report 1984*, p. 109.
81. Repetto, *Economic Equality and Fertility*, p. 70.
82. Ibid., p. 69.
83. Lappe and Schurman, "The Missing Piece", p. 55.
84. Ibid., pp. 55–63.
85. Ibid., see also "Working Women–Maternity Law", Ministry of Justice, Government of Cuba, 1975; Hugh Drummond, "And They Make House Calls", *Mother Jones*, May 1987, p. 16.
86. W. Indralal de Silva, "Ahead of Target: Achievement of Replacement Level Fertility in Sri Lanka Before the Year 2000', Asia–Pacific Population Journal, Vol. 9, No. 4, December 1, 1994, p. 14.
87. Bandarage "Women and Capitalist Development"; John C. Caldwell, Indra Gajanayake, Bruce Caldwell and Pal Caldwell, "Is Marriage Delay a Multiphasic Response to Pressures for Fertility Decline? The Case of Sri Lanka", *Journal of Marriage and Family*, Vol. 51, No. 2, May 1989, pp. 337–351; UNFPA, State of the World Population, 1993, p. 49.
88. T.N. Krishnan, "Population, Poverty and Employment in India" *Economic and*

AIDS, Pregnancy, and Poverty Trap Ever More African Girls

By Sharon LaFraniere

They met a year ago on the dirt road outside her aunt's house in this struggling township where houses are built from bound-together reeds and the only water comes from wells. Flora Muchave was 14. Elario Novunga was 22, nicely dressed and, Flora said, full of promises.

One stood out: Flora's family had been teetering on the edge of destitution since her father, a miner, died of AIDS in 2000. Elario said he would change that. "He asked me to have sex with him, and he guaranteed everything I would need," Flora recalled. "He said he would take care of everything for me."

He lied. Elario gave Flora the equivalent of about $4 and a baby, whose impending birth has forced her to drop out of sixth grade. Before Flora's mother died in May, apparently of AIDS, she forgave her daughter for ignoring her warnings about fast-talking men. But she sketched out a bleak future for her only daughter.

"Now," Flora recalled her sobbing from her deathbed, "you are going to suffer."

Flora Muchave's cautionary tale is nothing new; Africa claims the world's highest adolescent birthrate and the world's lowest share of girls enrolled in primary school.

But for the last 25 years, the trends had been positive. African girls, like girls elsewhere, were marrying later, and a growing percentage were in school.

The AIDS epidemic now threatens to take away those hard-won gains. Orphaned and impoverished by the deaths of parents, girls here are being propelled into sex at shockingly early ages to support themselves, their siblings and, all too often, their own children.

"AIDS is reversing the trends that were improving for girls," said Margie de Monchy, regional child protection officer for the United Nations Children's Fund. "We really have to look at the kinds of lousy choices—and sometimes no choices—that they have for survival."

With 12 million children orphaned in sub-Saharan Africa because of AIDS, suffering abounds among boys as well as girls.

But orphaned girls tend to fare worse, relief officials say, because they traditionally hold a lower status in African society, are more vulnerable to sexual exploitation and, for anatomical reasons, are more likely than boys to contract H.I.V.

In Zimbabwe, a new Unicef study has found that orphaned girls are three times more likely to become infected than are girls whose parents are alive. In Zambia, orphaned girls are the first to be withdrawn from school.

Sharon LaFraniere, "Aids, Pregnancy, and Poverty Trap Ever More African Girls," *The New York Times*, June 3, 2005. Copyright © 2005 by The New York Times. Reprinted with permission.

In Zambia's capital Lusaka, impoverished relatives order some orphaned girls as young as 14 out on the street at night, telling them they must earn their keep, a recent survey found. In Lesotho, a growing number of adolescent girls are forced to work as maids or prostitutes, Unicef researchers have reported.

"Orphaned girls are at the absolute margins," said James Elder, Unicef's spokesman in Zimbabwe. "They are the very bottom of the barrel. They are much more likely to engage in risky behavior just to survive."

Patrice Lumumba, on the Indian Ocean a three-hour drive north of the capital, Maputo, is by no means Mozambique's poorest township. Most of its houses of reeds or concrete are well built and neatly maintained. Most residents have some semblance of furniture, even if only a set of plastic chairs hauled out for guests.

But AIDS has hit hard here, like everywhere in southern Africa. One in every six people between the ages of 15 and 49 is infected with the virus in the surrounding Gaza Province. Of the town's 43,000 residents, 1,583 are orphans. One in four primary school students has lost at least one parent, according to Pedro Mausse, headmaster of the primary school.

Flora's parents furnished their two-room reed house, which has a corrugated metal roof, with a wardrobe, dishes and two upholstered chairs.

Flora said she remembers how her father's earnings from work in South Africa's kept the family supplied. After he died in 2000 at 36, she said her mother's earnings as a cook for a Bible school—the equivalent of less than $35 a month—did not go far enough.

She could no longer afford to hire a tractor or a pair of oxen to plow the family's two fields. "It was hard to get food and clothes and soap," said Flora, a short, plump girl with a ready smile, curly lashes and ebony skin.

The whole situation made her more susceptible to Elario's blandishments, she said. "Actually, I was cheated," she said, smiling in embarrassment, as she waited for donated food outside a Unicef-financed organization. "He is a big liar."

Flora's mother, Ester, was still working as a cook in a Bible school last October when a relative told her Flora was pregnant. "At first I denied it," Flora said. "Then I started to cry. Then she started to cry. She said: 'I warned you against this. Now you are going to find out for yourself.'"

Her mother's death on May 9 is vivid in Flora's mind. That morning, she said, Ester called Flora and her 7-year-old brother to her bedside and ordered than to eat breakfast.

"I am told you are not eating, that you are spending all your time crying," Flora recalled her saying, "Whether you cry or not, I am still going to die. And I don't know who will provide for you."

Although Flora's body is unwieldy after eight months of pregnancy she still looks like a typical adolescent. Her face is covered with acne, her black polyester blouse is frilly, her plastic thongs a cheerful yellow. But there is nothing childlike about her life anymore.

Her father's relatives have abandoned her and her brother because her mother kept her husband's possessions after he died, flouting the tradition that says that a man's relatives, and not his wife, should inherit his wealth. Her mother's sister, a widow with five children can offer little help.

So it was Flora who, one Wednesday in May, hauled home a 66-pound sack of unmilled corn, 7 pounds of beans and a quart of cooking oil from a Unicef-supported center run by Reencontro, a Mozambican charity that assists people with AIDS and orphans. The next day, she balanced a 55-pound pail of water on her head and trekked half a mile home from the township's well.

"There isn't anyone to help," she said, soaked to the skin from the pail's sloshing water as she struggled to set the bucket down. "The responsibility is in my hands, so I have to do it."

Workers for Reencontro are urging Flora to return to school, and Flora, who says she used to get good grades, is interested. "But I don't know who would pay for the textbooks," she said.

Flora is but one of 639 orphaned girls here identified by Reencontro.

Two years ago, a worker found Lisario Mariquele, already pregnant at 13, caring for her ailing mother and three younger siblings. Her father had died at least four years earlier, apparently of AIDS.

Although a younger brother had made it to third grade, Lisario had never been to school before. What she knew was chores: hauling water, cooking over an open fire, kneeling over a wooden bowl with a heavy stick and pounding kernels of corn into paste. Her work multiplied last year after her son was born and her mother died of AIDS.

One recent morning, Lisario stopped pounding corn long enough to chat, her arms and blouse spattered with white flecks of paste. Her son, Vincente, slept nearby on a dirty reed mat, anemic and plagued with diarrhea. The dirt yard around them was strewn with beer bottles, shoes, rags and other debris.

Her son's father is named João, she said. She never learned his last name or his age. She agreed to have sex, she said, because "he promised to take care of me."

"It was a mistake on my part," she said. When the baby was born, she tracked down João in a nearby township. She said he told her: "The baby is yours."

Under pressure from Reencontro, she has now enrolled in first grade. Every other weekday afternoon, she lashes Vincente to her back with a strip of cloth and hikes to the school, where a two-hour class for adults is held under a tree.

She is ill-equipped and unsure of herself there. One recent Wednesday, she had to borrow a pencil and a sharpener. She repeatedly checked her notes on elementary Portuguese, Mozambique's official language against those of a classmate.

"I learned a lot of things" she said the next morning hurriedly wrapping a cloth around her naked baby. "But I can't remember them now."

No More Little Girls

By Elisabeth Bumiller

Female Infanticide Among the Poor of Tamil Nadu and Sex-Selective Abortion Among the Rich of Bombay

If you gaze down at the village of Belukkurichi from the one-thousand-year-old Hindu temple that sits on one of the higher surrounding hills, the valley below takes on the lush, whimsical character of an illustration from a book of fairy tales. Clusters of coconut palms sprout up from the land, and little cars motor purposefully along roads that bisect the radiant green fields of cassava and sugarcane. Belukkurichi lies deep in the interior of the south Indian state of Tamil Nadu, far from the plains of Khajuron, and the moist landscape seems to have given the village a softness around its edges. At this distance the scene appears serene, and the life within it benevolent. If you come down from the temple, what you see at first does not entirely change that impression. Although the drab little mud huts are clustered on reddish dirt lanes strewn with garbage, most have electricity and two dozen of them have television sets. Many of Belukkurichi's three thousand villagers appear almost plump, and you understand why when you see them eat with great enthusiasm the mounds of rice that they mix with cool yogurt. Even the Harijans seem reasonably well fed and do not have the sunken, defeated look of those in the north.

As you approach the town, you soon come upon the signs of a healthy village commerce: bicycle-repair shops, sweet crackers for sale in glass jars, pigs rooting through fruit peelings, clumps of red bananas hanging from tea stalls. The village even has a small library, a primary school and an old movie theater. As you walk through, your ears are filled with the usual film music blaring from unseen radios. The literacy rate of the women who come to shop here is higher than the national average, and they do not veil their faces with fear and embarrassment before strangers. Both young girls and grown women pin strands of cream-colored jasmine blossoms in their hair.

And yet, in this valley and another beyond it, I learned, families sometimes poisoned their newborn daughters. In August 1987, I met four couples, all poor farm laborers, who told me that the hardships in their lives and the astronomical expense of marrying off daughters had forced them to murder their infant girls. "I don't feel sorry that I have done this," Mariaye, one of the four mothers, told me quietly, "Actually, I think I have done the right thing. Why should a child suffer like me?"

The four couples described the practice as not uncommon in the area. No one knew for certain, however, how prevalent female infanticide really was. Certainly it was not the custom of the majority, and most of the people in the valleys around Belukkurichi considered it wrong. But the phenomenon was sufficiently widespread

Elisabeth Bumiller, from *May You be the Mother of a Hundred Sons*, pp. 101–123. Copyright © 1990 by Random House, Inc. Reprinted with permission.

so that government-employed midwives who lived in the area told me they feared for a newborn's life if it was so unfortunate as to be the third or fourth girl born into a poor family of farm laborers. Such a family could not possibly afford the price of another girl's dowry, a custom which in Belukkurichi had spread to lower castes that had not observed it even a decade before. The birth of a daughter had become a devastating blow, one that a family believed could threaten its survival. At best, a family saw a daughter, as an investment with little return. She would never earn as much in the fields as a son, and her small contribution from day labor would end when she left her family after marriage. To some villagers of the valley around Belukkurichi, "putting a child to sleep," as they called it, seemed their only choice.

In some ways, female infanticide was the poor woman's version of another phenomenon among India's upper classes—the use of prenatal tests to determine the sex of a child. Statistics in India showed that after such a test, if the fetus turned out to be female, most women decided to abort. Obviously, both sex-selective abortion and female infanticide represent a kind of extreme behavior and my reaction to both was revulsion. I have decided to explore them here because I think they are revealing, if shocking, symptoms of the larger problem facing women in India.

I learned just how deep-rooted that problem was during my stay in Belukkurichi, when I witnessed the birth of a baby. I had been interviewing families in the area with Jaya Gokulamani, a community-development worker from the state capital of Madras. Although Jaya had lived in Belukkurichi on and off for a year and a half, she spoke an upper-caste Tamil, the language of Tamil Nadu. She had to remember to switch to the looser, less imperious local dialect when working among the villagers, for reasons that became apparent the day the baby was born. That morning we were near a government health center, a primitive building of concrete blocks squatting in the red dust. Midwives who worked in the health center told Jaya that a mother who had walked in an hour before was about to give birth, and they invited me, the foreign visitor, to watch in the delivery room. Never before had I seen a baby born, and when I saw the fat little eight-pound boy on the delivery table and then heard him cry out, I was moved to tears. For the first time in my life I understood something I had heard for so many years—that the birth of a child is both the most ordinary and the most extraordinary event in human experience. As I watched the midwives wash the blood off the baby, I marveled that such a healthy, perfectly formed creature had been produced by a poor village mother, a woman who had been deprived of proper nutrition and modern medical care. In this village especially, the birth of the baby seemed no less than a miracle.

A moment later, I was brought back to the realities of India. The health workers told the woman her baby was a boy, but when Jaya came in a few moments later, she smiled and congratulated the woman on her new pillai—the word in Jaya's upper-caste Tamil for "boy." But in the local dialect, *pillai* meant "girl." The woman now thought she had given birth to a daughter and was shocked.

"You told me it's a boy," she said accusingly from the delivery table to the midwives, who were tying up the baby's umbilical cord. "Are you lying to me?"

One of the midwives held up the baby for her to see. The mother smiled, relieved. "No one is lying to you," the midwife said, and then explained the different meanings of the word.

Afterward, the midwives told us that they knew for certain that the woman had murdered her second daughter. If the newborn had been a girl, they said, she would also have been killed.

It was the British who first documented the practice of female infanticide in India in the late eighteenth century, chiefly among upper castes in the north. In some areas, officials reported discovering entire villages without even one female child. Lalita Panigrahi, in her book *British Social Policy and Female Infanticide in India,* recounts the experience of James Thomason, a British official who in conversation with a group of landowners in eastern Uttar Pradesh in 1835 happened to refer to one of them as the son-in-law of another. "This mistake raised a sarcastic laugh among them," Panigrahi continues, "and a bystander briefly explained that he could not be a son-in-law since there were no daughters in the village. Thomason was told that the birth of a daughter was considered a most serious calamity and she was seldom allowed to live. No violent measures were however resorted to, but she was left to die from neglect and want of food." Panigrahi says that a chief reason for the murders was the exorbitant cost of dowries among the upper castes. Many families also faced enormous difficulties in finding their daughters good husbands from a limited supply of suitable bridegrooms. Not marrying off a daughter was unthinkable and brought disgrace on a family.

The British outlawed infanticide in 1870, and a century later, educated Indians believed that the practice, like sati, had all but died out That assumption was shattered in June 1986, when *India Today* published an explosive cover story, "Born to Die," which estimated that six thousand female babies had been poisoned to death during the preceding decade, in the district surrounding the town of Madurai in Tamil Nadu. Although it was impossible to know how accurate this estimate was, the magazine reported that the practice of female infanticide was prevalent there among the two hundred thousand members of a poor subcaste called Kallars, who fed their infant daughters the lethal oleander berries growing in their fields. "There is hardly a poor Kallar family in which a female baby has not been murdered sometime or the other during the last ten years," an agricultural worker named Muniamma told *India Today*.

People were stunned by the *India Today* story, although perhaps they should not have been. After all, neglect of girl babies was commonplace. Studies have consistently shown that girl babies in India are denied the same food and medical care that boy babies receive. They also suffer more from severe malnutrition. Girl babies die more often than boy babies, even though medical research has long found that girls are generally biologically stronger as newborns than boys. The birth of a boy is a time for celebration but the birth of a girl is often viewed as a crisis. "The women of the family spread the news rather like a family illness or calamity," the social worker and women's activist Tara Ali Baig wrote in her book *India's Woman Power*. In India, she observed, the belief was that boy babies "should want for nothing. They should be fed when they howl, be dandled and coddled by everyone in sight and when ill be surrounded by acute feminine anxiety." This pattern of discrimination continues through a woman's life, making India one of the few nations in the world where men outnumber women, and where the ratio of women to men has declined since the turn of the century. In 1901, the Indian census reported that there were 972 women for every 1,000 men; by 1981, the figure had fallen to 933 women for every 1,000 men.

After the *India Today* story appeared I decided I would try to investigate the subject myself. Female infanticide, however was clearly so sensitive an issue that I knew I was undertaking an ambitious and probably unrealistic task. When I called *India Today,* staff members confirmed as much and told me there had been such an outcry from the Kallar community in Madurai after the "Born to Die" story appeared that the magazine had been burned in the streets. They believed that no one would talk to me if I went there, and they suggested that I go to another area in Tamil Nadu where female infanticide was suspected, taking along a person who was known and trusted by the local people. (Female infanticide was not unique to Tamil Nadu. In October 1988, just a few months after I left India, *India Today* reported that in a cluster of a dozen villages in a remote western corner of Rajasthan, an estimated 150 newborn daughters were put to death each year; among the area's 10,000 people, there were said to be only 50 young girls.)

The *India Today* correspondent in Tamil Nadu gave me the name of Jaya Gokulamani, the rural-development worker, who he thought might be able to help me, I looked her up at her apartment in Madras and found a forty-four-year-old widow, a Brahmin, tall, commanding and softhearted. When I met her, she was working two afternoons a week as an announcer at the local racetrack. Her knowledge of the villagers in Belukkurichi, about an eight-hour drive from Madras, came from her role as a consultant to a Danish government health project in Salem District, of which Belukkurichi was a part. For a year and a half, Jaya had lived off and on in a two-room house in Belukkurichi, where her job had been to assess the work and the living conditions of the Indian government health workers in the area, and also to help the villagers administer a newly created "community welfare fund" that would pay for such things as roads and public latrines. It was not the sort of life she ever would have imagined for herself, but in a sense it was a modem interpretation of the widow's lot in India. Jaya would never remarry—it was not part of her culture, she said—but instead would devote herself, if not to charity, then at least to useful work. I also think the Brahmin in her—and there was a lot of it—enjoyed the power she had to change the villagers' lives. Jaya told me she was convinced that female infanticide occurred regularly in the area around Belukkurichi, and that she would be happy to take me there and work as my go-between and interpreter. (Tamil, one of the fifteen official languages of India,, has no resemblance to Hindi.) It would be difficult but relatively well-paying work for her, but I think the real reason for her enthusiasm was that she saw the potential for the exposure of a social evil in whatever I might write. A month before in Belukkurichi she had seen a ten-day-old baby girl die, and she was haunted by the knowledge that she had been unable to prevent it. "I want people to know about this she said firmly. The mother of the baby had herself died during childbirth, and the relatives had brought the healthy newborn to Jaya, She took care of the child for six days, but on the seventh day the mother's sister asked for the baby back. Jaya had been in the area long enough to fear the worst, so she told the woman she had some friends who could bring up the child. The woman said no, the baby belonged to her family. Jaya, with great misgivings, handed the child over. Three days liter, she saw the baby again—but this time the infant was blue and suffocating on the examination table of a local doctor. The child's two grandmothers had brought the baby in, saying the girl refused milk and was having difficulty breathing. The baby died as the doctor examined her. "The child had been so beautiful," Jaya said, "She looked like a doll. If she had been a son, it wouldn't have happened like that."

To reach Belukkurichi, Jaya and I drove southwest from Madras into the interior of Tamil Nadu, past soft green rice paddies and a roadside temple where Jaya stopped to offer a prayer to the south Indian goddess inside, Adhiparasakthi. The south has its own deities, languages, foods and customs. I am not the first to observe this, but the entire region really always seemed to me a different country from the north. Not only was the south cleaner, tropical and more luscious, but the people themselves seemed to reflect the gentleness of the landscape. Close up they appeared physically smoother and somehow sweeter than the villagers struggling with a harsh existence in Uttar Pradesh or Bihar. Historically, the south never had to defend itself from the waves of invaders like those who crossed the mountains from Central Asia into northern India, South Indians believe this has made them less aggressive and kept their culture "pure."

At the end of the day, Jaya and I reached the town of Salem. We checked into a hotel and the next morning made the one-hour drive to Belukkurichi, where we spent our days for the following week. We returned to the hotel in Salem every night, but we had lunch every day at the home of one of Jaya's friends in Beltukkurichi, a housewife whose husband was a local official. The meal was usually stewed beetroot, rice and yogurt, which we ate with our hands, and afterward, we all stretched out on mats on the floor and fell asleep in the afternoon heat Jaya had a whole network of contacts among families and health workers in the area, and through them we were tipped off to couples who had put their daughters "to sleep." Belukkurichi was about one hundred miles from the area in Tamil Nadu that *India Today* had investigated for the "Born to Die" story. Officials at child welfare agencies in Madras told me they had heard rumors of infanticide in the area around Belukkurichi, but they did not expect anyone to admit to it. But by the end of the week, after combing the large valleys around the village. Jaya and I eventually met the four couples who told us, after long conversations about the problems in their lives, that they had murdered their baby girls. In the interest of telling the most complete story, I asked them if I could use their names, and they agreed. I am still not sure why. I told them I wanted to publish the information in a book I was writing, and perhaps the prospect of appearing in print in a land as vague and distant as America did not worry them. Maybe the couples thought I was going to help them; my questions had been sympathetic, and Jaya, whom they all knew and liked, was a reassuring presence. She was horrified by what these parents had done, but she too saw the deaths as symptoms of much larger problems beyond the parents' control. She knew that the couples, despite their guilt, felt that their actions had been justified. Whatever the reasons for their admissions, I will protect the parents—on the remote chance that they might be prosecuted—by not naming the areas of the large valleys around Belukkurichi in which they lived.

All four couples worked on the land for a living, "but only Chinnaswami and Karuppai, an uneducated Harijan husband and wife who made less than a dollar a day between them, were desperately poor. They were thin, dark and sinewy, and most days they worried that they would not have enough to eat. I remember when I took their picture that they stared straight into the lens with intensely serious expressions, even more than other villagers as if believing that the camera might uncover their souls. Karuppai, the wife, wore a thin cotton sari, and Chinnaswami, her husband, had on a Western-style shirt and a worn, faded lunghi, the traditional cloth that men tied around themselves like a skirt. Both husband and wife were barefoot, and no one could doubt that they had worked in the fields all of their lives. Eight years before, they said, they had hired an old man who lived in the hills to kill their fourth daughter. He gave the day-old baby the sticky white milk of what the villagers called the erukkampal plant, a spindly, light-green bush that grew along the roadside. For his services, the parents gave the man a free meal. "We felt very bad," said Karuppai, the child's mother, who was nineteen years old when her daughter died. "But at the same time, suppose she had lived? It was better to save her from a lifetime of suffering." She spoke in a quiet, flat tone as we sat on the floor of a local doctor's house. I had expected a dramatic, anguished revelation; instead her admission was made in grim, simple detail I think this was partly because she was talking about an event eight years past, and also because she was nervous and terrified, Karappal's face was expressionless, and she sat very still. Jaya was herself uneasy interpreting my questions. By the end of the interview, the tension in the room was suffocating.

A second couple, Muthuswami and Rajeshwari, were from a slightly higher caste and made more money. But three years before, they had their second daughter killed, "Abortion is costly," Rajeshwari, the child's mother, explained, almost defiantly. "And you have to rest at home. So instead of spending money and losing income, we prefer to deliver the child and kill it," I honestly don't know if Rajeshwari saw no difference, other than the expense, between abortion and infanticide. Her words were shocking, and would be powerful fuel for an antiabortionist. Perhaps the harsh economics of her life had made her as callous as she sounded, but I suspect she was putting on an act and was too proud to let an outsider like me feel sorry for her. Her manner continued to be lively as she explained, as we sat at a local landowner's house; that she had waited twenty-four hours before killing her baby. "I was of half a mind to bring up the child," she said "I couldn't decide. But because of the problems she would face at a later stage, I decided to do it. And everybody else was in favor of putting the child to sleep, so I decided to go along." But it was the mother-in-law, not the mother, who gave the child the milk from the erukkampal plant.

A third couple, Mariaye and her husband, Natesan, both illiterate and from a low caste, had also stood back while Mariaye's mother-in-law had administered the milk to their third daughter two and a half years before. We were talking at the same landowner's house, "The child had breathing difficulties, and then froth came from her mouth," Mariaye told me slowly, "She became pale, and then she died." I didn't know what to say, so I said nothing. Mariaye's husband, Natesan, filled the silence. "It was a peaceful death" he said.

Of the four, the last couple I met, Muthaye and her husband, Mohanassundram, were the parents I understood the best, to the extent that I understood any of them at all. Or maybe it was just that I saw a glimmer of their tragedy that the others had not allowed me to see. They were low-caste field laborers, and they too had killed their second daughter. We spoke first at the doctor's house where we had talked with the first couple. Muthaye was twenty-four, a slip of a woman in a yellow cotton sari, with her hair in a simple ponytail that made her look like a schoolgirl instead of a mother who had been through the kind of trauma she had. Like most village women she was wearing her wealth: two nose studs, a pair of diamond and gold earrings, several gold toe rings. She remained utterly silent, with a serious, worried expression on her face, while her husband and mother-in-law did most of the talking. Her husband could have been any one of the thousands of young Indian men I had seen on the streets of small-town India: thin, with a little mustache, and an open, cheerful face that displayed an innocence mixed with a hard-learned savvy. He was twenty-nine years old and wore a Western short-sleeved shirt and a lunghi. His mother, Nallamma, had a wiry build, white hair, sun-leathered skin that crinkled around her eyes and the take-charge look of mothers-in-law across India. As she talked, her grandson, a little ten-month-old boy in a T-shirt that said "Freeport, Bahamas," gurgled and played on the floor.

Muthaye and Mohanasundaram had been married six years. Mohanasundaram had a fourth-grade education and made a dollar a day harvesting rice, peanuts and the tall stalks of the cassava plant, whose roots were dried and made into small, starchy granules of tapioca. His wife, because she was a woman, made fifty cents a day for the exact same work. They could not find jobs every day, but in a good year, with rain, the couple could bring home about $350 between them. Mohanasundaram's parents owned an acre of land, and this brought them about $250 a year, putting the total annual income of the family of four workers at $600, Although the four made less than India's average per capita income of $250 the family was not desperately poor. Everyone ate two meals a day—a warm cereal before leaving for the fields at eight in the morning, and a dinner of rice and perhaps cooked vegetables when they returned at five in the evening. They lived in a collection of smooth mud huts with thatched roofs, all very clean, under a cluster of coconut palms at the edge of a peanut field. They had a fresh-water well and several animals, including a cow, which Muthaye milked in the mornings. Life was hard, but the family was not living a hand-to-mouth existence. The acre of land gave them security, and unlike so many other villagers in India, they seemed to have a plan for the future.

This, in fact, was what had driven them to murder. Three years before, Muthaye had delivered her firstborn, a girl. A year later, when she was pregnant again the family decided—although it was not clear exactly who Mohanasundaram meant by "the family"—that should the second child be a girl, they would "put her to sleep." The reason, the mother-in-law and Mohanasundaram said, was that "we wanted a male baby." "When Muthaye felt her first labor pains, about noon one day, she was taken to the home of a dai in a nearby village. She delivered a little girl at four that afternoon. Three hours later she returned home with the child. The next morning at dawn, "the family" gave the newborn some cow's milk mixed with five sleeping pills they had bought from a pharmacist in town. This was done inside one of the huts as the mother-in-law and both parents watched. The baby, they said, fell fast asleep. Two hours later she had stopped breathing.

A few relatives were called for the funeral that day, and were told simply that the little girl had not lived. No other explanation was given and the relatives asked no questions. Possibly they suspected what had happened and knew not to press; possibly they really thought the girl had died a natural death, since it happened all the time. Ten days later, a government health worker came by on her usual rounds and asked about the child. The family said she had died because she refused her mother's milk. The health worker noted it down, made no accusations and left.

Through Jaya, I then asked Muthaye and Mohanasundaram how they had felt afterward. Like that of the first couple I met, their story had so far been unemotional and straightforward, "For a month we cried every day." Mohanasundaram, the husband, said "We felt bad, but bringing up girls is very difficult nowadays." Then the mother-in-law chimed in, "It was not wantonly done," she said. "We were not in a position to bring up the child." Muthaye, the mother of the dead child, said nothing and stared into space with a strained expression on her face. It was impossible to read her mind but I had the feeling that bringing up the murder of her daughter—which had happened only slightly more than a year before—was a nightmare for her. I wondered if she played the death over and over in her mind, or if she had forced herself never to think of it again.

Sensing my uneasiness, her husband moved on to explain the family finances. As part of a local bank savings program called the Marriage Saving Scheme, he had deposited 3,000 rupees—2,000 of his own, 1,000 borrowed—when his first daughter was a year old. This was the equivalent of about $250. The bank had promised, he said, that when his daughter was twenty-one, an age when he expected her to be ready for marriage, it would give him 23,000 rupees, or $1,700 an adequate dowry for his caste. Mohanasundaram explained that he would then ask for the same amount in dowry at the time of the marriage of his son, the ten-month-old who was gurgling at our feet. This was the common way that people like Mohanasundaram afforded dowries at all. Mohanasundaram felt that a second daughter would have ruined his financial plans and the family's future as well. Another 3,000-rupee deposit in the Marriage Saving Scheme for another girl would have been almost as much as he and his wife earned in a good year. They would have had to borrow all of the money, which would have put them in debt, probably for life. And yet without a dowry, Mohanasundaram almost certainly could not have married off the second daughter, which was his chief responsibility as her father, and a duty Hindus like himself believed was an essential part of a meritorious life. As an unmarried woman in rural India, his daughter would have been shunned for the rest of her life. Mohanasundarara told me he didn't like dowry, but that he felt he had no other choice.

Jaya and I went from the doctor's house with Muthaye and Mohanasundaram to their collection of huts, first piling into the car and then walking along a red dirt road under a blazing sun. When we got there, the family insisted we sit down on a charpoy in a patch of shade and have something to drink. The mother-in-law then directed a man who appeared to work for them to climb the trunk of one of the palm trees. The man scampered up, and with a big knife cut off several green coconuts, which came thudding down to earth. The man climbed back down, lopped off the heads of the coconuts, then presented Jaya and me with two each. Jaya took the first one, leaned back her head, opened her mouth, and poured the milk in directly from the coconut. I followed her lead. The milk was sticky and warm, but clear and not too sweet. I found it an oddly pleasant moment, sitting there in the shade enjoying the bounty of nature, as if I had not spoken to the family an hour before about what they had done to their second daughter, Jaya continued to talk to the family while I took pictures, Muthaye told us she was using no form of birth control, and that she was afraid of a sterilization operation because she was convinced it would mean a month away from her work.

As Jaya and I were leaving, I asked the husband where his daughter was buried. He pointed in the direction of our car, and then walked us down to the grave. It was an unmarked spot right along the road, with a beautiful view of the peanut fields and the hills above where the temple stood. The scene was so lovely that when I saw two women walking along the road carrying bags of rice on their heads, I got out my camera to take their pictures. One of the women was obviously pregnant, and Jaya went up to talk to her. She soon came back disgusted. "That woman has one son and two daughters," Jaya said, "She told me that if this one's a girl, she'll kill her."

Six hundred miles from Belukkurichi, Bombay rises up on the other side of India, a fetid megalopolis of twentieth-century skyscrapers, crumbling Victorian gentlemen's clubs and wooden shacks jostling for breathing space on a narrow island that extends south into the Arabian Sea. Calcutta has long been India's internationally famous urban disaster, but I came to feel that Bombay is catching up and in sight of surpassing it. The stench of Bombay's poverty is particularly hard to take because nowhere in India is there such an abyss between those who have and those who do not, Bombay is the nation's financial capital, industrial engine and the home of its film industry—in short, the source of most of India's wealth. A sliver of the population, the very rich, inhabit apartments overlooking the sea for which they pay five thousand dollars a month, yet more than half of Bombay's ten million people live in squatters' slums. Bombay is the chic woman in the latest silk salwar kameez but also the beggar who thrusts his leprous stump through her open car window when she stops at a light. Bombay is the "Queen's Necklace," the twinkling lights along the dramatic sweep of Marine Drive, and also the reeking swamp of raw sewage that greets visitors as they leave the airport after arriving on a direct flight from London. Bombay is the new industrial baron who hurries by the oxcart, and the elegant French restaurants not far from the street food of Chowpatty Beach. While Delhi is a political capital, like Washington, that goes to bed early, Bombay is up late, drinking imported Scotch on marble terraces open to humid breezes and the ripe smell of fish. Bombay is glamorous, exciting, decadent, appalling. Nowhere in India is money more important.

It didn't surprise me that Bombay had become, by the mid-1980s, the center of two new medical techniques used by the city's business class to avoid the birth of unwanted daughters. Both procedures were commonly referred to as the sex test; in the United States they would be recognized as either amniocentesis or chorionic villus sampling, two prenatal tests developed for the detection of genetic abnormalities in a fetus. In the Bombay of the mid-1980s, however, the tests were most often used to determine only the gender of an unborn child. Most people did not even know that the tests could diagnose birth defects. In India, between the years 1978 and 1982, estimates put the number of abortions of female fetuses after the "sex test" at 78,000. That, at least, was the figure presented at a 1986 government hearing on the subject and widely quoted in the press. I was never able to determine how the figure was calculated or its original source, and it seemed to me another Indian statistic that could never be verified. Undeniable, however, was the fact that the majority of Bombay's private gynecologists (84 percent of those surveyed, according to one apparently reliable government study) conducted the test solely to determine the sex of a child. Even those doctors with misgivings said they performed the test because it was the wish of their patients. This led to all kinds of philosophical arguments to justify the practice, usually couched in such lofty concepts as "the will of the people" and "freedom." "Democracy should permit one to have a child that one wants," said Shirish Sheth, who was the incoming president of the Bombay Obstetrics and Gynecological Society. Sharad Gogate, a gynecologist with a busy middle-class practice, told me that "once a woman finds out it is female, in 80 percent of the cases she is hell-bent on an abortion." He estimated that he had aborted one thousand female fetuses. I gave him a look of alarm, "Yes," he said, "I have to accept that"

I always linked the "sex test" and Belukkurichi's female infanticide in my mind, and my pursuit of both subjects overlapped. I first went to Belukkurichi in January 1987 but arrived in the village already sick with stomach problems and had to turn back the next day. Four months later I went to Bombay to talk to women aid doctors about the "sex test" and only after that did I finally return to Belukkurichi for the week-long stay. There are of course fundamental differences between the two practices—the most obvious being the use of technology—but the root of the problem is the same. Although that does not mean that they are equally deplorable, I found myself torn. Infanticide is one of the most heinous of crimes, and yet, although I have always been pro-choice, I was more appalled by the abortions. Most of the educated, well-off women of Bombay were of course trying to avoid the astronomical cost of dowries in India, but among the rich, who could afford the cost of any number of weddings, a stronger motive seemed to be to avoid the social embarrassment of having daughters but no sons.

Bombay feminists in any case settled on the sex-determination tests as one of their most important causes. In May 1988, when the legislature of the slate of Maharashtra, of which Bombay is a part, passed a law that banned the tests for the use of sex determination, they claimed their biggest victory—raising all sorts of questions in my mind about how one controls the practice without infringing on a woman's right to abortion. The cause had been led by the Women's Centre, the leading feminist group in Bombay, which in 1982 had brought out its first report on the use of amniocentesis for sex determination. Although feminists in other Indian cities sometimes dismissed prenatal sex determination as an elitist problem confined to Bombay's business class, the Women's Centre countered that the tests were common in other areas as well, most notably in Punjab, India's breadbasket. In fact, Punjab's rich farmland and Maharashtra's industry made the states the two most prosperous in India, and it was a depressing irony that the "sex test" proliferated amid such plenty. Prosperity, as in the case of the sati in Rajasthan, had not eliminated old customs but seemed to be promoting them in alarming new ways. If nothing else, the sex determination tests were a powerful example of what can happen when modern technology collides with the forces of a traditional society.

Feminists also warned that the tests were seeping down to the middle class and the poor. Although private Bombay doctors charged as much as $125 for the test, clinics had sprang up in working-class areas and slums that offered amniocentesis at cut-rate prices and played on the fear of dowry with such slogans as "Better 500 rupees now than 500,000 later," As far back as 1977, Bombay's Hurkisondas Hospital, a private institution catering to the middle and working classes, began offering amniocentesis at one of the cheapest rates ever, eight dollars, in its new Prenatal Sex-Determination Clinic. "This is the only institution in our country which is carrying out this humane and beneficial test with such a high accuracy of the results," the clinic's information sheet said. In the years 1978 to 1982, a study of the hospital by a Bombay women's organization found that of 8,000 women who came from all over India for the test, 7,999 wanted a son.

One muggy April morning in 1987, a year before the state legislature, banned the tests, I found Assumpta D'Sylva, a thirty-one-year-old Bombay housewife, quietly waiting outside a Hurkisondas Hospital examination room for her "sex test," in this case a chorionic villus sampling. For CVS, as it is called, doctors use a catheter to extract a few milligrams of placenta tissue which is then analyzed for any genetic defects. In amniocentesis, doctors extract cells from the amniotic fluid by inserting a catheter into the sac surrounding the fetus. Amniocentesis is normally performed from the sixteenth to seventeenth week of pregnancy, CVS around the tenth. Both procedures invariably disclose the sex of the unborn child. CVS, though considered less accurate than amniocentesis, has the advantage of predicting a child's sex at a much earlier date and thus eliminating the need for a difficult second-trimester abortion.

Assumpta D'Sylva already had two daughters, and if the child she was carrying turned out to be female, she would have an abortion. Her husband, Qsbert D'Sylva, ran a family business, installing industrial boilers, that he said was worth $400,000. Assumpta D'Sylva said it wasn't that she and her husband couldn't afford another girl, and it wasn't that they didn't love their daughters. She even insisted that her husband was "not so keen" on her decision to have the test because "another girl wouldn't make any difference to him." The decision, she said, was hers alone. She simply wanted a boy.

Assumpta D'Sylva was in fact the woman who had first described to me the standard exchange that a mother without sons often heard from her friends, "Our society makes you feel so bad if you don't have a son," she told me before the doctor called her in. "Especially when I go out for parties, people say 'How many children?' and I say, 'Two girls,' and they say, 'Oh too bad, no boy.' And I feel very bad." She was well dressed and not shy about talking to me, From her point of view, she was doing what was best. She felt she was to blame, after all for producing two daughters. When I reminded her that it is the man who determines the sex of a child, she said yes she knew that, but "I still feel sometimes that it's my fault, I just feel a lady has the capacity for carrying a boy." Her parents and gynecologist were against the abortion she might have; her husband, she insisted remained "neutral," although he seemed to me to be in complete agreement with her decision. He listened quietly as she spoke. "We do feel bad about it," he said, when I asked if he did, "but things have to go this way. You do feel looked down upon if you have two or three girls." Amazingly, she and her husband were Roman Catholics. "Being a Catholic, it's the only sin I commit," Assumpta D'Sylva said, "When this test is here and everybody is doing it, why shouldn't we have what we want?" Her tone was apologetic but casual. I could only think that her pregnancy was still so recent that it was not quite real to her, and that the technology had somehow sanitized the decision she had made. As I had with other women in India, I tried to put myself in her place and summon up the feelings that her society had forced upon her. But our worlds were too different, and her thinking was unfathomable to me.

In any case, "Why shouldn't I have what I want?" was the refrain I heard all week at doctors' offices in Bombay's pockets of affluence. Nowhere was this attitude more in evidence than at the clinic of Rustom Soonawala, a gynecologist for women from Bombay's leading business families. His patients also included some of India's top actresses, as well as Americans, Europeans and Saudis. His waiting room was like no other doctor's office I had seen in India: a marble floor, leather banquettes, recessed lighting, tennis magazines on the coffee table. It was a Sunday afternoon, and yet there were several pregnant women in his waiting room. One had arrived in a red Standard sports car, which was selling in India for $20,000. After a short wait, I was ushered in to see the doctor himself, a handsome and elegant middle-aged man whom I could easily imagine on one of those marble terraces overlooking the sea. He was a member of the country's most exclusive religious minority, a Parsi, one of the 90,000 people in India who worshiped the god Zoroaster. Dr. Soonawala seemed almost British in manner and outlook. He gave me a soft drink in a glass, engraved with his initials, and he listened carefully to my first question about his use of amniocentesis. He thought for a moment, then began very slowly.

"Until the attitude of the whole Asian community changes, where a male issue in the family is a must," he said, "we as scientists can help out the poor mother who year after year produces a baby until a boy is born." Dr. Soonawala said he performed "fifty to seventy" sex-determination tests per year, using either amniocentesis or chorionic villus sampling. Of those, he aborted about "twenty to thirty" female fetuses, simply because they were female.

"I'm not very happy about it," he said, "But you have to think that the child is not wanted," The desire for male children, he explained, was stronger among the business community—the very people who could afford to have girls. "I wouldn't completely blame them," Dr. Soonawala added, "because if they've established a business, they need somebody to carry on the business after them." I asked why a father could not turn a family business over to his daughter. That was not an option, Dr. Soonawala said because the daughter must be given away in marriage to another family. He then offered another reason for the necessity of sons: "Amongst the Hindu community," he said, "the funeral pyre has to be lit by a male," I thought about asking why a daughter could not light the pyre but decided that questioning thousands of years of Hindu tradition would be of no use. "It's a very peculiar situation," Dr. Soonawala admitted. "If you don't do it, you are creating an unhappy situation for the mother and child. And if you do it, you are discriminating on the basis of sex."

That morning I had gone to a regular meeting of the Bombay branch of the Indian Medical Association because I had heard that the discussion for the day was going to be whether there should be "sex determination for the termination of pregnancy." The prevailing opinion among the thirty or so doctors appeared to be yes, with reservations. It was hard not be cynical; for many doctors in Bombay, the sex-determination tests were a lucrative part of their business. About halfway through the meeting, a young woman came to the front of the room and introduced herself as Jayshree Patel, a gynecologist She began by asking her colleagues to think about why sex-selective abortion had become so popular in India. I settled in for an emotional speech opposing the sex test but was soon startled to hear Dr. Patel sum up by saying she was in fact in favor of sex-selective abortion. "It is the lesser of two evils," she said. "The worse of the two evils is the state that a woman is going to face until the day she dies."

The meeting continued with a presentation by Dr. Gogate, the obstetrician and gynecologist who later told me he had aborted one thousand female fetuses. Dr. Gogate spoke on the technical aspects of amniocentesis, concluding that the test should be used, but "judiciously" whatever that meant. After the presentation, I introduced myself to Dr. Gogate and he invited me to come to his office to see a chorionic villus sampling he was performing the next morning. I was there at eight, in time to see a thirty-six-year-old mother of three daughters laid out on an examination table. She was eight weeks pregnant with a fourth child. She could afford another girl, she later explained to me but then repeated what I had heard so often. "In India," she said, "every parent must have one son."

The room where the test was to be performed was hot, run-down and sour-smelling. Nurses and technicians crowded around the woman and made last-minute adjustments in the medical equipment. Someone gave me a surgical mask and asked me to take off my shoes. I found a spot behind the bustle, where I stood, feeling out of place and queasy from the strange odors and heat. Dr. Gogate inserted a thin wire tube up into the woman's uterus in order to suck a few milligrams of placenta tissue, which would then be transferred for analysis to a petri dish. As I watched the wire's journey on the screen of the ultrasound machine, I slowly became disgusted. It had been building all week, but I think seeing this woman with her legs spread on the examination table, so exposed and, in a sense, so violated by the forces of her society, caused something to snap in me. What right did India have, I thought, to take the newest technology from the West and use it for something as reprehensible as the slaughter of female babies?

"Slaughter" is an explosive word, and it was something of a dilemma to find myself suddenly thinking of the abortion of a female as "slaughter" when I had for years believed in a woman's right to end her pregnancy. If I thought of the abortion of a female fetus as "slaughter," then what was I to call the abortion of a male fetus? Was it intellectually consistent to be in favor of a woman's right to abortion yet opposed to sex-selective abortion? I honestly did not know what I thought. For the rest of my time in India, I made a small career out of posing the question, whenever the topic came up, to feminists, doctors, lawyers and friends. It would often provoke heated arguments, and there seemed no way out of the moral dilemma.

It annoyed me that although the feminists were doing the right thing in opposing sex-selective abortion, they were so unaware of the philosophical traps. They tended to be more emotional than rational in their arguments and the paradox was that some of their rhetoric could easily have been borrowed by right-to-life groups in the United States. Some Indian feminists routinely referred to sex-selective abortion as "female feticide," which made me wonder why they were not opposed to "male feticide" as well. Reports by the Women's Centre included incendiary phrases such as "large-scale killing of the female fetus." One 1986 magazine article about sex-determination tests they distributed from their files was entitled. "The Silent Scream," which also happened to be the title of the 1985 pro-life propaganda film in the United States claiming to show a twelve-week-old fetus writhing in pain as it was surgically aborted. The feminists argued that sex-selective abortion was illegal because it violated Articles 14 and 15 of the Indian Constitution, which guarantee no discrimination against women. They also argued that the unborn female fetus had "the right" to be born. (Indian courts have not ruled in general on whether a fetus has rights, although the law does recognize certain inheritance rights in favor of an unborn child.) Whatever the case, if the female fetus had "the right" to be born, should not the male fetus have the same?

What I eventually concluded was that the feminists' sloganeering was aimed more at emotional effect than at logical persuasion, and that it reflected the differences in the issue of abortion in India and the United States. Bombay feminists could freely make outrageous statements that seemed to threaten a woman's right to terminate her pregnancy because the right to abortion was not under siege in India as It was in the United States. Interestingly, India had never engaged in the debate over when life begins, perhaps because the Hindu classical texts had expressed three views on the subject: life begins at conception; life begins with the first movement of the fetus; and life begins with the first breath of the baby after delivery.

Abortion in India was illegal in most cases until 1971, but in August of that year the law was liberalized after only two hours of tepid debate at the end of the monsoon session of Parliament. This was a year and a half before the U.S. Supreme Court in *Roe v. Wade* legalized abortion in America, Although I found in my research that it was never stated as such on the floor of the Indian Parliament, the reason for the easy passage of the Indian abortion law was widely acknowledged to be the government's desperate desire for another method of family planning in a country whose population was expected to reach one billion by the year 2000, with the result that India would eventually surpass China as the most populous nation on earth. The current Indian law in fact permits abortion only under certain conditions, but these are so broadly interpreted as to make abortion available on demand before the twentieth week of pregnancy. (For example, as the law is written, an Indian woman may have a legal abortion if she says that her method of contraception has failed.)

Since then, Indian feminists have generally supported a woman's right to terminate her pregnancy by abortion but have criticized what they believe is the government's callous view of abortion as a tool of the state in carrying out population control. Abortion in India has become a symbol—rightly—for the neglect of women's health. For example, the Women's Centre says that 90 percent of abortions in India are performed by unqualified doctors, and that on average there are 68 deaths for every 1,000 abortions performed in India. This is a much higher death rate from abortion than in other poor countries, but my instincts told me it was not an exaggeration. (In the United States in 1987, there were a reported 4 deaths following the 1,588,000 abortions performed.) "A woman's health isn't taken into consideration," said Vibhuti Patel, one of the leaders of the Women's Centre. "Our major issue is safe abortion." The same feminists also opposed the mass use of the birth-control pill, criticizing it as another example of the government's desire to control women regardless of health. Feminists complained that village women were commonly given oral contraceptives without adequate examinations or follow-ups, and were largely unaware of the pill's side effects. Many feminists were also opposed to the methods of the government's population control program in general, arguing that the program was motivated solely by the desire to bring down the birth rate and not by any desire to better women's lives.

As I spoke to the feminists, I began to wonder if sex-selective abortion had ever been debated in the United States, where the ethical issues raised by advances in technology—such as genetic engineering—are more fully developed. I had noticed some references to American essays on the subject in the library of a medical research foundation during my trip to Bombay, and when I returned to Delhi I wrote a friend in Washington and asked her to try to locate the material for me. What she sent was fascinating: In the late seventies in the *New England Journal of Medicine,* in what was apparently one of the first explorations of the subject, a research group of the Hastings Center, a think tank for biomedical ethics in Briarcliff Manor, N.Y., concluded that amniocentesis for sex choice should be discouraged. But in a 'subsequent article—in the same journal, John C Fletcher, a specialist in bioethics at the National Institutes of Health and a co-director of the Hastings Center research group, changed his mind, apparently because of the same moral dilemmas I was experiencing. He argued that although "sex choice was not a compelling reason for abortion," it was nonetheless "inconsistent to support an abortion law that protects the absolute right of women to decide and, at the same time, to block access to information about the fetus because one thinks that an abortion may be foolishly sought on the basis of the information." It was a persuasive point of view, but one that is easier to hold in the United States than in a culture where tens of thousands of fetuses are aborted simply because they are female. After I returned from India, *The New York Times* discovered the issue in a front-page story on Christmas Day, 1988. Under the headline FETAL SEX TEST USED AS STEP TO ABORTION, Gina Kolata reported that in the United States, "many doctors are providing prenatal diagnosis to pregnant women who want to abort a fetus on the basis of sex alone." The story at first seemed to suggest that sex-selective abortion was taking root in America but later explained that the practice was chiefly confined to women from India and other parts of Asia who had settled in the United States and who were "most likely to ask openly for sex selection." If so, how could the United States stop the practice without infringing on abortion rights, as well as rights to certain medical procedures?

Ultimately, I decided that the question of whether it was intellectually consistent to be in favor of a woman's right to abortion yet opposed to sex-selective abortion had, for me, a different answer in the United States than in India. I can't resolve the contradictions and can only conclude that there are no universally applicable answers in this world. In the United States, although the principle of *Roe v. Wade* is under attack, abortion is still generally available until the twenty-eighth week of pregnancy; in effect, a woman does not have to give her doctor a reason for her decision. Although the idea of terminating a pregnancy simply because the fetus is female is morally repugnant to me, I believe that outlawing such a practice would fundamentally infringe on a woman's right to choose.

In India, I felt, the situation was different. The Indian abortion law, although broadly interpreted, did not, as it was written, give a woman an unconditional right to abortion. An Indian woman was permitted to have an abortion only under certain conditions, usually if her doctor determined that her pregnancy would cause "grave injury" to her "physical or mental health." Pregnancy as a result of rape was presumed to constitute grave injury to a woman's physical or mental health, as was a failure of contraception—the most frequently stated reason for abortion in India.

More important I think the shocking number of aborted female fetuses in India constituted so serious a problem that the state had an obligation to step in and protect its interests, as the legislature of Maharashtra had done in banning sex-determination tests. The language of *Roe v. Wade* may help explain what I mean. In the majority opinion, Justice Harry A. Blackmun wrote that although an abortion should be considered part of a woman's right to privacy, that right was not absolute, and at the third trimester, when the fetus had the potential to live outside the mother's womb, "the state interests as to protection of health, medical standards, and prenatal life become dominant." Laws are not made in a social vacuum but reflect the societies they govern, and in India, I think, the rights of the state became dominant when prenatal tests developed for the detection of generic abnormalities in an unborn fetus began to be so widely and grotesquely abused.

Not all Indian feminists agreed with this point of view. Some argued, as I had in the beginnings that any law to ban sex-determination tests infringed on a woman's freedom of choice. "I would not be surprised if some women do challenge the law on the grounds that they have a right to abort a female fetus." Indira Jaising, one of Bombay's leading lawyers, told me before the Maharashtra law was actually passed. Others thought India's population problem was the more important issue and saw an aborted female fetus as at least one less child. A few even argued, like the woman obstetrician I had heard speak at the meeting of the Bombay branch of the Indian Medical Association, that it would be more humane to abort a female fetus than to allow the child to enter a world full of such hardship for women.

Ultimately, the feminists sidestepped the abortion-rights issue by pushing for a ban on the "sex test" and not a regulation of abortion itself, even though the ban did, in effect, limit a woman's abortion right. But most feminists eventually came around to this approach.

Excerpts from **Burned Alive**

A Victim of the Law of Men

By Souad and Marie-Therese Cuny

I Was in Flames

I am a girl. A girl must walk fast, head down, as if counting the number of steps she's taking. She may never stray from her path or look up, for if a man were to catch her eye, the whole village would label her a *charmuta*. If a married neighbor woman, or an old woman, or just anybody were to see her out without her mother or her older sister, without her sheep, her bundle of hay, or her load of figs, they would right away say *charmuta*. A girl must be married before she can raise her eyes and look straight ahead, or go into a shop, or pluck her eyebrows and wear jewelry. My mother was married at fourteen. If a girl is still unmarried by that age, the village begins to make fun of her. But a girl must wait her turn in the family to be married. The oldest daughter first, then the others.

There are too many girls in my father's house, four of marrying age. There are also two half sisters, born of our father's second wife, who are still children. The one male child of the family, the son who is adored by all, is our brother Assad, who was born in glory among all these daughters. He is the fourth born. I am the third.

Adnan, my father, is not happy with my mother, Leila, for giving him all these girls. He is unhappy, too, with his other wife, Aicha, who also has given him nothing but girls. Noura, the oldest daughter, was married late when I myself was about fifteen. Nobody has yet asked for Kainat, the second girl, who is about a year older than me. I did overhear that a man spoke to my father about me, but he was told that I must wait for Kainat's marriage before I can marry. But Kainat may not be pretty enough, and is probably too slow at her work. I'm not really sure why she hasn't been asked for, but if she stays unmarried, she'll be the butt of the village jokes, and so will I.

It is a curse in my village to be born a girl. I have no memory of having played games or having fun as a child. The only freedom a girl can dream about is marriage, leaving your father's house for your husband's and not coming back, even if you're beaten. It is considered shameful for a married daughter to return home because she is not supposed to ask for protection outside her husband's house. If she does return to her father's house, it is her family's duty to bring her back to her husband. My sister was beaten by her husband and she brought shame on our family when she came back home to complain.

She is lucky to have a husband, though. I dream about it. Ever since I heard that a man spoke to my father about me, I have been consumed by impatience and curiosity. I know he lives three or four steps from us. Sometimes I can catch sight of him from the upper terrace where I lay the laundry out to dry. He must have a good job in the city because he never dresses like a laborer. He always wears a suit, carries a briefcase, and has a car. I'd like to see his face close up but I'm afraid the family will catch me spying. So when I go to get hay for a sick sheep in the

Souad and Marie-Therese Cuny, from *Burned Alive: A Victim Of The Law Of Men*, pp. 1–21. Copyright © 2004 by Hachette Book Group USA. Reprinted with permission.

stable, I walk fast hoping to see him nearby. But he parks his car too far away. From watching, I know about what time he comes out to go to work. So at seven o'clock in the morning, I pretend to be folding the laundry on the terrace or looking for a ripe fig or shaking out the carpets to get a glimpse of him driving off in his car. I have to be quick so I won't be noticed. What I do is climb the stairs and pass through the rooms to get to the terrace. There I energetically shake a rug and look over the cement wall, just slightly glancing to the right. If somebody notices me from afar, they won't guess that I'm looking down at the street.

When I see him, I realize I am in love with this man and this car! I imagine many things on the terrace: I am married to him and, like today, I watch the car go off into the distance until I can't see it anymore. But he'll come back from work at sunset and I will remove his shoes, and on my knees I will wash his feet as my mother does for my father. I will bring him his tea, and I'll watch him smoke his long pipe, seated like a king in front of the door of his house. I will be a woman who has a husband!

And maybe I'll even be able to put on makeup, get into this car with my husband, and even go into town and into the shops. I will endure the worst for the simple freedom of being able to go through this doorway to go out and buy bread! But I will not ever be a *charmuta*. I will not look at other men. I will continue to walk fast, erect and proud, but will not watch my steps with lowered eyes, and the village will not be able to say bad things about me, because I will be a married woman.

It is from this very terrace that my terrible story began. I was already older than my older sister was on the day of her wedding. I must have been eighteen, or maybe more, I don't know, and I both hoped and I despaired. My memory went up in smoke the day the flames engulfed me, but I have tried to reconstruct what happened.

Memory

I was born in a tiny village that, I'm told, was somewhere in the West Bank. But since I never went to school, I don't know anything about my country's history. I have also been told that I was born there in either 1957 or 1958, so I'm about forty-five years old today. Twenty-five years ago, I spoke only Arabic; I'd never been farther than a few kilometers beyond the last house on the dirt road. I knew there were cities farther away but I never saw them. I did not know if the earth was round or flat, and I had no idea of the world in general. What I did know was that we had to hate the Jews who had taken our land; my father called them pigs. We were forbidden to go near them, to speak or come in contact with them for fear of becoming a pig like them.

I had to say my prayers at least twice a day. I recited them like my mother and sisters, but I only learned of the Koran in Europe many years later. My only brother, treated like the king of the house, went to school, but the girls did not. As I've mentioned, where I come from, being born a girl was a curse. A wife must first produce a son, at least one, and if she gives birth to only girls, she is mocked. Two or three girls at most are needed for the housework, to work on the land, and see to the animals. If more girls are born, it is a great misfortune and they should be gotten rid of as soon as possible. I lived this way until about the age of seventeen without knowing anything except that I was valued less than an animal because I was a girl.

So, this was my first life, as an Arab woman in the West Bank. It lasted twenty years, and the person I had been there died. She is no more.

My second life began in Europe at the end of the 1970s in an international airport. I was not much more than suffering human flesh on a stretcher. My body smelled so much of death that the passengers on the plane that was taking me from Palestine to Europe protested. Even though I was hidden behind a curtain, my presence was unbearable to them. As I write about it now, I relive that moment: They tell me that I am going to live but I do not believe that and I wait for death. I even beg for it to take me. Death seems preferable to this suffering and humiliation. There is almost nothing left of my body so why would they want to keep me alive when I don't wish to exist anymore, either my body or my mind?

I still think about that today. It is true that I would have preferred to die rather than face this second life that they were so generously offering me. But, in my case, to have survived is a miracle. It allows me now to bear witness in the name of all those women who have not had this opportunity, and who keep dying for this one reason, that they are women.

I had to learn French by listening to people speak and by forcing myself to repeat the words they explained to me with signs: "Bad? Not bad? Eat? Sleep? Walk?" I answered by making signs of yes or no. Much later I learned to read words in a newspaper, patiently day after day. In the beginning I could only decipher short announcements, death notices, or brief sentences with a few words that I would repeat phonetically. Sometimes I felt like an animal that was being taught to communicate as a human. In my head, in Arabic, I asked myself where I was, in what country, and why I hadn't died in my village. I was ashamed to be still alive, although no one knew this. I was afraid of this life but no one understood.

I have to say all this before attempting to reassemble the pieces of my memory, because I want these words to be inscribed in a book.

I remember very little of my earliest childhood, and my memory is still full of gaps. The first part of my life is made up of images that are strange and violent, like scenes in a film for television. I have so much difficulty putting these images back in order that it sometimes doesn't seem real. For example, how could I forget the name of one of my sisters, or my brother's age the day of his weddings but yet remember everything about the goats, the lambs, the cows, the bread oven, the laundry in the garden, picking the cauliflowers, the squash, the tomatoes and figs … the stable and the kitchen … the sacks of wheat and the snakes? Or the terrace where I spied on my beloved? The wheat field where I committed the "sin"?

Sometimes a color or an object strikes me, and then an image will come back to me, maybe a person, or voices, or faces that all blend together. Often when I'm asked a question, my mind goes completely blank. I desperately look for an answer and it won't come. Or another image suddenly comes to me and I don't know what it corresponds to. But these images are imprinted in my head and I will never forget them. After all, you can't forget your own death!

My name is Souad. I am from the West Bank. As a child, with my sister, I look after the sheep and the goats because my father has a flock of goats, and I work harder than a beast of burden. I must have started to work at about age eight or nine and I saw the blood of my first menstrual period at about ten. Among us, they say a girl is mature or "ripe" when this occurs. I was ashamed of this blood because I had to hide it, even from my mother's eyes, and wash my pants secretly to make them white again, and then dry them quickly in the sun so the men and the neighbors wouldn't see them. Two pairs were all I had, I remember the paper I used for protection on these awful days when you are considered to have the plague. I would bury it, the sign of my impurity, in secret in the garbage pail. If I had cramps, my mother would boil sage leaves and give it to me to drink. She wrapped my head tightly in a scarf and the next day I had no more pain. It is the only medicine I remember and I still use it because it works.

In the early mornings I go to the stable, where I whistle using my fingers for the sheep to gather around me, and then leave for the pasture with my sister Kainat, the one who is about a year older than me. Girls are not to go out alone but should be accompanied by someone older. The elder serves as safeguard for the younger. My sister Kainat is nice, round and a little chubby, while I am small and thin. We get along well. The two of us would go with the sheep and the goats to the field, about a quarter of an hour's walk from the village, walking fast and with eyes lowered as far as the last house. Once we were in the field, we were free to say silly things to each other and even laugh a little, but I don't remember any real conversation between us. Mostly, we ate our cheese, feasted on a watermelon, and watched the sheep and especially the goats, which were capable of devouring all the leaves of a fig tree in a few minutes. When the sheep moved into a circle to sleep, we fell asleep in the shade, risking having an animal wander into a neighboring field, and suffering the consequences when we got home. If an animal tore up a vegetable garden or if we were a few minutes late getting back to the stable, we got a thrashing with a belt.

Our village is very pretty and green. There are many fruits, such as figs, grapes, lemons, and an enormous number of olive trees. My father owns half the cultivated parcels of the village, all his. He isn't very rich but he has possessions. Our stone house is big, and is surrounded by a wall with a large door of gray iron. This door is the symbol of our captivity. Once we're inside, it closes on us to prevent us from going out. You can enter by this door from the outside, but you cannot go out again.

Is there a key or is it an automatic system? I remember my father and mother going out, but not us. My brother, on the other hand, is as free as the wind. He goes to the movies; he goes out and he comes back through this door, doing whatever he wants. I would often look at it, this awful iron door, and say to myself, *I'll never be able to leave through there, never …*

I don't have a good sense of the village because I'm not able to go out when and where I please. If I close my eyes and make an effort, I can tell what I've seen of it. There is my parents' house, then the one I call the rich people's house a little farther on the same side. Opposite is the house of my beloved, which I can see from the terrace. You cross the road and there it is. There are also a few other scattered houses, but I don't know how many—very few anyway. They are surrounded by low walls or iron fences and the people have vegetable gardens like us. I've never been through the entire length of the village. I only leave the house to go to market with my father and my mother or to the fields with my sister and the sheep. That's all.

Until I was seventeen or eighteen, I had seen nothing else. I had not set foot a single time in the shop in the village near the house, but in passing by in my father's van to go to market, I would always see the merchant standing at his door smoking his cigarettes. The shop has separate entrances for men and women. The men use the one on the right to go in and buy their cigarettes, newspapers, and drinks, and on the left are the fruits and vegetables where the women shop. In another house on the same side of the road as our house lives a married woman with four children. She has the right to go out and she can go into the shop. I see her standing on the stairs of the fruit-and-vegetable side holding transparent plastic sacks.

There was a lot of land around our house that was full of vegetables we had planted: squash, cauliflower, and tomatoes. Our garden was separated from the garden of the neighboring house by a low wall that was possible to step over, although none of us ever did. Being closed in was normal. It would never have occurred to any of the girls of the house to cross this symbolic barrier. To go where? Once in the village or on the road, a girl all alone would very quickly be spotted and her reputation and the family's honor would be destroyed.

It was inside this garden that I did the laundry. There was a well in one corner, and I heated the water in a basin over a wood fire. I would take a bundle of kindling from the supply and would break the branches over my knee. It took some time to heat the water but I did other things while I waited. I swept, washed the ground, and saw to the vegetables in the garden. Then I did the laundry by hand and would lay it out on the terrace to dry in the sun.

The house was modern and very comfortable, but for many years we had no hot water in the bathroom or the kitchen. It had to be heated outside and carried in. Later on, my father had hot water installed and brought in a bathtub and shower. All the girls used the same water for washing, but my brother had the right to his own water, and certainly my father also.

At night I slept with my sisters on the ground on a sheepskin. When it was very hot we slept on the terraces, lined up under the moon. We girls were next to each other in a corner. My parents and my brother slept in another part.

The workday began early. At sunrise if not earlier, my father and mother would get up. When it was the time for harvesting the wheat, we would bring something to eat with us and everybody worked, my father, my mother, my sisters, and me, but not my brother. When it was time to gather the figs, we would also set out very early because they had to be picked one by one, without missing a single one. We put them into crates and my father would take them to market. It was a good half hour's walk with the donkey to a small town, really very small, and whose name I've forgotten, if I ever knew it. Half of the market at the town's entrance was reserved for produce and the merchants who were there to sell it. To shop for clothes, you had to take the bus to a larger town. But we girls never went there. My mother would go with my father. It was like this: She'd buy a dress with my father and then she'd give it to one of us. Whether you like it or not, you have to wear it. Neither my sisters nor I, nor even my mother, had anything to say about it. It was that dress or nothing.

Girls wore long dresses with short sleeves made of a type of cotton, a very warm material that pricked your skin. They were gray or sometimes white, or very rarely black. The collar was high and tightly fastened. Over this we had to put a long-sleeved shirt or a vest, according to the season. It was sometimes so hot that it was stifling, but long sleeves were required. To show a bit of arm or leg—or worse, any skin below the neck—brought shame. Under the long dress we wore the *saroual,* which are long baggy pants that are gray or white. Worn beneath these was a pair of underpants that were cut big like shorts and that reached above the stomach. All my sisters dressed like this, too. Women usually did not wear shoes, except sometimes married women, so we were barefoot all the time.

My mother was often dressed in black. My father wore a white *saroual,* plus a long shirt and the traditional red-and-white head scarf. My father! I can see him sitting under a tree on the ground in front of our house, his cane nearby. He is small and has a pale complexion with red splotches, a round head, and very mean blue eyes. One day he broke his leg in a fall from a horse and we girls were so pleased because it meant that he couldn't run after us as fast as before to beat us with his belt.

I see him very clearly, our father. I can never forget him. It is as if I carry a photograph of him in my head. He is sitting in front of his house like a king before his palace, with his red-and-white scarf that covers his bald red skull, he's wearing his belt and his cane rests on the leg folded under him. He is small and mean. He takes off his belt and he shouts: "Why have the sheep come back by themselves?"

He pulls me by the hair and he drags me on the ground into the kitchen. He strikes me while I kneel, he pulls on my braid as if he wants to pull it out, and he cuts it off with the big scissors used for shearing wool. I have hardly any hair left. I can cry, yell, or plead but I'll get only more kicks.

It really is my fault about the sheep. I had fallen asleep with my sister because it was so hot, and I let the sheep go off on their own. He hits so hard with his cane that sometimes I can't lie down on either my left or my right side because I am in so much pain. With the belt or the cane, I think we were beaten every day. A day without a beating was unusual.

I think maybe it was this time that he tied us up, Kainat and me, our hands behind our backs, our legs bound, and a scarf over our mouths to keep us from screaming. We stayed like that all night, tied to a gate in the big stable. We were with the animals, but were worse off than they were.

This is what it was like in our village. It was the law of men. The girls and the women were certainly beaten every day in the other houses, too. You could hear the crying. It was not unusual to be beaten, to have your hair shaved off and be tied to a stable gate. There was no other way of living.

My father, the all-powerful man, the king of the household, who owns, who decides, who strikes and tortures us! And he sits there calmly smoking his pipe in front of his house with his women, whom he treats worse than his livestock, locked up. A man takes a woman in order to have sons, to have her serve him as a slave like the daughters who will come, if she has the misfortune to produce any.

I often thought when I looked at my brother, who was adored by the whole family including me: *What more does he have? What makes him so special? He came out of the same belly as I did.* And I had no answer. That was just the way it was. We girls had to serve him as we did my father, groveling and with head lowered. I can also picture the tea tray. You had to bring even this tea tray to the men of the family with your head down, looking only at your feet, with back bent, and in silence. You don't speak. You only speak in answer to a question.

At noon, it's sugared rice, vegetables with chicken or mutton, and always bread. In my father's house, the garden gives us almost everything we need for food. And we do everything ourselves. My father buys only sugar, salt, and tea. There is always food to eat; the family lacks nothing for meals. In the morning I make tea for the girls, I pour a little olive oil onto a plate, with olives on the side, and I heat the water in a basin on the coals of the bread oven. The dried green tea is in a sack of tan cloth on the floor in a corner of the kitchen. I plunge my hand into the sack, I take a handful and put it into the teapot, I add sugar, and I return to the garden for the hot basin. It's heavy and I have trouble carrying it by its two handles, my back arched, so as not to burn myself. I come back into the kitchen and I pour the water into the teapot, slowly, over the tea and the sugar. I know that if I drop any on the floor, I'll be beaten. So I pay attention. If I'm clumsy, I shouldn't sweep it up, but rather collect it and put it back in the teapot. Then my sisters come to eat, but my father, mother, and brother are never with us. In this picture of tea drunk in the morning, sitting on the floor in the kitchen, I always see only sisters. I try to situate my age but it's difficult. I do know that the eldest, Noura, isn't married yet.

As for outside work, there is a lot of fruit. Grapes grow along the terrace, where I pick them. There are oranges, bananas, and mainly the black and green figs. And a memory that I'll never lose is of going out early in the mornings to pick the figs. They have opened a little with the evening coolness and they run like honey, the purest of sweets.

The sheep are the really heavy work. Take them out, lead them to the fields, watch over them, bring them back, cut the wool that my father is going to take to the market to sell. I take a sheep by its hooves and get it to lie down on the ground so I can tie it up and I clip the wool with the big shears. They are so big for my small hands that I have trouble using my hands after only a few minutes. And I milk the ewes while sitting on the ground. I squeeze their hooves between my legs and I pull the milk, which is used to make cheese. When the milk cools off you drink it just like that, fat and nourishing.

In general, I am incapable of organizing my memories by my age at the time, but I think my memory is about right, give or take one or two years, I am more certain of events around the time of Noura's marriage when I was about fifteen.

My sister Kainat is still at home, older by a year and not married. And then there is another sister after me whose name escapes me. I try to remember her name, but it doesn't come to me. I have to call her something in order to talk about her, so I'll call her Hanan, but may she forgive me because it surely isn't her name. I know she took care of the two little half sisters my father brought home after he abandoned his second wife, Aicha. I have seen this woman and I did not have ill feelings toward her. It was considered acceptable for my father to have taken her. He always wanted to have sons, but it didn't work out with Aicha, either. She gave him only two more girls, still more girls! So he dropped her and brought the two new little sisters home. That was considered the normal thing to do. Everything the men wanted to do was considered normal in this village, including my father's striking us with the cane, and all the rest. I couldn't imagine any other kind of life. Besides, I didn't really imagine anything at all. There were no precise thoughts in my head. In our childhood, we knew no play or toys, no games, only obedience and submission.

In any case, these two little girls live with us now and Hanan stays at home to take care of them, of that I'm sure. But their names, too, are unhappily forgotten. I just refer to them as "the little sisters." In my first memories of them, they are about five or six years old and they don't work yet. They are in Hanan's care and she very rarely leaves the house, except when it is necessary for picking vegetables in season.

In our family, the children are about a year apart. My mother was married at fourteen; my father much older than her. She has had many children, fourteen in all, she says. Only five are still living. For a long time I didn't realize what giving birth to fourteen children meant. One day my mother's father was talking about it while I served the tea. I can still hear his words in my ears: "It's good that you married young, you were able to have fourteen children … and a son, it's very good."

Even if I didn't go to school, I knew how to count the sheep. So I could count on my hands that there were only five of us, Noura, Kainat, me Souad, Assad, and Hanan, not fourteen. Where were the others? My mother never said that they had died but it was acknowledged in her usual comment: "I have fourteen children, seven of them are living." She included the half sisters with us five, since we never said "half sisters," always "sisters." It would seem that there were then seven others missing. But really nine were missing, if the half sisters weren't counted. Either way, many of the children she had borne were not still alive.

But one day I learned why there were only seven of us in the house. I can't say how old I was, but I wasn't yet at puberty, so I was less than ten years old. Noura the oldest is with me. I have forgotten many things, but not what I saw with my own eyes, terrorized, but not really aware that it was a crime.

I see my mother lying on the floor on a sheepskin. She is giving birth, and my aunt Salima is with her sitting on a cushion. There are cries from my mother and then from the baby, and very quickly my mother takes the sheepskin and she smothers the baby. She is on her knees. I see the baby move under the blanket and then it's over. I don't remember what happened after that, I just know that the baby isn't there anymore. That's all, and a terrible fear grips me.

So it was a girl that my mother suffocated at her birth. I saw her do it this first time, then a second time. I'm not sure I was present for the third one, but I knew about it. And I hear my sister Noura say to my mother: "If I have girls, I'll do what you have done."

Excerpts from Burned Alive

This is how my mother got rid of the seven girls that she had after Hanan, the last survivor. This was accepted as normal. I accepted it, too, but I was also terrified. These little girls my mother was killing were a little of me. I started to hide and cry every time my father would kill a sheep or a chicken, because I was trembling for my life. The death of an animal, like that of a baby, was so simple and so ordinary a thing for my parents, but it set off in me a fear of disappearing as simply and as quickly as these babies had. I would tell myself that it's going to be my turn one of these days, or my sister's. They can kill us whenever they want. Big or small, there's no difference. Since they've given us life, they have the right to take it.

As long as you live with your parents in my village, the fear of death is there. I'm afraid of going up on a ladder when my father is down below. I'm afraid of the hatchet that is used for chopping the wood, afraid of the well when I go for water. Afraid when my father watches the sheep returning to the stable with us. Afraid of the noise of a door at night, of being suffocated in the sheepskin that is my bed.

Sometimes, corning back from the fields with the animals, Kainat and I talk about it a little: "And supposing everybody's dead when we get home … And if our father killed our mother? A blow with a stone is all it would take! What would we do?"

"Me, I pray every time I go to the well because it's so deep. I tell myself that if somebody pushed me in, no one would know where I was. You could die down there, nobody will come looking for you."

That well was my great terror, and my mother's, too, I could feel it. And I was afraid in the ravines when I led the goats and the sheep back. The idea would loom up in me that my father could be hiding somewhere and that he was going to push me into the void. It would be easy for him to do, and I would be dead at the bottom of the ravine. They could even pile up a few stones on top of me and I would be in the ground and I'd be left there to rot.

The possibility of our mother dying preoccupied us more than the death of a sister because there were always other sisters. Our mother was often beaten just as we were. Sometimes she tried to intervene when my father beat us really viciously, and then he'd turn the blows on her, knocking her down and pulling her by her hair. We lived every day with the possibility of death, day after day.

It could come for no reason, take you by surprise, simply because the father had decided it. Just as my mother had decided to smother the baby girls. She would be pregnant, then she wasn't, and nobody asked any questions.

We didn't have any real contact with other girls in the village except to say hello and good-bye. We were never together, except for weddings. And the conversations were banal, about the food, about the bride, about other girls who we thought were pretty or ugly, or maybe about a woman we thought was lucky because she was wearing makeup.

"Look at that one, she's plucked her eyebrows …"

"She has a nice haircut."

"Oh, look at that one, she's wearing shoes!"

This would be the richest girl in the village, she wore embroidered slippers. The rest of us went into the fields barefoot, where we got thorns in our feet and would have to sit on the ground to take them out. My mother didn't have any shoes, either, and my sister Noura was married barefoot. The wedding ceremony consisted of only a few sentences exchanged. I was present at only two or three of these ceremonies.

It was unthinkable to complain about being beaten because that was just the way it was. There was no question about a baby being alive or dead, unless a woman had just given birth to a son. If this son was alive, then glory to her and to the family. If he was dead, they wept over him and the misfortune that had befallen her and her family. The males counted, not the females.

When I disappeared from my village later, my mother must not have been forty years old. She had given birth to fourteen children and only five were living. Had she smothered all the others? Nobody really cared because it was customary. I never knew what became of the baby girls after my mother smothered them. Did they bury them somewhere? Did they become food for the dogs? My mother would dress in black, my father also. Every birth of a girl was like a burial in the family. It was always considered the mother's fault if she produced only girls. My father thought so and so did the whole village.

In my village, if the men had to choose between a girl and a cow, they would choose the cow. My father repeated endlessly how we girls were not good for anything: A cow gives milk and produces calves. What do you do with milk and calves? You sell them and bring the money home, which means a cow does something for the family. But a girl? What does the family get from her? Nothing. What do sheep bring to us? Wool. You sell the wool and you get money. The lamb grows up, it makes other lambs, still more milk, you make cheese, you sell it and you bring home money. A cow and a sheep are more valuable than a girl. And we girls knew this very well because the cow, the sheep, and the goat were treated much better than we were and they were never beaten!

And we also knew that a girl is a problem for her father because he is always afraid of not being able to marry her off. And once she's married it is a cause for misery and shame if she leaves her husband, who's mistreating her, and dares come back to her parents' house. But as long as she is not married, the father is afraid that she'll stay an old maid and the village will gossip. For the whole family that is a terrible embarrassment because if an unmarried girl walks in the street with her father and mother, everyone looks at her and makes fun of her. If she's more than twenty years old and still in her parents' house, it is not normal. Everyone observes the rule of marrying the eldest daughter first and the rest in the order of their ages. But after the age of twenty, nobody makes allowances. A girl is expected to be married. I don't know how this worked in the big cities of my country but that's the way it was in my village.

Motherhood and Morality in America

By Kristin Luker

According to interested observers at the time, abortion in America was as frequent in the last century as it is in our own. And the last century, as we have seen, had its own "right-to-life" movement, composed primarily of physicians who pursued the issue in the service of their own professional goals. When abortion reemerged as an issue in the late 1950s, it still remained in large part a restricted debate among interested professional. But abortion as we now know it has little in common with these earlier rounds of the debate. Instead of the civility and colleagueship that characterized the earlier phases of the debate, the present round of the abortion debate is marked by rancor and intransigence. Instead of the elite male professionals who commanded the issue until recently, ordinary people—and more to the point, ordinary women—have come to predominate in the ranks of those concerned. From a quiet, restricted technical debate among concerned professionals, abortion has become a debate that seems at times capable of tearing the fabric of American life apart. How did this happen? What accounts for the remarkable transformation of the abortion debate?

The history of the debate ... provides some preliminary answers. Technological advances in obstetrics led to a decline in those abortions undertaken strictly to preserve the life of the woman, using the narrowly biological sense of the word *life*. These technological advances, in turn, permitted (and indeed forced) physicians over time to make more and more nuanced decisions about abortion and eventually brought to the fore the underlying philosophical issue that had been obscured by a century of medical control over abortion: is the embryo a person or only a potential person? ... Once this question is confronted directly, a unified world view—a set of assumptions about how the world is and ought to be organized—is called into play. ... World views are usually the product of values so deeply held and dearly cherished that an assault upon them is a deeply disturbing assault indeed. ... The abortion debate has been transformed because it has "gone public" and in so doing has called into question individuals' most sacrosanct beliefs.

But this is only part of the story. This chapter will argue that all the previous rounds of the abortion debate in America were merely echoes of the issue as the nineteenth century defined it: a debate about the medical profession's right to make life-and-death decisions. In contrast, the most recent round of the debate is about something new. By bringing the issue of the moral status of the embryo to the fore, the new round focuses on the relative rights of women and embryos. Consequently, the abortion debate has become a debate about women's contrasting obligations to themselves and others. New technologies and the changing nature of work have opened up possibilities for women outside of the home undreamed of in the nineteenth century; together, these changes give women—for the first time in history—the option of deciding exactly how and when their family roles will fit into the larger context

Kristin Luker, "Motherhood and Morality in America," *Abortion and the Politics of Motherhood*, pp. 192–215. Copyright © 1984 by the Regents of the University of California. Reprinted with permission by University of California Press.

of their lives. In essence, therefore, this round of the abortion debate is so passionate and hard-fought *because it is a referendum on the place and meaning of motherhood.*

Motherhood is at issue because two opposing visions of mother hood are at war. Championed by "feminists" and "housewives," these two different views of motherhood represent in turn two very different kinds of social worlds. The abortion debate has become a debate among women, women with different values in the social world, different experiences of it, and different resources with which to cope with it. How the issue is framed, how people think about it, and, most importantly, where the passion come from are all related to the fact that the battlelines are increasingly drawn (and defended) by women. While on the surface it is the embryo's fate that seems to be at slake, the abortion debate is actually about the meanings of *women's* lives.

To be sure, both the pro-life and the pro-choice movements had earlier phases in which they were dominated by male professionals. Some of these men are still active in the debate, and it is certainly the case that some men continue to join the debate on both sides of the issue. But the data in this study suggest that by 1974 over 80 percent of the activists in both the pro-choice and the pro-life movements in California were women, and a national survey of abortion activists found similar results.

Moreover, in our interviews we routinely asked both male and female activists on both sides of the issue to supply information on several "social background variables," such as where they were born; the extent of their education, their income level, the number of children they had, and their occupations. When male activists on the two sides are compared on these variables, they are virtually indistinguishable from one another. But when female activists are compared, it is dramatically clear that for the women who have come to dominate the ranks of the movement, the abortion debate is a conflict between two different social worlds and the hopes and beliefs those worlds support.

Who Are the Activists?

On almost every social background variable we examined, pro-life and pro-choice women differed dramatically. For example, in terms of income, almost half of all pro-life women (44 percent) in this study reported an income of less than $20,000 a year, but only one-fourth of the pro-choice women reported an income that low, and a considerable portion of those were young women just starting their careers. On the upper end of the income scale, one-third of the pro-choice women reported an income of $50,000 a year or more compared with only one pro-life woman in every seven.

These simple figures on income, however, conceal a very complex social reality; and that social reality is in turn tied to feelings about abortion. The higher incomes of pro-choice women, for example, result from a number of intersecting factors. Almost without exception pro-choice women work in the paid labor force, they earn good salaries when they work, and if they are married, they are likely to be married to men who also have good incomes. An astounding 94 percent of all pro-choice women work, and over half of them have incomes in the top 10 percent of all working women in this country. Moreover, one pro-choice woman in ten has an annual *personal* income (as opposed to a family income) of $30,000 or more, thus putting her in the rarified ranks of the top 2 percent of all employed women in America. Pro-life women, by contrast, are far less likely to work: 63 percent of them do not work in the paid labor force, and almost all of those who do are unmarried. Among pro-life married women, for example, only 14 percent report any personal income at all, and for most of them, this is earned not in a formal job but through activities such as selling cosmetics to groups of friends. Not surprisingly, the personal income of pro-life women who work outside the home, whether in a formal job or in one of these less-structured activities, is low. Half of all pro-life women who do work earn less than $5,000 a year, and half earn between $5,000 and $10,000. Only two pro-life women we contacted reported a personal income of more than $20,000 Thus pro-life women are less likely to work in the first place, they earn less money when they do work, and they are more likely to be married to a skilled worker or small businessman who earns only a moderate income.

These differences in income are in turn related to the different educational and occupational choices these women have made along the way. Among pro-choice women, almost four out of ten (37 percent) had undertaken some graduate work beyond the B.A. degree, and 18 percent had an M.D., a law degree, a Ph.D., or a similar postgraduate degree. Pro-life women, by comparison, had far less education: 10 percent of them had only a high school education or less; and another 30 percent never finished college (in contrast with only 8 percent of the pro-choice women). Only 6 percent of all pro-life women had a law degree, a Ph.D., or a medical degree.

These educational differences were in turn related to occupational differences among the women in this study. Because of their higher levels of education, pro-choice women tended to be employed in the major professions, as administrators, owners of small businesses, or executives in large businesses. The pro-life women tended to be housewives or, of the few who worked, to be in the traditional female jobs of teaching, social work, and nursing. (The choice of home life over public life held true for even the 6 percent of pro-life women with an advanced degree: of the married women who had such degrees, at the time of our interviews only one of them had not retired from her profession after marriage.)

These economic and social differences were also tied to choices that women on each side had made about marriage and family life. For example, 23 percent of pro-choice women had never married, compared with only 16 percent of pro-life women; 14 percent of pro-choice women had been divorced, compared with 5 percent of pro-life women. The size of the families these women had was also different. The average pro-choice family had between one and two children and was more likely to have one; pro-life families averaged between two and three children and were more likely to have three. (Among the pro-life women, 23 percent had five or more children; 16 percent had seven or more children.) Pro-life women also tended to marry at a slightly younger age and to have had their first child earlier.

Finally, the women on each side differed dramatically in their religious affiliation and in the role that religion played in their lives. Almost 80 percent of the women active in the pro-life movement at the present time are Catholics. The remainder are Protestants (9 percent), persons who claim no religion (5 percent), and Jews (1 percent). In sharp contrast, 63 percent of pro-choice women say that they have no religion, 22 percent think of themselves as vaguely Protestant, 3 percent are Jewish, and 9 percent have what they call a "personal" religion. We found no one in our sample of pro-choice activists who claimed to be a Catholic at the time of the interviews.

When we asked activists what religion they were raised in as a child, however, a different picture emerged. For example, 20 percent of the pro-choice activists were raised as Catholics, 42 percent were raised as Protestants, and 15 percent were raised in the Jewish faith. In this group that describes itself as predominantly without religious affiliation, therefore, only 14 percent say they were not brought up in any formal religious faith. By the same token, although almost 80 percent of present pro-life activists are Catholic, only 58 percent were raised in that religion (15 percent were raised as Protestants and 3 percent as Jews). Thus, almost 20 percent of the pro-life activists in this study are converts to Catholicism, people who have actively chosen to follow a given religious faith, in striking contrast to pro-choice people, who have actively chosen not to follow any.

Perhaps the single most dramatic difference between the two groups, however, is in the role that religion plays in their lives. Almost three-quarters of the pro-choice people interviewed said that formal religion was either unimportant or completely irrelevant to them, and their attitudes are correlated with behavior: only 25 percent of the pro-choice women said they *ever* attend church, and most of these said they do so only occasionally. Among pro-life people, by contrast, 69 percent said religion was important in their lives, and an additional 22 percent said that it was very important. For pro-life women, too, these attitudes are correlated with behavior: half of those pro-life women interviewed said they attend church regularly once a week, and another 13 percent said they do so even more often. Whereas 80 percent of pro-choice people never attend church, only 2 percent of pro-life advocates never do so.

Keeping in mind that the statistical use of averages has inherent difficulties, we ask, who are the "average" pro-choice and pro-life advocates? When the social background data are looked at carefully, two profiles emerge. The average pro-choice activist is a forty-four-year-old married woman who grew up in a large metropolitan area and whose father was a college graduate. She was married at age twenty-two, has one or two children, and has had some graduate or professional training beyond the B.A. degree. She is married to a professional man, is herself employed in a regular job, and her family income is more than $50,000 a year. She is not religiously active, feels that religion is not important to her, and attends church very rarely if at all.

The average pro-life woman is also a forty-four-year-old married woman who grew up in a large metropolitan area. She married at age seventeen and has three children or more. Her father was a high school graduate, and she has some college education or may have a B.A. degree. She is not employed in the paid labor force and is married to a small businessman or a lower-level white-collar worker; her family income is $30,000 a year. She is Catholic (and may have converted), and her religion is one of the most important aspects of her life: she attends church at least once a week and occasionally more often.

Interests and Passions

To the social scientist (and perhaps to most of us) these social background characteristics connote lifestyles as well. We intuitively clothe these bare statistics with assumptions about beliefs and values. When we do so, the pro-choice women emerge as educated, affluent, liberal professionals, whose lack of religious affiliation suggests a secular, "modern," or (as pro-life people would have it) "utilitarian" outlook on life. Similarly, the income, education, marital patterns, and religious devotion of pro-life women suggest that they are traditional, hard-working people ("polyester types" to their opponents), who hold conservative views on life. We may be entitled to assume that individuals' social backgrounds act to shape and mold their social attitudes, but it is important to realize that the relationship between social worlds and social values is a very complex one.

Perhaps one example will serve to illustrate the point. A number of pro-life women in this study emphatically rejected an expression that pro-choice women tend to use almost unthinkingly—the expression *unwanted pregnancy*. Pro-life women argued forcefully that a better term would be a *surprise* pregnancy, asserting that although a pregnancy may be momentarily unwanted, the child that results from the pregnancy almost never is. Even such a simple thing—what to call an unanticipated pregnancy—calls into play an individual's values and resources. Keeping in mind our profile of the average pro-life person, it is obvious that a woman who does not work in the paid labor force, who does not have a college degree, whose religion is important to her, and who has already committed herself wholeheartedly to marriage and a large family is well equipped to believe that an unanticipated pregnancy usually becomes a beloved child. Her life is arranged so that for her, this belief is true. This view is consistent not only with her values, which she has held from earliest childhood, but with her social resources as well. It should not be surprising, therefore, that her world view leads her to believe that everyone else can "make room for one more" as easily as she can and that therefore it supports her in her conviction that abortion is cruel, wicked, and self-indulgent.*

It is almost certainly the case that an unplanned pregnancy is never an easy thing for anyone. Keeping in mind the profile of the average pro-choice woman, however, it is evident that a woman who is employed full time, who has an affluent lifestyle that depends in part on her contribution to the family income, and who expects to give a child as good a life as she herself has had with respect to educational, social, and economic advantages will draw on a different reality when she finds herself being skeptical about the ability of the average person to transform unwanted pregnancies into well-loved (and well-cared-for) children.

---

* As might be imagined, it is not an easy task to ask people who are anti-abortion activists about their own experiences with a certain kind of unanticipated pregnancy, namely, a premarital pregnancy. Most pro-choice people were quite open about having had such pregnancies; ... their pregnancies—and subsequent abortions—were central to their feelings about abortion. Pro-life women by contrast, were deeply reluctant to discuss the topic. Several of them, after acknowledging premarital pregnancies, said that they did not want people to think that their attitudes on abortion were merely a product of their personal experiences. Thus we have no comparative figures about the extent to which the values represented here are the product of different experiences or just different opinions. We know only that unanticipated pregnancy was common among pro-choice women, and the interviews suggest that it was not uncommon among pro-life women. The difference in experience is, of course, that those in the first group sought abortions and those in the second group, with only a few exceptions, legitimized their pregnancies with a marriage.

The relationship between passions and interests is thus more dynamic than it might appear at first. It is true that at one level, pro-choice and pro-life attitudes on abortion are self-serving: activists on each side have different views of the morality of abortion because their chosen lifestyles leave them with different needs for abortion; and both sides have values that provide a moral basis for their abortion needs in particular and their lifestyles in general. But this is only half the story. The values that lead pro-life and pro-choice women into different attitudes toward abortion are the same values that led them at an earlier time to adopt different lifestyles that supported a given view of abortion.

For example, pro-life women have *always* valued family roles very highly and have arranged their lives accordingly. They did not acquire high-level educational and occupational skills, for example, because they married, and they married because their values suggested that this would be the most satisfying life open to them. Similarly, pro-choice women postponed (or avoided) marriage and family roles because they chose to acquire the skills they needed to be successful in the larger world, having concluded that the role of wife and mother was too limited for them. Thus, activists on both sides of the issue are women who have a given set of values about what are the most satisfying and appropriate roles for women, and they have made *life commitments that now limit their ability to change their minds.* Women who have many children and little education, for example, are seriously handicapped in attempting to become doctors or lawyers; women who have reached their late forties with few children or none are limited in their ability to build (or rebuild) a family. For most of these activists, therefore, their position on abortion is the "tip of the iceberg," a shorthand way of supporting and proclaiming not only a complex set of values but a given set of social resources as well.

To put the matter differently, we might say that for pro-life women the traditional division of life into separate male roles and female roles still works, but for pro-choice women it does not. Having made a commitment to the traditional female roles of wife, mother, and homemaker, pro-life women are limited in those kinds of resources—education, class status, recent occupational experiences—they would need to compete in what has traditionally been the male sphere, namely, the paid labor force. The average pro-choice woman, in contrast, is comparatively well endowed with exactly those resources; she is highly educated, she already has a job, and she has recent (and continuous) experience in the job market.

In consequence, anything that supports a traditional division of labor into male and female worlds is, broadly speaking, in the interests of pro-life women because that is where their resources lie. Conversely, such a traditional division of labor, when strictly enforced, is against the interests of pro-choice women because it limits their abilities to use the valuable "male" resources that they have in relative abundance. It is therefore apparent that attitudes toward abortion, even though rooted in childhood experiences, are also intimately related to present-day interests. Women who oppose abortion and seek to make it officially unavailable are declaring, both practically and symbolically, that women's reproductive roles should be given social primacy. Once an embryo is defined as a child and an abortion as the death of a person, almost everything else in a woman's life must "go on hold" during the course of her pregnancy: any attempt to gain "male" resources such as a job, an education, or other skills must be subordinated to her uniquely female responsibility of serving the needs of this newly conceived person. Thus, when personhood is bestowed on the embryo, women's nonreproductive roles are made secondary to their reproductive roles. The act of conception therefore creates a pregnant woman rather than a woman who is pregnant; it creates a woman whose life, in cases where roles or values clash, is defined by the fact that she is—or may become—pregnant.

It is obvious that this view is supportive of women who have already decided that their familial and reproductive roles are the major ones in their lives. By the same token, the costs of defining women's reproductive roles as primary do not seem high to them because they have already chosen to make those roles primary anyway. For example, employers might choose to discriminate against women because they might require maternity leave and thus be unavailable at critical times, but women who have chosen not to work in the paid labor force in the first place can see such discrimination as irrelevant to them.

It is equally obvious that supporting abortion (and believing that the embryo is not a person) is in the vested interests of pro-choice women. Being so well equipped to compete in the male sphere, they perceive any situation that both practically and symbolically affirms the primacy of women's reproductive roles as a real loss to them. Practically, it devalues their social resources. If women are only secondarily in the labor market and must subordinate working to pregnancy, should it occur, then their education, occupation, income, and work become potentially temporary and hence discounted. Working becomes, as it traditionally was perceived to be, a pastime or hobby pursued for "pin money" rather than a central part of their lives. Similarly, if the embryo is defined as a person and the ability to become pregnant is the central one for women, a woman must be prepared to sacrifice some of her own interests to the interests of this newly conceived person.

In short, in a world where men and women have traditionally had different roles to play and where male roles have traditionally been the more socially prestigious and financially rewarded, abortion has become a symbolic marker between those who wish to maintain this division of labor and those who wish to challenge it. Thus, on an intimate level, the pro-life movement is women's version of what was true of peasants in the Vendée, the part of France that remained Royalist during the French Revolution. Charles Tilly has argued that in the Vendée, traditional relationships between nobles and peasants were still mutually satisfying so that the "brave new world" of the French Revolution represented more loss than gain, and the peasants therefore resisted the changes the Revolution heralded. By the same logic, traditional relationships between men and women are still satisfying, rewarding, and meaningful for pro-life women, and they therefore resist the lure of "liberation." For pro-choice women, however, with their access to male resources, a division of labor into the public world of work and the private world of home and hearth seems to promise only restriction to "second-class" citizenship.

Thus, the sides are fundamentally opposed to each other not only on the issue of abortion but also on what abortion *means*. Women who have many "human capital" resources of the traditionally male variety want to see motherhood recognized as a private, discretionary choice. Women who have few of these resources and limited opportunities in the job market want to see motherhood recognized as the most important thing a woman can do. In order for pro-choice women to achieve their goals, therefore, they *must* argue that motherhood is not a primary, inevitable, or "natural" role for all women; for pro-life women to achieve their goals, they *must* argue that it is. In short, the debate rests on the question of whether women's fertility is to be socially recognized as a resource or as a handicap.

To the extent that women who have chosen the larger public world of work have been successful, both legally and in terms of public opinion and, furthermore, are rapidly becoming the numerical majority, pro-life women are put on the defensive. Several pro-life women offered poignant examples of how the world deals with housewives who do not have an official payroll title. Here is what one of them said:

> I was at a party, about two years ago—it still sticks in my mind, you see, because I'm a housewife and I don't work—and I met this girl from England and we got involved in a deep discussion about the English and the Americans and their philosophies and how one has influenced the other, and at the end of the conversation—she was a working gal herself, I forget what she did—and she says, "Where do you work?" and I said, "I don't." And she looked at me and said, "You don't work?" I said "No." She said, "You're just a housewife … and you can still think like that?" She couldn't believe it, and she sort of gave me a funny look and that was the end of the conversation for the evening. And I've met other people who've had similar experiences. [People seem to think that if] you're at home and you're involved with children all day, your intelligence quotient must be down with them on the floor someplace, and [that] you really don't do much thinking or get yourself involved.

Moreover, there are subtle indications that even the pro-life activists we interviewed had internalized their loss of status as housewives. Only a handful of married pro-life activists also worked at regular jobs outside the home; but fully half of those who were now full-time homemakers, some for as long as thirty years, referred to themselves in terms of the work they had given up when they married or had their first child: "I'm a political scientist," "I'm a social worker," "I'm an accountant." It is noteworthy that no one used the past tense as in "I used to be a social worker": every nonemployed married woman who used her former professional identification used it in the present tense. Since this pattern was not noticed during the interviewing, what the woman themselves had in mind must remain speculative. But it does not seem unreasonable to imagine that this identification is an unconscious bow to the fact that "just plain" individuals, and in particular "just plain housewives," lack the status and credibility of professionals. Ironically, by calling on earlier identifications these women may have been expressing a pervasive cultural value that they oppose as a matter of ideology. They seemed to believe that when it comes to making public statements—or at least public statements to an interviewer who has come to ask you about your activities in the abortion debate—*what* you are counts more than *who* you are.

Because of their commitment to their own view of motherhood as a primary social role, pro-life women believe that other women are "casual" about abortions and have them "for convenience." There are no reliable data to confirm whether or not women are "casual" about abortions, but many pro-life people believe this to be the case and relate their activism to their perception of other people's casualness. For example:

> Every time I saw some article [on abortion] I read about it, and I had another friend who had her second abortion in 1977 ... and both of her abortions were a matter of convenience, it was inconvenient for her to be pregnant at that time. When I talked to her I said, "O.K., you're married now, your husband has a good job, you want to have children eventually, but if you became pregnant now, you'd have an abortion. Why?" "Because it's inconvenient, this is not when I want to have my child." And that bothered me a lot because she is also very intelligent, graduated magna cum laude, and knew nothing about fetal development.

The assertion that women are "casual" about abortion, one could argue, expresses in a short-hand way a set of beliefs about women and their roles. First, the more people value the personhood of the embryo, the more important must be the reasons for taking its life. Some pro-life people, for example, would accept an abortion when continuation of the pregnancy would cause the death of the mother; they believe that when two lives are in direct conflict, the embryo's life can be considered the more expendable. But not all pro-life people agree, and many say they would not accept abortion even to save the mother's life. (Still others say they accept the idea in principle but would not make that choice in their own lives if faced with it.) For people who accept the personhood of the embryo, any reason besides trading a "life for a life" (and sometimes even that) seems trivial, merely a matter of "convenience."

Second, people who accept the personhood of the embryo see the reasons that pro-abortion people give for ending a pregnancy as simultaneously downgrading the value of the embryo and upgrading everything else but pregnancy. The argument that women need abortion to "control" their fertility means that they intend to subordinate pregnancy, with its inherent unpredictability, to something else. As the pro-choice activists ... have told us, that something else is participation in the paid labor force. Abortion permits women to engage in paid work on an equal basis with men. With abortion, they may schedule pregnancy in order to take advantage of the kinds of benefits that come with a paid position in the labor force: a paycheck, a title, and a social identity. The pro-life women in this study were often careful to point out that they did not object to "career women." But what they meant by "career women" were women whose *only* responsibilities were in the labor force. Once a woman became a wife and a mother, in their view her primary responsibility was to her home and family.

Third, the pro-life activists we interviewed, the overwhelming majority of whom are full-time homemakers, also felt that women who worked *and* had families could often do so only because women like themselves picked up the slack. Given their place in the social structure, it is not surprising that many of the pro-life women thought that married women who worked outside the home were "selfish"—that they got all the benefits while the homemakers carried the load for them in Boy and Girl Scouts, PTA, and after school, for which their reward was to be treated by the workers as less, competent and less interesting persons.†

Abortion therefore strips the veil of sanctity from motherhood. When pregnancy is discretionary—when people are allowed to put anything else they value in front of it—then motherhood has been demoted from a sacred calling to a job.‡ In effect, the legalization of abortion serves to make men and women more "unisex" by deemphasizing

---

† In fact, pro-life women, especially those recruited after 1972, were *less* likely to be engaged in formal activities such as Scouts, church activities, and PTA than their pro-choice peers. Quite possibly they have in mind more informal kinds of activities, premised on the fact that since they do not work, they are home most of the time.

‡ The same might be said of all sacred callings—stripped of its layer of the sacred, for example, the job of the clergy is demanding, low status, and underpaid.

what makes them different—the ability of women to visibly and directly carry the next generation. Thus, pro-choice women are emphatic about their right to compete equally with men without the burden of an unplanned pregnancy, and pro-life women are equally emphatic about their belief that men and women have different roles in life and that pregnancy is a gift instead of a burden.

The pro-life activists we interviewed do not want equality with men in the sense of having exactly the same rights and responsibilities as men do, although they do want equality of status. In fact, to the extent that *all* women have been touched by the women's movement and have become aware of the fact that society often treats women as a class as less capable than men, quite a few said they appreciated the Equal Rights Amendment (ERA), except for its implied stand on abortion. The ERA, in their view, reminded them that women are as valuable *in their own sphere* as men are in theirs. However, to the extent that the ERA was seen as downplaying the differences between men and women, to devalue the female sphere of the home in the face of the male sphere of paid work, others saw it as both demeaning and oppressive to women like themselves. As one of the few married employed pro-life women argued:

> I oppose it [the ERA] Because I've gotten where I am without it. I don't think I need it. I think a woman should be hired on her merits, not on her sex or race. I don't think we should be hiring on sex or on race. I think we should be taking the competent people that are capable of doing the job … I don't think women should be taking jobs from the breadwinner, you know. I still think that our society should be male … the male should be the primary breadwinner. For example, my own husband can-not hope for promotion because he is white and Anglo, you know, I mean white male. He's no, going to get a promotion. If he could get the promotion that others of different minorities have gotten over him, I probably wouldn't have to work at all. So from my own point of view, purely selfishly, I think we've got to consider it. On the other hand, if I'm doing the same job [as a man], I expect to get the same pay. But I've always gotten it. So I really don't think that's an issue. I see the ERA as causing us more problems than it's going to [solve] … As I see it, we were on a pedestal, why should we go down to being equal? That's my feeling on the subject.

It is stating the obvious to point out that the more limited the educational credentials a woman has, the more limited the job opportunities are for her, and the more limited the job opportunities, the more attractive motherhood is as a full-time occupation. In motherhood, one can control the content and pace of one's own work, and the job is *intrinsically meaningful*. Compared with a job clerking in a supermarket (a realistic alternative for women with limited educational credentials) where the work is poorly compensated and often demeaning, motherhood can have compensations that far transcend the monetary ones. As one woman described mothering: "You have this little, rough uncut diamond, and you're the artist shaping and cutting that diamond, and bringing out the lights … that's a great challenge."

All the circumstances of her existence will therefore encourage a pro-life woman to highlight the kinds of values and experiences that support childbearing and childrearing and to discount the attraction (such as it is) of paid employment. Her circumstances encourage her to resent the pro-choice view that women's most meaningful and prestigious activities are in the "man's world."

Abortion also has a symbolic dimension that separates the needs and interests of homemakers and workers in the paid labor force. Insofar as abortion allows a woman to get a job, to get training for a job, or to advance in a job, it does more than provide social support for working women over homemakers; it also seems to support the value of economic considerations over moral ones. Marry pro-life people interviewed said that although their commitment to traditional family roles meant very real material deprivations to themselves and their families, the moral benefits of such a choice more than made up for it.

> My girls babysit and the boys garden and have paper routes and things like that. I say that if we had a lot of money that would still be my philosophy, though I don't know because we haven't been in that position. But it's a sacrifice to have a larger family. So when I hear these figures that it take $65,000 from birth to [raise a child]. I think that's ridiculous. That's a new bike every year. That's private colleges. That's

a complete new outfit when school opens. Well, we've got seven daughters who wear hand-me-downs, and we hope that sometime in their eighteen years at home each one has a new bike somewhere along the line, but otherwise it's hand-me-downs. Those figures are inflated to give those children everything and I think that's not good for them.

For pro-life people, a world view that puts the economic before the noneconomic hopelessly confuses two different kinds of worlds. For them, the private world of family as traditionally experienced is the one place in human society where none of us has a price tag. Home, as Robert Frost pointed out, is where they have to take you in, whatever your social worth. Whether one is a surgeon or a rag picker, the family is at least ideally the place where love is unconditional.

Pro-life people and pro-life women in particular have very real reasons to fear such a state of affairs. Not only do they see an achievement-based world as harsh, superficial, and ultimately ruthless; they are relatively less well-equipped to operate in that world. A considerable amount of social science research has suggested, at least in the realm of medical treatment, that there is an increasing tendency to judge people by their official (achieved) worth. Pro-life people have relatively fewer official achievements in part because they have been doing what they see as a moral task, namely, raising children and making a home; and they see themselves as becoming handicapped in a world that discounts not only their social contributions but their personal lives as well.

It is relevant in this context to recall the grounds on which pro-life people argue that the embryo is a baby: that it is genetically human. To insist that the embryo is a baby because it is genetically human is to make a claim that it is both wrong and impossible to make distinctions between humans at all. Protecting the life of the embryo, which is by definition an entity whose social worth is all yet to come, means protecting others who feel that they may be defined as having low social worth; more broadly, it means protecting a legal view of personhood that emphatically rejects social worth criteria.

For the majority of pro-life people we interviewed, the abortions they found most offensive were those of "damaged" embryos. This is because this category so clearly highlights the aforementioned concerns about social worth. To defend a genetically or congenitally damaged embryo from abortion is, in their minds, defending the weakest of the weak, and most pro-life people we interviewed were least prepared to compromise on this category of abortion.

The genetic basis of the embryo's claim to personhood has another, more subtle implication for those on the pro-life side. If genetic humanness equals personhood, then biological facts of life must take precedence over social facts of life. One's destiny is therefore inborn and hence immutable. To give any ground on the embryo's biologically determined babyness, therefore, would by extension call into question the "innate," "natural," and biological basis of women's traditional roles as well.

Pro-choice people, of course, hold a very different view of the matter. For them, social considerations outweigh biological ones: the embryo becomes a baby when it is "viable," that is, capable of achieving a certain degree of social integration with others. This is a world view premised on achievement, but not in the way pro-life people experience the word. Pro-choice people, believing as they do in choice, planning, and human efficacy, believe that biology is simply a minor given to be transcended by human experience. Sex, like race and age, is not an appropriate criterion for sorting people into different rights and responsibilities. Pro-choice people downplay these "natural" ascriptive characteristics, believing that true equality means achievement based on talent, not being restricted to a "women's world," a "black world," or an "old people's world." Such a view, as the profile of pro-choice people has made clear, is entirely consistent with their own lives and achievements.

These differences in social circumstances that separate pro-life from pro-choice women on the core issue of abortion also lead them to have different values on topics that surround abortion, such as sexuality and the use of contraception. With respect to sexuality, for example, the two sides have diametrically opposed values; these values arise from a fundamentally different premise, which is, in turn, tied to the different realities of their social worlds. If pro-choice women have a vested interest in subordinating their reproductive capacities, and pro-life women have a vested interest in highlighting them, we should not be surprised to find that pro-life women believe that the purpose of sex is reproduction whereas pro-choice women believe that its purpose is to promote intimacy and mutual pleasure.

These two views about sex express the same value differences that lead the two sides to have such different views on abortion. If women plan to find their primary role in marriage and the family, then they face a need to create a "moral cartel" when it comes to sex. If sex is freely available outside of marriage, then why should men, as the old saw puts it, buy the cow when the milk is free? If many women are willing to sleep with men outside of marriage, then the regular sexual activity that comes with marriage is much less valuable an incentive to marry. And because pro-life women are traditional women, their primary resource for marriage is the promise of a stable home, with everything it implies: children, regular sex, a "haven in a heartless world."

But pro-life women, like all women, are facing a devaluation of these resources. As American society increasingly becomes a service economy, men can buy the services that a wife traditionally offers. Cooking, cleaning, decorating, and the like can easily be purchased on the open market in a cash transaction. And as sex becomes more open, more casual, and more "amative," it removes one more resource that could previously be obtained only through marriage.

Pro-life women, as we have seen, have both value orientations and social characteristics that make marriage very important. Their alter-natives in the public world of work are, on the whole, less attractive. Furthermore, women who stay home full-time and keep house are be-coming a financial luxury. Only very wealthy families *or families whose values allow them to place the nontangible benefits of a full-time wife over the tangible benefits of a working wife* can afford to keep one of its earners off the labor market. To pro-life people, the nontangible benefit of having children—and therefore the value of procreative sex—is very important. Thus, a social ethic that promotes more freely available sex undercuts pro-life women two ways: it limits their abilities to get into a marriage in the first place, and it undermines the social value placed on their presence once within a marriage.

For pro-choice women, the situation is reversed. Because they have access to "male" resources such as education and income, they have far less reason to believe that the basic reason for sexuality is to produce children. They plan to have small families anyway, and they and their husbands come from and have married into a social class in which small families are the norm. For a number of overlapping reasons, therefore, pro-choice women believe that the value of sex is not primarily procreative: pro-choice women value the ability of sex to promote human intimacy more (or at least more frequently) than they value the ability of sex to produce babies. But they hold this view because they can afford to. When they bargain for marriage, they use the same resources that they use in the labor market: upper-class status, an education very similar to a man's, side-by-side participation in the man's world, and, not least, a salary that substantially increases a family's standard of living.

It is true, therefore, that pro-life people are "anti-sex." They value sex, of course, but they value it for its tra-ditional benefits (babies) rather than for the benefits that pro-choice people associate with it (intimacy). Pro-life people really do want to see "less" sexuality—or at least less open and socially unregulated sexuality—because they think it is morally wrong, they think it distorts the meaning of sex, and they feel that it *threatens the basis on which their own marital bargains are built.*

These differences in social background also explain why the majority of pro-life people we interviewed were opposed to "artificial" contraception, and had chosen to use natural family planning (NFP), the modern-day version of the "rhythm method." To be sure, since NFP is a "morally licit" form of fertility control for Catholics, and many pro-life activists are very orthodox. Catholics, NFP is attractive on those grounds alone. But as a group, Catholics are increasingly using contraception in patterns very similar to those of their non-Catholic peers. Furthermore, many non-Catholic pro-life activists told us they used NFP. Opposition to contraception, therefore, and its corollary, the use of NFP, needs to be explained as something other than simple obedience to church dogma.

Given their status as traditional women who do not work outside of the home, the choice of NFP as the preferred method of fertility control is a rational one because NFP enhances their power and status as women. The NFP users we talked with almost uniformly stated that men respect women more when they are using NFP and that the marriage relationship becomes more like a honeymoon. Certain social factors in the lives of pro-life women suggest why this may be so. Because NFP requires abstinence during the fertile period, one effect of using it is that *sex becomes a relatively scarce resource.* Rather than something that is simply there—and taken for granted—sex be-comes something that disappears from the relationship for regular periods of time. Therefore, NFP creates incentives for husbands to be close and intimate with their wives. The more insecure a woman and the less support she feels from her husband, the more reasonable it is for her to want to lengthen the period of abstinence to be on the safe side.§ The increase in power and status that NFP affords a woman in a traditional marriage was clearly recognized by the activists who use NFP, as these two quotations suggest:

> The rhythm [method] is the most freeing thing a woman can have, if you want me to tell you the honest-to-God truth. Because if she's married to someone that she loves, and she ought to be, then you know [when she abstains] she's got a romance time, she's got a time when she doesn't have to say she has a headache. He's just got to know, hey, either we're going to have another baby and you're going to pay for it or we're going to read our books tonight. And once in a while we're going to get to read our books, that's the way I look at it. I think it's wonderful, I really do, it might not sound too romantic to people, but it is, this is super romantic.

> You know, if you have filet mignon every day, it becomes kind of disinteresting. But if you have to plan around this, you do some things. You study, and you do other things during the fertile part of the cycle. And the husband and wife find out how much they can do in the line of expressing love for one another in other ways, other than genital. And some people can really express a lot of love and do a lot of touching and be very relaxed. Maybe others would find that they can only do a very little touching because they might be stimulated. And so they would have to find out where their level was. But they can have a beautiful relationship.

NFP also creates an opportunity for both husbands and wives to talk about the wife's fertility so that once again, something that is normally taken for granted can be focused on and valued. Folk wisdom has it that men and women use sexuality in different ways to express their feelings of caring and intimacy: men give love in order to get sex and women give sex in order to get love. If there is some truth to this stereotype (and both popular magazines and that rich source of sociological data, the Dear Abby column, suggest that there is), then it means that men and women often face confusion in their intimate dialogues with one another. Men wonder if their wives really want to have sex with them or are only giving it begrudgingly, out of a sense of "duty." Wives wonder if husbands really love them of merely want them for sexual relief. Natural Family Planning, by making sex periodically unavailable, puts some of these fears to rest. Some women said their husbands actually bring them flowers during the period of abstinence. Though husbands were much less forthcoming on this topic, it would seem reasonable that a woman who has been visibly reassured of her husband's caring for her might approach the renewal of sexual activity with the enthusiasm of someone who knows she is cared for as a whole person, to the husband's benefit and pleasure.

Furthermore, a few mutually discreet conversations during our interviews suggest that during abstinence at least some couples find ways of giving each other sexual pleasure that do not involve actual intercourse and hence the risk of pregnancy. Given traditional patterns of female socialization into sexuality and the fact that pro-life women are both traditional and devout women, these periods of mutual caressing may be as satisfying as intercourse for some women and even more satisfying than intercourse for others.¶

---

§ One NFP counselor described a case to me in which a woman found herself unavailable for sex an average of twenty-five days a month in what seemed a deliberate attempt to use sex to control a spouse's behavior. But the interpretation of oneself as fertile (and hence sexually unavailable unless the spouse wishes to risk the arrival of another child) need not be either calculating or conscious. The more insecure a woman is in her marriage the more insecure she may be about interpreting her fertility signs, both because the insecurity in her marriage translates into a more general insecurity and because she may wish to err "on the safe side" if she is worried about the effects of a pregnancy on a shaky relationship.

¶ In short, these interviews were describing both "petting" and oral sex. Feminist literature has called to our attention the fact that traditional notions about sexuality are "male-centered": it is assumed that there will be insertion and that there will be a male ejaculation. Ironically, NFP—the birth control method preferred by the devout, traditional women we interviewed—may come very close to achieving the feminist ideal. Under NFP, the "rules" of "regular" sex are suspended, and each couple must discover for themselves what feels good. For a generation of women who were raised when long periods of "necking" and

The different life circumstances and experiences of pro-life and pro-choice people therefore intimately affect the ways they look at the moral and social dilemmas of contraception. The settings of their lives, for example, suggest that the psychological side benefits of NFP, which do so much to support pro-life values during the practice of contraception, are sought in other ways by pro-choice people. Pro-choice people are slightly older when they marry, and the interviews strongly suggest that they have a considerably more varied sexual experience than pro-life people on average; the use of NFP to discover other facets of sexual expression is therefore largely unnecessary for them. Moreover, what little we know about sexual practices in the United States (from the Kinsey Report) suggests that given the different average levels of education and religious devoutness in the two groups, such sexual activities as "petting" and oral-genital stimulation may be more frequently encountered among pro-choice people to begin with.**

The life circumstances of the two sides suggest another reason why NFP is popular among pro-life people but not seriously considered by pro-choice people. Pro-choice men and women act on their belief that men and women are equal not only because they have (or should have) equal rights but also because they have substantially similar life experiences. The pro-choice women we met have approximately the same kinds of education as their husbands do, and many of them have the same kinds of jobs—they are lawyers, physicians, college professors, and the like. Even those who do not work in traditionally male occupations have jobs in the paid labor market and thus share common experiences. They and their husbands share many social resources in common: they both have some status outside the home, they both have a paycheck, and they both have a set of peers and friends located in the work world rather than in the family world. In terms of the traditional studies of family power, pro-choice husbands and wives use the same bargaining chips and have roughly equal amounts of them.

Pro-choice women, therefore, value (and can afford) an approach to sexuality that, by sidelining reproduction, diminishes the differences between men and women; they can do this *because they have other resources on which to build a marriage*. Since their value is intimacy and since the daily lives of men and women on the pro-choice side are substantially similar, intimacy in the bedroom is merely an extension of the intimacy of their larger world.

Pro-life women and men, by contrast, tend to live in "separate spheres." Because their lives are based on a social and emotional division of labor where each sex has its appropriate work, to accept contraception or abortion would devalue the one secure resource left to these women: the private world of home and hearth. This would be disastrous not only in terms of status but also in terms of meaning: if values about fertility and family are not essential to a marriage, what supports does a traditional marriage have in times of stress? To accept highly effective contraception, which actually and symbolically subordinates the role of children in the family to other needs and goals, would be to cut the ground of meaning out from under at least one (and perhaps both) partners' lives. Therefore, contraception, which sidelines the reproductive capacities of men and women, is both useless and threatening to pro-life people.

The Core of the Debate

In summary, women come to be pro-life and pro-choice activists as the end result of lives that center around different definitions of motherhood. They grow up with a belief about the nature of the embryo, so events in their lives lead them to believe that the embryo is a unique person, or a fetus; that people are intimately tied to their biological roles, or that these roles are but a minor part of life; that motherhood is the most important and satisfying role open to a woman, or that motherhood is only one of several roles, a burden when defined as the only role. These beliefs and

---

"petting" occurred before—and often instead of—intercourse, NFP may provide a welcome change from genitally centered, male-oriented sexual behavior to more diffuse body-focused "female" forms of sexual expression.

** Kinsey's data suggest that for males the willingness to engage in oral-genital or manual-genital forms of sexual expression is related to education: the more educated an individual, the more likely he is to have "petted" or engaged in oral sex (Alfred Kinsey, *Sexual Behavior in the Human Male*, pp. 337–81, 535–37). For females, the patterns are more complicated. Educational differences among women disappear when age at marriage is taken into account. But as Kinsey notes: "Among the females in the sample, the chief restraint on petting … seems to have been the religious tradition against it." The more devout a woman, the less likely she is to have ever petted (Kinsey, *Sexual Behavior in the Human Female*, pp. 247–48).

values are rooted in the concrete circumstances of women's lives—their educations, incomes, occupations, and the different marital and family choices they have made along the way—and they work simultaneously to shape those circumstances in turn. Values about the relative place of reason and faith, about the role of actively planning for life versus learning to accept gracefully life's unknowns, of the relative satisfactions inherent in work and family—all of these factors place activists in a specific relationship to the larger world and give them a specific set of resources with which to confront that world.

The simultaneous and ongoing modification of both their lives and their values by each other finds these activists located in a specific place in the social world. They are financially successful or they are not. They become highly educated or they do not. They become married and have a large family, or they have a small one. And at each step of the way, both their values and their lives have undergone either ratification or revision.

Pro-choice and pro-life activists live in different worlds, and the scope of their lives, as both adults and children, fortifies them in their belief that their own views on abortion are the more correct, more moral, and more reasonable. When added to this is the fact that should "the other side" win, one group of women will see the very real devaluation of their lives and life resources, it is not surprising that the abortion debate has generated so much heat and so little light.

Abortion in American Medicine

A Recent History

By Lori R. Freedman

In 1995, Dr. Jane Hodgson, abortion provider and heroine in the movement to legalize abortion, wrote an editorial in the *British Medical Journal* reflecting on the period of legalized abortion in the United States. In it she lamented the problems that plagued abortion care-problems that, unlike antiabortion activism, were fostered within American medicine itself:

> The public should have been caught by medical leaders for the past 22 years that abortion is a necessary surgical service that should be available to whoever needs it. Abortion clinics should have been encouraged to occupy space in the large professional medical buildings, surrounded by other specialties, or, even better yet, to seek the protection of anonymity within hospital walls. Instead they have been forced into isolation as freestanding clinics. Removed from the mainstream of medical practice, they are more vulnerable to violence and harassment and less accessible to students and residents for the purposes of medical education. (Hodgson 1995: 548)

Dr. Hodgson's words represent the very heart of a prominent pro-choice argument for the integration of abortion services into mainstream health care. Integrationists want to see the medical profession use its muscle to protect and normalize abortion care. Yet, although increases in abortion training since Hodgson wrote her editorial have successfully changed the medical culture of some academic medical settings, little has changed in the overall organization of abortion services. This chapter examines the medical context of abortion practice since *Roe v. Wade*—both how the marginalization of abortion services came about, and solutions advanced by pro-choice advocates and medical constituencies to bring abortion in from the periphery.

Medical leaders have been present and influential in all major stages in U.S. abortion history, including the criminalization of abortion during the nineteenth century, the Illegal practice of abortion during the twentieth century, the legalization of abortion in 1973, and the persistent "abortion wars" that have followed. In each of these stages, the medical profession became interested in abortion at times when it assisted the professionalization project—that is, when it could be used to help legitimize its claims to power. Thus, abortion care has not always been "untouchable" by the mainstream. However, given the larger threats to medical autonomy after abortion became legal, abortion services seemed to garner support from mainstream medical associations only at moments when medical autonomy was threatened. Through examination of significant moments of abortion turf grabbing

---

Lori R. Freedman, "Abortion in American Medicine: A Recent History," *Willing and Unable: Doctors' Constraints in Abortion Care*, pp. 20–36. Copyright © 2010 by Vanderbilt University Press. Reprinted with permission.

and guarding, one can see that not only is the medical profession's development important to the history of abortion, but abortion is important to the history of the medical profession.

American medicine's relationship to abortion has been one marked by long-standing lethargy (Hodgson 1995), deep ambivalence (Joffe 1995), and even intentional avoidance (Halfmann 2003). Such characterizations should be unsurprising, as American medicine is not a monolithic entity. It is composed of disparate professionals with different political and religious leanings. However, the net effect of the medical profession's noncommittal orientation toward abortion care has been to thwart efforts by abortion rights advocates within medicine to legitimize abortion as a normal reproductive health need. Since abortion was legalized in 1973, the lack of mainstream institutional and organizational support for it (Joffe, Anderson, and Steinauer 1998; Joffe 1995) has ultimately resulted in the marginalization of abortion care into freestanding abortion clinics served by politically motivated physicians. Heated contention around abortion has surfaced within the medical profession periodically over the years, and as this book demonstrates, mainstream medical settings have responded by avoiding involvement with abortion whenever possible. Such avoidance might not be significant if abortion were not one of the most common surgical procedures performed on women of reproductive age (DeFrances and Hall 2007; Jones et al. 2008).

When those in the medical profession have not avoided the discussion of abortion, their positions on it have taken different forms. The most consistent message has been, "no one but us should do it." The medical profession has exerted considerable effort toward ensuring that abortion stay under the domain of physicians—and not the midwives of the nineteenth century or the "back-alley butchers" of the twentieth. The twenty-first-century struggle under way involves midlevel providers working through sanctioned legal and medical channels for the right to provide abortions (not always under the supervision of physicians) in order to expand the base of abortion providers.

Regardless of medicine's interest in maintaining abortion turf, recent decades witnessed a steady decrease in the number of physicians providing abortion in their private practices and hospitals and increased consolidation of abortion services into the socially insulated settings of abortion clinics and academic teaching programs. Although specialized abortion clinics, which provide 93 percent of abortions (Jones et al. 2008), are known to provide efficient and competent care, they are largely segregated from mainstream medicine and reflect the intense marginalization of the stigmatized, uphill battle of abortion practice. The physicians who do the majority of the abortion work in the United States often sacrifice the rest of the skills for which they were trained because multiple forces limit their ability to straddle both the world of mainstream medicine and the world of abortion care.

The Marginalization of Legal Abortion (1973–1985)

In 1973 *Roe v. Wade* legalized abortion nationally, and American medicine was faced with the job of determining how abortion care would be delivered. Had abortion been like any other procedure, without the moral tensions and gender politics that surround it, it would have been one more surgery that physicians would add to their repertoire to be scheduled in hospitals or sometimes done in their offices. If abortion had been legalized during our current era of hyperspecialized medicine, perhaps an outpatient model would have arisen regardless of the politics, but this trend in medicine had not become the norm until at least a decade later. Because abortion is (and has always been) wrapped in such contentious politics, it became an inadvertent trailblazer modeling specialization in outpatient care.

Outpatient abortion services rapidly expanded in the early to mid-1970s. While only thirteen thousand legal abortions were reported to the CDC for the year 1969 {Lindheim 1979), only three years after legalization 1.2 million procedures were reported (Ventura et al. 2000). Regardless of the fact that abortion quickly became and remained extraordinarily common, it was not seamlessly integrated into mainstream medical practice or education. After the *Roe* decision repealed abortion laws, hospitals did not increase their abortion services. Studies from the CDC and Alan Guttmacher Institute (which is now a major authority on national and international reproductive public health research and statistics, founded by the aforementioned physician activist) showed that in the aftermath of *Roe* a minority of doctors and hospitals were involved with abortion care (Jaffe, Lindheim, and Lee 1981: 32). Instead, abortion increasingly took place in clinics modeled after Preterm (one of the first large-scale abortion services, established in Washington, D.C., in 1971) and other legalized abortion services established in states that had already legalized abortion a few years before *Roe*. Typically, such clinics were physically removed from other medical institutions and specialized in abortion with counseling geared toward the social issues surrounding women's experiences with abortion similar to the one Carole Joffe's ethnography documented in the late 1970s (Joffe 1986).

A 1976 study of the responses of major medical associations to the change in abortion law found that twenty-two of the thirty-six responding groups, including the Association of American Medical Colleges, the Joint Commission on Accreditation of Hospitals, and the National Board of Medical Examiners, provided no guidelines regarding the standards of abortion care or recommendations that would normally be expected under such circumstances of major medical policy change (Jaffe, Lindheim, and Lee 1981:46). Therefore, abortion was not sanctioned as "normal" by these organizations, thus further challenging the legitimacy of abortion services.

The most influential physician organization, the AMA, had treated abortion as a low-priority issue during the legalization process. In this they lagged behind medical organizations, such as the American Public Health Association (APHA) and the American College of Obstetrics and Gynecology (ACOG), in demonstrating support for legalization, even declining to submit an amicus brief directly requested by *Roe v. Wade* attorneys (Halfmann 2003). AMA policymakers told Drew Halfmann (2003), who researched abortion policy trajectories in the United States and Britain, that abortion had not been a high priority around the time of *Roe* because of pressing issues related to soaring health care and malpractice costs and the newly emerging precursors to managed care. Statements made by the AMA on abortion were oriented toward protecting physicians' rights to abstain from performing abortions.

Indeed, the *Roe* decision itself was focused more on ensuring the autonomy of physicians than on ensuring the autonomy of women. The justices who authored the decision intentionally abdicated responsibility to physicians for the larger ethical and moral questions around abortion (Hunter 2006). They did this by insisting that the law protect the privacy of the patient-physician relationship, consistent with earlier contraceptive legislation. The justices held that members of the medical profession possessed health expertise, including the unique ability to decide when an abortion should be performed, and were therefore beyond the purview of legislation. The justices valued medical authority and regarded medicine as a body that should govern itself free from state influence (Hunter 2006). In this way, the legal opinion reflected the professional autonomy that physicians still enjoyed at that time and entrusted physicians, rather than pregnant women, with the moral authority to evaluate the necessity of abortion in each case.

Regardless of abortion's newfound legal status, physicians who had been providing abortions illegally were not readily absorbed into academic departments or residencies to share their skills after *Roe* passed (Joffe 1995). Instead, they remained associated with pre-*Roe* "back-alley butchers" and the controversy surrounding the legalization of abortion and received little support from the preeminent medical organizations. In Carole Joffe's interviews with physicians who provided abortion before and after legalization, providers recounted experiences of being denied surgical privileges at hospitals, skipped over for anticipated medical leadership positions, and excluded from medical societies (Joffe 1995). During these critical early years, academic institutions conducted little training or research in freestanding clinics, and prominent physicians rarely devoted time to working in them (Joffe, Anderson, and Steinauer 1998).

Over the decades since *Roe*, hospital abortion services have steadily decreased. In comparison to the way birth was subsumed and medicalized by the medical profession (Reissman 1998; Sullivan and Weitz 1988), abortion experienced almost the opposite trajectory. Abortion turf seemed to have lost its appeal as it was gradually excised from mainstream medicine, leading to the near-total segregation of abortion care to freestanding clinics. Although in 1976, hospital-based clinics accounted for two-thirds of all abortion providers and one-third of all abortion procedures (Forrest, Tietze, and Sullivan 1978), in 2005 they accounted for just one-third of providers and performed only 5 percent of abortion procedures (Jones et al. 2008). With only 2 percent of abortions taking place in physicians' offices, more than 9; percent of abortion procedures in 2005 took place in specialized abortion clinics dedicated almost exclusively to abortion and contraceptive services (Jones et al. 2008).

In summary, upon the rapid expansion of demand for abortion services after legalization, mainstream medicine largely avoided the job, and specialized abortion clinics arose to meet the need. Major medical associations and regulatory bodies were quiet during abortion policy change and implementation. In avoiding responsibility for abortion care, the American medical profession conveyed to those performing and seeking abortions that it was not sanctioned, normal medical work and that physicians were not professionally obligated to provide abortions.

The Consequences of Isolated Abortion Practice

Marginalization has had detrimental consequences for abortion care. While freestanding abortion clinics were (and still are) generally efficient at delivering quality reproductive health services, their visibility and isolation became a liability during the Reagan-Bush era with the rise of the loud and at times violent antiabortion movement. From 1977 to 2009, 41 bombings and 175 arson incidents were reported to the police, along with several hundred incidents of burglary, stalking, bomb threats, and anthrax threats. Since 1993, there have been eight murders and seventeen attempted murders of abortion clinic workers and physicians. Clinics have been regularly picketed, with patients and staff members harassed on their way in and out. Protesters successfully popularized imagery of dismembered fetuses on their signs. Ultimately, the antiabortion movement made enormous gains through media portrayals, violence, and obstructive theatrics. Faye Ginsburg, an ethnographer of abortion clinic life, writes about the violence at its peak, "This sense of marginalization and even danger was made stunningly apparent between March 1993 and December 1994 when five people-abortion doctors, clinic staff, and volunteers—were murdered by antiabortion extremists" (Ginsburg 1998: x). In 1994, as a response to this elevation of violence, the Freedom of Access to Clinic Entrances (FACE) Act was passed by the U.S. Congress and signed into law by President Bill Clinton. This provided legal protection to clinics and some degree of deterrence, as the incidence of violence and harassment notably declined.

In the 1990s and 2000s, legislative attacks surpassed violent ones as a means of disrupting or deterring abortion provision. Abortion has been in the courts continuously since it was legalized, as individual lawsuits were brought to whittle away at abortion rights. *Planned Parenthood of Southeastern Pennsylvania v. Casey* in 1992 was particularly significant because it ruled that state authority supersedes the physician authority granted in *Roe*. Hence, it allowed states to create laws affecting patient care. Each year hundreds of bills related to abortion care are filed across the country (Connolly 2005; Donohoe 2005). As of September 2009, thirty-two states have banned the use of state funds for abortion. Specific counseling is mandated in seventeen states, often to inform women of purported consequences of abortion that have been discredited in the scientific literature (breast cancer, mental illness). Twenty-four states require waiting periods, usually twenty-four hours, between the counseling appointment and the procedures. Parental consent and involvement laws exist in thirty-five states.'

Furthermore, a trend of what pro-choice organizations call TRAP (Targeted Regulation of Abortion Providers) laws followed in thirty-three states. These are laws designed to make abortion provision prohibitively cumbersome, and they generally apply only to abortion service facilities. While some were purportedly passed to make abortion safer (even though abortion clinics in general have a superb safety record), examples such as laws pertaining to the landscaping of the facility and some architectural requirements seem only to add cost with little benefit to patients (Rose 2007). Some TRAP laws require that registered nurses carry out functions for which, abortion providers claim, nurses are overqualified—even though nurses are in short supply (CRR 2007). Other TRAP laws authorize unannounced inspections of facilities when patients are present, compromising patient confidentiality (CRR 2007).

The isolation of freestanding clinics has been a problem in other ways beyond susceptibility to antiabortion intimidation by protests, violence, and TRAP laws. As early as 1979, abortion researcher Barbara Lindheim articulated her concerns about how confinement to this setting might compromise abortion services and education: "In spite of the generally excellent record of clinics, the estrangement of mainstream health providers from the provision of abortion is of concern. It hinders better integration of health services and makes the development of adequate referral and informational resources of abortion more difficult. By isolating some abortion providers, it decreases opportunities for the professional interaction vital for continuing education and professional self-regulation" (Lindheim 1979: 289). Just as Lindheim suggested, providers have had to advance abortion practice and research in isolation. In order to address problems related to such marginalization, abortion rights activists, including physicians, created the National Abortion Federation (NAF) in 1977. NAF offers practical support and holds conferences every year for abortion providers to share technical knowledge, research findings, and policy concerns. NAF fills the gap left by research institutions and governmental bodies that are normally involved with other medical and public health issues.

Since the 1990s, abortion rights activists and organizations have worked to undo this marginalization and all of its accompanying problems. Groups such as Physicians for Reproductive Choice and Health and Medical Students for Choice especially have called for integration of abortion into the rest of women's health care by mainstream medicine. These integrationists, like Jane Hodgson, argue that physicians could absorb some of the abortion clinic load into their general practices and effectively disperse the targets of violence, increase the number of abortion providers, and destigmatize the practice of abortion.

Integration has not been easy for a host of reasons, some of which are discussed in great detail in this book. A meta-theme affecting all aspects of medical practice, which lacks sufficient recognition by the integration movement, is the restructuring of medicine since the advent of managed care. Studies of physician employment characteristics have consistently demonstrated a trend toward larger group practices as well as significant increases in physicians working as wage and salaried employees without ownership stakes in the group, hospital, or HMO. The trend away from individual and small group ownership has reduced physicians' autonomy over what they do in their practices.

Even when managing bodies have no restrictions on abortion, the low cost of abortion is a further deterrent to integration. The cost of abortion has been suppressed since the 1970s because of the high efficiency of specialized clinics (some for-profit ones are derogatorily called "abortion mills"). Additionally, a combination of pro-choice philanthropy and volunteerism has subsidized abortion costs in nonprofit clinics in order to make abortion more accessible and affordable for patients. Thus insurance reimbursements are low, and physicians (or their business managers) feel they "lose" money by performing abortions when compared with what they would earn doing other procedures that take the same amount of time and resources. Thus, abortion clinics fit perfectly with the ever-increasing trend under managed care to contract out specialized work, saving managing bodies money. Therefore, under managed care, physicians (outside of abortion clinics and academia) often lack control over whether to include abortion in their practices for financial reasons in addition to ideological ones.

Abortion rights advocates, however, hopeful that motivated physicians can overcome these constraints, have focused on how to increase the supply of *willing* providers. In particular, medical student and resident training became a strategic focus of institutional (as opposed to grassroots) abortion rights activism during the 1990s, as it seemed the most clearly modifiable factor within medicine. Abortion training was not strong in residency curriculums after legalization, and it had become increasingly sparse as antiabortion controversy and violence escalated. Between 1985 and 1991, the proportion of ob-gyn residency programs that routinely offered training in first-trimester abortions decreased from 23 percent (Darney et al. 1987) to 12 percent (MacKay and MacKay 1995). Given that abortion was more common than hysterectomy, sterilization, or C-section (ACS 1993; Owings and Kozak 1998) during this period, the dearth of training in abortion care in ob-gyn residency programs became a concern to a wider audience beyond abortion rights advocates, most notably the Accreditation Council of Graduate Medical Education (ACGME).

Of additional concern, many physicians who had dedicated their careers to abortion since *Roe* were retiring, and in the increasingly hostile political climate, few were filling their shoes. In 1990, NAF organized a symposium to explore "key reasons underlying the lack of available abortion providers and to develop strategies to address this situation" (Joffe, .Anderson, and Steinauer 1998: 323). For the first rime ever, representatives were sent to a NAF event from ACOG (which cosponsored the symposium), the ACGME, and the Council on Resident Education in Obstetrics and Gynecology. The symposium concluded that several factors were contributing to the abortion provider shortage: "Among those noted were the 'graying' of abortion providers who had come of age in the pre-*Roe* era and had seen the ravages of illegal abortion, increasing anti-abortion harassment and violence, inadequate economic incentives for abortion work, and the social stigma and professional isolation that commonly accompanied abortion work" (Joffe, Anderson, and Steinauer 1998: 323). The professional isolation noted here refers to the fact that abortion providers frequently give up mainstream medicine (often not voluntarily) to work in abortion clinics. This means they sacrifice the majority of what they were trained for, such as preventive care, birth, and gynecological surgeries. Full-spectrum care necessitates working in a hospital setting and interacting with diverse personnel in addition to attending professional meetings with colleagues. Abortion clinic physicians, on the other hand, tend to have relatively less contact with other physicians.

Thus, at the same time that managed care redistributed power in U.S. medicine, abortion care suffered multiple blows. With abortion contention at its highest, antiabortion harassment, legislative attacks, increased professional isolation, and decreased abortion training in residency resulted in a declining provider base. The isolated, marginalized abortion services continued as such as they fit neatly into the newly dominating structure of medical subspecialization and outsourced care.

Mobilizing around Abortion: A Fight for Professional Authority

While the marginalization of abortion services has continued largely uncontested by the medical profession, three head-on conflicts over abortion regulation united major medical powers in recent years when medical authority has felt most threatened. These encounters to some extent represented a partisan political battle of pro-choice doctors against anti-abortion political constituents. But the ability of vocal pro-choice physicians to enlist wider support represents an unprecedented willingness of the professional associations to get involved and put their names behind abortion as an issue.

The first battle took place over training requirements. In 1995, after five years of research and consultation with residencies and other medical organizations, the ACGME approved new standards for residency education that would require training in abortion and the management of abortion-related complications, barring moral or religious objections from the individual resident or hospital. This unleashed a strong response from members of the U.S. Congress, who made every attempt to impede the new ACGME requirements. In a rare moment of medical mobilization, representatives from the AMA, ACOG, and a handful of other medical organizations defended the new standards (Joffe, Anderson, and Steinauer 1998). They were particularly vocal against governmental intrusion into the medical profession's private regulatory bodies. On June 14, 1995, a representative of ACOG, Dr. Frank Ling, argued before the House of Representatives: "Congressional override of the ACGME requirements would represent an unprecedented involvement in the private educational accreditation process. Never before has such an override of education standards been proposed. ... Congress is simply not equipped to make decisions about what is or is not appropriate medical care and training" (cited in Joffe, Anderson, and Steinauer 1998:326).

Accustomed to self-regulation in this regard, the major medical groups saw this as a flagrant intrusion of politics into their domain. The timing of this battle is interesting in that it occurred at the height of discontent with and moral outrage about managed care. Thus, while the medical profession had lost much control around how medicine is practiced, it held tightly onto its relatively intact ability to regulate its educational and training requirements. The ACGME mandate took effect January 1, 1996, but Congress made that mandate difficult to enforce by passing the Coats Amendment to the Omnibus Consolidated Rescissions and Appropriations Act of 1996 (Public Law 104-134), which ensures that "residency programs will be deemed accredited by the federal government, or any state or local government that receives federal funds, even if programs fail to comply with abortion training accreditation requirements" (Foster, van Dis, and Steinauer 2003:1777). Additionally, several states passed legislation prohibiting elective abortion in publicly supported institutions, which made it necessary for their residency programs to train residents at off-site abortion clinics to stay in compliance with the ACGME requirements (Foster, van Dis, and Steinauer 2003). Ironically, the fight with Congress over the ACGME mandate presented a professionalization opportunity similar to the one provided by the nineteenth-century criminalization of abortion. While a century earlier physicians rallied behind the campaign to criminalize abortion to build professional authority, here, too, in 1995 physicians rallied around abortion to strengthen their power, although they were on the opposite side of the issue.

The second case of medical mobilization around abortion took place a decade later. Major medical associations came together to oppose a Supreme Court ban on "partial-birth" abortion, a specific technique of second-trimester abortion that its opponents construed as inhumane (it is sometimes called D&X, for dilation and extraction, in the medical community). In this case, medical professionals strongly objected to governmental regulation of the surgical technique. Specifically, what was at stake was the fact that the law had no health or life exemption for the pregnant woman, meaning that the procedure would be banned even if a physician believed it to be the safest way to terminate a pregnancy for a particular case. ACOG offered a statement that in some cases D&X "may be the best or most appropriate procedure … to save the life or preserve the health of a woman," and several experienced abortion providers testified thus *(Gonzales v. Carhart* 2007). However, antiabortion physicians selected by the Bush administration argued both that it was inhumane and that it was never necessary. Interestingly, these physicians had never performed such abortions because of their political positions on the issue, but the testimonies of physicians who were experts in abortion care were deemed too biased to be credible, making for a particularly problematic construction of expertise characteristic of the Bush era. Bioethics lawyer Alta Charo concluded in an editorial: "The Court then argued that since medical opinion is divided about D&X, Congress has the authority to invade the doctor-patient relationship and substitute blanket judgment for individualized medical judgment concerning the best care for a particular patient. Although regulation of the drugs and devices marketed for use in medical care has long been accepted, legislative restriction of doctors' individual medical judgment is far more contentious" (Charo 2007: 2127). It is noteworthy that this nearly scathing response was found in arguably the most prestigious medical journal in the United States, the *New England Journal of Medicine*. It was presented in a special edition with other like-minded editorials, including one entitled "The Intimidation of American Physicians: Banning Partial-Birth Abortion" (Greene 2007). Dr. Michael Greene writes: "The decision to pursue a second-trimester abortion is never taken lightly and usually results only after anguished discussions among the patient, her loved ones, and her health care providers … the last thing a provider needs is to have to worry that the procedure could potentially evolve into a criminal act if a fetus in breech presentation should slip out intact through a partially dilated cervix. But this is exactly the situation created by the partial-birth abortion bill" (Greene 2007: 2128). Greene was not alone; other physicians shared his fears of accidentally breaking the law and facing prosecution. One physician I interviewed panicked when scheduling a second-trimester abortion procedure at her hospital, scared that she might be prosecuted as she second-guessed the distinction between a "normal" second-trimester abortion and a "partial-birth" abortion (see a more detailed account in Chapter 5), while another worried that "they could manipulate the wording to get rid of first-trimesters too." Thus, the ban resulted in the insecurity of physicians vis-a-vis the government in a way that is reminiscent of earlier years of illegal abortion practice.

The third and most recent incident was sparked by an ACOG (2007) report entitled "The Limits of Conscience Refusal in Reproductive Medicine." It relates to "refusal" or "conscience" clauses in legislation that have popped up throughout the United States. These clauses protect both individuals and institutions from legal liability when they abstain from abortion provision or a variety of things they find objectionable (contraception, sterilization, emergency contraception, etc.). The "right to refuse" has been extended in practice to giving referrals and information as well (Curlin et al. 2007). The ACOG report stated, "Physicians and other health care professionals have the duty to refer patients in a timely manner to other providers if they do not feel that they can in conscience provide the standard reproductive service that patients request" (ACOG 2007: 5). In doing this, ACOG took a firm stance on a politically inflammatory matter. Its claims assert that physicians have a professional obligation to their patients related to contested aspects of reproductive health care.

The report generated a response from Health and Human Services Secretary Mike Leavitt—former governor of Utah appointed by George W. Bush in 2005—in the form of a press release in which he made explicit his disappointment in ACOG's new policy, going so far as to call on the American Board of Obstetrics and Gynecology (ABOG) responsible for physician certification and licensing to reject the policy and "protect the conscience rights of physicians." In a letter Leavitt wrote to ABOG that was included with the press release, he stated, "I am concerned that the actions taken by ACOG and ABOG could result in the denial or revocation of Board certification of a physician who—but for his or her refusal, for example, to refer a patient for an abortion—would be certified." Thus, in December 2008, in the final weeks of Bush's presidency, he signed into law an additional "conscience" protection for health-care practitioners who violate ACOG's referral requirement policy. Seven states filed lawsuits against

Health and Human Services as a response, and soon after President Barack Obama took office, his administration began working to revoke the Bush rule, citing concerns over health-care access (Sorrell 2009).

These three incidences mark significant points of recent contact between governing and medical authorities over abortion. While the politics of abortion are the driving force behind these debates, it is notable that the medical profession has had relatively little interest in direct involvement with abortion care until the government threatened medical autonomy. In these cases, physicians did not overtly embrace the politics of reproductive rights, but they did argue on behalf of the quality of abortion care. These battles represented something vital to the profession, their last vestige: control over the content (if not the business) of medicine.

Today: Abortion Training and the Provider Shortage

Finding physicians who are willing to provide abortions in the current political and medical context can be challenging in some parts of the country, especially rural areas. Abortion rights advocates within medicine have focused on improving abortion training in residency programs because increasing the supply of physicians means improving access to abortion for patients. Since the ACGME mandated abortion training in residency in 1996, a study showed that 46 percent of residencies-up from 12 percent before the mandate (MacKay and MacKay 1995)—claim to offer "routine training" in abortion (Almeling, Tews, and Dudley 2000), but the same study showed such low rates of residents getting trained that it brought that study's definition of "routine training" into question (Landy and Steinauer 2001).

Routine training and *opt-out training* are terms used to indicate that abortion training is included within the normal curriculum of a residency program and that if a resident does not want to be trained in abortion care, he or she must actively choose not to participate. Although residency programs must comply with the ACGME mandate, most new programs appeared to be offering "opt-in" training, meaning that the resident would need to use his or her elective period to go to a local Planned Parenthood or other off-site outpatient clinic for training. Such abortion clinics can provide thorough training because of the high patient volume; however, when routine training in abortion is integrated into other hospital services, abortion may be viewed less politically and more as a normal part of a spectrum of ob-gyn services. This reasoning implies that the normative function of medical authority extends from residency to resident, not just from physician to patient. Indeed, a study of the effect of training on provision in one state found that "the more integrated and extensive the training, the more likely the graduate is to provide abortions" (Steinauer et al. 2003: 1163). This suggests two things: first, more abortion training makes residents more confident in their abortion skills, and second, more training normalizes the highly stigmatized and contested procedure. The former is expected, but seeing as abortion is a somewhat simple surgery compared with the many learned during residency, normalizing abortion seems to be the more significant accomplishment of increased training.

Recent years have witnessed a steady increase in both programs with routine (now up to 51 percent) and opt-out (39 percent) training (Eastwood et al. 2006) as well as increased resident participation in the abortion training (Steinauer et al. 2007). A national survey of ob-gyns regarding their experiences in abortion training during the 1990s showed that graduates trained after the ACGME requirements went into effect were more likely to perform abortions (Steinauer et al. 2007). This finding indicates that the official policy change (and the programmatic changes that resulted from it) increased their acceptance of abortion practice.

Regardless of improvements in training, the overall number of providers continues to decrease nationally, though the decline has slowed its pace. The number of providers declined by 14 percent from 1992 to 1996, 11 percent from 1996 to 2000, and only 2 percent from 2000 to 2005 (Jones et al. 2008). In 2005, 69 percent of metropolitan counties in the United States and 97 percent of nonmetropolitan counties had no abortion provider at all (Jones et al. 2008). Medication abortion—also known as the French abortion pill or RU-486, approved in 2000 for use in the United States—has slowly changed some of the culture of abortion care such that it now accounts for 13 percent of procedures (Jones et al. 2008), but the vast majority of these are performed in abortion clinics and not integrated into primary care or rural health care at the rates that pro-choice advocates initially hoped (Joffe and Weitz 2003; Shochet and Trussed 2008). Physicians are not in short supply for most urban abortion clinics, but rural clinics and those in conservative semi-urban areas struggle to find physicians and often rely on physicians who are willing to commute by airplane part-time. Therefore, the provider shortage is predominant in rural and conservative towns.

Summary

After *Roe v. Wade* legalized abortion in 1973, services expanded rapidly, but largely at the margins of medicine. Mainstream medicine had little response and grew decreasingly involved with abortion care, sending the message that abortion was not a normal part of women's health care, that it was political and separate. In its marginalization, abortion care was vulnerable to the ideological contention surrounding it, which brought harassment, legislative barriers to care, professional isolation, and little support for training new providers. At the same time, managed care was revolutionizing the structure of medicine and in the process decreasing physician autonomy such that physicians were less able to provide abortions within their general practices even if they wanted to. Finally, as a specialized service, the abortion clinic model fit neatly into the managed care model, which was increasingly contracting out specific services to save money.

By and large, major medical professional organizations were passive about how marginalization was affecting abortion services. However, they became active around abortion at key moments when conservative political attempts to suppress abortion affected the profession's ability to regulate the technical and educational content of medicine. In order to protect their ability to control the parameters of abortion training (ACGME mandate), surgical technique (partial-birth abortion), and professional obligation (limiting conscience clauses), medical associations were willing to involve themselves with abortion once again.

Pro-Life Nation

By Jack Hitt

It was a sunny midafternoon in a shiny new global-economy mall in San Salvador, the capital city of El Salvador, and a young woman I was hoping to meet appeared to be getting cold feet. She had agreed to rendezvous with a go-between not far from the Payless shoe store and then come to a nearby hotel to talk to me. She was an hour late. Alone in the hotel lobby, I was feeling nervous; I was stood up the day before by another woman in a similar situation. I had been warned that interviewing anyone who had had an abortion in El Salvador would be difficult. The problem was not simply that in this very Catholic country a shy 24-year-old unmarried woman might feel shame telling her story to an older man. There was also the criminal stigma. And this was why I had come to El Salvador: Abortion is a serious felony here for everyone involved, including the woman who has the abortion. Some young women are now serving prison sentences, a few as long as 30 years.

More than a dozen countries have liberalized their abortion laws in recent years, including South Africa, Switzerland, Cambodia and Chad. In a handful of others, including Russia and the United States (or parts of it), the movement has been toward criminalizing more and different types of abortions. In South Dakota the governor recently signed the most restrictive abortion-bill since the Supreme Court ruled in 1973, in *Roe* v. *Wade*, that state laws prohibiting abortion were unconstitutional. The South Dakota law, which its backers acknowledge is designed to test *Roe* v. *Wade* in the courts, forbids abortion, including those cases in which the pregnancy is a result of rape or incest. Only if an abortion is necessary to save the life of the mother is the procedure permitted. A similar though less restrictive bill is now making its way through the Mississippi Legislature.

In this new movement toward criminalization, El Salvador is in the vanguard. The array of exceptions that tend to exist even in countries where abortion is circumscribed—rape, incest, fetal malformation, life of the mother—don't apply in El Salvador. They were rejected in the late 1990's in a period after the country's long civil war ended. The country's penal system was revamped and its constitution was amended. Abortion is now absolutely forbidden in every possible circumstance. No exceptions.

There are other countries in the world that, like El Salvador, completely ban abortion, including Malta, Chile and Colombia. El Salvador, however, has not only a total ban on abortion but also an active law-enforcement apparatus—the police, investigators, medical spies, forensic vagina inspectors and a special division of the prosecutor's office responsible for Crimes Against Minors and Women, a unit charged with capturing, trying and incarcerating an unusual kind of criminal. Like the woman I was waiting to meet.

I was on my sixth cup of coffee when I spotted my contacts—two abortion rights advocates who work in the region and a local nurse who had heard this young woman's story. They entered the lobby surrounding another

Jack Hitt, "Pro-Life Nation," *The New York Times*; April 9, 2006. Copyright © 2006 by The New York Times. Reprinted with permission.

woman like Secret Service agents. A quick glance let me know that I shouldn't make a premature appearance. Even as I retreated to some large sofas, I could hear the Spanish flying—words of comfort, of being brave, of the importance that others understand what is happening in El Salvador. At last the retinue approached. I was not quite ready for what I saw. The woman, I had been told, lived in a hovel in a very poor part of the town. Somehow that had put a certain picture in my head. I don't know, call it sexism. I just didn't expect to see a tall and strikingly beautiful woman with the kind of big grin that could very well appear in one of those full-page ads you might see in an airline magazine inviting people to "Vacation in El Salvador!"

We chatted briefly about the one thing I knew we had in common—malls—before we went up to a quiet hotel room, where she and I could talk. One intermediary acted as our interpreter. I agreed to call her by her initials, D.C.; she is afraid to be identified by name, though she did agree to be photographed. (While it was impossible to confirm every detail of her story, I did later see legal records that corroborated her description of events.) D.C. sat down, and now that we were ready to talk about her experience, she started to cry. She wiped her eyes several times with a paper napkin. She spent a few minutes folding and twisting it. D.C. crossed her ankles and stared down at the shrinking napkin, now tightly compacted into a large pill. Then she began to tell me her story.

> *I worked in a clothing factory two years ago. I have a son, 7 years old. Well, when I found out I was pregnant, I didn't know what to do. I told my friend. She told me if I was going to have it, I needed to think about that. I had a child already. I told the father. He said he didn't want another child. He didn't want to deal with problems like this. My mother told me she would kick me out if I ever got pregnant again.*
>
> *I started talking to my friend. Every day was so hard. I cried, and I didn't do anything, I didn't want to see anybody, and I didn't sleep. My friend told me to go to a man, and he gave me some pills. I was two months pregnant He said that I could put them in my vagina. I did, and after that I just bled a couple of times. Two months more went by. I was still pregnant. I cried and didn't know what to do. When I was about four months along, my friend told me one of her friends lived near a house where there was a woman who did abortions. I felt so worried. I didn't know what to do, whether I should go talk to the woman. But then one day, I went.*

With the signing of the Chapultepec Agreements in Mexico in 1992, El Salvador's civil war came to an end. As the nation turned away from its violent years, there were calls from both sides of the political divide that it was time to re-examine certain social issues. One of them was abortion. The country's abortion law, like the law in most Latin American countries at the time, was already a near-ban with only a few exceptions, specifically in cases of rape, serious fetal malformation and grave risk to the mother's life. For decades, the law was rarely discussed, and enforced quietly and somewhat subjectively. Once the issue was raised in the political arena, though, Salvadorans discovered that a brand-new kind of discourse on abortion had emerged in Latin America.

In El Salvador, a mostly Catholic country, abortion first surfaced as a potent political issue in 1993, when conservative members of the Assembly proposed that Dec. 28, the Catholic Feast of the Holy Innocents, be declared a national day to remember the unborn. In 1995, the FMLN—the former guerrilla force that had transformed itself into the country's main left-wing party—supported a very different proposal in the National Assembly. The proposal addressed a variety of women's issues, including domestic violence and rape. It also contained a provision to extend the abortion exceptions to include cases in which the mother's mental health was threatened, even if her life was not. This liberalizing proposal was rejected, but it provoked a debate, which in turn had the effect of raising the political heat around the subject of abortion.

Also in 1995, Pope John Paul II appointed a new archbishop for San Salvador, Fernando Sáenz Lacalle. Archbishops in El Salvador inherit a potent history. During the civil war, many members of the clergy in El Salvador were proponents of liberation theology, a liberal—some would say radical—evangelical doctrine of social justice. The movement was despised by the country's right-wing leaders. In 1980, in a hospital chapel, Archbishop Óscar Arnulfo Romero, a proponent of liberation theology, was shot and killed by a right-wing death squad while celebrating Mass. His replacement, Arturo Rivera Damas, was also a supporter of liberation theology.

The pope's appointment of Lacalle 11 years ago brought to the Archdiocese of San Salvador a different kind of religious leader. Lacalle, an outspoken member of the conservative Catholic group Opus Dei, redirected the country's church politics. Lacalle's predecessors were just as firmly opposed to abortion as he was. What he brought to the country's anti-abortion movement was a new determination to turn that opposition into state legislation and a belief that the church should play a public role in the process. In 1997, conservative legislators in the Assembly introduced a bill that would ban abortion in all circumstances. The archbishop campaigned actively for its passage.

"The ban was part of a backlash," I was told by Luisa Cabal, the legal consultant for Latin America at the Center for Reproductive Rights, an abortion rights organization based in New York. The proposed bill, Cabal said, was a result of "the church's role in pushing for a conservative agenda." With the archbishop's vocal support of the ban and conservative groups fully energized, opposition soon became difficult. Any argument in favor of therapeutic abortion was met with a religious counterargument.

Julia Regina de Cardenal runs the Yes to Life Foundation in San Salvador, which provides prenatal care and job training to poor pregnant women. She was a key advocate for the passage of the ban. She argued that the existing law's exception for the life of the mother was outdated. As she explained to me, "There does not exist any case in which the life of the mother would be in danger, because technology has advanced so far." De Cardenal was particularly vehement in responding in print to her opponents. As she wrote in one Salvadoran newspaper column in 1997, "The Devil, tireless Prince of Lies, has tried and will continue to try to change our laws in order to kill our babies."

Positions on the strengthened ban essentially split along party lines, at least at first. "The majority of our leadership came out in opposition," Lorena Peña, an FMLN representative in the Assembly, told me. But the FMLN held only a minority of the seats in the 84-member Assembly, and they were unable to stop the bill. The proposal to ban all abortions passed the Assembly in 1997 and became the law of the country in April 1998.

"But that was not enough," de Cardenal later wrote in an article recounting the victory. In 1997, her foundation also proposed a constitutional amendment that would recognize the government's duty to protect life from the time of conception.

A proposed constitutional amendment in El Salvador has to pass two important votes. It must be accepted by a majority in one session of the Assembly and then, after a new election, ratified by a two-thirds vote in the next Assembly. During the first vote, in 1997, FMLN legislators stood against the amendment but they were outvoted, and the amendment passed the first round.

In January 1999, as the issue headed toward the second vote in the Assembly, Pope John Paul II visited Latin America. "The church must proclaim the Gospel of life and speak out with prophetic force against the culture of death," he declared in Mexico City. "May the continent of hope also be the continent of life!" De Cardenal says that the pope's visit re-energized supporters of the constitutional ban. As the vote neared, her group rolled out a series of radio ads in favor of the amendment and presented legislators with a petition of more than 500,000 signatures. At one demonstration, members of the group sprinkled the National Assembly with holy water. To punctuate her campaign, de Cardenal arranged to have two pregnant women come to the Assembly and have ultrasounds publicly performed on their fetuses.

The leadership of the FMLN, afraid that the party would be trounced in the coming elections if they were on the record as opposing the amendment, freed its deputies from their obligation to follow the party's position and urged them to vote with their consciences. When the final vote was taken, the amendment passed overwhelmingly.

The legislative battle and its outcome did not escape the attention of leaders of anti-abortion groups in the United States. Rev. Thomas J. Euteneuer, the head of Human Life International, based in Virginia, is intimately familiar with the campaign in El Salvador and says that there are lessons for Americans to learn from it. For one thing, as Euteneuer sees it, the Salvadoran experience shows that all moves to expand abortion rights are pushed through by "elite" institutions of government (the U.S. Supreme Court, for example); by contrast, Euteneuer contends, when the laws are tightened, a grass-roots campaign is inevitably responsible. "El Salvador is an inspiration," he told me recently, an important victory in what he called "the counterrevolution of conscience."

Today, Article 1 of El Salvador's constitution declares that the prime directive of government is to protect life from the "very moment of conception." The penal code detailing the Crimes Against the life of Human Beings in the First Stages of Development provides stiff penalties: the abortion provider, whether a medical doctor or a back-alley practitioner, faces 6 to 12 years in prison. The woman herself can get 2 to 8 years. Anyone who helps her can get 2 to 5 years. Additionally, judges have ruled that if the fetus was viable, a charge of aggravated homicide can be brought, and the penalty for the woman can be 30 to 50 years in prison.

> *D.C.: When we got to the woman's house, there was so much disorder. It was all a mess. We talked, and she felt my stomach and said: "Yeah, I can do it. Come back in four days." I asked how she would do it, and she said, with a probe.*
>
> *On that day, I came in and was told to lie down. It was not even a bed. There was just so much disorder. She asked me to take off my clothes, and she put a shirt on me. She came with a piece of cloth and put it underneath my nose, and I felt a little numb. She came back with a long wire, like a TV antenna. It was not like a doctor's instrument it was just a wire tube with another wire inside it. She put some oil on it and told me to breathe deeply.*
>
> *She put it in. And she was scraping around I was supposed to be asleep. But I felt pain. I told her it hurt. She said, "Yeah, we're almost done." But she kept scraping around, and I said: "No, no, stop. It's hurting me." Then she said, "It's done."*
>
> *She said I would have a fever and I should not go to the doctor or they would report me. That night everything was O.K. So I went to sleep.*

"Back-alley abortion" is a term that has long been part of the abortion debate. In the United States, in the years since *Roe v. Wade*, it has come to seem metaphorical, perhaps even hyperbolic, but it happens to conjure precisely D.C.'s experience. And it's easy in El Salvador to find plenty of evidence that D.C.'s story is neither isolated nor the worst case. A report by the Center for Reproductive Rights offers this grim list of tools used in clandestine abortions: "clothes hangers, iron bars, high doses of contraceptives, fertilizers, gastritis remedies, soapy water and caustic agents (such as car battery acid)." That list is meant to disgust a reader in the same way that imagery of mangled fetuses is meant to when employed by those who oppose abortion. But the criminalization of abortion in the modern age, in El Salvador at least, is not so simple as a grim return to the back alley. For the most part, the new law has not resulted in a spike in horror stories of painful and botched clandestine procedures.

To begin with, when a woman might face jail time for an abortion, she's less likely to discuss her pregnancy at all. According to a study on attempted suicide and teen pregnancy published last year by academics at the University of El Salvador, some girls who poison their wombs with agricultural pesticide (its efficacy being a Salvadoran urban legend) would rather report the cause of their resulting hospital visit as "attempted suicide" which is not as felonious a crime nor as socially unbearable as abortion. "They don't want to be interviewed about abortion," Irma Elizabeth Asencio, one of the study's authors, explained to me. "They know they have committed a crime."

Abortion as it exists in El Salvador today tends to operate on three levels. The well-off retain the "right to choose" that comes of simply having money. They can fly to Miami for an abortion, or visit the private office of a discreet and well-compensated doctor. Among the very poor, you can still find the back-alley world described by D.C. and the others who turn up in hospitals with damaged or lacerated wombs. Then there are the women in the middle; they often rely on home-brewed cures that are shared on the Internet or on a new underground railroad that has formed to aid them.

"I keep two telephones in my purse," I was told in El Salvador by one woman who wished not to be identified because her work is illegal. I'd heard of her through an abortion rights advocate, and I asked to meet her in person. "One phone is for work and personal matters," she went on to explain in fluent English. "The second one is for the other thing." Although she doesn't work directly in women's health care, her job keeps her traveling and in contact with people working for health groups and women's rights groups who do outreach throughout the country. "I would estimate that there are about 20 people who are working in different and specific places who have this phone number," she said. They pass it along when they think it is necessary.

And so when the phone rings, she has to decide whether the woman seeking an abortion is legitimate or not. On occasion, she has turned off the phone after a suspicious call. "You need to be careful, especially when the people who call are young people," she said. "One day they think one thing and the next day another thing. And they know your information." Her practice is first to find out the crucial facts of the pregnancy; then, if she decides she's willing to help, she calls a doctor she knows who lives in a neighboring country.

"When I'm calling the doctor, I never say on this telephone, 'Someone needs an abortion,'" she told me. "Rather, I might say, 'We have a situation here.' When we talk about the details, like how many weeks along she is, the doctor might ask me, 'What time is it?' I might say it's 8 o'clock, meaning the patient is eight weeks along." After all the details are worked out in code, the doctor flies in. The abortion—usually nonsurgical—is performed without charge.

"No one ever learns the doctor's name or where she's from," she said.

A doctor who works this underground circuit also agreed to meet me and discuss abortion. She seemed terrified the entire time we spoke. She constantly glanced around the cafe where we had coffee with an interpreter. She ended every paragraph with a plea not to reveal any details that might identify her. But she said she wanted to explain how abortions are done in El Salvador. Most women with some education or access to the Internet quickly learn about misoprostol, she said. It is an ulcer drug that, when inserted in the vagina, can provoke contractions and cause bleeding that looks, in an emergency room, just like a miscarriage.

"I show people how to put the misoprostol in and tell them that when they go to the hospital just to say, 'I started bleeding,'" this doctor explained. "There is no way that can be detected." The only problem, she went on to say, was that "some women go right to the hospital when there's initial staining." Then, if a doctor or nurse finds a half-dissolved pill during a pelvic exam, they are obliged to call the police.

According to nearly a dozen doctors and nurses I interviewed in San Salvador, there has been a decline in the incidence of harrowing coat-hanger/pesticide-type abortions in the time since the law was passed. (No official national statistics were available.) But the doctors I spoke to also noted—again, anecdotally—that there were still consistent numbers of pregnant women coming to the hospital with unexplained bleeding. The consensus was that more and more women were learning about misoprostol. In El Salvador, misoprostol is sold under the name Cytotec. Type that word alongside "abortion" into Google, and it becomes apparent that the old back alley of witch doctors with coat hangers could be deserted soon, replaced by online dealers peddling ulcer drugs.

In some ways, D.C.'s personal story is a transitional tale between an old world and a new one. She apparently tried the misoprostol abortion but got the wrong information about the dosage. Her later desperation and confusion about how the drug worked is what drove her, at last, into the house of a traditional back-alley abortionist.

> D.C.: *At 2 a.m., I started to shake. I had a fever and convulsions. My mama came, and I told her I was cold. She put more clothes on me. The next day I was fine and went to work. I started to feel bad pain but kept working. That night another fever came, and shaking. Mama said she was taking me to the doctor, and I said no. That night I began to convulse again and the pain was stronger. I didn't go to work the next day. I went to the bathroom and bled heavily.*
>
> *Two days later, on Friday, even my hands and feet were hurting. My kid was sick, he had a cold. I took my son to the doctor, who asked if it was me who was there to see him. I said it was my child, and he said, "You're yellow, like hepatitis." Then I was crying because he touched me on the stomach and liver and it hurt a lot. He asked me if I was sure I was O.K. because I looked bad. When I left the clinic, I couldn't walk. My sister went to look for a cab.*
>
> *Several days later, I was back at the doctor. They did some tests and called an ambulance. At the hospital they asked me what I had. I didn't want to say. I said I felt bad. They did tests on my urine, blood and lungs and found I had a severe respiratory infection. They did an ultrasound and found my kidneys, lung and liver were infected. And the ultrasound showed something else. They asked me: "Why do you have a perforated uterus? What have you done?" Then they did a vaginal exam, and it was the most painful thing for me in the world. They put something in me, and I cried out. They had two doctors holding me down. They said they knew I had had an abortion because my uterus was perforated and big and they would have to operate immediately. All I remember was going to the operating room, and then I don't remember anything because for the next six days I was in a coma.*

"When we get a call from a hospital reporting an abortion," said Flor Evelyn Tópez, "the first thing we do is make sure the girl gets into custody. So if there is not a police officer there, we call the police and begin to collect evidence." Tópez is a prosecutor in the district of Apopa in San Salvador, a part of town noted for its poverty, crime and gang violence. She is a compact and tense woman. She wears a beautiful silver cross around her neck with smaller matching crosses for earrings. Her hair is pulled into a tight narrow bun across her head, held in place by small plastic flowers. Her gaze beams from steady eyes, each haloed in cobalt mascara.

Nationwide, after the ban came into effect in 1998, the number of legal cases initiated nearly doubled, according to a study published in 2001 by the Center for Reproductive Rights. Today the number of abortion cases investigated each year averages close to 100, according to Luz McNaughton and Ellen Mitchell, policy consultants with Ipas, an abortion rights advocacy group in Chapel Hill, N.C., who gathered the statistics for a study to be published later this year by the American Journal of Public Health. In 2004, the most recent year for which any statistics are available, there were 93 investigations of people associated with a clandestine abortion. In 2003, there were 111 investigations; in 2002, there were 85. (El Salvador's population is 6.5 million, roughly that of Massachusetts.) The vast majority of charges are brought against the woman or the provider. In a few cases, the boyfriend or mother or someone else who has helped out is also charged. Typically, the woman can avoid prosecution altogether if, after she is arrested, she names the provider.

When the woman is first detained, the form of custody can vary. Wandee Mira, an obstetrician at a hospital in San Salvador, told me that she had seen "a young girl handcuffed to her hospital bed—with a police officer standing outside the door." In El Salvador, a person accused of a major crime is typically held in jail in "preventative detention" until the trial begins. Tópez, who said she had prosecuted perhaps 10 or 15 abortion cases in the last eight years, said that she took the severity of the case into account and sometimes argued for substitutive measures instead of jail," like house arrest, while the accused was awaiting trial. My impression was that Tópez was emphasizing such relative leniencies as house arrest instead of detention, as well as suspended sentences for women who report the abortionist, because, like most people, she was uncomfortable with the inevitable logic that insists upon making a woman who has had an abortion into a criminal. Even Regina de Cardenal, whose group was instrumental in passing the ban, could not quite square the circle.

"I believe the woman is a victim," de Cardenal told me. "The criminals are the people who perform the abortions." When pressed about the fact that the law she helped pass does treat the woman as a criminal, she said: "Yes, it's part of the law of our country. Because the woman has murdered her baby—and that's why she is sent to jail. But I believe that the woman who is sent to jail remains a victim of the abortion doctor, the abortionist, who knows exactly what he is doing."

In the United States, this conundrum is only beginning to emerge, as it did on "Meet the Press" in October 2004, when Tim Russert, the host, asked Jim DeMint, a South Carolina Republican representative then in the middle of what turned out to be a successful campaign for the U.S. Senate, to explain his position in favor of a total ban on all abortion procedures. DeMint was reluctant to answer Russert's repeated question: Would you prosecute a woman who had an abortion? DeMint said he thought Congress should outlaw all abortions first and worry about the fallout later. "We've got to make laws first that protect life," he said. "How those laws are shaped are going to be a long debate."

Russert refused to leave the congressman alone. "Who would you prosecute?" he persisted.

Finally DeMint blurted, "You know, I can't come up with all the laws as we're sitting right here, but the question is, Are we going to protect human life with our laws?"

In El Salvador, the law is clear: the woman is a felon and must be prosecuted. According to Tópez, after a report comes in from a doctor or a hospital that a woman has arrived who is suspected of having had an abortion, and after the police are dispatched, investigators start procuring evidence of the crime. In that first stage, Tópez has 72 hours to make the case to a justice of the peace that there should be a further investigation. If enough evidence is collected, she presents the case before a magistrate to get authorization for a full criminal trial before a judge.

During the first round of investigations, police officers interview the woman's family and friends. "The collecting of evidence usually takes place where the events transpired—by visiting the home or by speaking with the doctor at the hospital," Tópez said. In some cases, the police also interrogate people who work with the woman. Tópez added that that didn't happen very often because, she said, "these are women who don't work outside the home." (Indeed, the evidence suggests that the ban in El Salvador disproportionately affects poor women. The researchers who conducted the Journal of Public Health study found that common occupations listed for women charged with abortion-related crimes were homemaker, student, housekeeper and market vendor. The earlier study by the Center for Reproductive Rights found that the majority were domestic servants, followed by factory workers, ticket takers on buses, housewives, saleswomen and messengers.)

As they do in any investigation, the police collect evidence by interviewing everyone who knows the accused and by seizing her medical records. But they must also visit the scene of the crime, which, following the logic of the law, often means the woman's vagina.

"Yes, we sometimes call doctors from the Forensic Institute to do a pelvic exam," Tópez said, referring to the nation's main forensic lab, "and we ask them to document lacerations or any evidence such as cuts or a perforated uterus." In other words, if the suspicions of the patient's doctor are not conclusive enough, then in that initial 72-hour period, a forensic doctor can legally conduct a separate search of the crime scene. Tópez said, however, that vaginal searches can take place only with "a judge's permission." Tópez frequently turned the pages of a thick law-book she kept at hand. "The prosecutor can order a medical exam on a woman, because that's within the prosecutor's authority," she said.

In the event that the woman's illegal abortion went badly and the doctors have to perform a hysterectomy, then the uterus is sent to the Forensic Institute, where the government's doctors analyze it and retain custody of her uterus as evidence against her.

> *D.C.: After I came out of the coma, they moved me to the maternity hospital. My brother visited and asked me if the police had come to ask me questions. He said the police had come to our house and they had interrogated our relatives and neighbors. They had gone to where I worked. They asked everyone a lot of questions about me and who I was and if they knew whether I was pregnant and whether I'd had an abortion.*
>
> *When I got home, the prosecutor came to see me, and he asked lots of aggressive questions. He talked to me like I was a criminal. I didn't want to answer because I was scared. He said if I didn't answer, even though I was in bad physical shape, he would put me in jail. He wanted me to tell him who the father of the child was and the name of the person who had done this to me. I didn't know her name. Then he made a date for me to come to the prosecutor's office.*

Doctors in El Salvador now understand that it is their legal duty to report any woman suspected of having had an abortion. Abortion rights advocates point out that Salvadoran law also spells out a conflicting responsibility: the doctor's duty to keep the patient's medical information confidential. What this blurring of medical and legal obligations means, in practice, is that doctors have to choose for themselves what to do. The result is a country in which some doctors eagerly report women, some eagerly search for loopholes to avoid having to report and some simply want to stay out of trouble.

"Many doctors are afraid not to report," says Mira, the obstetrician I spoke to. This fear is heightened for doctors, she explains, by the fact that nurses also have a legal duty to report abortion crimes but are often confused about their obligation of confidentiality. So doctors are afraid that the nurses will report them for not reporting. "The entire system is run on fear," Mira said.

One morning, I got permission to hang out all day at Hospital National de Maternidad, a large public hospital in San Salvador, and talk with doctors there. Somehow the Salvadoran government learned of my visit, and the federal Ministry of Health dispatched an "escort" to accompany me the entire day. The chief of the OB/GYN residents was Carmen Vargas, a young doctor with a fondness for eyeliner and lipstick. Like that of many doctors in El Salvador, her sense of the whole issue is that, regardless of what she might think personally, the law obligates her to turn women in. In the last year or so, she reported one young woman herself and was present when another was reported. For Vargas, the cases were pretty cut and dried. "When we see physical evidence, we are required to report," she explained, "because the doctor and the institution can be charged."

The physical evidence in a case can be supported by other clues. Vargas said that in medical school she read in a gynecological textbook, published in the late 1990's in Chile, that the doctor should listen carefully to the patient's story. If the woman is "confused in her narrative," Vargas said, that could well indicate that she'd had an abortion.

Vargas offered me an example. "Last year, in March, we received a 15-year-old who came referred from a hospital in an outer area," she said. "She had a confused patient history. She had already been operated on and had a hysterectomy and had her ovaries taken out. She was in a delicate state, on respiratory assistance in intensive care. The doctors there said they had seen a perforation in the space beneath the cervix.

"This was around Eastertime last year, and the prosecutor's offices were closed," Vargas said. She had not seen any of the evidence herself, she said, but saw that the other doctors "had tried to call the prosecutor's office, but it was closed. I came in, and on the chart what was pending was to call the police. So I called them."

Vargas remembered that the police interviewed her but asked only general questions. "The hard part was when I was called as a witness," she said. "That lasted a whole day. That was really ugly, and it was first time I ever testified. They asked me if I had noticed anything suspicious or if I had heard anything about the girl."

Vargas told the prosecutor that the girl's stepfather "asked me not to call the prosecutor's office because it would be better for the girl if I didn't call." She fixed me with a look. "I didn't think it was for the girl that he was asking me not to call." Vargas said her hunch was that the man was abusing his stepdaughter, and she said that she felt that she was doing the 15-year-old a favor by turning her in for felony abortion.

"It's a hard question as to whether I did the right thing," she said. "I think part of it is not right, from the point of view that you can expose the life of the patient, and because it can cause women not to seek care. But at the same time, I felt I did the right thing. I suspect she was abused in her own house. I felt like it was helping her get away from a possible bad situation."

As it happened, I located this particular patient, who resolved her case without going to jail. Two of the activists I met made contact with her by cellphone. At first the family agreed that I should meet this young woman, but at the last minute the stepfather intervened. He said he didn't think his stepdaughter should tell her story. After that, no one answered our calls.

> D.C.: *At the prosecutor's office, I met a woman. She said if I talked, I might have a chance to stay free. She said there was no worse punishment than that I couldn't have any more children. So why not talk? Why defend this person? So she gave me another date to come back and talk. I told my mama, but she said that if I told them who the woman was, the woman could take revenge on my family. I didn't know what to do. But I decided to stay free and so I told her everything.*
>
> *I went back to work, and everybody knew what I had done because the police had come. I was scared because I didn't know what they would say about me. A lot of people wouldn't talk to me, but some people said: "Here's my little girl! My little girl has come back!" I felt good. They loved me and they said, "It was a mistake, and everybody makes mistakes."*
>
> *Later the prosecutor called again and told me I would need to go to court and hear from the judge whether I would be free or go to jail.*

A policy that criminalizes all abortions has a flip side. It appears to mandate that the full force of the medical team must tend toward saving the fetus under any circumstances. This notion can lead to some dangerous practices. Consider an ectopic pregnancy, a condition that occurs when a microscopic fertilized egg moves down the fallopian tube—which is no bigger around than a pencil—and gets stuck there (or sometimes in the abdomen). Unattended, the stuck fetus grows until the organ containing it ruptures. A simple operation can remove the fetus before the organ bursts. After a rupture, though, the situation can turn into a medical emergency.

According to Sara Valdés, the director of the Hospital de Maternidad, women coming to her hospital with ectopic pregnancies cannot be operated on until fetal death or a rapture of the fallopian tube. "That is our policy," Valdés told me. She was plainly in torment about the subject. "That is the law." she said. "The D.A.'s office told us that this was the law." Valdés estimated that her hospital treated more than a hundred ectopic pregnancies each year. She described the hospital's practice. "Once we determine that they have an ectopic pregnancy, we make sure they stay in the hospital," she said. The women are sent to the dispensary, where they receive a daily ultrasound to check the fetus. "If it's dead, we can operate," she said. "Before that, we can't." If there is a persistent fetal heartbeat, then they have to wait for the fallopian tube to rupture. If they are able to persuade the patient to stay, though, doctors can operate the minute any signs of early rupturing are detected. Even a few drops of blood seeping from a fallopian tube will "irritate the abdominal wall and cause pain," Valdés explained. By operating at the earliest signs of a potential rupture, she said, her doctors are able to minimize the risk to the woman.

One doctor, who asked to remain anonymous because of the risk of prosecution, explained that there are creative solutions to the problem of ectopic pregnancies: "Sometimes when an ectopic pregnancy comes in, the attendant will say, 'Send this patient to the best ultrasound doctor.' And I'll say, 'No, send her to the least-experienced ultrasound doctor.' He'll say, 'I can't find a heartbeat here.' Then we can operate."

This doctor also told me that there are ways to avoid reporting an abortion. "I can only say what I saw when I examined the patient," the doctor said. "If I can see lacerations or cuts, I cannot say what that means if the patient says, 'I have done nothing.' I can describe what I saw, but I cannot say she has or has not had an abortion."

The doctor pondered a hypothetical situation: "If the patient says, 'Yes, I did it, but please keep that between us'?" There was a pause. "I keep that promise. The confidentiality right is more important than the legal duty to report."

D.C.: A month later, I got my exact court date. I spent the day crying and crying. I took the bus from work to the court. I didn't tell my mom where I was going because she would want to come. I didn't know what was going to happen. I just told one friend, and she was waiting for me. I got there, and the judge began the proceeding, and he said I would go free, that what they were going to do was look for the person who had done this to me and that I had no reason to go to jail. I was so happy, so very happy.

In prosecutors' offices in El Salvador, as in prosecutors' offices anywhere, longer sentences are considered better sentences. "The more years one can send someone away for," I was told by Margarita Sanabria, a magistrate who has handled several abortion cases, "the better it is for the prosecutors." She cited this motivation to account for what she has observed recently: more later-term abortions being reclassified as "aggravated homicide." If an aborted fetus is found to have been viable, the higher charge can be filed. The penalty for abortion can be as low as two years in prison. Aggravated homicide has a minimum sentence of 30 years and a maximum of 50 years.

The issue of proving viability after an abortion is a tricky one, of course. There is no legal standard. But many of the people I talked to in El Salvador, including Tópez, the prosecutor, said there was a rule of thumb: if an aborted fetus weighs more than 500 grams, or a little more than a pound, then you can argue that the fetus was viable. When I mentioned this to Judge Sanabria, she said she wished she had known more about the rule before. She recalled one case, that of a 20-year-old mother named Carmen Climaco, whose abortion of a fetus estimated at 18 weeks had been recast by the prosecutor as aggravated homicide. The judge admitted that if she had known this rule of thumb, she might not have sent the case to trial. "I feel bad about it," she said.

But the case did go to trial, and the prosecutor won a conviction for aggravated homicide. At trial, the evidence included lifting Climaco's fingerprints from the fetus, which was found under her bed. The prosecutor's accusation was infanticide by strangling.

The women's prison where convicted murderers are sent is in the outer district of Tonacatepeque. I visited it in January. It's an old, creaky facility that inspires the kind of dread that comes of seeing concertina wire and much-painted cinder blocks, made all the creepier by a paint choice of baby-boy blue. Inside the first gate is a neutral area. It's filled with almond trees that provide a flickering shade on a hot winter afternoon. All the women are kept in a deeper jail, walled off inside. Through a small window, I could see an open area crisscrossed by laundry lines and arrayed by different women lying around smoking.

I was there to see Carmen Climaco. She is now 26 years old, four years into her 30-year sentence. She has three children, who today are 11, 8 and 6 years old. We talked about them for a while. Since she was the only person in the family who worked, her children's financial situation is precarious; they now stay with their grandmother.

Climaco said she lives for their visits, which are brief and come only twice a month. She was dressed in red jeans and a white polo shirt. We sat with an interpreter in the half-shade in green plastic yard chairs. Climaco had a paper napkin with her that she folded and folded into a familiar-looking pill. She had light brown hair, and occasionally a smile steadied her trembling lips.

"I became pregnant at a time when my smallest child was in the hospital," she said. "I never thought I could get pregnant because I had been sterilized. Suddenly I saw two doors shutting at the same time. There was nothing I could do. My mother said she'd toss me out of the house if I got pregnant."

Her story came out in fits and starts. She said that she was innocent and had never done anything illegal. Then she said, "I keep asking God to pardon me for what I've done." She said that the day it happened, she felt dizzy and collapsed at home. She woke up covered in blood. "I stood up and it felt like something fell out of me." It took her a while to understand just what had happened. "I put my hand on its throat to see if it was moving," she said, "which is why my fingerprints were found on its neck."

I spent the better part of an hour watching Carmen Climaco's face, listening to her whimpering pleas to Jesus Christ for forgiveness and tiny prayers to me to believe in her innocence. Like anyone serving time in prison, she has inhabited the details of her story to the point that they no longer sound true or false. She has compressed her story into a dense, simple tale of innocence—she just woke up covered in blood—to hold up against the public accusation of baby-strangling. I kept looking at her face, incapable of seeing the innocent girl she described or the murderer the prosecutor sent to prison. The truth was certainly—well, not in the "middle" so much as somewhere else entirely. Somewhere like this: She'd had a clandestine abortion at 18 weeks, not all that different from D.C.'s, something defined as absolutely legal in the United States. It's just that she'd had an abortion in El Salvador.

Excerpts from **Men and Abortion**

Losses, Lessons and Love

By Arthur B. Shostak, Gary McLouth, and Lynn Seng

Although no one seems to give them a thought, as many as 600,000 males annually—from downy-cheeked teens to gray-haired fathers—"do time" in the waiting rooms of the nation's 500 or so abortion clinics.[1]

Generally ill-at-ease, the men sit apprehensively and embarrassed among a much larger group of girlfriends, sisters, and mothers. Striking in their diversity, the *men* who wait also are set apart by their lack of macho self-confidence and their dour solemnity. ("Nobody, *but* nobody, cracks any jokes in there," a 24-year-old cab driver recalled.)

When we started thinking about them, after having done time ourselves among them, we wondered:

Who are these men? How typical are they of all American males?

Why are they there? What motivates them to come along for the abortion appointment?

How do they feel about the pregnancy, the decision to terminate, the loss of fatherhood, their role, the female's role, and the future of the relationship?

What do they think of pro- and anti-abortion arguments? Of the nature of the fetus? Of the right to an abortion on request, for any reason whatsoever?

How much power do they want in the decision to terminate a pregnancy?

Whom do they turn to for advice, support, and solace? How many talk to male friends? Parents? Abortion clinic counselors?

What happened at the clinic? How many felt good or bad about it? Why?

Could the experience have been a better one for them? What abortion clinic reforms, if any, do they endorse—and why?

Arthur B. Shostak, Gary McLouth, and Lynn Seng, from *Men and Abortion: Losses, Lessons and Love*, pp. 2–20, 183–193, 195–208. Copyright © 1984 by ABC-CLIO Inc. Reprinted with permission.

How intent are they on not being abortion repeaters? What sorts of reforms do they think might lower the number of abortions?

We also wondered about the role of "significant others" in this situation:

How does the public feel about the role men should have in abortion decision making? Do men and women think alike here, or do the sexes differ in their viewpoints?

How do lawmakers and jurists treat the role men should have in abortion decision making? What legal rights, if any, do men have in a contested abortion?

Above all, we wanted to learn how the men who wait respond to the *entire* situation—from the news of the conception through the months that follow the abortion; what the range of their feelings was during their ordeal, especially through the obvious fact of relationships' strengthened, weakened, or broken by this trial.

Two ensuing years of field research involving 30 abortion clinics from New England to California are now beginning to reveal some provocative answers to these questions.[2]

Of our 1,000 male respondents from the 30 clinics we studied, 60% were single, 18% were married, 12% were "living together," and 10% were formerly married men (87% of the married men, by the way, were accompanying their wives). Even among the singles, the relationships were relatively stable (22% of the single men were engaged and 57% were dating their partner on a steady basis). Thus, it was not surprising that waiting room males show genuine concern about the well-being of their lover, fiancée, or wife, many interrupting clinic staffers with anxious questions about the woman at every opportunity.

The men in our sample also reflected the age distribution of all abortion patients, one-third of which were under 20 years of age (see Table 2.10.1). The ages of men in our sample were concentrated in the youngest age categories with those 21 or younger comprising 35% of the sample, and those 22–25 making up 30% of the sample. Given their youthfulness, 27% were still in college or a trade school—which is about the average for American males over 18.

Because more financially secure couples tend to use a private physician rather than a public abortion clinic, the waiting room crowd included few professionals, a more representative number of white-collar workers (20%), and slightly more blue-collar-workers (35%) than is usually found among males in general. Nearly half were Protestants, a third were Catholic and 15% reported no affiliation. Finally, in rounding out this profile, the men who wait in abortion clinics reflect the black/white distribution in America (10% and 87%, respectively), while slightly understating the proportion of Hispanics (1.5%) and Asian-Americans (0.8%) (see Figure 2.10.1).[3]

Given these demographic characteristics (which are similar to the U.S. population with the exception of the younger age), as well as the commitment of these men to the relationship and to the female they have accompanied to the clinic—what do *they* think and feel about the unusual situation in which they find themselves? When we

Table 2.10.1 Comparison of Clinic Male Respondents (1983) with Female-Abortion Patients (1980)

	1,000 male respondents	Female Abortion Patients*
Unmarried	82%	79%
White	87	70
Under 20	35	30
Attended or graduated college	45	34
Had a previous abortion	25	33

*Source: Stanley K. Henshaw and Kevin O'Reilly, "Characteristics of Abortion Patients in the United States, 1979 and 1980," *Family Planning Perspectives*, January/February 1983.

gave them a chance to write anything they wished which would capsulize the matter, many took the opportunity to share thoughts like these:

> I have two small great and beautiful children, but we really can't handle a third right now—it would really hurt us. (*Married, 29, Catholic, white*)

> I feel helpless, poorly informed, and put in a "typical" male role. (*Married, 33, Catholic, white*)

> I can now understand the importance of birth control. I now have a deeper respect for being able to have sex with a woman. (*Single, 20, Christian, college student, white*)

> I wish it wouldn't seem like we're doing something dirty. (*Married, 30, Protestant, white*)

> Killing the fetus may be crime but child abuse and neglect is a bigger crime, I feel. (*Single, 26, Protestant, engineer black*)

> My strongest concern is for my relationship with my fiancée—emotionally and mentally I believe she will never feel the same about me, herself, children and life in general. I have already experienced some neglectfulness and deep-seated guilt on the part of my fiancée. ("*Living-together," 27, Protestant, electronics technician, white*)

> It has opened my eyes to life and love. (*Single, 26, Protestant, machinist, white*)

> I think the men should be allowed to be in the room while surgery is being performed. Also, allowed in the waiting room. This procedure is just as important as childbirth in my mind. Thank you for the opportunity to voice my opinion, because I feel very strong about the procedure. (*Single, 22, Christian, car salesman, white*)

Over and again, in hundreds of such written comments, and in long, vivid personal interviews, we were reminded of the extraordinary nature of this confusing and troubling experience—perhaps the least well known and least understood of any challenges in a man's life.

Barren Bookshelf

For every kind of good reason imaginable, researchers in abortion scholarship have been preoccupied with the female, the fetus, the state, the church, the ethical questions, and other such controversial aspects. Not surprisingly, therefore, when we used a computer search system to assay the content of 279 recent (1963–1984) examples of relevant sociological research on abortion, some 239, or 85%, dealt with women, or the fetus, or the state, etc.—anything except the men involved. Of the 40 articles linked to our subject, nine concentrated on the male experience in countries abroad, and only six (three by Art Shostak, one of this book's co-authors) shared any new field research in the American context.[4] A scholar in 1979 concluded in exasperation that this type of literature "often totally disregarded the male role, reported it in an implicit or covert manner, or at best reported through the perceptions of the man's partner."[5]

Fortunately, a search of unpublished doctor dissertations, masters theses, and graduate student papers unearthed eight field research reports, all of which we use extensively in the chapters that follow. Each has the strength of focusing in depth on a small group of males (60–126) at only one or two clinics, and testing a carefully honed hypothesis. We incorporate the conclusions of these studies to sharpen the information gathered in our survey of 1,000 males in 30 abortion clinics around the country.[6]

Figure 2.10.1 Profile of 1,000 Clinic Male respondents

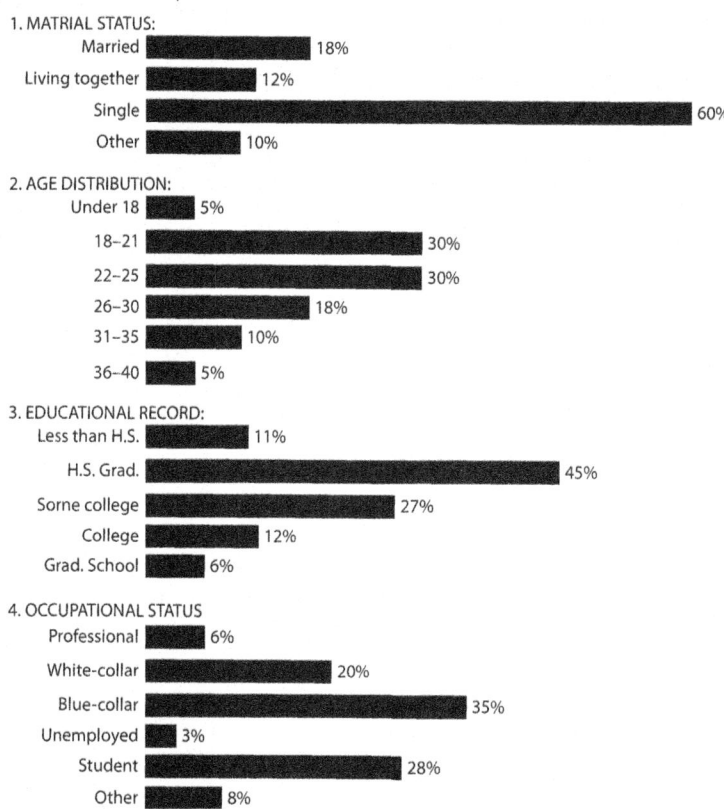

Intent on taking help from every possible source, we expanded our literature search far beyond conventional boundaries. Abortion clinic personnel, for example who had often never heard of the eight Ph.D., and M.A. field research items, were excited about having read something of relevance in one or another of the major mass-circulation women's or men's magazines. Prodded by leads as vague as these, we eventually located "men and abortion" feature articles in *Esquire*; *Glamour*, *Hustler*, *McCall's*, *Mademoiselle*, *New York Times Magazine*, and *The Progressive*.

Characteristically strong on human-interest vignettes, but weak on data, statistics, and typologies, the magazine essays were especially valuable for revealing what circulation-seeking publishers believed the public wanted to know about our subject *Esquire*'s writer, for example, advised readers in 1981 that abortion was "a far greater dilemma for men than researchers, counselors and women have even begun to realize."[7]

Another useful lead provided by the counselors involved three pamphlets which 62% of our 30 clinics give or sell (at cost) to waiting room males. Authored by current or former abortion counselors, the pamphlets try to sensitize male readers to their *own*, as well as to the women's, varied emotional and spiritual needs in the clinic and in the weeks and months following the abortion. Unique in being based on hundreds of individual and group counseling sessions conducted by their authors, the three pamphlets lack any research data, a deliberate omission in keeping with their nonacademic, practical character. We found them especially helpful as a touchstone of sorts, a validity check on the feedback we were getting from our 1,000 waiting room men. (Two of the pamphlet authors are counselors at clinics cooperating with our study, and both also are contributors to this book.)[8]

Given the preoccupation of abortion scholarship with the world of women, we dared to hope a few items in the bookshelf might pay men at least passing attention. We were not disappointed. Much was written about the thoughts and feelings of abortion patients concerning their boyfriends, lovers, fiancés, and husbands. In the hands of social scientists such as Luker, Zimmerman, Smetana, and Gilligan, these second hand accounts of what male sex partners were experiencing as interpreted by their women shed unique and valuable light on our subject.

Figure 2.10.1 continued

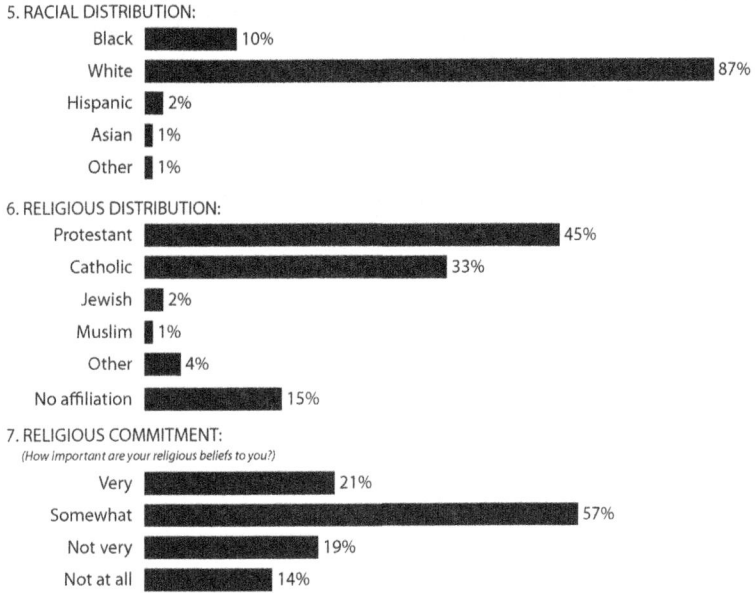

Finally, we would be seriously remiss not to mention two very special, very exacting, and very sparse resources that made a distinct contribution.

The first involved the statistical reports of large-scale public polling projects, such as the 1965–1982 set of abortion questions asked of 1,500 Americans by the National Opinion Research Corporation (NORC), and the 1963–1982 abortion surveys of the Gallup Corporation. We also were fortunate in gaining the cooperation of *Glamour* magazine and the University of Connecticut's Institute for Social Inquiry, both of which ran special computer tabulations of their abortion polling data at our request. Similarly, the Drexel University Survey Center included some of our abortion questions in two 1983 phone surveys of the Philadelphia public, and ran the computer analysis for us that we designed. Data of this rich and varied nature helped clarify the attitudes and values of the public in general, and of males and females in particular.

Our second very special, exacting, and all-too-sparse resource involved the fictional and poetic recreation of the male experience. Relevant writers included novelists John Barth (*The End of the Road*), William O'Rourke (*Idle Hands*), Richard Brautigan (*The Abortion*), and Theodore Dreiser (*An American Tragedy*); short-story authors such as Marian Ellison; Ernest Hemingway, and Alice Walker; and poets Adrienne Rich and Anne Sexton, among others. Evocative and engaging, this small selection of fine writing added soul and substance to the bare numbers of public opinion polls, and augmented the drama we experienced in scores of intense discussions with waiting room men.

Finding Out for Ourselves

Intent on expanding the inadequate research base of knowledge in this matter, we identified six target groups and a data-gathering strategy for each:

1. *Males who accompany their sex partners to an abortion* were invited by staffers at 30 abortion clinics to complete our questionnaire; 1,000 men eventually did so. (The 30 clinics were located through the 1981–82 and 1982–83 directories of the National Abortion Federation, a composite list of 243 providers all of whom were invited to participate in our research.)

2. *Males who do not accompany their sex partners* were sought through media appeals (radio talk shows, etc.), public forum appeals, and requests for cooperation placed in men's movement newsletters; 18 eventually responded and completed our questionnaire.[9]
3. *Males willing to discuss the aftermath of an abortion* were located through phone numbers they provided on the questionnaires distributed in the abortion clinics; 75 were interviewed by phone or in person.
4. *Clinic representatives* were asked to "guesstimate" the percentage of clients accompanied by sex partners, the percentage of such males who request counseling, and other items on which none usually collect statistics. They also were asked to describe the services available for waiting room males, and their future plans for any such services, a request eventually honored by 26 of our 30 cooperating clinics.[10]
5. *Clinic counselors* were interviewed at length in a dozen locations from coast to coast, and five chose to supplement these focused discussions with essays they wrote especially for this volume.
6. *Abortion activists,* such as Bill Baird of the pro-choice camp and Joe Scheidler of the anti-abortion bloc, were interviewed in person or by phone, and each cooperated in the preparation of a profile on their actions, attitudes, and values.

This six-part data collection effort took the better part of two years, and resulted in our making new friends across the country and gaining a much broader understanding of the man's abortion experience.

At the very heart of the entire project was our main data-gathering tool, a five-sided, three-page questionnaire of 102 questions. The questionnaire was pretested on small groups of waiting room males whose answers highlighted gaps and ambiguities in our early drafts.

The final version focused on several different areas: We asked the respondents to reconstruct their attitudes and behaviors both when they learned of the pregnancy and during the decision-making period. We then asked questions about the actual abortion, and also had the men look ahead and speculate about the impact of the abortion on their relationships with their female partners. We explored their moral and political views about abortion, and paid special attention to their thoughts about the fetus, the loss of fatherhood, and the allocation of decision-making power between themselves and their partners. We also asked half of our group which, if any, of six possible clinic services for males they would utilize, and why.[11] Finally, we gave the men an opportunity to use their own words to answer two open-ended questions: "How could this entire experience be a better one for you?" and "Do you have any other thoughts you care to add about any aspect of the experience?"

Processing the Data

Each questionnaire was first examined for any handwritten answers or comments (as found in 55%), and then all were turned over to a key puncher for transfer of their 102 answers to a set of five data punch cards. After being rigorously examined for (rare) keypunch errors, the 4,500 cards were run in a statistical program handled by our two methodologists, Jan Harrington, and later, Dr. Joan Spade.[12]

Sharing the Findings

Before beginning our writing, we deliberately sought a hearing from a wide range of concerned audiences and gained much from the lively discussion our data generally provoked. We spoke on TV talk shows and radio call-in shows in 15 states (via phone hook-ups), along with pro-choice forums (vigorously attended by anti-abortion activists), a statewide (New Jersey) N.O.W. forum on abortion policies, a Washington, D.C., forum of a national men's organization ("Tree Men"), and various campus forums (Hartwick College, West Chester State College, Drexel University, among others). Especially helpful was the time spent sharing findings and reform ideas with the entire staff of two very different clinics, one with an avowed feminist orientation (and a disinclination to help us get surveys done in their waiting room), and the other, a full-service women's health center which was of major assistance to our survey collection effort.[13]

Influenced by these direct exchanges of data, insights, and recommendations with varied groups of adults, we made three policy decisions of major consequence for this book. First, we decided to write for the largest possible audience—the kind we had had in our TV, radio, and forum appearances—as well as abortion clinic staffers, partisans, and the like. Second, we decided to keep the writing as clear and cogent as possible. All statistical tables have therefore been held to a minimum, and the jargon of specialists has been translated into conventional English. Third, we decided to go beyond a cut-and-dried presentation of the findings. Instead, we build on this material to highlight reform possibilities endorsed by many of our 1,000 men—reforms we regard as worthy of sustained trial and sensitive assessment.

Limitations of the Project

As our data come only from males inclined to cooperate with us, we have no way of knowing what the experience meant for others in the clinic waiting rooms too embarrassed, embittered, indifferent, or self-contained to complete our questionnaire. Similarly, while we secured and analyzed 18 surveys from men who did not go along to the abortion appointment, we would have preferred a much larger number—though this is an extraordinarily difficult type of respondent to draw into research cooperation. And while we invited (and re-invited) over 300 clinics (243 NAF members and over 60 non-NAF clinics) to assist in circulating our questionnaire, we would have preferred participation from many more than the 30 that finally joined us.[14] Above all, given the absence of any scientific knowledge of waiting room males in general, and our inability therefore to pursue a random or representative sample of this universe, we have had to settle for a sample of convenience, an "available sample" of a previously unmeasured aggregate. Accordingly, we make no claim for the representativeness of our findings, and urge utmost caution in generalizing beyond the 1,000-male cohort itself

Summary

We were struck during our own abortion experiences by certain stark and regrettable features of the scene—the absence of any helpful preparation for the experience; the embarrassment and sense of uselessness men felt during their clinic vigil; the wish to talk about it versus the social pressure to tell no one; and the need to appear supportive regardless of one's own ambivalence and heartache. We began to ask if it *had* to be like this, if there wasn't a better way for 600,000 males annually to help their partners and themselves meet the abortion challenge.

Finding very little in the research literature, we spent over two years gathering data, conducting interviews, and exchanging ideas with concerned audiences. Our book shares statistics and human-interest material from 1,000 waiting room men and scores of clinic staffers, data that make clear a remarkable similarity in the attitudes of Catholic and non-Catholic males, a poignant difference in the attitudes of white and black males, a striking increase in post abortion discomfort, and other provocative findings. Guided by front-line insights, we now can make a case for pragmatic and promising reforms of the *entire* situation—from pre- to post-abortion—as it can all be done better, to the substantial gain of men and women alike.

PROFILE

We have chosen Daniel as our beginning interview deliberately and wholeheartedly. His story illustrates much about lessons, losses, and love, even as if is also representative of major concerns of our other men.

Daniel

A lot of it is a blur. I couldn't give you a daily account. I went to work and didn't even know what I was doing. I could have cut myself accidentally … I work with knives so much.

It was one of the only times in my life where I realized I was involved, but I didn't have the ultimate say. I wasn't really in favor of it at the time, but I realized it was … a woman's decision.

I didn't want to get married, but I wanted to make it comfortable for her, adoption or whatever, but I didn't want to see a life end. Is that it? I'm not sure. I had been against abortion and still am, but a man's position is secondary. It has to be in that decision, it involves someone else's body. That's my primary justification. It makes me feel helpless, having a certain conviction and realizing it doesn't matter in practical terms. It doesn't bother me that people have a choice, but it bothers me because I don't like it [abortion].

My relationship is stronger, better now. It was the first major crisis that tested our feelings. There was initially a sense of resentment on my part, but, again, respecting her right to make the decision made me realize the resentment was a gut reaction.

I resented the fact that I was stuck with the situation and her decision, and the responsibility and commitment to the situation. I resented the fact that regardless of whose body it was in, it was my kid, too.

Working it out was mostly due to what she said and did. She just couldn't face it—the responsibility. If she'd had the child, she couldn't give it up, but the responsibility was too great for her. But, I was willing to lessen the burden as much as I could … by taking financial responsibility. I was even toying with the idea of being a single father. I was probably being a bit idealistic at the time. I was willing to give it a try.

In that kind of situation does a man have any rights? To take my baby and bring it up as a single father? If not, it is unfair, especially in this day and age of modern medicine which can prove paternity. […]

I have always found it difficult to talk about my deepest personal problems. When I was 14, my father died. It was an incredible emotional crisis. I never discussed it with anyone, including my family who was going through the same thing.

It's like how you choose the Pope. They're in that room up there and when they finally make the decision, the smoke goes up. That's how you know everything is okay. I know close friends of mine sensed from my attitude that something was wrong and I know they could tell when it was okay again, but I never verbalized what was going on. Now that I think about it, it was kind of an insult that I didn't open up to them.

I went through a period where I intellectualized this intangible thing into a part of my life and now I've made it intangible again. I went through a heavy guilt period even before the abortion had taken place. I think I felt guilty just because of things I ignored. For a short while we didn't practice birth control. We were lazy for a while and then it happens and you end a potential life, kill something.

It taught me a lot of lessons. How you have to be smart. Like the old "it couldn't happen to me" thing is a lot of crap. Not just in terms of sex, but how you deal with your life. […]

It's so easy when you watch the news on TV. It's so unreal and also removed from your life. This situation occurs and you realize you're part of the world. It made me feel part of a much larger body of people, those who had experienced abortions.

It's hard to imagine people allowing themselves to go through an abortion repetition. I know men who have and I can't see how they do it. It certainly made me stop and think. Maybe men are conditioned to not even care about it. It's even weirder that a lot of women don't either. I find that more appalling. But, you find you can prevent it and we do now by the pill.

The clinic was very bizarre. Here I was in this packed waiting room, standing room only by the time we left, the combination of people ... groups of women supporting one woman friend. I saw a young 14-year-old whose father was with her. Despite the situation, I respected him. It must have been tough.

I saw several couples. Every man in there had the same look on his face—wanting desperately to be someplace else.

I really wanted to support my girlfriend, but I didn't know what was happening. I'd read pamphlets and she'd told me about it. But I hadn't thought about not being with her. I got up automatically and went to the door and the attendant stopped me. It really pissed me off. It's like my mother says women's problems.

I waited and read every magazine I could find. I had bought a science magazine to read and in that issue they had a report with pictures on a special process—amniocentesis. I forced myself to look at it, but it was a real blow. I didn't say anything. We had already made the decision and I didn't want to rehash the argument there. I didn't need to see that, or maybe I did. Somebody could have hit me over the head with a sledgehammer.

How can you suggest changes, how can you make it easier? In the Soviet Union, they've made it an everyday thing. Like everyone has one. It wouldn't make it easier for me.

I took it solely as my fault that she was pregnant. I did it to her. I see now it's ridiculous. Why I felt that way, I'm not sure.

Fatherhood is a good thing; I want to be one.

The fetus, even to this day, took on a kind of other-world identity. I couldn't see it, I couldn't feel it. My girlfriend could. That's the biggest difference in that a woman experiences it in such a tangible way. A man's bonds are only emotional. A woman's bonds are both.

It's a wound you can't see or feel, but it exists. It heals, though. You go through the process of finding ways to deal with it. Guilt is pointless; it's like self-flagellation. You can pout about it or get over it. If it hadn't healed, I couldn't live with this woman now. It's finally something that happened in my life and I've had to keep going.

The hardest period was three or four days prior to the abortion. In a small way I felt relief the minute we stepped out of the clinic, although the guilt was there. Have you read Anne Sexton's poem about abortion? There's a line—something like—"Someone who lived is gone." I read it and that's how I felt about it and still do. It's someone who didn't get a chance ... This is good for me. I've thought about it a lot.

In the clinic no one came around to talk to us, like the brochure said.

But I didn't seek out anybody either, so it's partially my fault. I probably wouldn't have said anything in the group discussions anyway, knowing me.

It would be a hard experience to go through watching it, not that I wanted to see it, but I wanted to be with her. They create a situation where she has to go through something alone. I did, too, but it was all a total head trip in the waiting room. [...]

It brought our relationship down to earth from just romanticism and idealism. Before, we were just, two people living together, off on different tangents. The abortion brought us into one, helped us grow together in more cooperation. We could go on ignoring whose turn it was to do the laundry, but the abortion forced us to define our relationship and roles.

    Daniel's keen sense of powerless involvement and uncompensated loss forced him to seek resolution. Although he could have chosen resentment and guilt, he sought healthier altitudes of understanding and love. Daniel's level of concern and energy resonated throughout our other personal interviews. These men continually reminded us, indeed, implored us to focus on the human particulars of our material along with our statistical data.

    Daniel like all of our 1,000 men, did not run from his pregnant girlfriend, or from us, or from himself. Unfortunately, many Americans expect a man in his situation to take the easy way out. Daniel chose responsibility, however, and in this society of legally defined choice, such young people model a mature approach to our freedoms and responsibilities.

Daniel had crisscrossed the country from Ohio to Oregon to New York City, alternating college and a variety of odd jobs. In Baltimore he met a woman with whom he began living, and took a job as a full-time chef at a downtown restaurant. He appeared to be enjoying his relationship, his work, and his life when, shortly before Christmas 1982, her pregnancy forced him to reexamine everything.

Notes

1. In 1983 it was estimated that 1,600,000 legal abortions took place. Our 30 clinics believe 85% of their patients told the natural father of the pregnancy. Combining these figures, we believe about 1,360,000 men are involved annually in the abortion drama. As for the reliability of the 85% guesstimate, it is important to note that Bracken Hachamovitch, and Grossman found 87% of 489 women had told their partners of their decision to seek an abortion (1974); Melamed's 1975 research on 188 abortion patients indicated 85% had told their partners of the pregnancy, and 83% of the decision for abortion. Michael Bracken, Moshe Hachamovitch, and Gerald Grossman, "The Decision to Abort and Psychological Sequelae," *Journal of Nervous and Mental Disease* 158 (1974): 157; L. Melamed, "Therapeutic Abortion in Midwestern City, *Psychological Reports* 37 (1975): 1144.

    Dr. Roger Rochat, director of the Centers for Disease Control (Atlanta) indicated in October 1983 that final figures for 1981 and 1982 had not yet been tabulated. After noting that not all abortions are reported to health authorities, he suggested that a final figure for any year would probably be 20% higher than any number listed (1980 = 1,300,000), UPI, "Abortions Set Records, But Rate of Rise Slows." *The Patriot* (Banisburg, Pennsylvania), October 10, 1983, p. A–2.

    Our 30 clinics also reported only 50% of their patients were accompanied by males, for a tally of over 600,000 waiting room men. The 85% and 50% figures are "guesstimates" from 30 clinics that may or may not be representative of the nation's 520 such institutions. Unfortunately, no national data could be found with which to compare our estimates. For conventional statistics on the clinics, see Stanley K. Henshaw, "Freestanding Abortion Clinics: Services, Structure, Fees," *Family Planning Perspectives* 14 (September/October 1982): 248–256. When we phoned the Alan Guttmacher Institute on July 13, 1983, and asked if the nation's leading source of abortion data had statistics on males, a very cooperative Communications Associate, Barbara Parks, indicated no such data existed (except with reference to family planning matters). When we phoned the National Abortion Federation with the same question, they sent a xerox copy of a 1981 *New York Times* feature column that focused on Art's research (Dova Sobel, "Man's Role In Abortion Decision," *New York Times,* November 9, 1982; p. B–12). While the Guttmacher Institute does have its own directory of clinics, we were told it will not share this address list for scholarly research.

2. Naturally, we sought a much larger sample of the nation's 520 clinics. We mailed a request for research cooperation to every clinic listed in the 1980–81 and 1982–83 *Directory* of the National Abortion Federation, a total of 243 clinics. Unfortunately, 199 never replied, 16 were not at the address given, and only 25 elected to cooperate with our research. It would appear that no source in the country at this time has a complete and publicly available directory of the nation's abortion providers, and *all* abortion statistics, therefore, remain estimates subject to unknown error.

3. In 1980, the last year for which national data are available, 79% of all abortion patients were unmarried (as were 82% of our respondents), 67% had no previous abortion (75% of our men), 70% were white (87% of our men), 34% have attended or graduated from college (45% of our men), and 30% were under 20 (35% of our men). While the matchup is generally close, it would seem that we over-sample white males or that proportionately fewer black males accompany patients to the clinics; only future research will clear this up. For data on abortion patients, see Stanley K. Henshaw and Kevin O'Reilly, "Characteristics of Abortion Patients in the United States, 1979 and 1980," *Family Planning Perspectives* 15 (January/February 1983); 5–16, See also Howard Ory, *Making Choices* (New York: The Alan Guttmacher Institute, 1983).

4. We searched Social Science Citation Index and Sociological Abstracts on April 1, 1984. We found 239 citations on "women and abortion" and 40 on "men and abortion" for the years 1963–1984 in *Soc Abstracts,* and 271 and 29 in SSCI with complete overlap.

5. Mark Randall Smith. "How Men Who Accompany Women to an Abortion Service Perceive the Impact of Abortion Upon their Relationship and Themselves." Iowa City, Iowa: The University of Iowa, 1979, p. 13.
6. In addition to the Smith Ph.D. thesis cited above, we used research by Arden Arbel Rothstein (1974), Robert Barry Lees (1975), Michael Finley (1978), Kristine Larae Rotter (1980), Karen Deborah Brosseau (1980), William Marsiglio (1983), and June Hill-Falkenthal (1983). See references in footnote #1 for Chapter 2 for the complete citation; space restrictions precluded having a Bibliography.
7. Linda Bird Francke. "Men and Abortion." *Esquire* (January 1981): 60. As recently as 1966 a reform activist characterized the entire subject as "... the dark secret of society. It has been relegated for so long to the darkest corners of fear and mythology that an unwritten compact virtually requires that it remain untouched and undiscussed." Lawrence Lader. *Abortion*. Indianapolis: Bobbs-Merrill, 1966, p. 1
8. The contributors are Roger Wade and Peter Zelles; the third author is Ann Baker. See elsewhere among the footnotes for the complete citations.
9. A wide variety of efforts were made to secure respondents; e.g., Art and Gary made radio talk show appearances in the phone-question format and several more listeners later requested and completed questionnaires (WKVI, Seattle, WA; WXPN, Philadelphia, PA; etc.). An article by journalist Tim Harper in a Madison, Wisconsin, community newspaper (*Isthmus*) produced ten requests in February, 1983, for our questionnaire, and a note about the project that Art had inserted in a national men's movement newsletter (*Transitions*) attracted two questionnaire requests. Similarly, another such note inserted in the newsletter of the Pittsburgh men's collective secured cooperative requests from two readers.
10. Two clinics declined to attempt such guesstimates; a third withdrew its cooperation after providing a small number of completed waiting room surveys; and a fourth ignored repeated requests for completion of the survey form.
11. We drew here on the pioneering research of sociologist William Marsiglio of Ohio State University and remain very much in his debt. Only the second bloc of 500 men were asked to designate their choice of six possible clinic reforms, as this question came to our attention *after* we had gathered our initial 500 surveys.
12. Invaluable in this connection is a methodological critique prepared at our request by Dr. Joan Spade, which is offered in the book's appendix.
13. Reproductive Health and Counseling Clinic of the Crozer-Chester Medical Center, led at the time by Artis Ryder, gave the kind of sustained, sensitive, and unstinting support without which this research would not have been possible.
14. In an effort to reach clinics outside of the *NAF Directory* a search was made of abortion clinic ads in the telephone yellow pages of several cities (Atlanta, GA; Baltimore, MD; Los Angeles, CA; and others). Thirteen requests for research cooperation were mailed on February 24; 18 more on March 4, and six more on March 7. Unfortunately, nine of the clinics were no longer in operation (to judge from "order expired" stamps on the return mail), and 23 chose not to respond al all. We did, however, earn the cooperation of five clinics in this way.

Our 30 cooperating clinics contributed as few as two and as many as 101 surveys each, with only seven responsible for 5 to 12% of the total. Indeed, only two (Reproductive Health, PA, 12%, and Hillcrest Clinic, MD, 13%) actually made up more than 10% of the 1,000 cases. The spread, in short, was thin across a large number, making it unlikely that the characteristics of any one clinic's clientele biased our data in any particular way.

Climate of Opinion: Male and Female Attitudes

We are in the middle of a collective American history in which the established configuration of sexual roles is shifting, cracking, glacially yielding to a different configuration. For women, the movement has been occurring long enough that one can discuss it confidently. For men, the movement is so incipient that one wonders, sometimes, if one is hearing the sounds of actual change or merely the echoes of women's voices, or simply the murmurs of dreams.

Peter Filene, *ed., Men in the Middle* (Prentice-Hall, Englewood Cliffs, New Jersey, 1981, p. 28).

Table 2.10.2 Attitude toward Legality of Abortion, by Sex, 1975, 1981

"Do you think abortions should be legal under any circumstances, legal under only certain circumstances, or illegal in all circumstances?"

	1975		1981	
	Male	Female	Male	Female
Legal under all circumstances	20%	22%	22%	23%
Legal under only certain circumstances	54	53	54	50
Illegal in all circumstances	22	23	19	24
No Opinion	4	4	5	3

Source: *The Gallup Poll (Vol. Two). 1978 (April 1975), p. 509; The Gallup Poll, July 1981, Report No. 190 (May 1981), p. 18.*

Table 2.10.3 Attitude toward Legality and Morality of Abortion, 1982

"Abortion should be	legal	illegal	not sure	
	62%	31%	7%	Date: 1/82

"If you personally believe abortion is wrong, do you think it should be illegal?"

Is not wrong	Is wrong but should not be illegal	Is wrong and should be illegal	Not sure
44%	22%	27%	7%

Source: *AP/NBC Survey, released on 1/82, 8/82.*

Table 2.10.4 Abortion Attitude Resoluteness, by Sex, 1982

"How firm are you about your opinion on abortion? Would you say you are—	Males (612)	Females (841)
Very likely to change?	3%	2%
Somewhat likely to change?	15	10
Somewhat unlikely to change?	25	20
Very unlikely to change?	58	68

Source: *General Social Survey, NORC; Codebook, 1982. p. 159*

If we are to understand the experience of 1,000 men who sit and wait, we must explore the climate of public attitudes and opinion that shapes and informs that experience, the world of views that count.

Some 75% of our respondents spoke to no one other than their sex partner before reaching a decision about the pregnancy and its resolution. Given this restriction of dialogue, they leaned heavily on their impression of what "everyone feels" and what "we all know." But how do the sexes actually view the legalization of abortion? And its morality? On the different reasons (health related or otherwise) offered by women seeking abortions? And, do the

Table 2.10.5 Attitude Toward Start of Life, by Sex 1973, 1975, 1981

"Some people feel that human life begins at the moment of conception. Others feel that human life does not begin until the baby is actually born. So you yourself feel that human life begins at conception, at the time of birth, or some point in between?"

	1973		1975		1981	
	Male	Female	Male	Female	Male	Female
Anti-abortion answers:						
At conception	55%	73%	58%	74%	55%	67%
At quickening						
Pro-choice answers:						
When the unborn baby can survive if born early					11%	9%
At birth	20%.	8%	20%	9%	21%	14%
Don't know or no opinion	N.D.	N.D.	N.D.	N.D.	13%	10%

Source: The 1973 and 1975 Gallup data are from Judith Blake, "One Supreme Court's Abortion Decisions and Public Opinion in the United States," *Population and Development Review*, 3, 1977, pp. 55–56. The 1981 data are from *The Gallup Poll*, Report No. 190, July 1981, p, 19.

attitudes of the sexes suggest a consensus is emerging, a convergence in viewpoints independent of gender? Above all, how does any or all of this influence the men who sit and wait?

Public Judgment: Pro-Choice or Anti-Abortion?

While the American public agrees by two-to-one that the public good is adequately served by legalized abortion-on-request, many men and women remain considerably troubled by critical moral questions. Their unease explains much of the strained atmosphere of clinic waiting rooms.

Americans worry about the alleged personhood of the fetus. Some deny the reasonableness of elective surgery as a fall-back birth control option. And many doubters fear that abortion reform undermines tight-knit nuclear family values and traditional-sexual morality. Some go on to indict the women's movement and the Supreme Court for viewing the abortion option as "fundamentally involving a conflict among the rights of individuals, quite apart from their rights and obligations as family members. Yet such an atomistic view of society conflicts with the way these people see the world."[2] Accordingly moral censure and political opposition persists in those of either sex with a special commitment to the culture's more traditional morality values.[3]

Reasons for Abortion: "Hard" and "Soft"

People appear curious about why a female or a couple wants to terminate a pregnancy, and their curiosity is seldom neutral. Instead, there is a decided tendency to play judge and jury; to rush to judge the wholesomeness, reasonableness, and just plain good sense of this or that explanation offered by abortion seekers. As made clear by national

Table 2.10.6   Attitude toward Reasons for Abortion, by Approval Percent, 1965, 1972, 1976

	1965	1972	1976
"Hard"			
Health danger to mother	73%	87%	91%
Rape	59	79	84
Defect	57	79	84
"Soft"			
Too poor	27%	49%	53%
Single	18	43	50
Married; no more children desired	16	49	46

Source: National Gallup Polls, as reported in Raymond Tatalovich and Bryon W. Daynes, The Politics of Abortion: A Study of Community Conflict in Public Policymaking (New York: Praeger, 1981), p. 118.

Table 2.10.7 Attitude toward Reasons for Abortion, by Approval Percent, by Sex, 1982

	Male (615)	Female (832)
"Hard"		
Health danger to mother	93%	91%
Rape	88	86
Defect (fetus)	85	84
"Soft"		
Too poor	52%	52%
Single; doesn't want a child	49	49
Married; wants no more children	51	47

Source: General Social Survey, NORC 1982 Codebook, pp. 154–155.

polling data that predates the 1973 legalization decision, the public insists all explanations or reasons are *not* equally worthy.[5] Some are far less acceptable than others—these being the ones most often cited by waiting room males!

Between 1965 and the mid–1970s, for example, the public showed a decided tendency to approve reasons over which a female had little or no control ("hard"), and to disapprove of abortion situations where the choice was much more optional ("soft"). Typical of the polling used to measure these attitudes is this six-item question from NORC's General Social Survey, a question employed with some slight variation from 1965 through 1982:

"Please tell me whether or not *you* think it should be possible for a pregnant woman to obtain a *legal* abortion—

1. If there is a strong chance of serious defect in the baby?
2. If she is married and does not want any more children?
3. If the woman's own health is seriously endangered by the pregnancy?
4. If the family has a very low income and cannot afford any more children?
5. If she became pregnant as a result of rape?
6. If she is not married and does not want to marry the man?"

Between 1965 and 1976, the NORC survey showed a sweeping increase in approval, though almost 50 percentage points continued to separate highly acceptable from barely tolerated reasons for an elective abortion (see Table 2.10.6).

When examined two years later, the NORC data confirmed a long-term trend; three-fourths or more of the respondents in 1978 favored abortion for the top three "hard" reasons, while less than half were favorable when "soft" reasons were offered.[6] In 1982, the picture was very much the same: the "hard" reasons won approval by 92%, 87%, and 85%; the "soft" by only 52% (low income), 49% (married), and 49% (single).[7]

As for male and female attitudes, the 1982 data reflect a convergence profile true of earlier years as well—men and women see eye-to-eye in this matter, as is shown in Table 2.10.7. All of this suggests that waiting room males confront a judgmental public generally twice as accepting of "involuntary" as of "voluntary" excuses for an abortion; a public consistent in its ranking over time and across the sexes, though, also, a public capable of making more refined judgments along critical lines of demarcation (sweeping approval or disapproval; pick-and-choose; and hard reasons only).

Summary

When as many as a million or more American men annually learn a pregnancy they share may end in abortion, the largest number choose to keep it to themselves: only one in four of our 1,000 waiting room males talked with anyone besides their sex partner before the decision was made. Instead, the males silently process their subjective notions of what "everybody knows," of what "everybody feels," of what the climate of general opinion seems to recommend.

To judge cautiously, then, from public opinion data, males who sit and wait may wrestle with three critical attitude clusters:

1. *Both sexes generally support the legalization of abortion on request;* neither sex, however, considers this an unqualified right, and both males and females respect the regulatory role of the state in this matter.
2. *Both sexes generally support the right of the prospective parents to decide the fate of the fetus;* neither sex, however, believes any and every reason offered to explain a termination decision is comparably worthy and morally acceptable.
3. *Both sexes generally subscribe to the same or similar attitudes toward abortion;* neither sex, however, agrees with the other about when human life ("personhood") begins—males, in particular holding a more pro-choice attitude than females.

These ambivalent views undoubtedly take their toll on waiting room men sensitive to the public's uncertainty and remorse about abortion.

Notes

1. "Two-thirds of a national sample agree that any woman who is pregnant should be able to decide whether or not she wants to have an abortion." Market Opinion Research, "New Attitudes about Government Involvement in the Abortion Issue," p. 2, Washington, D.C.: National Abortion-Rights Action League, 1981. "On abortion, 75% said that the decision to have an abortion should be left to a woman and her doctor." Witt and Evans, "Poll Shows Little Change in Opinions." *Philadelphia Inquirer,* June 7, 1981, p. 15–A. "Two out of three Americans think abortion should be a matter for decision solely between a woman and her physician." Anonymous, "The Gallup Poll Surveys Abortion" *Philadelphia Evening Bulletin,* September 5, 1972, p. 10.

2. Peter Skerry, "The Class Conflict Over Abortion." *Public Interest,* Summer 1978, p. 81. "If we accept for the sake of argument that abortion *is* a moral issue, then the nature of the class conflict over abortion is more apparent. Scientific knowledge and analytic skills are simply not as capable of informing this issue as they are certain others, such as pollution or nuclear power. The members of the knowledge class ... are thereby really not any better equipped to deal with the matter of abortion than are the "members of any other group." (p. 84)
3. Typical of those with anti-choice attitudes are evangelical conservatives who, in a 1980 poll, were 41% in favor of banning all abortions versus all voters (31%). Allan J. Mayer et al. "Evangelical Politics," *Newsweek,* September 15, 1980, p. 36. Donald Granberg has found that opposition to abortion may reflect a more general political conservatism, especially in terms of opposition to divorce, sex education, dissemination of birth control information, premarital sex, and pornography. Issues of personal morality appear *the* major source of difference in attitudes between anti-choice and pro-choice activists. Donald Granberg, "Pro-Life or Reflection of Conservative Idealogy? in Analysis of Opposition to Legalized Abortion." *Sociology and Social Research* 62 (1978): 414–429. On the attitudes of Catholic males in our sample, see Arthur Shostak, "Catholic Men and Abortion, *Conscience* (January/February 1984): 5–6.
4. Jerry Adler and John Carey, "But Is It A Person?." :*Newsweek,* January 11, 1982, p. 44.
5. See in his connection, Benjamin I. Page and Robert Y. Shapiro, "Changes in Americans' Policy Preferences, 1935–1979." *Public Opinion Quarterly* Spring (1982): 31; Judith Blake, "The Supreme Court's Abortion Decisions and Public Opinion in the United States." *Population and Development Review* 3 (1977): 55–56; Judith Blake, "Abortion and Public Opinion: The 1960–1970 Decade," *Science* 171 (February 12, 1971): 540–549; Alice S. Rossi, "Public Views on Abortion," in Alan F. Guttmacher, Sr., ed., *The Case for Legalized Abortion Now,* pp. 26–53. Berkeley, Calif: Diablo Press, 1967; Lucky M. Tedrow and E. R. Mahoney, "Trends in Attitudes toward Abortion: 1972–1976." *Public Opinion Quarterly* 1979: 181–189; Theodore C. Wagenaar and Ingeborg W. Knot, "Attitudes toward Abortion: A Comparative Analysis of Correlates for 1973 and 1975," *Journal of Sociology and Social Welfare* 4(6, July 1977): 927–944.
6. Helen Rose Fuchs Ebaugh and C. Allen Haney, "Shifts in Abortion Attitudes: 1972–1978," *Journal of Marriage and the Family* (August 1980): 493.
7. Sharon N. Garnrtt and Richard J. Harris, "Recent Changes in Predictors of Abortion Attitudes." *Sociology and Social Research* 66(3, April 1982); 324.

Men—What Do They Want?

To be responsible for oneself, it is first necessary to acknowledge what one is doing. The criterion for judgment thus shifts from goodness to truth when the morality of action is assessed not on the basis of its appearance in the eyes of others, but in terms of the realities of its intention and consequence. ... The needs of the self have to be deliberately uncovered.

Carol Gilligan, *In a Different Voice* (Cambridge, Massachusetts, Harvard University Press, 1982, pp. 83, 84).

In addition to the impersonal climate of public opinion, our background analysis of the male abortion experience includes the highly personal process of developing a moral core, of forming the moral center of one's being.

How have clinic waiting room men earned their moral resolutions? How do they make moral decisions? And what are their central moral concerns? Above all, how does their moral frame-work compare with that of their sex partners? And how significant is any disparity, or convergence, in their respective moral domains?

These questions received especially helpful treatment from the field research and analysis of Carol Gilligan, a cognitive psychologist who, in 1982, authored an aptly titled book, *In a Different Voice*.[1] From our reading of Gilligan's work, we have gained a clearer understanding of the moral background of our 1,000 waiting room men.[2] A campus-based counseling psychologist Arnold Medvene, closes this chapter with some thoughts of his on two distinct approaches males seem to take to the abortion challenge. His clinic-derived insights complement Gilligan's line of analysis, and shed new and valuable light on the innermost thoughts of waiting room males.

One Morality Or Two?

As Gilligan critiques prevailing wisdom in this matter, she attempts to correct eminent male psychologists (such as Erikson, Freud, Kohlberg, Levinson, McClelland, Piaget, Valient, and others) who may seriously mislead their readers. For a variety of reasons these men have treated both sexes as if they were one, and have created the erroneous impression that only one moral way of being exists.[3] On the contrary, Gilligan asserts, there are two very different moral ideologies, one male, one female. And this duality explains much of the dissimilarity in the abortion experiences of men and women.

Drawing on 10 years of her own field research (including a rare pre- and post-abortion study of 21 women, and a study of 144 individuals—72 males—in which she asked about conceptions of self and morality), Gilligan began to distinguish two ways of speaking about moral problems, two modes of describing the relationship between the other and the self. As she reconstructed the socialization experience of the sexes, males take from childhood an Ethic of Abstract Rights; females, an Ethic of Caring and Intimacy. While males tend to define moral problems in terms of rights and rules (the "justice approach"), females define moral problems in terms of an obligation to exercise care and avoid hurting others.[4]

Males grow up preoccupied with winning and holding the respect of significant others, especially their childhood peers and parents. Later, the respect of employers and co-workers becomes comparably important. Females, however, are socialized to look for approval by satisfying the needs of others *first*, even while struggling not to entirely betray their own needs. Males learn that respect is earned through struggle through taking a "proper" stand. Females are socialized instead to demur, to focus on gaining and holding intimate relationships rather than on asserting or defending abstract rights and rules.[5]

At a time, then, when a rapid decision must be made about an unwanted pregnancy, the male relies on his Ethic of Abstract Rights. Many, however, perhaps for the first time, struggle to balance a moral absolute—"the baby must live!"—against a newly discovered contradiction—"My sex partner has a right not to go through with the pregnancy; it's *her* body!"

Females, in turn, struggle to achieve an "understanding that gives rise to compassion and care."[6] Reared to want to sacrifice themselves to protect the unborn child, they must learn, with their sex partner's help, how to protect their *own* rights as well.

Both males and females alike are compelled to recognize that there are life situations in which it is impossible to avoid hurting others.

Keeping One's Distance versus Gaining Intimacy

Along with its emphasis on unavoidable hurt, Gilligan's analysis illuminates the tension between abortion clinic couples who move toward, and yet, also away from one another in often erratic ways, barely understood by either of them.

For the male, much of the difficulty derives from his emotional reticence and macho pose which helps bottle up his feelings. Raised to respect a stiff-necked Ethic of Absolute Rights, many men seem to view morality dilemmas (such as the abortion question) as primarily a matter of what they think life and society owe their hapless pregnant sex partner. Since the U.S. Supreme Court has twice decided the fairness question in favor of an unfettered right to an abortion on request (1973, 1983), certain males conclude the "right thing" for them to do is repress any emotions or thoughts of their own in the matter. They assure their sex partner that *anything* she wants is okay with them ("If only she wouldn't be so upset!").

Females look elsewhere for moral guidance. They make little, if any, use of the male insistence on absolute right and wrong. As their childhood taught them to view morality in terms of caring, and resolving conflicting responsibilities, they focus on making and holding onto loving attachments. Many males in contrast, are preoccupied with "making it." "Power and separation secure the man in an identity achieved through work, but they leave him at a distance from others who seem in some sense out of his sight."[7] So pervasive is this male drive for prowess that many view the female emphasis on gaining emotional attachment as perilous: Intimacy is thought to pose a "danger of entrapment or betrayal, as being caught in a smothering relationship or humiliated by rejection and deceit."[8]

Females, sensitized to a different world view, follow a script complete with its own ethic and moral preoccupations. Many come to see the distancing ways of males as perilous, as posing a danger to females of unwanted isolation, loneliness, rejection, and deceit.

Each sex seeks to counter threats seemingly posed by the other threats neither sex actually perceives itself posing. Males remain suspicious of opportunities to lose themselves in love relationships. Many prefer to guard their options, to keep their distance by playing the field. Females are deprived thereby of deep romantic relationships, and endure the heartache of searching for a White Knight. Each sex, ironically, actually needs more of that which it thinks it fears the most—males need *more* emotional investment; females, *less* emotional dependency ("… we know ourselves as separate only insofar as we live in connection with others, and we experience relationship only insofar as we differentiate other from self.").[9]

Achievement of the ability to be intimate is regarded by Gilligan as indispensable if the maturing male is to mitigate excessive isolation. Intimacy, she contends, is "… the critical experience that brings the self back into connection with others; making it possible to see both sides to discover the effects of actions on others as well as their cost to the self."[10] For this reason, intimacy is "the transformative experience for men through which adolescent identity turns into the generativity of adult love and work"[11] and, for this reason, abortion clinic counseling for males should be dramatically revised and expanded to include intimacy-gaining skills.

Gilligan's insights, in sum, could guide counseling in the direction of more and more empathy between the sexes. It is important here to emphasize the explanatory power of her two-mode approach. If Gilligan's understanding of sex-specific moral domains is sound, much of the inability of the sex partners to understand one another becomes itself more understandable and far more amenable to reform than has been previously considered or imagined. Waiting room men may be capable of achieving far more moral and personal growth from their experience than is presently understood. As one of Gilligan's female respondents explains, "Abortion, if you do it for the right reasons, is helping yourself to start over and do different things."[12]

Arnold Medvene, Counseling Psychologist

In my psychotherapy experiences with men facing abortion, their resolution of loss revolves around two pivotal issues: (1) openly confronting and working with one's emotional experience, and (2) disclosing these feelings and emotions on an intimate level with others to work against the sea of isolation and personal withdrawal that men often experience following this benchmark emotional event.

As a male therapist my goal is to form a strong therapeutic alliance with my brother to fully examine the male experience, issues of trust, openness, decision making, power, separation, control, equality, and feelings of anger, sadness, hurt, and loss are central themes which are explored without judgment or evaluation. My purpose is greater clarity and understanding of the male dilemma so men can truly make free choices, and not be fettered by cultural beliefs, traditions, and values that define what a man really is.

Abortion is a male crisis of vulnerability. At a time when he wishes to be omnipotent there is a pervasive sense of powerlessness and helplessness. Abortion brings the man close to forces of life and death and shatters his fantasies of invulnerability. Unwanted pregnancy demands that a man confront an experience for which he has limited resources and skills. This sense of helplessness and frustration leads to bewilderment, anxiety, loss of self-esteem, and despair. A highly significant life happening is occurring, yet it is one often responded to by little or no emotion by the male.

Since Western male culture places strong emphasis on growth, competence, and overcoming adversity, there is little understanding of and support for an inward emotional glance that says to the man, "trust your feelings, share your feelings, expand your feelings, be your feelings." This emotional denial of natural grief responses is energy draining, and often leaves the male exhausted and feeling without reserves or resources. Living does include sadness, hurt, and pain. The capacity to reach inside and touch that part of oneself and not shrink away from painful thoughts and feelings is a beginning to fully living.

The men I work with are essentially *Personalizers* or *Controllers* in their abortion experience. I will list the kinds of responses and reactions each group brings to therapy as they better try to understand their way of coping with a highly significant life event. Their capacity to heighten self-awareness, to explore and extend previously surface-level ideas and feelings, to trust another person with their doubts, fears, anxieties, humor, anger, and feared humanness is an indication of their self-acceptance and capacity to be intimate in a personal relationship.

Personalizers

1. Acknowledge the abortion as an intense emotional experience.
2. In-depth exploration of their feelings.
3. Integration of thoughts and feelings about this loss, and how it corresponds to other transition points in their lives.
4. Respond to the woman in terms of her feelings, values, and self-experience.
5. Struggles with being too female-identified, and fear losing the respect and admiration of their male friends.
6. Embarrassed by having too many feelings.
7. Cherish individuality for both sexes.
8. Mood swings are common.
9. Loving and affectionate to the woman and feel a keen sense of loss in their life together.
10. Creative problem solvers.
11. Search for meaning in their experience.
12. Try to maximize this experience as a benchmark in their adult development.
13. Feel guilty that the woman pays such a high price for their mistake; feel guilt about destroying life; feel anger at failed birth control.
14. View powerlessness and helplessness as a means toward greater self-awareness.
15. Struggle with their male-conditioned response to blame the woman and to hold her responsible for their problems.

Bob

I don't find myself scarred from it. It's been reduced to another of life's problems. It is now resolved. I have been to Nam, and I know the sense of power from looking down the barrel and deciding on a life. The abortion of a fetus is lower on the scale of phenomena. But I no longer use absolutes—all or never. I think the controversy over abortion is based on poorly-defined absolutes.

I found out on long-distance while she was out of town. She was very elated. She loved the idea of being pregnant. She determined that on approval from me she'd have the baby. ... I got caught up in the idea from her effervescence. My reaction was conditioned by hers. I had a lot of reservations, but I said, "Why not?"

Was I willing to sacrifice to be a good father? I came from a broken home, I had been denied a lot and I was looking for a lot. As a father I didn't know if I'd be able to sacrifice my ambitions to give and cater to it. And an absentee father is not my idea of a good one. It is a conundrum for me ... She wasn't self-sacrificing enough for children. Ideas, not realities of nurturing and daily routine of raising a child, were what she had.

I accept that conception is the beginning of life. Whatever you want to call it. It's human, of humans. What degree of responsibility do we as a society have to women, to embryos? I believe we have to protect the rights of those who are developed. On the other hand, abortion should not be used as a birth control device.

It should be used as an emergency tool rather than a standard birth control device. The ideal, of course, is birth control. In that absence we need abortion to cover technical or use failures. Funerals are for the living; so, too, are abortions. It's cultural. I can't see the fetus as a cultural human being, although it has the potential from conception.

There was a sense of fantasy about the whole thing as we worked it out over the phone. ... I don't remember who was first, but we began to talk about not going ahead with marriage and children.

It was peace and calm after we reached the decision. It was right and we felt it. I probably felt more at peace than she did. The idea of having a human being inside her was awesome to her, "Little Johnny's gone," she'd say in public as a spoof, but there was a cutting sense of loss.

I wasn't ready to marry before the pregnancy and I wasn't ready afterward. She knew that and eventually it became a determining factor in the decision ... I sense that she feels rejected, especially after the abortion because I could have supported the decision to have the kid and she'd not have changed. I'd be a father—last month [January 1983].

Rita

I'm very intrigued that men are shocked at my opinion of them. Two male friends were upset with me because I said they didn't care about pregnancy or abortion. They said they had feelings, but what do they have beyond that?

I've had my own abortion experience. ... Being pregnant was absolutely mind blowing in a primitive way. I mean, it (sex) really worked! Afterward, I talked to a lot of women about what it felt like. Men seemed to be out of that whole ballpark. They listened sympathetically, but the men never talked about their regrets, or their connections to the pregnancy or the abortion.

Bob was so out of touch with what being pregnant was like that he never asked how I felt, only what did I want to do. He wasn't in love, didn't want a baby, but he said he'd marry me to make it honest, I suppose. One morning I woke up and realized my relationship was a fraud and that marriage and pregnancy didn't go together. I had to take over by myself.

When I said I was getting an abortion, Bob said, "Whatever you want to do ..."

The irony of the whole thing was that I thought I could get support from anyone but him. I could not do it with a man—my sister, mother, friends, but no man I know is open enough to share something as heavy as pregnancy and abortion.

I don't know how men feel about pregnancy. My feelings are strong about being pregnant. I was overjoyed. I still want it more than a husband, or a ranch house, or anything.

... he had no understanding of what I had been through and what I had to go through right afterward, even though I told him. Bob did all the gesturing, but we never sat down and talked. For him it was over. He went on about his job, I wanted to move out. He showed no emotion about breaking up. I never slept with him again and we never discussed the abortion, although I ran into him several times after I moved out.

I've been seeing a new man for awhile and he's pretty nice, but we don't really talk about sex or birth control. Except one night when we were first going out, he said to me "If you never want another abortion, you'd better stop playing Russian roulette with your birth control pills, because I have no intention of marrying you."

I always feel like I have to protect my man. Saying, "I don't want to ruin your life." If I imagine telling him that I'm pregnant, I think of soft candlelight and wine, breaking the news gently, I'd want to reassure him. Why do I feel that way?

Controllers

1. Hard to be in a supportive, non-starring role.
2. Angry and resentful about their loss of control and sense of powerlessness.
3. View the experience as a power struggle with a winner and a loser. It is a test case of who is more dominant and forceful.
4. Tend to focus on solutions and make the problems concrete and solvable to move away from their feelings.
5. View the woman in an impersonal and objectified way.
6. Tend to denigrate her being to render her powerless and insignificant.
7. Fear being stigmatized and losing esteem among other men.
8. View abortion as right of wrong—no feelings involved.
9. Ambitious, acquisitive and view self-disclosure as a threat.
10. Resist shared decision making with the woman as she is seen as less competent and too emotional.
11. Insensitive to feelings—theirs and the woman's.
12. Tend to trivialize the meaning of the experience for self and the other person.
13. Feel outside and peripheral to an internal experience.
14. Feel isolated and wary of the interest of other people.
15. Restless overactivity.

Personalizers try to look at their experience of loss as a way to know themselves in greater depth. Their journey is one of authenticity and enrichment though this trip encompasses grief, anger, pain, and sadness. These men often choose growth over safety and, in doing so, risk the security, power, and influence endemic to being male in our culture. Their capacity to travel unfamiliar roads connotes a great deal of inner wonder and a willingness to be pioneers in the male experience.

Controllers are basically angry with the woman having the abortion as she is seen as a threat to their control, power, and dominance. These men use a great deal of energy in emotional denial, and their reluctance to grieve produces a sense of safety and security; but it also fosters severely restricted personal growth. Coming to terms with their feelings of sadness, hurt, and pain is a way to be whole and not split off from themselves, and it is their quintessential developmental task in this experience.

We cannot really hide from our pain as it is a part of life. But when we begin to face the meaning of our feelings, we can learn a great deal about how to live and the meaning of life. George Bernard Shaw once wrote that "Heartbreak is life educating us," and our ability and courage to trust and explore within allows us to live as fully as we can.

PROFILE

Although we discussed abortion with a number of articulate women and formally interviewed a select few, we have presented on interviews as a matter of thematic and editorial strategy. The climate of opinion chapter, however, has explored the male and female domains and whet our appetites to see how the perspectives offered in the chapter might apply in a given male-female situation.

Bob and Rita were interviewed on separate occasions. Each talked sincerely and openly about their abortion experiences with the other one. The parallel split interview format demonstrates many tenets of male and female domains, contrasts, comparisons, and conflicting perceptions.

	Father's Advice for Daughter/Son	Mother's Advice for Daughter/Son
Have an abortion	20%/17%	23%/19%
Have the baby; give it up for adoption	13%/12%	23%/22%
Have the baby and keep the child; or seek custody of it	21%/6%	14%/5%
Marry and keep the child	13%/26%	6%/11%
None. Would leave it entirely up to her/him	17%/19%	19%/22%
Other	17%/19%	20%/23%
	(N=605)	(N=8,076)

Source: *A Report on American Families from the Editors of Better Homes and Gardens*, May 1983, pp. 136–137.

Parental Advice

Only one survey we found in the abortion research literature explores the kind of advice parents think they would offer an unmarried son or daughter trying to decide how to resolve an unexpected pregnancy. Drawn entirely from white, middle-class, well-educated "mainstream" respondents, the survey has highly restricted generalizability. Nevertheless, to judge from our encounters with waiting room males, the advice profile below is one in broad general use, almost regardless of race, class, or style of life.

Sex-role stereotypes are obvious above, the men urging their sons to do the "right thing" and marry the girl (26%), even while advising against any new-fangled notion of single male parenthood (6%). In contrast, they would advise their daughters to undertake single parenthood (21%) rather than marry the "s.o.b." who "knocked her up" (13%). Women, in turn, are far less endorsing of single parenthood for either gender, and also think very little of the marriage option. Instead, unlike the men, they urge the adoption route, or, slightly more often, the abortion resolution.

Sharp distinctions between fathers and mothers in the advice they would offer a son or daughter confronting pregnancy may go far in explaining why only 11% of our 1,000 waiting room males actually took their parents into their confidence—and weighed their advice in reaching a resolution of the pregnancy: Only one other source of advice—the clergy—was less seldom used by waiting room males.

Notes

1. Carol Gilligan. *In a Different Voice: Psychological Theory and Women's Development*, Cambridge, Mass.: Harvard University Press, 1982.
2. To be sure, Gilligan focused entirely on female respondents (29 expectant mothers, 21 of whom were interviewed again at the end of the year following their choice of the abortion option). We alone are responsible for this effort to apply her theorizing to the male partner in the abortion experience.
3. Gilligan contends these men devised models of human development in which women appeared deviant or morally stunted. See, in this connection, Phyllis Chester, *About Men*. New York: Simon and Schuster, 1978.
4. Gilligan cautions on page 2 that the gender linkage to the two themes "is not absolute, and the contrasts between male and female voices are presented here, to highlight a distinction between two modes of thought and to focus a problem in

interpretation rather than to represent a generalization about either sex." See in this connection Raye H. Rosen and Lois J. Martindale, "Sex Role Perceptions and the Abortion Decision," *Journal of Sex Research* 14 (November 1978): 231–245.

5. Gilligan's model of women's moral reasoning appeals to responsibilities, rather than to rights. Women are thought to fear isolation, rather than aggression, and to emphasize caring for others before oneself. An admiring critic concludes this line of analysis "builds a moral megaphone that enables us to hear women's voices with all their complexity and integrity." Judith Kegan Gardiner "Morality on a New Scale." *In These Times,* October 20–26, 1982, p. 19.
6. Gilligan, op. cit., p. 165.
7. Ibid., p. 163.
8. Ibid., p. 42.
9. Ibid., p. 63.
10. Ibid., p.163
11. Ibid. p. 163. Mark Gerzon concurs, and advises that "a crisis in masculinity is also an opportunity. It compels us to find new maps of the world we live in. It encourages us to find wise traveling companions. It inspires us to learn to read the compass of our heart … men want access to what they have forfeited: intimacy, nurturance, friendship, mutuality." Mark Gerzon, *A Choice of Heroes: The Changing Faces of American Manhood,* Boston: Houghton Mifflin, 1982.
12. Gilligan, op. cit., p. 78. For a dissent from Gilligan's perspective, see Judith O. Smetana, *Concepts of Self and Morality: Women's Reasoning about Abortion,* op. cit. For a negative view of gender convergence, at least in the marketplace, see Rachael Flick, "The New Feminism and the World of Work." *The Public Interest* (1983): 33–44. For a skeptical view of Gilligan's perspective, see Carol Tavris, "Women and Men and Morality." *New York Times Book Review,* May 2, 1982, pp. 14–15; Anne Colby and William Damon; "Listening to a Different Voice: A Review of Gilligan's *In a Different Voice,*" *Merrill-Palmer Quarterly* 29 (October 1983): 473–481.

Reform Possibilities

In this closing section of our book, we are preoccupied with the single most compelling question we have: "How could it be done any better?"

We are sensitive to the major reasons offered in defense of the status quo; for example, "The female, after all, is *the* patient, and *must* be our major concern!" "Funds are in short supply, and *must* go to subsidize the abortions of indigent women." "Men in our waiting room never complain, at least, not that we have heard." "Until the anti-abortionists stop threatening our clinic's very existence, we cannot be distracted by *any* new reform efforts." Each of these arguments was made repeatedly, only to have many speakers later note that certain clinic staffers *were* troubled by their relative neglect of male partners, by the number of relationships that seemed to flounder after an abortion (perhaps unnecessarily) and by the increasing incidence of male repeaters.

[Later in this book] we explore the standing of men in the law, and discuss how, since the 1973 Supreme Court legalization of abortion-on-request, men have had no rights in a contested abortion situation. Special attention is paid to three legal reform possibilities: spousal consent requirements; spousal foreknowledge requirements; and the revision of child support requirements—the pros and cons of which are laid out for the reader's own assessment.

[Later in this book] we move rapidly through a large number of reforms that bear on the preclinic phase of the experience. For example, we discuss the role of sex education courses in secondary schools, the impact the media could have, the contribution that might be made by the men's movement—and the women's, as well—among many more such potential sources of aid.

[Later in this book] we focus on the clinic day experience. Drawing on many reform ideas suggested by our 1,000 men, and on programmatic changes espoused by our contributing abortion counselors, we outline several practical, low-cost, and promising changes in clinic realities. Should these soon earn an experimental trial, we might finally achieve the sensitive and rewarding quality of services for men favored by many clinic staffers.

After traveling across the country in 1980 and visiting numerous clinics from coast to coast, journalist Linda Bird Francke concluded many such providers were "increasingly becoming disturbed because they offer little besides free cups of coffee to the men who sit and wait."[1] Perhaps the time has finally arrived to go further—much, much further.

Notes

1. Linda Bird Francke, *The Ambivalence of Abortion,* p. 158, New York; Dell, 1978. See also Linda Bird Francke, "Abortion and Men," op. cit., pp. 58–60; Carole Joffe, "What Abortion Counselors Want from Their Clients," *Social Problems* 26, 1 (1978): 112–121.

Enlisting Men in Support of Reproductive Freedom

By Alexander Sanger

Antoine stands on the sidewalk outside the Margaret Sanger Clinic of Planned Parenthood of New York City on a hot, humid July morning. He has dropped off his girlfriend for an abortion and is waiting to take her home. He wears a windbreaker that is zipped halfway up despite the heat. A social worker tells him that she works at the clinic and is talking to his girlfriend and asks him if he wants to come inside to discuss his girlfriend's decision. Antoine shakes his head and murmurs, "No." The social worker and I wonder whether Antoine is armed and doesn't want to go through the metal detectors at the clinic entrance. The social worker gently persists and asks if he wants to talk about the abortion. Antoine declines again: "That's her business. It ain't mine." When we relay the conversation to his girlfriend inside, she says "Typical. He thinks he's being respectful. All I want is for him to talk to me and deal with our relationship."

Do Males Need Reproductive Freedom?

Just as my grandmother framed birth control as a woman's issue, reproductive rights advocates have framed abortion as a woman's issue. Men and women alike have long viewed birth control and abortion this way as well. But framing the issues of reproductive freedom as women's issues does not help garner male support because it doesn't provide satisfactory answers to a male's questions: When is abortion my business? Why should I support women's reproductive rights? What's in it for me? Don't I have reproductive rights too? Why should a woman's rights prevail over mine?

To get the support of males, reproductive rights advocates must address and support male reproductive interests. Just as women are more than wombs, men are more than inseminators. Men's reproductive interests and rights derive, as women's do, from their role in human evolution. Women's reproductive rights derive from the importance to women of controlling their own reproduction. Natural selection favored those women who did. The genes of women who controlled their reproduction had a better chance of being passed down than those of women who did not, because the women who controlled their reproduction had a better chance of surviving childbirth, as did their children. This chapter will argue that it is of equal importance for men to control their own reproduction and to have the right to do so. Men like women, need reproductive freedom to achieve reproductive success.

Alexander Sanger, "Enlisting Men in Support of Reproductive Freedom," *Beyond Choice Reproductive Freedom in the 21st Century*, pp. 145–161. Copyright © 2005 by Public Affairs, a Member of The Perseus Books Group. Reprinted with permission.

Humanity needs both men and women to be reproductively successful. It is not in women's interest to make reproductive freedom their exclusive preserve.

Before we can try to define the extent of male reproductive freedom, we need to see what a man's reproductive interests might be. Even though males and females have different biological roles, the essential male reproductive interest is the same as a female's successful procreation. Men will not achieve reproductive success unless mother and child survive childbirth and the child survives to adulthood to reproduce.

Therefore, men like women need to control the timings, spacing and number of children to maximize their offspring's chance of surviving and being healthy and prosperous. For men this involves more, however, than just using contraceptives so that births can be spaced and timed, although this is part of a successful strategy. Men, like women, need a complete reproductive strategy that involves finding and choosing the right mate, then their mate's having a successful pregnancy and a problem-free birth and then years of upbringing for the child.

The biological differences between males and females mean that each sex will have divergent reproductive and sexual strategies to accomplish this biological goal. The battle of the sexes is over the control of reproduction.

Each sex battles among itself and against the other sex for this control. But for men the process is fraught with special challenges. Because women generally do the choosing, men have to compete with each other to reproduce. Alas, not all men get chosen. Men therefore compete often violently among each other for dominance and high status. In an attempt to try to improve their chances of being selected, men will either try to control women directly by force or will indirectly try to attract women by controlling resources or by other means of demonstrating their reproductive fitness. Males have evolved to have sexual and other characteristics that demonstrate and communicate their health and genetic fitness in a myriad of ways. But since males get selected for not only their genetic fitness, but also their social standing, resources, kin network and parenting abilities, they need to demonstrate these also. Conspicuous displays of wealth or family ties are done for a biological purpose.

Next, men have to try to exercise influence over whether and when a particular partner conceives a child. But men have fewer options than women to prevent pregnancy and childbirth. Other than sterilization, the sole male methods of contraception are the condom and withdrawal. Both are evident to the woman. A woman has more power to control whether or not she gets pregnant and can do so without the male knowing or controlling what her decision is. Furthermore with abortion a woman can control whether or not she gives birth. The battle of the sexes so far looks like a rout for the females.

After childbirth the scales tip towards the males somewhat. Parenting presents a fundamental quandary for men. During and after pregnancy and childbearing men have more immediate opportunities than women to find another mate and parent another child. Parenting reduces a man's opportunities to take this path towards another reproductive success. A man has to make a choice between investing in parenting one child, or proceeding to reproduce with another person. Women because of their investment in the pregnancy have less of a choice.

The battle of the sexes for control of reproduction becomes even more of a rout for the females because of the male's basic biological problem that even if he succeeds in the competition and gets selected to mate, he has absolutely no assurance (until the advent of DNA testing) that he is the genetic father of the children that his "mate" produces. This is the problem of paternity uncertainty. Natural selection favors men who know who their children are. If a man devotes the time, resources, and energy to parent his children, it is more likely that his genes will get passed own. If he unknowingly parents some other man's children, he is helping some other man's genes, not his own, to get passed down. So how does a man improve his chances here?

Men have evolved to have a variety of strategies for ensuring their reproductive interests and achieving reproductive success. These include trying to prevent other men from having access to their mate or else trying to have sex with a variety of other female partners in the hopes of fathering a child. These are not mutually exclusive strategies and men often pursue a combination of these strategies. But so do women, hence the paternity problem for men. Men have responded by using the law as their weapon.

Laws restricting a woman's reproductive freedom by restricting access to birth control and abortion, or by increasing the penalties for a woman's adultery, are efforts by men to tilt the playing field so that they will be able to pursue their strategies while not allowing women the same leeway to pursue theirs. There are costs, however to men when they restrict women's reproductive freedom: their own freedom is also restricted and their potential reproductive success is threatened. Therefore, men who have more status, and thus more reproductive chances, will be less likely to want to restrict women's reproductive freedom. A high-status male, who has many prospects for mating, is less threatened by a female's ability to control her mating and reproduction than a low-status male who has fewer prospects. The low-status male will get chosen less, if at all, for mating and must make the most of his few opportunities. He will want to invest in parenting and, if married, will want to preserve the marriage for the benefit of the children. Reproductive freedom is viewed by low-status men, and by their partners as well, as a threat to their marriage and to the well-being of their children.

The uneven biological playing field forces us to confront the issue of how we can get men of every status to support reproductive freedom for women when it may not be in their immediate interest. At the same time we must ask the extent to which certain male reproductive-interests should be enshrined as male reproductive rights. In order to recognize male interests and freedoms, we must admit that male efforts to win the battle of the sexes are not necessarily inimical to women's interests. The solution to these knotty issues will come when we find a way for men and women to unite in some common reproductive strategies for their mutual benefit. If this is possible, then perhaps we can enlist men in support of women's reproductive freedom, and enlist women in support of men's.

How can we get men of every status to support reproductive freedom? I believe only by eliminating paternity uncertainty. Technology in the form of condoms and DNA testing now allows this. While condom use is not totally effective in preventing pregnancy, it will go a long way towards letting men control when they are going to father a child. DNA testing can give men certain proof, after the fact, that the child they are parenting is actually their genetic child (while the percentage of time this happens is relatively small, on the order of ten percent or less, the fear is substantially greater). Paternity certainty will have enormous implications. It should level the playing field, should lead to changes in men's and women's reproductive strategies and should lead to more co-operation and partnership between the sexes in childrearing. It could, if advocates of reproductive freedom position it properly, lead to increased male and female support for reproductive freedom, since men will have the same interest as their partners in controlling pregnancy and childbirth to obtain the optimal reproductive result for them.

Women's reproductive freedom will get increased political support when it is seen as being in a man's interest as well as a woman's. The same is true of men's reproductive freedom. It will gain in support when it is seen as being in women's interests. While since *Roe* we have seen increased restrictions in women's reproductive freedom imposed by legislatures and permitted by the courts, we have also seen increased restrictions on a man's reproductive freedom. Both men and women should view this with alarm.

Male Reproductive Interests Do Not Automatically Translate into Male Reproductive Rights

The Supreme Court in its birth control and abortion cases ruled that both women and men had a fundamental right to decide whether or not to have a child. However, the courts have been more willing to restrict a man's rights than a woman's, even where there was no conflict between their wishes.

For example, some courts have ordered men behind on child support payments not to have any more children. In the summer of 2001 the Wisconsin Supreme Court approved a lower court ruling that David Oakley, a father of nine, who owed $25,000 in child support, could be ordered not to father any more children while on probation "unless he could prove to the court that he could support all of them." While the court took note of Oakley's past record of abusing his children, the court justified the sentence not on abuse grounds but on the sole ground of Oakley's "abysmal history" of non-payment of child support. The court asserted that the court order did not deprive Oakley permanently of his constitutional right to procreate since "he can satisfy the condition of his probation by making efforts to support his children as required by law." One judge in the majority stated that he supported the order because the defendant intentionally refused to pay child support. If the defendant had been indigent and unable to pay child support, the judge said, he would have joined the dissent and permitted the defendant to have more children.

The dissenting judges argued that the ruling "wrongly supports an economic test for would-be parents," adding, "The right to have a child has never been rationed on the basis of wealth. The majority has essentially authorized a judicially imposed 'credit check' on the right to bear and beget children." The dissent also noted that this ruling placed a terrible burden on a female that the defendant impregnated—either she gets an abortion or alternatively she has a child and the defendant goes to prison for contempt of court. All of the court's four male judges were in the majority, and all of the three female judges were in the minority.

In a similar ruling in Ohio in September 2002, a trial judge in Medina County initially ordered bachelor Sean Talty to avoid having children since he was $38,000 behind in child support for two of his six children. However, Judge James Kimbler, after hearing arguments from Talty's lawyer that everyone, even a deadbeat dad, had the right to have children, ordered the defendant to "take reasonable efforts to avoid conception." The judge allowed that Talty would not violate his probation if he could prove that he tried to use birth control but it failed (one wonders how the defendant would prove this).

The courts of Wisconsin and Ohio apparently have the view that being poor, or a deadbeat, disqualifies a man from having children. No court has said the same about women. So long as poor women do not abuse their children, they are entitled to have children and to go on welfare to get support for them. That in fact is what the welfare system is designed for. The Wisconsin and Ohio courts view poor men as having lesser "reproductive rights" than poor women, even when the right asserted by the men did not conflict with or affect a woman's right. In fact, Sean Talty's reproductive interests coincided with those of his current girlfriend, who was the mother of two of his children. She was not pleased with the verdict and complained: "It took me ten years to get two and I would like to have more."

In May 2002 a court in Louisville, Kentucky, took a more jaundiced view of the reproductive rights of a deadbeat dad and ordered him not only to stop having children but also not to have any more sex. The defendant, Luther Crawford, age forty-nine, had fathered twelve children by eleven different women and owed $74,000 in back child support for three of those children. It was not revealed how much child support he owed, if anything, for the others. Crawford was unemployed, blind in one eye, had heart disease and high blood pressure, and on the whole did not appear to be much of a reproductive "catch." Despite these handicaps he had been in some ways a reproductive success, even though there was no evidence presented on how well his children were doing. The no-sex sentence was part of a plea bargain that reduced Crawford's jail time for non-payment of child support. At a subsequent hearing Crawford's lawyer argued that even if Crawford had a vasectomy, he would still be in violation of the court order if he had sex. The court reconsidered, withdrew its order, and sentenced Crawford to one year in jail, thereby preventing him from having sex with women and impregnating them at least for that year. Judge Tom McDonald said; "I can't order you to be a loving father, but the law requires you to financially support them, and you have failed miserably."

Being in jail has proven to be an obstacle for non-sexual male reproduction, even with new artificial insemination techniques and overnight mail. William Gerber, an inmate serving a 100-year sentence in Mule Creek State Prison in California under that state's three strikes law, having been convicted of discharging a firearm, making terrorist threats, and using narcotics, wanted to impregnate his wife, age forty-four, by sending a sperm specimen to her by overnight mail that she could use for artificial insemination. Conjugal visits were not permitted for prisoners serving life sentences. Gerber unsuccessfully petitioned the prison authorities for permission to procreate by mail. The Ninth Circuit Court of Appeals, by a six to five decision, upheld the prison authorities, saying that Gerber's right to procreate was fundamentally inconsistent with his status as a prisoner. Even though Gerber and his wife both wanted children, the court ruled she had no right to have a child by mail with her male.

These decisions involving men's reproductive rights come perilously close to reinstating eugenics as a valid principle for government regulation of reproduction. The courts are willing to abridge a man's reproductive rights even when there is no apparent conflict between the man's reproductive interests and his partner's. Oakley's girlfriend and Gerber's wife both wanted to have children, and perhaps so did Luther Crawford's next girlfriend. Even though the courts paid lip service to a man's reproductive rights, they ruled that the compelling state interests of requiring men to support their children, of preventing child abuse, and of preserving the integrity and purposes of the penal system were sufficient to prevent these men from having more children.

These important state interests are applied differently, however, to men and women. The courts are much more likely to constrict the reproductive freedom of men than they are of women. A man can be ordered not to have children if he cannot or will not support them; a woman cannot be. A man in jail cannot father a child but a woman can bear a child (she may not be able to have an abortion, however, depending on where she is incarcerated). Courts appear to be stricter on men with a record of child abuse, than on women with one.

The case of Darlene Johnson is illustrative. A month after Norplant was approved in January 1991, a California judge, Howard Boardman, presided over Johnson's sentencing. She had been found guilty of three counts of child abuse. Johnson was twenty-seven, the mother of four and eight months pregnant with her fifth. She had a prior criminal record and faced up to seven years in jail. Judge Boardman gave her a choice—seven years in jail or, as an alternative, one year in jail with an additional three years of probation plus having Norplant inserted in her arm. She elected the latter. The defendant's appeal of the sentence was never resolved because she violated other terms of her probation and was jailed.

Clearly at the time, Johnson was not a fit mother to her existing children and needed help. The children were going to be removed from her no matter what the sentence. And no matter which option the defendant took, she would lose her ability to have more children for the duration of the sentence—for seven years if jailed, assuming no conjugal visits, and four or five years if on probation. In fact, the Norplant/probation option would enable her to have a child sooner than the jail sentence, if she desired. What was galling to those of us who opposed the sentence was the blatant use of regulating and preventing fertility as a criminal deterrent, as well as threatening by implication a longer jail sentence unless she agreed to Norplant. Surely an alternative would be to say to the defendant that, unless she were deemed a fit mother, any children she did have would be removed from her care.

The fear that a person, male or female, may commit child abuse on an as-yet-unborn child is hardly a valid reason to forbid that person from having that child. The sentences imposed on the men above were harsher than that imposed on Darlene Johnson. She could have children at the end of her probation; the men's sentences were open ended. If they were never able to become financially solvent and meet their child support obligations, they would never be able to legally have more children. In each of these three cases these men clearly had something to offer since their girlfriends wanted to become pregnant with them. Since it appears that the men were supporting some of their children or had deliberately refused to even though they had the means, these cases represent an elitist, eugenic view that reproduction is only for men of means.

Male and female reproductive interests can conflict. This can occur when a woman wants a child and the man does not, and vice versa, the woman does not want a child and the man does. When these conflicts occur before pregnancy and cannot be resolved, either party can take steps to find a new partner. When these conflicts occur after the woman is pregnant, then the couple must try to resolve it privately. Often the disagreement boils over in the clinic. Leslie Rottenberg, the director of social services in the Margaret Sanger Clinic of Planned Parenthood of New York City, reported that, when a couple comes in, together, in half the cases the woman wants the child and the man doesn't and in the other half it is the opposite. When it is the woman who wants to have the child, the most common response from the man is: "It isn't fair. I should have a say if I am going to be a father." Rottenberg explains as tactfully as possible that he had a choice before he had sex. In her experience, men separate sex from potentially becoming a parent whereas women do not. As a result of this perceived unfairness, men can get violent not only towards their partners but also the staff at the clinic. In the summer of 2003 a man burst into the clinic despite the extensive security and demanded to see his wife, who he thought was there for an abortion. He wanted to stop the abortion and to have the child. He put the clinic supervisor in a choke hold and after not getting any information out of her, said, "I'm not done with you yet." He left the clinic peacefully. We don't know which patient he was there to see, or even if she was there.

Other men want to be sure they are not going to be a father. One day in 2003 at the Margaret Sanger Clinic, a woman originally from Bangladesh, who had had an abortion a week earlier came in with her boyfriend. She was nineteen, he was twenty-eight. She clearly adored him. His feelings for her were somewhat less ardent. They both came from the same province in Bangladesh, but his family was the most prominent in the province while hers was of a significantly lesser status. A marriage between them was unthinkable in their society as was having a child out of wedlock. The purpose of the visit was for the man to examine the girl's medical chart to be sure that she had had the abortion. With her permission he looked at the chart and they left the clinic together. There would be no child to interfere with his and his family's plans for his future.

Occasionally disagreements over childbearing end up in court. When a disagreement goes into court, the legal system will examine each party's reproductive interests to see if they rise to the level of reproductive rights. In most, if not all, cases, this will mean the interests of the female will become reproductive rights and will prevail since she alone bears the health risks of a pregnancy. Because of this the courts have ruled, correctly, in my view, that a woman has a right to make her own childbearing decisions, as well as the right to preserve her health and life. This is the current state of the law in the United States and in most other countries where abortion is legal. A husband's permission for a wife's abortion is required in several countries, mostly in the Middle East and Asia, including Egypt, Saudi Arabia, and Syria, thus giving a husband veto power over his wife's abortion.

Despite the clear holding to the contrary of the U.S. Supreme Court in *Planned Parenthood v. Casey* in 1992, American men persist in going to court to try to stop their wife's or girlfriend's abortions. In 2002 John Stachokus asked a court in Pennsylvania for, and got, a temporary injunction to prevent his former girlfriend, Tanya Meyers, from having an abortion. The two had broken up when she was eight weeks pregnant, and Meyers decided to end the pregnancy. Before the judge could read the *Casey* decision, find that Stachokus had no legal leg to stand on, and reverse himself, Meyers miscarried, thereby ending the proceedings.

If the polls are any guide, the American public supports the idea that husbands have reproductive rights, even when they conflict with their wives'. The Gallup Poll of January 2003 reported that 72 percent of those polled supported the husband of a married woman being notified if his wife decides to have an abortion. In an earlier nationwide poll conducted by the *Washington Post* in 1992, 63 percent of respondents supported a wife having to get her husband's legal permission before having an abortion. A later *Los Angeles Times* poll in June 2000 found that 49 percent of respondents favored a woman getting the consent of the "biological father" before having an abortion. These results are recognition that the husband, and to a lesser extent the biological father, have reproductive interests at stake when a woman decides to terminate a pregnancy. Whether or not his interests become a right is another matter.

I have argued that women have reproductive rights because the rights are of benefit to not just women but to humanity. Men can only have reproductive rights if it can be established that these rights too will be of benefit to humanity, not just to men. When there is not a conflict with a woman's reproductive rights, American courts recognize in theory a man's reproductive rights. However they wrongly, in my view, use broader grounds to restrict these rights than they would for a woman, citing poverty and the potential damage to current or future children if they were to permit some men to procreate at will. When there is a conflict with a woman's rights, the courts currently give precedence to the woman's rights. The courts recognize that giving a man an equal right in effect gives him veto power over a woman's decision and, in the context of a pregnant woman, this would mean that, if the couple could not agree on an abortion, she would give birth.

There is not much dissent currently from the proposition that a man and woman must jointly agree on becoming pregnant. However, while the law prohibits rape, it does not directly prohibit the woman from saying she is using birth control when she isn't or removing sperm from a used condom and impregnating herself. Mutual consent to pregnancy has not always been the norm. Traditional moral and religious principles said that a wife must submit to her husband in every way including sexually and in the decision to have children. Roman law required that a husband consent to his wife's abortion, on the theory that the child was his property. Roman law is one vote away in the U.S. Supreme Court from being permitted in the United States. The Supreme Court in *Casey* overturned Pennsylvania's law that required a husband's notification before an abortion is performed, but only by a five to four vote. The court noted that the vast majority of women, in fact about 95 percent, did tell their husbands and those that did not either were experiencing marital difficulties, feared violence or abuse against them or their children, or were pregnant as the result of an affair. The court stated that for women in abusive situations "a spousal notification requirement enables the husband to wield an effective veto over his wife's decision." The court added that a woman does not give up her liberty over her body and childbearing decisions when she marries.

The *Casey* court did recognize that the husband has an interest in his wife's pregnancy, but said it was not enough of one to override her interests. For example, the court said that this interest would not permit laws that would require a wife to notify her husband before she used birth control or smoked while pregnant or underwent surgery that might affect her reproductive organs. The court ruled: "A State may not give to a man the kind of dominion over his wife that parents exercise over their children."

Given that in the United States a husband's lack of legal power over his wife's reproductive decisions hangs by one vote in the Supreme Court, this issue is sure to return to the state legislatures and then to the court. Since the legislatures and the court should examine the respective reproductive interests of the husband and wife in considering any such legislation, we need to see if there is any biological basis for a man's reproductive interests to take precedence over his partners.

Men's and women's reproductive strategies are intertwined in order to successfully propagate the human race, but they are also often in conflict. Men, who are traditionally in control of governments, have often created laws to further their reproductive interests. Have these laws been a success from the male point of view? Or from humanity's point of view? That is the issue. If not, then these laws cannot stand. To the extent that these laws harm humanity, which I submit they do, then they are wrong and immoral.

Why Males Need Reproductive Strategies

Males, like females, need reproductive strategies in order to advance their reproductive interests. At all stages of the reproductive process, from mating to pregnancy to childbirth to parenting, they are competing with other men and for the attention of women. Men and women have co-evolved strategies, each trying to control the process.

While women and men each compete for mates and are selective, in general women set the ground rules for reproduction. Men have evolved in some ways differently than women because of this. Everything else being equal, men have a harder time getting chosen to mate than women do. Males must compete for this honor on a variety of levels. Biologist Joan Roughgarden of Stanford University argued that the social selection aspects of reproduction are as important or even more important than the sexual selection aspects: "Female choice attempts to identify males who will deliver on their promises of parental care ..." Thus in order to get selected by the females, males have to let the females know that they in fact have what women need, including resources like genetic fitness, family status, wealth, ability to provide physical strength, parenting ability, and willingness to bond as a couple. Roughgarten said that women select men more for parenting than good genes. Whatever the playfield might be, men often end up competing with each other for resources and compete in demonstrating all the desired characteristics that females seek in order to get selected by them.

Not every male measures up or can win in these competitions and not every male is inclined to parent, and therefore not every male gets chosen by a female to mate. Hence not every male will parent a child. Successful men will often have successive mates and children by them, as will some successful women. More men than women will have large numbers of children, and conversely more men than women will have no children. Men who in fact have children have on average more children than women who have children. In most societies men with resources have more children than those men with fewer resources. In other words, male reproductive success varies more than female reproductive success, and higher-status males of almost every species have more reproductive success than lower-status males.

Men of different status will adopt different reproductive strategies. Professor Patricia Adair Gowaty of the Institute of Ecology of the University of Georgia described how the forces of natural selection affect the selection of strategy. Since not all males are freely chosen by females to mate, the males not freely chosen will be able to pass down their genes only by trying to manipulate or control female choice through forced copulation and other strategies of control. Natural selection will favor males who succeed in doing this, because they will actually pass down their genes. However, this strategy may lead to harm to women since they lose control over their reproduction. In this case natural selection will favor the females who resist the males' efforts to control reproduction and who reassert their own control.

The rejected males can either give up, and not reproduce, or alternatively can stay in the game. Since force or control didn't work, these men can get chosen only by trying to attract those females who successfully resisted their previous overtures by employing a fallback stratagem exchanging resources such as food, shelter, and protection in exchange for reproduction. This bargain may harm some females because they are giving up control over reproduction, and again natural selection will again favor the females who resist and insist upon controlling their reproduction. Gowaty concluded that those females who succeed in resisting these male overtures will be able to choose mates "based on honest signals of intrinsic male quality." Gowaty concluded, "Thus, within population mating tactics will almost always vary ... Mating systems variation thus can be seen fundamentally as a function of how much control of their own reproduction females have."

Under Gowaty's theory, males will engage in three types of mating strategies—the control strategy, the exchange of resources strategy and a strategy of demonstrating their fitness. The control strategy used to be the domain of kings and tyrants who captured women and kept them as slaves or in harems. It could be reproductively rewarding. In February 2003 the first measurable example of how well this strategy could succeed was discovered when geneticists measured the Y chromosomes of men currently living in the nations comprising the former Mongol Empire created by Ghengis Khan in the thirteenth century. Geneticist Chris Tyler-Smith of Oxford University discovered eight hundred years later that:

> ... 8% of the men dwelling in the confines of the former Mongol empire bear Y chromosomes that seem characteristic of the Mongol ruling house.
>
> If so, some 16 million men, or half a percent of the world's male population, can probably claim descent from Genghis Khan.

Few men today or in the past can attain the reproductive success of Genghis Khan. The Khan family success was due to a vast network of harems established in conquered territories. Instead of using conquest and control, most men compete in the battle of the sexes by using the other two strategies—exchanging resources or demonstrating fitness and character, or some combination thereof. There are many exceptions to and variations of these Darwinian and Gowatian rules, but in general women, if they escape the male control strategy, control human reproduction. Women control reproduction not because they are necessarily smarter, but because they have to. Natural selection has favored and does favor women who take control of the reproductive process. Women who have the traits that enable them to do this will pass these traits down to their daughters, and they will become more prevalent in the population.

Men have used a variety of strategies, short of harems, to try to take back control of reproduction from women. They seek to take control because they want to insure their own reproductive success and not leave their success up to their partners. Thus laws prohibiting abortion are an attempt by men to take control of reproduction. Men wrote laws, such as the early American abortion laws, where abortion would be permitted only when physicians, then all male, permitted it. German physicians admitted the same thing to my grandmother after World War I when they opposed laws legalizing birth control. They wanted to force women to come to male doctors for abortion and keep male control over the future of the German race. As wrong as these laws were, these men were not acting irrationally. They were trying to tilt the evolutionary scales in their favor. It was a fight over power—reproductive power.

With or without laws restricting a woman's reproductive options, men still have to compete to reproduce. They need strategies to reproduce successfully, just as women do. Not all men will be chosen, and in general high-status men have more reproductive success than low status men. Men therefore compete for status and resources. Even so, women have evolved to control the process of choosing a mate, and men have responded with a variety of strategies to try to level the playing field and even to tip it in their direction. Natural selection has favored women who control reproduction since they give birth at times and with partners who will help them and their child.

Natural selection also favors men who control their reproduction. What gives men evolutionary fits is the fact that they have never been able to be sure that the children they are parenting are theirs. This is the problem of paternity uncertainty.

Excerpts from **This Common Secret**

My Journey as an Abortion Doctor

By Alan Kesselheim and Susan Wicklund

Chapter 1

A woman's life can really be a succession of lives, each revolving around some emotionally compelling situation or challenge, and each marked off by some intense experience.

Wallis Simpson, Duchess Of Windsor (1896–1986)

When I drove into Grandma's driveway, all I could think about was how she would react. I had started out to tell her many times over the last few years. On so many visits I had meant to have that conversation but had never found a way. Something had always intervened. Some other errand had always come up. I had found a way not to face her judgment.

It didn't matter that I was rock solid in my resolve and in my chosen profession. This was my grandma. My Flower Grandma. What she thought of me mattered a lot, and I had no idea how she'd take it.

It was February of 1992, a Saturday afternoon. The next day the *60 Minutes* segment I'd done with Lesley Stahl would air. Grandma never missed *60 Minutes*. I had to tell her before she saw it—before she saw her oldest granddaughter talking about the death threats and stalking and personal harassment my family and I were enduring.

The harassment wasn't the issue that mattered now. It was the fact that I was, as a physician, traveling to five clinics in three states to provide abortion services for as many as one hundred women every week, and that I had been doing this work for four years already.

I wasn't at all ashamed of my career. In fact, I always considered it an honor to be involved in reproductive choices, this most personal and intimate realm for women. I just never felt the need to make it public. Very few of my family and friends were aware of what I did.

Within a day, however, everyone I had grown up with, everyone who knew my family, and every member of my family would know the truth. Would I be isolated and ostracized? Would I get support or condemnation?

I pulled off the highway and into the drive leading to the house I'd grown up in. Mom and Dad still lived in the white, two-story, wood-frame home.

Dad had worked as a precision machinist in the town of Grantsburg, ten miles away. His love had been the gunsmithing, hunting, and fishing he did in his free time. My three siblings and I had always been included. We

Alan Kesselheim and Susan Wicklund, from *This Common Secret: My Journey as an Abortion Doctor*, pp. 1–33, 174–191. Copyright © 2008 by Public Affairs, a Member of The Perseus Books Group. Reprinted with permission.

were as competent with firearms, field dressing a deer, or catching a batch of sunfish as anyone in the area. Dad was retired now and not feeling well. It was painful to watch him, the strong man who starred in my memories, struggling with simple tasks.

Mom was retired too, from her elected position as clerk of court for our county. She was the one everyone—especially women—turned to for advice and support. Mom had been instrumental, many years earlier, in starting a shelter for victims of domestic abuse. In her job she had seen so many situations in which women and children had nowhere to go for help. It was just like Mom to tackle a need that everyone else ignored.

I grew up in the unincorporated village of Trade Lake, Wisconsin, a small gathering of about six houses, several of which were the homes of my relatives. The only business left was one small gas station/grocery store. When I was a kid, there had been a feed store and creamery and a meat market, but those had been gone for better than thirty years. Only rotten shells of buildings remained.

Even now, Trade Lake is a very rural place. People still raise chickens in backyards, drive tractors to the little grocery store. Chimneys puff wood smoke in the winter.

The small river that wound its way through our yard came into view. Behind it were the woods where I'd built forts and climbed oak trees with my sister. She and I each had a horse and spent the bulk of our summers out of doors. Grandma and Grandpa had lived just down the road. We picked mayflowers every spring with Grandma. In the summer we fished with Grandpa for sunfish and crappies using cane poles baited with worms dug out of the garden.

Mine had been a good childhood. This was a safe place. Turning into the driveway had always been a good thing—a coming home. This time was different.

I felt myself sweating under my coat. My racing heart pushed against my throat. I had to reveal something to my dear grandma that could change everything she believed and loved about me.

Grandma had moved into a trailer house in the backyard of the family home. Grandpa had died fifteen years earlier, and Mom wanted her mother even closer—just steps across the yard. I saw the clothesline hung with rugs, the twine still strung up on the porch to hold the morning glories that filled the railings in the summer.

Flower Grandma. My daughter, Sonja, gave her the name when she was three and there were too many grandmas to keep track of. Sonja spent many days baking cookies with her great-grandmother and playing outside, just as I had as a young girl. She ran back and forth constantly between the houses of her two grandmothers. This grandma always had flowers growing in every nook and cranny inside and out.

Flower Grandma she became, and Flower Grandma she stayed. Before long my entire extended family called her Flower Grandma, and even her friends at the local senior center fell into the habit.

I coasted to a stop at the bottom of the slope. I sat there long enough to take a deep breath and fight back a few unexpected tears. I didn't know where the sadness came from. The car engine ticked. I was alone, vulnerable, aching. Was I longing for those simple childhood days, whipping down the hill on my sled? How far I'd come from that.

I peeled myself out of the car, shed my coat, and left it on the seat. It was unusually warm for February in Wisconsin. The hardwood forest was all bare sticks and hard lines. I knew it would soon be time to tap the maple trees and cook the syrup we all loved on Grandma's Swedish pancakes.

I turned and deliberately moved up the steps to the trailer house. I was terrified of what Grandma would say, but there was no avoiding this moment.

The big door was already open by the time I got to the top step. Out peeked her welcoming smile. She was giggling.

"Hi, Grandma!"

"Oh my goodness! What a surprise! What a sweet, sweet surprise! Did I know you were coming today?"

I hugged her in the doorway, held her tight, stepped inside.

"Did you somehow know I was making ginger snaps?" she teased as she set a plate full on the kitchen table. She poured me a glass of milk, and I sat down on the wooden chair next to hers, I tried to bury myself in the smell of her place, a mixture of ginger cookies, Estée Lauder perfume (the one in the blue hourglass bottle always on her dresser), and home permanents. She and Mom always gave each other perms, trying to get just the right curl in their hair. The smell never left the place.

I think she sensed that I had come to talk about something important. I started talking a few times about other, inconsequential things; then, finally, I plunged in.

"Grandma, you know I work as a doctor."

"Of course. And we are all so proud of you."

"Yes, but I don't think you know the whole story. I'm a doctor who works mostly for women, helping women with pregnancy problems."

Flower Grandma hesitated just a second, pushed back her chair, stood, and held out her hand for me to follow. She went to sit in her rocker, the same one sitting in my living room today. The rocker I have sat in so many hours since. The rocker I sit in right now, writing this down and trembling as I do.

She seemed distant. I moved to the old leather hassock beside her. She took my hand and placed it on top of one of hers, then covered it with her other one. Our hands made a stack on the arm of the rocker—old skin, young skin. We sat in silence a minute. She turned to look directly at me.

Her eyes, framed by gentle wrinkles, were full of some deep trouble.

After a moment, she stared straight ahead and started to speak. Slowly. Deliberately. In a very quiet voice. At the same time she began stroking my hand. It was as if the gentle stroking was pushing her to talk.

"When I was sixteen years old, my best friend got pregnant," she said. A chill went through me.

"I always believed it was her father that was using her," she went on, "but I never knew for sure. She came to my sister, Violet, and me, and asked us to help her."

While I listened, thoughts whirled through my head. Stories I had read of women self-aborting and dying of infections when a safe, legal option was not available. The women who came to the clinics where I worked, many of whom still had to overcome huge difficulties to end an unwanted pregnancy.

It isn't uncommon to have patients confide in me that prior to coming in for an abortion, they had used combinations of herbs to try to force a miscarriage. These home remedies can be extremely dangerous and have caused the deaths of many women.

I felt myself tighten and withdraw, anticipating what Flower Grandma was going to tell me. I wanted to see her eyes, but she kept them straight ahead. And she kept stroking my hand. So soft. I only wanted to think about those hands. Hands embracing and caressing mine—strong, gentle, soft.

"The three of us were so naïve. We knew very little about these things, but we had heard that if you put something long and sharp up there, in the private place, sometimes it would end the pregnancy."

In spite of myself I conjured the modest room: a dresser in the corner with a kerosene lamp and maybe a hairbrush or hand mirror beside it. I saw three young, scared girls, still children, acting on old wives' tales and whispered instructions.

My stomach turned. Was this my grandma? Was I really here in her trailer house hearing this? I could barely breathe. She kept talking, all the while stroking the top of my hand, her eyes looking off into space, traveling back in time. Occasionally a pat-pat with her hand would break the rhythm of the stroking. Such old skin, full of brown age spots and paper thin. Stroking my hand in perfect measure with her words.

Please just stop, Grandma. Don't tell me anymore. Just hold my hand, and let's talk about what you'll plant in the spring. Tell me about the oatmeal bread you baked yesterday. Are there many birds coming to the bird feeder? I was flushed all over. And still she stroked, while she talked. Pat-pat, stroke.

"We closed ourselves, the three of us, in one of the bedrooms late one morning. We didn't talk much, and she didn't ever cry out in pain. It took a few tries to make the blood come. None of us spoke. We didn't know what to expect next, or what to do when the blood kept coming. It was all over the sheets. All over us. So bright red. It was awful. It just wouldn't stop."

She was still stroking my hand. I was shaking uncontrollably. I stared at the African violets under the plant light, trying to make them the focus of my attention. Her voice was a monotone, never a pause.

"We put rags inside of her to try to stop the bleeding, but they soaked full. We all three stayed in her bed. We just didn't know what to do."

My hand was trembling so hard it was all I could do to keep it on top of hers. She grasped it briefly, held it tight, patted it a few times, and then went on.

"We stayed there together, unable to move, even after she was dead. Her father found us, all three of us, in the bed. He stood in the doorway, staring. No words for a long time. When he did speak, he told my sister and me to leave and that we were never, ever to speak of this. We were not to tell anyone, ever. Ever."

She stopped stroking my hand and sat still before turning to look directly at me. "That was seventy-two years ago. You are the first person I have ever told that story. I am still so ashamed of what happened. We were just so young and scared. We didn't know anything."

Terrible sadness welled up inside me. And anger. I couldn't picture my grandma as someone responsible for the death of anything, much less her best friend at the age of sixteen. She had carried this secret all her life, kept it inside, festering with guilt and shame.

I wondered if the pregnancy was indeed the result of incest. Would it have made a difference? What were friends and family told about the death? What had they actually used to start the bleeding? What had the doctor put on the death certificate as the cause of death?

I knew, through the patients I had met, that no one has to look very far into their family history to find these stories tucked away, hidden from view. But it didn't lessen the shock of finding it here, so close, in the heart of my own family.

Flower Grandma sighed and held my hand tight. Tears welled in her eyes.

"I know exactly what kind of work you do, and it is a good thing. People like you do it safely so that people like me don't murder their best friends. I told you how proud I am of what you do, and I meant it."

Chapter 2

- In 1930, illegal abortions were recorded as the cause of death for 2,700 women, 18 percent of all maternal deaths in that year.
- Before 1973 and the passage of *Roe* v. *Wade,* an estimated 1.2 million women had illegal abortions in the United States yearly. As many as 5,000 died each year as a result.
- Between 1973 and 2002, more than 42 million legal abortions were performed.
- Risk of death during childbirth is eleven times higher than the risk of death from legal abortion.

Flower Grandma is gone now. So is my mother. I can share the story my grandmother kept inside from the time she was a young girl. Her story and hundreds of others like it desperately need to be told. We need their legacy so we don't forget, and to remind ourselves that every family has a similar tale somewhere in its history.

It has been my privilege and honor to hear many women's stories and to participate in their unfolding. As a young woman, the idea that I might be in such a position would have seemed far-fetched indeed. No, actually, it would have seemed impossible.

In April 1980 I was a twenty-six-year-old mom living in Wisconsin, raising a daughter alone, working part-time at a VFW bar and part-time in a natural foods co-op. I was on welfare, medical assistance, and food stamps. My post-high school education consisted of a handful of community college classes, none of which it together or qualified me for anything, with one exception.

I had given birth to my daughter at home just north of San Francisco, where her father and I were living. To prepare for the event, I took birthing classes, which led to an interest in midwifery. Since Sonja's birth, I had been involved in many births, both in homes and in hospitals, volunteering as an advocate for women in labor.

I knew from my own experience how empowering it was for women to be informed. With that information, women feel secure about expressing their needs. Their active participation changes the entire dynamic. I loved the energy of those births. By the late 1970s, however, midwives were being prosecuted for practicing medicine without a license, so I had resorted to teaching birth classes in an effort to optimize the hospital experience for women.

Sonja's dad, David, and I had gone our separate ways, having fundamental differences in lifestyles. I had yearned for the rural life again and wanted Sonja to grow up knowing her grandparents. David was a jazz musician who needed and craved the big city life. When it came down to it, I couldn't live on the road following a musician around, and he couldn't imagine a life full of chopping wood and hunting deer. Our breakup had been amicable, and David continued to be very committed to Sonja even after I moved back to the Midwest in 1979.

On Easter Sunday 1980 I was invited to a gathering of people on the West Bank of Minneapolis. The host roasted a lamb in an open pit and provided traditional Greek wine. It was the first really warm day of spring. I was wearing a piecework skirt I had sewn, a pink V-necked T-shirt, and Birkenstock sandals. I fit right in. Sonja, nearly three, was having a blast running around with all the other kids.

I began talking with a man perhaps twenty years older than I. We sat on the grass drinking red wine and soaking up sunshine. An occasional dog streaked through the chaos.

It was one of those conversations that avoided the common superficialities. Hal questioned me about my interests and skills and background. He wanted to know what made me happy what frustrated me. Did I like travel, or was I a homebody? He wanted me to tell him about Sonja's birth and about the training I had as a midwife. He asked about what I liked to read. What my parents did. What my fears were, and my dreams.

I told him how much I loved the contact with women and what satisfaction I got from teaching birthing classes. I felt I could communicate the information effectively and in a way most of the women understood. My collection of books on pregnancy and birth and midwifery and early childhood development was growing rapidly and I was devouring them. I missed the chance to be involved in home births now that I was back in the Midwest.

I also talked about my dreams of somehow making a difference, a real difference, in peoples' lives. I didn't know what or how or when that might happen, but I knew I would not be content to work in the local grocery store or VFW all my life. I wanted more diversity. More challenge. More adventure.

It seemed as if we'd been there most of the afternoon when Hal looked at me and said, "It is clear that you need to go to medical school. You would be a great doctor."

"*Me?!* Be a doctor?"

I hugged myself across my belly tipping over into the grass and laughing until I cried. He had to be out of his mind! Sonja came running up and jumped on me, I curled up tighter, still laughing.

The idea was preposterous. The logistics alone would be impossible.

We went on with the day, enjoying the sunshine and good food and music. Local musicians kept pulling out instruments and playing them late into the night. It was only much later that I learned Hal worked as a career counselor at a nearby federal prison.

Crazy as it was, in the weeks following the party, Hal's suggestion kept echoing in my thoughts. I knew my life was on hold, waiting for some nudge, some direction. By mid-May, Sonja and I had moved into a tent in a goat pasture. We were helping some friends with a building project. Living right on site seemed like a good idea.

Summer went on, full of building fences, tending gardens, moving rocks for a foundation but the seed Hal had planted that Easter Sunday wouldn't go away. The idea of college and then medical school seemed far out of my reach. I had absolutely no money to pay for tuition or child care for Sonja. I didn't know if I could even handle the academic challenges. Imagining myself in the role of a doctor was outrageous.

The biggest mental and emotional hurdle I was struggling with was wrapped up in becoming part of the medical community. True, my childhood family doctor had always been kind, someone I looked up to. But he was almost a neighbor, and he was a man. Men were doctors. Women were nurses.

That stereotype wasn't insurmountable, but there was something else I had to deal with. Something much more visceral and daunting. The memory of my own abortion, in 1976, in Portland, Oregon.

When I became pregnant, politics and *Roe v. Wade* were the furthest things from my consciousness. I didn't engage with the political and social issues.

At that time I rented a house with four roommates, including David. I had no money and juggled three jobs: waitressing, cleaning horse stalls, and growing alfalfa sprouts. David played local gigs with jazz musicians in bars and clubs. No part of me was ready to be a mother, and I felt no emotional connection to the pregnancy. I learned from a community health clinic that I could get an abortion just blocks from where I lived.

I called the clinic and made an appointment, but learned that the abortion cost $350, an impossible amount of money, more than I made in a month. All of my roommates pitched in to help me come up with the necessary cash.

The doctor's office was on the second floor of a large building. David came with me. Protesters outside carried signs, tried to talk to us. I was so preoccupied, so anxious, that I only remember them as an annoyance, a hassle.

The first thing they wanted in the tiny office was my money. Pay in advance, all of it, in cash. I was so frightened and unaware. What was supposed to happen? No counseling took place, no explanation of procedures or options; no one tried to understand my circumstances or answer my questions.

In another tiny room a nurse told me to undress and lie down on the table.

"What are you doing?" I wanted to know.

"Just be still," she said. She sat in front of me and put a cold speculum into my vagina. I could feel tugging and pulling, but no real pain. She was done quickly, took out the speculum, and then told me to get dressed.

"Am I done?" I asked.

"Done?" she slapped the words at me. "No. I just put something into your cervix that will make it open up for the abortion. You should leave now and come back at three this afternoon."

I still had no idea what to expect.

"What's happening?" David kept asking when we left. "What are they going to do?" I couldn't deal with his questions. I had no answers. I had been told nothing, knew only that I had to hold on to my resolve until this was over.

I dropped David off at the house and drove on in our VW bus to work for a few hours, spraying flats of alfalfa seeds and bagging sprouts. I kept cramping, fighting against the pain and anxiety that threatened to overwhelm me. The time dragged.

When we returned, the same woman took me back to the small room, again had me get undressed, and used the speculum to examine me. She removed something she had put inside me earlier, but was impatient with me when I asked questions.

I was moved into a much larger room. It seemed huge, filled with machines and trays of exposed instruments and syringes and needles. Two other women came in. They had me strip naked, lie on a table, and put my feet in stirrups. They put a paper sheet over my upper body and told me to lie still. Then all three of them walked out. No advice, no preparatory explanation, no squeeze of the hand. For a long time I lay there in that vast, cold room, utterly exposed and as vulnerable as I'd ever been in my life.

Finally, the door opened, and a very large man, the doctor, came toward me. I remember looking down over my legs at him, aware of how physically exposed I was.

He said nothing, didn't even tell me his name, asked no questions, but abruptly started to work. An emotional claustrophobia enveloped me. I could feel myself starting to panic.

"What are you doing?" I asked. "Please tell me what you are doing!"

I could feel instruments inside me, a harsh invasion and pain I hadn't expected. "Is it supposed to hurt?" I pleaded.

"Shut up and lie still!" His voice was rough, angry, as if I had no right to intrude. I started to squirm away from him, trying to make him stop long enough to talk to me.

"Please," I pleaded, "Please just tell me what you are doing. Stop. Talk to me. Please!"

He called for nurses to come hold me down.

The claustrophobia grew and grew, the pain kept coming, and I writhed and fought as nurses grabbed my arms and shoulders. I heard myself scream. Tears ran past my ears and into my hair. Then they injected something into my arm, and I faded away from the nightmare.

When I woke, my face was stuck to a Naugahyde couch. I was in a very small room, alone. I struggled up groggily and went to the door. Locked. Panic rose up again, but all I could do was sit and cry until someone let me out.

"If you have problems, go to an emergency room," was the sum total of advice I was given as I went out the door.

Something terrible had been done to me. I felt abused and violated and beaten, I did not feel that I had made a bad choice, that I had done a bad thing. But I knew something bad had been done to me. All I wanted, then, was to escape.

I remember sitting on the dark staircase in our house that weekend and calling my mother, telling her what had happened, "I wish I could be with you," she kept saying. I could hear her voice tremble over the phone, almost two thousand miles away I wished I had talked to her earlier. I wished I had allowed her to support and comfort me.

After David and I were married and had moved to California, I became pregnant again. He was still playing sax, and I was waitressing, but this time was different. As much as I hadn't felt attached to the earlier pregnancy, this time I felt an immediate connection. I knew I wanted this baby.

My problem, and it grew more and more worrisome as the pregnancy advanced, was that I was terrified of doctors and clinics and hospitals. My abortion experience had scarred me. I simply couldn't relinquish control over my body to someone who might treat me as badly as I had been treated in Portland. The thought of being in a sterile hospital room with my feet in stirrups and no one I loved nearby was horrifying.

Friends talked about the possibility of having a home birth with a midwife. As soon as it sank in that this was a real alternative, I jumped on it. The connection I made with our midwife, Nan, was immediate and wonderful.

The pregnancy and the birth were both completely normal. In stark contrast to my abortion experience, during Sonja's birth I was surrounded by people I loved and who loved me. I was in my own bed, in my own home, the tiny apartment we rented. And I knew exactly what was happening, both because of my own research and because my questions were honored and answered.

Chapter 3

Desperate Measures Used to End Unwanted Pregnancies:
- Use of sharp object like coat hanger or knitting needle
- Acalding water baths
- Massive doses of herbal concoctions, such as black cohosh teas
- Douches with lye
- Cleaning fluids, boiling water
- Excessive exercise

Now, three years after Sonja's home birth, I was considering the possibility of entering a medical career; a profession that held real terror for me, as well as fascination and challenge. It would mean I could attend home births as a physician and educate women about alternatives. It would mean that I could support Sonja.

Since the breakup of my marriage, providing for Sonja had become a major preoccupation and necessity. I knew that public assistance was a temporary boost, but I didn't want that to become my permanent solution.

In the end, what tipped the scales was the realization that if I actually pulled this off, I could make sure my patients were treated differently than I had been—with respect and decency. The memory of my own abortion troubled me, but it also hardened my resolve. I refused to let one bad doctor dictate a decision over my life direction.

By the beginning of July going to college was sounding like a challenge I wanted to accept. I made a trip to the University of Wisconsin at River Falls and went to the financial aid office to see what the possibilities might be. I was greeted by encouraging, knowledgeable people who helped me through the landscape of forms and formalities needed to apply for college and for student loans.

I enrolled in August. I hadn't declared any long-term intention, but I was at least going to get started. Sonja and I gave up our wall tent and moved two hours south, into a trailer house next to the river just blocks from campus. Our first morning I set her in a red Radio Flyer wagon piled high with books and extra clothes and snacks. I dropped her off at the day care on campus and began college full-time.

My declared major was sociology. I still didn't know if I could handle the hard sciences. I hadn't studied physics or chemistry in high school. How dare I have the audacity to think I could even *be* a doctor?

The first quarter was all it took to boost my confidence. I took chemistry and math, along with biology, psychology, and English, and came out with a 4.0 GPA. By the end of the first year I was on a roll and loving every bit of it. I went to summer school to do the equivalent of a year's worth of physics and continued with excellent grades and increasing optimism.

Sonja went with me everywhere. In warm weather I pulled her around campus in the red wagon. During the winter months she burrowed into a nest of blankets in a box mounted on a sled. She came with me to biology lab and counted fruit flies through the dissecting scope. She loved the poster of the human skeleton and learned the names of all the bones with me. When she fell off the porch and broke her arm, she walked beside me into the emergency room holding her arm.

"I think it's the radius," she told the doctor, and she was right.

The second winter we lived in a drafty farmhouse outside of town. It had no running water, and our electricity was limited to one extension cord that ran in the door from a junction box outside, but it was rent-free. The owners wanted someone there to keep vandals out. Every evening Sonja would sit on the couch, cuddled up in a sleeping bag and cutting out paper snowflakes, while I built a fire in the wood stove. I would stoke that stove for hours, using the wood my father and sister had hauled down from home, 120 miles away. Even at that, it was all I could do to get the heat up to fifty degrees. By the end of winter, every inch of wall space was covered in paper snowflakes.

But I was happy being a student. Chemistry, biology, physics, all the course work I had feared—from photosynthesis to physics in everyday life, I kept having ah-hah! moments. I aced course after course.

I was happy, too, because I'd met a man named Randy. Actually, I'd known Randy slightly back in high school. He had been a senior when I was a freshman, and I remembered him for his successful crusade to abolish the student dress code. We met again when I was home visiting and working at the local food co-op. He was working as a heavy equipment operator.

We started spending weekends together whenever possible. I loved Randy's genuine honesty, his dependability, and his solid commitment to people and the causes he believed in. He was the only person I trusted with my true medical aspirations.

Most important, Randy fell head over heels in love with Sonja. The feeling was mutual. Almost from the start, Sonja started calling Randy "Randad."

It wasn't until I'd finished two years of school, and was fueled with newfound confidence, that I felt able to articulate my ultimate goal to my family and friends: I was going to be a doctor.

My mother was encouraging and proud and promised to do all she could to help. There was no money to help with expenses, but she could pitch in with child care. My father was skeptical but knew enough not to say it out loud. Maybe he was worried about where he'd have to haul wood to next. I could feel the sideways looks of aunts, uncles, and cousins, very few of whom had gone past high school.

Higher education had never been a part of our extended family expectations. Mom would have loved to go to college and law school, but the times and circumstances did not allow it. Dad had only finished eighth grade, but he had enrolled in machinist school on the GI bill after serving in World War II. He had earned a GED many years later, along with some of his brothers. Dad and all five of his brothers served in the war.

After three years I earned my bachelor of science degree in biology and was accepted into medical school. Another move for Sonja, but this time we joined a married couple with two kids. The husband was in the same program I was, and the wife was in nursing school. We shared childcare responsibilities, along with meals and bedtime stories. And, as Sonja pointed out, you just had to turn up the thermostat to make it warmer.

Most weekends we drove down to be with Randy. I studied nonstop, but Randy and Sonja had their standard routine. They'd make a trip to the dump, buy groceries, do chores, then head off on the round of family visits to grandmas and aunts and uncles. Randy built Sonja a sandbox in the yard, where she played for hours.

It didn't take long in medical school to see that even though women were allowed in, it was a system run by and for men. Most of the lecturers and attending physicians were men. All the deans and department heads were men.

There were times when it was all I could do to keep my mouth shut. Other times I was not able to contain myself and took actions that almost got me expelled. One incident that put me toe to toe with the medical school hierarchy still makes me shudder.

It was the first morning of a third-year medical student rotation in obstetrics and gynecology. We met in a lecture hall for a discussion of pelvic anatomy with the attending physician. He told us that the best way to learn pelvic anatomy was to do an exam on a relaxed pelvis and that a woman under general anesthesia was ideal. We were led to the operating room suite and were told we would all be performing pelvic exams on five or six women and then discussing our findings.

It dawned on me that these were women admitted for a variety of operations or procedures. A gallbladder surgery, perhaps, or breast lumpectomy or knee surgery. I suspected that the patients hadn't been told they would be undergoing pelvic exams by eight or ten medical students while under general anesthesia.

My suspicion was confirmed. I was absolutely appalled and walked up to confront the attending physician.

"So we're all doing pelvic exams on this patient?" I asked.

"Yes."

"Without her permission?"

He stared at me.

"We're all really supposed to do this?"

"Quit asking questions," he said. "Scrub in and get with the program."

I refused, turned around, and went directly to the department head.

"I can't believe we are expected to do this," I said. "It is a terrible violation."

"These women have come to a teaching hospital," he replied. "They understand that medical students are present and need to learn. They'll never know it anyway."

"Are you proud of this teaching institution?"

"Of course," he replied.

"Then you'll have no problem when I go to the local paper and discuss this teaching practice."

I knew very well that this could mean the end of my medical education, but if this was what it meant to become a doctor, I had no desire to go any further. After a heated discussion, the department head agreed to put a halt to pelvic exams on anesthetized women, and I agreed not to go to the papers with the story.

In spite of the fact that almost half of the women in this country have an abortion at some time in their reproductive lives, abortion was not acknowledged, discussed, or described during my ob-gyn rotation. When I asked to be taught the procedure, I was met with total resistance. It was simply not a program option. This refusal only made me more determined.

Shouldn't a physician be able to at least intelligently discuss all the options for women with unplanned pregnancies?

I was finally able to arrange, on my own, an elective reproductive health rotation at another institution. There I was able to learn about the various methods of abortion and observe procedures.

Memories of my own abortion kept creeping in, memories too painful to talk about, but I had been in enough medical situations by then to realize that my experience was not the norm. I was anxious to see how procedures were done in a legitimate, well-run clinic.

The first abortion I saw during that rotation was for a woman who was halfway through her pregnancy. The fetus had an abnormality incompatible with life. It had started out as a very planned and wanted pregnancy. When the abnormality was diagnosed through an ultrasound, the woman chose to end the pregnancy instead of going full-term, delivering the baby, and having it die immediately.

Most abortions done at this stage are for similar reasons, or to save the life of the mother, but knowing the circumstances did not soften the visual reality of a twenty-one-week fetus. Seeing an arm being pulled through the vaginal canal was shocking. One of the nurses in the room escorted me out when the color left my face.

Not only was it a visceral shock; this was something I had to think deeply about.

I had been about eight weeks pregnant when I had my abortion. I knew from my embryology classes in the first year of medical school that an eight-week embryo is about the size of my thumbnail. It cannot feel pain or think or have any sense of being. I have never regretted that abortion.

Confronting a twenty-one-week fetus is very different. It still cannot feel pain or think or have any sense of being, but the reality is, this cannot be called "tissue." It was not something I could be comfortable with. From that moment, I chose to limit my abortion practice to the first trimester: fourteen weeks or less.

Over the next six weeks I met eight to ten women in the clinic almost every day, women who had come to end pregnancies for a variety of reasons. For some it was financially motivated. Others had educations to finish or careers they had just started. Some were in abusive relationships and did not want that connection to the man. There were women with chronic illnesses whose lives would be in jeopardy if the pregnancy continued. And there were women carrying fetuses with genetic abnormalities or anomalies incompatible with life. Many had been using a form of birth control that failed.

Never once did these decisions seem easy or casual. Every one was the product of tremendous personal struggle. Anyone who claims otherwise is either very ignorant or unkind or both. Anyone who says that women use abortion as a method of birth control or as a simple matter of convenience should spend a day in a clinic where abortions are performed. No honest person would ever make that statement again.

Equally important and revealing is the fact that women who have abortions come from every level of education, every income bracket, and every age from puberty to menopause. They are Catholic and Jewish, Protestant and Buddhist, agnostic and atheist. Every race and every ethnic group. Every possible woman. They are, in truth, our sisters, aunts, grandmothers, music teachers, neighbors, and best friends.

By the end of six weeks I had become steadfast in my belief that abortion has to be legal and available for all women, even when the pregnancy is into the second trimester. Women cannot be forced to bear children they are unable to care for physically, financially, or emotionally. Women cannot be forced to continue with a pregnancy that may cost them their lives. The bottom line, as expressed by my friend Liz Karlin, is, "Women have abortions because they want to be good mothers."

What struck home more than anything during that rotation was how drastic and tragic it would be to have this choice taken away from women. By the end of it, I had learned that abortions could be performed with compassion and respect, just as I had suspected. It was an experience I had been denied, but one I vowed not to deny any woman who became my patient.

From there I went on to another elective rotation in Salt Lake City, Utah, to study infertility in vitro fertilization, and embryo transfer. It might initially seem strange for a doctor who wants to do abortions to enroll in both those rotations. But true choice is a matter of understanding and weighing all the options, and then being free to carry out the most appropriate one.

While I was leaning toward a specialty in some aspect of women's reproductive health, I was still weighing other options. I found genetics fascinating, for instance, and was intrigued by the career possibilities in forensic pathology.

Before I had learned to do abortions and was still early in my training, I met a woman whose circumstances illustrated the life-and-death reality of choice. I didn't know it then, but her case would be the turning point in my medical career.

When I encountered her, I was one of many students, interns, and doctors doing prenatal care in a low-income clinic. Most of my time was spent getting initial information from patients, keeping charts, taking medical histories—the grunt work of the process.

This woman, when I first saw her, wouldn't look at me directly. She seemed heavy with defeat. She moved slowly and spoke slowly. I was the first person in the system she had seen. I began working on her chart, getting her ready for the exam, "I can't have this baby," she blurted out.

"What do you mean?"

"I can't have it," her voice was hushed, frightened. "He'll kill it if I do."

"Who? Who will kill it?"

"My man. The county already took my two girls because he beat them. I already lost my two girls. I can't lose another. He'll kill it. I know he will!" She was looking at me now, beseeching, her voice strident.

"Have you had counseling?" She shook her head. "There are shelters for abused women. Places you can get help, where you can get away from him." She kept shaking her head.

"I can't have this baby. He'll kill it."

I began making inquiries over the next few days. The social service agencies were aware of the case, knew the history, but couldn't be mobilized. They wouldn't agree to take the child after birth until there was evidence of abuse. The woman had no money. $350 for an abortion might as well have been $350,000.

When I saw her again, I asked her about adoption, but she adamantly refused.

I felt completely helpless. This woman's predicament seemed insurmountable. The rest of the medical personnel in the clinic were no help. I saw her periodically throughout her pregnancy. Eventually she stopped pleading with me, but in her eyes I read deep fear and reproach, I was her first connection to the clinic, the one she chose to confide in, a person she thought had real power, and I was impotent.

The night she delivered was incredibly busy on labor and delivery. I scurried from patient to patient, prepping, comforting, coaching, assisting doctors. Her birth was one of many, an uncomplicated procedure lost in the confusion of a hectic night. Her "man" was not there. She had no visitors.

When we sent her and the baby on their way in a taxi two days later, she wouldn't meet my eyes.

"Be safe," I said, as I closed the cab door. She rode away, out of my life. I thought about her from time to time, but things careened on. Only the present demands stayed in focus.

Nearly a week later my pager went off, and all I could hear was my name and the words "emergency room." When I walked through the swinging doors, there she was again. I saw her holding her infant son. ER staff surrounded her, trying to get her to hand over the baby, but she was holding the limp body tightly.

When she saw me, she held it out, shaking with emotion. "It's your fault!" she cried. The baby, this infant, just born and already dead, lay across her arms like an accusation, "It should never have been born." The woman's face was twisted in anguish and hatred. "It's your fault."

I stood with my hand over my mouth, frozen in place. Now I was the one unable to meet her eyes. I felt a surge of mingled guilt and frustration and anger. Guilt for not being more persistent in finding her the help she had asked for. Frustration with a system that doesn't protect the weakest and poorest and most vulnerable. Anger at the father for all the obvious reasons. I also felt utterly inadequate.

For a long time I felt it was indeed my fault. Her face haunted me. Her words echoed in my head. Even now her face still confronts me. At that moment I knew with absolute certainty that I had to learn to do safe, legal abortions. I had to be able to offer that service to my own patients. Abortion is about life: quality of life for infants, children, and adults. Everywhere and in every sense of the word. Life, not death.

Chapter 11

Shortly before the trial of Michael Griffin for the 1993 murder of Dr. David Gunn, former Rev. Paul Hill and 33 others signed what has become known as the "defensive action statement." ...

We, the undersigned, declare the justice of taking all godly action necessary to defend innocent human life including the use of force. We proclaim that whatever force is legitimate to defend the life of a born child is legitimate to defend the life of an unborn child. We assert that if Michael Griffin did in fact kill David Gunn, his use of lethal force was justifiable provided it was carried out for the purpose of defending the lives of unborn children. Therefore, he ought to be acquitted of the charges against him.

Frederick Clarkson, "Justifiable Homicide: The Signers," Intelligence Report 91 (Summer 1998)

Deeply Private, Incredibly Public

Irony, if not blatant hypocrisy, is everywhere in the realm of abortion clinics and women's reproductive health. Sexuality is a universal drive, no matter what your ethics are, and a pregnancy is irrefutable. It forces people to confront weaknesses, to face the inconsistencies of their beliefs, conflicts of lifestyle, the disconnect between a public persona and private reality or it provokes the powerful temptation to deny and rationalize, to escape that confrontation, whatever it takes.

Sometimes the brazenness of the hypocrisy takes my breath away in clinics and in protests, we see it every day.

Kathleen was forty-two years old and a model of perfection. Hair, nails, clothes done up as if she were prepped for a high-profile job interview. When I came into the room and asked my standard question, "Are you absolutely sure you want this abortion?" she squared her jaw and glared at me.

"Of course I don't want to have an abortion. I HAVE to have an abortion." She held an oversized purse on her lap, kept fumbling with the latch.

"Why? Is someone forcing you?"

"No one is forcing me. I just CANNOT have a baby now. I know it's murder and should not even be legal, but I HAVE to have an abortion."

"So," I spat back, "if you think this is murder, do you think I am a murderer?"

"Of course you are"

"Do you think I should go to jail for doing abortions?"

"Yes, I do."

I couldn't believe I was hearing this. I felt sick with outrage and disbelief. Maybe I had misunderstood. I asked her again.

"So, you think this should be illegal and that I should go to prison for murder, but you also want me to do an abortion for you?"

"Yes" she said, without blinking an eye.

Everything inside me turned upside down, I had never encountered anything like this.

"I need to step out of the room a minute," I said. I got off my stool and headed for the door.

"You can't leave," she barked. "I want an abortion. It is my right, and you have to do it."

"I have rights, too," I replied, and I slipped through the door. Flashes of the final scene in the movie *If These Walls Could Talk* ran through my head. In the movie, a couple comes to an abortion clinic, supposedly for an abortion. The woman's partner accuses the doctor of being a murderer, then pulls out a gun from a hand bag and kills her. It is a scene burned into my memory.

I paused and took a deep breath before going to talk to the clinic administrator. After I relayed the conversation, I asked that someone else tell the patient that we would not be providing the abortion. There was no way I could do it.

The counselor who had visited with Kathleen earlier went into the room. Within twenty seconds the conflict was loud enough for everyone on the floor to hear.

"I will NOT leave! It is my RIGHT to have an abortion and I am staying until it is DONE!"

Brief silence.

"NO! I will NOT get dressed until I have the ABORTION!"

We heard a loud thump, the patient slamming her fist onto a desk. The clinic administrator called the front desk guard to escort her out. If that didn't work, we'd have to call the police.

"I am going to sue that doctor and this stupid clinic!" the woman yelled. I imagined everyone in the waiting room cringing. I literally hid in the staff lounge until she was gone.

At the end of the day all the staff gathered in the empty recovery room.

"I'm sorry I couldn't confront that woman," I apologized. "It doesn't happen often, but once in a while someone comes along who I simply can't deal with."

We talked about the danger a patient like that could present. From that time on, we established a clinic policy that prevented patients from bringing purses, bulky coats, or bags with them beyond the waiting room.

One of the most galling realities is the lack of consistency within the medical community. In Montana, as in other places, I was repeatedly attacked by anti-choice factions in editorials and letters to the editor. Statements containing false medical information and misleading "facts" went unchecked. Only one physician in Bozeman publicly supported me. The rest either were silent or professed to be against abortion, knuckling under to antichoice pressure. Yet more than once I was asked to perform a secretive abortion after hours for a girlfriend or wife of a local doctor.

I remember meeting one such doctor at eight PM in the quiet hallway outside my office.

"Thank you for seeing us tonight," he said, shaking my hand. He looked up and down the empty hall. "This is just so awkward, you know."

I kept my thoughts to myself, focused instead on the woman by his side. When I didn't respond, he continued. "Well, at least there's an accountant's office nearby I can always say we were going there if someone sees us tonight. They work late sometimes, don't they?"

Then there are the patients who come to us, admitting they have been against abortion, but struggling with the uncomfortable fact that they are now the victims of unwanted pregnancies. Suddenly, for them, the black-and-white parameters turn a decided shade of gray

Early in my career, in a Midwestern clinic, I saw a twenty-two-year-old single mother in the waiting room whom I recognized as one of the group of protesters who had recently chained themselves together with bike locks, blocking the clinic entrance in an attempt to close us down. She had been sitting against the side doors, pounding her fist in a rhythmic way doing her best to mimic a heartbeat. Thump thud. Thump thud. Thump thud. At the same time she screamed, "Mommy, don't kill me!"

What was she doing in our waiting room? Was she a spy, gathering information? Would she open the doors and let in a flood of protesters? Was she faking a pregnancy in order to find out more about our facilities?

It became clear that she was actually there for an abortion. Unbelievable. The initial reaction from all the staff was anger and disbelief. How dare she expect us to take care of her? Did she take us for fools?

Our most seasoned counselor volunteered to talk with her. The two of them stayed cloistered in the room for perhaps an hour before the counselor reappeared with a look of determination and amazement on her face.

"She really is pregnant and really does want an abortion. I think we should help her, but I also think each of us needs to talk with her first. She should know how we feel about this. More important, she needs to understand the impact she has had on our lives and the lives of our other patients."

There was a lot of resistance from the staff, myself included. The counselor persisted, telling us to be forgiving and understanding and to allow this woman the chance to learn the truth about us and about abortion.

"You never know," she said, "This young woman might end up being an ally. Even if she doesn't, it will be pretty hard for her to go back to the protesters.

"She knows now that things aren't so ethically clear and simple as she was led to believe. Those pat answers aren't working for her. Forget that she was a protester, and listen to her with an open heart."

When I went in to see her, I started with a straightforward question: "Do you believe abortion should be legal?"

"Well, yes, I guess so. Yes. I do. Well, now I do. But I didn't before ... ," she stumbled over the words.

"What has changed your mind?" I asked.

"This is my second pregnancy. The first time I got pregnant I came here to get an abortion, but the people out front stopped me and promised to help me if I had the baby. They told me I might die in here and that you were awful people that just wanted to kill babies."

I kept listening and prodding her to tell me more.

"They said they'd pay for my prenatal care and give me baby clothes and diapers and all that."

"So you had the baby?" I asked.

"Yes. And I really love him, but he's only five months old, and I am really having a tough time taking care of him. I have to work, but I'd like to go to the community college. I don't know how I could possibly do it with two kids."

"So what happened to the people that promised to help you?"

"All they gave me was a layette set and two boxes of diapers. That's it. They were all friendly and took me to church and wanted me to demonstrate with them, but they really haven't helped me at all with anything. I feel like all they cared about was that I didn't have an abortion."

"But after all the things they told you about us, how do you know who to believe? How could you even dare to come here?" I asked.

"I talked to my aunt. She's a nurse and told me a lot of things I didn't know. I trust her, and she said I should trust you. She said this was a good clinic and that I'd be safe."

I leaned back in my chair, thinking hard about the next thing on my mind. "Tell me," I looked her in the eye. "Are you ever going to protest outside an abortion clinic again?"

"Absolutely not," she replied without hesitation.

"And if your best friend got pregnant and came to you for advice, what would you tell her?" I wasn't going to let up.

"I'd be her friend no matter what. It would be up to her, but I wouldn't try to talk her out of an abortion like I would have last year."

We talked a bit longer. I told her I believed that everything happens for a reason, and that she and I were both learning lessons in forgiveness and understanding.

After the abortion, that young woman became a pro-choice advocate. She kept in contact with us. Every time she stopped in, she expressed gratitude for our care and for our ability to see who she really was.

Not all encounters with patients who have been strongly anti-choice end this way. I have had patients who admit that they have been protesters, but rather calmly and rationally explain why they need to end a pregnancy in spite of their beliefs. We give them accurate information and perform safe, legal abortions if they choose to go forward. Some of those same women are back out in front of the clinic protesting within a week of their procedure.

Mostly I'm able to ignore and minimize the impact of protesters, but a few of them make the hair stand up on the back of my neck. Mostly they are men: people who will never experience the personal, agonizing trauma of an unwanted pregnancy but who preach their version of truth, bully patients, and emanate hatred. I'm utterly convinced that, for these people, the abortion issue is not about morality but about power and control. Control over women's lives. Nothing I've observed in them shows any sincere concern or sympathy for children or families.

The first time I saw Chet Gallagher was in Fargo, North Dakota. He was aggressive with patients and staff, swaggering around on the sidewalk in front of the building as if it were his domain. When patients approached he'd shout in their faces. "You'll die in there," he pointed to the doors. "Your baby will scream in pain. You'll never be able to have another child!"

If a young woman was accompanied by her boyfriend, Gallagher would get in his face, too. "Be a man," he'd yell. "Don't let her do this."

Over the months we learned that Chet Gallagher had been a police officer, a person hired to uphold the law. That he had once been in charge of protecting the public seemed absurd. Here he was breaking laws left and right, racking up many arrests. Over time, he has become one of the national leaders in the anti-choice movement. He now claims to have been arrested more than a hundred times and calls himself a lay minister.

During my years in Bozeman I was targeted by several local men who were obsessed with my clinic. One of them was particularly rabid. He was eventually arrested for trying to burn down the building where my offices were located. Before that, however, he stalked me, put up "wanted" posters with my picture on them, and repeatedly harassed people associated with any aspect of family planning or reproductive health.

At one point he burst into a mother/daughter seminar sponsored by a local medical practice. The weekend session was devoted to fostering family communication and discussing issues of puberty. He rampaged around the room, ranting about teen sex and abortions. He accused the facilitators of fostering promiscuity and loose morals. The facilitators finally had to call the police before the man would leave.

The same man stood up and disrupted church services where some of my employees worshiped, telling the minister and congregation that they were sinners for allowing baby killers in their midst.

The most blatant hypocrisy takes place outside clinics, but inside it isn't uncommon to witness fateful intersections between patients that force them to face their decisions rather than keep them hidden.

One day I heard two very audible gasps in the outer waiting room when a couple of women, both patients with appointments for abortions, came face to face.

"WHAT are YOU doing here?" one of them said.

"I don't know," stammered the other. "What are YOU doing here?"

They stared at each other, both at a loss. The receptionist quickly stepped in and signaled them to follow her to a more private area.

"If the two of you know each other and would like to talk privately, we can provide you with a quiet space. Or one of you can reschedule if you'd like."

They chose to talk. They stayed in there a very long time.

It turned out that they were coworkers at a Catholic school. One of them was an administrator, the other a teacher. No doubt they had each hoped to keep their secret safe and go on with life. The public face they presented to the world could remain unchanged, except for their chance meeting. No doubt they had some rationalizing and explaining to do, but when they came back out, they both seemed resolved and under control.

Both women stayed for their procedures. In fact, they scheduled their follow-up exams for the same day so that they could carpool for the three-hour drive. I have little doubt, given their positions, that they still publicly denounce abortion and tell their students abortion is a grievous sin. Except for their awkward encounter, they might have avoided any confession at all.

For the most part, my knowledge of personal hypocrisy is protected by my commitment to confidentiality. The insights that come to me stay locked up tight by necessity. Occasionally, though, an opportunity comes along to call on someone to live up to public statements.

The first time I turned the tables on the local "crisis pregnancy center," I had a patient in the clinic who really did not want an abortion but who had no resources to cover the costs of prenatal care or childbirth. She was single and without insurance coverage but made just enough money to be ineligible for state assistance. She already had outstanding bills at the hospital and with the local ob-gyn practice. No doctor would see her without payment up front.

We were willing to do the abortion for a reduced rate or for free if necessary. But she really didn't want an abortion. Once I understood her situation, I went to the phone and called the local "crisis pregnancy center."

"Hello, this is Dr. Wicklund."

Dead silence. I might as well have said I was Satan.

"Hello?" I said again. "This is Dr. Wicklund."

"Hello," very tentatively, followed by another long silence.

"I need help with a patient," I said. "She came to me for an abortion, but she really doesn't want one. What she really needs is someone to do her prenatal care and birth for free."

"What do you expect us to do?"

I let that hang for a minute.

"Well, maybe this is your chance to save a baby. Isn't that your mission? Here you are. My suggestion is that you find her the care she needs, or she will be forced to have an abortion."

"But no one does free, prenatal care and births."

"How about Dr. Abott? He is always publicly preaching about the evils of abortion. Why don't you call him and see if he'll put his money where his mouth is? Tell him I am willing to do the abortion for free, but it won't be necessary if he can match my offer."

In this case, it worked. Dr. Abott provided her prenatal care and birth without charge, although he reminded her of his noble gesture at every visit. The young woman came by several times to let us know how things were going.

"He always moans about being tricked into the deal," she told us. "Then goes off on these tirades against abortion."

Not surprisingly, the people who pay the greatest price in the abortion war are always the ones without power, without resources, without advocates, the most vulnerable of our culture. Poor women in the United States are four times as likely to have an unwanted pregnancy than affluent women. They are five times more likely to have an unintended birth and three times more likely to have an abortion. The correlation between poverty and unwanted pregnancy is stark.

Too often poor women become pawns in the battle—used while they serve a purpose and abandoned the moment their usefulness ends. People like Martina Greywind.

Fargo, North Dakota. 1992. Martina Greywind is a local figure, one of those people everyone averts their eyes from on the street. Her hands are weathered, her hair disheveled. Her face is creased with the lines of her life's trials—winters spent sleeping on heat grates and mattresses of newspaper, repeated physical abuse, excessive alcohol and drug use. You'd guess she was fifty, but she is twenty-eight years old.

She regularly sniffs paint. Her face is often flecked with gold from spray paint cans. She is no stranger to jail.

She is pregnant and wants an abortion. She has already given birth to six children, cares for none of them. For weeks she has been maniacally sniffing paint, not simply to get high but in hopes that she will provoke a miscarriage.

Now she is in jail again, charged with recklessly endangering her fetus, sentenced to an ironic nine-month term. She makes no secret of her desire to obtain an abortion.

In her cellblock two members of the Lambs of Christ are also incarcerated, held for their illegal actions against the local clinic. They hound her with rhetoric. "Don't kill your baby," they shout. "We will help you. Your baby will be loved."

Martina tells them to leave her alone, that it is none of their business, but they persist. For weeks I am kept abreast of the case through clinic staff. I make it clear that I'm willing to come to Fargo if Martina is able to have an abortion.

The story makes local daily headlines: "Greywind Still Wants Abortion." The *New York Times* picks up the story. Her plight is featured on the *Today Show.*

When a local resident offers to cover Greywind's abortion costs, the Lambs of Christ accuse the clinic of bribery. They raise $11,000 and offer it to Greywind if she will continue her pregnancy. She rejects them.

Then Martina is sentenced to thirty days of rehabilitation in a state hospital more than a hundred miles away. Authorities refuse to transport her for medical appointments, saying it is a waste of taxpayer money. By the time she returns, it will be too late for an abortion. A last-minute court order delays her rehabilitation sentence for a few days.

Martina requests a leave for a clinic appointment. It is granted for Sunday. The clinic is normally closed on weekends, but the staff agrees to be available. I will fly in from Milwaukee. When the antis get wind of this, they go wild. Desecrating the Sabbath, they cry. We will stop this!

They go to court for an injunction, claiming Greywind is mentally incompetent. They are rejected.

I follow the drama from afar. It becomes clear to me that there is no way we will succeed on the publicly announced day. Too much fervor has built up. The antis will stop at nothing.

"We have to change the day," I tell the administrator by phone.

"But it's already Thursday," she says. "We have to go to court to do that. There isn't time."

"We need to try," I persist "Otherwise it'll be a circus, a standoff, and Martina will be trapped in the middle."

The clinic administrator goes to the city attorney. "Lives are at stake here," she tells him. "If we go ahead on Sunday, there is no telling what might happen."

He agrees to try, but the presiding judge is away on vacation. Finally we reach the judge by phone and get his verbal agreement. The court order is filed seconds before the office closes on Friday. We can only hope that the antis haven't gotten wind of the change.

On Friday night, after a full day of clinic in Milwaukee, I fly to Fargo. Before boarding the plane I call Sonja.

"Hi Sonja. How was school today?" We talk about the day. I try to sound reassuring, but Sonja knows something is up. "Listen, I won't be able to get home tonight. I have to fly to Fargo for a special case. I'll be home by tomorrow afternoon, okay?" I can hear the disappointment in her voice, but she bucks up as she always does. "I'm sorry sweetie. It's important, or I wouldn't go. Tell Randy what's going on. I love you."

It is nearly midnight when I slip in the back door of a Fargo hotel and register under a false name. My sleep is restless, but at six-thirty AM I meet a van at the back door. The clinic director and lab tech are already in the vehicle.

At the same time, two volunteers drive to the garage at the Fargo jail. Martina climbs behind the back seat and hides under blankets. They make their way to the clinic.

The Lambs of Christ still in jail somehow get the word and raise the alarm, but they are too late. Martina is already inside the clinic offices by the time protesters start swarming around outside like angry insects. Police cars pull up. The media arrives, sniffing the next headline.

Inside, Martina and I sit in a small room. I turn a radio on to help drown out the shouts and commotion from the street.

"How are you holding up?" I ask her.

"I'm tired. I just want this to be over," she replies quietly.

She reminds me of a rag doll. Pliable. Soft. Plain. No grit or fight left in her. I want to take her home and try to make everything better for her, but I know I am not being realistic. We move forward.

"Are you absolutely sure this is what you want to do?" I ask.

She just nods, but her head is down, and she is not looking at me. I wait for more. She nods again. Still I say nothing. Finally she raises her head and looks at me.

"Yes," she says in a very soft voice.

The staff wants me to hurry. They are justifiably afraid of the growing crowd and mounting tension outside.

But Martina and I move at our own pace. We are together in a different realm, oddly serene. The procedure goes well, but instead of moving her to the recovery room right away, I just roll my stool up beside her and place my hand on her arm. We are both silent. We each shed tears we don't acknowledge. I feel the weight of her life, the fatigue in her bones. I stand; our eyes meet.

The news appeal swirling around Martina dries up and disappears in no time. Within days the charges against her are dropped, and she is released.

Her "protectors" no longer find her useful. They claim they were tricked and misled by the clinic, as if they ever had a right to be part of Martina Greywind's decision. Never once, before or after her abortion, do they make any genuine attempt to change the circumstances of her life. She slips back to the streets, becomes anonymous again, a cultural pariah.

The ultimate and most threatening expression of hypocrisy comes from the segment of the "pro-life" movement that believes murdering abortion doctors is "justifiable homicide." The biblical commandment "Thou shalt not kill" is conveniently glossed over in their ends-justify-the-means philosophy. They spout religion, they pay homage to godliness, they call themselves god-fearing, yet they find it in their hearts to commit murder, arson, and violence of every kind against doctors and clinics.

I remember the first time I saw Sonja shrink away in horror from someone who innocently announced their devotion to Christianity. To her, Christians were the people who called me a killer and who publicly agitated for the murder of her mother.

Until the courts ordered them to cease, the justifiable homicide crowd maintained a website listing every known abortion provider in the country, along with addresses, phone numbers, information about other family members, photos, and personal profiles. It was called the Nuremberg File, and it was nothing less than a detailed hit list. If a doctor was wounded or killed, that entry would be highlighted in a different color on the site, as if to check off a job well done.

Seeing myself and my family listed on that website threw a dark shadow across my basic assumption of human goodness.

The Male Partner Involved in Legal Abortion

By A. Kero, A. Lalos, U. Högberg, and L. Jacobsson

This study comprises 75 men who have been involved in legal abortion. The men answered a questionnaire concerning living conditions and attitudes about pregnancy and abortion. Most men were found to be in stable relationships with good finances. More than half clearly stated that they wanted the woman to have an abortion while 20 stressed that they submitted themselves to their partner's decision. Only one man wanted the woman to complete the pregnancy. Apart from wanting children within functioning family units, the motivation for abortion revealed that the desire to have children depended on the ability to provide qualitatively good parenting. More than half the men had discussed with their partner what to do in event of pregnancy and half had decided to have an abortion if a pregnancy occurred. More than half expressed ambivalent feelings about the coming abortion, using words such as anxiety, responsibility, guilty, relief and grief. In spite of these contradictory feelings, prevailing expectations concerning lifestyle make abortion an acceptable form of birth control. A deeper understanding of the complexity of legal abortion makes it necessary to accept the role of paradox, which the ambivalence reflects. Obviously, men must constitute a target group in efforts to prevent abortions.

Introduction

Studies investigating men in abortion situations are extremely rare. Most studies of legal abortion are focused on the women and when abortion and contraception are discussed, attention is mostly centred on the role and responsibility of the woman. Hospital staff often meet only the woman and not the man in cases of legal abortion, which can result in the risk of abortion being regarded solely as a female issue. Thus, the participation of the man remains largely invisible. However, many women have stated that they are influenced in their decision about abortion by the man and one of the most frequently stated reasons for terminating a pregnancy is related to the partner (Torres and Darroch Forrest, 1988; Törnbom et al., 1994; Skjeldestad, 1994; Holmgren, 1994; Söderberg et al., 1997; Johansson et al., 1998).

Many of the legal abortions carried out occur in established relationships (Swedish Ministry of Health and Social Affairs, 1983; Holmgren, 1988; Törnbom et al., 1994). One of very few studies carried out in Western countries that included both women and men showed that the majority of those who had legal abortion had good

A. Kero, A. Lalos, U. Hogberg, and L. Jacobsson, "The Male Partner Involved in Legal Abortion," *Human Reproduction*, vol. 14, no. 10, pp. 2669–2675. Copyright © 1999 by Oxford University Press. Reprinted with permission.

socio-economic positions and were in relatively established relationships. Many couples had no children but the majority planned to have children in the future. Nevertheless, many women felt alone when making the decision to have an abortion and they also had to take responsibility for contraception (Jacobsson et al., 1980). Other studies including only women also show that many women make the decision to have a legal abortion more or less on their own (Trost, 1982; Holmgren, 1988). In contrast, another study of both women and men concluded that few women seemed to be alone in their decision (Graff-Iversen and Kristoffersen, 1990). Furthermore, a study on 60 men who accompanied their partners to the hospital showed that the men considered themselves responsible, along with the partners, for preventing unwanted pregnancies and choosing abortion (Rothstein, 1977). However, abortion studies usually ignore the involvement of the man or examine it only indirectly, i.e. the women are asked about how they regard their partners' attitude and participation and how they are influenced by them. Therefore, roles and reactions of men in connection with unwanted pregnancy and legal abortion remain a virtually unexplored and neglected field.

Ambivalence during the early stages of pregnancy and towards parenthood is a known phenomenon among expectant mothers (Uddenberg, 1974; Holmberg and Uddenberg, 1993). A study of prospective parents showed that the ambivalence among both men and women appeared in conflicting views regarding children as constituting the meaning of life or the loss of freedom. The view that children represent loss of freedom was more obvious among men (Wikman et al., 1993). Ambivalence also existed among women applying for abortion (Trost, 1982; Allanson and Astbury, 1995; Hamark et al., 1995; Törnbom et al., 1996). For example, one study showed that 44% of the women were in doubt about the abortion decision when the pregnancy was initially confirmed and 30% when the abortion was due (Husfeldt et al., 1995). Another study found that the most common thought for abortion among women was that continuing the pregnancy would jeopardize their future and the most common theme against abortion was that they really wanted to have children some day (Allanson and Astbury, 1995).

The primary aim of this study was to increase knowledge and understanding of the abortion situation by making the men/impregnators' views visible. Therefore, psychosocial background and current living conditions of the men and their attitudes and feelings about pregnancy and legal abortion were studied. A further aim was to investigate whether there are any differences between men with previous experience of legal abortion and those without.

Materials and Methods

This study on men is part of a larger project which included a questionnaire completed by women and an interview study involving both men and women. The entire study was carried out at the University Hospital, Umeå, Sweden which has a catchment area with about 160,000 inhabitants. The questionnaire study was performed at the Department of Obstetrics and Gynaecology between February and November 1995. Two experienced social workers asked 250 consecutive Swedish-speaking women applying for legal abortion if they would be willing to participate in the study. Seventeen of the women came with their partners to the clinic and those men were personally asked about participation in the study. Women who came without a partner were asked to give a questionnaire to the men by whom they had become pregnant. Information about the study and a prepaid envelope were enclosed with the questionnaire. In all, 51 of the participating women ($n = 221$) and 28 of those who dropped out ($n = 29$) did not want to give a questionnaire to the man involved so the maximum number of men who might have participated was 171. However, it is impossible to know how many women actually gave the questionnaire to the man. Seventy-eight men actually answered the questionnaire, which is 46% of the maximum number possible. As it was impossible to identify the men, they could not be sent a reminder to complete the questionnaire. Two of the men answering questionnaires had partners who chose to continue their pregnancies to full term and another one's partner turned out not to be pregnant. These three questionnaires were excluded from the analyses, which therefore finally included 75 men. In only six cases the pregnancy had passed the 12th week.

The questionnaires covered the men's own judgement about psychosocial background, current living conditions, partner relationship, use of contraceptives, decision-making process, motives for abortion and questions about emotions in connection with the pregnancy, the current abortion and possible previous abortions. The questionnaire was semistructured, self-administered and contained 49 questions, mainly with given response options.

Questions about emotions in connection with the pregnancy, the current abortion and previous abortions gave the respondent the possibility to choose more than one response option, allowing the possible occurrence of contradictory feelings to be expressed. Answers other than the given response alternatives could also be supplied. In order to avoid the dichotomy and the valuation which are built into expression of positive and negative feelings, feelings in this study were classified as positive or painful. The answers were divided into three categories: those containing only positively charged words, those containing only words expressing pain and those containing both positively charged words and words expressing pain. The question about motives for having an abortion was open-ended in order to allow the respondents to express themselves freely. In a follow-up question the respondents were subsequently asked to state the most important motive and in the analyses the answers were divided into categories. Analyses of data and choice of categories were (triangulated) made by the two social workers together with the supervisor.

Non-Participants

This study relied on the assistance of pregnant women applying for legal abortion. This resulted in answers from 78 men, constituting 46% of the maximum number of men who were possible participants.

However, the corresponding drop-out of 54% cannot be considered real since some women probably did not give the questionnaire to their partners, meaning that many men never got a chance to decide whether or not they wanted to participate in the study. Since the men were not patients, it was impossible to identify them, and consequently to ask or remind them to send in the completed questionnaire.

Thus, a traditional analysis of the non-participants was not possible to do. However, it was possible to analyze whether there were any significant differences between the female partners of responding and non-responding men. The group of women whose partners answered the questionnaire ($n = 74$) was compared with the group of women who clearly stated that they did not want to give a questionnaire to their partner ($n = 47$ since four out of these 51 women had been excluded because they were not pregnant or had decided to continue the pregnancy), and the group of women who took a questionnaire for their partner but where the partner did not respond ($n = 90$). The groups were compared for a large number of variables such as age, civil status, education, personal finances, children, partner relationship, attitudes and feelings in connection with pregnancy and abortion, the partner's attitude to the current abortion and experiences of previous abortions. The results of these analyses show that the groups of women exhibited more similarities than differences. Some differences were found between the group of women whose partners answered the questionnaire and the group of women who did not take a questionnaire for their partner. The latter more frequently stated that they did not have a firm relationship with the man they were pregnant by or that they were more dissatisfied with the relationship ($P < 0.001$). These women also had a lower educational level ($P < 0.05$). There were fewer differences between the group of women whose partners participated in the study and the group of women who took a questionnaire for their partner, who failed to reply. The group whose partners did not reply had a lower educational level ($P < 0.05$) and more often thought that most men consider that it is the woman's responsibility to prevent unwanted pregnancy ($P < 0.01$). The results of these analyses show that there are no essential differences between the women whose men participated in the study and the women whose men did not participate. However, it was uncertain whether these similarities among the women could be extended to the men.

Statistics

Statistical analyses were performed using the SSPS statistical package. Discrete variables were compared with the χ^2 (exact test). A P value of < 0.05 was considered as statistically significant.

The study was approved by the Ethics Committee of the University of Umeå.

Results

Psychosocial Characterization

The median and mean age for the men was 29 years, range 18–50 (one missing). The corresponding figures for the pregnant women were a median age of 25 years (mean = 27), range 15–47 years. Men with previous experience of abortion had a median age of 35 years, range 19–50 (mean = 36) and the median and mean age for the others were 27 years, range 18–46 ($P < 0.001$). Table I shows the living conditions of the men. The majority were married or co-habiting in relatively long-lasting relationships with the pregnant woman. Most of them were employed and slightly more than a quarter was studying. A total of 84% were pleased with their occupation and more than 70% regarded their financial situation as good; 11% were very worried about it (data not shown). Half the men already had children, and 34% had children with the pregnant women. Three quarters of the married and co-habiting men and a quarter of the single men had children ($P < 0.001$). All except five had grown up in Sweden and one third of all men adhered to some religious belief.

A total of 89% of the men had a partner relationship and all except two were pleased with their relationship (Table I); 67% of these men said that the pregnancy had not had any influence on the relationship, 21% said that the relationship had been influenced positively while 12% felt it had had a negative influence. One man was unsure whether he was the prospective father. All men except six considered their sexual life in positive terms. Sixty-three per cent of the men declared that the couple had not used any contraceptive methods at the time of conception and four men did not know if contraceptives were used.

A total of 75% of the men were involved in legal abortion for the first time while 25% had had a previous experience. There were more similarities than differences concerning psychosocial factors between those who had and those who had not experienced abortion previously (Table 2.13.1). Significant differences were found between the groups concerning age (see above), duration of the relationship, evaluation of sexual life and whether or not they had children. Men with previous experience of abortion were older compared with men involved in abortion for the first time ($P < 0.001$) and more often lived in long-term relationships ($P < 0.05$) than those involved for the first time (Table I). Men with previous experience of abortion more often had children with the pregnant women ($P < 0.001$) and had children more than twice as often as the men in the other group ($P < 0.001$). However, men involved in their first abortion were more satisfied with their sexual life than men with previous experience of abortion ($P < 0.05$).

Men Accompanying the Women to the Hospital

Seventeen men accompanied their partners to the hospital and could therefore be asked in person to participate in the study. One of them refused to participate and two were excluded because the partner of one decided to continue the pregnancy to full term and the partner of the other was found not to be pregnant. Thus, 14 of the men who accompanied their partners to the hospital were included in the study. These men differed from the rest of the men concerning employment, attitudes to abortion and use of contraceptives. They were more often at home, i.e. not in paid employment, were students or unemployed ($P < 0.01$), they more often used only positively charged words in relation to the current abortion ($P < 0.05$) and none had used contraceptives during the relevant intercourse/s ($P < 0.01$) compared with men not accompanying the woman to the hospital.

Motives for Legal Abortion

Every second man (56%) stated that they had talked to the woman before she became pregnant about what they should do in the event of pregnancy. Twenty-six of these men (60%) said that they had decided with their partner to have an abortion. No differences were found in this case between men with and without experiences of previous abortions.

Table 2.13.I. Psychosocial characterization of the men responding to the questionnaire (n = 75; values are percentages)

	Total (n = 75)	First abortion (n = 56)	Previous abortion (n = 19)
Civil status			
Single	44	48	32
Married/cohabitant (with the pregnant woman)	56	52	68
Duration of present relationship			
<6 months	17	20	10[a]
≥6 months <3 years	28	34	11
≥3 years	44	34	74
No partner relationship	11	12	5
Children			
0	50	61	16[b]
1–2	33	28	47
3–5	17	11	37
Children with the pregnant woman			
0	66	79	32[b]
1	10	11	5
2	14	6	37
3–5	10	4	26
Education level			
Completed elementary school	9	9	11
Completed senior high school	62	61	63
Completed university studies	29	30	26
Professional status			
Employed	56	50	74
Student	26	31	10
Unemployed/others	18	19	16
Present economic situation			
Income too low	11	12	5
Income only just meets needs	17	16	21
Income meets most needs with care	69	68	74
Income meets all needs	3	4	0
Emotional conditions during childhood			
Very good	48	48	48
Good	27	29	21
Rather good	17	14	26
Bad	8	9	5
Opinion about partner relationship			
Very satisfied	54	56	53
Satisfied	23	21	26
Rather satisfied	9	7	16
Not satisfied	3	4	0
No partner relationship	11	12	5
Opinion about present sexual life			
Satisfied	64	70	47
Rather satisfied	23	20	32
Not satisfied	8	3	21[a]
No sexual life	5	7	0

[a] $P < 0.05$, [b] $P < 0.001$, compared with first abortion group.

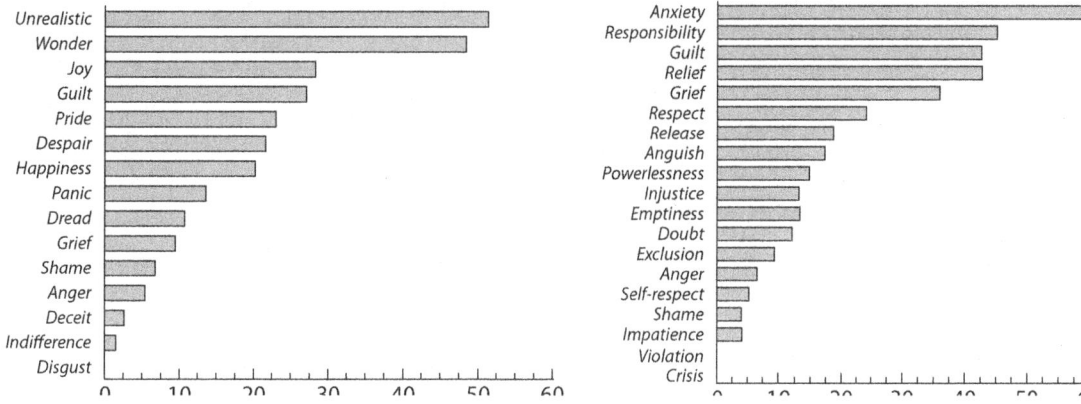

Figure 2.13.1. Words expressing the men's initial feelings about the current pregnancy (n = 74). Information missing for one man (see Table 2.13.2).

Figure 2.13.2. Words expressing the men's feelings about the expected abortion (n = 75).

Among all men, 64% stated in clear terms that they wanted the woman to have an abortion and 27% said that they did not take any specific standpoint but left it to the woman to decide. Five men said that they had not at the time of the questionnaire study decided whether to support an abortion or not. In total, 48 men who thought that the women should have an abortion were asked about the motives behind their standpoint. However, 11 of the 25 men who had answered either that they left the decision to the woman or that they had not taken any standpoint answered this question. Thus, 59 men declared motives for having legal abortion.

The primary motive for being in favour of an abortion was given by 30% as family planning; either they already had all the children they wanted or it was not the right time to have children. Half of these men had children. The other half, consisting mainly of students without children, provided more background to their standpoint, and said that they gave priority to other things, principally their studies, or that they were unable to offer a child a caring environment in their current circumstances; 19% gave reasons related to insecure relationships with the woman while 12% gave socio-economic motives. Next in order came motives related to age (12%), mainly a feeling of being too young; 10% stated as the first reason for the abortion that they had no time for an extra child: their work and existing children already took all their time. Four men stated motives concerning health.

Analysis of psychosocial factors and the stated primary motives for abortion revealed very few links. All those who gave planning as their motive enjoyed economic prosperity while none of those living under more strained economic circumstances stated that as a motive ($P < 0.01$). Half of the 19 men who were studying declared that they gave priority to their studies and 25% believed they were too young. Among the 41 employed men the motives were more varied. A quarter of them stated planning reasons and another quarter stated reasons related to insecure relationships. Men without children gave motives related to the relationship nearly twice as often as men who already had children. All men under 20 years of age gave age or socio-economic motives. At ages between 20–30 years, planning and reasons related to the relationship were predominant, while the predominant motive for the over 30 year olds was the planning. An obvious trend was found with increasing age. The older men less often gave socio-economic reasons, fewer reasons related to the relationship and more motives related to problems of combining professional work/housework with existing children. No man with previous experience of abortion gave motives relating to the relationship as a reason for having the abortion, while 11 in the other group stated this as their primary motive ($P < 0.05$). Apart from this, no differences between motives given for abortion could be found among men with and without previous experience of abortion.

Table 2.13.2. Initial feelings related to the pregnancy in relationship to feelings related to the abortion (n = 74)[a]. Values are numbers of men

Initial feelings related to the pregnancy	Feelings related to the abortion			Total
	Only positive	Both positive and painful	Only painful	
Only positive	5	9	6	20
Both positive and painful	2	21	7	30
Only painful	3	13	8	24
Total	10	43	21	74

[a] *Information missing for one man who did not want to answer the question about feelings related to the pregnancy.*

Feelings Connected with Pregnancy and Abortion

Figure 2.13.1 gives the words the men could choose from, that would best reflect their initial feelings towards the current pregnancy. The most frequent words were unrealistic, wonder, joy, guilt and pride. Contradictory feelings appeared among 41% who chose both positively charged words and words expressing pain. A third of them (32%) chose words which only characterized pain such as unrealistic, despair, guilt, panic and dread while 27% chose only positively charged words such as joy, pride and happiness.

Figure 2.13.2 gives the words the men could choose from, that would best correspond to their feelings about the coming abortion. The most frequent words were anxiety, responsibility, guilt, relief and grief. Fifty seven per cent chose both words that were positively charged such as responsibility, relief and release and those that reflected pain such as anxiety, guilt, grief, anguish and powerlessness; 29% chose only words charged with pain and the remaining 13% chose only positively charged words. No differences in feelings regarding the pregnancy and the abortion were recorded between men who had children and men who did not. Furthermore, no differences could be found concerning feelings and attitudes to pregnancy and abortion between men who had and who did not have previous experience of legal abortion.

Table 2.13.2 shows the men's initial feelings related to the pregnancy in relationship to feelings related to the abortion. More than a quarter (28%) had experienced both positive and painful feelings related to both the pregnancy and the abortion. A quarter of the men (25%) who chose only positively charged words to describe their initial feelings related to the pregnancy also chose only such words to describe their emotions related to the abortion. On the other hand, the same situation could be described in that half of those with only positive feelings towards the abortion initially had only positive feelings related to the pregnancy (Table 2.13.2). Another separate analysis revealing the complexity of the abortion situation shows that 45% of the men who only expressed positive initial feelings towards the pregnancy also stated clearly that they wanted the woman to have an abortion (data not shown). Furthermore it was found that 64% of the men who expressed only painful feelings related to the abortion nevertheless wanted the woman to have an abortion (data not shown).

Among the 19 men who had experience of previous abortions, eight had been involved in at least two abortions. Those men were asked about their feelings related to the previous abortion/s. The words the men could choose from were almost the same as those in Figure 2.13.2. The words anxiety and anguish were excluded and the words depression and regret were added. About half the men chose such words as relief, guilt and grief when describing their emotions regarding previous abortions. About 30% chose words such as powerlessness, responsibility and emptiness while about 20% chose words such as shame, release, regret, and exclusion. Many of these words were the same as the words the men used about their feelings with reference to the current abortion (Figure 2.13.2). When confronted with either the current or a previous abortion no man used the word 'crisis'. Eleven of the men with experience of previous abortions described these experiences with both positively and painfully charged words. Four expressed only positive feelings and three chose words that only characterize pain.

Discussion

Men are usually invisible in abortion studies and hardly ever considered as a target group in the effort to prevent legal abortions in Western countries. To increase the understanding of the complexity of an abortion situation, it is of great importance that men involved in abortion should also become visible. However, it is ethically difficult to contact these men, as they are not patients. Thus, it is impossible to know how many men actually received the enquiry to participate in the study. In the present study women applying for abortion were asked to answer a questionnaire and thereafter to decide whether they wanted to participate in a prospective interview study. The women were also asked to give a questionnaire to the man they had become pregnant by. This procedure may have increased the stress on several women which in turn could mean negative influence acting on the possibility of the men participating in the study. In addition, we do not have any information about the men's proficiency with Swedish language. Furthermore, an American study has found an over-representation of domestic violence among women applying for abortion who did not want to involve their partner (Glander et al., 1998). Taking into account the delicacy of the issue *per se*, the participation frequency of about one in two is understandable. Whilst the participating men are not a statistically representative group for all men involved in abortion, they nevertheless represent a group that is of great interest, since they make visible 75 Western men involved in legal abortion.

The majority of the men were married/co-habiting and lived in functioning and relatively long-lasting relationships. Three quarters of them had children. More than half were employed, about a third were students and the remaining men were mainly unemployed. The majority were financially in a good position. Thus, the abortion situation for the vast majority did not equate to poor psychosocial conditions. On the whole, these results correspond with the results from a similar study conducted at the same department 20 years ago (Jacobsson et al., 1980). More similarities than differences were found between those who had and those who had not experienced legal abortion previously. Characteristic of the 19 men with previous experience of abortion was that they were older than the others and that they more often lived in long-term relationships and more often had children.

The majority of the men clearly stated that they wanted the woman to have an abortion. The predominant motives behind the men's standpoint regarding abortion involved various aspects of planning. Either they wanted to postpone parenthood until they had achieved an acceptable socio-economic standard or they already had the number of children they wanted. For some men the difficulty of combining employment with housework and satisfactory parenthood was a reason for wanting to limit the number of children. Unreliable relationships, i.e. problematic or newly established relationships constituted the second most common reason for abortion. This corresponds to results in other studies among women (Holmgren, 1994; Törnbom et al., 1994; Söderberg et al., 1997) and in one study among both women and men (Jacobsson et al., 1980). Furthermore, it has been shown that the intention to have children is dependent on the fulfilment of certain prerequisites and that the desire to have a child tends to decrease as a function of the number of children and the duration of the relationship (Willén and Montgomery, 1996).

Family planning and motives for abortion reflect living conditions and expectations about lifestyle, which in our postmodern society implies that most women and men adapt so that they can combine professional careers and housework with quality good partnership and parenthood. In Sweden divorces are common and men and women are expected to be economically independent. The Swedish parental insurance system is based on previous income from employment, which leads to a lifestyle where having a job necessarily comes before parenthood. In this study, men's thinking in the abortion situation was dominated by the idea that apart from wanting to have children in functioning family units, children should be desired and entitled to good care. Naturally, putting these opinions into practice requires careful family planning; thus the decision to have an abortion can be regarded as a rational choice. The fact that more than half the men had talked with their partner before she became pregnant concerning what to do in the event of pregnancy, and more than 50% had decided to have an abortion if a pregnancy should occur, must be interpreted to mean that legal abortion is regarded by many people as an acceptable form of birth control. This is in accordance with the conclusions from another Scandinavian study (Knudsen, 1997). In the work to prevent induced abortions, it is not sufficient only to give information about contraceptives and sexuality. The conditions for bearing and bringing up children in a modern society must be focused on since a good living standard and stable relationship do not ensure that a pregnancy will be accepted or wanted.

The fact that the majority of the men in this study regarded legal abortion as a possible solution to an unplanned pregnancy does not imply that they experienced their standpoint regarding abortion as easily conceived and uncomplicated. The decision process involves a large number of factors that concern the desire for a child, the partner, living conditions and the 'right time'. The decision to have a legal abortion also involves considerations at an existential and ethical level. It is well known that these circumstances can evoke ambivalence in women. In the present study it is clearly shown that ambivalence in connection with pregnancy and abortion also exists among men. One example of this complexity is that initially more than a quarter experienced only positive feelings when they became aware of the pregnancy. Among these men, nearly half wanted the woman to have an abortion. Obviously, strongly positive feelings can be experienced about pregnancy/ fertilization even if one is mentally prepared for abortion.

More than half the men chose both positively and painfully charged words to describe their feelings in connection with abortion. More than half the men with previous experience of abortion expressed these experiences in the same way. It is interesting to note that no man chose the word crisis to describe his experiences in connection with either the current or previous abortions, though more than half had contradictory feelings. Abortion as a solution to the problem of an unwanted pregnancy was expressed in such words as relief, release and responsibility but simultaneously the consequences of the choice were expressed in such words as anxiety, anguish, grief and guilt. This gives a picture of a person as one who can contain and live with paradoxes. In order to comprehend the complexity of the abortion situation, it is necessary to be open to the idea of paradoxes. We know about the ambivalence that arises in connection with pregnancy and legal abortion but the openness to paradoxes, which that ambivalence reflects, is often lacking as our thinking to a great extent is based on dichotomization. This dichotomization becomes obvious when ambivalence, for example, is shown as the occurrence of both positive and negative feelings (Törnbom et al., 1996) or when emotional pain is described as negative feelings (Lazarus, 1985; Adler et al., 1990; Dagg, 1991). The consequence of designating some feelings as negative is that important aspects in the abortion situation are not given a positive value and risk being regarded solely as something problematic or threatening. If the paradoxes in connection with abortion become visible, men and women have a better chance of recognizing themselves, which is an important prerequisite if the work to prevent undesired pregnancies is to succeed. In this context, it is of great importance that further studies include long-term experience and psychological integration of legal abortion among both men and women.

Acknowledgments

The authors would like to thank social worker Katarina Bergström for professional assistance in conducting the study. The project has been supported by The Swedish Council for Social Research (project 94–0178) and the Swedish National Institute of Public Health.

References

Adler, N.E., David, H.P., Major, B.N. *et al.* (1990) Psychological responses after abortion. *Science,* 248, 41–44.

Allansson, S. and Astbury, J. (1995) The abortion decision: reasons and ambivalence. *J. Psychosom. Obstet. Gynecol.,* 16, 123–136.

Dagg, K.B. (1991) The psychological sequelae of therapeutic abortion—denied and completed. *Am. J. Psychiat.,* 148, 578–585.

Glander, S.S., Moore, M., Michielutte, R. *et al.* (1998) The prevalence of domestic violence among women seeking abortion. *Obstet. Gynecol.,* 6, 1002–1006.

Graff-Iversen, S. and Kristoffersen, M. (1990) The role of the male partner in contraception and the decision of abortion. *Tidsskr. Nor. Laegeforen.*, 110, 1497–1500.

Hamark, B., Uddenberg, N. and Forssman, L. (1995) The influence of social class on parity and psychological reactions in women coming for induced abortion. *Acta Obstet. Gynecol Scand.*, 74, 302–306.

Holmgren, K. (1988) Time of decision to undergo a legal abortion. *Gynecol. Obstet. Invest.*, 26, 289–295.

Holmgren, K. (1994) Abortion ethics—women's post abortion assessments. *Acta Obstet. Gynecol., Scand.*, 73, 492–496.

Holmberg, K. and Uddenberg, N. (1993) Ambivalence during early pregnancy among expectant mothers. *Gynecol. Obstet. Invest.*, 36, 15–20.

Husfeldt, C., Hansen, S.K., Lyngberg, A. *et al.* (1995) Ambivalence among women applying for abortion. *Acta Obstet. Gynecol. Scand.*, 74, 813–817.

Jacobsson, L., Lalos, A., von Schoultz, B. *et al.* (1980) Women applying for legal abortions and their male partners. *Läkartidningen*, 77, 537–564.

Johansson, A., Nguyen, T.N., Tran, Q.H. *et al.* (1998) Husbands' involvement in abortion in Vietnam. *Studies in Family Planning*, 4, 1–14.

Knudsen, L.B. (1997) Induced abortions in Denmark. *Acta Obstet. Gynecol. Scand.* (Suppl.), 164, 54–59.

Lazarus, A. (1985) Psychiatric sequelae of legalized elective first trimester abortion. *J. Psychosom. Obstet. Gynaecol.*, 4, 141–150.

Rothstein, A.A. (1977) Men's reactions to their partners' elective abortions. *Am. J. Obstet. Gynecol.*, 128, 831–837.

Skjeldestad, F.E. (1994) When pregnant—why induced abortion? *Scand. J. Soc. Med.*, 1, 68–73.

Söderberg, H., Andersson, C., Janzon, L. *et al.* (1997) Continued pregnancy among abortion applicants. *Acta Obstet. Gynecol. Scand.*, 76, 942–947.

Swedish Ministry of Health and Social Affairs (eds) (1983) Swedish official statistics; family planning and abortion. Experiences of a new law. Report from the Committee of Abortion of 1980. *Stockholm Allmänna förlaget*, 31, 177–207.

Torres, A. and Darroch Forrest, J. (1988) Why do women have abortions? *Family Planning Perspectives*, 4, 169–176.

Trost, A-C. (ed.) (1982) *Abort och psykiska besvär (Abortion and emotional disturbances)*. Thesis. Uppsala University, Vasteras International Library, pp. 108–109.

Törnbom, M., Ingelhammar, E., Lilja, H. *et al.* (1994) Evaluation of stated motives for legal abortion. *J. Psychosom. Obstet. Gynecol.*, 15, 27–33.

Törnbom, M., Ingelhammar, E., Lilja, H. *et al.* (1996) Repeat abortion: a comparative study. *J. Psychosom. Obstet. Gynecol.*, 17, 208–214.

Uddenberg, N. (1974) Reproductive adaptation in mother and daughter. A study of personality development and adaptation to motherhood. *Acta Psychiatr. Scand.* (Suppl.), 254, 61–79.

Wikman, M., Jacobsson, L., Joelsson, I. *et al.* (1993) Ambivalence towards parenthood among pregnant women and their men. *Acta Obstet. Gynecol. Scand.*, 72, 619–626.

Willén, H. and Montgomery, H. (1996) The impact of wish for children and having children on attainment and importance of life values. *Journal of Comparative Family Studies*, 3, 499–518.

The Fertility Doctor Meets the Pill

By Maragret Marsh and Wanda Ronner

Shrewsbury, Massachusetts, 1944. Biologists Hudson Hoagland and Gregory Pincus establish the Worcester Foundation for Experimental Biology, one of the nation's first independent research organizations. Among its clients is a Chicago pharmaceutical company called Searle.

Sonta Barbara, California, 7952. Wealthy feminist Katharine Dexter McCormick seeks introduction to Gregory Pincus with an eye to funding the development of a birth-control pill.

Brookline, Massachusetts, 1953. John Rock joins forces with Pincus to develop an oral contraceptive.

John Rock's seventh decade—he turned sixty in March 1950—would turn out to be one of the most challenging, and fulfilling, of his professional life. Changes in the way medicine was practiced in the postwar period, combined with the childbearing frenzy of the baby boom era, helped to make his infertility clinic the most prominent in the nation, as young couples filled its waiting rooms. In growing numbers, Rock's colleagues from around the country invited themselves to observe the clinic's operation with an eye to replicating its success in their own cities. And young doctors from across the nation and around the world sought positions as fellows to advance their careers. Just as his fertility clinic was bursting at the seams, Rock launched his now-famous collaboration with biologist Gregory Pincus on the development of the oral contraceptive. His work on what became known simply as "the pill" brought him international attention as well as new allies and opponents.

In retrospect, John Rock and Gregory Pincus seemed to be such an odd couple that those who told the story of the pill in later years believed their collaboration had to have been an accident. Much has been made of the seeming incongruity of Rock and Pincus using the same hormone for opposite purposes and not even realizing it until they met—by fate or by chance—at just the right moment. Almost everyone who has written about the two men tell one or another version of the happenstance story. As one writer put it, their coming together was "one of those haphazard, inscrutable accidents that spangle the history of science." And a 2002 television series on science and sexuality based an entire program on what the show's writers called the "serendipity" of this encounter.

The general outlines of the fateful meeting story go like this. In the early 1950s, Gregory Pincus began work on the birth-control pill, but he was in a quandary about exactly how to proceed. Then, as luck would have it, he happened to run into John Rock at a conference, not having seen him for decades. To their mutual amazement, they discovered that Pincus in Worcester was engaged in animal research on progesterone as a potential contraceptive,

Margaret Marsh and Wanda Ronner, "The Fertility Doctor Meets the Pill," *The Fertility Doctor: John Rock and the Reproductive Revolution*, pp. 139–151. Copyright © 2008 by Johns Hopkins University Press. Reprinted with permission.

just as Rock in Brookline, using the very same substance for cases of infertility, had accidentally discovered that the hormone prevented ovulation. What a shock! Rock was finding in women what Pincus believed he had achieved in rabbits, and the world would never be the same. It's a great story. It's just not true. Rock and Pincus, although they were not close friends, were professional acquaintances of long standing who were very familiar with each other's work. Rock had made his first appearance in Pincus's correspondence in 1937. A year after that, when Miriam Menkin interviewed with Rock, he hired her principally because she had worked for Pincus on superovulation in rabbits. And Rock's embryo and ova studies were inspired by Pincus's animal studies on ovulation, in vitro fertilization, the manipulation of ova, and embryo implantation. The men had, in short, followed each other's work for years. Once Pincus began work on the pill, it would have been much more surprising, given the convergence of their interests, if the two men hadn't gotten together than that they did.

So, how did the story get started? Its genesis may lie in the many ways Pincus and Rock were polar opposites—in their personalities, upbringing, and career paths. Rock was Catholic; Pincus, Jewish. Rock was socially ambitious and had married into Boston's upper crust; Pincus took pride in his immigrant heritage. Rock was smooth; Pincus had a decided edge to him. Rock was part of the establishment; Pincus was something of an antiestablishment scientific entrepreneur.

Pincus would become the driving force behind the pill's development. Without his organizational brilliance, scientific acumen, and entrepreneurial persistence, the pill never would have made it from lab bench to the physician's drug closet. But Rock, who in later years would call himself the "stepfather" of the pill, would in the end become nearly as important to the project as Pincus.

Gregory Pincus, born in 1903, grew up in Woodbine, New Jersey, an immigrant Jewish farming community in the southern part of the state. He attended Cornell's agriculture school intending to follow the footsteps of an uncle into agronomy, but in college he became more interested in other areas of biology. He earned his PhD at Harvard in 1927, after which he took a postdoctoral research position in England at Cambridge University. In 1930, Harvard offered him an assistant professorship in biology. Brilliant and original, with a dazzling research agenda, he was also viewed by some of his colleagues as a publicity hound. In the mid-1930s, after reporting that he had succeeded in producing "immaculate conception" (parthenogenesis) in female rabbits, he allowed himself to be profiled in Collier's, a popular national magazine. The author of the article, J. D. Ratcliff, was the one who speculated that the eventual outcome of Pincus's work would be a reproductive future for humans in which men were no longer necessary, maybe not even desirable. Ratcliff predicted a future in which "the mythical ... Amazons ... [would come] to life" and create a "world where woman would be self-sufficient; man's value [would become] precisely zero,"

This article sounded the death knell of Pincus's Harvard career. In those days, Harvard preferred its researchers to be notable, not notorious. Its leading professors may have personified old-family New England arrogance, but they wished to seem, if not to be, modest about their professional triumphs. To engage in media self-promotion was a cardinal sin. Brilliance was not enough. Harvard did not grant him tenure, which meant he lost his job.

He was shocked, but maybe he shouldn't have been. Even some of his admirers wondered, in historian James Reed's words, whether his "experiments were too complex to be carefully controlled or easily reproduced." University politics and anti-Semitism also came into play. William Crozier, Pincus's department chair and mentor, had troubles of his own at Harvard and could not help his young protege. Harvard's new president, James Conant, viewed Crozier as an "empire builder" and saw to it that Crozier's department was cut out from under him and his power in the university destroyed, Crozier and his supporters believed that the university's action against Pincus was aimed at them just as much as at Pincus. And Harvard was not immune to the virulent Ivy League anti-Semitism of the era. In Reed's words, the whole sad saga reflected "prejudice against [Pincus] as a student of Crozier and as a self-advertising Jew who published too soon and talked too much." Maybe he would have been denied tenure anyway, and the fatherless rabbits only sealed his doom.

Harvard gave Pincus a paid research leave at Cambridge University for the academic year of 1937-1938, but after that he was out of a job. To his dismay, despite the best efforts of both Crozier and the influential William Castle at the University of California at Berkeley, another of the young scientist's supporters, Pincus received no offer of a position in the United States. War in Europe loomed, and Pincus was eager to get home, but he needed a job. His very career as a scientist imperiled, he was rescued by Hudson Hoagland at Clark University in Worcester,

Massachusetts. Hoagland offered him a position as a visiting professor in his laboratory and provided the desperate scientist with a research base. Unfortunately, Hoagland had little else to give—no salary and no faculty perquisites. Luckily for Pincus, a wealthy benefactor, fellow scientist Lord Nathaniel Rothschild, stepped in to provide two years' salary.

This was not the career that Pincus had envisioned, but in the end, it gave him the freedom he craved. Together, he and Hoagland moved on to create an entirely new scientific enterprise. Hoagland, like Pincus, was an entrepreneur at heart whose ambition was to build his own research empire at Clark. Clashing regularly and rancorously with the university administration, he became fed up, so he and Pincus decided to strike out on their own in the late 1930s. They founded the Worcester Foundation for Experimental Biology (WFEB), an independent research laboratory, locating it in Shrewsbury and incorporating in 1944.

At the time, theirs was a daring undertaking. This was more than a decade before the federal government, under the aegis of the National Institutes of Health and the National Science Foundation, would become the principal funding source for science in the United States. The two scientists had no safety net. Although some of their research was conducted under grants from foundations, their most profitable relationships were with the burgeoning pharmaceutical industry, for which they developed new processes to produce compounds and performed animal testing on existing ones.

As it happened, their timing was excellent; they caught the first wave of the new era of antibiotic and steroid therapy. Pharmaceutical companies, in fierce competition for patents and profits, were developing scores of new chemical compounds and seeking advice on how to synthesize others. The WFEB was prepared to provide biological expertise in both these arenas. One of these companies was G. D. Searle and Company, still a family-owned and operated business. Pincus began regularly performing scientific studies for them as early as 1939. However, by the early 1950s, his relationship with the company had become rocky at best. In fact, Searle and Pincus in 1951 nearly had a fatal break. Having invested a half-million dollars in various Pincus enterprises, Searle—in the person of research director Al Raymond—came close to pulling the plug permanently on Pincus and the Worcester Foundation.

The crisis came over the synthesis of cortisone, which had recently been own to treat severe rheumatoid arthritis. Cortisone was a treatment, not a cure, and its side effects would soon become evident, but the fact that men and women who had not been able to lift their arms without pain were now able to move freely and go about their daily lives was indeed a medical miracle. But it was a miracle available only to a few at first, because it was difficult and expensive to synthesize the drug.

If a way could be found to synthesize cortisone cheaply and simply, enormous profits would follow. In the late 1940s, Searle and other American pharmaceutical companies raced to see who could figure out how to produce large quantities of hydrocortisone at a moderate cost. Pincus, under contract to Searle, had figured out a synthesizing process based on perfusion. On the plus side, he could produce large quantities. On the minus side, this was a very expensive way to manufacture the product. But almost as soon as they had purchased, at Pincus's urging, this expensive equipment, Searle was beaten out by a rival pharmaceutical company. Upjohn's researchers had discovered a much simpler—and more important, cheaper—method than Pincus had devised. Pincus had promised, lavishly as usual, and Pincus had not delivered.

Searle, a small company that invested selectively in only a few new drugs at a time, had lost this race in an expensive way. On behalf of the Searle Company, Al Raymond was furious. "You haven't done a thing to justify the half- million that we invested in you," Raymond told Pincus. "Your record as a contributor … to the Searle Company is a lamentable failure, replete with false leads, poor judgment, and assurances from you that were false." Profoundly shaken at the time, Pincus remained unsettled and worried for a long time, because his survival as a research entrepreneur depended on his relationship with companies such as Searle.

Pincus knew he could not afford to burn his bridges to Searle. Fortunately, Al Raymond soon recovered from his outburst. Searle lost out on cortisone, but it had now become interested in what would become an equally promising avenue of investigation, the testing of synthetic sex hormones. Although a still wary Raymond was not about to invest any big money in Pincus right away, he did contract with him for animal studies on some new compounds.

In the early 1950s, in fact, both Pincus and Rock were testing the same product— benzelstilbestrol, an estrogen that Searle hoped to market under the brand name Monozol. It is not clear for what purpose Pincus was testing the product, but Rock was using it, and several other synthetic estrogens, for female endocrine and fertility disorders. Letters between Rock and researchers at Searle document his and Pincus's familiarity with each other's complementary animal and human testing of similar products. The two men also occasionally communicated directly with each other about the effectiveness of compounds they were both testing, for Searle and other pharmaceutical companies.

Pincus was not conjuring an idea out of thin air when he began to investigate the possibility of hormonal contraception. In 1947, when the National Research Council (NRC) created its Committee on Human Reproduction, it had asked John Rock to set its research agenda, and hormonal contraception was one of the items on his list. And several historical accounts of the development of oral contraceptives have shown how, almost from the moment that estrogen was discovered, scientists began to speculate about hormonal contraception. Actually developing such an agent, however, was a different matter. And since most of the early research into hormonal contraception took place in Central Europe, notably by Austrians Ludwig Haberlandt and Otfried Fellner, working separately, the extent to which Americans were aware of such investigations is unclear.

As long ago as World War I, the idea had begun to take shape. In 1919 Innsbruck, Austria, gynecologist Ludwig Haberlandt transplanted the ovaries of pregnant rabbits into rabbits who were not pregnant. The transplanted ovaries, he claimed, rendered the other rabbits sterile. Haberlandt suggested that such animal transplants into women might also render them "temporarily sterile." Of course, such a technique would hardly have mass appeal. Haberlandt knew it and looked toward other methods. By 1927 he was trying oral preparations of cow corpora lutea on rabbits and full ovarian extracts on mice. He later teamed up with a Hungarian pharmaceutical house to develop an oral preparation, which would be called Infecundin, for possible human use. Throughout this period, European and American laboratories were keeping the abattoirs of Europe busy with requests for the thyroids, pituitaries, ovaries, and testicles of cattle and sheep slaughtered for food, so he would have no problem with supply. Although the evidence is not clear, the product may have been briefly placed on the market just before Haberlandt's death in 1932.

Another Austrian, Otfried Fellner of Vienna, was also experimenting with the ovaries of pregnant cows in the 1920s, and by the end of the decade he had produced injectable extracts and an oral preparation he called Feminin, both of which rendered rabbits and mice sterile. The idea of what Haberlandt initially called "temporary sterilization" did not appear to elicit much immediate interest. Scientists in the United States—Leo Loeb and William B. Kountz at Washington University in St. Louis, who were experimenting on the hormonal sterilization of guinea pigs; William Makepeace and his colleagues at the University of Pennsylvania, who demonstrated the contraceptive properties of progesterone in rabbits; and Pincus, who showed that estrogen injections in rabbits caused the destruction of ova in the fallopian tube—were apparently unaware of their Austrian counterparts' work.

Given the politics of the 1930s, with the rise of Nazism and fascism throughout Europe, producing an injectable hormonal contraceptive could have had chilling consequences. Envisioning the potential appeal to eugenicists does not require much imagination. Medical and legal antipathy toward contraception in the 1930s also played a role, as did concerns even then within the medical profession about the potential health risks attendant on the long-term use of estrogen. And let us not forget the career lesson that scientists could draw from Pincus's experience—tamper with cherished ideas about sexuality and reproduction, even if only with bunnies, and be exiled to Worcester! Whatever the combination of reasons, American scientists did not pursue the idea of hormonal contraception, not even after both estrogen and progesterone had been synthesized, and in spite of clear evidence that American couples were employing whatever methods they could find to control the size of their families in the Depression-era 1930s.

Although American scientists steered clear of hormonal contraception in the years between World Wars I and II, they eagerly embraced general research on hormones in the 1930s and early 1940s. Especially during and immediately after World War II, the major focus of hormonal research was the corticosteroids that control adrenal function. Competition to synthesize such hormones was fierce, as shown by the Searle Company's fury when Gregory Pincus led them down the wrong path.

It is not a coincidence that the same companies competing to develop cortisone products were also involved in creating other hormonal compounds. As the story of the oral contraceptive unfolds, its relationship to the intense competition among the pharmaceutical "houses" (as they were often called because most had roots as family-owned businesses) becomes an important part of the narrative. For that reason, it is important to understand the emerging and increasingly intertwining relationships of scientists, clinicians (especially at research institutions), and pharmaceutical companies in transforming medical research, including that of Pincus and Rock, in the 1940s and 1950s.

When historians of medicine speak of the mid-twentieth century as the era of "triumphal medicine," they are generally referring to the explosive development of antibiotics. During these years, one magic bullet after another was discovered, synthesized, and put on the market. It began with the discovery of sulfa drugs, the first antibacterials to be marketed as anti-infective agents in the 1930s; they provided a major impetus to the search for similar drugs. World War II dramatically increased the demand for even more effective agents to cure infections and treat disease.

Penicillin, the antibacterial properties of which were discovered by Alexander Fleming in 1928, was isolated and purified in 1940 in Howard Florey's laboratory at Oxford University by Florey, Ernst Chain, and Norman Heatley. The first successful human use was in 1941. By 1944, nineteen American drug companies were producing penicillin, and the major pharmaceutical houses had come to recognize that their prosperity and competitive edge would increasingly depend on the development of an ever-growing pharmacopoeia. But they wanted drugs they could patent, not simply manufacture. As economic historian Peter Temin asserted, during the 1940s and 1950s, the industry changed dramatically, from "a fairly typical manufacturing industry to one based on the continual progress of technical knowledge. New drug development—particularly new products that unlike sulfanilamide and penicillin could be patented and then exclusively marketed by the company that created them—became central to the good health of the companies.

These dramatic changes provided the scientific and economic climate that allowed Hudson Hoagland and Gregory Pincus to build a research enterprise independent of a university structure. Working on contract for several companies, in the 1940s they were involved both in the development of new processes and in the animal testing of new compounds that came directly from the companies. Just as wartime needs helped to spur the development of penicillin, they prompted scientists to study adrenocortical function, attempting to understand its role in physical and mental stress, and to find chemical ways of countering those stresses.

In a war-torn world in which the medical priorities were for agents that could heal the wounded soldier and prevent the able ones from succumbing to physical and mental deterioration, the study and use of the sex hormones, while not exactly ignored, were relegated to the back seat. But the civilian uses of antibiotics and steroids, and the hopes of finding newer and ever more useful ones, outlasted the war. Interest in the sex hormones—especially in their potential to enhance fertility—was reinvigorated during the baby boom. In the postwar years, millions of young American men and women avidly embraced marriage and family life, marrying earlier than their parents and grandparents and choosing larger families over smaller ones. The advent of the baby boom in the United States spurred fertility research and treatment on a large scale, even if no major advances in the pharmacological treatment of infertility would appear until the 1960s.

Most scientists and clinicians who were interested in hormonal research in this period were interested primarily in treating infertility, not developing hormonal contraception. But in some ways, the two went together. That was certainly how Rock had viewed the study of fertility. And so, when Rock came to collaborate with Pincus, he viewed this work as simply another aspect of his life's work on problems of reproduction.

He did not back into contraceptive research inadvertently, even if he had for many years tried to be careful in his public professions of support for birth control. By the time Rock began his collaboration with Pincus, he had already become more overt in expressing his views. He still favored early marriage and early parenthood, assuring "newly married couples" that they "will be happier parents if they have their children young." But he also believed that once a couple decided their family was complete, they should have access to a full range of contraceptive options. After all, he had seen first hand the results of too-frequent childbearing combined with too-few resources. Since he believed that rhythm worked only rarely and that sexual abstinence weakened a couple's love, he became ever more willing to act as a public advocate of contraception. But he never subscribed to the feminist belief that birth control should serve as an instrument of women's autonomy, a tool to enable her to reject or limit childbearing in favor of a career or personal fulfillment. Rather, he was an outspoken family man who maintained that happiness in marriage depended on a couple's ability to support and enjoy as many children as they could emotionally and financially afford.

In Rock's mind, there was no contradiction between his lifelong commitment to alleviating infertility and his growing commitment to the converse. In the late 1940s, he had become more active in the NCMH. And just after World War II, when the NCMH and Planned Parenthood Federation jointly asked the NRC to oversee a research program in reproductive science and medicine, the NRC created the Committee on Human Reproduction in 1947, with Rock as a founding member.

Widely considered the nation's leading expert in the field of human fertility and endocrine disorders, Rock agreed to set the committee's agenda in that field. His 1948 position paper reiterated his frustration with reliance on animal studies to explain human reproduction. In terse outline form, he derided the scientific understanding of female fertility as "surprisingly obscure … Little is known of human reproductive physiology, biochemistry, and hormonology [sic]. Dependence on zoologic analogy is heavy and unsafe." In his judgment there were only about six "fairly good" sterility (his word) clinics in the United States and about the same number of "endocrinologic" clinics. For the most part, he said, the endocrine clinics "occasionally" produced good research and were "steadily improving." He had no kind words for the clinics that focused only on sterility. There, "the research work, with few exceptions, is purely clinical, unscientific, and not worth much."

As befitted a director of a fertility and endocrine clinic, Rock's priorities were the support of research in such institutions and development of a new generation of basic and clinical researchers. His proposed program of contraceptive research included the study of hormonal "suppression [of] ovular maturation, ovulation, or conjugation," which were also three areas of high priority in studying the promotion of fertility. In other words, understanding more precisely how human ova grew and matured; tracing the process of ovulation, tubal migration, and fertilization itself; and comprehending the hormonal, enzymatic, and other factors promoting or inhibiting the implantation of the fertilized ovum were critical both to promoting and to preventing pregnancy.

Rock provided his colleagues with a full research program, which included hormonal contraception. But it was all for nothing. The committee had been created to develop a research agenda for which the Planned Parenthood Federation of America and the NCMH would serve as the fund-raising arms. The arms were unable to carry the burden, and within four years, the committee had dissolved and researchers sought other funding sources.

And so, after all is said and done, it was not the drug companies, not Pincus (who was already interested but would have needed funding, and Searle wasn't ready knowingly to fund the development of an oral contraceptive), not Rock, but two feminist icons—Margaret Sanger and Katharine Dexter McCormick—who were determined to use that hormonal research to devise a way for women to control their own reproductive lives. One of them was both willing and able to pay for it.

Margaret Sanger, still the first lady of birth control in the minds of most Americans, had loathed the idea of changing the name of what she considered her own American Birth Control League to the Planned Parenthood Federation. She was right to be offended. The name change did reflect the stirrings of a growing societal consensus on the use of contraceptive measures, but it was not a feminist consensus. Sanger, whose name had been synonymous with the birth-control movement for half a century, consistently maintained that access to birth control on an unfettered, democratic basis was both a fundamental right of all women and the foundation of social progress. Even as she traveled from youthful radicalism to political conservatism, she never swerved from those separate but linked convictions. It was her passionate conviction that birth control would free women from having to bear unwanted children and, almost as important, allow them to enjoy sex without worrying about pregnancy. She insisted, and rightly so, that the name "Planned Parenthood" did not convey the idea of contraception as a means of women's empowerment. Without denying that she and McCormick both believed that impoverished women in the developing world stood in greatest need for a simple and safe contraceptive, for her to say that the poor should have fewer children did not conflict with her belief that fewer children would lead to women's autonomy and general prosperity.

Existing contraceptives prevented pregnancy, but few methods offered complete security. The two most popular methods—condoms and withdrawal—required the active engagement of the male partner, and men sometimes viewed them as impediments to their full satisfaction. For some, a condom formed a barrier to pleasure. Withdrawal required a man to control his responses, not always an easy thing to do. Religious and political opposition to contraception remained strong in some religions and in some parts of the country. The Catholic Church vehemently opposed contraception. In several states, including John Rock's Massachusetts, it was illegal for physicians to provide birth-control information or devices. Indeed, as late as 1960, thirty states would still have laws that in some way restricted the advertisement or the sale of birth-control devices.

Until the prospect of a birth-control pill emerged, Sanger's preferred contraceptive was the individually fitted diaphragm, because it was female controlled. But to obtain a diaphragm, a woman had to visit a physician. (In Europe, nurses fitted diaphragms, but not in the United States; to garner medical support for the diaphragm, Sanger had to agree that physicians would prescribe and fit the devices.) Katharine McCormick, who would fund the development of the pill, left no record of her own sexual attitudes, but when she became involved in birth control, she made it clear that male-controlled birth control was her only priority in funding contraceptive research. Although her biographer believes that Katharine's husband was impotent as a young man, others have suggested that his mental illness led her to decide to remain childless. If so, since he would not have been able to take responsibility for contraception, preventing pregnancy would be up to her. In the 1930s, she had even smuggled diaphragms into the United States for Sanger's clinics.

Except within the Catholic Church, cultural opposition to birth control was receding by the late 1940s and early 1950s, in part because such organizations as Planned Parenthood began to persuade the public that birth control was a sensible way to plan a good-sized family and not a feminist plot to overthrow the conventional roles of the sexes. Such attitudes about family planning emerged during World War II and became entrenched in the baby boom era that followed.

In the 1950s, with couples marrying and having their families at young ages, compared with their parents and grandparents, there was bound to be a demand for reliable contraception once they had their three, four, or five children. After all, by then a wife was usually just over the age of thirty, with at least fifteen years of potential fertility still ahead. These couples whose fecundity fueled the baby boom wanted children *and* they wanted to make sure that once they had as many as they wanted, they could stop having them. By 1950 John Rock had spent more than a quarter-century trying to make it possible for the infertile to have the children they often so desperately wanted, but he also witnessed the desperation of women who could never stop having children, even though their economic, emotional, or physical situations worsened with every new birth.

Not only was he used to seeing infertility and overfertility as two sides of a single issue, but by 1950 his ideas about contraception had also become compatible with those of most Americans, if not with his church's hierarchy. In 1949 he had even coauthored a book endorsing birth control. In later years, Rock would use the specter of world overpopulation to justify his demand that the Catholic Church approve the pill, While "the population bomb" was not an excuse for him—he really did believe that the world was endangered by overpopulation—he nevertheless made it clear to friends, colleagues, the medical students he taught, and the couples he counseled that contraception was likewise for the ordinary couple who wanted to space their children and to stop having them altogether whenever the optimal number of offspring, whatever that was for a particular couple, had been reached.

Go Forth and Multiply

Faith and Family Planning

By George D. Moffett

Mexico

Padre Alberto Marquez Aquino's church, a cinderblock rectangle held up by poured-concrete beams, is as nondescript as its address: the corner of Avenues 508 and 518 in the sprawling western reaches of one of the world's largest cities.

On this Saturday morning, the neighborhood of Maria Madre de la Iglesia is relaxed. Mothers cluster to gossip while toddlers orbit the pack like tiny revolving moons. Across the street, half a dozen teenage boys hunch over a broken bicycle. Diagonally across from the church, which bears the neighborhood's name, Videocentro does a brisk trade renting movies like *Lethal Weapon* and *Ghostbusters.*

The neighborhood also bears reminders this day of the troubles faced by a country in which rapid population growth has outpaced economic performance, leaving millions unemployed and anxious. A white banner hung from the churchyard fence announces meetings for A Better Way, Mexico's branch of Alcoholics Anonymous.

Padre Marquez's church is a haven for the several hundred parishioners who comprise of a corner of this 30,000-person community of bureaucrats and gardeners, small merchants and mechanics. They come to praise God and confess their sins, to marry and mourn their dead. And, as on this day, to celebrate the rites of passage that demarcate often difficult lives. A special mass has been held to mark the fifteenth birthday of Teresa, dressed for the occasion in a formal, turquoise taffeta dress. Following the service, she is the center of attention in the small courtyard that abuts the church. Four brothers, uncomfortable in ill-fitting tuxedos, act dutifully as attendants while family and friends look on admiringly and an uncle captures the event on videotape. It is a moment of genuine pride and happiness.

A granite statue of Christ Jesus looks on from an adjacent grassy plot demarcated by a dozen poplar trees and rows of pansies and geraniums, bedraggled but still cheerful in the lukewarm January sun. To the right of the statue is a low-slung building that houses the parish's administrative offices. There, secretaries answer phones and type letters under the gaze of two figures who have shaped the Catholicism of modern Mexico. One is a virgin. The other has stern advice for those who aren't.

The virgin is Mary, possessor of a virtue the Church has long considered more conducive to the quest for spiritual perfection than marriage. Legend has it that in 1531, just a decade after the Spanish came to Mexico, she appeared to an Indian on his way to a mission. She asked him to build a church to her memory and performed the first miracle

George D. Moffett, "Go Forth and Multiply: Faith and Family Planning," *Critical Masses: The Global Population Challenge*, pp. 224–259. Copyright © 2000 by Penguin Group (USA) Inc. Reprinted with permission.

in the New World. She is considered a mother to the Americas and a symbol of the arrival of Christianity in Mexico, the West Indies, and Central America. Her virginity is one of the highest ideals in Catholicism.

The other figure is Pope John Paul II. A color photo of the peripatetic pontiff shows him stepping off an Aero-Mexico jet during his first visit to Mexico, his white robes blending into fluffy winter clouds behind. On his first papal trip, he retraced the route taken by the first Christian evangelist to the New World, Christopher Columbus, to Mexico and the Dominican Republic. He visited Guadalupe's basilica and pledged to be a voice for the poor and oppressed. When he warned that economic and political rights should never be allowed to take precedence over human rights, few of Mexico's faithful missed the point: Catholics should not use hard economic times as an excuse to resort to modern methods of contraception to limit the size of their families.

In 1979, the year of the papal visit, only 18 percent of Mexican women were using contraceptives. Fifteen years later, at 59 percent, Mexico has one of the highest contraceptive prevalence rates in the developing world.

In a small office lined with wooden bookcases, Padre Marquez, a keeper of the faith, says the pope is right.

"We have to respect nature because that's the voice of God, and we cannot alter it. These principles the Church teaches can be seen very clearly by people who have the Christian faith, by people who are pure and understand the dignity of the person. We have to learn to look at how we're going to live life. Are we going to live it righteously or go through life doing what our urges prompt us to do? Do you have sex when you want kids or because you like it?"

Marquez has been a priest for over twenty years. A stalwart, he is popular in this community where the Church retains a strong hold on the peoples' affections and loyalties. He speaks as a man who has no doubt about the Church's position on contraception but who understands the struggles of those who do. He also grasps the surprising fact, borne out by a large body of anecdotal evidence, that despite the Church's well-publicized views on the subject, very many Catholics do not understand the large area of permissibility that enables Catholics to space children and to use natural means of contraception to limit family size.

"The problem regarding the use of contraceptives is that many people don't know what the Church really says," says the soft-spoken cleric. "Many people think that the Church says they should have a lot of kids. Others think that Catholicism is totally against any type of contraception and family planning. Maybe 10 percent know what the Church really feels. And because they don't understand what the Church doctrine is, they don't even think about it, and they do what they want to do. Some feel guilty, but most are simply ignorant of the Church's true position."

As the senior priest of Maria Madre for the past seven years, Marquez has spent dozens of hours talking to parishioners about birth control. His main target has been engaged couples. In sessions before marriage, he tells them about the Church's position, about the requirements of successful marriage, and about managing a domestic economy. A doctor talks about sexual relations. The point is reinforced by examples of couples for whom "natural" family planning methods—various forms of periodic abstinence such as the rhythm method—have worked.

"Too many people think natural forms of birth control don't work. If they really understood that natural methods do work, they would not use artificial contraceptives."

He has no way of knowing how many obey because most no longer confess to using modern contraceptives. But he is worried that the battle is being lost.

"There's an element of laziness. There's a certain discipline associated with natural methods that people are unwilling to accept." The real problem, he says, is "the atmosphere of technology" that has bred trust in artificial means to achieve what is now an almost universal goal in Mexico: smaller families.

"When I can talk with people about this personally, they usually understand. The problem is that we can only reach so many people. But the publicity and advertising about artificial contraceptives and the need to limit families reaches everybody. People are hearing it from all sides: governments, contraceptive manufacturers, schools. Can the Church compete with this? I'm not sure we can win, but we're trying."

A sketch of Don Quixote hangs on one wall between two bookcases. If Padre Marquez knows the feeling of an uphill cause, he also has no doubt that the cause is right.

"Using artificial contraceptives is a sin. Sin isn't just performing the act of using artificial contraceptives. It's what you think. You can have a wife who uses a pill or an IUD, but if she's not aware that it's a sin, it's not a sin. When she comes to me, I ask: Did you know it was a sin? If she says no, it's not a sin even though it's all wrong. All sins are forgiven so long as they know they're wrong and try to correct them. Even abortion can be forgiven under such circumstances if the person feels sincerely repentant."

"It's a problem, but it happens in all different areas of life," Marquez says of the spreading apostasy on the subject of birth control. "People take drugs, people are unjust, people will disobey. The mission of the Church is to tell people what's right, but there are always going to be people who will go against that."

Guadelupe is one of those people who do.

If the statistics are accurate, the thirty-two-year-old mother of two represents what Mexico has become: a nation of Catholics who believe themselves faithful despite a breach over the essential issue of contraception.

When they were married in San Jose de los Cedros, a small mountain town on the outskirts of the capital, Guadelupe and her husband, Santiago, nodded when the priest informed them that it was their duty to have all the children God sends. The first one, Julio, now fifteen, came almost immediately.

Then Santiago decided to go back to school to earn an accountant's degree. After calculating that it would be impossible to support a second child on a student's budget, Guadelupe made a fateful decision. After talking to her husband and her doctor—but not her priest—she began using an IUD.

"I was just sixteen when I had my first child. I wasn't sure what to do next, and I was very afraid. So I talked to my doctor. He recommended using an IUD. We didn't talk about religion; I was aware of what the Church said. But I was sure it would be better to use an artificial contraceptive because I knew 'natural' methods wouldn't work the way the Church said. I knew my husband wouldn't abstain on the days we weren't supposed to have sex."

Like millions of Mexican women, Guadelupe insists that the decision to use artificial contraceptives has not compromised her loyalties to the Church. "I agree with the Church on everything else," she says, "I still think of myself as a good Catholic. But I can't agree on the subject of birth control. I can't believe that the fact that I only want two children makes me a bad Catholic."

Two years ago a second child, Edgar, was born. After consulting with her husband again, she decided to have a tubal ligation, closing off the possibility of further births. Later, she told her parish priest. He told her that what she had done was a sin then said that what's done is done.

"I told him I don't care because I don't want to have any more kids. To bring kids into the world and not be able to give them proper food and clothing is not right. I know I'm supposed to do what God wants. But I don't see God. I haven't heard him tell me to have more children. So I feel I've done the right thing. I'm sure that God cannot be angry with me because I want to have only the children I can educate.

"Things are difficult here. A majority of people are having hard times. Jobs are hard to come by. For me, the issue is education. You can't give your kids a good education if you have too many of them. With only two kids, we can get them further along in school, and that's what's going to make it possible for them to have good jobs.

"The Church should accept what the people use because there are so many poor people, and the Church doesn't help them. The Church says not to use contraceptives, that it's a sin, but they don't come here and say, I see you have all these kids, and I'll help you.

"I'm still a Catholic," says the namesake of her country's patron saint. "But birth control is a whole different issue." If there is any institution that symbolizes conservative resistance to the use of modern contraception, it is the Roman Catholic Church. The opposition is so powerful that, when surveyed in 1992, one distinguished group of academics and government officials judged that changing the Vatican's position was one of the most urgent measures needed to solve one of the world's most urgent problems: rapid population growth.

But as the case of Guadelupe illustrates, the reality behind the perception is changing fast. Across Mexico and around the Catholic world, a historic transformation of lay attitudes toward contraception is taking place as the relentless pace of modernization is forcing millions of believers to revise their ideas about what is morally correct and religiously acceptable. In Latin America, where half the world's 800 million Catholics reside, this transformation has already produced significant demographic changes: A continent that used to be the object of gloomy demographic predictions, similar to those now made about Africa, is now a notable, if not uniform, family planning success story.

"In terms of attitudes toward family planning, Latin America is like Berlin after the Wall came down," says Paul Burgess, a former priest and Vatican official, who is an expert on population issues. "It's a whole new era."

At least since the sixteenth century, the Catholic Church has approved the concept of "responsible parenthood," meaning that it is acceptable for Catholic couples to limit births for legitimate medical, economic, and social reasons. The main sticking point is the means, and it is over the question of using "modern" contraceptives that the issue between Rome and the Catholic faithful worldwide has been joined. In many individual countries, Catholics use contraceptives at rates equal to or higher than do adherents of other faiths. Of those who do not, religion is usually now the main reason. Meanwhile, despite pressure from the Church, governments in most Catholic countries are now committed to family planning and have invested large sums of money to make contraceptives widely available.

In Mexico, the magazine *Excelsior* recently sampled public attitudes on a range of matters in which the Church's views have long held sway. Among other things, 93 percent of respondents said that they approved of family planning, while only 7 percent disapproved.

On the matter of specific contraceptive choice, public attitudes in Mexico and across Latin America are also largely at variance with the teachings of the Church. Despite the Church's 1975 ban on sterilization, 20 percent of Latin American couples of reproductive age use sterilization, and the proportion is rising fast, according to one UN study. Fully one fourth of reproductive-age married women in Brazil are sterilized, one third in Panama and El Salvador, and 40 percent in Puerto Rico, the highest rate in the world. And these trends show no sign of leveling off. Among women in their later thirties and early forties, the figures are higher still.

As for the pill, banned in the Church's definitive 1968 encyclical *Humanae Vitae,* only northern and western Europe surpass Catholic Latin America in its use. Together, the pill and female sterilization account for two-thirds of all contraceptive use in Latin America and the Caribbean.

The defection from Church strictures even extends to the baseline issue of abortion, which, in the face of the widespread use of contraceptives, has become a more crucial litmus test of fidelity. In Mexico, as in most Latin American countries, induced abortion is illegal, permitted only if the life of the mother is endangered or if a woman is a victim of rape or incest. Even so, in a 1991 Mexican Gallup poll, 75 percent of respondents said the decision whether to have an abortion belongs to the woman alone (40 percent) or should be made by the couple together (35 percent). The poll showed that 43 percent of women and a surprising 54 percent of men believe that women should not have to consult the Church when deciding whether to have an abortion.

In practice, the Church's partial success in restricting the availability of contraceptives, and thus increasing the number of unwanted pregnancies, has resulted in higher rates of abortion throughout Latin America. A quarter of all pregnancies in Latin America have been intentionally aborted during the past two decades, compared with estimates of less than 10 percent in Africa and between 15 and 20 percent in South and Southeast Asia, according to the International Planned Parenthood Federation. In an U.S. survey conducted by the Alan Guttmacher Institute in 1987, Catholic women were found to be 30 percent more likely to have an abortion than Protestant women.

The diminishing influence of religion on fertility is also suggested by the fact that the gap between desired fertility and actual fertility—that is, the percentage of unwanted births—is higher in Latin America than any region of the globe. Among women in Latin America who do not want children and who do not use contraceptives, only a small minority cite religious beliefs as their reason for not practicing family planning, according to the IPPE.

Latin America, of course, is not the only predominantly Catholic region swept by the revolution in contraceptive use. The use of modern birth control devices is widespread in other Catholic nations, testifying to the prevalence of what Pope John Paul II has described as the "contraceptive mentality." The prime example lies outside the pope's front door. Italy, where condoms can be purchased within sight of the Vatican, has the highest contraceptive prevalence rate (nearly 80 percent) and the lowest fertility rate (1.3 children per woman) ever recorded. According to the World Health Organization, the country's birthrate has declined by half since the early 1960s. It now produces fewer children in relation to its population than any country in the world.

Nor is Catholicism the only religion buffeted by the contraceptive revolution. Millions of Muslims have responded as well by accenting a more permissive side of their theology. In the process, they have removed one barrier to reducing fertility in the Muslim crescent of South Asia and the Arab world, where birthrates are among the highest in the world. There are signs of change even in that bastion of religious fundamentalism Iran, where a belated recognition of the economic consequences of runaway population growth has led government officials to begin aggressively promoting family planning.

The ethics of reproduction are also changing in Hindu nations. Like most of the world's major faiths, Hinduism is pronatalist and patriarchal. Sons are extremely important, among other reasons, because males are responsible for the funeral rites that ensure the survival of the souls of the departed. In rural Nepal, the emphasis on sons has been so great that couples traditionally have as many as six children to ensure two surviving sons, according to research conducted by the Ford Foundation's James Ross.

But in Nepal, as elsewhere, new factors have altered the calculus of reproduction. With less and less agricultural land to divide among heirs, the economics of having large families has been altered. As a result, religious considerations that favor large families have taken a backseat to the necessity of having fewer children who can be educated for salaried jobs. The trend toward smaller families in Nepal has been abetted by the increasing availability of health care services, which have raised child survival rates, and by the provision of basic family planning services by the government.

"In all religions, there are strong culturally pronatalist values, but they are amenable to variation," says Ross, who is the Ford Foundation's representative in Bangladesh.

In nearly every region of the world, similar circumstances have prompted millions of believers to separate their reproductive decisions from their religious faith.

The recent dramatic growth of urban areas has been one powerful catalyst for change. In the face of the idle hours of unemployment, shacks made from scrounged debris and the brutal environment of exploding mega-slums, the admonition of one recent pope that "large families are most blessed by God" has lost much of its appeal.

The evolving role of women has also had a large effect, as the gradual expansion of economic and educational opportunities has catapulted millions of women out of traditional roles that are often reinforced by religious doctrines.

Conservative religious teachings have also lost ground to the full-scale public information campaigns mounted by scores of government and private family planning agencies, which have relentlessly spread the new gospel of smaller families to the remotest corners of the world.

Bruce Harris is head of the Mexico City office of Covenant House, a Catholic charity that helps street children. His observation on Latin America has universal application. "It's simple," he says, "With more kids, more mouths to feed, and an urban economy that's not growing at a rate where kids can be absorbed into it, you'll have an excess number of kids who won't have enough to eat. If you're living on the edge of survival, economic decisions outweigh the Church."

Demographers and other academic experts have debated for years just how—or even whether—religious beliefs influence reproductive behavior.

During the 1950s and 1960s, the conventional wisdom was that Church doctrine made a big difference in fertility rates and contraceptive practices. This commonsensical-sounding notion of "particularized theology" held that couples whose religion banned abortion and contraceptives and promoted large families were likely to have more children.

Nowadays, demographers are much less certain whether this cause-and-effect relationship actually exists and are much more inclined to attribute the high birthrates of earlier eras to factors other than religion. In fact, women may have had their own reason for wanting larger families, a desire that was far more prevalent in pre-modern rural societies. Or large families may have simply resulted from the fact that modern contraceptives were unavailable.

Joseph Chamie is a UN official whose book, *Religion and Fertility*, examines the influence of religious beliefs on reproductive behavior in Lebanon.

"Forty years ago, it seemed that if Catholics had higher fertility than Jews, religion must be the reason," he says. "The problem is that correlations don't prove causality. Very few people have eight or ten kids because of religion."

In fact, the synergism between religious belief and fertility is complex. To understand it, it is necessary to make a distinction between the direct and indirect influence religion has on reproductive behavior.

Most researchers doubt that there has ever been a strong direct correlation between Church policy and individual family planning decisions. If they are right, plummeting fertility in the Catholic world (and elsewhere, for that matter) may have little to do with the declining influence of the Church. Modernization, urbanization, higher levels of education, expanding economic opportunities for women, and the sheer availability of contraception may be more important factors.

Bolivia and Peru are cases in point. According to recent studies, a majority of women in these countries use "natural" methods of contraception—not because the Church tells them to but because they can't obtain more modern methods. The fact that 90 percent of Peruvian and Bolivian women say they do not want another child is stronger evidence that fealty to the Church is not their primary motive. Indeed, Peru has the highest level of unmet demand for modern contraceptives in the world.

Research conducted in 1987 by the Mexican Institute for Family and Population Research confirms the absence of any significant direct Church influence on reproductive behavior. The study examined factors that form attitudes and shape behavior on the subject of family planning. The key variable turned out to be the relationship women had with their sexual partners. Out of 1,500 women interviewed, only one cited the Church's position as her reason for not using artificial contraception.

Evidence from Colombia reinforces the point. A survey there questioned sexually active women who said they did not want to become pregnant yet did not use artificial contraception. Fewer than one in 200 cited religious beliefs as their reason for not practicing family planning. Similar conclusions, based on anecdotal evidence, come from a series of interviews the Mexican Institute conducted with Mexican women whose reproductive years predated the widespread availability of modern family planning methods.

"Women have always wanted family planning in this country; they have always wanted to stop having so many children," says the Institute's Susan Pick de Weiss. "But women were afraid to talk about it. It wasn't socially acceptable … It's not that *attitudes* have changed. It's *behavior* that's changed because now it's possible to get information about family planning and access to contraceptives."

"There has never been a period when a majority of Catholic women took the Church's position on birth control seriously. The Church's position has never been a determining factor for most women," adds Frances Kissling, president of the Washington-based Catholics for a Free Choice. "What has changed is sexual attitudes and the availability of contraceptives."

The evidence suggests, then, that the direct influence of religious doctrine on individual reproductive decisions is weak. But indirect or oblique influence is another matter, and in many countries, this has been sufficient to slow the transition from high to low fertility. One example of such influence is the way religious authorities have restricted access to modern contraceptives, often through direct intervention in the political process. Their main targets have been sterilization, which is restricted in most Catholic and Islamic nations, and abortion, which is widely practiced but legally banned except to save the life of the mother in the Catholic nations of Eastern Europe, in Francophone Africa, and everywhere in Latin America except for Cuba and Nicaragua.

But even temporary birth control methods have come under religious censure. The Church has attacked the pill, IUDs, and other modern contraceptives for being "abortifacients," since on very rare occasions they act to prevent implantation of a fertilized egg. In lieu of such "artificial" means, it has promoted "natural" methods like breastfeeding and periodic abstinence, which have a higher failure rate.

Limits on contraceptive choices can also be self-imposed for religious reasons. Two American scholars published research in the late 1980s indicating that American Catholics have a somewhat greater tendency to use the anonymous condom rather than IUDs and diaphragms, which require the intervention of a physician.

Another example is the influence religion has on the cultural values that bear on fertility, including attitudes toward children, family size, and the role of women in society. Sylvia Marcos, a clinical psychologist from Cuernavaca and director of the Mexican branch of Catholics for the Right to Decide, explains, "The Church is a determinant in a larger sense than just faith. The morals of Mexico are Catholic morals. It's not that people have religious attitudes, but that it's a Catholic, pronatalist culture with no public life for women."

This phenomenon can manifest itself in ways that seem contradictory. One Mexican doctor explains that in her small village, fear of using contraceptives often outweighs the fear of getting pregnant.

"There's less stigma for a girl who has premarital sex without contraceptives and gets pregnant than one who uses contraceptives and doesn't. If you use birth control, people assume you're sleeping with several people."

The Mexican Institute, for its part, found in research conducted in 1990 that religious values did have a significant bearing on the sexual behavior of Mexican adolescents. At least one important personality trait—submissiveness—was distinguished between teenagers who had sex and those who did not, between those who used contraceptives and those who did not, and between those who got pregnant and those who did not.

"The strong influence of the Church is indirect. It's cultural and educational. The submissiveness is a kind of passiveness, a lack of initiative, a tendency to obey authority—men, adults, parents, the Church. It's in this sense that the influence of the Church is important—this submissiveness and the guilt it teaches us we should have," says the Institute's de Weiss.

"We are taught that we should obey what is expected of us and not think in terms of what we need," de Weiss continues. "We are expected to be traditional in our ways. One aspect of this is to have sex for reproductive reasons, not to have sex for pleasure.

"An enormous amount of the education we get and the motivation we have in our day-to-day actions is based on guilt. If I don't do this, I get punished. If I do this, I get rewarded. We are not internally controlled in our actions but more externally controlled, and one of the external factors is the guilt. And I think that is transmitted through the Church."

In the Muslim world, the line between religion and conservative social traditions is harder to draw. But the effect of Catholic values has its counterpart. Despite the pressures of overcrowding in cities like Cairo and Algiers, couples are still urged by families and friends to have children early and often.

"The normal thing is, after you get married, people begin to ask: Any good news? Anything coming along yet?" says one young Cairene, who decided to delay her first pregnancy.

High fertility rates are buttressed by the less-than-egalitarian view of women that prevails in many Muslim nations. Attitudes toward marriage (early), divorce (easy for a man; nearly impossible for a woman), and polygamy (permitted conditionally in the Koran and still legal even in more modernized Muslim countries like Egypt) reinforce a woman's dependence on children for status and economic security. In Muslim societies, as in most third world societies, the primary role of women is to serve and obey men and to bear them children.

The strength of such attitudes has forced family planning agencies to be highly sensitive to religious opinion and cultural views, A new employee's manual issued by Egypt's Ministry of Health containing instructions on dealing with patients, for example, strikes a fine balance between the sacred and profane in making the case that mothers should breastfeed as a means of spacing births: "She will please her God, who has ordained breastfeeding. She will [also] protect her baby's life and get rid of fats accumulated during pregnancy, thus preserving her figure."

In Latin America, family planning agencies have also had to base their arguments for child-spacing on the need to protect the health of mother and child, without reference to limiting family size. In several notable cases, including Colombia, they have made a virtue of necessity to gain the reluctant acquiescence of Church authorities. They have argued that if the Church is serious about stopping abortion, then Church officials must back—or at least not publicly oppose—family planning to reduce the number of unwanted pregnancies.

The strongest influence religion has on slowing the transition to low fertility is among poor and uneducated women in rural areas. The example of one woman living in a village in rural Bangladesh illustrates the point.

Influenced by the steady drumbeat of family planning messages broadcast by the government and endorsed by the country's Muslim hierarchy, the woman decided to get sterilized, but without her husband's permission. "A few days after she was sterilized, she slipped and fell down and has not felt well since," notes Sidney Ruth Schuler and Syed M. Hashemi, the two researchers who interviewed her. "Her husband consulted the local *maulavis,* and she became worried about whether she would receive a proper burial. She recalled that a month after her sister-in-law was sterilized, a goat died all of a sudden. She confided to the interviewer her fear that punishment might suddenly be meted out to her as well."

"There is punishment for not seeking one's husband's permission," she told the researchers. "Sin I have committed, no doubt, and my heart throbs constantly with premonitions and fears."

The woman's experience illustrates what Schuler and Hashemi describe as the struggle taking place in rural Bangladesh between "traditional" and "modern" views of the religious status of contraception. This struggle remains intense in rural and poor settings. But there is now abundant evidence that the resistance of religion and tradition give way quickly in the presence of opportunities for higher education and gainful employment

Fertility rates are relatively low in Muslim countries such as Tunisia and Turkey that provide greater access for women to education and jobs, according to one study. Rates remain high in Muslim nations where such opportunities are largely unavailable, such as Algeria and Pakistan. The results suggest that fertility rates are a function not so much of religion as of education and employment. These secular concerns influence age at marriage, equality within marriage, and the confidence to use family planning services.

The conclusion that socioeconomic factors outweigh religion when it comes to reproductive choices is supported by another study, conducted in Bangladesh. The research showed no significant differences in the use of contraceptives between Muslims and Hindus at higher levels of education. At lower levels of education, contraceptive use among Hindus was significantly higher than among Muslims.

Whether they like it or not, the world's major religions have had to take steps to accommodate the contraceptive revolution that has swept the world since the 1960s. In many ways, Islam has adapted more gracefully to these changing circumstances.

There are differences of opinion among Islamic leaders over the propriety of modern family planning methods. But these tend to be verticals between conservatives who cling to old ways and liberals who believe that the religion needs to be responsive to changing circumstances. In the Catholic Church, the division is more strictly horizontal as parishioners and many local clerics, faced daily with the grim consequences of rapid urbanization and population growth in Latin America and Africa, have parted ways with the strict mandates of Rome.

"Is the Roman Catholic Church against family planning?" asks the former priest Paul Burgess. "If by the Church you mean the hierarchy and the bishops in Rome, the answer is yes. If by the Church you mean the clergy and the laity, the answer is no. At the level where it counts, the Catholic Church practices birth control."

The history of the Catholic Church's position on contraception can be divided into two distinct phases. During the first, which lasted until the Reformation in the sixteenth century, a rigidly restrictive doctrine evolved in response to one set of historical circumstances, including the plagues and famines lasting through the Middle Ages that decimated Catholic populations in Europe.

"We are not dealing with a doctrine invented by man," said Pope John Paul II of the teaching. It is a doctrine "written by the creative hand of God in the nature of the human person."

The second phase has been one of a halting, reluctant, limited accommodation to another set of historical circumstances: the improving status of women, greater scientific knowledge of the reproductive function, the rise of the birth control movement, and the population crisis itself—the combination of which has produced a slight relaxation in the Church's absolute standard.

The Church's dim view of contraception began as a reaction to the sexual dissipation of the Roman empire, where the Church was born. It drew strength from the Genesis injunction to "go forth and multiply," prompting one early pope to insist that procreation was not merely good but sacred, since it furthered the work of God. Grounded on the point, early Catholic theologians concluded that procreation could be the only legitimate reason for conjugal intercourse. To survive in the face of the pagan vices of the Greco-Roman world, writes former Vatican official Francis X. Murphy, "the Church had to insist on the value of life and its transmission and the positive aspects of love and human dignity."

The next intellectual building block was supplied by St. Augustine, who in the fifth century posited the notion that dominated all of Christianity until the twentieth: that contraception was evil since it violated the primary purpose of marital intercourse—namely, to produce children. In Augustine's scheme, contraception was an instrument of the sin of lust, turning the wife into a "harlot" and the husband into an "adulterer." Couples who used an "evil appliance" to stop contraception, Augustine warned, were guilty of mortal sin. The first actual papal injunction against birth control, issued by Gregory IX in 1230, reflected a further concern that contraception opened the door to promiscuity, threatening the sanctity of marriage. The first papal legislation on the subject, enacted by Gregory X in 1272, voided a marriage that was entered into with the intention of not having children.

By the advent of the modern age, the fundamental premise of the Church's position was firmly in place: that sexual intercourse was not legitimate without reproductive intent. As a result, the Church's first reaction to the growing practice of contraception, championed by the birth control movement that originated in nineteenth-century England and America, was defensive.

"Any use whatsoever of matrimony exercised in such a way that the act is frustrated in its natural power to guarantee life is an offense against the law of God and nature, and those who indulge in such are branded with the guilt of grave sin," a defiant Pope Pius XI declared in a landmark encyclical in 1930.

The document makes clear that the Churches pronatalism was not entirely disinterested. It is the duty of Christian couples, it said, "to raise up … members of God's households that the worshipers of God and of Our Savior may daily increase." But in one of the first compromises of its kind, the same Pope Pius XI recognized the legitimacy of intercourse during the infertile period, if not for family planning then at least as a means of satisfying the secondary ends of marriage: "mutual aid, the cultivation of mutual love, and the quieting of concupiscence."

Two decades later, in 1951, Pope Pius XII went further, recognizing the legitimacy of natural family planning under certain circumstances but within the context of a general obligation on the part of married couples to have children. Pius endorsed the principle, implied in earlier Church teachings, that acceptable medical, economic, and social grounds exist for avoiding procreation. The position, which still pertains, is as close as the Church has ever come to legitimizing family planning.

The high-water mark of dissent occurred when, spurred by the advent of the pill and runaway population growth in the developing world, a movement formed within the Church to legitimize all forms of contraception. In 1963, during the Second Vatican Councils, Pope John XXIII bowed to the gathering forces of change and agreed to create a commission to review the Church's position on family planning. After deliberating for two years, a body of sixty-four laymen and theologians endorsed a plan to revise Church policy by allowing the use of artificial contraceptives. Of the fifteen cardinals who took part in the final session, only six voted to maintain the Church's hard-line position. The commission even prepared an explanatory note laying the intellectual groundwork for what would have been a historic turnabout, comparable to those made by the Church in earlier years on the subjects of slavery and usury.

"They left convinced that the position was going to change," explains Father Murphy, whose reports from Vatican II were published in *The New Yorker* under the *nom de plume* Xavier Rynne. But at the last minute a small group of conservative bishops intervened with Paul VI, who had acceded to the papacy after John's death in 1963. They convinced him that to change positions after so long would undermine the Church's magisterial authority. "If the Church had been wrong, what would that mean for the souls sent to Hell for violating the ban?" one Spanish Jesuit asked, getting to the heart of the matter.

After a long period of deliberation, during which one cardinal personally entreated the pope not to create "another Galileo case" by keeping the Church out of sync with the times, the pontiff decided to close the door on reform. In a strongly worded encyclical, *Humanae Vitae,* issued in 1968, he categorically reaffirmed the Church's prohibition on all but natural forms of contraception. The Church's teaching is founded on nothing less, he said, than "the inseparable connection, established by God and unable to be broken by man on his own initiative, between the unitive and the procreative meanings" of the conjugal act.

The ban on artificial methods was reaffirmed in 1992 in the first new universal catechism issued by the Church since the mid-sixteenth century. In 1993, it was again reaffirmed in the encyclical *Veritatis Splendor*, issued by Paul's successor, John Paul II, who early in his papacy attacked the "irrational control of births preventing the access of new mouths at the banquet of the Lord."

Like the pope, defenders of *Humanae Vitae* see the ban on artificial contraception as part of a larger war against the onslaught of materialism, secularism, and sexual permissiveness. Defenders also insist that the Church is not ignoring the real problem, which is not rapid population growth but political and economic systems that inequitably distribute the world's resources.

"We can't take a mechanistic approach to the solution of poverty and finding jobs," explains one Mexican Church official. "We can't lump all this into the population bottle. We can't say that if we just give enough people enough pills and IUDs that somehow justice will suddenly emerge. We've had family planning programs in Mexico for twenty years. We've reduced fertility rates. But our people still do not have more jobs, are not wealthier, do not have better jobs than when fertility rates were higher."

But in other quarters, *Humanae Vitae* was greeted with consternation, opening the door to a dissident view that is now so widespread within the Church as to bear quasi-legitimacy in the eyes of many Catholic clerics and laity. Twenty-five years later, one priest describes the encyclical as "probably the papacy's most controversial ... and also probably its most ineffective document."

When *Humanae Vitae* was handed down, hundreds of theologians and Catholic scholars around the world respectfully but firmly dissented. A majority of the national bishops' conferences "mitigated" the encyclical by pointing to another Church doctrine—freedom of conscience—that confers upon Catholics the right to make their own decisions. A large minority of bishops at a 1980 synod on the family, meanwhile, asked that the encyclical be reconsidered.

Many clerics and lay Catholics have challenged the notion, advanced by the Church for centuries, that contraception violates "natural law," a controversial concept that is usually interpreted to mean whatever the authorities in Rome say it means. Others now protest that in an era of AIDS and in the face of the vast number of unsafe abortions resulting from unwanted pregnancies in Catholic countries each year, the Church's views on contraception are at variance with its own doctrine regarding the sanctity of human life.

Another objection has been the element of confusion that, critics charge, continues to surround the Church's position. Since the 1920s, it has been known that a woman can get pregnant only three days or so of every month. Such knowledge has rendered meaningless the notion that every conjugal act should be open to the transfer of life. If, say the critics, it is acceptable to take advantage of such long infertile periods, as the encyclical indicates, then it is disingenuous to insist, as *Humame Vitae* also does, that all sex acts remain open to the transmission of life. And if economic and educational considerations constitute valid moral reasons for limiting family size—a notion first legitimized by the Church in the sixteenth century—then why does it matter whether natural or artificial means are used? *Why*, in short, is one form of contraception (natural) a form of obedience to the law of God, while another (artificial) is a sin, when the usual motive behind the use of either—child-spacing and family limitation—is acceptable to the Church?

The answer, given overwhelmingly by Catholics around the world, reflects significant global value changes that have left the Church and its adherents a crucial impass. Church officials show no signs of backing down, individual Catholics continue to use modern contraceptives at rates equal to or higher than non-Catholics. The issue is joined and no compromise is in sight.

While Roman Catholicism is restrictive at the top and permissive at the bottom, just the reverse is true in Muslim nations, where birthrates are among the highest in the world.

Mohammad Sayyid Tantawi's office overlooks one of the infamous landmarks of Cairo: a cemetery, the "City of the Dead," which is home to half a million living Cairenes. A government-appointed *mufti*, or religious scholar, he speaks with authority as a keeper of doctrine for the world's 850 million Sunni Muslims.

"Islam provides no opposition to controlling birth. There is no Koranic verse which forbids family planning," says the bearded cleric. "I personally, if I were to have a meeting with the pope at the Vatican, would explain to him that the Shari'a of Islam does not forbid family planning as long as the couple sees that there is a necessity for it."

Across town, inside an ornate 300-year-old mosque, three wizened sheikhs ponder the same subject while waiting for the start of afternoon prayers.

"Contraception is killing," says one, as his bearded colleagues nod in agreement, "Because God the Almighty is the one who creates the being, so we do not kill it."

"The only people who say contraception is okay are the sheikhs of the government," proclaims another, in an obvious reference to Tantawi. "All other sheikhs say it's sacrilegious. The Koran says you can't limit the size of your family."

Just what is and what is not allowed under Muslim law, it seems, is a matter of debate. Throughout the 1,400-year history of Islam, the world's second-largest faith, children have been considered one of the greatest blessings of God. The religion's long tradition, based on the Prophet Muhammad's injunction to "marry and have children"—the Islamic equivalent of the Genesis admonition to "go forth and multiply"—is one reason why large families have been the rule in Muslim nations. But in the Muslim world, as in Catholic nations, old teachings are bumping up against the hard realities of population trends that have fundamentally altered daily life. The result has been a sweeping redefinition of permissible reproductive behavior that has opened the door to family planning progress in Muslim countries around the world.

The implications of high birthrates in the Arab world dawned first among politicians, whose jobs depend on keeping up with spiraling demands for jobs, food, and housing. More than three decades ago, Tunisia's president Habib Bourghiba warned of "a human tidal wave that is implacably rising, rising more quickly than our capacity to support ourselves."

"What good is it to increase our agricultural production and our mineral wealth if the population continues its anarchic and demential growth?" Bourghiba asked rhetorically as he established the region's first successful family planning program.

Thirty years later, the logic of family planning extends even to that bastion of Shiite orthodoxy, Iran. When they seized control of the country from the Shah in 1979, the country's Islamic rulers sneered at birth control, condemning it as a Western plot. Fifteen years later, with twice the population but the same fixed, oil-based annual income, the mullahs have caught the spirit. With the zeal of converts, they have erected the structure of a family planning pro-gram that includes everything from aggressive public education to free vasectomies to financial disincentives for couples having over three children.

As the case of Indonesia, the Muslim world's greatest success story, demonstrates, translating the desire to slow population growth into a successful family planning program involves more than creating a government bureaucracy. It also requires winning the support of the country's Islamic establishment.

"You can't disregard the fact that you have to get Islamic support," says Aziza Hussein, who should know. She is the founder and chairperson of the Cairo Family Planning Association, a leading private group that has devoted long hours to cultivating clerical support for Egypt's family planning efforts. "If Islamic leaders know the size of the problem, they have to back family planning," Hussein says. "Because Islam says you have to do what's in the interest of the community."

Such support has been forthcoming in many Islamic nations because, with the Koran silent on the subject of family planning, the issue has essentially been a matter of local option.

Tantawi explains, "When it comes to rituals, they are required to be performed the same way in Egypt as in Saudi Arabia. But there is nothing in the Koran about family planning, so in these matters, we improvise.

"Family planning is permitted in the Islamic Shari'a whenever there is a necessity for it. And this question varies from one circumstance to another, from one state to another. Where family planning might be a duty in Egypt, it could be unnecessary in Libya, for example, because Libyans' area is greater than that of Egypt, and its population is only 4 million. A *fatwa* (religious edict) there would be different than a *fatwa* here, even if set by the same man."

Another reason for Islam's adaptability is that the faith contains parallel traditions, one that provides an elaborate justification for large families, the other of which, now in vogue, justifies precisely the opposite. The first tradition stems from the notion, a tenet of nearly every major faith, that children are the gifts of God and that it is a religious duty to multiply. For generations, the sacred admonition to "marry and multiply, for I will make a display of you on the Day of Judgment" has been reinforced by secular circumstances—namely, the need for many children to earn and protect wealth, gain honor, and demonstrate a man's virility. If it is right to propagate, then the reverse is also true: that to thwart pregnancy—even for economic reasons—is to thwart the will of God and to doubt his ability to provide.

"What creature living on earth does not God look after?" asks one of the Egyptian sheikhs. "You do not kill your children for the fear of poverty, because God provides."

The resistance to family planning stems also from the fatalistic notion that, with or without contraceptives, God will settle the issue of family size.

"To God is ownership of the skies and heaven," says another of the sheikhs, "God can make a woman pregnant or make a man sterile. It is all God's decision."

An entirely different strain of Islamic thought is elucidated in Tantawi's 1989 *fatwa*, which has been indispensable to the Egyptian government's efforts to slow the country's population growth rate. The more-liberal view laid out in the *fatwa* draws on the Koran's counsel to parents to have no more children than they can provide for physically and economically. The corollary—that preventing economic hardship nurtures piety—also speaks to the burden of large families on parents. "The most grueling trial," the tradition of the Prophet has it, "is to have plenty of children with no adequate means." Nor are weak multitudes advantageous to the prosperity of Islam itself, as one official statement issued by the *mufti* proclaims. "Such a multitude cannot be considered as a source of pride for the noble Prophet, peace be upon him. On the contrary, Islam abhors and despises such a multitude as pointed out by the Prophet … You will be in great numbers, but you will be worthless like the bubbles of water driven ahead by torrents."

The most important tenet of this more permissive interpretation is its endorsement of contraception, based on the Hadith, or commentaries on the Prophet written by Muhammad's contemporaries, including Jabir Ibn Abdullah: "We used to practice coitus interruptus *['azl]* during the time of the Prophet. The Prophet came to know about it but did not forbid us. If this were something to be prohibited, the Koran would have forbidden us to do it."

Using argument by analogy—the third source of law after the Koran and the Hadith—Muslim scholars have reasoned that if *'azl* was acceptable to the Prophet, modern contraceptives are acceptable today.

An earlier *fatwa,* handed down in 1964, elucidates the context in which the issue of contraception has been re-evaluated. In an earlier period in history, it notes, Muslims had to multiply to generate the manpower needed to defend Islam against powerful adversaries. "But now," it says, "we find that conditions have changed. We find that the density of population in the world threatens seriously to reduce the living standards of mankind to the extent that many men of thought have been prompted to seek family planning in every country, so that the resources may not fall short of ensuring a decent living for its people."

Although family planning has been the subject of debate among Islamic scholars for centuries, the more permissive view has been buttressed by the impact of unprecedented population growth rates.

"Fifty years ago, the *mufti* would have said that family planning is infidelism and paganism, going against the will of God. Talking about family planning would have been impossible," says Tantawi. "But the world has changed in the past fifty years more than it has in the thousand years before. Fifty years ago, the population of Egypt was 6 million and there were 6 million *fedans* of land. Today there are 60 million Egyptians and the land is still 6 million. So family planning is necessary. You must take the measures by which you minimize the numbers of population so that Egypt can progress."

But if such adaptability has enabled governments like Egypt to harness the Muslim establishment to its policy of reducing population growth, the message has been slow to trickle down to the local mosque *imams,* or preachers, many of whom—to the consternation of family planning agencies—still counsel that limiting family size contravenes the will of God.

The problem, explains Abdel Omran in his book *Family Planning in the Legacy of Islam,* is that with family planning acceptable in Islam only by implication, the latitude for disagreement is wide. "It's not like prayer, which you have to do. In Islam, family planning is permissible, but it's optional. That opens the door to controversy. Islam is definitely not a hindrance to family planning, but grassroots Muslim leaders sometimes oppose family planning because of their own misunderstanding."

The traditional, anti-modernist outlook of many local *imams* has been reinforced by the resurgence of Muslim fundamentalism, which views family planning as a Western plot to weaken Islam by keeping Muslim nations underpopulated.

"The correct interpretation [of Islam on family planning] will win out in the end," says Tantawi. "The people who have brains are aware of it. Thanks be to God, the people who have brains are becoming more numerous than those without."

On January 30, 1993, news of an unusual incident crossed the Associated Press news wire. It concerned the death of an Italian housewife, Carla Ardenghi. Stricken with cancer, the twenty-eight-year-old Ardenghi decided to stop treatments during her pregnancy to protect her unborn child. Eight hours after the baby's premature birth, Carla Ardenghi died.

"Every day in my life is another day for the child I have inside," reads an entry from her diary, released by her husband.

Ardenghi's death, which was front-page news in Italy, triggered a lively public debate over the terrible ethical dilemmas involved in weighing the life of a mother against that of an unborn child. Inside the Vatican, it was an easy call. One Church spokesman praised Ardenghi posthumously for her "heroic" decision not to have an abortion, a decision, said another, that has given meaning to "all of our lives." A month earlier, the Vatican beatified Gianna Beretta Molla, advancing to the *verge* of sainthood another Italian woman who died in 1962 after giving birth.

The Vatican's swift, unqualified response to Ardenghi's death provides an instructive glimpse of the Church's continuing determination to stem the global tide of apostasy on matters of abortion and contraception. Having lost the battle for the hearts and minds of the vast majority of Catholic faithful, Church leaders, by the mid-1970s, had adopted the only available alternative strategy, stepping up efforts to win their governments with the objectives of keeping abortion illegal, modern contraceptives scarce, and sex education out of the classroom.

"In terms of [contraceptive] practice, Catholicism has little influence at the parochial level," says Thomas Merrick, senior population adviser at the World Bank in Washington. "But politically the Church is a force in Latin America. At that level, the Church has often been a player in the question of whether or not a country should have family planning."

In spirited attacks, Latin American bishops have scorned the relentless inroads made by family planning agencies as a form of "contraceptive imperialism" designed to impose alien traditions on their countries. In Mexico, Church officials have denounced family planning as a "smokescreen" intended, according to various interpretations, to keep Mexico's population low to slow the rate of immigration to the United States; to contribute to the prosperity that would enable Mexicans to buy more consumer goods from the United States; or simply to keep Mexico weak. One particularly blunt papal message juxtaposes the "culture of death," which equates contraception with drugs and murder, with the "culture of life," championed by the Church.

Beyond mere rhetoric, Church leaders have skillfully capitalized on their formidable influence in Catholic countries. In the unusual case of Mexico, the Church has pressed its case from a position of newfound strength. For decades, successive Mexican governments have shunned the Church, refusing to recognize it officially and barring clerics from voting or holding land. Relegated to the political sidelines, Church officials were unable to mount any significant resistance to the establishment of the country's ambitious family planning program that was begun in the early 1970s.

But worried by the gathering strength of two opposition parties that have close ties to the Church, President Carlos Salinas de Gortari, the head of Mexico's governing Revolutionary Independent Party (PRI) moved in 1991 to broaden Catholic support by restoring the Church's legal position.

"It was clear to the PRI that if it wanted to maintain political power, it would need a stronger constituency," says a Mexican source familiar with the workings of the party. "If it recognized the Church at the official level, it would be likelier to say good things about the PRI in time for the next election."

The deal, closed in 1992, brought Mexico into the community of more than sixty nations that maintain diplomatic ties with the Vatican. Although it merely formalized a tacit arrangement, it gave the Church—and other religions recognized under the same statute—its first free access to Mexican radio, television and the press.

The political power of the Church had been demonstrated two years earlier after lawmakers in the Mexican state of Chiapas, in a surprise move, sought to decriminalize abortion for poor and single women and in cases where the decision had the consent of both husband and wife. Faced with such an unprecedented threat, Church leaders sprang into action. Priests were instructed to preach against the measure. One influential local bishop warned that women who sought abortion would be excommunicated. Within two weeks, 200,000 signatures were gathered against the measure, forcing the legislature to back down.

A year later, the Church again flexed its political muscle when it pressured the provisional governor of the state of San Luis Potosi to expel Mexfarn, the twenty-seven-year-old affiliate of the IPPF, for corrupting the morals of young people and encouraging abortion—charges that Mexfam has hotly denied.

"This could not have happened two years ago," says Mexfam's president, Alfonso Lopez Juárez. "This is possible now because of the new courage the Church has, to be more bold and to act more officially against things which are against its doctrine. I think the situation is radically changed now from two years ago because of Mexico's recognition of the Church."

The Church's new assertiveness has been encouraged by the papal *nuncio,* or ambassador, dispatched after diplomatic relations with Mexico were officially restored in 1992. As the eyes and ears of the pope and the dispenser of papal perks, including promotions and membership on prized Vatican commissions, the *nuncio* has had the clout to convince local bishops to hold the government's feet to the fire on the issues that matter: abortion, contraception, and sex education.

"Before relations with the Vatican were resumed, individual bishops had much more latitude in terms of the extent to which they hewed to the Vatican line," says a Mexican source who asked not to be identified. "Now that the *nuncio* is here to bring the commands of Rome, they have to be more publicly vigilant and not let deviations arise within the Catholic community.

"The *nuncio* is saying to the bishops: Don't you think you should be commenting to the government and preaching to the people about the increased use of money by the government for family planning? Don't you think you should be insisting on more money for natural family planning? Don't you think you should be decrying the attempt to bring abortion into the country?"

The elevation of the Church's status has also energized the work of socially conservative private groups, including Pro-Vida (Pro Life), a shadowy, twenty-year-old organization that has been on the front lines of efforts to restore lost Catholic virtues to Mexico.

One Mexican official likens Pro-Vida to the Heritage Foundation in Washington, which was ideologically close to the Reagan administration during the 1980s without actually being a part of it. Another Mexican, a journalist, compares Pro-Vida to the American gun lobby, which has great influence even though its views are out of sync with those of the vast majority of Americans.

Working with other socially conservative private groups and frequently with the tacit support of Church officials, Pro-Vida has used newspaper and radio advertisements and direct lobbying to put heat on local government officials to ban sex education for adolescents, whose birthrates remain high and who have been largely overlooked in the otherwise successful twenty-year Mexican campaign to lower birthrates.

"In Chiapas and elsewhere, Pro-Vida and the Roman Catholic Church were working hand in hand. They were lobbying with the quiet support of the Church," notes Edgar Gonzales, a Mexican journalist who has written extensively about Pro-Vida.

One recent newspaper advertisement paid for by Pro-Vida accuses Mexico's education minister of "pushing young people toward sexual promiscuity, which lays a foundation of falsehood and corruption" and for refusing to ban advertisements encouraging the use of condoms. The ad refers to birth control pills as "mini-abortions."

Meanwhile, encouraged by their victory in expelling Mexfam from San Luis Potosi, Pro-Vida lobbyists have started targeting other Mexfarn chapters armed with a logic that has befuddled family planners.

"Contraception is one step away from abortion," Pro-Vida's president, Jorge Serrano Limon, told the *Miami Herald*. "It encourages couples to have sexual relations for reasons other than having children. Then, when the contraceptives fail, a woman may feel she has no recourse but to abort."

Some Mexican family planning administrators acknowledge privately that the campaign against family planning and sex education is making it harder to operate. They say that local field workers now worry about being excommunicated by the Church. Meanwhile, board members of groups like Mexfam, often prominent personalities in the

Mexican business and government establishment, have been stung by the adverse publicity blaming family planning for the corruption of public morals. After one recent ad campaign, the chairman of Mexfam stepped down, insisting that Mexfam adopt a lower profile. Following a summit meeting arranged in 1992 between Mexfam and Pro-Vida, Mexfam agreed to be less explicit in future advertising about how to use contraceptives.

"The problem is that we need support from boards, governments, heads of schools, and they are now scared by the Church," notes Lopez, who says one third of his time is now: spent warding off attacks and publishing rebuttals. The consequent, he says, is that Mexfam has to channel its resources and energy to fight an adversary that was not in the arena two years ago, or that was present but not on the offensive. The Church knows that it can't change attitudes toward contraception, so the goal is now to harass family planning organizations and to have the government ban Mexfam in every state, says Lopez.

Nor is Mexfam the only object of the Church's interest. In countries around the Catholic world, Church officials have capitalized on local circumstances to slow the spread of artificial contraception. When Peru mounted its first serious effort to erect a family planning program in the 1980s, the archbishop of Lima publicly warned that women who used artificial contraception risked not going to heaven.

In Brazil, pressure from the Church has deterred the government from providing federal funding for family planning services altogether. During a 1991 visit, Pope John Paul II condemned the country's privately operated family planning programs as "gravely illicit" and urged couples to have more children to help remedy a national shortage of priests.

In Poland, where the Church's decision to back the Solidarity labor movement marked the beginning of the end of four decades of communist rule, its political influence has been translated into social policy. Family planning programs set up under the communist government have been weakened. Some oral contraceptives have been banned. Those remaining lost their government subsidy, making them too expensive for many women to use. In 1990, sex education in Polish public schools was replaced with classes in Catholicism.

"With little in the way of a private family planning network and with virtually no government support, contraceptive information and services are now almost nonexistent," notes a recent report issued by Population Action International. "With safe abortion services also disappearing, Polish couples, most of whom prefer small families, face an impossible dilemma."

In the Philippines, meanwhile, where fertility is twice the East Asian average, family planning is only slowly recovering from cutbacks pressed by the Catholic Church in the aftermath of the key role it played in the 1981 revolution that overthrew Ferdinand Marcos. Under pressure from the Church, family planning budgets and staff were cut by a third, while the government of Marcos's successor, President Cory Aquino, shifted from an aggressive policy of limiting births through family planning to one that emphasized "the improvement of the quality of human life." The new policy abandoned references to the responsibility of the state to achieve demographic goals. Following a dialogue between Church and government leaders in August 1990, the Church agreed to the principle that in a pluralistic society couples should have access to contraceptives. In return, the government agreed to prohibit contraceptives that induce abortion. But the deal was short-lived. In October, the Church issued a pastoral letter that attacked the government's family planning program and urged the government's 7,000 health workers to exercise their freedom of conscience to subvert it.

After the 1992 election of Fidel Ramos, a Protestant who is a strong advocate of family planning, the Church stepped up its attack, staging "down with condom" prayer rallies and challenging the constitutionality of the country's family planning program in the Supreme Court. Church leaders also produced a copy of a 1974 study by the U.S. National Security Council that they said proved that "demographic imperialism" was behind Washington's financial support for the Philippine family planning program. The document, prepared during the Nixon and Ford administrations, said that rapid population growth could contribute to political instability in several strategically important countries, including the Philippines, and recommended family planning assistance.

The Philippine Church's "guiding principles" on population matters urge parents to bring children into the world "generously" and decry "the attitude that selfishly avoids the procreation of offspring solely because couples do not want to bear the responsibility that comes with having a child."

The Roman Catholic Church's most notable political successes occurred in 1984, when the Reagan administration announced that it was withdrawing funding from UNFPA and IPPF, and later, on the eve of the 1992 UN Conference on Environment and Development (UNCED) in Rio, when the Vatican delegation and allied negotiators succeeded in keeping population off the final Earth Summit agenda.

At Rio, Church representatives capitalized on the conviction of developing nations that Northern consumption patterns, not third-world population growth, was the primary cause of global environmental degradation. In the run-up to the Rio conferences, Southern nations held the population issue hostage to Northern concessions on foreign aid and global economic reform, other issues championed by the Church. Tapping into such discontent, representatives of three Latin American nations took the lead during the fourth and final preparatory committee of UN member nations—or "prepcom," for short—in watering down the draft language on population that was ultimately approved at Rio.

As one UN official who was present at the fourth prepcom explains, agreement had been reached between the UNCED secretariat and representatives of the "Group of 77" developing nations on language calling for the right of couples to determine the size and spacing of their families and to have access to the information and means to do so. But as the prepcom dragged on, the language was quietly altered, a phrase here, a phrase there, until all mention of family planning was deleted.

High Dowry Demands Causing Issues in Society, Islamic Scholar Says

By Ayesha Al Khoori

Abu Dhabi, March 11, 2014

Experts are urging families and couples to agree on a reasonable dowry and focus on the future relationship of the marriage.

Last week, The National reported on a study issued by the Department of Family Guidance at Sharjah Sharia courts showing that among the problems faced by 2,557 families were demands for high dowries.

Sheikh Sediq Al Mansouri, an Islamic scholar, said dowries, the transfer of funds from the groom to the bride's family, were a basic right in Islam.

"It is a symbol of commitment, it is an honouring gift from the man to show the woman he wants her," he said.

However, demands for high dowries are creating issues in society, said Mr Al Mansouri.

"As long as there is agreement between the bride's family and the groom's. There are many procedures in a marriage nowadays including the wedding. Some people can afford it, but others see it as a problem," he said.

The dowry did not matter, and what was more important is finding "comfort and love in each other", and that in itself is a blessing, he said.

Quoting the Prophet Mohammed, he said: "The best of [dowries] is the simplest [or most affordable]."

Mr Al Mansouri said: "Allah will grant his blessing towards them, and will give them intimacy and love that every couple need," he said. "If the dowry is low, the husband is happy, he starts the relationship at ease. He does not overwhelm himself [with finances]."

High dowries also resulted in a new rising phenomenon, "divorce before consummation", the study revealed.

The dean of the College of Sociology at the University of Sharjah, Ahmed Al Omosh, said that these kinds of divorces deeply affected brides.

"She feels frustrated, her dream has ended. Not many men will consider remarrying her and will prefer an unwed one," he said.

He also asked that families and newly married couples focus on the emotional aspect of a marriage.

"Awareness is needed, for the sake of happy marriages these wedding trends need to vanish. They are temporary and bring temporary happiness, and the couple begin their life in debt," he said.

He said the dowries had distorted the idea of a marriage in the Arabian Gulf and Arab region.

"[Families] used to look for a conservative man and one that is compatible, nowadays people look for materialistic trends. Weddings have become a 'propaganda', an industry on their own, and girls are falling into their nets," he said.

Spinsterhood, young men in debt, and marriage from foreigners are some of the after-effects of high dowries, Mr Al Omosh said.

Ayesha Al Khoori, "High dowry demands causing issues in society, Islamic scholar says," *The National*. Copyright © 2014 by Syndigate Media, Inc. Reprinted with permission.

Section Three

What Are We Really Creating?

Introduction

What Are We Really Creating?

By Catherine Marrone

The third section of this Reader should be regarded as anything but the final part of Reproduction, because it is here that most students truly begin to conceptualize Reproduction as a matter of considerable social, political and technological importance. Our ability to manage our reproduction has meant that many of us will postpone it, leading in some cases to age-related infertility and, consequently, to the need for donated eggs and sperm and wombs. The ability to test and transfer (in cases like the Pre-implantation Genetic Diagnosis) provides us with opportunities to select gender and genetic traits, and to ensure that children are born free from disease. Just as technology provides great opportunity for advancement and improvement on endless fronts, so does it often set the stage for exploitation and for the unavoidable stratification that will surely come with such advancements. Some of the most significant questions in this context begin to loom: Who will be in charge of reproduction—science, the government, or the family? How will the fertility industry change what reproduction looks like and how families come to be?

And we must ask, both in the beginning of the class and later at the end, what will happen to the meaning of motherhood—and fatherhood—if what can occur naturally, in many cases, becomes wholly contrived, re-calibrated and ultimately a detached scientific and medical enterprise. Maybe we ought not worry about this, since reproduction seems at its core inevitable and based on "natural" imperatives. Maybe human reproduction is one "activity" we just expect will remain an expression of freedom and choice and that we will continue to welcome the assistance of Science and Industry to help protect and guarantee this basic human need. I would argue, however, that Reproduction is the very place that we need to stop as a society to ask the important questions: What is it about reproduction that we feel so entitled to? What is it about children and their social meaning that causes us to sometimes forget that when we reproduce we create unique individuals? We often reproduce with little insight as to the reasons why—and do so while heavily burdening, perhaps, our "creations" with all of our individual, cultural, and generational expectations for what "they" can bring.

The Right to Control Fertility

Sterilization and Contraception

By Robert Blank and Janna C. Merrick

Reversible Long-Term Fertility Control Techniques

The increased incidence of divorce and remarriage of many of the individuals who chose contraceptive sterilization between the 1960s and the 1980s, along with an apparent change of priorities that led some to seek restoration of their fertility, shifted research emphasis to the development of reversible techniques. If is unlikely that a "perfect" fertility control technique will ever be found that meets all conceivable demands. This section focuses on some of the new methods that are currently available.

Contraceptive Implants for Women

Subdermal hormonal implants are a form of programmed medication. Surgically implanted rods or capsules containing the contraceptive steroid meter it into the surrounding tissue and maintain the blood level in the desired range; they are effective for approximately five years (Sivin, Sternand and Diaz 1992).

Norplant, the most extensively tested implant, was developed by the Population Council and has been manufactured by Leilas Oy in Finland since 1983. It has been used by more than 1.8 million women in fifty-one countries (McCauley and Geller 1992, 3). Six 3.4 cm silicone rubber capsules, each about the size of a match, are filled with the synthetic progestin levonorgestrel, which suppresses ovulation and causes thickening of the cervical mucus, thus inhibiting sperm penetration. After administration of a local anesthetic, the capsules are surgically implanted in a fanlike manner under the skin of the upper arm. The procedure lakes approximately ten minutes and leaves no visible marks. Because the progestin is released slowly and in low doses and because the implant contains no estrogen, the risk of overdosing and the risk of strokes and blood clots associated with same formulations of contraceptive pills are substantially reduced (McCauley and Geller 1992, 8).

Norplant has a high rate of effectiveness and high continuation rates. The pregnancy rate is 0.2 per 100 woman in the first and second year of use. The percentages of women who still have the implant one year after insertion range from a low of 76 percent in Scandinavian countries to 99 percent in Sri Lanka (Singh, Viegas and Ratnam 1992; McCauley and Geller 1992, 10–13). For this reason, Norplant is welcomed by family planning clinics, which have long had to deal with the problems of education and compliance posed by techniques that require self-administered, daily maintenance. Norplant and other subdermal implants are a convenient and, perhaps, safer alternative to the pill

---

Robert Blank and Janna C. Merrick, "The Right to Control Fertility: Sterilization and Contraception," *Human Reproduction, Emerging Technologies, and Conflicting Rights*, pp. 63–80. Copyright © 1995 by CQ Press. Reprinted with permission.

(see Laurikka-Routte and Haukkamaa 1992 for a discussion of Progestin ST 1435). The availability of this option may lead to a reduction in the number of tubal ligations performed in the United States.

One problem with Norplant is that the capsules are non-biodegradable and therefore must be surgically removed upon expiration. Clinical trials of biodegradable systems that eliminate the need for removal are now under way. One biodegradable implant, Capronor, consists of a single rod, containing up to 26 mg of levonorgestrel, inserted under the skin of the arm or hip for eighteen months (Darney et al. 1992). Because the walls of the implant break down when exposed to tissue fluids, removal is not necessary unless the patient wishes to discontinue use before using up all of the levonorgestrel. Capronor is being developed by the Research Triangle Institute and is expected to be available on the market in the mid-1990s.

Intracervical Devices and Other Methods for Women

The intracervical contraceptive device (ICD), which is inserted in the cervical canal, has undergone successful preliminary trials in Britain (Kate, Lancet and Shiber 1986). The main part of the mushroom-shaped device is a hollow cylinder made of inert polycarbonate plastic containing a nontoxic silicone rubber valve that prevents the ascent of sperm, while allowing exit of menstrual flux. The cap, attached to the cylinder, prevents penetration of any sperm cells that may have gained access to the area between the cervical walls and the cylinder. The device is inserted and removed with a specially designed inserter and is kept in place by two anchors of stainless steel on the outside of the cylinder.

Another form of intracervical devices is now being developed in Finland. A relatively constant level of levonorgestrel is released from a Silastic reservoir that is inserted in the cervical canal and held in place by horizontal arms located in the uterine opening. Researchers are attempting to refine the design to reduce the unacceptably high rate of expulsion (Rastsula 1988).

Research is still being conducted on the Silastic vaginal ring, which the Population Council predicts will be available for worldwide distribution in the mid-1990s. One variation being tested releases a combination of levonorgestrel and estrogen that virtually stops ovulation. The ring is designed to stay in place for up to three weeks. The woman then removes it for one week and reinserts it herself. The same ring can be used up to six months. Another variation being investigated is a low-dose vaginal ring that releases only levonorgestrel. Although it does not slop ovulation, it suppresses conception by making the cervical mucus impermeable to sperm for the two months it is in place (Liskin and Blackman 1987).

The cervical cap was approved for general use by the FDA in May of 1988. This small, thimble-shaped, rubber barrier contraceptive fits tightly across the cervix, thus preventing sperm from entering the uterus (Shihata and Gollub 1992). It has been shown to be 85 percent effective in preventing pregnancy, a rate comparable to that of the diaphragm but significantly lower than that of long-term subdermal implants. The cap is inserted by the woman and remains for up to sixty hours at a time, but problems remain concerning fit and dislodging (Klitsch 1988).

Fertility Control Methods for Men

Despite the popularity of vasectomy, the number of men electing this procedure has been steadily declining in the United States since the 1970s. Although most research on reversible methods continues to focus on the fallopian tubes, a number of vas deferens occlusion devices have been investigated since the mid-1970s (see Martinez-Manautou et al. 1991). These techniques include: reversible valves or devices that can be switched on or off to regulate passage of sperm through the vas deferens; occlusion plugs and prosthetics similar to the removable silicone plugs used by women; and a variety of clips, injectables, threads and copper devices. Most of them never reached the stage of clinical evaluation, however, and those that did proved to be either ineffective or not sufficiently reversible.

One device that holds promise as an effective, yet reversible, sterilization technique for males has been tested in primates. The Shug consists of two elongated silicone plugs (each approximately 25 mm to 30 mm in length) that are hollow except at the tip and are connected by a 5 cm nylon thread. To implant the Shug, two holes are punctured in the exposed vas deferens. Metal styli are then inserted into each plug, and the plugs are pushed through the holes into the vas deferens. The connecting thread remains partially outside the vas deferens, thus not only holding the plugs in place but allowing for removal of the Shug when reversal is desired. Removal is accomplished by exposing the vas deferens where the plugs are located and pulling the thread with a forceps. Two separate primate experiments showed that the device completely prevents sperm transport during a seven-month period. Moreover, upon its removal, all of the primates ejaculated sperm at normal concentrations and of normal motility. According to one group of researchers, these results "indicate the potential contraceptive use of the device and encourage its validation in men" (Zaneveld el al. 1988, 527).

Voluntary Sterilizations: The Legal Context

The majority of sterilizations performed in the United States are voluntary. In the 1960s and 1970s, largely as a result of the development of less intrusive, safe and effective sterilization procedures, as well as changes in the attitudes of the medical profession and the general public, a substantial effort was made to legalize voluntary sterilization. Legal action concerning voluntary sterilization for fertility control is a relatively recent development; eugenic sterilization, however, has been the subject of statutory and case law since the turn of the century (Kevles 1986).

Voluntary sterilization is now legal in all fifty states. In the first half of the twentieth century, states were hesitant to allow its use for fertility control. In a few states, it was illegal for a physician to perform sterilization for any reason other than the legally defined eugenic indication or a medical necessity. Most states had repealed their restrictions on contraceptive sterilization by 1960; Connecticut, Kansas and Utah did not do so until the early 1970s. In those states, the restrictions resulted in inequities in access to the procedure. The age-parity formula, which stated that the woman's age times the number of her live children had to equal 100 or 120, denied the option to women who had few (or no) living children. There were also requirements that the person seeking sterilization consult at least two physicians and obtain consent of the spouse and that the procedure be performed only in a licensed hospital.

There is considerable variation in the states' voluntary sterilization statutes; in general, however, the requirements fall in four categories:

1. Age requirements for sterilization candidates
2. A waiting period (usually thirty days between obtaining consent form and performance of sterilization)
3. Consent of spouse
4. Second-opinion consultation

In spite of these restrictions, most adults in all fifty states now have the option to undergo contraceptive sterilization.

In addition to the states legislative actions, several court decisions have struck down some of the most constraining legal restrictions. In *Hathawa v. Worcester City Hospital* (1973), a U.S. court of appeals held that the city hospital's refusal to permit use of its facilities for sterilization operations violates the constitutional rights of a woman seeking a tubal ligation for contraceptive purposes. The court held that the Constitution protects the individual's right to both therapeutic and elective sterilizations.

In *Avila v. New York City Health and Hospitals Corporation* (1987), the Bronx County Supreme Court ruled that an institution receiving federal funds and performing sterilizations may not arbitrarily prevent a mentally competent and freely consenting individual from having the operation. Moreover, the state courts have jurisdiction to determine whether the institution's refusal to perform the requested operation is arbitrary. However, in *Chrisman v. Sisters of St. Joseph of Peace* (1974), a suit against a hospital operated by a religious order, a U.S. court of appeals held that the hospital's receipt of federal funds under the Hill-Burton Act of 1946, which provided government grants and loans for the construction and modernization of medical facilities, tax-exempt status and regulation by the state did not constitute sufficient public involvement to require the hospital to make sterilization available. In *Ponter v. Ponter* (1975), the New Jersey Superior Court granted Judith Ponter's right to be sterilized despite her husband's objections. In *Carey v. Population Services International* (1977), the Supreme Court invalidated New Jersey's statutory limitation on a miner's access to contraceptives. It held that this right extended to all forms of birth control, presumably including sterilization.

Although these statutes and court decisions have clarified the legal right to obtain sterilization for fertility control in some jurisdictions, there are still some restrictions on the availability of voluntary sterilization. Publicly supported hospitals cannot refuse to perform sterilizations, but in most states, they still can establish their own policies regarding waiting periods, physician consultation and spousal consent. Furthermore, the 1973 Church Amendment (named for Sen. Frank Church) to the Hill-Burton Act gives private hospitals the right to deny sterilization on moral or religious grounds without loss of federal support for programs such as Medicare. In July 1980, the National Conference of Catholic Bishops affirmed the existence of a ban on the performance of tubal ligations, including therapeutic sterilizations, in Catholic hospitals. Such procedures can be performed only for "grave reasons extrinsic to the case." The restrictions imposed by hospitals have little impact, however, because at present, most sterilizations are done on an outpatient basis—often in a clinic or in the physician's office. But because physicians can also impose their own restrictions on those they consider eligible, in some localities certain categories of persons, especially minors, have difficulty obtaining voluntary sterilization. Many physicians, especially in states that have not addressed the question of minors, require that the patient be over the age of 21, be married and have spousal or parental consent. Some states require waiting periods ranging from seventy-two hours to thirty days (the same as the waiting period for all federally funded sterilizations) to minimize the possibility that a person might change his or her mind after the procedure is completed.

Insurance policies vary in their coverage of sterilization operations. Many policies treat contraceptive sterilization as a medical procedure, whatever its motivation; others distinguish between medically indicated and elective sterilization and reimburse only the former. Some policies specifically exclude non-therapeutic sterilization. Obviously, this consideration might discourage or even prevent individuals with limited financial resources from seeking voluntary sterilization. Because Medicaid coverage for sterilization is a matter of state, not federal, jurisdiction, there is wide variation; about one-quarter of the states exclude coverage for elective sterilization.

Involuntary or Nonconsensual Sterilization: The Continuing Controversy

Early in the twentieth century, interest in sterilization was prompted by its possibilities for achieving societal control; individual choice was not a consideration. Legislators were influenced both by medical theories that menial illness was inherited and by social, elitist theories stemming from social Darwinism (Kevles 1986). Since the 1930s, nonconsensual sterilization has been used as a means to achieve population control, reduce societal burdens, minimize genetic defects in the population and as a punitive device for criminals and other undesirables; it has also been motivated by racism. Sterilization performed with the informed consent of the subject now enjoys widespread support in the United States, but sterilization performed without regard for individual choice arouses considerable controversy. Sterilization, no matter how high-minded when voluntary, is subject to abuse.

It should be noted that the term *nonconsensual* has at least two meanings. It can refer to sterilization that is not voluntary because the patient is legally incompetent to exercise informed consent. The parents of a mentally retarded woman who petition the court for permission to have her sterilized are seeking to substitute their consent for hers. This type of involuntary sterilization is always problematic because it is difficult to determine what the subject would choose if he or she were capable of informed consent. The term can also refer to sterilization that is compulsory: A person who is legally capable of informed consent is coerced to be sterilized; consent is not even requested.

Federal Government Involvement in Sterilization

The federal government funds approximately 10 percent of all sterilizations annually. It is the primary source of funding for poor women, affording them the option to exercise control over their fertility. In the fiscal year of 1987, the federal and state governments together spent $412 million on fertility control services for women who might not otherwise have been able to obtain them (Forrest and Singh 1990, 6). Almost all publicly funded sterilizations are paid for by Medicaid (88 percent in 1987); thus the costs are shared by the state and federal governments. Although most of these applications are voluntary and based on the informed consent of recipients, the government's involvement has aroused suspicion and been the subject of criticism. This should not be surprising, given the history of eugenic sterilization in the United States in the early twentieth century, the mistrust of many groups to state intervention (even if it is intended to be beneficial for the recipients) and instances of coerced sterilization. Welfare workers threatened recipients with a loss of benefits unless they agreed to be sterilized (Nsiah-Jefferson 1989, 30). Women were allegedly sterilized without their knowledge while they were, ostensibly, in the hospital for an abortion or some other operation (Mains and Poggi 1990, 284). Such reports continued to surface, even after passage of the Family Planning Services and Population Research Act of 1970 made sterilization available in federally funded clinics. The Court alluded to them in its decision in *Relf v. Weinberger* (1974):

> Although Congress has been insistent that all family planning programs function on a purely voluntary basis, there is uncontroverted evidence in the record that minors and other incompetents have been sterilized with federal funds and that an indefinite number of poor people have been improperly coerced into accepting a sterilization operation under the threat that various federally supported welfare benefits would be withdrawn unless they submitted to irreversible sterilization. Patients receiving Medicaid assistance at childbirth are evidently the most frequent targets of this pressure (at 1198).

Prior to 1973, the Public Health Service (which in 1953 became part of the Department of Health, Education and Welfare, or HEW, which was renamed the Department of Health and Human Services in 1979) funded sterilization, along with other family planning services for the poor, under a number of programs. The regulations imposed on state and private agencies receiving these federal grants simply required that all services, including sterilization, be "voluntary" and shall not be a prerequisite to eligibility for or receipt of any other service or assistance from or to participation in any other program of the entity or individual that provided such service or information (42 USC 300, A-5). After reports of abuse, HEW issued final regulations for sterilization procedures February 6, 1974, whose enforcement was to be deferred at the request of the Court until March 18, 1974. These regulations permitted the sterilization of persons under the age of 21 and persons legally incapable of giving informed consent under certain conditions that included a waiting period of at least 72 hours between provision of written consent and performance of sterilization and a warning about the risks and the irreversibility of sterilization. Welfare recipients also had to be informed, prior to giving consent, that their benefits could not be withdrawn should they refuse to undergo the procedure.

Almost immediately, court action was initiated to enjoin implementation of the HEW rules. On March 15, 1974, Judge Gerhard A. Gesell of the U.S. District Court for the District of Columbia, in the combined cases of *Relf v. Weinberger* and *National Welfare Rights Organization v. Weinberger*, held that they were inconsistent with the statutory requirement of voluntariness.

> No person who is mentally incompetent can meet these standards, nor can the consent of a representative, however sufficient under state law, impute voluntariness to the individual actually undergoing irreversible sterilization (at 1202).

For this reason, the court permanently enjoined HEW from providing federal funds for the sterilization of individuals who were under the age of 21 or whom the courts had determined to be incompetent to give informed consent.

This injunction held until 1977, when the Court of Appeals for the District of Columbia vacated the order of the lower court in *Relf* and ruled that HEW had statutory authority to define a federal standard of voluntariness. The department subsequently published its proposed rules in the *Federal Register* and invited written comments as well as the voicing of opinions at public hearings that were held throughout the United States. In November 1978, it issued final regulations concerning sterilization performed under programs and projects funded by its Public Health Service and Social and Rehabilitation Service.

Significantly, the regulations, which became effective on February 6, 1979, prohibit federal funding for the sterilization of persons under the age of 21, institutionalized persons and persons legally incompetent to give informed consent. The regulations also prohibit the overt or implicit threat of loss of welfare or Medicaid benefits as a consequence of non-consent and prohibit the performance of hysterectomies for purposes of sterilization under federally funded programs. Sterilization on the basis of substituted consent is not permitted. Informed consent cannot be obtained while a person is in labor or under the influence of alcohol or drugs or immediately before or after an abortion. The informed consent form must be signed by the person seeking sterilization, the person who obtains the consent, the physician performing the sterilization and an interpreter, if one is necessary. Complete information concerning the risks, side effects and irreversibility of sterilization, as well as alternative methods of contraception, must be given in the patient's own language, both orally and in writing. A waiting period of at least thirty days is required.

The regulations were attacked on several grounds. Liberal critics argued that they did not go far enough in preventing coerced sterilization of the poor and protecting their rights (Petehesky 1979). They also pointed out that the cutoff of federal funding of abortion and the cutback of prenatal service for poor women leaves sterilization as the only option for some of them. According to the Committee to Defend Reproductive Rights, poor women are sterilized at disproportionately higher rates than non-poor women (1985, 1). For example, in the 1970s, sterilization rates for women who were on welfare were 49 percent higher than those for women who were not. Moreover, women of color have been sterilized in higher proportions than white women: 20 percent of black women, 24 percent of Native American women, 22 percent of Chicanas and 37 percent of Puerto Rican women were sterilized in 1979, compared with 16 percent of white women (1935, 2).

Conservatives contended that reports of abuse had been exaggerated and that the effect of the stringent regulations and arbitrary judgments by administrators was to deny sterilization to many indigents. They asserted that although the 1979 regulations' criteria of minimum age and minimum number of children were reasonable prerequisites for sterilization in order to reduce the "regret potential" for patients, the imposition of overly strict restrictions on women who were on public assistance prevented them from obtaining their desired form of fertility control. Most of the criticism was leveled at the thirty-day waiting periods, which was viewed as paternalistic (in that it required women to delay their choice and to be guided by what authorities deemed best for them) and as reflecting a failure to acknowledge the plight of most poor women. Critics also argued that it might also subject a woman to the risk of having two surgeries if she consented to a postpartum sterilization but delivered prematurely before expiration of the thirty-day limit then had to return for a sterilization (Chi, Gates and Thapa 1992).

State Legislative Action

The 1979 federal regulations have done little to reduce the frequency of nonconsensual sterilization because they apply only to operations subsidized by federal funding. Most cases of nonconsensual sterilization fall within the jurisdiction of the states, not the federal government. The states' policies regulating the sterilization of those deemed incapable of giving informed consent are inconsistent and often contradictory.

Since 1980, an increasing number of state legislatures have demonstrated renewed interest in nonconsensual sterilization statutes. Table 3.1.5 lists the twenty-one states that, in 1988, had statutes permitting nonconsensual sterilization; it indicates the diversity of their general provisions. Four states permit nonconsensual sterilization of

Table 3.1.1 State Legislation for Nonconsensual Sterilization, 1988

State	Person sterilized		Initiator			
	Institutionalized only	Anyone	Administrator	Parent or guardian	*Procedural safeguards*	*Court order required*
Arkansas		X		X	X	X
California		X		X	X	X
Colorado		X		X	X	X
Connecticut		X	X	X	X	X
Delaware		X	X		X	
Georgia		X		X	X	X
Idaho		X	X	X	X	X
Kentucky		X				
Maine		X	X		X	
Minnesota		X	X	X	X	X
Mississippi	X		X		X	
New Hampshire		X		X	X	X
North Carolina		X	X	X	X	X
North Dakota	X		X	X	X	X
Oklahoma	X		X		X	
Oregon		X	X	X	X	
South Carolina	X		X		X	
Utah		X	X		X	X
Vermont		X	X	X	X	X
Virginia		X	X	X	X	X
West Virginia		X	X	X	X	X

Source: Adapted from Association for Voluntary Surgical Contraception 1988.

institutionalized persons only; the institution's superintendent is usually the official required to initiate the request. Seventeen states permit sterilization of persons in the community as well as those in institutions. In fourteen states, parents or legal guardians can initiate sterilization proceedings; in Virginia, the spouse or "next friend" also has that authority. Those sterilized usually include the menially retarded or mentally ill and, in a few states, epileptics. The Delaware statute authorizes sterilization of habitual criminals.

Although all but seven states require a hearing prior to sterilization, the procedural safeguards vary considerably from state to state. Four states require only an administrative hearing, usually conducted by the director of the state department that has jurisdiction over public institutions. Nine states require a full judicial hearing prior to the performance of sterilization.

They also grant the right to counsel to the person who is to be sterilized, the right to be present and to cross-examine witnesses and the right to receive a full record of all testimony, both written and oral. Eight states substituted consent by the parent or guardian; several states also require such consent by the spouse of the person to be sterilized. Fourteen states require a court order before the sterilization can be performed.

These nonconsensual sterilization laws are evidence of the move away from a eugenic rationale. Only in four states does the legislation require eugenic or hereditary grounds for sterilization; the laws of three of them require other grounds as well. Increasingly, the statutory standards for sterilization include references to "the inability to care for and support children," the "best interests of the person" or the "welfare of society."

Judicial Action on Nonconsensual Sterilization

In recent years, the most conspicuous activity regarding nonconsensual sterilization has been centered in the courts and has focused on two questions: (1) Are the state statutes constitutional? and (2) In the absence of express statutory authorization, do the courts have jurisdiction to approve petitions for the sterilization of persons who are incompetent? The courts' response to the first question has generally been a qualified yes. Although the courts have not always agreed in their response to the second question, they have increasingly assumed jurisdiction by issuing orders allowing sterilization but within strict parameters.

The Constitutionality of State Statutes

The courts have tended to agree that nonconsensual sterilization statutes are constitutional, following the precedent of *Buck v. Bell* (1927), in which the Supreme Court upheld eugenic sterilization. The majority opinion included Justice Oliver Wendell Holmes's dictum that "[t]hree generations of imbeciles are enough." They have, however, gradually narrowed that precedent by ruling that specific statutes lack necessary due process elements, such as the right to counsel, to a hearing or to an appeal. In these cases, the courts have usually left it up to the legislatures to rewrite the laws to include both procedural and substantive protections for the targets of sterilization. In *Lulos v. State* (1990), an Indiana appellate court held that a guardian's petition for sterilization of an incompetent adult should be granted upon "clear and convincing evidence that the judicially appointed guardian brought the petition for sterilization in good faith and the sterilization is in the best interest of the incompetent adult" (at 174). The appeals court ruled that the trial court erred in using a more stringent standard of proof than the Indiana law dictated when it denied the petition for nonconsensual sterilization.

In *North Carolina Association for Retarded Children v. North Carolina* (1976), a U.S. district court left standing the right of a slate legislature to enact sterilization laws but only in certain circumstances. The court explicitly dismissed eugenic bases for mandating sterilization and rejected specific provisions of the North Carolina statute. It pointed to substantial medical opinion that sterilization might be desirable as a last resort and in relatively extreme cases. Sterilization might be warranted in cases where there were clearly identifiable genetic defects and a "significant probability" that offspring would inherit them. Cause for sterilization might also be established if a mentally retarded person were incapable of discharging the responsibility of parenthood because of the inability to create a non-detrimental environment for his or her progeny. Other indications for sterilization, the court noted, included a person's inability to understand that the natural consequence of sexual activity is a child, a person's desire not to have children, combined with the inability to use other forms of birth control and, in rare cases, a medical determination that sterilization would be in the best interests of either the mentally retarded person or the state, or both.

Using a somewhat different rationale, the Oregon Court of Appeals, in *Cook v. State* (1972), upheld as constitutional an Oregon statute that authorized involuntary sterilization. The court approved the sterilization of a 17-year-old girl on the grounds that if she were to have children, they would most likely be neglected and become wards of the state because she was incapable of caring for them. The court ruled that it was therefore proper to sterilize her. In *Motes v. Hail*, County Department of Family and Children Services (1983), however, the Supreme Court of Georgia declared that the state statute permitting the involuntary sterilization of mentally incompetent persons was unconstitutional because it denied those persons the right to procreate.

Equitable Jurisdiction of the Courts to Order Sterilization

Before 1980, with few exceptions, the courts generally ruled that they did not have authorization to order the permanent sterilization of incompetent persons if there had not been an express legislative grant of such power. Higher courts that assumed jurisdiction in such cases include the Supreme Court of Alaska *(In the Matter of C. D. M.,* 1981), as well as those of Colorado *(In the Matter of A. W.,* 1981), Iowa *(In the Matter of Guardian ship of Hayes,* 1980), New Hampshire *(In the Matter of Penny N.,* 1980), New Jersey *(In the Matter of Grady,* 1981), Washington *(In the Matter of Guardianship of Hayes,* 1980) and Wisconsin *(In the Matter of Guardianship of Eberhardy,* 1981). Although the signals coming from the courts are not always consistent or unequivocal, there is a clear indication that courts are increasingly accepting what most of them had previously perceived as legislative role: In the absence of authorizing statutes, they are assuming jurisdiction in matters that concern the sterilization of those incapable of giving consent. In *Conservatorship of Valerie N.* (1985), the Supreme Court of California invoked the jurisprudence of fundamental rights to invalidate a California statute that prohibited the sterilization of menial and retarded persons. In a long majority opinion, from which there was strong dissent by Chief Justice Rose E. Bird, Justice Jose Grodin argued that the statute "impermissibly deprives developmentally disabled persons of privacy and liberty interests protected by the Fourteenth Amendment ... and ... the California Constitution" (at 771–772). By denying the option of sterilization to an incompetent woman, the statute deprived her of her only realistic opportunity for contraception and consequently restricted her chances for self-fulfillment. "Since the right to elect sterilization as a method of contraception is generally available to adult women in this state, the restriction [of that right] must be justified by a compelling state interest" (at 774).

Despite the increased acceptance by the courts of their jurisdiction to approve petitions for nonconsensual sterilization in the absence of authorizing statutes, there is a hesitancy to order irreversible sterilization, except under extreme circumstances. For instance, although the appellate court in *Wentzel v. Montgomery General Hospital, Inc.* (1982) concluded that "circuit courts, acting in pursuance of their inherent *parens patriae* authority have subject matter jurisdiction to consider a petition for an order authorizing a guardian to consent to sterilization of an incompetent minor" (at 1253), it rejected the petition for the hysterectomy of a 13-year-old girl on the grounds that the evidence did not support such drastic action.

The Irreversibility Assumption

The availability of safe and effective sterilization techniques that offer a high rate of reversibility, along with long-term subdermal implants, will create a climate of increased social pressure for nonconsensual sterilization. Sterilization no longer represents the permanent destruction of a person's reproductive capacity caused by conventional surgical sterilization but rather a less intrusive and presumably temporary cessation of fertility. From a purely technical standpoint, nonconsensual sterilization is more easily justified under such circumstances. These same innovations that promise to make sterilization less invasive technically, however,, also threaten to increase the frequency of its use for eugenic or social control purposes by eliminating the most objectionable aspect of invasion—irreversibility.

Just as advancements in sterilization techniques in the 1890s helped rationalize compulsory sterilization, current innovations with regard to reversible procedures will make them a less objectionable means of solving social problems. Courts that have refused to order sterilizations or have vacated lower court orders for sterilization have consistently emphasized the irreversible nature of the procedure. In a 1974 case, *In the Interest of M. K. R.*, the Supreme Court of Missouri disallowed the sterilization of a woman with an IQ of 50. Judge Fred Henley explained that this "routine operation would irreversibly deny to a human being a fundamental right, the right to bear or beget a child" (at 470, emphasis added). He argued that the jurisdiction to exercise the power to deprive a person *permanently* of this right may be conferred only by a special statute.

Similarly, in *Relf v. Weinberger* (1974), Judge Gesell of the U.S. district court flatly stated, "Sterilization of females or males is irreversible" (at 1199). The court rejected the federal government's attempts to sanction

> one of the most drastic methods of population control—the involuntary irreversible sterilization of men and women—without any legislative guidance.... We should not drift into a policy, which has unfathomed implications and which permanently deprives ... citizens of their ability to procreate without adequate legal safeguards (at 1204).

This argument echoes Justice William O. Douglas's opinion In *Skinner v. Oklahoma* (1942):

> The power to sterilize, if exercised, may have subtle, far-reaching and devastating effects ... There is no redemption for the individual whom the law touches. Any experiment which the State conducts is to his irreparable injury. He is *forever* deprived of a basic liberty (at 541, emphasis added).

Similar conclusions were reached by a U.S. district court in *North Carolina Association for Retarded Children v. North Carolina* (1976), when it voided parts of the North Carolina sterilization statute: "Sterilization is a drastic procedure, almost impossible to reverse in females and difficult and uncertain to reverse in males, that is intended to be permanent" (at 454). Such a drastic measure, said the court, requires that a heavy burden of proof be placed on those who institute proceedings for sterilization: "The burden of proof put upon the petitioner [by the North Carolina Supreme Court] that the evidence must be clear, strong and convincing strongly protect against predictive error" (at 458). In *Wyatt v. Aderholt* (1974), a federal district court defined sterilization as "any medical or surgical operation or procedure, which results in a patient's permanent inability to reproduce" (at 1384).

Rosalind Petchesky has taken a strong stand against the practice of involuntary sterilization in the United States, basing her argument on the assumption of irreversibility. Sterilization is a procedure that

> renders a person permanently unable to bear children.... While the ethics of a biomedical procedure are never determined by technology alone, the virtually irreversible nature of surgical sterilization makes the choice a more drastic one than it might be otherwise. (1979, 29).

As she cogently explains in her defense of thirty-day waiting periods, although they are frequently a source of inconvenience, women need to understand fully the ramifications of having their "bodies and reproductive capacities ... irrevocably altered" (36).

Although Petchesky's assumption of irreversibility was generally accurate in 1979, the question here is the extent to which her argument is undermined by the availability and use of technically reversible procedures, particularly subdermal implants. She argues that the ethics of a biomedical procedure are not determined by technology alone, but technology plays a major role in defining the context of decision making and the range of choices available. Petchesky notes that the permanency of sterilization makes the choice a more drastic one than it might otherwise be. This implies that when reversible techniques become available, the choice will become less drastic. The question is, how much less so?

With the emergence of reversible procedures, will the courts be prompted to reconsider their opinions and allow reversible techniques to be used, or will they attempt to devise a basis other than irreversibility to reject these new procedures? At the least, the emphasis will have to be shifted to practical irreversibility in the cases they are examining.

Such methods as Norplant may be technically reversible, but once they are applied involuntarily to a mentally retarded person, or a mother on welfare, it is unlikely that they will be reversed, no matter how effective the reversal procedure. Control over fertility is taken out of the hands of the method's user and placed in the hands of specialists in the health care profession. Only a health care professional (most likely, a physician) has the ability to remove the implant or reverse the procedure. In contrast, control over the use of the pill, condom, diaphragm and, to a lesser extent, the IUD is retained by the user. Whatever strategy the critics adopt to challenge technological advances in reversible means of fertility control, their task in demonstrating the dangers of nonconsensual compulsory sterilization will be made more difficult by the abolition of the assumption of permanency.

Reducing the Economic Burden: Sterilizing Welfare Recipients

The economic motivation for nonconsensual sterilization is not a new one. In *Buck v. Bell* (1927), the superintendent of the State Colony for Epileptics and Feeble Minded for the State of Virginia testified that there would be a great savings to the state if girls like Carrie Buck could be sterilized and released, rather than institutionalized during their childbearing years. Much of the controversy over federal funding of sterilizations and the resulting HEW regulations of 1979 was provoked by assertions of widespread coerced sterilization of women on welfare (Docksai 1981, 10). Pressure to reduce rising welfare costs combined with moral indignation over some well-publicized welfare abuse cases, led to the introduction in some state legislatures of measures authorizing the sterilization of women on welfare after they had had a specified number of illegitimate children. Although none of these measures has yet been passed, they continue to have the support of many state policy makers.

Opponents of the sterilization of mothers on welfare charge that it is the fundamental right of every woman to bear children and that sterilization often precludes that choice. They agree that the exercise of this right by these women might impose a financial burden on society but argue that the state exists primarily to protect the interests and rights of all socioeconomic groups. The court in *Relf v. Weinberger* concluded that maintenance of the state's fiscal integrity is not a compelling interest when a fundamental right, like procreation, is held in the balance. The opponents argue that any intervention that limits the procreative choice of women on public assistance is not only a wholesale violation of the woman's rights but an obvious attempt to eliminate whole groups of people by terminating their fertility.

The argument of many who advocate limiting the procreative choice of women on public assistance plays into the hands of the critics. Dwight Ingle (1973), for instance, argues that the quality of the gene pool is deteriorating because the birth rates of the educated middle class are increasing more slowly than those of the uneducated poor, and that the survival of society therefore demands intervention in the area of reproduction.

Although coerced, irreversible sterilization is antithetical to the principles of a free society, encouragement of the use of reversible methods has some merits, which must be balanced against the costs. Many children born to women on welfare are unplanned and unwanted, as evidenced by the figures on abortion among these women—approximately 300,000 per year before the Hyde Amendment ended federal funding of abortions in 1978. If the premise is correct that these women wish to control fertility but have an understandable aversion to permanent sterilization, then providing access to reversible techniques that allow the woman to have ultimate control for reversal might be an appropriate solution.

The availability of reversible fertility control techniques makes it easier for many persons to rationalize their use by women on welfare and, ironically, increases their potential for abuse because they are perceived as a less extreme intrusion. Reversibility might facilitate the passage of statutes similar to the measures introduced in many state legislatures but defeated because of the irreversibility of conventional techniques.

Reversibility has raised some yet-unanswered questions. Who ultimately has the power to reverse sterilization? Although the removal of subdermal implants is likely to be a relatively simple and inexpensive medical procedure, it must be performed by a trained health care professional and thus will entail an expense. Should the government provide welfare recipients, who have undergone sterilization, the opportunity, and the funding, for its reversal? Under what conditions is reversal warranted? Is there a real likelihood of reversal for most women whose sterilization was funded by governmental programs as long as they remain on welfare, or must they get off welfare before reversal can be considered? These questions must be resolved if policy makers are to view reversible sterilization as a possible way of reducing the expenditure of scarce public resources in response to the taxpayers' demands to cut government spending.

Women and the Dilemmas of Modern Motherhood

By Liza Mundy

"Your Numbers Look Good"

Lunchtime in downtown Washington. Spezie, a crowded restaurant specializing in upscale Italian for the downtown power diner. The woman across from me: a friend of a friend. I'll call her Melanie. She prefers not to be identified by her real name, because all of this is still tentative and ongoing. She is wide-eyed, freckled, uncosmeticized, likable, humorous, smart, self-deprecating, slender, married. She looks thirty-five but is forty-two. In much of her story she typifies the modern fertility patient, who when she begins treatment swears, "I will never do IVF."

Melanie grew up in a working-class town in the mid-Atlantic region. Summers, as a teenager, she held down two jobs. Having worked hard to get into a top-flight university, having done well there and pursued her MBA afterward, Melanie pursued what is, for her, extremely satisfying public service work in the nonprofit sector. Melanie is number two in her office, and has been number two for several years. Being number two is in some ways harder than being number one; being number two means taking care of the administrative scutwork number one doesn't bother with; it means running the office when number one is away; it means striving to be good enough to be, someday, number one herself. Among other things, being number two has meant that there has not been a natural opportunity to have a baby. Nevertheless, she has always wanted children; so three years ago, when she was thirty-nine, she and her husband decided they'd better get started.

It was, she thinks now, about three years too late.

She did get pregnant naturally. At least, that's what the blood test confirmed. The pregnancy turned out to be a blighted ovum, something she had never heard of but would soon became all too familiar with. "Blighted ovum" means that the sperm fertilizes the egg, but the embryo never develops, and instead halts as an empty sac, a not-fetus, a missed opportunity. A blighted ovum is a form of miscarriage. Sometimes it is voided naturally by the body, and sometimes, as in Melanie's case, it is scraped out of the uterus by a procedure known as dilation and curettage. After that unpleasant experience—knowing that even this unsuccessful pregnancy had taken months to achieve—her gynecologist proposed that she take clomiphene citrate, a low-level, orally administered fertility drug, commonly known as Clomid, that would stimulate her ovaries to make sure they were still expelling a monthly egg. This is known as the Clomid challenge; it's a diagnostic test of the female reproductive system, like something a mechanic would perform on an engine.

A challenge! Excellent! Melanie took the Clomid.

Liza Mundy, "Women and the Dilemmas of Modern Motherhood," *Everything Conceivable: How the Science of Assisted Reproduction Is Changing Our World*, pp. 24–59. Copyright © 2008 by Random House, Inc. Reprinted with permission.

"Your numbers look good," her gynecologist told her afterward, which was sort of like saying, "Here is a yummy liver bit" to a well-trained dog. It was the kind of comment to which she has been programmed to respond.

Numbers looking good is how Melanie has lived her life. Her numbers have always looked good, and she has worked hard to make those numbers look better. If her numbers looked good, then clearly treatment would eventually work. Melanie decided to ratchet things up a notch. On her doctor's recommendation she visited a private fertility clinic, where she tried intrauterine insemination (IUI), often regarded as the natural next step after Clomid. IUI involves injecting a concentrated dose of sperm directly into a woman's uterus, to increase the odds of fertilization. IUI usually also involves taking a stronger drug, aimed at persuading the woman's body to produce more than a single egg each month. A drug like this must be injected. Melanie found herself sitting in her bathroom every night, palms sweating, flicking the vial to dispel air bubbles, sure that she would be the one patient to die of an embolism. Night after night she made the injection. Morning after morning she woke up with bruises on her thigh. She was hooked now. She was engaged. She was trying.

"It was my makeup," she says now. "There hasn't been anything I've wanted that I haven't gotten. It's awful but it's true."

Problem was, the shots weren't working. Or maybe they were. It was hard to know. She would go into the doctor's office for the ultrasound tests that would tell whether her Graafian follicles, the fluid-filled cysts where eggs grow and mature, were enlarging in response to the drug. But the nurse was reticent and Melanie couldn't make out what was happening on the ultrasound screen. The night came when she was supposed to take the "trigger" shot: another drug, one that causes the eggs to be released. But now—finally—the doctor was on the phone and, without saying what was wrong, told her just to take her trigger shot and "have sex with your husband." It wasn't worth coming in for the insemination procedure. Apparently what had looked like a follicle wasn't. Or something.

Melanie decided she hated that doctor. So she went to a hospital practice, where women queue up when the door opens at seven. There is little privacy in a hospital. That part was bad. But she happened to get a terrific young female doctor who fully understood what she was going through. They decided it was time for full-blown IVF, which months earlier Melanie had considered unthinkable, but now seemed like a natural transition. Again Melanie would take the shots to stimulate her ovaries. This time, the eggs would be surgically removed before the hormones could cause her own ovaries to ovulate, and fertilized with her husband's sperm through IVF. Following this regimen Melanie produced thirteen eggs, which was good, and about half of those eggs were fertilized, which was also promising. The best two embryos were transferred, and a blood test confirmed she was pregnant. One morning she joined the women lining up for the big eight-week ultrasound. She sat there in her paper gown while other elated women emerged saying things like "It's twins!" to their beaming partners. She went in and found out that what was growing inside her was … a blighted ovum.

It was the day before Thanksgiving. Melanie and her husband were supposed to spend the holiday with her in-laws, who lived in another state. Her husband—figuring somebody had to go—went. She stayed in their apartment, curled up in a little ball Her blood tests were continuing to come back normal. "I'm just old," she says now. "If we had started when I was thirty-six or thirty-seven, I'm sure we would have a child. There's nothing aside from age that's wrong with me."

How Women Got Here: A Brief History of Female Infertility

And yet "age" is a diagnosis few foresaw thirty years ago, when reproductive technology experienced a quantum leap forward. In fact, when one of the first IVF clinics in the United States opened, there was an age limit for female patients. In the early 1980s, no woman older than thirty-five was accepted into the Jones Institute for Reproductive Medicine. IVF was seen as a technology for the younger woman, recently married, who wanted a family and because of specific physiological problems couldn't have one naturally.

"We limited our cases at first to those women who had had their Fallopian tubes removed," explains Howard Jones, elegant and white haired, who today happens to be wearing a fuchsia shirt that a British colleague literally gave him off his back at a meeting when Jones admired it. Sitting in his capacious office in Norfolk, Virginia, Jones, now in his nineties and semiretired, describes the first group of patients treated in the Jones clinic, which is affiliated with Eastern Virginia Medical School. Back then, he says, the clinic wanted to maximize the chances of pregnancy, and also wanted to be sure this new technique, IVF, was responsible for any children that were conceived. If a woman got pregnant who had no Fallopian tubes at all—no natural passageway between ovaries and uterus, no way for an egg to slip through so that fertilization could occur naturally—then success could be due only to science. And if IVF worked for tubeless women, presumably it would work for other young women who suffered from tubal blockages. These were considered the target group for a new therapy that some doctors still viewed as freakish, irrelevant, a kind of unimportant scientific parlor trick.

And there were many such women. Among women, infertility has always existed. Contrary to popular belief, female infertility is not a new condition that has been inflicted as punishment on career women who have dallied overlong in fulfilling their reproductive duty. Historically and today, female infertility often results from tubal scarring, the result of pelvic infections that can be due to any number of causes, including sexually transmitted diseases but also childbirth itself. In fact, childbirth is a frequent cause of infertility in third-world countries, where, ironically both fertility rates *and* infertility rates tend to be highest. Other common causes of infertility are fibroids, or large uterine growths; endometriosis, a painful condition where the menstrual lining grows outside the uterus; and hormonal imbalances, such as polycystic ovarian syndrome (PCOS), that interfere with ovulation. All these conditions have waxed and waned over time. In this country there is less infection now than formerly, thanks to condoms and antibiotics, but there are more ovulatory problems, owing in part to the nation's obesity epidemic as well as other, contradictory trends: there is a form of PCOS—you could call it the Upper East Side version—that comes from being too thin.

In addition, as Margaret Marsh and Wanda Ronner outline in *The Empty Cradle: Infertility in America from Colonial Times to the Present,* there has always been infertility imposed on women by outside forces. In the nineteenth century, double standards for sexual behavior caused many virgin brides to suffer pelvic pain not long after their wedding night; visiting their doctor, they learned that they had contracted gonorrhea, and with it infertility, from their new husbands. In the twentieth century, fads for reproductive surgery prompted the gratuitous removal of organs. One contemporary doctor, David Keefe, remembers training with a gynecologist who, every time he removed a woman's uterus during a hysterectomy, held it up and said, with relish: "Another brick for the villa." Keefe himself was deeply affected by a young woman he knew growing up, who was diagnosed with a cancer called vaginal clear-cell adenocarcinoma. During pregnancy the girl's mother had been given diethylstilbestrol, or DES, a drug widely prescribed in the 1950s and '60s by doctors who believed, wrongly, that it would prevent miscarriage. Instead, it had devastating effects on female fetuses. Some DES daughters, like the young woman Keefe knew, would die of cancer; others would grow up to find their own reproductive organs malformed. A coalition of scientists, the Collaborative on Health and the Environment, organized by a women's health group at Stanford University medical school, is attempting to discover whether other forms of female infertility are the result of the chemical revolution—whether plastics and other chemical compounds are affecting human reproduction in subtle ways. The U.S. government has also launched a major project, Life Study, that will track the fertility of a thousand men and women, to evaluate the reproductive effects of the tens of thousands of chemicals that are now a routine part of our sleeping, eating, and working lives.

Let it not be forgotten either that some have always unfairly blamed women for creating their own barrenness, through book learning and ambition. Excessive education "is accountable for much of the sterility and physical degeneracy of American womanhood," tut-tutted doctor and social commentator Horace Bigelow in 1883; he was appalled by the trend of women attending colleges in substantial numbers, which, he believed, led to "a want of reverence for her special vocation," motherhood. His concerns were shared by Harvard physician Edward H. Clarke, who wrote in 1873 that female "sterility" was caused by education of women, which diverted energy from the womb to the brain, leaving women with "monstrous brains and puny bodies."

And naturally there have always been folk willing to peddle a solution. "A baby in every bottle" is what Lydia Pinkham, purveyor of a nineteenth century "vegetable compound," promised women who drank her fertility tonic. A poster from the time shows a chubby baby sitting in a bottle, and a woman guzzling tonic while a man—her husband? her doctor?—looks fiercely on. For many years, as Marsh and Ronner also document, the field of fertility cures was populated both by quacks and by genuine healers: one early surgeon, suspecting women were infertile because their cervical openings were too small, created a vogue for surgical enlargements of the vagina, done with a scalpel, often without anesthetic. During the twentieth century, some real strides began to be made: surgery got better and in some cases may even have helped. Equally important, doctors discovered the reproductive hormones. Chief among these pioneers was John Rock, whose midcentury experiments with estrogen and progesterone would famously lead to the birth control pill, but also—with less notice—to advances in fertility treatment. Women now could be given drugs that in some cases would regulate their ovulation and result in much-wanted pregnancies. As early as 1942, Rock achieved the first reported attempt at IVF (it is not clear whether fertilization occurred), but never transferred an embryo. An article in *Look* prompted hundreds of women to write to Rock begging to be guinea pigs in his research, including one who wrote that life was "empty and useless without children."

Rock would later comment that he found infertile women who wanted babies far more willing to subject themselves to experiments than fertile ones who wanted contraception. And of course, Edwards and Steptoe found no end of eager subjects. When Louise Brown was born, Robert Edwards remarked that IVF signaled "the end of the beginning:" the end of gory interventions and the beginning of something like effective treatment for millions of women worldwide.

The End of the Beginning

In the United States, the first IVF child was born in 1981 thanks to the work of two Joneses: Howard and his wife, Georgeanna, who both had distinguished careers caring for the infertile. Howard Jones was a gynecological surgeon who had collaborated with Robert Edwards during a stay Edwards made in the United States. Equally eminent, Georgeanna Jones was a reproductive endocrinologist (an ob-gyn who specializes in treating infertility) who had much success with gonadotropins, the hormonal drugs that stimulate ovulation. The Joneses themselves had three children and an extremely close marriage. In 1977—forced to retire from Johns Hopkins University, which had a mandatory retirement age of sixty-five—they were persuaded to take over the department of obstetrics and gynecology at Eastern Virginia Medical School. They happened to move there on the day Louise Brown was born in England. During the hullabaloo, a television reporter asked Howard Jones whether a test-tube pregnancy could be achieved in the States. Jones replied that it could, easily. Asked what it would take, he replied, "Money."

The next day, the Joneses received a call from a former patient who had had a child thanks to a drug regimen of Dr. Georgeanna Jones's devising. The grateful woman wanted to fund the first U.S. IVF clinic. She offered $5,000 to purchase a microscope and an incubator. Other benefactors followed, and within a few months, the Joneses had $25,000, which, amazingly, was enough to set up an IVF lab. Women, it should be noted, have always driven infertility research, not just with their bodies but, when they had some, with their money. Edwards and Steptoe also owed part of their success to the fact that a California woman stepped in to underwrite their controversial IVF project, after other, more conventional funders bowed out.

Money also came from unlikely sources: When the Norfolk clinic was being established, it was bitterly opposed by pro-life groups, who—leery of any work involving human embryos—wanted to stop IVF before it got started. A Virginia pro-life organization tried to prevent the medical school from obtaining the "certificate of need" required by the state to set up any new clinic. Having failed at that, pro-life groups continued to send letters and organize protests. When the Norfolk *Virginian-Pilot* ran an editorial erroneously saying that the Joneses were forcing patients to get prenatal testing and to agree in advance to abort any abnormal pregnancy, Georgeanna Jones sued the paper's parent company for $5.5 million, and plowed the money from the settlement back into the clinic. Still, the pro-lifers exacted some concessions: in the early days, the clinic promised that all embryos would be used, and that none would be disposed of.

In those days, the Jones clinic attracted staffers who would go on to become the architects and in some cases the superstars of the field, along with colleagues in countries such as Australia, England, and France. Among the first generation was Lucinda Veeck (later Lucinda Veeck Gosden), a young scientist who helped advance the field of embryology by, among other things, producing a picture atlas of human embryos. Another was Zev Rosenwaks, a reproductive endocrinologist who, like Veeck Gosden, would later move to the Manhattan clinic affiliated with Cornell University and New York–Presbyterian, where he trained many in the next generation of doctors. In the United States, IVF clinics were created at a few medical schools, including the one at Yale University, where psychotherapist Dorothy Greenfeld was hired to monitor the mental health of patients and make sure they weren't driven crazy by treatment. The Jones clinic had a waiting list as soon as it opened, and Yale found itself inundated by patients who had to wait as long as eighteen months for an initial appointment.

This was despite the fact that in the 1980s IVF success rates were still excruciatingly low. As few as 5 or 6 percent of "cycles"—single rounds of treatment—resulted in a child. There were many reasons for this. One was that doctors were at the mercy of the female body rhythm. After their own failures using synthetic hormones, Steptoe and Edwards maintained—wrongly—that IVF would not work if the woman took drugs to boost her egg production. So doctors followed the natural ovulatory cycle of every patient: taking her temperature, doing blood tests, and otherwise endeavoring to detect that unseen moment when a single, mature egg slips out of the ovary. If they tried to retrieve the egg too soon, it would be immature and unusable. Too late, and it would have disappeared. This meant coming in the middle of the night, slogging in during snowstorms, banging on the hospital door to be admitted. Eventually, Georgeanna Jones decided to try using gonadotropins. She found that Steptoe and Edwards were wrong, and that drugs did work for IVF. This made it easier to control the release of the eggs, which meant that egg retrievals could be done during the day, when, as one doctor put it, "lab staff were fully awake."

Then there was the challenge of equipment: everything—everything—had to be invented or improvised. When Steptoe and Edwards were conducting their initial IVF experiments, they had to transport human eggs, human sperm, and human embryos back and forth between Oldham, where the hospital was, and Cambridge, where the lab was. They did this by putting a specimen in a sealed tube, and tucking the tube into a pouch that had been surgically created in the skin of a living rabbit. "It was pretty crude by today's standards," says Arthur Leader, who knew Steptoe and Edwards and went on to help develop the field in Canada. "It's a testimony to the hardiness of the human eggs and embryo that they survived." Even when incubators became available, scientists had to teach themselves how much carbon dioxide, oxygen, and nitrogen were needed to approximate the makeup of the female body. The same was true of culture media, the viscous mix in which specimens are contained and grown: it was trial and error, figuring out how to duplicate the rich, ever-changing environment an embryo experiences as it travels from the Fallopian tubes into the uterus.

In the beginning, nothing was known for certain. What size needle best retrieves eggs? How thin is too thin? Doctors in some cases made their own tools, while embryologists worried about every substance every instrument was made of. They kept the lab dark, says Lucinda Veeck Gosden, because they knew that light can affect the DNA in many cells. "We were always worried about toxic substances, anything you could smell, perfumes, construction fumes, somebody opens the door, you smell isopropyl alcohol. They can be extraordinarily toxic."

One of the most profound retardants was the fact that in the United States, there was no funding for human embryo research from the federal government, the world's most powerful engine of scientific and medical advancement. There was no way to test the effect of equipment or medications or light on the embryos that science was creating. Instead, doctors had to put the embryos into the uterus, and wait until a child was or was not born. IVF itself *was* the experiment. In Britain, the situation was more coherent: there pro-life groups also protested IVF, but government and scientific leaders made a serious effort to resolve the conflicting viewpoints, and found a way to regulate the field while letting it move forward. Members of Parliament were invited to peer through microscopes at eight-cell embryos. One member, Baroness Mary Warnock, was commissioned to draw up regulations. In Britain, it was decided that research could be done on human embryos for fourteen days after the embryo was created and that every IVF lab must be licensed, every procedure approved. A list of clinics and the procedures they perform is published annually. "That did an enormous amount, I think, to satisfy both MPs and the public that there weren't horrific Frankenstein scientists hiding in dark corners, making human-ape hybrids and I don't know what else," recalls Dame Anne McLaren, an eminent biologist whom I interviewed in a medical building at Cambridge University while she, tiny and amiable and birdlike, sipped water from a laboratory beaker.

In the United States, IVF got its start during the presidency of Ronald Reagan, a conservative politician presiding over an administration in which little money was available for any reproductive research. As for *human embryos:* well, bioethicists met; commissions agonized. Pro-life organizations quietly lobbied. Women's groups were otherwise occupied. In a weird stalemate, it was decided that embryo research might be federally funded, if approved by a certain advisory board. The board was formed, briefly, but soon was deliberately disbanded. You could apply, but there was nobody to apply to. As early as the mid-1970s, a scientist named Pierre Soupart submitted a request to the National Institutes of Health (NIH), asking for federal funding to research IVF embryos in his lab at Vanderbilt University. He died without receiving a reply it was truly a Kafkaesque situation, until in 1995 two Republican members of Congress, Roger Wicker of Mississippi and Jay Dickey of Arkansas, proposed a formal law that no government funding could be used for research that involved the destruction or endangerment of human embryos. Jay Dickey is no longer in office, but the so-called Dickey-Wicker amendment is passed every year as part of the Department of Health and Human Services appropriations bill; it has become a conservative touchstone.

In late 2005, Phyllis Leppert, a veteran NIH staffer, stood before a group of doctors and tried to find a diplomatic way to describe the effect of that ban. This group of doctors was interested in the still open question of the health of IVF children; under discussion was the effect of culture media on embryos that are living and excreting and growing and developing in it. Nobody—nobody—knows what the effect of the medium might be on the children conceived therein. "Anything funded by the federal government—that includes CDC, NIH, FDA—we have to follow the Dickey-Wicker amendment, which says that we cannot fund any research on human embryos, and that has been an incredible—what shall I say—*constraint*," said Leppert, a sensible-looking woman who rose to speak with real passion, the frustration of decades fueling her outburst. "And make no mistake about it, Congress watches, every day."

This ban on embryo research meant that no federally funded experiments could be conducted on the safety or efficacy of IVF, even as the field itself was surging ahead, unfunded and unregulated. Or, one should say, self-regulated: many among the still small circle of IVF doctors were members of the American Fertility Society, which would later become the American Society for Reproductive Medicine. Using money from the drug company Serono, they started an unofficial, unpublicized, ad hoc registry of the children conceived by IVF. The purpose was simple: to stave off malpractice suits. "We wanted a registry and Serono wanted a registry in case there was a bad outcome; in case your kid had a cleft lip, and you would sue the clinic, this way we would know that the number of cleft lips were three percent of the country," says Alan DeCherney, a cheerful, forthright man and former president of the society. According to DeCherney, at one point the National Institutes of Health approached the doctors about maintaining a government registry tracking child health, but "the only way they could do it was if the same pediatrician examined every kid, which was impractical and too expensive."

Getting at the Germ Line

But in the early days of IVF, what was really holding the field back was a technical problem having to do with women's tendency to protect their genetic offspring. Men, the thinking goes, like to spread their genes around indiscriminately, while women like to make sure their genes, and their genetic offspring, are well protected and carefully nurtured. At least, this is the really pretty reductive view of human behavior set forth by evolutionary psychology, a school of thought that sees many human actions as explainable by the drive to ensure the survival of the individual gene line.

And it's true: in women, that trove of genetic material known as the human germ line is protected to the point of being excruciatingly hard to get at. Human beings have two kinds of body cells. One kind are somatic cells: the ordinary body cells that make up the skin, the heart, the eyeballs, the blood, the hair. The other kind are germ cells, Germ cells are the unique, specialized cells devoted to human reproduction; they are the only cells capable of dividing their woven strand of forty-six paired chromosomes into twenty-three single ones, then fusing with another germ cell from another human body to develop a new human being.

Germ cells are, in short, the sperm and the egg.

For the purposes of IVF—for any purpose, really—the male germ line is absurdly easy to get at. In fertility clinics, men are given a pornographic magazine and sent to a small room to produce a sperm sample, which is processed in the lab. A small amount is then dropped into a culture dish in the vicinity of a waiting egg, which the sperm set upon and push around for some time, harrying the egg to and fro in their frantic effort to penetrate it, continuing the contest long after a single sperm has won. Meanwhile, getting at the female germ line is—or was—hell. For most of a woman's life, eggs, known as oocytes, are immature cells that lie resting in the ovary, a small organ, well protected, nestled behind other abdominal organs. One and sometimes two eggs come to maturity once a month, at which point the follicle, or pocket, in which the egg is growing swells with fluid. Although eggs are the largest cell in the body, they are, nevertheless, cells, and invisible to the naked eye. A doctor cannot simply open the belly, spot an egg, and tweeze it out.

What doctors had to do in the late 1970s for women with pelvic scarring was to inflate the woman's abdomen with carbon dioxide gas to perform a surgery—laparoscopy—under general anesthesia. Passing a telescope into the abdomen, the doctor would free the ovary from its scar tissue, insert a retrieval needle through a cut near the belly button, and, looking directly at the ovary and the follicle, puncture the follicle and remove its fluid. In the early 1980s, pelvic ultrasound allowed the ovary and follicle to be seen from outside. Once the results were brought to the lab, the staff would hope to find a pearly sphere—the oocyte—standing out against the bloody mess that is follicular fluid. Because of all the scar tissue from previous infections, half the time there would be no egg; "a woman went through a surgical procedure and anesthetic and got nothing to fertilize," recalls Arthur Leader.

To advance the field, what was needed was a better way of getting at that stubbornly inaccessible female germ line. It was a little like coal mining or oil exploration. Different extraction methods were tried. At one point a small, spring-loaded gun was in vogue. "You would measure the distance from the skin to the ovary," Leader remembers, "and you would fire a needle, and hopefully hit only the ovary. It didn't last very long. Nobody got hurt, thank God, but people didn't feel comfortable firing this needle into anybody."

Because these procedures required that the patient be put under anesthetic, they had to be done in an operating room. In hospitals, IVF labs had to fight for space with specialties that were better established. Lab staff ended up rushing around with dishes of culture media, from the operating room to wherever the lab happened to be grudgingly located by the hospital administration, frantically pushing the buttons on elevator panels, terrified lest the egg be lost or dropped.

In the mid-1980s, doctors began to suspect it might be possible to get at the germ line from within—to take a fifth-column approach to egg retrieval. They wondered if it might be possible to insert a needle up through the wall of the vagina, rather than down through the abdomen, while using an ultrasound wand inserted into the vagina (vaginal ultrasound was developed in Europe in 1985) to get a more complete view of the ovaries. It made so much sense. When the ovary is stimulated with fertility drugs, its larger and heavier than normal, and lies almost on top of the vagina, meaning that if you could travel through the back of the vagina with your needle, you had only about a half inch to go.

The prospect of putting a needle through the vaginal wall made some doctors nervous, because of the potential for infection, but nevertheless it was tried. The technique worked—so well that by 1987, it had taken off. In many ways this medical advance was the tipping point for fertility medicine. It transformed the field, gave it momentum, made so much else possible. It enabled not only more reliable retrieval of eggs, but also the donation of eggs from one woman to another. And the donation of eggs to science: vaginal retrieval would help advance therapeutic cloning and with it stem-cell research. Before too very long, the female germ line would become an engine driving not just fertility medicine but medicine, period. The female germ line would become one of the world's most sought-after natural reserves, essential to stem-cell research, one of the most hyped and controversial fields of medical and scientific endeavor. One day, it is hoped, the human egg, which exists to create a child, may become the vehicle for curing the diseases that accompany old age. It would therefore become a potential and potentially quite profitable fountain of youth: coveted, contested, bought, sold, shipped, argued over, freely sacrificed, stolen, traded, and sometimes obtained by ruse.

In the short term, what vaginal egg retrieval did was enable the explosive growth of IVF. Suddenly, human eggs were so much easier to get at, and as fertility drugs became more powerful and refined, there were more and more eggs to get at simultaneously. The beauty of it was that with vaginal retrieval you didn't have to put a woman under heavy anesthetic. You weren't really doing surgery. A woman could be given local anesthetic, and the egg retrieval could be carried out In ten minutes. IVF could be done—well, IVF could be done anywhere. It could become an outpatient procedure. Fertility clinics no longer had to be located in hospitals. All you needed was a couple of offices, some equipment, and a small lab, which could be attached to the retrieval room, with a window for passing specimens back and forth. "What it did was, it took IVF out of the operating room," says Leader. "It could be done now in any facility. It could be in an office building. A mall."

A mall! Why not? Fertility clinics were indeed set up in malls, discreetly, so as not to attract pro-life protests. There they remain. Human life can be created in labs in the most nondescript locations. There is one clinic near my house in Arlington, Virginia, located on the upper floor of an office building in a small strip mall, not far from a cluster of ethnic restaurants, a dollar store, and a Goodwill charity outlet. Clinics could now be run as private, profit-making enterprises. They could be set up as chains. They could advertise their services directly to patients, a development many academic, hospital-based doctors deplored, and still do, as diminishing the dignity of the profession. "The money ruined a lot of things," says Robert Nachtigall, lamenting colleagues who have left hospital practices affiliated with medical schools, and the research they promote and sponsor, in favor of the lucrative private sector. Somewhat ironically, the very profitability of the field served to impede its development: What research is done by private practices often is not shared, because of the competitive nature of the marketplace. Private practices that hit upon successful protocols guard them, "much like the forceps that [ob-gyns] guarded back in the eighteenth century to keep their competitive advantage," as Arthur Leader observes. And without the U.S. government funding and directing research, there was less of an effort—compared to fields such as cancer research—to develop standards that could improve success rates for all. Patients were paying for procedures whose quality varied markedly from provider to provider.

And they were paying a lot. Just over $12,000, on average, for a single procedure, though at some sought-after clinics, the bill could be closer to $50,000. Because infertile women—and men—were willing to pay anything. They were willing to go through IVF over and over again, submit to an unfolding series of procedures that doctors began to experiment with in the next several years. In 1986, there were 41 IVF clinics in the United States, according to an early industry registry. By 1998, that number would rise to more than 300, an increase of more than 700 percent. Ten years later there would be more than 400 clinics. Between 1968 and 1990, the number of annual office visits for infertility would increase from 600,000 a year to 2 million. Reported cases of impaired fertility would rise, from 4.9 million in 1988 to 7.3 million in 2002.

"Age of the Female Partner, Age of the Female Partner, Age of the Female Partner"

Part of the reason for the explosion was the steady improvement in treatment; part was pent-up demand from patients with infertility of a traditional sort. But part was the fact in the late 1980s and the '90s, a new kind of patient began to make her presence known. By the 1980s, feminism was well established, if eternally under assault. Professional aspirations for women were normalized; women graduating from college often were expected to work, attend graduate school, or both. Employers depended on these women, and they expected women to stick around once they were hired. Maternity leave was by no means a given. Neither were flexible workdays. Women responded by not taking maternity leave and by not asking for flexible workdays. They responded—to a complex set of incentives, including the fact that their partners and husbands were really liking this extra paycheck thing, this high-earning spouse, this chance to endlessly dine out and travel—by not having children, yet.

The new arsenal of reproductive technologies—the ones invented to help women *not* have children—would in some ways create a natural demand for the next reproductive technology, the one invented to help them have children once they were ready. "Controlling your reproduction" would become, for some, a three-decade continuum. Between 1973 and 1980, according to the Alan Guttmacher Institute, the rate of abortion in America almost doubled, rising from 16.3 to 29.3 abortions per 1,000 women. It would remain there for all of the 1980s. As for the Pill, as early as 1967, more than 6 million women were using it. In 1960, the average American woman had 3.6 children. The fertility rate thereafter began to fall steadily, until in 1970 the average woman had 2.5 children. In 1975, the average American woman had just 1.77 children. Not until 1989 would the fertility rate edge back up to 2.0, where it has hovered ever since.

It's not that women weren't having babies. Well, some weren't; rates of childlessness have also increased markedly. But the ones having children were having fewer, and—crucially—they were starting their families later. At this time the age of first childbirth also began an inexorable climb. Since the mid-1990s, each year the average age of the first-time American mother has been higher than it was the year before, a pattern that has continued to this day and that has been replicated in other first-world countries. For some women the new paradigm worked; when desired, the children obediently materialized. For others it did not. And so doctors began seeing women like Melanie: bright, hardworking women who had wanted children all their lives; who had struggled to achieve in a workplace that was not geared to working mothers; and whose infertility was due to the fact that when the time finally seemed right, the timing itself was wrong. Now there were women sitting in fertility clinics who were fit; who ran marathons; who did yoga; women astonished to find out that getting pregnant was going to be even harder than making partner in their law firm had been. Now, thirty-eight is the average age at the Jones Institute, where the cutting-off point once was thirty-five. There is no cutting-off point anymore.

And the thing was, you couldn't tell who was going to end up in a clinic and who wasn't. Doctors couldn't tell—still can't tell—which women are going to become infertile and at what age. For sure, scientists began trying to get some handle on it: They studied the Hutterites, a religious sect in which contraception was not practiced and women had children until they couldn't have children any longer. What they found is this: In her late twenties, a woman's fertility undergoes an initial, modest decline. There is a steeper decline at about thirty-seven. Or rather, there *can* be a steep decline at thirty-seven. The decline is far more severe in some than in others, and it starts in some earlier than in others. Before thirty-five, most women are fertile. After thirty-five, women enter a period of extreme variability. A woman may remain fertile for ten years, or she may undergo a precipitous drop in her ability to conceive; her childbearing days may be over. As a rough gauge, doctors assume that infertility usually sets in ten years before menopause, which begins, on average, at age fifty-one.

According to one study published in *Human Reproduction*, 75 percent of women who begin trying to conceive naturally at age thirty will succeed within a year. At age thirty-five, about 66 percent will conceive within a year, and 44 percent at age forty. Failure is by no means the norm, even after forty. It just becomes much more likely. After forty, women undergo a terrible division into two camps: those who can, and those who can't. You can see these two camps eyeing each other warily in offices and coffee shops and street corners everywhere: the happily pregnant, and the miserably still-trying. At forty-five, 87 percent of women are infertile.

Why does female fertility drop, and why is it so variable? Scientists everywhere are trying to come up with the cause of reproductive aging, as well as a reliable test to predict when it will happen and even, someday, to reverse the process. All signs point to the egg. According to the most widely accepted scientific theory, a woman is born with all the oocytes she will ever have. She has the most eggs while still in utero: at twenty weeks, a female fetus has about six to seven million oocytes in her tiny, newly formed ovaries. Massive numbers are quickly lost, however, so that at birth, about one to two million oocytes remain. The process continues; eggs die off, so that at thirty-seven a woman has something like 25,000 oocytes resting in her ovaries, and by the time she is fifty-one, she has only about 1,000 left.

A thousand may seem like a lot. But the older the egg, the less likely it is to work. Patricia Hunt, a reproductive biologist who studies aging, suspects the problem has to do with the way an egg undergoes meiosis, which is the process of dividing its forty-six chromosomes—the stumpy, loglike structures on which the genes are located—in half. Meiosis is something both sperm and egg must do before they come together. For reasons no one knows, meiosis in eggs begins almost immediately, when a girl-child is still in utero and her oocytes have only recently come into existence. The process then stops, and doesn't resume until the girl-child is mature and the egg is fertilized, years and years later. So eggs sit in suspended animation, their chromosomes awaiting the chance to sort themselves, for many years, even many decades. The older the egg, the less able it seems to be to finish dividing properly. And if an egg doesn't divide properly, the number of chromosomes in the resulting embryo may be unequal: the embryo may have forty-five or forty-seven chromosomes, instead of the normal human complement of forty-six. Where there should be a pair of chromosomes there may be one or three, a condition known as aneuploidy that is either bad or fatal. This is why the chances of having a child with Down syndrome—an extra chromosome 21—increase with maternal age. It's also why the chances of miscarriage rise as a woman gets older.

And more and more women are suffering miscarriage: according to the National Center for Health Statistics, the United States has seen a rise in miscarriage rates. Up to now, scientists have assumed that miscarriage rates are pretty much constant worldwide; while early pregnancy loss is notoriously hard to detect, rightly or wrongly it has always been estimated that roughly the same number of pregnancies miscarry in different countries and cultures. Some miscarriages are caused by infection, smoking, and other external influences, but the majority, scientists believe, are due to chromosomal abnormalities that doom the pregnancy from the start. Miscarriages are "nature's way" of ending a pregnancy that was never meant to be, as doctors invariably tell the devastated women undergoing them. For the first time, the miscarriage rate among American women has begun to rise, as more pregnancies are begun at later ages and more embryos are chromosomally compromised. More and more women, like Melanie, are experiencing the disappointment of getting pregnant only to lose the pregnancy, over and over.

And so it is that reproductive endocrinologists find themselves sitting across from patients, drawing the same dreary chart every day: the curve of female fertility. Little drop at twenty-nine, big drop at thirty-five or thirty-seven. They find themselves sitting across from women who, while smart and well educated, are surprised to learn that just because you are still menstruating doesn't mean you are still ovulating, and just because you are still ovulating—that is, producing a mature egg every month—doesn't mean the egg will work. They are seeing more and more women whose diagnosis is "diminished ovarian reserves," or—what often amounts to the same thing—"unexplained."

Keep in mind that older women are *not* the women most likely to be infertile. That distinction still belongs to poorer women and less well-educated ones, and to minorities. "Non-Hispanic blacks and other race women, high school dropouts, and high school graduates are significantly more likely to be infertile, and significantly less likely to have ever sought medical treatment to get pregnant or prevent miscarriage," notes one report. In fact, according to the National Survey of Family Growth, while infertility among women over thirty-five increased by 6 percent between 1996 and 2002, women under twenty-five reported a striking 42 percent rise in impaired fertility, for reasons nobody understands, from 4.3 percent of women to 6.1 percent.

But older women tend to be the ones able to afford IVF treatment, or to have insurance coverage, or both, so they are overrepresented among patients. They also attract more than their share of controversy. It is inevitably assumed that women over forty find themselves infertile because of a series of deliberate choices. If you do an online search for "women" and "delay childbirth," you will find any number of news articles and op-eds in which it is assumed that pregnancy delay is something women have single-handedly brought about—something women have *chosen*—and that it has nothing to do with, for example, reproductive dawdling on the part of indecisive male partners or active discouragement from bosses. The age of first childbearing among males has risen at the same rate as among women, yet this trend of men choosing to delay child-fathering has attracted little public hand-wringing.

The great problem is that older women are the least likely to be helped by treatment. They are the ones most likely to be spending $12,000 for an IVF cycle and getting nothing for their money. "You know the old real estate adage: location, location, location. Well, in IVF, its age of the female partner, age of the female partner, age of the female partner," says Marcelle Cedars, a reproductive endocrinologist who has been working in the field since before IVF began. Doctors can almost gauge how treatable a situation is by looking at the woman's birth date. If a couple comes in and the woman is thirty-two and suffering from endometriosis, that's better than if the woman is forty-one and has no ailment anybody can identify. Studies show that among ART patients who are forty years old and using their own eggs, there is a 25 percent chance of pregnancy over the course of three IVF cycles. The chances diminish to around 18 percent at forty-one and forty-two, 10 percent at forty-three, and zero at forty-six.

In 2005, a group of doctors at Cornell surveyed IVF patients over forty-five who had attempted to conceive using their own eggs. Among women between forty-six and forty-nine, not one got pregnant using her own eggs. Not one.

"Fat, Slutty, Old, Smokers"

And yet aging has remained a weirdly taboo topic among women's reproductive rights groups, who have not served their constituency well in this area. There has been an energetic muddying of the waters by some old-line women's groups, which have preferred either to ignore the facts or, in some cases, to deny them. When it comes to the consequences of aging, the same groups who encouraged women to use mirrors to collectively inspect their cervixes, and even taught them how to cobble together jars and aquarium tubing to pump out their menses, seem to regard rather differently any effort to acquaint themselves with the details of other reproductive organs.

The most notorious clash came in 2001, when the American Society for Reproductive Medicine (ASRM) decided to devote $50,000 to an infertility awareness campaign. The goal was to point out to men and women alike the effects of any number of lifestyle issues: smoking, obesity, sexually transmitted disease, and age (though, in the eternally unfair way of the world, age does not affect male fertility nearly as much as it affects female fertility). It was a pretty delicate message to sell. "Infertility patients thought we were saying they were fat, slutty, old, smokers," says ASRM spokesman Sean Tipton. But by far, the most controversial message was that of age.

This was surprising to the architects of the campaign. You wouldn't think sharing a few facts would be that inflammatory, says Marcelle Cedars, who practices at the world-class infertility clinic at the University of California, San Francisco, and who was in charge of the panel on reproduction and aging. "We knew it would be a hot potato," says Cedars, a working mother with a deep commitment to reproductive health. "We could tell that it was going to be so controversial, there was a push from some people on the committee to drop it. I'm like, 'You can't drop it. It's the most important factor in infertility for people of this generation. We can't *not* talk about it.'" So the committee approved an advertisement that showed a baby bottle in the shape of an hourglass, to communicate the idea of time running out. It wasn't a big campaign. The ads ran on metro buses in four cities. But *Newsweek* picked up on the topic with a cover story on reproductive aging; and all hell broke loose.

The opposition came from the National Organization for Women (NOW), co-founded by the late Betty Friedan. It should be pointed out that Friedan was no enemy of family life. In *The Feminine Mystique,* she posits the reasonable suggestion that women deserve a place in public life, and that they also deserve the intimacy and love afforded by children. But the current NOW president, Kim Gandy, saw the ASRM campaign as an attempt to bully women into having babies early. "I don't think we need to be putting that pressure on younger women," Gandy told CNBC. To Katie Couric, then host of the *Today* show, Gandy said that "what is essentially a scare campaign is extraordinarily ill-advised."

Fertility doctors were nonplussed.

"We were shocked. We thought [NOW] would be allies, you know, because we're empowering women," says Robert Stillman, a doctor at Shady Grove Fertility who was also on the committee, and who quickly realized that all in all the outrage was a good thing: it leveraged the tiny publicity campaign into something much bigger. Ultimately, ASRM was so energized that it decided to run the ads again, on a larger scale. "Women are, once again, made to feel anxious about their bodies and guilty about their choices," Gandy wrote in an editorial. But she eventually stopped commenting, out of a reluctance, a NOW spokesperson said, to provide the fertility awareness campaign any more free press.

Still, the conflict underlines the fact that while doctors who advocated for better contraception and abortion rights are seen by many feminist groups as natural allies, fertility doctors have been marginalized. Any effort to educate women—and men—about consequences of delayed childbearing is seen by some feminist leaders as tyrannical, oppressive, retrograde. Just as the hullaboo over the ASRM campaign was dying down, *Creating a Life: Professional Women and the Quest for Children*, Sylvia Ann Hewlett's 2002 book about the reproductive consequences of aging, was similarly attacked, from roughly the same quarters, as antifeminist. Increasingly, this is a challenge for the reproductive rights movement: there is a formidable swathe of women, now, who are lying on gynecological examining tables with their feet in stirrups undergoing the hysterosalpingogram—a terrifically painful procedure in which dye is forcibly injected into the Fallopian tubes to see if they are open—and rethinking everything they were led to believe about the ability to choose when to conceive.

"Boy, are they pissed," says Robert Nachtigall succinctly, after thirty years of working with fertility patients in San Francisco. Or as one fortysomething patient put it, speaking from behind the closed door of her San Francisco law firm, contemplating the birth of her own IVF-conceived, egg-donor child: "I didn't grow up thinking that I'll have a baby this way."

"All we were trying to do was give women information," says Marcelle Cedars, still stung by the way a major women's group turned on her. "We're not *telling* them to have children. We're not telling them you should have children before having a career. We're telling them that if having children is a priority for you, its something you should factor in. What I hate is women who show up in my office at forty, and say, I never knew this."

Why Don't You Just Adopt?

During the same period, a traditional solution for infertility, domestic adoption, was undergoing changes of its own. Adoption is a complicated topic, as fraught and controversial as anything else involving family making, and a full exploration is beyond the scope of this book. But it seems fair to say that during the second half of the twentieth century, developments were taking place that would propel more would-be parents away from adoption agencies and into medical clinics. The pool of U.S. children available for adoption was shrinking and the process for adopting them becoming more expensive, laborious, and daunting, making fertility treatment that much more appealing, at least as a solution of first resort. More bluntly: there were fewer white babies, and those who were available became harder to get.

According to Marsh and Ronner, there have never been enough adoptable children in the United States to meet the demand of infertile couples. Even so, the supply used to be larger than it is now, and adopting them used to be, for better or worse, more informal and streamlined. In generations past, parentless children were sometimes seen as miniature servants; for infertile couples in colonial times, the void was filled, in part, by taking in children as apprentices and household helpers. In the late nineteenth century there were actual "orphan trains" that carried children around the country, stopping at cities where orphans would be "put up" for adoption, displayed on platforms for viewing by members of the community, who often regarded them as sources of farm and household help, preferred boys to girls, and didn't have to jump through many hoops to take them home. In the early twentieth century the process became more formal, with the creation of maternity homes where unmarried women could bear their children, receive medical care, and surrender the newborns after birth. Couples who wanted to adopt a child had to apply, but "the application was literally one page long," recalls Paige McCoy Smith, a spokeswoman for the Gladney Center for Adoption, one of the oldest U.S. adoption agencies.

The 1970s brought a major change in adoption procedures, and changes, too, in the number of babies available. In prior decades, young unmarried mothers were often pressured by their families, and by social services, to relinquish their babies even when they wanted to keep them. That painful phenomenon is movingly explored in Ann Fessler's 2006 book, *The Girls Who Went Away: The Hidden History of Women Who Surrendered Children for Adoption in the Decades Before Roe v. Wade*. After *Roe*, women could more easily end problematic pregnancies; moreover, the pressure to relinquish lessened as single motherhood became more accepted. With abortion legal and birth control safer, more reliable, and readily available, fewer unplanned pregnancies came to term, and the babies born were more likely to be kept by the women who bore them. "What we started seeing in the eighties and nineties is a decline in the number of women making the decision to place a child for adoption," McCoy Smith says. "A dramatic decline."

A government study confirms this. In the early 1970s, 9 percent of unmarried mothers relinquished their children for adoption. By 1988, the rate was just 2 percent. The decline was most marked among white women, who—contrary to popular belief—have always provided the majority of adoptable babies.

According to the study, before 1973, 19 percent of children born to single white women were placed for adoption. That percentage fell to 8 percent in the period between 1973 and 1981, and it had dropped to just 3 percent by 1988. The relinquishment rate among black women has never been high; it has hovered around 2 percent. Hispanic women have never been very willing to relinquish babies. According to government researchers, women are more likely to relinquish children if there is a high "opportunity cost" to raising that child: if the child endangers some other part of her life—such as a career, education, marriage, or social status—the woman is more likely to give the child up for adoption. At least she used to be. According to the Evan B. Donaldson Adoption Institute, just 13,000–14,000 U.S. women now voluntarily relinquish infants for adoption each year.

At the same time, the number of parents seeking adoptive children was beginning to rise. Demand was increasing even as supply was on the downswing: "Now, for every one call from a birth mother, I receive six to ten phone calls from prospective adoptive parents," says McCoy Smith, who stresses that her agency is always—eventually—able to find a child for qualified parents. And the ethics were evolving. Before the 1950s, adoption was carried out secretly, and adoptive children were rarely told the truth of their origins. After midcentury a generation of adoptees began to protest. Adults who had been adopted as children began to argue that secrecy was traumatic and corrosive; that there was, or should be, no stigma surrounding adoption; that children deserved to know the truth of their origins and if possible the identity of their birth parents.

That movement had an enormous impact on the way domestic adoption happens. Now openness is the norm. Now the birth mother has much more control over where, and with whom, her child is placed. "In the past, when the birth mother would deliver the child, the adoptive parents were already selected by the agency," says McCoy Smith. "Now the birth mother has the option of selecting her parents based on criteria she provides." It's a better system, most believe; a birth mother who feels good about the adoption is less likely to try and reclaim the child afterward. But, McCoy Smith allows, it makes some parents nervous. It also makes the process more expensive. The average Gladney adoption takes a year, and costs at least $20,000. Even with agencies that can carry out adoption more cheaply, competition cannot be avoided. Would-be parents compete with other would-be parents; they assemble scrapbooks, describe their marriages and homes, pay for the birth mother's health care and, in some states, expenses. Some eschew agencies altogether, placing ads in newspapers and striking up independent agreements with a birth mother. All of these arrangements are closely monitored by the courts. For a judge to release a child for adoption, most states require that intended parents undergo a criminal background check, a home study by a licensed clinical social worker, and other formal evaluations. Part of the purpose is to find out how parents plan to deal with the fact of the adoption when talking to the child.

If a parent said in the home study that they did not intend to tell the child of his or her adoption, that, according to McCoy Smith, "would be a real red flag. That tells us: what's your issue with adoption?"

So Why Don't You Just Half Adopt? The Dawn of Egg Donation

Meanwhile, surprisingly early on fertility medicine proved able to deliver a compromise solution: sort of like adoption, and sort of like having your own biological offspring. Assisted reproduction could offer, to this group of older women, a way to salvage something from an unforeseen situation. The chance to—well, to adopt half a baby, in a sense, and gestate that baby and experience childbirth and breast-feeding, and control fine's diet and alcohol intake and cigarette smoking and all the other pings that cannot be controlled, or not so easily, if the child is being gestated by another. Fertility medicine offered the woman who cannot conceive using her own eggs the opportunity to conceive using the eggs of another.

Egg donation is one of the fertility procedures that turned out to be more doable than anyone had anticipated. As early as 1984—just three years after the birth of the first U.S. IVF baby, Elizabeth Carr—Sanford Rosenberg, a doctor practicing in Richmond, Virginia, was confronted by a patient suffering from premature ovarian failure, meaning that her eggs had stopped being viable well before the normal age. The patient asked whether her sister's eggs could be used in the IVF procedure instead of hers.

Rosenberg had no idea whether they could or they couldn't. Nobody knew what was possible in terms of trading eggs between women. Rosenberg called Zev Rosenwaks, a leader in the field; according to Rosenberg, Rosenwaks replied that there seemed to be no reason not to try. A baby was born, genetically the child of one sister and gestated by the other. Elsewhere, doctors performed scattered procedures using eggs scrounged from patients who were undergoing their own infertility treatment and had excess eggs, or women who had undergone hysterectomies and happened to have a mature egg in their ovaries when they were removed. Somewhat to everyone's surprise, many of these procedures worked. An infertile woman could rather easily be given drugs to prepare her uterine lining to receive an embryo conceived from the eggs of a different woman.

"Who knew that all you would need would be estrogen and progesterone to get the uterus to work?" says Richard Paulson, chief of the fertility clinic at the University of Southern California medical school and a pioneer of what has become a fast-growing area of fertility treatment: egg donation to older women. Who knew that a woman's body would willingly take in a little genetic alien? That the womb itself was willing to adopt? Could such a thing be done on a wider scale? Not right away. When eggs were being retrieved under surgical conditions, it was not practical, or ethical, to have a stranger undergo surgery for another stranger. At the outset, you couldn't do egg donation en masse.

And then, all at once, you could. Once again, it was vaginal egg retrieval—the new ease of getting at the female germ line—that allowed egg donation to become routine treatment. In 1987, Paulson and several other doctors in Southern California recruited a group of women to be formal egg donors. These were early adopters in the high-tech birth arena, open-minded women willing to allow their eggs to be removed and fused with sperm from a stranger, to produce children who, while related to them and their own children, would be raised in households other than their own. These women weren't birth mothers. They did not fit the social profile of someone relinquishing a living child. They were married women with children—women considerably older than most egg donors now—who knew how important their own families were to them and were glad to help someone else attain the same happy state. They were, as the pleasant saying went, "women helping women."

Doctors were making up the rules as they went along. There was no medical playbook here. There were no government guidelines. What was normal? What was wrong? Who knew? Paulson's group decided that egg donors, to be accepted into their program, had to be finished with their own childbearing. At the time, it was unknown whether egg donation might affect a donor's own fertility, or interfere somehow with a later pregnancy, so they admitted only donors who did not want more children, in case there were adverse effects. Another rule was that egg donors were not paid, or not much, because to pay them seemed coercive, and felt too much like buying a human being. These early donors "were altruistic, motivated," says Paulson, who sometimes shares a PowerPoint presentation on the history of egg donation with medical students for whom the early days must seem as remote, and as faintly absurd, as the U.S. invasion of Grenada.

Another rule, at first, was that Paulson's group would not accept infertile patients older than forty. Nobody knew whether the body of a fortysomething infertile woman could properly gestate a fetus. If a woman's own eggs had deteriorated, what about the rest of her reproductive apparatus? Instead, egg donation was performed on younger women who had suffered premature ovarian failure. Pretty quickly, though, the rule was relaxed. When some women waiting for egg donors turned forty-one, Paulson and his group decided to see what would happen if these women were allowed to stay in the program. They found that in this case age hardly mattered. Infertile women over forty could get pregnant; thanks to egg donation, they could gestate a baby as successfully as anybody. Women who were forty-two, forty-three, forty-four, forty-five. "Lo and behold, they got pregnant at the same rate as women under forty," says Paulson. "This was the light bulb. Oh, I get it: The problem must not be in the uterus. The problem must be in the egg." Egg donation underscored what doctors were already learning about female fertility: what mattered was not the age of the patient, but the age of the egg.

In 1990, Paulson and colleagues published a paper in the *New England Journal of Medicine*, "A Preliminary Report on Oocyte Donation Extending Reproductive Potential to Women over 40." This paper prompted a snowstorm of controversy in the medical academy and the popular press. Concerns centered not on egg donation per se, but on the ethics of older motherhood. Regular old-fashioned mainstream ob-gyns were concerned, pragmatically, that older mothers might suffer more complications in childbirth, which in fact they do. In papers with titles such as "Increased Maternal Age and the Risk of Fetal Death" and "Advanced Maternal Age—How Old is Too Old?" doctors noted that the older the mother, the more likely she is to experience preeclampsia, gestational diabetes, hypertension. The older the mother, the more likely her child is to be premature, small, or—this does happen—dead.

And then there was the reaction of reproductive rights advocates. The feminist camp was split. There has always been a school of feminism that tends to view fertility medicine as one more way in which an oppressive patriarchy forces women to bear children against their will. These theorists, whom Richard Paulson refers to as "lunatic ultra feminists," had an easy time of it. Like many conservative skeptics, they could and did reject egg donation to older mothers as unnatural: "violations of nature" are often a deal breaker for Far Right and Far Left alike. But there is another line of feminist reasoning that says that egg donation to older women makes women more like men and therefore is a good and liberating breakthrough. Enabling women to become parents in their late forties is a kind of Title IX for the body, a gender equity measure that permits women to become parents at the age when many men do. After all, actuarial tables show that women live longer than men do, so isn't it more ethical for a woman to become a parent at forty-eight than for a man to do so? This is Paulson's view: "I am a feminist, and as a feminist I take great issue with the fact that [the lunatic ultra feminists] call themselves feminists," he said during an interview in his academic office.

Controversy or no controversy, Paulson and his group kept going. It was kind of the opposite of the limbo: how high can you go? In 1993 they published a paper reporting egg-donation pregnancies in women over fifty. In these cases, it was often necessary to give women drugs to reverse menopause and restore the hormones for supporting a pregnancy. At first, Paulson says, their fiftysomething patients tended to be women who had been infertile their whole adult lives, women who were always one step behind—or rather ahead of—the technology. He offers the hypothetical example of a woman born in 1943 whose tubes were blocked at age ten by a ruptured appendix and who for most of her life was regarded as hopelessly infertile. "When she was thirty-five years old in 1978, Louise Brown was born, and she thought perhaps there would be hope for me yet," Paulson explains, describing the sort of woman who did in fact make up about 50 percent of his older patients. "Then in 1983 when she was forty, IVF technology was starting to percolate into clinics in the States, but they were only taking women under forty. In 1988, she was 45 and her eggs were not going to work. Then she turns fifty and the technology of egg donation was now available. She finds that technology has finally caught up with her, and at the age of fifty, she can go in and have a baby."

This, however, is one of the many areas in reproductive medicine where the borders of "normal" are very hard to locate. Because the other 50 percent of his patients had not been infertile all their lives. They had just gotten started late. As more older women presented themselves for treatment, not just in Southern California but everywhere, clinics had to develop mathematical formulas and ad hoc age-related guidelines, which they are constantly revising and making exceptions to. Some practices have decided that they will not accept any couple whose combined age is more than, oh, say, 100. Others are willing to go further: "The combined age should not exceed 110, and I wouldn't do a single woman over 50, though God knows I might change that in a few years," one Los Angeles doctor, Vicken Sahakian, told me in 2004, snatching a conversation between treatments in his Wilshire Boulevard practice, where there is a separate waiting room for celebrities, a land of reproductive green room. Sahakian acknowledged that he once treated a couple where the woman was sixty-four and the man was sixty-eight (they were using a surrogate). His staff were mad at him, he says, and when that pregnancy miscarried, "I refused to do it again with the frozen embryos. I said, 'I really can't do this anymore.' They took the embryos and went somewhere else."

Paulson and his group decided that fifty-five was a quasi-physiological limit for a female patient carrying her own pregnancy, the age at which the risks outweigh the benefits. Even within those parameters, the experiments produced extraordinary results. As early as 1993, Paulson and colleagues published an article in *Human Reproduction*, "Quadruplet Pregnancy in a 51-Year-Old Menopausal Woman Following Oocyte Donation." Just fifteen years after the birth of Louise Brown, assisted reproduction was able to make a menopausal woman pregnant with four babies simultaneously. According to the paper, the woman underwent "selective reduction" to reduce her pregnancy to twins.

The new normal: a fifty-one-year-old having twins.

And it was. It was the new normal. Around the world, a certain species of doctor/scientist/self-promoter was learning that a sure way to garner headlines—aside from fake claims of having cloned a baby—was to impregnate the "world's oldest mother." In 1994, Severino Antinori, an Italian embryologist practicing at a time when Italian fertility medicine was notoriously permissive, reported getting sixty-two-year-old Rosanna Della Corte pregnant. Taking pregnancy into the seventh decade! Clearly, that was going too far. "Antinori is a crazy guy," says Paulson, who himself was working well within the confines of what seemed acceptable: just sitting there in Long Beach, adhering to his first-half-of-the-sixth-decade limit. Then, one day, a woman named Arceli Keh walked into Paulson's office. Keh said she was fifty. Paulson thought she looked older but figured that every person ages differently. So he treated her, successfully, using donated eggs. He released her to a gynecologist, who presently called to let him know that Keh was in fact over sixty. "I said, watch her like a hawk," says Paulson, who was relieved when Keh, who developed gestational diabetes, delivered a healthy baby by C-section.

Paulson felt that ethically he had to write the case up for publication in a medical journal. But he needed to know the scope of his achievement. So he contacted Antinori to find out exactly how old Della Corte had been. Turned out that Della Corte was sixty-two years, six months, and two weeks on the day of delivery, while Arceli Keh was sixty-three years old and nine months. Turns out that he, Richard Paulson, feminist, normal guy, bona fide academic, had created the world's oldest mother! By mistake! His old mother was older than Antinori's old mother! So he wrote for the journal *Fertility and Sterility* an article titled "Successful Pregnancy in a 63-Year-Old Woman," which described the case and followed with a discussion of the difficulties of setting reasonable age limits on motherhood. After raising the question of whether there should be a law declaring how old is too old for a woman to give birth, Paulson reviewed the reasons why there should not. If there were a law, he pointed out, doctors would have to card their patients, and you know how easy fake IDs are to make. Plus, what would that do to doctor-patient trust? Plus, what if a fraud were committed: would the doctor be sent to jail? How unimaginable is that? He concluded, inevitably, that "the decision as to when and how to procreate is best left to the patients and their physicians."

In short, like so many others in every arena of reproductive technology, he fell back on choice.

The New Old Mother

Before long, "world's oldest mother" would become a staple of news bites, a reliably interesting and borderline sick category, like "worst-dressed actress at the Oscars" or "most-divorced country singer." "Retired lecturer, 67, set to be oldest mother, and its twins!" said a 2004 article in *The Times* of London, describing the Romanian woman who may or may not be the actual "world's oldest mother" (though it turned out to be a singleton, not twins). This would be Adriana Iliescu, who in her Web photos really does look startlingly old, frail and wrinkled and bleak-looking, possibly because Botox and hair highlights are harder to come by in Eastern Europe than they are in Los Angeles. Before long, to make headlines a woman who was moderately old had to possess some other distinction, as in "California woman in her 50s gives birth to second child," a headline that appeared in 2005 in the *Orange County Register,* which, like many newspapers, adopted a jolly, who'd-a-thunk-it tone in describing Carolyn Pelcak, who, having given birth via IVF at fifty-two, decided to do the same at fifty-five, after which, the article quoted, "the single mom is loving every minute of it."

Then there was "Woman, 55, Gives Birth to Grandchildren," the headline in the *Washington Post,* profiling a woman who delivered triplets in Richmond, Virginia, while acting as a surrogate mother for her own daughter. Or "Great-Grandmother Becomes One of the Oldest Women in the World to Successfully Give Birth," the careful headline on the 2006 press release in which an online casino called Nine.com rewarded its "Gambler of the Week" award to Janise Wulf, of Redding, California, who at sixty-two—diabetic, blind from birth, the mother of eleven children, grandmother of twenty, and great-grandmother of three—used IVF to conceive her twelfth child. Her husband was forty-eight. Nine.com treated the feat as funny, noting that "Gambler of the Week" awards are reserved for "those who take risks by doing something unusual, risky, heroic or foolish."

Small wonder that by now the categories are finely parsed, the superlatives elaborately qualified. In 2004, when Aleta St. James, the "energy healer" whose newborn twins are, of course, featured on the website that offers her up for speaking engagements, gave birth at fifty-seven, she had to settle for being "the second oldest woman in the United States to give birth to twins."

As for over-forty moms: who cares anymore? A little more than ten years after the publication of Paulson's "preliminary report" on fortysomething mothers, a parade of high-profile women, many of them actresses facing the professional dry spell that Hollywood imposes on the talented but no longer nubile, have made fortysomething motherhood seem almost—natural. Jane Seymour, forty-four. Susan Sarandon, forty-six. Geena Davis, twins at forty-seven. Holly Hunter, twins at forty-seven. The late Wendy Wasserstein, a premature daughter at forty-eight. The woman in the cubicle next to you—well, giving birth at forty-five just feels normal now, doesn't it?

You can conceive at forty-eight, can't you? Using your own eggs?

This is what many people now assume. Ironically, the parade of ART-assisted older mothers has served more than anything to cloud the waters of reproductive accuracy. Infertility awareness campaigns notwithstanding, the medical profession is hard at work blurring its own message. Even now that "biological clock" has become a grim cliché, women can be forgiven for not knowing exactly when the alarm bell goes off.

The real ethical issue isn't older mothers. It's the fact that many celebrity older mothers, who inevitably benefit from the publicity surrounding their darling newborn, or newborns, tend to leave out the pesky detail of having had help. Aleta St. James, bless her self-promotional heart, thanks her egg donor in the course of tirelessly telling her story of New Age determination and late-in-life childbearing. But she's the exception. How should one think about the don't-tellers? Should closeted egg-donor moms be outed? For the sake of collective education and reproductive truth telling? What would be the thinking feminist position here? Example A in this bioethical essay question might be Joan Lunden, the trim former anchor *of Good Morning America*, who, after raising one family in the usual window of time, remarried a younger man and decided to do it all again. (This is a common pattern: many fifty something mothers are women who have married a younger man and want to "give him a child," a situation that in and of itself is a little hard to know what to think about.) In so doing, Lunden secured her place on magazine covers not one but two years in a row. Lunden "had" twins in 2003 at fifty-two; two years later she had "twins again!" as *Good Housekeeping* trumpeted on its cover. The double whammy of coverage must have been a welcome boost to Lunden's career, which includes a book on childhood nutrition, and, inevitably, a stint hosting a reality show.

In a series of interviews on her "miracle babies," Lunden acknowledged using a surrogate to carry the babies, a woman she warmly thanked. She would not, however, comment on whether she also used an egg donor, despite the fact that she clearly—unless these truly were miracle children—must have done so. Her reticence was for the benefit of "all the other people who are calling and writing me now, wanting to do this," she said piously when *Ladies' Home Journal* had the temerity to ask her whether she used an egg donor. "I don't want them to feel that they can't achieve what we have if they can't produce their own eggs. I want everybody to understand that however they make their families doesn't make any difference."

Huh? If doesn't make a difference how you make your family, why not go ahead and say how you made your family? Could it be that not acknowledging egg donation is something a public woman does because she wants the public to think of her as young?

And how to feel about that warm and likable late-in-life mom Elizabeth Edwards, wife of former North Carolina senator and Democratic presidential candidate John Edwards? During the 2004 campaign, when he was running for vice-president, the Edwards's young children, Jack and Emma Claire, were one of the few reliably cheerful sights on the campaign trail. Charmingly reminiscent of John-John and Caroline, they enhanced John Edwards's Kennedyesque air of youth and vigor. And yet their means of conception was nothing if not edgily modern: After the Edwardses' teenage son, Wade, was killed in a car accident in 1996, the grieving Edwardses, who also had an adult daughter, decided to conceive again. When she bore Emma Claire and Jack, Elizabeth Edwards was forty-eight and fifty, respectively. In 2004, an article in *Slate* speculated on what doctors had been discussing as a certainty: the younger Edwards children were most likely conceived using egg donation. Elizabeth Edwards has declined to address this or to acknowledge using IVF, saying only that she had some help from "shots," and that to say more would not be "ladylike." John Edwards, in keeping with the way of the world, does not appear to have been asked.

The *Slate* article provoked a barrage of e-mails to the Fray, the magazine's tetchy repository for reader response. Many thought it was wrong to invade the Edwards family's privacy. But was it? And if so, why? Its true, families who use fertility medicine are not obliged to reveal every detail of treatment, and if public people choose not to comment on family matters, maybe they have good reason. Maybe they don't want their children to suffer any stigma. Then again, wasn't it precisely "stigma" that provided the rationale for secrecy back in the days of hiding the truth about adoption? Wasn't it just this idea of stigma that adoptive children were battling? While hardly rising to the level of a campaign issue, the question did offer Edwards the opportunity to be of service to other women, and to their children, and dodging it may have misled some into thinking a fiftysomething pregnancy can be accomplished easily.

"You need a huge section [in the book] talking about the biology of reproduction," I was earnestly told by Fady Sharara, a Virginia reproductive endocrinologist who gets very exercised on the subject of well-known women who are in the closet about having used an egg donor. Sharara was one of the doctors who went on record as saying Elizabeth Edwards likely used egg donation to have those lovely, much-loved children. To Sharara, honesty in these matters *matters,* because he is the one left cleaning up the mess created by minor little half-truths and ladylike omissions. "Women are clueless, *clueless,"* he said. "They come in at forty-four, forty-seven, and don't know why they aren't getting pregnant." The day I spoke with him he said that a fiftysomething woman had recently called him from rural southwestern Virginia, expecting that fertility medicine could produce for her a biological child. She was incensed to learn that it can't. She felt he had wronged her. In just thirty years, ART itself has become part of the problem: in persuading women that they can safely wait, assisted reproduction is creating for itself a new-patient base.

"If It's Not Going to Be Mine, Couldn't it Not Be Both of Ours?:" The Marital Politics of Egg Donation

"I wish I had known some of this ahead of time," says Melanie over lunch, still trying to make sense of her own uncertain journey into the hardest parts of treatment. Having once sworn that she would never even try IVF, Melanie is considering using a donor egg. This is the kind of "choice" now facing women: When should I abandon all hope of a biological connection to my baby? When should I give up on ever seeing my own features reflected in the face of my child? At forty-two? Forty-three? Forty-four? Melanie is looking for any small hint, any piece of data, any test result that might offer an answer. Meanwhile, more and more fertility practices are offering egg donation as the natural next step of treatment, an automatic transition in an ongoing medical process. "We've seen over the past couple of years, moving couples quickly into donor egg, almost as a standard of care," worries one therapist. "Donor egg for these couples is a last-minute switcheroo, snatching victory from the jaws of defeat," agrees Robert Nachtigall.

And patients are left wondering: What will it feel like, giving birth to a child who is genetically related to my husband, but not genetically related to me?

"I think about this all the time," says Melanie, who, after she had endured the second blighted ovum—or was it the third? There have been so many—decided that old-fashioned adoption would suit her fine. No more injections. No more bruises. No more blood tests. No more miscarriages. Tired of the physical toll treatment was taking, she decided that she would be glad to adopt a child domestically. She would be glad to adopt a child internationally. She would willingly adopt a special-needs child. She and her husband had the means; they could afford to give a child, any child, plenty of resources and love. At least, this was the way Melanie saw it, and so she came home one day and said to her husband: "Let's adopt."

"We haven't exhausted our options," her husband replied.

Who knew that Melanie's husband would be the one propelling them toward egg donation? If it's not going to be mine, couldn't it not be both of ours?" she asked when they were discussing what to do next. Her husband replied, "I can't believe you wouldn't want to at least try to have a child that's ours."

Ours?

"That," she says now, "shocked me more than anything."

And so now it's Melanie's husband who is urging her to continue with egg donation. While genetic connection matters to him, he cannot see, she says, that it should matter so much to her. After all, she'll be carrying the child. She'll bear the child, deliver the child, breast-feed the child, bond to the child. Melanie is not so sure it will be that easy. She doesn't think she would have the same ambivalence about adoption. Adoption, she thinks, would be clear-cut. Adoption would be straightforward. With adoption, she and her husband would be equally unrelated to the child. Moreover, adoption seems more honest. She worries that egg donation would feel—to her—like a public lie.

"I would feel like a fraud, like I'm going through this whole process with something that's not really mine," she speculates. "This wouldn't be my biological child, so why am I going through this whole charade?" What, she worries, if she doesn't love the child? What if she does love the child, but in a different way than she might have loved a child related to her? Would such a child feel like her child? Would it feel like more of her husband's? Would he have more authority? Would he have more say?

What about their marriage? Melanie and her husband have had to work through a disagreement that many couples never imagine confronting. "I don't think he's ever going to be comfortable with adopting, and I have to respect that. That's where his boundary is," she says now. Their marriage was strained, but emerged, she thinks, stronger. Adoption: out, for now. Egg donation: possible. So they talked to the fertility practice about their available egg donors.

What they found was that the logistics and ethics of egg donation have changed enormously since Richard Paulson and his colleagues were making up the rules in Long Beach, California. "Women helping women" is no longer an ethical guideline; it's an advertising hook in every college newspaper and neighborhood pennysaver. The initial guidelines have been jettisoned. Now egg donors are young; the majority have not begun their own families. Now egg donors are paid. They're paid a lot. And because they are paid a lot—because there's good money to be made—private commercial agencies have gotten involved in procuring donors. Unlike adoption agencies, egg-donation agencies do not have to be licensed. They are not charitable. They are not run by churches or nonprofits. They are businesses. Yet unlike real estate agents, egg brokers do not have to take written exams or obtain certification. Real estate agents are dealing with houses; egg brokers are dealing with the essence of life, the most sought-after human cell in the world. And they are eagerly recruiting donors, with campaigns so slick that many medical practices can no longer hold their own against the Tiny Treasures and Loving Donations and Creating New Generations of the world. "We're out-advertised, out-hustled," says Richard Paulson, acknowledging that even USC now often must get its egg donors through profit-making agencies. Some of these donors are young enough to give Paulson pause. How young is too young to surrender your eggs to another? Paulson personally draws the line, or tries to, at twenty-one.

"I struggle with these things," says Paulson. "I would so like this to be women helping women."

Melanie struggled too. At first, she and her husband looked through the thin notebook provided by their hospital practice, which recruits many of its Caucasian donors from rural Pennsylvania, there being a shortage of white donors in Washington, D.C., a majority African-American city with a high demand for donors of all races. Problem was, there weren't many donors in the book, and they weren't very well presented. Whereas every Sunday newspaper carries advertisements from private clinics and for-profit agencies that maintain fancy databases of donors. So Melanie and her husband checked out one of these private clinics with an enormous egg-donor program. "Each one was numbered, and had a little bio," Melanie remembers, and there was a wealth of information about each donor's achievements and aspirations.

Melanie had more relationship surprises in store. She and her husband had different donor-selection priorities. While Melanie was looking at donors' weight and hair color, hoping for a child who would resemble her and her husband, her husband was drawn to one thing: height. "The donor he was completely obsessed with was about six feet tall," Melanie says now, laughing. "I'm like 'Look at me! I'm not six feet tall!' He's like 'What if we have a boy?' I'm like 'What if we have a girl?' We start calling her the Green Giant. We'd look at other profiles, and then I'd be like 'Oh, we're back with the Green Giant.'"

So who gets to choose?

Both. Neither. Melanie talked her husband out of the Green Giant and they picked a donor who satisfied both of them. They paid about $20,000 to get treatment started. Only after they had paid did the fancy private clinic initiate psychological and physical testing of the donor. This was Melanie's introduction to the fact that many for-profit egg brokerages don't do the major testing of donors—testing for disease, family medical history, and fertility potential—until that donor has been selected. It isn't cost-effective to test a donor who won't ever get chosen. In truth, most huge databases of donors aren't as huge as they seem. Often, as in Melanie's case, the first donor doesn't pass some aspect of screening. The donor they had selected had alcoholism in her family, parents who were serious, active drinkers, and now that donor was no longer a candidate. Would they like to pick another?

Who Doesn't Have Children?

By Susan L. Lang

> 'Tis fate that flings the dice, and as she flings
> Of kings makes peasants, and peasants kings.
>
> —John Dryden, *"Jupiter Cannot Alter the Decrees of Fate"*

In this chapter, we'll look at the kinds of trends some researchers have found in women's lives that seem to be linked with higher rates of childlessness. How do such factors as age at marriage, careers, a woman's orientation to traditional vs. nontraditional values, and finances play out in a woman's life in regard to having children? Which factors are most influential? What kinds of events steer women away from the baby track?

Older women say they know very few women who never had children—mostly just single women who never married and a few wives they assumed couldn't get pregnant. Many people mention an aunt, their grade-school teachers, and older, traditional college professors—especially those at women's colleges. Women under fifty, on the other hand, know scads; and the younger the women, the more they know.

Among famous people, actress Katharine Hepburn always comes to mind as the epitome of a fiercely free spirit, too independent to be bound by any man or child. Helen Gurley Brown and Gloria Steinem are thought of next: the first a magazine mogul who glamorizes the sexiness of marriage without motherhood; the other, just as glamorous herself, a crusader for women's rights. Other celebrities who've never had kids include Diane Sawyer, Dolly Parton, Betty White, Marlo Thomas, Oprah Winfrey, Ann Beattie, and Elizabeth Dole. Brilliant minds and past pioneers who took the road less traveled include Jane Austen, Emily Dickinson, Georgia O'Keefe, Amelia Earhart, Beryl Markham, Lillian Hellman, Emily Brontë, George Eliot, Virginia Woolf, Simone de Beauvoir, and Anaïs Nin (who had one stillbirth pregnancy). Researchers talk of two kinds of childless women. One-third are the "voluntary" and two-thirds are the "involuntary"—those who chose to be child free vs. those who couldn't have children for reasons beyond their control.

But women's lives don't come in clear black or white packages. Take Randy. ... She married and divorced in her twenties, and knew she didn't want children then. At thirty-seven, she remarried and quickly found herself pregnant with a baby she still wasn't ready for and so she obtained an abortion. A few years later she thought she was pregnant and felt ready, but it turned out she wasn't pregnant. She wanted a baby then, but for medical reasons had to have a hysterectomy. She is both voluntarily and involuntarily childless.

What "kind" of woman doesn't have children? Broadly speaking, marriage is the strongest link: in general, married women do and single women don't ...

Susan S. Lang, "Who Doesn't Have Children?" *Women Without Children: The Reasons, the Rewards, the Regrets*, pp. 51–61. Copyright © 2002 by Susan S. Lang. Reprinted with permission.

Intriguingly, though, the later a woman marries, the less likely she is to have a child. This sounds like it would be obvious, except that it holds true for women throughout their prime baby-making time. For example, a teen bride has a higher likelihood of becoming a mother compared to a woman who marries in her early twenties; and an early twentysomething bride is more likely to have a baby than a late twentysomething bride.

When Kathleen Kiernan of the Family Policy Studies Center in London looked at women born between 1936 and 1940, she found that only four percent of the teenage brides born between those years never had children. That rate doubled for women born at the same time who married between twenty and twenty-four, doubled yet again for women who married between twenty-five and twenty-nine, and doubled again for brides between thirty and thirty-four! Even though all these ages are the prime ages for childbearing, late twentysomething brides were *four* times as likely to never have children as teen brides.

Of course, fertility nose dives in the late thirties, so the pattern becomes understandable here: when women from the same cohort married for the first time between thirty-five and thirty-nine, half remained childless; of those married after forty, three out of four never had children.

Kiernan found the same pattern for American, British, and Welsh women, as well as for women today who are in their thirties and seventies, and even women born in the 1860s.

What's going on here? Since fertility is still very high well into the thirties, physiological factors can generally be ruled out, Kiernan suspects that the same social and psychological factors that prompted the women to postpone marriage in the first place may be related to their higher rates of childlessness. Indeed, childless women tend to be more educated and have higher-status jobs than their "childed" counterparts. So, instead of marrying, these women were getting more education and climbing career ladders. Perhaps children eventually became a lower priority as time went on, or were unimportant in the first place. It's difficult to know which came first; it's the old chicken-and-egg conundrum.

Kiernan also found two puzzling relationships when she looked at women who had been married at least ten years. Only children were twice as likely to be childless than women with siblings. Even stranger, women who had gotten their first periods before the age of thirteen were more likely to be childless decades later. The real connection here, Kiernan suspects, is that, curiously, only children tend to get their first periods earlier. This relationship had been recognized before but not understood, and why it is so remains unexplained. Kiernan postulated that only children may have more gynecological and obstetrical problems in their family histories, which is why they were only children in the first place. Or maybe since only children are disproportionately represented among the voluntarily child free, their presence in the overall childless population skews the percent of only children among all the childless.

What else distinguishes the childless/child free from others? Although childless couples tend to be much less religious than couples with children, the research on childlessness and specific religions has been conflicting. One study found that nonreligious and Protestant women had the highest childlessness rate; another study found the highest rate among Baptists and Methodists, with Catholics trailing close behind. Yet another study found no link with religion at all.

Researchers have also found significantly high percentages of childless women in urban areas and in the West and Northeast, which makes sense. Careers are clustered in these areas, and alternative lifestyles are more tolerated.

What else is linked to childlessness? How traditional or untraditional a woman is may play an important role. In the past, only very nontraditional women defied the overwhelming norm to marry and have children. Although some women harbored an unexpressed lack of desire to mother, most didn't really consider children a choice and became "reluctant mothers" and often resentful mothers who have felt deprived and robbed of their freedom and self-identity by motherhood. Many such women were found among the mothers of the women interviewed for this book and in other studies of childless women, including Jean Veevers' landmark study of voluntary childless couples. Hopefully, far fewer women who feel that way are becoming mothers in the freer social climate that allows choice in the realm of children.

Women with nontraditional streaks are probably more likely to remain childless. A 1987 University of Virginia analysis suggested, for example, that a woman's childbearing future is strongly connected to her traditional vs. nontraditional view of motherhood. Women don't decide about children by weighing the costs vs. benefits but rather by paying attention to their symbolic outlook. Whereas traditional women are most apt to become homemakers and mothers, "liberated" women will "strive for success, freedom, and occupational achievement," says sociologist Steven Nock. Although many of these women will eventually become mothers, too, Nock suggests that they're likely to view parenting in much the same way as fathers do; unlike traditional mothers, these women devote less of their primary time and attention to mothering. Although Veevers and others have found that voluntarily child-free women don't consider themselves nontraditional, other than by deviating from the norm of having children, childless women do tend to be more nontraditional in terms of sex roles; their relationships and roles regarding housework, decision-making, finances, etc, are more egalitarian. About half the women interviewed for this book generally considered themselves nontraditional.

With women facing so many more choices these days, it's no wonder that so many—especially career women—are confused and ambivalent about whether and when to have a baby. To find out how such women do decide whether or not to have children, New York University sociologist Kathleen Gerson, author of *Hard Choices: How Women Decide about Work, Career, and Motherhood* (1985) studied sixty-three career women of the baby-boom generation, ages twenty-seven to thirty-seven.

How the women felt early in life about becoming mothers had very little to do with whether they actually ended up mothers or not, Gerson found. Rather, she found four prominent interrelated factors that pulled women away from having children:

1. Unstable marriages or relationships. This is "one of the most powerful and disorienting events" that trigger a chain reaction away from motherhood. Gerson found that as male support falls away, women's romantic notions about having a baby quickly fade.

Sometimes, women think they've found "the" relationship that will eventually lead to a baby carriage only to find themselves single again a few years later. Feeling suddenly stranded, such women become determined to be more self-reliant, Gerson found. They may pour themselves into a career or other kinds of self-development. Plans for children get put on hold until a good relationship comes along. In the meantime, women discover new talents or hidden interests they hadn't tapped before. Time ticks on and new experiences and opportunities weave their way into women's lives. Without a relationship that lends itself to having a baby, many women's work commitments grow stronger.

Ellen, the forty-seven-year-old therapist, fits this profile. After getting her master's degree, she taught high school for five years and married at twenty-seven, The marriage was never strong enough to withstand children and Ellen knew it: "I knew I didn't want to stay in that marriage so I never tried to have children then."

By the time she divorced five years later, "everyone was having babies. I wasn't in any serious relationship, though, so I didn't really think about having children then. I always wanted to be in a good relationship rather than just have a child," So Ellen decided to pursue her dream profession and went back for another master's degree in psychotherapy. For the next decade or so, she plunged into her work. It wasn't until she remarried at forty-two that she could think about having a baby. But it was too late. After two years of a harrowing infertility experience? Ellen let go of her dreams for a child at age forty-five.

2. Feeling that a baby would be too much of a financial strain. This also plays an important role in moving a woman away from motherhood, even when she has a stable relationship. If having a child is viewed as a potential economic hardship, a woman may postpone a pregnancy. But that seemingly minor and temporary decision seems so inconsequential at the time, just "a mere postponement of an ultimate decision in favor of motherhood," Gerson says. "The final result, however, was often the opposite of this early expectation."

For example, Diane, a forty-three-year-old middle manager at a large corporation, said:

> I always assumed as a young girl that I'd marry and have children. When I married at twenty-five, though, my husband wasn't financially ready for a child, so we decided to wait. It turned out he wasn't the right person for me anyway, and we divorced four years later.

Ever since then, although Diane has been continually in and out of relationships, even one that lasted ten years, she's never been in a situation again that would be appropriate for children. She's grateful she wasn't burdened with being a single mother which she knows she certainly would have been had she had a child during her first marriage. What's eerie, though, is that the unforeseen consequences of postponing a baby at twenty-six or twenty-seven resulted in permanent childlessness for Diane, a condition she never expected or planned for.

Postponement for financial reasons also motivated Dolores, now aged sixty-five, although unlike Diane, she's been married for forty-two years. She met her husband at the age of twenty-one while working as a secretary for a mail-order house. It was the late 1940s and everyone was having babies; she assumed she would, too.

> When we got married, he didn't make that much as an accountant, and we'd say, well, when he makes $100 a week, we'll have a baby. We couldn't afford it at the time, we lived in a basement apartment, but we still figured we'd have a child sometime. Then we thought we'd wait until he made $150, then $200 a week, and it kept escalating, and that was it. We kept putting it off until finally we said, we're satisfied. The feeling to have a child just faded away.

3. Turned off to staying home. Career women especially postpone children because the thought of staying home to care for them sounds boring and lonely and feels like a demotion. "Motherhood threatened to impose not only isolation, but also, and perhaps worse, personal denigration. This perceived danger prompted some respondents to reject domesticity and potentially motherhood as well," reports Gerson. Janice, a forty-four-year-old married attorney, said:

> I think I'd be miserable staying home with a child; I'd miss being in the outside world, miss the excitement and challenge of my work. But if I were going to have a child, I'd want to do it right and be the best mother I could. I think it's too important to leave to a hired caregiver, at least for the first few years. But I don't really want to do it.

Such women typically view children as a trap and tend to devalue domestic life; they derive their identity and self-worth from their careers and so plunge themselves into their work. If circumstances don't switch them back to the baby track, their desire for children tends to wane somewhere in their late thirties and early forties while their careers provide for them their greatest source of self-esteem and satisfaction.

4. Career opportunities. Most intriguing in Gerson's work was her finding that work opportunities play a crucial role in determining a woman's childbearing decision. When career women decided to have a baby, Gerson found, it was not out of some deep-felt, abstract "mothering need," but rather as a function of two factors. First, a nurturing, stable relationship had to be in place. Second, when work became more frustrating than pleasurable, home began to look like a haven. "Many women chose motherhood not to fulfill deep-seated emotional needs, but rather as the best option among a number of unappealing alternatives," In other words, when work gets boring, feels like a dead end, or just simply loses its lustre and all-important meaning in life, the thought of having a child begins to glitter. "Domestic pastures" look greener and the sanctity of home more fulfilling. The "right" time, Gerson found, was consistently linked to job dissatisfaction.

Ann, for example, had already been divorced twice by age twenty-eight. That's when she went back to school for an MBA degree and worked long yet fulfilling hours as a personnel manager for a large corporation. Before she remarried at thirty-five to a man who didn't want children, she decided to have her tubes tied before the wedding:

> If I had not been sterilized then, I might have wanted to have children in my late thirties. That's about when I decided my career wasn't fulfilling and I would just as soon stay home. Having children would validate my not working.

Women given promotions or new job opportunities at critical times, on the other hand, would feel reinforced in their choice to pursue their career, thereby keeping the thought of pregnancy on a back burner.

Gerson points out that "those with declining aspirations [at work] focused on the liberating, nurturing, and fulfilling aspects of mothering, but these upwardly mobile women stressed instead its potentially negative consequences …"

Linda, for example, remembers always loving children, but the idea of having her own felt like a trap, and besides, she kept getting better and more exciting jobs. She started out in early education at a day-care center, and then became director of a local head-start operation. She married right after college at twenty-two and is still married to Ed seventeen years later:

> I think we assumed we'd get to having children, but every time things got real regular and predictable, one of us, usually me, did something to change it—usually a better job. I thought I'd be a good mother, but it never seemed like enough to do with my life. It was just something women were stuck with, having families and being mothers, and not anything that I considered at the time worthwhile or interesting.

At twenty-eight, she was offered a wonderful opportunity to head up her state's cancer association in a city three hours from where Ed worked. They had a commuter marriage for a year or so, and when Linda accidentally got pregnant, their relationship was at an all-time low.

> He hated his job, it was very expensive having two residences, and my new job was really exciting. He was feeling very martyred, having to commute to see me in an old car that kept breaking down. I loved what I was doing, he hated what he was doing. We could barely talk, so we decided it wasn't the best time to have a child. I was twenty-nine. I remember feeling really disappointed but had an abortion anyway.

Ed then got a job in the same city as Linda for two years. When he got an even better job an hour away, they commuted again for a year. Then Linda got an even better job in the state capital as the director of staff development for a state agency. She now commutes three hours on weekends to their custom-built house perched on a wooded hilltop.

> I've always been back and forth about whether to have a baby or not. Then, as I got older, it seemed like it was getting too late to get started. The last time we talked about it seriously, a few years ago, we both realized we were happy with what we were doing.

The connection between work dissatisfaction and dropping out to have a baby is perhaps highlighted best by Lisa's story. She remembers always loving children. She babysat for years and worked with children in camps, hospitals, and adoption agencies. At twenty-four, she married and worked full time at an adoption/foster-care agency. At twenty-six, she decided to have a baby.

> I thought I really wanted a baby. I worked with babies, I adored babies, and I always imagined I was going to have six children. When my husband and I got involved, we assumed we'd have children. He was the first man I met who seemed interested in settling down and having a family, and that was important to me.

> After two years, I announced I wanted a baby. Work was draining and putting a strain on us. I'll never forget what he said; "Do you want a baby or do you just want to stop working?"

> It had never occurred to me to stop working for no reason. I was brought up to think you stopped working if you had a baby, but otherwise you worked. Yes, I wanted to stop working and thought that the way to do it was to have a baby.

Lisa quit working, started painting, and put off getting pregnant temporarily. Two years passed, and she felt very content painting, housekeeping, camping every weekend, and traveling all summer. People kept asking her, "Well, aren't you going to have your baby now?"

> And I thought, I like this too much to have a baby. I no longer had a need to have a child. I don't know what those needs were that fostered wanting one. I suspect they were wanting this loving creature who adores you back, and it's a very warm, wonderful, responsive relationship. But I had that with my husband and didn't need it from a child.

Lisa, now forty-six, has not worked at a paying job since. She would have had a baby to quit her job had her husband not suggested that she merely quit first and "wait and see." She had a tubal ligation at thirty-five and has never regretted it.

So who doesn't have babies? Obviously, women who feel they don't have the right relationship as well as women who clearly know they don't want to mother. But many women don't have children because of the consequences of decisions made long ago.

"Neither chance circumstances nor individual personalities determined the paths these women took as they made decisions that shaped the direction of their lives," Gerson points out. Women make decisions based on information they have at the time. They can only guess what the future consequences of those decisions will be.

Says Gerson: "Even the most carefully calculated choices often had unintended consequences that led to unanticipated directions. Change occurred not simply because people wished it to, but more fundamentally because seemingly static, discrete, inconsequential decisions had only dimly perceived long-term consequences"

In other words, some women don't have children because of fate and fortune. As their life histories unfold, they face critical turning points of choice and action. They make decisions—however minor, ambiguous, or conflicted—the best way they can, with the information at hand. Some choices, however, may lead women unknowingly down paths with unexpected consequences, of which never having children may be one.

Dropping Sperm Counts

The Science and Politics of Male Reproductive Health

By Cynthia Daniels

In 1992, a team of Danish researchers reported a drop of more than 40% in sperm count rates worldwide over the previous fifty years. They noted as well an almost fourfold increase in rates of testicular cancer in men and a doubling of genital birth defects in baby boys. Others noted a decrease in the male-to-female birth rate; it seemed that fewer baby boys were being born. In the ten years to follow, these claims would be among the most highly disputed in both science and politics. It would seem that these measures would be simple to assess: Had testicular cancers increased or declined? Had sperm counts risen or fallen? Had the proportion of baby boys gone up or down? How was it possible that we didn't know or hadn't noticed? But no one seemed certain about the state of men's reproductive health. The lack of historical attention to male reproductive health meant that there were few baseline measurements to recall, little information about the extent to which such reproductive ailments had afflicted men in the past. Neglect throughout the twentieth century meant that there were few tracking systems to assess the simplest measures of male reproductive health.

When such issues spilled over into public consciousness, as they did in the ten years, following the Danish team's initial report, the response displayed many of the elements of public panic, with deeply conflicted responses in the scientific community, the media, government agencies worldwide, and the general public. Some declared a crisis of epic proportions—the "feminization" or "chemical castration" of men and the potential end of the human race. Others denied such claims as social and scientific hysteria. At one extreme, claims of a monumental health crisis appeared to eclipse scientific reason. At the other, the doubts with which these measures were met appeared to exceed reasonable scientific skepticism.

What was at stake, it seemed, was more than just male reproductive health but masculinity itself. This failure to agree on even the simplest measures of male reproductive health is evidence not only of the difficulty of tracking rates of disease or disability but also of cultural barriers to the recognition of the potential reproductive vulnerabilities of men and the volatile nature of any suggestion of male reproductive failure.

Social, scientific, and political controversies surrounded male reproductive health disorders at the end of the twentieth century. These controversies, as well as the public response, were informed by the second element of reproductive masculinity—the presumption of the invulnerability of the male reproductive body. This presumption has led, first, to a historical lack of attention to male reproductive problems and now to conflict-ridden responses to such issues. Ultimately, appropriate attention to these problems, including simple assessments of the level of risks men truly face, hardly seems possible until this second presumption of reproductive masculinity is challenged as well.

Cynthia Daniels, "Dropping Sperm Counts," *Exposing Men: The Science and Politics of Male Reproduction*, pp. 31–71. Copyright © 2008 by Oxford University Press. Reprinted with permission.

The "Diseases of Men"

> There is no question but that those afflictions peculiar to the male have been more neglected, less fully understood, and more frequently treated "for what there is in it," rather than a desire to benefit the patient, than was ever true of the diseases of women. We believe that today fully as barbarous, slipshod, and dishonest work is being done in this class of affections as was ever to be observed in gynic disease. Diseases of men have ever been the fruitful field of the quack and the charlatan. (1891 editorial in the *Journal of the American Medical Association*)

Historically, the singular focus of reproductive medicine on the female reproductive system was paralleled by a concurrent neglect of the male system. Men, it seemed, with their peripheral role in human creation, had elementary reproductive systems that needed no special study or medical attention. Like a simple mechanical instrument, the male system either worked or it didn't. Because women were seen as primary in reproductions problems of fertility were typically assumed to be female in origin. The vulnerable female system stood in contrast to the virile male system, despite nineteenth-century appeals by some physicians that "there is no part of the body that so quickly and painfully resents incompetency and tinkering as does the genitourinary apparatus of the male."

While the field of gynecology grew throughout the nineteenth century, there was little similar development in andrology—the study of the nature and diseases of male reproduction. As a result, reproductive sciences in the nineteenth and early twentieth century focused primarily on the diseases and disorders of female reproduction through the development of gynecology and obstetrics. The science of reproduction focused primarily on the "management" of women. Although the term *andrology* made a brief appearance in the professional medical lexicon in the late nineteenth century, it was then absorbed (and virtually disappeared) into the field of urology for more than fifty years. The term *andrology was* not reintroduced into medical terminology until 1951, when it was coined by a professor of gynecology in Germany. The first medical journal to address the field *(Andrologie)* was not established until 1969. Although an informal medical association of physicians and researchers focusing on male reproductive health was active in the United States from 1969 onward, not until 1975 was the American Society of Andrology founded. As medical historian Nelly Oudshoorn has rightly observed, "It was only in the late 1970 was that scientists and clinicians established andrology as a medical specialty devoted to the study and medical treatment of male reproductive bodies ... today, andrology is still a small and marginal profession compared to gynecology."

By the year 2001, the International Society of Andrology (founded in 1981) had thirty-six national societies and more than eight thousand members worldwide. Still, this was a far cry from the size and scope of medical associations, schools, and centers dedicated to the study and treatment of female reproduction. As earlier chapters have suggested, the initial assessments of male reproductive health focused either on male "underproduction" or on "overproduction"—either treatment of male infertility or, even more marginally, control of male fertility through male birth control methods.

As the one of the earliest analysts of male infertility observed:

> Now, when a man is unable to beget children by his wife, although his virility is unimpaired, he is said in common parlance to have a cold nature. To my mind, however, it would be more apt to say that no living animalcules will be found in the seed of such a man, or that, should any living animalcules be found in it, they are too weakly to survive long enough in the womb. (Leeuwenhoek, Letter to the Royal Society, London, March 30, 1685)

Despite Leeuwenhoek's early investigations and concerns, male fertility has been a subject historically understudied. As previous chapters have suggested, ancient physiologists and philosophers proposed different theories of sperm production. One medical historian recounts: "Aristotle thought semen arises from the brain, Hippocrates wrote that semen was transported to the testicles via the arteries behind the ears, and Plato considered that semen originates from the spinal cord." Reproductive disorders of the male system received only limited attention, and not all of this positive. In 1585, Pope Sixtus V apparently decreed that "all marriages in which men do not have two testicles in the scrotum should be dissolved." One of the first clinical practices to treat male reproductive ailments was not established until 1905.

Although the field of andrology has expanded considerably, basic functioning of the male reproductive system remains somewhat of a mystery. As researcher Richard Sharpe put it in 1992:

> We can't monitor sperm production. All we can do is look at the end product. It's like investigating the production of a motor car by looking at whether it's come out of the factory or not, and whether it's got doors on back to front, but not being able to go inside the factory to see where in the production cycle something has gone wrong.

Very few studies have been conducted on the general population of men to determine average sperm counts over extended time periods or even correlations between sperm counts and actual male infertility. Sperm shape and movement appear to be as important as count or, as one news headline personified the findings, "Shapely Swimmers Win Fertility Race!" Sperm count may vary from day to day or week to week, but we're not certain by how much or for what reasons. Sperm count may decrease with age, but it's unclear at what rate. Counts appear to vary by season and by geography, but not enough data exist to determine predictable patterns. Although we know, for instance, that heat slows sperm production, sperm counts are not necessarily lower in tropical climates. We have, therefore, few baseline estimates for establishing what is normal for men, despite the fact that, technically speaking, collecting semen from the male body is relatively easy.

Historically, semen analysis has relied on subjective measures taken by lab technicians who were trained to count sperm under a microscope and observe abnormalities, like dual heads or missing tails. Technicians simply placed sperm samples under a microscope equipped with a grid screen, counted the number of sperm in each grid, and extrapolated total sperm count from this sample. They also assessed normal versus abnormal structure and noted levels of sperm movement. At the end of the twentieth century, sperm was microanalyzed through more objective computer-aided assessment measures. Sperm samples are now videotaped under a microscope, and sperm shape, size, and speed are assessed with standardized computer assistance.

In contrast to earlier assumptions of the male body as machinelike and sperm as relatively invulnerable to harm, researchers have noted that sperm are apparently fairly fragile—sensitive to both temperature and movement. Evaluation must take place within two hours of being "produced." Samples are prewarmed in an incubator or on a warming plate before being placed under a microscope. Technicians are warned to avoid "vigorous shaking" of the sample to avoid damage to the sperm. If sperm were "produced" by the female body, researchers might have said they were "delivered," but mechanical and production metaphors seem to dominate in studies of men's sperm count.

As the media response to reported drops in sperm count will illustrate, male sperm count, despite its questionable relationship to male fertility, is still considered a primary sign of one's manhood; consequently, low sperm counts typically carry with them stigmas of "unmanliness." As a result, it is not always easy to find willing donors to study, male participants are subject to a level of sexual surveillance not typically experienced by men: They are asked to refrain from ejaculation at least two days before producing a specimen and may be asked for an "ejaculation calendar" (because sexual frequency may have an effect on sperm levels). They may be asked about alcohol, cigarette, and drug use or be monitored for such use during the study period. As a result, sperm count studies are typically not drawn from the general population but from men who have some other motivation for participating (sperm donors, couples at fertility clinics, or men working in toxic environments) or from men already under state surveillance *(in prison or in the military)*.

Sperm Count Crisis: Scientific Evidence (or Not?)

In the 1980s, Danish pediatrician Niels Skakkebaek noticed an alarming trend in the school-aged boys he saw in his pediatric practice. A surprisingly high number of them were appearing with malformations of the genitals or with one or both testicles undescended—conditions that could lead to sterility or higher rates of testicular cancer as they grew older. Skakkebaek had already noted a dramatic rise in testicular cancer rates for men. Denmark had the highest rates in the world—nearly one in a hundred men in Denmark would be diagnosed with the disease in their lifetimes. By the mid-1980s, Skakkebaek had documented in his practice a relationship between abnormal cells in the testes, low sperm count, and adult testicular cancer, and he and his colleagues began to investigate this relationship.

Along with other Danish scientists, Skakkebaek had also noticed the difficulties sperm banks were having in recruiting adequate sperm donors, some centers reporting that they had to test ten men to find one good donor. He suspected a relationship between rising rates of cancer and falling sperm count rates. With a group of other researchers, Skakkebaek decided to initiate a preliminary study of sperm quality as the simplest measure of the health (or failure) of the male reproductive system. Their first preliminary study of male airport workers in Denmark found that 50% had abnormal forms of sperm, much higher rates than expected.

To see how widespread this trend might be, the Danish team then collected evidence from all of the sperm count studies they could find that had been conducted worldwide between 1938 and 1990 and combined data from almost 15,000 men to examine long-term sperm count trends. Although varying in their methodology, most of these studies had been conducted to assess sperm quality because of the rise of artificial insemination and sperm banking. Skakkebaek and his associates found a greater than 40% drop in sperm count over the fifty-year period. They noted as well that data from the United States and Europe indicated that testicular cancer had increased "twofold to fourfold over the past fifty years." Because the rates of testicular cancer had risen fairly dramatically over a short time period and sperm counts had dropped in a similar time frame, Skakkebaek and his associates suggested that the cause was "probably due to environmental rather than genetic factors." In conclusion, they suggested that "some common prenatal influences could be responsible both for the decline in sperm density and for the increase in cancer of the testis.... Whether oestrogens or compounds with oestrogen-like activity ... or other environmental or endogenous factors damage testicular function remains to be determined."

Despite the cautious conclusions of Skakkebaek and other major researchers, critics immediately attacked research findings suggesting any decrease in sperm counts by questioning both the validity of sperm count drops and any association with environmental estrogens. The aggregated studies upon which the Danish team based their findings were questioned on a number of levels: Geographical variation might account for the apparent decline; methodological differences might have skewed the research; subject selection might have produced the appearance of a decline, when in fact there was none. Follow-up analyses sought to take these critics' questions into account.

Some researchers suggested that changes in research methods over the same time period might have skewed the sperm count numbers. Because the sixty-one original studies were conducted before the advent of standardized techniques for semen analysis, critics argued that sperm evaluations could have varied as much as 40% upward or downward, depending on the quality of equipment and the subjectivity of technical readers. The *New England Journal of Medicine* ran a 1995 editorial questioning the validity of the studies' methods and evidence: "The men in these studies ranged in age from 17 to 64 years, the duration of abstinence was for the most part neither controlled nor recorded, and the mean sperm concentration varied threefold." In addition, most studies relied on a single sperm sample, when sperm count levels can vary "two to fourfold" in a single week for an individual man, even under "disciplined conditions of abstinence." Any of these elements could have skewed sperm count assessments up or down, although it was not clear that any one of these complicating factors would have systematically created the appearance of a sperm count decline.

Researchers also looked more carefully at the original sixty-one studies examined by the Danish team. Studies controlled for abstinence time, age, percent of men with proven fertility, and specimen evaluation methods confirmed the decline in sperm density for the United States and northern Europe but noted that not enough data were available to assess sperm count rates for non-Western countries. In 1996, a prominent group of nineteen scientists issued a statement that "several aspects of male reproductive health have changed dramatically for the worse over 30 to 50 years ... [including a] striking decline in sperm counts in the ejaculate of normal men."

Yet critics contested these conclusions and argued that sperm count rates vary by geographical location and that comparisons between East Coast and West Coast or First World and Third World countries could create the appearance of a decline that didn't exist. Researchers Harry Fisch and E. T. Goluboff of Columbia Presbyterian Hospital in New York disaggregated the original sixty-one studies, first eliminating all those containing fewer than a hundred subjects. Of the remaining twenty studies, they found that all of the studies before 1970 were from the United States, and 80% of these were from New York City, which, they argued, has typically higher sperm counts than other locations. In contrast, 80% of the studies conducted after 1970 were from locations with typically lower counts—Europe and five Third World countries. Others argued that these geographical variations might be due to ethnic differences between cities, with some evidence that Chinese men have naturally lower sperm counts than white, African-American, or Hispanic men. These conclusions were limited by the fact that they were drawn on only twenty of the original sixty-one studies. Nevertheless, many welcomed this study. As one commentator reported, "There is no longer a need to feel impotent in the face of mass extinction."

Sperm count studies multiplied across the globe. Declines were found in the United States, Pakistan, Germany, Hong Kong, Sweden, and Belgium. One study of four European cities cited significant geographical variations in sperm count, with the lowest sperm counts for Danish men, followed by French, Scottish, and Finnish men. French researchers found that the sperm count of men in Paris had declined 2–3% every year from 1973 to 1992, along with increases in the percentage of abnormal sperm and decreases in sperm concentration and motility. A study of more than 48,000 Canadian men showed similar declines. Danish scientists found that 43% of army recruits tested in one study had sperm count levels low enough to lead to decreased fertility. Studies that held geography constant seemed to confirm the decline.

Others suggested the data on sperm count drop could be skewed by subject selection. Over the forty-year period, most studies of sperm quality have been conducted at fertility clinics or on sperm donors-men with either especially low or especially high counts. If the early studies came from fertility clinics and the later ones from sperm donors, that difference might also create the false appearance of a decline. Follow-up studies tried to hold subject selection constant. One study collected semen from men who were seeking fertility treatment with their partners at the University of Southern California Medical Center in Los Angeles. Sperm counts of these men, compared with semen collected in a 1951 study, showed only a 1% decline. Researchers in Australia said that sperm donors in Sydney remained "as fertile as ever," with no decline between 1983 and 2001, and no decline in sperm counts was found in one study of donors in Seattle. It would be reasonable to assume, researchers suggested, that if there had been a drop in sperm count worldwide, this would be reflected in a decrease in the counts of sperm donors.

Other critics looked at male infertility rates, under the assumption that if sperm counts had been dropping, then male infertility should be rising, but there was no apparent drop in male fertility during the past fifty years. On the contrary, studies suggested that "time to pregnancy"—the number of months it takes a couple to achieve conception—had improved. As a *Lancet* commentary accompanying the report of study suggested: "At present, the near-panic sometimes expressed in the lay press about the effects of environmental pollution on sperm quality and male fertility is not justified." Such studies of time to pregnancy provided ammunition for those who questioned the validity of sperm count studies more broadly, even though researchers also noted that any decline in male fertility might have been compensated for by improvements in techniques for predicting ovulation and achieving conception over the same time period. Nevertheless, stories such as "Potent News" in the *Milwaukee Journal Sentinel* reported that "the virility of American men hasn't changed much in the past four decades."

Countering such hopeful sentiments, others warned that the natural overabundance of sperm in a man's semen is no reason to be complacent about male fertility. Even if they were in decline, sperm counts still remained, on average, well above the level needed for male fertility. But as researcher Richard Sharpe of Scotland noted, "If we are being exposed to something that is having this effect and we don't know what it is, then we don't know whether we've reached the bottom of that decline, ... If we were to come along in another 50 years' time and find our sperm counts had fallen by another 50 percent then we would be extremely concerned."

Data from the sixty-one studies on the nearly 15,000 men examined over five decades, burdened as they were by methodological difficulties, didn't seem to be able to resolve the question of dropping sperm counts. Studies conducted on thousands of men in the 1990s didn't seem to hold definitive answers either, although much of the research confirmed Skakkebaek's original conclusions. The evidence, while still contested, seemed to suggest that sperm counts had decreased, at least in some parts of the globe, over the preceding fifty years.

Male Reproductive Deformations

While debate continued on the question of sperm count drops, others explored the evidence presented by Skakkebaek and his colleagues of a substantial increase in malformations and diseases of the male reproductive system. Hypospadias is a developmental malformation in which the urethra opens on the underside of the penis or on the perineum. This malformation can lead to male infertility or a range of health problems. Reports had suggested increased rates of this malformation from the 1960s to the 1980s. Researchers also reported increases in cryptorchidism—a condition in which one or both of the testicles fail to descend. Undescended testes had been suspected as a cause of increases in testicular cancer in men, as well as a cause of male infertility. Two U.S. studies showed increases in this condition. As researchers framed the discussion, both hypospadias and cryptorchidism represented forms of "feminization" of the male body.

In addition, Skakkebaek had noted a dramatic increase in testicular cancer rates. In follow-ups to the Danish team's original observations, researchers documented in young men an increase of testicular cancer, the most common form of cancer in men age 15–44, with a peak incidence between the ages of 18 and 35. Some studies found that rates of testicular cancer had increased worldwide, with the highest incidence in Denmark, Switzerland, and New Zealand. One research group reexamining the evidence concluded that the evidence was overwhelming that testicular cancer incidence had "increased rapidly" in virtually all countries studied. In the United States, testicular cancer rates among white active-duty servicemen 17 to 44 increased by 61% from the 1970s to the 1990s. Reports in the *Journal of the National Cancer Institute* confirmed that testicular cancer had increased by 51.2% in white men between 1973 and 1996.

Critics challenged these numbers as well, with scientists such as Stephen Safe arguing that the evidence showed not a comprehensive increase but changing demographic distributions in these disorders before 1985. Rates of hypospadias and cryptorchidism, he argued, had not changed or had actually decreased in some areas since 1985. Although increased rates of testicular cancer appear to be relatively undisputed, critics like Safe suggested that geographical variations in rates remained unexplained and were unlikely to be due to environmental exposures. Despite such criticisms, the evidence seemed fairly clear that these two disorders, as well as rates of testicular cancer, had increased dramatically over a relatively short time period and that these increases were not limited to a single geographical area.

"Bye, Bye, Baby Boys"

Researchers also saw changing birth sex ratios as one indicator that male reproductive health may be affected by environmental toxins. A 1976 explosion at a chemical plant in Seveso, Italy, exposed residents to high levels of dioxin (TCDD). Parents with the highest blood levels of the toxin produced no baby boys for the next seven years. In the general Seveso population in the nine years that followed the explosion, the rate of birth for baby boys dropped to half. Interestingly, the study found that TCDD exposure had a greater impact on men than on women. Females, the study found, were "insensitive to the effects of TCDD" and gave birth to both male and female children if the fathers were non-exposed men. On the other hand, the young men in Seveso who were exposed to relatively low levels of TCDD before or during puberty continued to produce disproportionately female children later in life. For these men, dioxin exposure seemed to permanently affect the sex ratio of the children they fathered.

Initially, following conception, all embryos are female. Between six and nine weeks of gestational age, hormonal stimulation typically begins the process of sexual differentiation. Historically, birth rates are skewed slightly in favor of boys (on average 106 males to 100 females). Little or no androgen stimulation can either stop male development or produce a "feminized" male that may appear female at birth. Estrogen or estrogenic chemicals, if delivered to the developing embryo at this stage, have been shown to disrupt sexual development in clinical animal studies. Incidents like the Seveso accident seemed to suggest that the same process could be produced in humans. Researchers turned to broader studies of sex birth ratios.

Throughout the late 1990s, researchers found a decrease in male births in Denmark, the United States, and Canada. In 1996, researchers in Denmark found statistically significant declines in male births from the 1960s to 1995. Researchers again suggested that toxic exposures in utero may have caused increased miscarriage rates for male fetuses or sex transformation in utero. In 1997, researchers in Canada documented a declining male birth rate from 1970 to 1990, with a loss of 2.2 male births per thousand. Researchers in the United States also found a decline in male births from 1970 to 1990, with a loss of one male birth per thousand. As the U.S. researchers suggested:

> Such small changes ... can have profound implications for large populations, where hundreds of thousands or millions of births occur each year. For example, the reported statistically significant decrease of 2.2 males per 1,000 births in a country the size of Canada with an annual average of 333,159 births represents a cumulative decline of about 8,600 male births since 1970. During the same period, the U.S. decline of 1 male birth per 1,000 corresponds to approximately 38,000 male births.

Studies of male agricultural workers exposed to herbicides and pesticides have shown statistically significant increases in birth abnormalities in their children, and such birth defects seem to disproportionately affect their male children. Additional studies that examined the sex ratio patterns of workers exposed to dioxins have found significant evidence that male birth rates have declined for these workers. And studies of men exposed to the pesticide dibromochloro-propane (DBCP) also found that those men not rendered infertile by the exposure produced three times as many girl children as expected in the years following exposure.

Some researchers argue that the male fetus is more vulnerable to harm from paternal exposures than the female fetus—more likely to be miscarried, more likely to have sexual development disrupted, more likely to have future fertility affected, and more likely to be born with birth defects as a result of in utero exposures. Evidence also appears to indicate that fathers are more vulnerable to toxic harm than mothers in the sense that they are more likely to pass on to the developing fetus damage from such exposures, even if those exposures occur long before conception. As the authors of one comprehensive study concluded, "It appears that the male fetus is more vulnerable to paternal exposures that take place prior to conception and that may be linked with birth defects."

Still, there is no clear causal relationship between environmental toxins and changing sex ratios. Sex ratios can be affected by a wide range of factors, including race (male births are lower in black populations), parental age (older parents produce more girls), use of fertility drugs, and decreased stillbirth rates (stillbirth rates are typically higher for male babies and so reduced stillbirth rates will produce an increase in male births). In some occupational studies, sample sizes may be limited; in some environmental research, sex ratio effects are significant but small; research on some environmental accidents shows no change in sex ration in their aftermath; little is known, cross-culturally or historically, about what may be natural fluctuations in human sex ratios, Yet, animal studies clearly indicate that certain chemical exposures can change birth sex ratios. Some argued that the evidence was strong enough to consider sex ratio changes a "sentinel health indicator"—a red flag signaling that an "avoidable" factor is having a significant impact on human health, a flag that shows the need for public intervention. Yet others saw it as one more instance of "environmental hysteria," this time combined with male reproductive panic.

On sperm count rates, male reproductive disorders, reproductive cancers, and sex birth ratios, there seemed to be little agreement and limited human data. But animal research, which documented some of the same problems in wildlife species, provided additional support for those who argued that male reproductive health was in trouble.

Wildlife Studies: Turtles, Panthers, Alligators, and Fish

In the 1980s, prominent scientist John McLachlan and a team of researchers at the University of Texas dramatically demonstrated the estrogenic qualities of the toxin PCB. By painting the outside of turtle egg shells with the chemical, they were able to reverse the sex of neonates developing inside from male to female. Clinical research such as this, as well as evidence from wildlife research on alligators, panthers, birds, and fish, lent support to the thesis that male reproductive health was in trouble and seemed to confirm suspected environmental causes. Many of the disorders of men were also found in animals in the wild.

Since the 1960s, scientists had documented the effects of pesticides on the reproductive systems of wildlife. During the 1970s and 1980s, research on birds and fish in the Great Lakes basin found "male birds growing ovarian tissue, and female birds growing excessive oviduct tissue; male fish not reaching full sexual maturity; and hermaphroditism in fish." Researchers suspected high levels of chemical pollutants were contributing to poor reproductive outcomes for eagles, herring gulls, and terns living off the lakes. Meanwhile, beginning in the 1980s, British biologists discovered "intersexed" fish downstream from sewage outfall pipes in northern England and suspected that residues of birth control pills were washing into water supplies. One in twenty fish, researchers found, were hermaphrodites—containing the genitals of both sexes. Experiments showed that male fish placed at the mouth of the outfall pipes became hermaphrodites with exposure to the effluent, literally changing their sex. In 2002, scientists continue to report the "feminisation" of fish downstream of sewage plants in England, as one reporter put it, "changing the sex of half the fish in Britain's lowland rivers." They have since discovered hormone-disrupting chemicals in four of every ten samples tested in the rivers of England, reduced fertility, and "widespread sexual disruption" in fish. The source of this disruption remains in dispute, with some arguing that it is due to the sewage "tainted" by hormones excreted through the urine of women using birth control pills, and others that a component of plastics, nonylphenol, might be responsible for the estrogen-like effects.

In 1994, researchers led by Louis Guillette of the University of Florida reported alligators born with dramatically decreased penis size and undescended testes in Lake Apopka, Florida. Lake Apopka had been polluted with DDT by chemical runoff from nearby farms and a chemical spill at an adjacent chemical company in 1980. In the immediate aftermath of the spill, 90% of the alligators disappeared. The remaining alligators survived but showed signs of toxic damage, including reproductive dysfunction. More than ten years later, researchers found female alligators with abnormal ovarian growths, juvenile males with depressed testosterone levels, and adult males with "poorly organized testes and abnormally small phalli." Guillette went on to find similar symptoms in lakes considered to be "non-polluted" in Florida and suspected the cause might be background levels of chemical contaminants.

Animal research suggested that hormonal exposures can have an impact on reproductive development not just in the aftermath of toxic spills but at extremely low dosages. Biological scientist Fredrick vom Saal argued that changes in the functioning of the prostate, glandular development in fetuses, and sperm production can be caused by tiny changes in hormone exposure:

> To most people if I said there's only a millionth of a gram of it here you'd say, "How can it do anything?" A millionth of a gram of estradiol [the female hormone] in blood is toxic. The natural hormone is actually operating at something like a hundred millions times lower than that ... We experimentally elevated estradiol levels in mouse fetuses during the period when their reproductive organs were forming. And what we did was we experimentally elevated estradiol by one tenth of one trillionth of a gram of estradiol in a milliliter of blood. We estimate that we're increasing estradiol by about one molecule of estradiol per cell in the body. ... The consequence of this is that at the end of the first day of development of the prostate in the male fetuses we could see dramatic change in the sprouting of prostate glands. We rendered the prostate abnormally enlarged, and this was detectable within twenty-four hours of the beginning of its embryonic development. And when we looked at these treated animals as adults, that difference had persisted. They had abnormally enlarged prostates that were hyper-responsive to hormones.

In 1995, scientists also reported reproductive disorders in the endangered Florida panther, only thirty to fifty of which survived in the wild. The panthers had been captured and tracked since the 1970s. By the 1990s, studies showed an increase in genital malformations. Researchers found that cryptorchidism (undescended testes) had "increased exponentially in male cubs since 1975," from about 15% to 90% of the population in 1995. Increased rates of sterility were also found among the male panthers. And more than 75% of the male panthers' sperm "exhibited severe deformity," compared with 20–25% in other wild cat species. Panther researchers argued that the cats were bioaccumulating mercury and pesticides by eating raccoons as their major source of food. Raccoons ingest a high level of toxins from the aquatic food chain, and according to researchers, such toxins disrupted the endocrine systems of the panthers who ate them.

Animal studies are often problematic as predictors of human risk and as such have been reasonably subject to scientific skepticism. Thalidomide, for instance, is a notorious human reproductive toxin, but animal studies showed few signs of teratogenicity. Yet for reasons of human ethics, experimental studies on animals as well as evidence from wildlife studies often provide the only avenue for predictors of risks to humans. Although animal studies are clearly not definitive of risks to humans, they nevertheless provide invaluable data on potential risks to human health.

By the turn of the twenty-first century, many were convinced that human and animal studies together confirmed symptoms of a deteriorating male reproductive system. They suspected the source lay in environmental exposures of males either in utero or after birth. Debate began over a range of possible causes.

Causes

Researchers theorized a number of causes, with environmental chemicals at the top of the list. But a wide range of other causes were considered as well: the use of plastic diapers on boys, increased rates of sexual activity, the shift from boxer to jockey shorts, the rise of male obesity and dietary changes in men, increased use of drugs and alcohol, the shift from factory to sedentary work, maternal use of drugs during pregnancy, the use of hard bicycle seats, even the advent *of* feminism and the decline of war!

Some researchers argued that increased levels of sexual activity for young men since the 1960s might have lowered sperm count over the decades. Men who engage in frequent sex have lower sperm counts than other men. But in reexamining past sperm count studies that controlled for frequency of ejaculation, researchers found no association between increased sexual activity and sustained dropping sperm counts. It seemed that sexual frequency did not increase dramatically enough to change aggregate sperm counts.

Others looked at the shift from boxer shorts to jockey shorts as a potential source of the sperm count drop; snug underwear, by holding the testicles closer to the body, might increase testicular temperature and cause a drop in sperm counts. As one news report put it, "tight pants" and "tight underwear" should be avoided by anyone concerned with his sperm counts. Another warned men that "long hot baths and a fondness for tight trouserings are particularly dangerous." But researchers found no such temperature increase in men tested wearing boxers or briefs.

Attention in the 1990s shifted also to the use of plastic diapers for not only leaching plastics into the environment after use but also increasing scrotal temperature. A team of scientists in Germany found that plastic diapers increased the scrotal temperature in boy babies and possibly damaged their long-term ability to produce healthy sperm. The scientists placed forty-eight babies in disposable diapers and cotton diapers with tiny heat monitors that recorded scrotal temperature every thirty seconds for twenty-four hours. Temperature in the plastic diapers was one degree Celsius higher than in cotton and, because increased temperature can decrease adult male fertility, the scientists speculated that increases in the temperature of male babies might have similar effects. Lending additional credence to the theory, the authors of the report speculated that sperm count drops seemed to correspond with the development and distribution of plastic diapers worldwide after World War II. But the one-degree increase didn't seem to be enough to cause long-term testicular damage. And, as might be expected, the thesis came under immediate attack from the diaper industry: "We believe the study is scientifically flawed and unsound. The conclusions are irresponsible, inappropriate and unreliable." Or as one Australian report put it, "Nappy manufacturers … condemned the research's methodology and conclusions,"

Other researchers suggested a diet low in folic acid could cause low sperm counts. In studies of rats where folic acid was withdrawn, sperm counts dropped by 90%. But it was not clear why men's diets, across the world, would have so suddenly changed in the same direction to cause a drop in folic acid and related decrease in sperm production.

The most convincing evidence seemed to lie in environmental causes. Debates over the causes of male reproductive health problems were galvanized in 1996 by the publication of *Our Stolen Future* by Theo Colborn, Dianne Dumanoski, and John Peterson Myers, which argued that many of the reproductive ailments documented since the 1970s could be caused by the introduction of estrogenic chemicals into the environment. Estrogenic chemicals are compounds that are not estrogens but mimic their function and disrupt the endocrine system once introduced into the human body. Colborn, Durnanoski, and Myers argued that pesticides, herbicides, and plastic compounds could have such effects, producing higher rates of cancers in both men and women, increased birth defects, and decreased sperm production. During the 1970s, researchers had examined the estrogenetic effects of a range of pesticides. DDT seemed to have similar effects on reproductive systems, and researchers suspected other pesticides, such as trichloroethylene (TCE) and/or polychlorinated biphenyls (PCBs), as well. Many studies focused on the association of sperm counts with toxic exposures. A study of 225 farmers who attended an infertility clinic in Argentina found associations between sperm count levels and exposure to insecticides, herbicides, and fungicides. A study of 1,001 men in four European cities found associations between sperm defects and stress, "occupational posture," and metal welding.

In the late 1980s, U.S. scientists accidentally discovered the estrogenic qualities of plastics. In unrelated research, researchers noticed that cells stored within sealed plastic tubes were strangely reproducing, as if they had been exposed to estrogens. They discovered that the plastic tubes were the source of the problem. Hormonal effects in the wild or in human populations, some argued, might be produced by the introduction of plastic compounds into the environment since the 1960s. In 1999, a study suggested that phthalates, a solvent used to make plastics flexible, may have estrogenic qualities. Researchers administered the chemical to female rats; their exposed male offspring produced far less testosterone and developed reproductive abnormalities and testicular tumors, even after very low exposure levels.

Others criticized the focus on environmental causes and argued that men's "lifestyle" factors—drinking, smoking, obesity, and hormonal drug use—might be the cause of the decline. As one researcher put it, "You see all these risk factors, yet men blame some environmental factor when they should blame themselves." But little research focused on these risk factors. One suspects that researchers finding a decline in female fertility might be quick to examine the drug and alcohol use of women, but few studies examined this association in men. Instead, most studies of men focused not on male behavior or even the exposures of men as adults but on maternal transmission of harm to the developing male fetus.

Many researchers found the evidence on the sperm count drop, as well as associations with environmental estrogens, if not decisive, then convincing. Animal studies had been used many times before to justify regulatory action, and animal studies in this case seemed to prove at least the damaging reproductive effects of pesticides, plastics, and solvents on males. But this time it seemed that animal studies and historical evidence were not enough. Again, critics launched sharp, at times virulent, attacks against the arguments that environmental toxins were placing male reproductive health at risk.

Once again, scientist-critic Stephen Safe questioned not just the evidence but the theorized association with environmental estrogens. For one, Safe argued, the presumed timing of the sperm count drop didn't seem to correspond with the introduction of chemicals into the environment. In reanalyzing data from the Danish study, Safe found that most of the sperm count decline had occurred before 1960, with little decline from 1960 to 1990. This seemed counterintuitive, given increasing uses of chemical pesticides during the later period. Safe also argued that exposure to industrial estrogens was minuscule compared with the average intake of estrogens naturally found in foods. As Safe himself colorfully suggested, "Just because Denmark has a problem and a few alligators in a swamp below a Superfund site develop small penises doesn't mean our sperm counts are going down or our reproductive success has declined. I just don't think we should extrapolate." Safe and others argued that reproductive disorders in the wild, particularly among limited populations of Florida panthers, could be due to simple inbreeding.

Media commentaries supported Safe's research and argued that the sperm count scare could be attributed to "chemophobes' fact-butchering." As commentator John Belau graphically put it, "Whereas man-made chemicals used to be characterized as the Grim Reaper [in cancer scares], they're now a stand-in for Lorena Bobbitt." While scientific debate continued, media coverage of the issue reflected the two extremes of alarm and disbelief. By the 1990s, public discourse on the debate had in large part already been constructed by these two extremes.

Media Coverage: The Emasculation of Men

Male reproductive health concerns broke into the news in 1992, in the aftermath of the publication of the Danish study in the *British Medical Journal*. The report set off a series of alarms and debates in the media, almost exclusively focused on sperm count drops, with relatively little attention to the other disorders reported. The level and intensity of media reports suggested that this was a debate not just about a potential human health problem but about masculinity itself. Sperm were, in essence, "little men" weathering an assault of social, technological, and environmental forces. Sperm counts represented not only a measure of one's manhood but also the symbolic measure of a nation's strength and well-being.

Like the controversies in the scientific and political communities, media coverage swung between alarm on the one hand and vigorous denial on the other. At both extremes were common themes that suggested the representational value of male reproductive health debates.

Personification

Often stories personified sperm as tiny beings with will and intention. Sperm were either "sluggish" or "vigorous" swimmers. Sperm were also cast as Casanovas who "seduce young women." Many reports reflected the sentiments of a tongue-in-cheek editorial in the *San Francisco Chronicle,* "Dealing with Heir Loss," which proclaimed: "Here's a new crisis that dwarfs all the others into insignificance." Noting the symbolic meaning of sperm counts, Arthur Hoppe noted, "When we approach a pretty young woman, tip our hat and inquire, 'Do you come here often?', it's those 250,000 spermatazoa doing the talking. Yes, sir, it's they who make a man a man." One environmentalist magazine published a story accompanied by a cartoon image of a personified sperm wearing a USA baseball cap turned backward and shedding worried sweat from its brow, as it plummets down a sloping scale of sperm counts over time.

Sperm were sometimes described as warriors in stories like "Sperm under Siege" or "Sperm Wars"—consistent with highly prized ideals of manhood. Masculine characterizations of sperm were reinforced by militaristic language that portrayed them as the tiniest soldiers, fighting off threats from toxic chemical assaults. In a *New Yorker* article on the sperm crisis, Lawrence Wright's characterization of the reproductive process is replete with war images: "It takes a healthy army to achieve conception," he argues. "The head carries the pay-load—a compressed molecular dollop of DNA—surrounded by a helmet of enzymes that will help it break down the wall of the egg." An early report of low sperm counts, he says, "reads like a casualty report from some devastating battlefront." Sperm are first on the front lines: "Altogether, the sperm is an elegant testament to form following function. It is pure purposefulness—the male animal refined into a single-celled, highly perishable posterity-seeking rocket." Though not a war against women, it is certainly a war against the female hormone estrogen ("the most likely villain"). Sperm may be under siege, but they are heroically fighting the good war—a war in which they have suffered casualties but in which they are sure to prevail.

Other stories employed boxing metaphors to describe sperm's fight for survival. Such language reinforced associations of male reproduction with the physical prowess and aggression of traditional masculinity. An article in *Mother Jones* was titled "Down for the Count," and a Reuters story reported that "modern living is hitting men right where it hurts the most, with sperm counts falling more quickly than anyone thought."

Ironically, even when sperm are pictured as miniaturized beings, their production over a 72-day period within the male body is never cast as a form of gestation. Rather, the male system is a machine—an industrial production facility, a plant or factory where sperm is "built" on a conveyer belt. As one reporter characterized the spermatic factory, "The toxicants affect sperm production—a conveyor-belt process that takes place in the huge bundles of tubules in the testicles, taking about 10 weeks to manufacture each sperm." Such portrayals deflected the notion that real men were being harmed. Men didn't need care; the male machine needed structural repair.

When not portrayed in human terms, sperm were often referred to as an endangered species. Again recalling associations with traditional masculine roles, hunting metaphors abound in such stories—the "hunt was on" for the causes of the sperm count decline, as if sperm were being tactically stalked by an assailant. Another article jokingly (?) concludes with a recommendation to establish a "Sperm Protection Agency." Whether human or animal, sperm appear to have volition of their own—an independent will separate from their male maker. Like the -Florida panther, sperm faced the threat of extinction. If sperm were endangered, it was because the human testis was "an organ at risk."

Feminism

What was apparently placing this organ at risk was not just environmental toxins but, some stories suggested, the feminist movement. Dropping sperm counts were a sign that men were losing the sex wars. One supposedly comical editorial, for instance, suggested that the sperm count decline might be due to a "sinister development in the sex war ... a sperm strike of epic proportions" launched by men fed up with "the invasion of the cackling sisterhood into every sphere of their lives." In another swipe at feminism, one report of a study of college men suggested that the reduction in male students' sperm counts was proportional to the rise of the number of women in universities over the past fifty years. As a story titled "That Feminine Touch" put it, women (represented by the female hormone) were apparently responsible not just for invading male workplaces or colleges but for undermining the very procreative power of men.

Even reports of the potential damages done by polyvinyl chlorides (PVCs) were framed as part of a war of women against men. As one piece comically framed it, "Barbie kills sperm dead. ... The next time you open your wallet and contemplate your credit cards, be aware that you are looking at vinyl. Actually, it's the same stuff that comprises the weird bodies of Barbie and Ken Dolls. It's going to be a long bitter debate."

If feminism was not to blame for the decline in sperm counts, it might be at least partly to blame for the public panic about sperm count evidence. Journalist John Berlau, a critic of the evidence, suggested that feminist activists might welcome the reported associations: "In a twisted way, some in the environmental movement seem to welcome the alleged link between chemicals and male reproductive disorder." Feminist advocates, like former congresswoman Bella Abzug, had been trying to get Congress to ban chlorine for its supposed links with breast cancer, to no avail. "But now that manhood is threatened," Abzug told *New York Magazine,* "We should do much better. I mean, these men don't want to go around with shrinking penises."

This was not just a story about environmental hazards. It was Barbie against Ken, Bella Abzug against the congressmen. It was college girls emasculating college boys. Some even suggested that the "absence of involvement of men in war" might be responsible, presumably because peace might depress testosterone in men. In its most extreme characterizations, it was the pacific androgynous politics of feminism undermining the testosterone-producing war machine. As a result, men were looming "intersexed."

Maternal Transmission

Research released in 1993 indicating that estrogen exposure during pregnancy might damage male fetal reproductive functions led to a series of news stories on the issue. Richard Sharpe and Niels Skakkebaek, in an article published in *Lancet,* suggested that the increase in women's consumption of cow milk during pregnancy might be responsible for such exposures because cows had been increasingly treated with the female hormone. In a front-page story, *USA Today* focused primarily on "estrogen passed from pregnant mothers to their sons."

Many news stories stressed the mediation of harm though the maternal body. As Sharpe was quoted as saying, "I have absolutely no doubt that this is the most important time of your life, certainly if you're a male." Reporters emphasized that "if even a small amount of an extraneous synthetic estrogen slips across the mother's placental boundary at a critical moment and invades the body of a developing fetus, it can have a devastating impact on male sexual development." Researchers referred to the "adverse prenatal factors" that later handicap sperm production in the adult male. Others suggested that estrogen-mimicking chemicals "block testosterone in the womb, disrupting sexual development" and "feminizing male fetuses." Men's sperm-producing capacity was "crippled at birth."

It was not men who were at risk but the "male fetus." Encased in the uterus, there was nothing the male fetus could do to avoid chemical emasculation. Men were vulnerable only by virtue of their captive position inside the female body. Such stories shifted focus from the vulnerabilities of the male body to the culpability of the pregnant body. Perhaps mothers were once again responsible, if only by passive transmission, for the problems of men.

Assault on Manhood—The Feminization of Men

The most disturbing effect of exposure to estrogens was often said to be the blurring of the divide between men and women—the production of the "intersexed," the "feminized male," the "hermaphrodite." As men became "more like women," the dissolution of the boundaries between them produced disease and "weakness." It was this presumed feminization of men that had produced testicular cancer, lower sperm counts, and; increased rates of "abnormal" development in men.

Men were not just experiencing male-specific reproductive problems but were being *turned into women*. Chemical exposures produced "gender bending," as men with low sperm counts or with genital malformations were somehow cast as deformed women. The feminization of men followed the "feminization" of men's work. As one story in *Esquire* magazine put it, with a play on men's weakened economic position, men were subject not just to downward mobility but now to "downward motility." Reduced sperm counts threatened not only to throw male fertility into jeopardy but also to undermine manhood itself: "Reduce our sperm count? Why in no time we'll be a nation of pallid, Jell-O-spined wimps, watching Wheel of Fortune rather than Monday Night Football and asking strangers for directions."

The theme of feminization was especially evident in stories on wildlife research. Fish and alligators with malformations of the genitals were not called just deformed but "feminized." Penis size was also cast as a measure of one's manhood. As one PBS report, entitled "Teeny Weenies," on the discovery of alligators with reduced penis size reminded men, "In Britain's Lake Apopka, size does matter." Research on fish in Great Britain also reported with alarm that "proportionately, a man now produce [sic] only about a third as much sperm as a hamster" and that the world is more likely to end with a "wimp" than with a "bang." In 1993, a BBC documentary depicted the issue as an "assault on the male" and dramatized it by showing film of scientists skulking through the Florida swamps in search of baby alligators with tiny penises and images of hermaphrodite fish.

With titles like "That Feminine Touch" and "The Gender Benders" throughout 1994 and 1995, news stories suggested that environmental toxins were "emasculating" both men and wildlife. The well-regarded science publication *Nature* titled a story "Masculinity at Risk" and called "urgently" for more research on the subject. News reports of studies on the association between plastics and sperm counts were reported with headlines like "Common Pollutants Undermine Masculinity."

Some stories declared, "You're only half the man you used to be" with sperm counts lower than those of your grandfathers. Others warned of impending male "impotence" (wrongly named because impotence does not refer to potency but to erectile function). Stories suggested men were threatened with "chemical castration" or "sterilization" (also wrongly named, because sterilization implied a zero sperm count).

The disorders of the male reproductive system were characterized not as male disorders but as forms of feminization. One might expect this sort of language if males were growing ovarian tissue or men were developing breasts (but even in this case wouldn't they still be *men* with ovarian tissue, *men* with developed mammary glands?). But the language of feminization and emasculation was frequently used not just when males developed "female" organs but when men experienced male reproductive disorders—when sperm counts were dropping, when men were reported to have increased rates of testicular cancer or genital malformation.

Stories of impending crisis were followed quickly by speculation about the possible causes of such a drop. Most stories suggested that chemical pollutants were the prime suspect, but other themes seemed to suggest that the "softening" of the world had led to a weakening of men. Stories speculated about a possible link of male health problems to "too much drinking," "tight pants," or an increase in male stress. Others suggested that the decline might be due to too much TV watching resulting in cathode-ray tube radiation and could correspond to the rise in television viewing. As one letter to an editor suggested, "I would venture to suggest that, among the small percentage of people who forgo television will be found many families that enjoy a higher-than-average birth rate." Or perhaps the modern comfort of indoor heating was to blame, with some suggesting that the higher indoor temperatures might depress sperm production. News stories reported that "sperm cells are the most delicate in the male body" and subject to damage from toxins at fairly low levels of exposure. Men, no longer invincible, were failing in the manufacture of their most important product.

Others suggested "desk work" was to blame or work in which men spent long periods of time sitting—airline pilots, taxicab drivers, or bus drivers. Sitting presumably increases the temperature of the testis, and heat may cause reduced sperm production, the speculation went. Perhaps the drop was a consequence of the decline of the industrial economy and rise of the service industry—the "feminization" of men's work. Perhaps men were biologically unfit to perform sedentary service jobs. The male reproductive system, often likened to industrial production, perhaps was revolting at the shift to desk work. Yet others suggested the toxins of industrial employment might be equally hazardous. Men exposed to pesticides in chemical production, men exposed to car exhaust in indoor parking garages, or men working in tunnels might also be at risk. Shame still accompanied stories on men's loss of fertility from environmental toxins. A personal account of a Hispanic male worker in California, presumably rendered infertile by chemical exposures at work, reported: "He doesn't want his name used. I don't want people to know," he says in Spanish, "that I am not a man.'" Low sperm counts produced not just health problems but "pathetic male ineffectuality."

Nationhood

Manhood was also tied to nationhood. A nation's sperm count was a measure of its national virility. Stories compared the sperm counts of various nations in Olympic competition terms. Finnish men could "stand tall," while American men "faced extinction." Western sperm counts could "plummet" as Third World sperm counts remained unchanged. Sperm were often given nationalist status. In the United States, men were facing "The Gelding of America." An article in *The Futurist* included a pull-quote that "developing countries may see widespread infertility, falling birthrates." A "sperm count chart" illustrated the threat with two sharp lines in dramatic decline, one marked "Americans" and one marked "Europeans." Soon, developed countries might be out populated by more virile Third World nations. A 2000 study by University of Southern California scholars finding no change in U.S. sperm counts brought welcome headlines in newspapers. As the *New York Times* reported, "American Sperm, as Hardy as Ever."

Reports of falling sperm counts and birth rates in Scotland led to panicked reports that "there is something rotten in the state of the nation" and that a "draining life force" had produced a "lack of national virility." By contrast, three stories reported the results of a study published in the *British Medical Journal* that found Finnish men "way above average" in their sperm counts. As news stories recounted, "the mighty men of Finland are walking tall these days" and "the men of Kuopio [Finland] are the spermiest in the world." In apparent international sperm rivalry, Glasgow's *Herald* reported the "first ever" survey of sperm counts in a random study of healthy young men that found that 43% of Danish army recruits have sperm count levels low enough to lead to decreased fertility. "Paradoxically," the report went on, "scientists at Glasgow Royal Infirmary's test tube baby clinic turned to Denmark for sperm donors last autumn when confronted with insufficient domestic supply to meet demand." Perhaps the Danes should be turning to the Scots.

Representing their nation, men who retained high sperm counts were truly men—the "spermiest" Finnish men could "walk tall" because they had superior sperm counts, while man-made chemicals were threatening not just men but "American manhood."

Global Doom

The loss of masculinity and decline of worldwide sperm counts led in some quarters to predictions of catastrophe and global doom—not just reduction of male fertility (for which there was still very weak evidence) but the end of the human race. As one story put it, "Imagine a future in which the male sperm count drops, universally, to zero. The sap runs out for Homo sapiens." Religious revelations laced through such reports suggested dropping sperm counts as the beginning of worldwide apocalypse: "The revelation of a striking decline in human sperm number and quality has rung alarm bells world wide. Could the Western male become sterile in the next century?" Or perhaps, as one editorial jested: "It's the Good Lord trying to tell us something." One prominent British mystery novelist, P. D. James, was inspired to write a futuristic novel in which all men had become sterile.

Many stories cautioned of a "disaster" in the making or of "terror on the trouser front." The *USA Today's* front-page headline, "Sperm Count Slide," suggested that such a decline might continue down that slippery slope toward extinction. More general accounts of spreading alarm over the possibility that environmental chemicals might be damaging male health were presented with headlines like "Scientist reveals nightmare vision of infertile race," with images of a "barren planet" whose inhabitants become extinct and "it could be all over for the male of the species." In advocacy pieces, environmental organizations declared: "The sperm count of our species is in serious decline!" and "U.S. men face extinction" as a result of "chemical castration." "If current trends continue," one report cautioned, "U.S. males will be sterile by 2020."

News reports painted a picture of an "infertile race," a "barren planet," a species in decline. It "could all be over for the male of the species" and for the human race as well. The end of manhood apparently meant the end of the human race. The world was ending with a "wimper" and not a bang. As one story entitled "Goodbye Macho Man?" put it: "A dramatic fall in sperm count has triggered a hunt for causes—and fears for all humankind."

Others reported the drop in sperm counts as an "impending catastrophe." "It is not a good time to be a sperm," reported one journalist. "Most reproductive scientists now agree: Western men's sperm counts are falling—and fast. With the quality of sperm also in rapid decline, and with sperm defects already responsible for a quarter of all cases of infertility, some even expect that male infertility will become the norm by the end of the next century." The commentator concluded that "any man who suspects he has a fertility problem should not consider it a shameful reflection on his manhood." Rather, men can follow a twelve-step plan to increase their fertility, including avoidance of cigarettes, alcohol, and drugs; reducing hazardous exposures at work; exercising regularly; eating more fruit and vegetables; and reducing stress.

Taken together, these themes strike the note of panic for modern manhood. With manhood already in crisis from loss of jobs and the rise of the feminist movement, stories like these were made easy to believe. In this context of a crisis in masculinity, government agencies sought to respond to the sense of panic created by the evidence that male reproductive health was at risk. Although the themes in the popular press did not determine the policy response or the response of the scientific community, they more explicitly expressed the underlying anxieties and concerns that informed these. Representations in the media give us a window into the symbolic meaning of these debates for broader questions of masculinity.

Regulating Men

What has been the political response to controversies over evidence that male reproductive health was in trouble? In the political process, male reproductive health concerns were subsumed, and sometimes eclipsed by broader concerns about the impact of endocrine disruptors on human health. Activists raised concerns about increasing rates of breast cancer, birth defects, and other human cancers presumably produced by environmental estrogens. The earliest attention to the issue in the U.S. congress came as a result of activism on two fronts. First, advocates focused political efforts on representatives from districts where research showed pollutants had had a significant impact on wildlife, most notably in the Great Lakes states. In 1991, the senators from Michigan and Wisconsin held hearings on the question of endocrine disruptors, with the prompting of Theo Colborn, who had headed most of the research in this area. Colborn focused on the association of PCBs with birth defects as well as the "feminization" of the offspring of pregnant rats exposed to dioxin.

On a second front, advocates focused on the possible links between endocrine disruptors and the rise in breast cancer rates. In 1993, the U.S. House of Representatives sponsored hearings primarily on breast cancer as a possible outcome of endocrine disruption, with secondary attention to the sperm count drop. In 1993 and 1994, eight bills were introduced into the House and Senate related to endocrine disruptions, all of which focused on further research on the question and testing of chemicals for their broad hormonal effects. In 1996, Congress mandated that the EPA report on the impact of environmental estrogens on women's health. The political drive behind this and other bills was concern about breast cancer. The two senators (Alfonse D'Amato and Daniel Patrick Moynihan) who were chief sponsors of major legislation were from New York, where research showed clusters of breast cancer in communities on Long Island. As political scientist Krimsky has noted, "The activism of Long Island women organized around the issue of breast cancer was a key factor in focusing D'Amato's attention on the issue of estrogenic chemicals and ultimately in winning his support for the screening program." Advocacy by women's organizations produced an increase in funding for breast cancer research from $5 million in 1990 to $500 million in 1995.

In 1996, Congress passed two major acts that addressed the issue and set the framework for future policy developments. The Food Quality Protection Act (FQPA), passed unanimously in 1996, gave the Environmental Protection Agency the authority to require data from chemical companies on the endocrine effects of the pesticides they produced. Congress also passed an amendment to the Safe Drinking Water Act that required the EPA and the Department of Health and Human Services to develop a screening program to determine whether chemicals found in drinking water had estrogenic effects on humans. At the time, the pesticide industry was deeply engaged in more threatening battles with environmental organizations attempting to ban all pesticide residues from food products. To the industry, the provisions of the act were fairly moderate, giving the EPA three years to determine whether certain substances have "an effect on humans that is similar to an effect produced by naturally occurring estrogen[s]."

The FQPA had mandated that the EPA develop a screening program to determine whether chemical substances had an effect on the hormonal system. Of the 87,000 compounds the EPA estimated to be in use, few had been studied for their hormonal effects. By 1998, the EPA estimated that for only 50 to 100 chemicals were there sufficient data for the EPA to proceed to formal hazard assessment. The EPA recommended that another 500 to 600 compounds "proceed directly to testing." The rest lacked sufficient data for the EPA to make a formal assessment of risk. Initial screening of these compounds would lead to sorting chemicals up through a tiered testing *system*. Compounds would be tested for their effects not just to estrogen but to androgen and thyroid hormones. But testing systems themselves were still not yet developed. By the year 2000, the EPA reported that there were still "no adequately validated routine screens or tests for determining whether a substance may produce an effect in humans similar to an effect produced by a naturally occurring estrogen or any other naturally occurring hormone."

Of great political significance was a report released in 1999 that had been commissioned by the EPA to assess the state of the knowledge on endocrine disrupters. In 1995 the EPA had sponsored a workshop to identify a research program to address risk assessments and environmental effects of endocrine disrupters. The majority of the more than ninety scientists and environmental health professionals present agreed that the "endocrine disruptor hypothesis was of sufficient concern to warrant a concerted research effort." Through the National Academy of Science, a board of experts was commissioned by the EPA and the Department of Interior in 1995:

> To review critically the literature on hormone-related toxicants in the environment; identify the known and suspected toxicological mechanisms, and impacts on fish, wildlife, and humans; identify significant uncertainties, limitations of knowledge, and weaknesses in the available evidence; develop a science-based conceptual framework for assessing observed phenomena; and recommend research, monitoring, and testing priorities.

The committee was composed of seventeen members, many of whom had been active in research on the issue. It included, for instance, Stephen Safe of Texas A & M, one of the most vocal critics of the evidence, as well as Louis Guillette, who had directed much of the research on Florida alligators. The intent of the committee was to provide a consensus statement on evidence. Yet years of internal disagreement delayed the committee's work. As reports in the media observed, the committee was "dogged by ... deep disagreements." The committee could hardly agree on the definition of the term *endocrine disruptor* itself, finally settling on the more neutral term *hormonally active agent* (HAA). Neither could it agree on the significance of wildlife studies, the agents that might be causing visible effects, or the possible associations between laboratory studies on animals and human health problems. Such fundamental disagreements produced a committee that could come to consensus on very little. As the committee's final report, *Hormonally Active Agents in the Environment* (HAAE), stated:

> It became clear as the work of the committee progressed that limitations and uncertainties in the data could lead to different judgments among committee members with regard to interpreting the general hypothesis, determining appropriate sources of information, evaluating the evidence, defining the agents of concern, and evaluating environmental and biologic variables.

Specifically on the question of a sperm count decline, the evidence, the report concluded, was simply unclear: "With respect to the end point most closely studied, sperm concentration, retrospective analysis of trends over the past half-century remain controversial." In such studies, the committee argued, "*it* was impossible to control for all confounding factors ... due to limitations in the original data sets." The failure of past studies to control for such confounding factors and geographical variation made knowledge of sperm counts uncertain.

"In fact," the committee concluded, "within single study centers and populations, considerable local variation has been demonstrated, with some studies suggesting a decline, and others no change, or even a possible increase in sperm concentration over the past 20 years." Given the limitations of past data and the lack of current data, the report concluded "No analysis to date can prove or disprove a uniform global trend in sperm concentration." Perhaps, the report suggested, studies of sperm concentration "may not be the appropriate question for study."

The report confirmed that laboratory studies of animals exposed to a range of pesticides and other chemicals clearly showed that such exposures could cause "reproductive and developmental abnormalities." These effects had been shown across animal populations and appeared to be dose-responsive. But some committee members challenged their significance for human health. As the report put it, "Although it was clear that exposures to HAAs at high concentrations can affect wildlife and human health, the extent of harm caused by exposure to these compounds in concentrations that are common in the environment is debated." What was missing, it argued, was conclusive "low dose" human data.

The report confirmed increases in rates of hypospadias, cryptorchidism, ism, and testicular cancer in men. Increasing rates of testicular cancer had been found in the United States, Canada, and six European countries, particularly for men born after 1950. In the United States, testicular cancer in white men, for instance, had increased by 2.4% each year from 1973 to 1994. This increase, the report suggested, could be related to growing rates of hypospadias or cryptorchidism in boys, both of which elevate risks of testicular cancer. But it concluded that none of these conditions could be definitively "linked to exposures to environmental HAAs at this time." It also affirmed significant studies of changing birth sex ratios, particularly in the aftermath of accidental exposures to TCDD, but noted that "the causes of the declines in sex ratio is [*sic*] yet unknown."

Internal disagreements within the committee were, in part, produced by the nature and complexity of the problem. The end points to examine were wide-ranging, from birth defects to childhood neurological problems, adult fertility issues, and cancers and other medical disorders Scientists were brought together from a wide range of disciplines, often with different research regimens. Yet research on other environmental toxins seemed to face the same complexities with less internal conflict and more success, which suggests that additional cultural forces were at work in this environmental debate.

Released in 1999, two years after its planned completion date, the report called for prospective studies and recommended only that "wild-life and human populations continue to be monitored for adverse developmental and reproductive effects." Such prospective studies would take years to complete. Media critics of the endocrine disruptor thesis used the report to dismiss all concerns about their effect on the environment. As commentator Michael Fumento, writing for *American Spectator*, put it, the report contained "enough scientific conclusions to box the cars of the endocrine alarmists."

Within the scientific committee, debates over the evidence appeared to go beyond simple lack of data. So deep were the disagreements that they seemed to throw into question accepted scientific methods of evidence, observation, and extrapolation. Committee members could not agree on the methodologies underlying such research: "of the value of different kinds of evidence obtained by experiments, observations, weight-of-evidence approaches, and extrapolation of results from one compound or organism to others, allowable sources of information and criteria for arriving at meaningful conclusions and recommendations" Resistance to evidence of male vulnerability came in the form not only of questioning the data but also of doubting the very scientific methods that produced the evidence in the first place.

What standard is used to judge the causality of an association? In general, scientific causality is judged by "the strength of the association, the presence of a dose-response relationship, specificity of the association, consistency across studies, biological plausibility, and coherence of the evidence." It appeared that most of these conditions were met through conducted on animals in the lab, yet these studies didn't seem to meet the criteria for affirming significant risks to the human population.

Almost years after Skakkebaek's original observations, there was to agreement on whether human fertility rates were in decline, what the cause of wildlife abnormalities might be, whether there might be an association between environmental toxins and breast or testicular cancers, or whether sperm counts had fallen or were continuing to fall. It seemed that a higher level of proof would be needed to justify public recognition of male reproductive disorders, as well as any governmental interventions to "protect" men. In the meantime, there were hardly any men's organizations publicly demanding action on falling sperm counts or rising rates of male reproductive disorders. And such debates were politically loaded, implicating not just the profits of the plastics and chemical industries and the reputations of competing scientists, but dominant norms of masculinity.

Paradoxes of Reproductive Masculinity

Some might say that the skepticism about claims of male reproductive risks was similar to that facing all environmental struggles—no more divisive, say, than debates over global warming. But an additional set of cultural meanings appears to be attached to this debate. This was a debate not just about the evidence but about manhood. Assumptions of masculinity were implicated in the belief or rejection of the evidence that male reproductive health was at risk. Gendered norms of manhood intensified the response in both directions, with sharply critical attacks at one extreme and predictions of global doom at the other. Indeed, in the end, the question was not whether male reproductive health was at risk at all, but how the perception of risk was obscured by these norms of masculinity.

Evidence of reproductive risk was deeply entangled with the second presumption of reproductive masculinity—the idea that men are less vulnerable than women to the harms of the outside world. The male body has been codified as relatively invulnerable to risk. The evidence suggested that this was no longer assured. The male reproductive system was cast as a machine, a factory that produced the goods necessary for human reproduction. As a machine, not an organic biological unit, the male body was presumably steeled against harm. Evidence of men suffering the "assaults" of environmental chemicals threw this presumption into question. The fact that this assault was not just on the male body but on the reproductive functions of men added insult to the injury. Men who were fragile or weakened were "more like women," with bodies vulnerable to external dangers.

Two stages of response characterized the social reaction to evidence of male weakness and vulnerability. First, evidence that threatens to disrupt presumptions of masculinity was met with highly charged responses of panic and denial Overreaction to the evidence suggests that signs of male risk socially implicate deeper norms of masculinity. Assumptions of male risk potentially throw into question not just gender but all of social order, producing predictions of global doom. If the strength and virility of the male body was no longer assured, if we could not count on the biological distinctions between men and women to hold firm, if the protectors of the nation needed protection, then where was the foundation of social order? If men presumably protected the vulnerable, then who would be left to protect the men? Evidence so loaded with meaning for broader understandings of masculinity (and by implication femininity) elicited reactions of social denial—subjecting evidence of risk to inordinately high standards of scientific proof.

When evidence of male risk and vulnerability was strong enough to overcome this social and scientific resistance, it was met with social responses of *deflection* and *reinstatement*. Arguments that the risk to men was transmitted through the maternal body during gestational development helped to shift attention away from the vulnerabilities of men. Threats to the male body were seen as transmitted through the maternal body, which mediated and delivered toxic risks to the male fetus, men "crippled at birth." Men were at risk not because the male body was inherently vulnerable but by virtue of their captive position inside the female body. In this way, assumptions about the nature of men's vulnerability were qualified by the mediation of harm through the maternal body.

The social processes of deflection functioned to reinstate the idea that men were neither needy nor dependent, nor were they the appropriate subject of state protection or surveillance. To publicly acknowledge the risks of the male body was to suggest that perhaps men were the ones in need of state protection, perhaps even more so than women. Male fetuses might be at greater risk than female fetuses—more likely to be lost during pregnancy, to be born with significant birth defects, or to eventually pass along defects to their own children. The harm that men suffered in utero or as adults might be more severe and long lasting than that suffered by women. Perhaps men would need to be subject to the surveillance of the state—tracking rates of diseases and disorder, monitoring sperm counts for signs of illness or decline. The social risks of acknowledging male vulnerability to harm seem to eclipse the real health risks suffered by men.

Politically, masculinity faced a catch-22. To recognize the risks of men and the vulnerabilities of the male reproductive body was to threaten presumptions of male domination, yet to fail to recognize them was to put real men at further risk of real damages to their health and their ability to father children. Where were the men's organizations demanding attention to these issues and regulatory action by the state, or at least clarification of the nature and extent of the risks? As long as male reproductive function was symbolic of manhood and male vulnerability was a source of shame, few men would stand up to demand public attention to the issue. Scientists, physicians, and politicians fed this reservoir of shame by their reluctance to adequately examine questions of male reproductive health.

In the end, this is a story not about the "gender wars" but about the price men pay for gender privilege. Do we *know* whether men's reproductive health is at risk? We know only that the question will be forever clouded in a social order reluctant to face the vulnerabilities of men or determined to deny them.

The paradox of masculine privilege would also frame discussions of male virility as social and economic forces pushed questions of male infertility into the public light. The development of technologies of artificial insemination would make it possible (and in the U.S. context, profitable) to address the health needs of men suffering from infertility. Yet the growth of a multimillion-dollar industry in sperm banking would threaten to disrupt the third presumption of reproductive masculinity the assumption of male virility—and would be met with similar social resistance.

Male fertility and, specifically, the quality of a man's sperm would come define manhood and supersede the identity of the man. Like a production line turning out widgets that are, of course, more important than the machine, men in the sperm banking industry, representing in microcosm the ideal qualities of all men, would be measured by the "quality" of their sperm.

In re: Baby M

Case 537 A.2d 1227, New Jersey Supreme Court 1988

The opinion of the Court was delivered by Wilentz, C. J.

In this matter the Court is asked to determine the validity of a contract that purports to provide a new way of bringing children into a family. For a fee of $10,000, a woman agrees to be artificially inseminated with the semen of another woman's husband; she is to conceive a child, carry it to term, and after its birth surrender it to the natural fattier and his wife. The intent of the contract is that the child's natural mother will thereafter be forever separated from her child. The wife is to adopt the child, and she and the natural father are to be regarded as its parents for all purposes. The contract providing for this is called a "surrogacy contract," the natural mother inappropriately called the "surrogate mother."

We invalidate the surrogacy contract because it conflicts with the law and public policy of this State. While we recognize the depth of the yearning of infertile couples to have their own children, we find the payment of money to a "surrogate" mother illegal, perhaps criminal, and potentially degrading to women. Although in this case we grant custody to the natural father, the evidence having clearly proved such custody to be in the best interests of the infant, we void both the termination of the surrogate mother's parental rights and the adoption of the child by the wife/stepparent. We thus restore the "surrogate" as the mother of the child.

We find no offense to our present laws where a woman voluntarily and without payment agrees to act as a "surrogate" mother, provided that she is not subject to a binding agreement to surrender her child. Moreover, our holding today does not preclude the Legislature from altering the current statutory scheme, within constitutional limits, so as to permit surrogacy contracts. Under current law, however, the surrogacy agreement before us is illegal and invalid.

I. FACTS

In February 1985, William Stern and Mary Beth Whitehead entered into a surrogacy contract. It recited that Stern's wife, Elizabeth, was infertile, that they wanted a child, and that Mrs. Whitehead was willing to provide that child as the mother with Mr. Stern as the father.

"In re Baby M," New Jersey Supreme Court Case 537 A.2d 1227. Copyright in the Public Domain.

The contract provided that through artificial insemination using Mr. Stern's sperm, Mrs. Whitehead would become pregnant, carry the child to term, bear it, deliver it to the Sterns, and thereafter do whatever was necessary to terminate her maternal rights so that Mrs. Stern could thereafter adopt tie child. Mrs. Whitehead's husband, Richard, was also a party to the contract; Mrs. Stern was not. Although Mrs. Stern was not a party to the surrogacy agreement, the contract gave her sole custody of the child in the event of Mr. Stern's death. Mrs. Stern's status as a nonparty to the surrogate parenting agreement presumably was to avoid the application of the baby-selling statute to this arrangement. Mr. Stern, on his part, agreed to attempt the artificial insemination and to pay Mrs. Whitehead $10,000 after the child's birth, on its delivery to him…

The history of the parties' involvement in this arrangement suggests their good faith. William and Elizabeth Stern were married in July 1974, having met at the University of Michigan, where both were Ph.D. candidates. Due to financial considerations and Mrs. Stern's pursuit of a medical degree and residency, they decided to defer starting a family until 1981. Before then, however, Mrs. Stern learned that she might have multiple sclerosis and that the disease in some cases renders pregnancy a serious health risk. Her anxiety appears to have exceeded the actual risk, which current medical authorities assess as minimal. Nonetheless that anxiety was evidently quite real, Mrs. Stern, fearing that pregnancy might precipitate blindness, paraplegia, or other forms of debilitation. Based on the perceived risk, the Sterns decided to forego having their own children. The decision had special significance for Mr. Stern. Most of his family had been destroyed in the Holocaust. As the family's only survivor, he very much wanted to continue his bloodline.

Initially the Sterns considered adoption, but were discouraged by the substantial delay apparently involved and by the potential problem they saw arising from their age and their differing religious backgrounds. They were most eager for some other means to start a family.

The paths of Mrs. Whitehead and the Sterns to surrogacy were similar. Both responded to advertising. The Sterns' response following their inquiries into adoption was the result of their long-standing decision to have a child. Mrs. Whitehead's response apparently resulted from her sympathy with family members and others who could have no children (she stated that she wanted to give another couple the "gift of life"); she also wanted the $10,000 to help her family.

Both parties, undoubtedly because of their own self-interest, were less sensitive to the implications of the transaction than they might otherwise have been. Mrs. Whitehead, for instance, appears not to have been concerned about whether the Sterns would make good parents for her child; the Sterns, on their part, while conscious of the obvious possibility that surrendering the child might cause grief to Mrs. Whitehead, overcame their qualms because of their desire for a child. At any rate, both the Sterns and Mrs. Whitehead were committed to the arrangement; both thought it right and constructive.

The two couples met to discuss the surrogacy arrangement and decided to go forward. On February 6, 1985, Mr. Stern and Mr. and Mrs. Whitehead executed the surrogate parenting agreement. After several artificial inseminations over a period of months, Mrs. Whitehead became pregnant. The pregnancy was uneventful and on March 27, 1986, Baby M was born.

Not wishing anyone at the hospital to be aware of the surrogacy arrangement, Mr. and Mrs. Whitehead appeared to all as the proud parents of a healthy female child. Her birth certificate indicated her name to be Sara Elizabeth Whitehead and her father to be Richard Whitehead. In accordance with Mrs. Whitehead's request, the Sterns visited the hospital unobtrusively to see the newborn child.

Mrs. Whitehead realized, almost from the moment of birth, that she could not part with this child. She had felt a bond with it even during pregnancy. Some indication of the attachment was conveyed to the Sterns at the hospital when they told Mrs. Whitehead what they were going to name the baby. She apparently broke into tears and indicated that she did not know if she could give up the child. She talked about how the baby looked like her other daughter, and made it clear that she was experiencing great difficulty with the decision. Nonetheless, Mrs. Whitehead was, for the moment, true to her word. Despite powerful inclinations to the contrary, she turned her child over to the Sterns on March 30 at the Whiteheads' home.

The Sterns were thrilled with their new child. They had planned extensively for its arrival, far beyond the practical furnishing of a room for her. It was a time of joyful celebration—not just for them but for their friends as well. The Sterns looked forward to raising their daughter, whom they named Melissa. While aware by then that Mrs. Whitehead was undergoing an emotional crisis, they were as yet not cognizant of the depth of that crisis and its implications for their newly-enlarged family.

Later in the evening of March 30, Mrs. Whitehead became deeply disturbed, disconsolate, stricken with unbearable sadness. She had to have her child. She could not eat, sleep, or concentrate on anything other than her need for her baby. The next day she went to the Sterns' home and told them how much she was suffering.

The depth of Mrs. Whitehead's despair surprised and frightened the Sterns. She told them that she could not live without her baby, that she must have her, even if only for one week, that thereafter she would surrender her child. The Sterns, concerned that Mrs. Whitehead might indeed commit suicide, not wanting under any circumstances to risk that, and in any event believing that Mrs. Whitehead would keep her word, turned the child over to her.

The struggle over Baby M began when it became apparent that Mrs. Whitehead could not return the child to Mr. Stern. Due to Mrs. Whitehead's refusal to relinquish the baby, Mr. Stern filed a complaint seeking enforcement of the surrogacy contract. He alleged, accurately, that Mrs. Whitehead had not only refused to comply with the surrogacy contract but had threatened to flee from New Jersey with the child in order to avoid even the possibility of his obtaining custody.

The court papers asserted that if Mrs. Whitehead were to be given notice of the application for an order requiring her to relinquish custody, she would, prior to the hearings leave the state with the baby. And that is precisely what she did. After the order was entered, the process server, aided by the police, in the presence of the Sterns, entered Mrs. Whitehead's home to execute the order. Mr. Whitehead fled with the child, who had been handed to him through a window while those who came to enforce the order were thrown off balance by a dispute over the child's current name.

The Whiteheads immediately fled to Florida with Baby M. They stayed initially with Mrs. Whitehead's parents, where one of Mrs. Whitehead's children had been living. For the next three months, the Whiteheads and Melissa lived at roughly twenty different hotels, motels, and homes in order to avoid apprehension. From time to time Mrs. Whitehead would call Mr. Stern to discuss the matter; the conversations, recorded by Mr. Stern on advice of counsel, show an escalating dispute about rights, morality, and power, accompanied by threats of Mrs. Whitehead to kill herself, to kill the child, and falsely to accuse Mr. Stern of sexually molesting Mrs. Whitehead's other daughter.

Eventually the Sterns discovered where the Whiteheads were staying, commenced supplementary proceedings in Florida, and obtained an order requiring the Whiteheads to turn over the child. Police in Florida enforced the order, forcibly removing the child from her grandparents' home. She was soon thereafter brought to New Jersey and turned over to the Sterns.

The Sterns' complaint, in addition to seeking possession and ultimately custody of the child, sought enforcement of the surrogacy contract. Pursuant to the contract, it asked that the child be permanently placed in their custody that Mrs. Whitehead's parental rights be terminated, and that Mrs. Stern be allowed to adopt the child, i.e., that, for all purposes, Melissa become the Sterns' child.

Soon after the conclusion of the trial, the trial court announced its opinion from the bench. It held that the surrogacy contract was valid; ordered that Mrs. Whitehead's parental rights be terminated and that sole custody of the child be granted to Mr. Stern; and, after hearing brief testimony from Mrs. Stern, immediately entered an order allowing the adoption of Melissa by Mrs. Stern, all in accordance with the surrogacy contract.

II. INVALIDITY AND UNENFORCEABILITY OF SURROGACY CONTRACT

We have concluded that this surrogacy contract is invalid. The surrogacy contract conflicts with laws prohibiting the use of money in connection with adoption. The prohibition of our statute is strong. The evils inherent in baby-bartering are loathsome for a myriad of reasons. The child is sold without regard for whether the purchasers will be suitable parents. The natural mother does not receive the benefit of counseling and guidance to assist her in making a decision that may affect her for a lifetime. In fact, the monetary incentive to sell her child may, depending on her financial circumstances, make her decision less voluntary Furthermore, the adoptive parents may not be folly informed of the natural parents' medical history.

Baby-selling potentially results in the exploitation of all parties involved. Conversely, adoption statutes seek to further humanitarian goals, foremost among them the best interests of the child. The negative consequences of baby-buying are potentially present in the surrogacy context, especially the potential for placing and adopting a child without regard to the interest of the child or the natural mother.

The surrogacy contract's invalidity, resulting from its direct conflict with the above statutory previsions, is farther underlined when its goals and means are measured against New Jersey's public policy. The contract's basic premise, that the natural parents can decide in advance of birth which one is to have custody of the child, bears no relationship to the settled law that the child's best interests shall determine custody. The fact that the trial court remedied that aspect of the contract through the "best interests" phase does not make the contractual provision any less offensive to the public policy of this State.

The surrogacy contract guarantees permanent separation of the child from one of its natural parents. Our policy, however, has long been that to the extent possibly children should remain with and be brought up by both of their natural parents. That was the first stated purpose of the previous adoption act. While not so stated in the present adoption law, this purpose remains part of the public policy of this State. This is not simply some theoretical ideal that in practice has no meaning. The impact of failure to follow that policy is nowhere better shown than in the results of this surrogacy contract. A child, instead of starting off its life with as much peace and security as possible, finds itself immediately in a tug-of-war between contending mother and father.

The surrogacy contract violates the policy of this State that the rights of natural parents are equal concerning their child, the father's right no greater than the mother's. "The parent and child relationship extends equally to every child and to every parent, regardless of the marital status of the parents." N.J.S.A. 9:17–40. The whole purpose and effect of the surrogacy contract was to give the father the exclusive right to the child by destroying the rights of the mother.

Under the contract, the natural mother is irrevocably committed before she knows the strength of her bond with her child. She never makes a totally voluntary, informed decision, for quite clearly any decision prior to the baby's birth is, in the most important sense, uninformed, and any decision after that, compelled by a pre-existing contractual commitment, the threat of a lawsuit, and the inducement of a $10,000 payment, is less than totally voluntary. Her Interests are of little concern to those who controlled this transaction.

This is the sale of a child, or, at the very least the sale of a mother's right to her child, the only mitigating factor being that one of the purchasers is the father. Almost every evil that prompted the prohibition on the payment of money in connection with adoptions exists here. The differences between an adoption and a surrogacy contract should be noted, since it is asserted that the use of money in connection with surrogacy does not pose the risks found where money buys an adoption.

First, and perhaps most important, all parties concede that it is unlikely that surrogacy will survive without money. Despite the alleged selfless motivation of surrogate mothers, if there is no payment, there will be no surrogates, or very few. That conclusion contrasts with adoption; for obvious reasons, there remains a steady supply, albeit insufficient, despite the prohibitions against payment. The adoption itself, relieving the natural mother of the financial burden of supporting an infant, is in some sense the equivalent of payment.

Second, the use of money in adoptions does not produce the problem—conception occurs, and usually the birth itself, before illicit funds are offered. With surrogacy, the "problem," if one views it as such, consisting of the purchase of a woman's procreative capacity, at the risk of her life, is caused by and originates with the offer of money.

Third, with the law prohibiting the use of money in connection with adoptions, the built-in financial pressure of the unwanted pregnancy and the consequent support obligation do not lead the mother to the highest paying, ill-suited, adoptive parents. She is just as well-off surrendering the child to an approved agency. In surrogacy, the highest bidders will presumably become the adoptive parents regardless of suitability, so long as payment of money is permitted.

Fourth, the mother's consent to surrender her child in adoptions is revocable, even after surrender of the child, unless it be to an approved agency, where by regulation there are protections against an Ill-advised surrender. In surrogacy, consent occurs so early that no amount of advice would satisfy the potential mother's need, yet the consent is irrevocable. The main difference, that the unwanted pregnancy is unintended while the situation of the surrogate mother is voluntary and intended, is really not significant. Initially, it produces stronger reactions of sympathy for the mother whose pregnancy was unwanted than for the surrogate mother, who "went into this with her eyes wide open." On reflection however, it appears that the essential evil is the same, taking advantage of a woman's circumstances (the unwanted pregnancy or the need for money) in order to take away her child, the difference being one of degree.

The point is made that Mrs. Whitehead agreed to the surrogacy arrangement, supposedly fully understanding the consequences. Putting aside the issue of how compelling her need for money may have been, and how significant her understanding of the consequences, we suggest that her consent is irrelevant. There are, in a civilized society, some things that money cannot buy. In America, we decided long ago that merely because conduct purchased by money was "voluntary" did not mean that it was good or beyond regulation and prohibition. Employers can no longer buy labor at the lowest price they can bargain for, even though that labor is "voluntary," or buy women's labor for less money than paid to men for the same job, or purchase the agreement of children to perform oppressive labor, or purchase the agreement of workers to subject themselves to unsafe or unhealthful working conditions. There are, in short, values that society deems more important than granting to wealth whatever it can buy, be it labor, love, or life. Whether this principle recommends prohibition of surrogacy, which presumably sometimes results in great satisfaction to all of the parties, is not for us to say. We note here only that, under existing law, the fact that Mrs. Whitehead "agreed" to the arrangement is not dispositive.

[The court concluded by ruling that the best interest of the child justified awarding custody to Mr. and Mrs. Stern. Further, the court ruled that Mrs. Whitehead should have visitation rights.]

The Curious Lives of Surrogates

By Lorraine Ali and Raina Kelley

Thousands of largely invisible American women have given birth to other people's babies. Many are married to men in the military.

Jennifer Cantor, a 34-year-old surgical nurse from Huntsville, Ala., loves being pregnant. Not *having* children, necessarily—she has one, an 8-year-old daughter named Dahlia, and has no plans for another—but just the experience of growing a human being beneath her heart. She was fascinated with the idea of it when she was a child, spending an entire two-week vacation, at the age of 11, with a pillow stuffed under her shirt. She's built perfectly for it: six feet tall, fit and slender but broad-hipped. Which is why she found herself two weeks ago in a birthing room in a hospital in Huntsville, swollen with two six-pound boys she had been carrying for eight months. Also in the room was Kerry Smith and his wife, Lisa, running her hands over the little lumps beneath the taut skin of Cantor's belly. "That's an elbow," said Cantor, who knew how the babies were lying in her womb. "Here's a foot," Lisa smiled proudly at her husband. She is, after all, the twins' mother.

It is an act of love, but also a financial transaction, that brings people together like this. For Kerry and Lisa—who had a hysterectomy at the age of 20 and could never bear her own children—the benefits are obvious: Ethan and Jonathan are healthy six-pound, 12-ounce boys born by C-section on March 20. But what about Cantor? She was paid, of course; the Smiths declined to discuss the exact amount, but typically, surrogacy agreements in the United States involve payments of $20,000 to $25,000 to the woman who bears the child. She enjoyed the somewhat naughty pleasure of telling strangers who asked about her pregnancy, "Oh, they aren't mine," which invariably invoked the question, "Did you have sex with the father?" (In case anyone is wondering, Lisa's eggs were fertilized in vitro with Kerry's sperm before they were implanted on about day five.)

But what kind of woman would carry a child to term, only to hand him over moments after birth? Surrogates challenge our most basic ideas about motherhood and call into question what we've always thought of as an unbreakable bond between mother and child. It's no wonder many conservative Christians decry the practice as tampering with the miracle of life, while far-left feminists liken gestational carriers and prostitutes who degrade themselves by renting out their bodies. Some medical ethicists describe the process of arranging surrogacy as "baby brokering," while rumors circulate that self-obsessed, shallow New Yorkers have their babies by surrogate to avoid stretch marks. Much of Europe bans the practice, and 12 states, including New York, New Jersey and Michigan, refuse to recognize surrogacy contracts. But in the past five years, four states—Texas, Illinois, Utah and Florida—have

Lorraine Ali and Raina Kelley, "The Curious Lives of Surrogates," *Newsweek*. Copyright © 2008 by Newsweek. Reprinted with permission.

passed laws legalizing surrogacy, and Minnesota is considering doing the same. More than a dozen states, including Pennsylvania, Massachusetts and, most notably, California, specifically legalize and regulate the practice.

Today, a greater acceptance of the practice, and advances in science, find more women than ever before having babies for those who cannot. In the course of reporting this story, we discovered that many of these women are military wives who have taken on surrogacy to supplement the family income, some while their husbands are serving overseas. Several agencies reported a significant increase in the number of wives of soldiers and naval personnel applying to be surrogates since the invasion of Iraq in 2003. At the high end, industry experts estimate there were about 1,000 surrogate births in the United States last year, while the Society for Assisted Reproductive Technology (SART)—the only organization that makes an effort to track surrogate births—counted about 260 in 2006, a 30 percent increase over three years. But the number is surely much higher than this—in just five of the agencies NEWSWEEK spoke to, there were 400 surrogate births in 2007. The numbers vary because at least 15 percent of clinics—and there are dozens of them across the United States—don't report numbers to SART. Private agreements made outside an agency aren't counted, and the figures do not factor in pregnancies in which one of the intended parents does not provide the egg—for example, where the baby will be raised by a gay male couple. Even though the cost to the intended parents, including medical and legal bills, runs from $40,000 to $120,000, the demand for qualified surrogates is well ahead of supply.

Another reason for the rise in surrogacy is that technology has made them safer and more likely to succeed. Clinics such as Genetics & IVF Institute In Virginia, where Cantor and the Smiths underwent their IVF cycles, now boast a 70 to 90 percent pregnancy success rate—up 40 percent in the past decade. Rather than just pulling an egg into a petri dish with thousands of sperm and hoping for a match, embryologists can inject a single sperm directly into the egg. The great majority of clinics can now test embryos for genetic diseases before implantation. It's revolutionizing the way clinics treat patients. Ric Ross, lab director at La Jolla IVF in San Diego, says these advances have helped "drop IVF miscarriage rates by 85 percent."

IVF has been around only since the 1970s, but the idea of one woman bearing a baby for another is as old as civilization. Surrogacy was regulated in the Code of Hammurabi, dating from 1800 B.C., and appears several times in the Hebrew Bible. In the 16th chapter of Genesis, the infertile Sarah gives her servant, Hagar, to her husband, Abraham, to bear a child for them. Later, Jacob gathers children by the maids of his wives Leah and Rachel, who raise them as their own. It is also possible to view the story of Jesus' birth as a case of surrogacy, mediated not by a lawyer but an angel, though in that instance the birth mother did raise the baby.

The most celebrated case of late, though, resulted in the legal and ethical morass known as the "Baby M" affair. Mary Beth Whitehead, age 29 in 1986, gave birth to a girl she had agreed to carry for an infertile couple. But Whitehead was also the baby's biological mother and tried to keep her after the birth, leading to a two-year custody battle. In the end, she was denied custody but awarded visitation rights. As a result, surrogacy agreements now almost always stipulate that the woman who carries the baby cannot also donate the egg.

But even as surrogacy is becoming less of a Jerry Springer spectacle and more of a viable family option for those who can afford it, the culture still stereotypes surrogates as either hicks or opportunists whose ethics could use some fine-tuning. Even pop culture has bought into the caricature. In the upcoming feature film *Baby Mama,* a single businesswoman (Tina Fey) is told by a doctor she is infertile. The businesswoman then hires a working-class gal (Amy Poehler) to be her surrogate. The client is a savvy, smart and well-to-do health store chain executive while Poehler is an unemployed, deceitful wild child who wants easy money.

When Fey's character refers to her surrogate as white trash we're supposed to laugh. "I just don't understand how they can think that," says surrogate Gina Scanlon of the stereotypes that influenced the film. Scanlon, 40, is a married mother of three who lives in Pittsburgh. Scanlon is also a working artist and illustrator who gave birth to twin girls for a gay New Jersey couple 18 months ago. The couple—a college professor and a certified public accountant—chose Scanlon because she was "emotionally stable," with a husband and children of her own. Unlike egg donors, who are usually in their 20s, healthy women as old as 40 can serve as surrogates; Scanlon two weeks ago underwent an embryo transfer and is now pregnant again for a new set of intended parents. "Poor or desperate women wouldn't qualify [with surrogacy agencies]," she says. As for the implication that surrogates are in it only for the money, she notes that there are many easier jobs than carrying a baby 24-hours a day, seven days a week (and most jobs don't run the risk of making you throw up for weeks at a time, or keep you from drinking if you feel like it.) "If you broke it down by the hour," Scanlon says wryly, "it would barely be minimum wage. I mean, have [these detractors] ever met a gestational carrier?" And even if they have, how would they know?

Very little is understood about the world of the surrogate. That's why we talked to dozens of women across America who are, or have been, gestational carriers. What we found is surprising and defies stereotyping. The experiences of this vast group of women—including a single mom from Murrietta, Calif., a military spouse from Glen Burnie, Md., and a small-business owner from Dallas—range from the wonderful and life-affirming to the heart-rending. One surrogate, Scanlon, is the godmother of the twins she bore, while another still struggles because she has little contact with the baby she once carried. Some resent being told what to eat or drink; others feel more responsible bearing someone else's child than they did with their own. Their motivations are varied: one upper-middle-class carrier in California said that as a child she watched a family member suffer with infertility and wished she could help. A working-class surrogate from Idaho said it was the only way her family could afford things they never could before, like a $6,000 trip to Disney World. But all were agreed that the grueling IVF treatments, morning sickness, bed rest, C-sections and stretch marks were worth it once they saw their intended parent hold the child, or children (multiples are common with IVF), for the first time. "Being a surrogate is like giving an organ transplant to someone," says Jennifer Cantor, "only before you die, and you actually get to see their joy."

That sense of empowerment and self-worth is one of the greatest rewards surrogate mothers experience. "I felt like, what else am I going to do with my life that means so much?" says Amber Boersma, 30, of Wausau, Wis. She is blond, outgoing and six months pregnant with twins for a couple on the East Coast who could not bear children on their own due to a hysterectomy, Boersma, married to a pharmaceutical rep, is a stay-at-home mom with a 6-year-old girl and 4-year-old boy, and a college graduate with a communications degree. "Some people can be successful in a major career, but I thought I do not want to go through this life meaning nothing, and I want to do something substantial for someone else. I want to make a difference."

Then there's the money. Military wife Gernisha Myers, 24, says she was looking through the local San Diego Penny Saver circular for a job when she saw the listing: "Surrogate Mothers Wanted! Up to $20,000 Compensation!" The full-time mother of two thought it would be a great way to make money from home, and it would give her that sense of purpose she'd lacked since she left her job as an X-ray technician in Phoenix. In 2004 Myers and her husband, Tim, a petty officer third class in the Navy, were transferred from Arizona to California. Ever since, she missed bringing home a paycheck, helping other people—and being pregnant She loved the feel of her belly with a baby inside, and the natural high that comes from "all those rushing hormones." So last fall she signed with one of the many surrogacy agencies near the 32nd Street Naval Station, where her husband is assigned. Her grandmother was not pleased with Myers's decision. "She said, 'Gernisha! We just do not do that in this family'," recalls Myers. "My uncle even said he was disgusted. But you know what? I'm OK with it because I know I am doing something good for somebody else. I am giving another couple what they could never have on their own—a family."

Like Myers, military wives are largely young stay-at-home moms who've completed their own families before they hit 28. IVF clinics and surrogate agencies in Texas and California say military spouses make up 50 percent of their carriers. "In the military, we have that mentality of going to extremes, fighting for your country, risking your life," says Jennifer Hansen, 25, a paralegal who's married to Army Sgt. Chase Hansen. They live in Lincoln, Neb., and have two young kids, and Chase has been deployed to Iraq for two of the past five years. "I think that being married to someone in the military embeds those values in you. I feel I'm taking a risk now, in less of a way than he is, but still a risk with my life and body to help someone." Surrogate agencies target the population by dropping leaflets in the mailboxes of military housing complexes, such as those around San Diego's Camp Pendleton, and placing ads in on-base publications such as the Military Times and Military Spouse. Now surrogate agencies say they are solicited by ad reps from these publications. Military wives who do decide to become surrogates can earn more with one pregnancy than their husbands' annual base pay (which ranges for new enlistees from $16,080 to $28,900). "Military wives can't sink their teeth into a career because they have to move around so much," says Melissa Brisman of New Jersey, a lawyer who specializes in reproductive and family issues, and heads the largest surrogacy firm on the East Coast "But they still want to contribute, do something positive. And being a carrier only takes a year—that gives them enough time between postings."

Dawne Dill, 32, was a high-school English teacher before she married her husband, Travis, a Navy chief, and settled in Maryland. She's now a full-time mother with two boys of her own, and is carrying twins for a European couple who prefer to remain anonymous. Dill is due in May. The attraction of surrogacy for her, apart from wanting to feel useful, was that the money could help pay for an occupational-therapy gym for her older son, who is autistic. "We're thinking of building the gym in our basement so he can get to it whenever he needs," says Dill. She worried that having an autistic child might disqualify her as a surrogate, but fortunately the agency was unconcerned. "They said because I was not genetically related to the twins, that it was just not an issue, and my IPS [intended parents] never brought it up to me personally. I assume they're OK with it, but maybe think it's too touchy of a subject to discuss openly with me," says Dill. As a prepartum gift, the couple sent Dawne and her husband to the Super Bowl.

Military wives are attractive candidates because of their health insurance, Tricare, which is provided by three different companies—Humana, TriWest and Health Net Federal Services—and has some of the most comprehensive coverage for surrogates in the industry. Fertility agencies know this, and may offer a potential surrogate with this health plan an extra $5,000. Last year military officials asked for a provision in the 2008 defense authorization bill to cut off coverage for any medical procedures related to surrogate pregnancy. They were unsuccessful—there are no real data on how much the government spends on these cases. Tricare suggests that surrogate mothers who receive payment for their pregnancy should declare the amount they're receiving, which can then be deducted from their coverage. But since paid carriers have no incentive to say anything, most don't "I was told by multiple people—congressional staff, doctors and even ordinary taxpayers—that they overheard conversations of women bragging about how easy it was to use Tricare coverage to finance surrogacy and delivery costs and make money on the side," says Navy Capt. Patricia Buss, who recently left the Defense Department and now holds a senior position with Health Net Federal Services. The subject of Tricare surrogacy coverage is becoming a hot topic throughout the military world; on Web sites such as militarySOS.com, bloggers with sign-on names such as "Ms. Ordinance" and "ProudArmyWife" fiercely debate the subject.

Surrogacy is not just an American debate—it is global. Thanks to reproductive science, Gernisha Myers, who is African-American, is now 18 weeks pregnant with the twins of Karin and Lars, a white couple who live in Germany. They are one of many international couples who turned to America to solve their infertility issues because surrogacy is not allowed in their own country. Couples have come to the United States from many countries, including Iceland, Canada, Franca, Japan, Saudi Arabia, Israel, Australia, Spain and Dubai in recent years. Although some couples are now turning to India for cheaper fertility solutions—yes, even surrogacy is being outsourced at a tenth of the price—the trend has yet to diminish America's draw as a baby Mecca.

Karin and Lars picked Myers after they read her agency profile. Myers says that the psychological screening is one of the most grueling, invasive and odd parts of the process. "The [questionnaire] asked some weird questions, like 'Do you think about killing people sometimes?' Or 'Would you want to be a mountain ranger if you could?' Or 'Do you find yourself happier than most?' But when they asked 'Are you afraid you're going to get attached to the babies?' I said, 'In a way, yes, even though I know they're not mine.' They said, 'Believe it or not, some GCs [gestational carriers] never feel any kind of bond.' I found that hard to believe back then, but now I know what they're talking about I don't feel that motherly bond. I feel more like a caring babysitter."

Myers's psychological detachment has a lot to do with the fact that, like most carriers today, she's in no way biologically related to the baby inside her—the legacy of the "Baby M" case. The most recent significant case involving a surrogacy dispute, *Johnson v. Calvert* in 1993, was resolved in favor of the intended parents, and against a surrogate who wanted to keep the baby. John Weltman, president of Circle Surrogacy in Boston, says that parents who work with a reputable agency have a "99 percent chance of getting a baby and a 100 percent chance of keeping it." But up until just about two years ago, Weltman says every single Intended parent asked, "Will she [the carrier] try and keep the baby?" Now, he says, a third of his clients don't even mention it.

That doesn't mean that it's gotten any easier for the surrogate to give up the baby. Most gestational carriers say it is still the hardest part of the job, and some have a rougher time than others. Gina Scanlon recalls the days after the birth of her first pair of surrogate twins: "When you go home it's so quiet," she says. "The crash comes. It's not the baby blues. It's not postpartum depression. It's that the performance is over. I was practically a celebrity during the pregnancy—someone was always asking me questions. After I had them, no one was calling. Now nobody cares. You're out. You're done. It's the most vain thing. I felt guilty and selfish and egotistical."

Stephanie Scott also found that life after surrogacy was not what she expected, especially since everything hummed along so nicely when she was pregnant seven and a half months in, she was feeling great—all except for those damn nesting urges. The stay-at-home mom tried to stay out of the baby stores and avoid those sweet pink onesies and baby booties shaped like tiny ballet slippers—but it was near impossible to resist. Her mind-set should have served as a warning. Although she knew the baby in her swollen belly belonged to a couple on the East Coast, she hadn't prepared herself for that biological surge that keeps stores like Babies 'R' Us in business. "I showed up to the delivery room with six months' worth of baby clothes" admits Scott, 28. "They ended up being my gift to the baby's intended parents. Sort of like a baby shower in reverse. I know, it's weird." But that was nothing compared to the childbirth, "When she was born, they handed her to me for a second," she says. "I couldn't look, so I closed my eyes tight, counted 10 fingers and 10 toes, then gave her away. I cried for a month straight. I was devastated."

The baby Scott gave birth to is now 3, and photos of the toddler come twice a year, on the child's birthday and Christmas. Scott says she thinks things would have been different had she been counseled more by the agency on attachment issues, but it was a small and less than professional operation (and there are plenty of those in the unregulated world of surrogacy agencies). It's one of the reasons Scott opened her own business in Dallas, Simple Surrogacy. "I would never just throw a girl out there like that. Surrogates need to know what lies ahead."

Any comprehensive road map of surrogacy should include not just potential attachment but an entire pull-down sheet on the second most difficult area of terrain: the relationship between surrogate and intended parent. The intentions and expectations of both parties are supposed to be ironed out ahead of time through a series of agency questionnaires and meetings. What kind of bond do they seek with one another—distant, friendly, close? Do they agree on difficult moral issues, like abortion and selective termination? And what requests do the IPs have of potential carriers? The parties are then matched by the agency, just as singles would be through a dating service. And the intended parents—or parent—are as diverse as the surrogates: gay, straight, single, married, young and old. Much of the time it works, even though it does often resemble an experiment in cross-cultural studies. "In what other world would you find a conservative military wife forming a close bond with a gay couple from Paris?" says Hilary Hanafin, chief psychologist for the oldest agency in the country, Center for Surrogate Parenting. And a good match doesn't necessarily equal a tight connection like that of Jennifer Cantor's and Lisa Smith's. Christina Slason, 29, who delivered a boy in January for same-sex partners from Mexico City, felt as the couple did—that a close relationship was not necessary. "We agreed that we would keep in touch, but neither of us felt the need to really bond," says Slason, a mother of three who lives in San Diego with her husband, Joseph, a Navy corpsman. "We were there to have a baby, nothing more. We were all clear on that."

But things are not always that clear. For Joseph, a single father from Massachusetts who asked to be identified only by his first name for privacy reasons, the process of finding a suitable surrogate on his own was frustrating, particularly when the first match got cold feet and pulled out. Intended parents Tamara and Joe Bove were troubled when the carrier for their triplets refused to go on bed rest even when a doctor advised her the babies' lives would be at risk if she did not: "She had delivered monstrously large twins vaginally before, even though one of them was breech. So she was kind of surprised that this could happen to her and just wouldn't cooperate." Tamara was plagued with worry. "Our plan was to keep in touch even after the babies were born, but then she stopped listening to the doctors. But you still have to keep acting like everything is fine because she's in control until the babies are born." (Despite Tamara's worries, the triplets were born healthy at 31 weeks via a C-section.)

Control, not surprisingly, is a sore point. A favorite pastime among surrogates—most of whom join support groups at the request of their agencies—is sharing stories of the most bizarre IP requests they've heard. One military surrogate was told if her husband was deployed anywhere in Asia, she was not to have sex with him when he returned for fear that he was unfaithful and carrying an STD.

Jennifer Hansen, the surrogate from Nebraska, says she had a few requests from her intended parents that were odd to her "as a Midwestern girl." Hansen says she's been asked not to pump her own gas. "They believe it leads to miscarriage," she says. "I've also been asked to change my cleaning supplies to all green, natural products. I'm a Clorox girl, and have no idea where to even buy these products. So they just box them up and send them to me from California." What most surrogates don't realize, according to Margaret Little, a professor of philosophy at Georgetown University and fellow at the Kennedy School of Ethics, is that the contracts governing their conduct during the pregnancy are not enforceable. She does have to surrender the baby once he's born, but cannot be forced to have (or not have) an abortion, or to obey restrictions on what she can eat, drink or do. The intended parents' only recourse is to withhold payment; they cannot police her conduct. "Surrogacy raises important red flags," Little says, "because you are selling use of the body, and historically when that's happened, that hasn't been good for women."

On the other hand, other agencies reported that some concerned surrogates have pumped and shipped their breast milk to the intended parents weeks after the birth out of fear that the newborn will not build a strong immune system without it.

As for Jennifer Cantor, resting at home last week after delivering Jonathan and Ethan, she intends to stay in touch with the family whose lives are now inextricably bound up with hers. Before returning to their home in Georgia. Lisa and Kerry brought the twins for a visit with the stranger who bore them, and with Cantor's daughter, Dahlia, whose relationship to them doesn't even have a word in the language yet. Lisa described her babies as "the true meaning of life … absolutely perfect." Next time they're hoping for girls. They're also hoping to find someone like Cantor—who, however, does not plan to be a surrogate again, much as she enjoyed it. She is relieved that she can sit normally and put her arms around Dahlia again, without a big belly in between them. She was happy that she had been able to fulfill her dream of bearing a child for someone else. "It was exactly," she said last week, "the experience I imagined it would be."

Breaking the Silence

By Ann Fessler

You asked me why I agreed to be interviewed and I think it was because you were here, because you came here and it spoke to me—that's all. There's still that voice in me that says, "Who would be interested? No one cared then, why would they care now?" I was abandoned when it was right in everybody's face, so I still believe that nobody cares. My personal struggle is to get beyond thinking I'm not worth caring about I am here, I do exist Maybe by adding my two cents I can help other moms who feel the way I do. Maybe they will find someone who cares.

—*Suzanne*

In JUNE OF 2002, I began tape-recording the oral histories of women who surrendered a newborn for adoption between the end of World War II, in 1945, and the 1973 passage of *Roe v. Wade,* which legalized abortion throughout the nation. These years were a time of enormous change for young women as barriers to equality and independence broke down. For the young men and women growing up in the postwar years, especially those of the baby-boom generation, this liberation from the past also applied to sexual behavior. And though premarital sex was certainly not a new phenomenon, it became increasingly common among those who had no plans to marry. For women born after 1949, the odds were that they would have sex before they reached age twenty.

Despite the increase in the number of young people having sex in the 1950s and 1960s, access to birth control and sex education lagged far behind. Fearing that sex education would promote or encourage sexual relations, parents and schools thought it best to leave young people uninformed. During this time, effective birth control was difficult to obtain. In fact, in some states it was illegal to sell contraceptives to those who were unmarried. The efforts to restrict information and access to birth control did not prevent teens from having sex, however. The result was an explosion in premarital pregnancy and in the numbers of babies surrendered for adoption.

Though sexual norms were changing among the young, the shame associated with single pregnancy remained. The social stigma of being an "unwed mother" was so great that many families—especially middle-class families—felt it was simply unthinkable to have a daughter keep an "illegitimate" child. These women either married quickly or were sent away before their pregnancy could be detected by others in the community. Between 1945 and 1973, one and a half million babies were relinquished for nonfamily or unrelated adoptions.

Ann Fessler, "Breaking the Silence," *The Girls Who Went Away,* pp. 7–23. Copyright © 2006 by Penguin Group (USA) Inc. Reprinted with permission.

I've tried to explain to my kids that it wasn't like it is today. Nobody knew that much about birth control. What used to bother me a lot was I knew lots of girls who were having sex; they just weren't caught. If you were caught, somehow you were different, and you needed to be horrified and shamed. I was thinking. "But everybody's doing it. Why am I a bad person now?"

It was just totally, totally different. You didn't keep your child. You didn't. I knew one girl who got married and immediately divorced afterward. At least that would keep the people who talk at bay.

—*Laurinda*

Just about everyone who lived through this era has a memory of a girl from their high school, college, or neighborhood who disappeared. If she returned, she most likely did not come back with her baby but with a story of a sick aunt or an illness that had kept her out of school. If her peers doubted her story, they probably did not challenge her directly. They simply distanced themselves. According to the prevailing double standard, the young man who was equally responsible for the pregnancy was not condemned for his actions. It was her fault, not their fault, that she got pregnant.

This was in that period of time when there wasn't much worse that a girl could do. They almost treated you like you had committed murder or something.

—*Toni*

The girls who went away were told by family members, social service agencies, and clergy that relinquishing their child for adoption was the only acceptable option. It would preserve their reputation and save both mother and child from a lifetime of shame. Often it was clear to everyone, except the expectant mother, that adoption was the answer. Many of these girls, even those in their twenties, had no other option than to go along with their families or risk being permanently ostracized. For them there was generally little or no discussion before their parents sent them away. Those who went to maternity homes to wait out their pregnancies often received little counseling and were totally unprepared for either childbirth or relinquishment. They were simply told they *must* surrender their child, keep their secret, move on, and forget. Though moving on and forgetting proved impossible, many women were shamed into keeping their secret.

As soon as the time was near and we were going to do this interviews all these physical things started happening. My jaw doesn't want to open and my lungs are all tight. I thought, "I wonder why I can't open my mouth." Then I realized, I'm supposed to be silent. I'm not supposed to tell this story. The secrecy has dominated everything. It's so powerful and pervasive and the longer you keep a secret the more power it takes on.

—*Diane IV*

I've never really felt like I could talk to anybody about it. You know, society has this picture—you hear about people giving their babies away. That whole terminology is just so misleading. I didn't give him away, I think one of the reasons I don't talk to some people about it *is* because they are so judgmental. Quite frankly, it's not that society can't understand; it's that they won't understand. People choose to not understand.

—*Carole II*

Afterward I never told, unless it was somebody I was very, very close to. I never opened up to anyone unless I felt that they would accept me. I felt like I lived a lie because people didn't really know me. I was afraid that people would not accept me if they knew the truth. It was something that I carried with me for thirty-five, thirty-six years.

—*Carol I*

The secrecy has, in part, allowed some of the old myths about women who surrendered babies to survive. One assumption was that they were women who were having a lot of sex with a lot of different young men. In fact, a majority of the women I interviewed became pregnant with their first sexual partner, some from their first sexual experience.

I'm being very honest with you by saying I was a very late bloomer. When I got pregnant, it was the very first time I had ever had sex. Very first time. I'm sure I probably didn't even like it. I went all through high school and never had sex.

My parents' generation, that greatest generation, thought it didn't happen to nice girls. You just have to know that's what society and parents felt: nice girls didn't get pregnant. But nice girls do get pregnant, and nice girls get pregnant now. People saw us as loose women. Well, I wasn't a loose woman! It wasn't that way for me. I didn't sleep around. But that's the label. That is absolutely the label. Oh well, I could be called worse things. I could be called a liar. I could be called a cheat.

—*Cathy II*

Another prevailing myth is that these women were all eager to surrender their child and be free of their problem. The assumption that these babies were unwanted by their mothers is ubiquitous. The act of relinquishment seemed to confirm this, since it is commonly believed to be a personal decision made by the mother based on her lack of interest or desire to parent—a decision that is independent of social, family, and economic pressures. This misguided and simplistic notion has been hurtful not only to the mothers but also to many adoptees who believe that they were thrown away. Over the years, I have had many conversations with adult adoptees who say, "She didn't want me. Why should I want to know her?" They clearly have no idea how infinitely more complicated their mother's circumstances were and a short conversation could not possibly explain it. This book is partly a response to their comments. It is a story best told by the mothers themselves, and best understood within the context of the time period.

Chances are the baby wasn't unwanted. It was a baby unwanted by society, not by mom. You couldn't be an unwed mother. Motherhood was synonymous with marriage. If you weren't married, your child was a bastard and those terms were used. I think I'm like many other women who thought, "It may kill me to do this, but my baby is going to have what everybody keeps saying is best for him." It's not because the child wasn't wanted. There would have been nothing more wonderful than to come home with my baby.

—*Glory*

Nobody ever asked me if I wanted to keep the baby, or explained the options. I went to the maternity borne, I was going to have the baby, they were going to take it, and I was going to go home. I was not *allowed* to keep the baby. I would have been disowned. I don't even know if they had programs to help women and children back then. I don't know what was available. I was made to feel very ashamed of the situation that 'I had created for myself" and for my mother and for my family and friends, so I felt all those avenues were closed. I guess maybe I had to convince myself that I didn't give him *away; I* gave him a way to have two parents, a way to have a home. Maybe that's a cop-out on my part. I don't know, but that's the only way I can live with it

—*Joyce I*

> I never felt like I gave my baby away. I always felt like my daughter was taken from me.
>
> —*Pollie*

Yet another myth in common currency is that these women did move on and forget. In truth, none of the mothers I interviewed was able to forget. Rather, they describe the surrender of their child as the most significant and defining event of their lives. Given the enormous number of women involved and the impact the surrender had on their lives, not to mention the lives of their parents, their subsequent partners and children, the fathers of their babies, and the surrendered children, it is remarkable that so little is known about these mothers' experiences even now, decades later. This silence has also kept many of these women from learning about one another and understanding that their feelings of loss were normal and consistent with thousands of other mothers who had surrendered children.

> I am shocked at how much it has impacted my life, I really tried to move on and forget, I tried to do what they said, but it didn't work. I was convinced that there was something wrong with me. There *must* be something wrong with me. It was supposed to work; everybody said so. But it didn't. No matter how many degrees I got, how many credits I had, how many years I worked, I was empty.
>
> —*Glory*

> The surrender was the beginning of a long cycle that colored my entire life. Your identity is formed in your teen years and if you take on this identity of a worthless, horrible, guilty person, then that's going to affect you your whole life. Guilt was always such a pervasive part for me. Not that I was sexual, or not that I was pregnant, but that I let somebody take my child. That's the guilt.
>
> People talk about the worst thing that could happen to you is to lose a child. And no one talks about that in terms of a birth mother. What do they think that is for her? Why would it be any different? It's in your cells, and in your guts, and in your consciousness, and in your heart.
>
> —*Diane IV*

As I listened to story after story, what impressed me so powerfully were the commonalities in the women's experiences. How the surrender was not only a deeply personal experience that affected the life of each woman but also a profound collective experience. Taken together, these experiences offer evidence of the lack of individual choice and the pervasiveness of surrender as a social phenomenon. For most of the women I interviewed, it was not a question of choice but of doing what society demanded–a demand that society has never folly acknowledged.

> You know, it was such a long time ago and I started thinking, "Just let it go. Just let it go and move on," yet I couldn't, and I can't. It's a big issue to those who lived it. There are women out there who lost their firstborn child and never got to grieve. I can't even put it into words. It's a weird thing, this whole adoption thing where people think that someone could just hand their child over and it will be okay. Obviously it's not. We're still alive. We're still here. We haven't died. Our issues are every day. We live this every day. Every day.
>
> —*Suzanne*

DOROTHY II

I was fifteen that summer. And I was in love with the Rolling Stones. My girlfriend Patty and I spent a lot of time listening to their music. One day my brother came home with his best friend. He introduced me to this guy and I remember being singularly unimpressed. But I noticed he stared at me in a way that no other guy before had. And it frightened and fascinated me all at once.

Meanwhile, I went on with my life as a Rolling Stones fan. And he started calling the house. He would call and ask for my brother. And we began to play this voice game where I would sound more and more seductive and he would sound more and more interested. And so that's how we began. Then one day when he called, he actually asked me out. It was my first real date. I felt safe because he was my brother's friend. I don't even remember what we did that first time—probably drove around in his car. He had a baby blue '57 Chevy that was his pride and joy. He spent a lot of time talking about the car and all these little gadgets he had attached. And I kind of liked riding in that car. I felt really important. I'm fifteen years old and I'm thinking, "Wow, this is what dating is like."

Then one night he decided we should go parking. I thought it was just gonna be a make-out session. But the very first time, he was already pushing me back in the seat and I remember thinking, "Boys are a handful," then thinking, "Well, he's nineteen, maybe that has something to do with it." And I think the very first time we went parking I began to be afraid. That this was going in a direction I was either not ready for or in some way I felt threatened by. And yet something else took over—a kind of fatalistic inability to say no. And I am not sure to this day why this happened. I've wrestled a lot with that.

I began to be very secretive with my family, and not tell them I was meeting him. I can't remember the first time we actually went all the way. I don't remember how many dates, in other words, it took. But I do remember feeling betrayed, because he refused to wear a condom. I remember saying, "I don't wanna do this, because I don't want to get pregnant." And he said, "Well, I promise you, you won't get pregnant." And I said, "How are you gonna manage this?" He said, "Well, I'm going to pull out," and he explained what that meant. So he stopped trying to convince me and just took over and sort of pushed me back, and again I felt unable to act. I was stunned, dazed. I could not say no.

It was very quick. I was not even sure that it had happened. It didn't hurt terribly—it just felt a little uncomfortable. There was this wet feeling between my legs and I said, "Was that it?" He was unable to speak for a few minutes. And then he said yes. Then he said, "You're mine now," and I think in my whole life that is one of the moments when I was the most afraid. In my whole life. Even now, to this day. That feeling of being *owned* was horrifying. And that's when I began to think, "I don't want to see this person ever again."

I began to make excuses not to see him. He was very possessive. I think we carried on for another month or so, and then I skipped a period. I was terrified. And I was just, I remember feeling like I was falling down this hole. I was just falling and falling and everything was spinning. And I thought, "No, not me. Why me?" My first love, and it wasn't even a love. Why me?

I didn't know what to do. I was very ashamed. This was not something that good girls did. Because I came from a very kind of poor family, I was more acutely aware than most people, maybe, about reputations and how easily they are lost. I knew from the experience of living in that small town that girls who got pregnant really lost their ability to have any kind of decent life. It was over for you. Your best hope in those days was to marry the boy and have done with it, and in the years to come hope that people would just forget it. The thing was, I was fifteen. I didn't love this boy. This was 1966—abortion wasn't an option. I mean, we didn't even think about it.

He said, "I've told my mother" and his mother wanted to talk to me. Her answer was "You're gonna get married." She said, "We'll help you get through this, *but* you have to marry him." And I said, "I'm not really ready for marriage." It's one thing to deal with being pregnant, and quite another to deal with being someone's wife. They said I was selfish. They called me some terrible things.

I finally realized I had to tell my own mother because I knew she was my only ally. So he and I took my mother out to Carvel's, which is this little ice cream place in town. And I remember being really afraid of how she would react. I was the one child of her four who just might make it through school, might make it out of our little town.

It turned out that I couldn't tell her. We were sitting in Carvel's in the parking lot, and he had gone in and bought us all banana splits. As soon as I saw mine, a wave of nausea just swept over me, I had to escape from the Chevy. I ran to the back of the parking lot, and I threw up. My mother was sitting in the back of this car watching me getting sick. And I saw the two of them talking from my vantage point and I realized he was telling her.

She got out of the back of the car and walked toward me. I felt so afraid and I started crying. I remember thinking, "Please, Mom, you're all I have. Just stick by me." And I waited, and I watched her walk to me. And she just put her arms around me and said, "It's okay, babe. Because no matter what, we'll get through this together." We cried in each other's arms for about ten minutes, I guess. And finally she waved him away. She waved him away. She said, "Just go."

And she and I walked home from Carvel's. We took this road, this detour that was one of our favorite walking spots. It was along the Housatonic River and it was a road that was lined with these wonderful weeping willow trees. It was the most beautiful place I think in our town at that time, at least for me. We walked with our arms around each other's waist. The willow trees were blowing in the wind and we hardly talked at all. By the time we got home, I knew that she was gonna watch out for me, and that she was gonna make sure that everything was okay.

I had to start school. I was going to school and throwing up in the bathroom—I was absent chronically during that month of September. By then I was about six or eight weeks pregnant, I guess. It became difficult to go to school at all. I decided to go see my priest and tell him about it. He was the only male authority figure that I trusted.

I talked to my priest and he said, "You know, there *is* a way, Dorothy." And I said, "Well, I can't imagine what that is because I don't want to marry him." And he said, "Well, I wouldn't advise you to marry him anyway, because he isn't a Catholic."

I didn't understand a lot of things about the Catholic religion. I was a convert and had only been officially a Catholic for maybe three years by the time I got pregnant, I didn't understand a lot of the details-things like you can't many a non-Catholic. I said, "So you're saying marriage isn't even an option for me? Is that what you're saying?" He said, "Unless you can find a good Catholic man who would be willing to adopt the child, no, we can't accept your marriage." On the one hand, I was glad, because this gave me ammunition to tell his mother, "I'm sorry, it's against my religion," of all things.

But the worst part was yet to come. He said, "You know what purgatory is? We've talked about that." And I said, "Yeah, I know what purgatory is," And he said, "We can't baptize your baby if you have her out of wedlock. So if you don't marry a Catholic man there's only one other option, or your baby's going to stay in purgatory when she dies. She can never be baptized into the Church."

I was devastated. Here I am, fifteen-years old, having to deal with the metaphysical complications of what happens to a soul when it passes from this earth if I don't do the exact right thing at this moment. I said to him, "Well, what would *you* do?" Like I was six-years old, I said, "What would you do? He said, "I would give the baby to a family who could take care of those things. A Catholic family—a good Catholic family." I said, "You mean adoption?" And he said, "Yes, I think that's your only out in this situation. You don't want to ruin your reputation. We can find a place for you to spend the last few months of your pregnancy. There's no reason for you to feel embarrassed or go through the pressure that you're currently facing with your boyfriend's mother."

I was sort of enamored of the idea of running away, sure. He made it sound like this place he was going to send me to was a country club. He said, "There will be other girls like you. You'll be able to talk and have fun for the last few months of your pregnancy, no one will bother you, and you will be able to make an informed choice." He said, "Nothing is final till it's final but I think you'll do the right thing." And that was just the first time I heard "do the right thing" in that whole nine-month period.

So I went home after that long meeting and tried to explain to my nonreligious mother what purgatory was, and how my child would end up there if I didn't give her away. She finally just gave up on trying to understand, and said she respected this priest. She said, "If the priest says you should go away to this place, then I think you should go. 'Cause I don't have an answer for you, babe. I'll help you if you want to stay here, but I don't have an answer for you."

So for me the easiest thing to do was to go away. It was a running away; it was a place where I really thought I could go and think. But before I could go there a social worker had to get involved. And it was explained to me that the state of Connecticut would be paying my tuition at this home for unwed mothers called St. Agnes. I was told it was located in West Hartford, and that they would take care of bringing me there. I could stay until my baby was born and then come home. They would take care of the adoption and I wouldn't have to worry about anything. Sounded wonderful, but it was very hard for me to say good-bye to my mother. I had never been away from home except for an overnight visit to a friend's house. I was devastated to be away from her.

She had said, "Write me letters. You won't feel as lonely." So I did. And that started my little pattern. Every night before I went to bed, I would write my mother a love letter. I think she kept them for most of her life. And it kept me in touch with the one person who really loved me.

And I just, to this day, cannot get over that feeling of loneliness and abandonment and being in that place with so many young people. Everybody I saw was just a kid. I noticed one thing very quickly at St. Agnes, and that was that nobody wanted to talk about what was going to happen to them at the end of their pregnancy. They really wanted to live in the moment. They didn't want to talk about "going over" that became a metaphor for the birth. We would come to breakfast in the morning and we would look around to see who wasn't there, "Oh, she went over last night. She went over." That meant she had gone to St. Francis Hospital and had her baby. We would envy that person because she was out of jail, so to speak. But we were a little afraid, because we didn't know what this was all about.

I remember that one of my best friends at St. Agnes was a girl named Brenda, who was like a movie star. She just was very glamorous and had long blond hair. She was one of those people who didn't really look pregnant. She just had a little belly and she looked *great*. We were all so envious of her. When she went over, we were all very interested to know what she had. After Brenda's four days, she came back to say good-bye to all of us. Being so popular, she almost had to. She held court in one of the rooms on the second floor, and we were all allowed to go in. We asked her all kinds of questions. "What was it like? What was it like?"

She had changed. In just those four days. She was very mature in a way that frightened me. She was not the same person. She looked fabulous, but she looked about four years older. She didn't want to talk about the details and we thought that was kind of curious. If Brenda didn't want to talk about it, it must not be good. She said she had a little boy, and she had said goodbye to him, and she hoped he had a better life. But that's all she would say. She said good-bye to us all, and we were a bit chastened after that. We all went upstairs. And that night I remember not many of us had dinner. We were just very, very worried. There were a group of us that were all due around the same time, and we kind of bonded. One by one, we went over.

By the time I was in my third false labor, they decided to induce me. I had no one there to hold my hand. I had no one, I didn't even know who was going to deliver me. It was the loneliest thing I've ever gone through in my whole life. The loneliest.

The baby was born at seven o'clock. I had only been in labor maybe seven hours, I guess. And most of it I don't remember. I woke up at about seven-thirty, maybe seven-forty-five, and I was in the recovery room. There was this nurse changing my sanitary napkin. I looked down and my stomach had caved in. I no longer had a child in there. I looked at the nurse and I said, "What happened?" She said, "You've had your baby," in a very kind of businesslike matter-of-fact way. She wouldn't look at me. And I tried to get her to meet my eyes, because I wanted to ask her all these questions. It was a very important moment for me. "I had the baby?" And she was just very—she was doing her job, and I said, "Well, what was it?" And she said, flatly, "It was a girl." I said, "Oh, it was a girl."

I remember thinking I wished it was a boy, because boys can't have children, I thought, "I gave birth to a little girl who's going to have to go through this, that poor little thing." I had always thought boys had it better than women. All my life, you know? And that whole experience made me feel even more so that it's the girls who get punished, the girls who suffer through all of this stuff, and the girls who can't talk about it.

But, of course, once I got used to the idea that it was a girl—which took me all of twenty seconds—I wanted to see her immediately, and they said, "You can't. We have to take you back to your room, and in the morning when they bring the children around for feeding time, you can see her." I said, "What's feeding time?" Because it sounded like the zoo. And she said, "Well, the hospital is on a feeding schedule, and they bring the children at ten and two," and something else—I forget. I thought, "Oh my gosh, I have to wait until ten in the morning to see my child?" And they said, "Well, that's the way we do things here." I said, "Well, where is she now?" "Well, she's in the nursery. They're taking good care of her."

They took me upstairs to this room. It was a room with four beds. Two of the beds were empty and one had one of my friends in it. She had delivered three days earlier. The next day would have been her last day. When I came in, she was awake. By then it was maybe eight-thirty, nine o'clock, 'cause it was dark outside. She said to me, "Dottie, is it you?" I said, "Yeah! How are you?" I was all happy. I was in the euphoria that—right after birth you have this euphoria, "I'm done, I'm done!" She was in the throes of post-partum depression already. I could sense that this was a serious *down* that she was on. She said she had had a boy, and she said, "Tomorrow's my last day of seeing him, and then I gotta go home."

I couldn't even relate to that sadness at that moment. I felt bad, but at the same time I couldn't relate. I said, "Oh, I can't wait till the morning, because I'm going to see my daughter. I had a little girl!" We were at opposite ends of this spectrum of grief. I hadn't seen it yet, she had already and it was very hard. She said to me, "Dottie, I have one bit of advice for you before they bring her; don't get attached," I said, "Oh, I won't I just wanna see her and count her toes and make sure she's okay." I was always a kind of brave kid, and thought, "I can do this."

Well, when they brought her I wasn't prepared. All that pain and all those months of waiting were nothing compared to what I felt when they put her in my arms. When I saw her for the first time, I knew what real love really was. And I've never been the same since that moment. I remember her cuddling up against my neck, and I held her as close as I could, and the feeling of her little face just nuzzling my neck, and I thoughts "Oh my God, if s a real, live person." And I loved her so much. I thought I loved my mother, I thought I loved my friends, I thought I loved Mick Jagger, but this was something else. This was like looking at another version of myself. I never thought you could feel like that in the whole world. And then I wondered, "What am I supposed to do now?"

I held her, and the first thing I did was unwrap her. I wanted to see her entire body. She was very tiny. She had the most beautiful, perfect little toes. I remember counting them, and I thought, "Well, this is what everybody said I would do." I did exactly what everybody said. I looked at her little fingers, and I remember caressing every single inch of the fingers and toes, and saying, "This is really her. This is really Tracy." And I started to talk to her, and to say, "I love you. You're just so beautiful." I started talking baby talk. And I remember her turning her face into my neck and nuzzling. I just knew it was her way of recognizing me. I thought, "She knows me!" And I called across to my friend, who was seeing her son for the last time—at the same time that I was seeing my daughter for the first. She was in grief and in tears. I said, "She knows me! She knows me!" And she couldn't speak She couldn't even be glad for me. And I just looked back at my child, and I thought, "In three days, I'm gonna be her."

Finally, on the third day, I had to say good-bye. I remember being very out of it, and not being able to come up with the right words. I felt somehow that whatever I said to her was really significant—that if I didn't say the exact words that it would somehow curse her. And I have no reason for this except for, possibly, it was the influence of the medication. But I told her to be a good girl. That I would never forget her. And to understand that I just did what I thought was best. And to forgive me.

When it was over, the last thing I remember was that little pink blanket. That little shred of pink blanket that I could see over the nurse's white shoulders going out the door. And that's the last time I saw my daughter.

The next couple of weeks were horrifying. I got sick. They didn't know what was wrong. They wanted to do an emergency exploratory laparoscopy. I guess at one point I was in critical condition. So during that couple of weeks of recovering from the surgery, that's when the real loss of my daughter hit me. I was able to think at that point. It was then that I felt seriously depressed.

The person who drove me home from the hospital happened to be the social worker. Again, me trying to think the best of people, I thought she was just being kind. Then I remembered she wanted me to sign that piece of paper. And, sure enough, halfway home, she pulls over by this little lake. She had taken the scenic route. I guess she thought that would make it easier. She pulls over and brings out her little briefcase. My mother was in the backseat. I think she had picked up my mother before she had come to get me. And again I thought this was so kind of her, but it turns out she needed my mother's signature. That's why. It wasn't anything altruistic at all.

So I'm in the front seat with the social worker. My mother's in the backseat. And out come the papers. She said, "We need you to sign these so we can place your baby." I said, "You know, I really don't think that I can sign these papers. I really don't think I can do this. I really don't want to do it now—I'm just coming out of this surgery," And she said, 'Well, look. The baby's been in foster care this whole time. You haven't bonded with her at all." She said, "As far as we're concerned, she's only known the foster mother at this point. The adoptive family is waiting for her. And why would you want to just do this to *them?* They've been waiting ail this time while you were sick to get this done." On the one hand, I was outraged that I should care that they were waiting, and on the other hand, that was the deal I had made. As young as I was, I understood what making a deal with the devil means: you just can't win.

So my mind is racing, trying to think up ways to get out of this. And I said, "Well, I really need to see her one last time because then I'll know for sure." And, of course, I was planning on making a break for it. She refused to tell me where the baby was. She said, "I'm not at liberty to disclose that." And I said, "Well, have you seen her? How do you even know she's all right?" She said, "Oh, she giggles and coos and she's happy as heck." She didn't say "Heck." She said, "She's very happy. She's a happy baby, and she's ready to go with her new family."

I said to myself, "Well, she's got it all sewn up good and proper, doesn't she?" Everything I could think of, she had an answer for. And as things got a little tense, and I was about to say, "No. I'm not gonna sign these," she said, "You know, the state paid for you to go to St. Agnes. That's quite a bit of money that we put out in good faith. Do you have the money to pay for that?" I said, "No." I looked at my mother, and I said, "Mommy, what am I going to do?" And she said, "Babe, I don't know. We don't have any money." I wanted to know from an attorney—I wanted to know from somebody what my rights were. But for every question I asked this woman I got the answer that I didn't want to hear: that I had no rights. That I had already given her away. That it was the best thing. And that it was all my fault. Somehow, it was all my fault that things weren't going well. And that I needed to just go home and I would forget about it and I would be fine.

We sat there for a long time, wrangling back and forth, and she wore me down. I was still sick, I still had not recovered. I was very weak and needed to lie down. She wasn't moving that car until I signed those papers. I remember almost grabbing them from her at one point and saying, "All right, I'll sign them." I remember just scrawling my name and handing them back to my mother and my mother signed. The social worker took the papers, put them in her briefcase and we drove to my house without saying one more word. And life for me was never the same.

That fall I went back to school. I was a junior in high school but all I cared about was escaping. I couldn't concentrate—it was very difficult. I realized that I could find escape in drugs and, later, in alcohol. And that began a lifelong problem, with trying to realize you can't bury your emotions. You just have to talk about them. So for about fifteen years, I smoked pot really heavily. I drank. I couldn't hold a job. I didn't know what I wanted. I remember just being really wild and not caring about anything. I was courting death, certainly. This went on for years.

I never had another relationship with a boy; I would never let anyone close enough to me. I no longer associated pleasure with sex. I associated death and pain and loss with sex. At some point I cleaned up enough to get a job, and I met my ex-husband in the late eighties. By then I was, like, thirty-six or something. And he taught me to enjoy sex, which I'm really grateful for. Before the age of thirty-six, I did not know how to enjoy sex. I also noticed another phenomenon: I couldn't talk about what had happened to me, about my daughter and giving her up, because every single person I told the story to judged me. Not one single person said, "I know how you feel. If I were in your spot I would have had a hard time." Every single person judged me.

The Give and Take of Adoption

By Barbara Katz Rothman

The institution of adoption is the embodiment of all of our deepest cultural contradictions about motherhood. Shame, secrecy, and gentility: the stigma of inappropriate, "illegitimate" fertility and the stigma of infertility. Pride, pleasure, and responsibility: adoption as a moral solution, both to illegitimacy and to infertility; doing a good deed in giving up a baby to those who can "better care for it," and doing a good deed in taking in a baby "as one's own." The recognition of the social relationship of parenthood: the forging of the bonds of family out of legal rather than blood ties. The continuing concern with the "seed," the endless pseudo-science reports about how adopted children are "not the same." The fascinating convolutions of class relations: rich people adopting poor people's children and hiring other poor people to care for them. The business of adoption: the brokers, the fees, the black market, the gray market, and the white-baby–only market, the international wheeling and dealing in children.

If we could come to understand adoption, perhaps we could come to understand motherhood.

To adopt is to fake as one's own; to adopt a child is to make of that child one's own child. When we think of adoption that is what comes to mind: the waiting arms, the welcoming parents. But for every pair of welcoming arms, there is a pair of empty arms. For every baby taken in, there is a baby given up.

If we can make ourselves believe that babies arrive in the world at birth, if we can make ourselves ignore the meaning of pregnancy, then we can ignore those empty arms. We can tell a woman who will be giving a baby up not to see it or hold it, so that she won't miss it. We can tell her not to "bond" with the baby, but to give it up right away. But if we recognize the absurdity of dismissing months of physical intimacy, then we have to recognize that adoption is also someone's loss: perhaps a chosen loss, perhaps even a full-hearted relinquishment, but always a loss.

Recognizing the reality of the relationship that is ending takes nothing away from the reality of the relationship that is about to start. This is not a zero-sum game. The question is not, should not be, and need not be "Who is the real mother?" We can acknowledge the ongoing grief of a woman who has given up a baby: without saying that that makes her the real mother, or more the mother than the adoptive mother or father who gives ongoing love and care. A woman, who has carried a baby in her body is a mother. Her motherhood is part of who she is, who she will always be to herself, if not to the child. She may give up the child, give up its care, give up its responsibility, ending forever the relationship. Yet she is changed by what she did, by her mothering of that child. It shapes her.

And a woman who adopts a child is the mother of that child. There is no question in my mind but that adoptive parents are true, real parents to their children. Parenthood is a social relationship, not a genetic connection. Adoption is not a second-best, almost-your-own way of making a family. Adoption is what all parenthood is: an intimate social

Barbara Katz Rothman, "The Give and Take of Adoption," *Recreating Motherhood: Ideology and Technology in a Patriarchal Society*, pp. 125–139. Copyright © 1989 by Barbara Katz Rothman. Reprinted with permission.

relationship. A woman—or a man—who raises a child is the parent of that child. Her motherhood, too, is part of who she is, who she will always be. She, too, is changed by what she does, shaped by her mothering of that child. And a man who raises a child becomes part of that child and his fatherhood becomes part of his identity, changes him, shapes him.

Because I believe it is the intimacy, the relationship that makes a parent and not the genetics, I fully recognize *both* the adoptive relationship *and* the loss that is the birth mother's—and it is the unique loss the birth *mother* feels that I address. I am not able to use the gender-neutral language "birth parent" that I saw so often in reading the social science literature about adoption. What, after all, is a "birth father"? If it is not to be genetics that ultimately determines parenthood, but nurturance, then a genetic father who does not nurture is not, in a sense that is meaningful to me, a father, a parent. On the other hand, I am comfortable with the gender-neutral "adoptive parent," because any adult, man or woman, can be the parent, the nurturer of a child. But in adoptive families, no less than in those formed by birth, it is predominantly women who do primary parenting, who "mother," and it is adoptive mothers who feel their motherhood most threatened by the motherhood of the birth mother.

We need a way of recognizing the significance of both of these women's relationships to the child and, more important, the significance of the child to both of these women. Children know who their parents are, understand the social, psychological parents to be "real." But unrequited love is real, too: the birth mother feels the significance of the child, even when the child would not know her, when she means nothing to the child. That someone else is mother to her child does not crate the birth mother as a mother: the motherhood of one woman does not cancel out the motherhood of the other.

Under the best of circumstances, the women themselves can recognize the sharing chat has gone on. It's been expressed in the heartfelt poetry of birth mothers and adoptive mothers:

> Our child
> Can never be not yours
> Nor not ours.
>
> …
> Thank you for
> Caring deeply,
> For trusting enough
> To place your babe into a small secure ark,
> To float into the rushes of life
> Without even a Miriam at watch
> To tell you where
> His growing path will be.
> We honor that trust,
> And we shall love and cherish him
> As strongly and surely as you do.
> —Chris Probst

And-from the other side of the giving, from a birth mother to her child:

> I loved you and still do
> But I can't let that love in my life.
> I gave you life so your mother could love you.
> I signed papers that said I was "Abandoning" you,
> But with love,
> With the knowledge that a family waited for you,
> Waited with joyous outstretched arms.

I've seen the joy of families with special babies
Like you.
It is matchless,
I've no regrets.
    —Anon.

But rarely is the giving and taking done under the best of circumstances, and all too often there are regrets:

Sign the paper here
We need your heart and soul
And your reward is
DOIN TIME
You will forget
You can have other children
Don't be selfish
You won't regret
You have nothing to offer.

…
In the night we feel
Sorrow, the twisting, churning
Of nothingness
The madness of giving, and not
Knowing to whom
No one ever told us
About
DOIN TIME.
    —Helen Garcia

    The grief of the birth mother is there because grief is a fully normal response to loss. Some regret may be part of grief, the feeling of sorrow following loss. But regret also implies a feeling of being sorry for some act, some choice of one's own. Grief may be inevitable in life, but by acting wisely, with foresight, we think we can avoid regret. The birth mother without regrets may express and come to terms with her grief. The loss is there, but she can live with it, take satisfaction in the joy she created, the life she created and gave away. The birth mother with regrets feels punished for her choice, feels she is eternally "Doin Time."

    In Garcia's poem we hear the pressure the birth mother experiences: pressure, forced chokes, and ultimately regret. It is not this choice that leads to the regret, but the *force*. We also hear regret in the stories of women who would have chosen to give a baby up, but were forced away from that, into raising the child or to abortion, and of women who would have chosen abortion but were forced into raising the child or to adoption. Regret will be a theme in the lives of women wherever we are without power to make the choices we need to make for ourselves.

    The reality is that birth mothers do not always give up their children with a deep sense of the rightness of what they are doing, but because they are pressured into it. Birch mothers who give up babies for adoption suffer the powerlessness of their youth, of the stigma of their inappropriate fertility, and most often they suffer the powerlessness of poverty as well.

    If we step outside the psychological dynamics of adoption, if we look for a moment at the class relations in adoption, some ugly facts emerge. "Poor countries export children to rich ones, black parents to white, poor parents to better off." And if we take a thoughtful look at the mechanisms established for facilitating, adoption, we can also accurately say that "adoption agencies are a system for redistributing children from the poor to the middle classes." Thirty-two-year-old attorneys living in wealthy suburbs do not give up their children to nineteen-year-old factory workers living in small towns. Whether we look at the birth mothers who go through adoption agencies and compare them with the adoptive couples who go home with their babies, or look at the open marketing of babies as practiced via newspaper ads and brokers, we see that adoption is as much a class issue as it is anything else.

Adoption in America is a competitive market situation. In her 1980 exposé *The Baby Brokers* Lynne McTaggart traced the very open selling of white babies. Want ads are placed in economically depressed towns. Brokers want cash only for certain transactions. International trafficking in babies is rampant. Certainly this system sits side-by-side with the very legal, very open, very legitimate work done by the adoption agencies. But the agency system operates in its own chaos, and creates its own marketing. At one of the well-respected, genteel, long-standing adoption agencies in New York my husband and I were told that there was a sliding scale for adoptions, going up to $9,000 for people earning $70,000 a year. That money, we were told, was most certainly not to be thought of as purchasing a baby. It was a fee to cover the costs of the agency's services. And although there were homeless newborn non-white infants within walking distance of where we sat, the "boarder babies" abandoned in New York City hospitals, the agency did not work with the city: the city does not pay its bills. Those babies, the babies of women of color who were not sophisticated enough, well enough, or "together enough" to get themselves to the agencies that would handle black babies, well, those babies would go into the foster care system. The city itself reflects no urgency in placing those children for adoption.

Children are commodities in a competitive market, and the ironies abound. Potential adopters with the most resources—two parents, solid income—can get the "cream of the crop," the healthy, white newborn. Older, single, or in any way disadvantaged prospective parents find themselves on a waiting list for the leftovers: older children, children with known disabilities, children who have been in and out of foster care. "The most difficult children tend to be placed in situations which have more than usual stress and fewer than usual resources. While this paradox is widely acknowledged, the competitive nature of the adoptive situation in the United States makes it inevitable."

McTaggart concluded that the new adoption business, the brokering of babies—and I would add the even newer business of brokering "surrogate" services to create babies to order—"magnifies what is wrong with the old one, most particularly the roles assigned to each member of the adoptive triangle: the child as merchandise, the biological mother as manufacturer, the adoptive parents as potential customers." The true miracle of adoption is that out of all this ugliness, beautiful families are formed. Once the brokers, the wheelers and dealers leave, children cease to be merchandise and people forced into the role of purchasers are able to grow into parenthood. It is not only the birth mothers who are abused: this system punishes everyone. "It is only the most extreme manifestation of the way we abuse the rights of unwanted children, disregard the needs of teenagers in the area of sexuality and fertility, and punish those people who cannot produce their own children."

But while all of the members of the adoption triangle are made to suffer, they do not suffer equally. The last group, the ones who are infertile, have social power that the others lack. Infertility, after all, does happen to rich people, to white people, to well educated people, and adoption may be their only choice if they want to share the joys of childrearing. Unwanted pregnancies may happen to rich, white, well-educated women, too—but adoption is rarely their only choice. If they make that choice, those are the birth mothers most likely to have no regrets, whatever their sense of loss may be. It is the young, uneducated, poor birth mother who is most likely to feel the pressure, the loss of choice. The system is weighted heavily against her, as her ability to create something precious is turned into her liability.

Solving Problems with Problems

There is an enormous difference between what works on an individual level and what works as a social policy. As a public policy, adoption cannot be the long-range solution for infertility, even though it obviously works for many individuals. It does not work as a social policy because it makes us dependent upon the grief of one group of people to solve the problems of another group of people.

In a better world, in the world I would want us to have, there would be virtually no women giving up babies: contraception, abortion, and the resources to raise her own children would be available to every woman. But in a better world, we would also devote our energy to solving infertility, solving it on its own terms, curing physical problems with physical solutions, and, most important, preventing these physical problems wherever possible. Safer contraception, a cleaner environment, better preventive health-care services—these would go a long way toward avoiding infertility in the first place.

While attention has focused on the infertility of wealthy whites, in-fact infertility, like virtually all illness and disability, is class and race related. Poor people and people of color are much more likely to be infertile. For people of color, adoption, informally arranged through families or more formally through agencies, remains available. The complexities of race relations in the United States make it very difficult, and often, entirely inappropriate, for white people, of whatever economic status, to adopt black babies. An all-white family in an all-white community, however much love it offers, cannot meet the social needs of a child growing up black in America. The inflexibility of the system, however, leaves children without any permanent placement. I am not persuaded that it is better for a child to be unplaced than to be placed in an "unmatched" family.

With economic justice and an end to racism, with a feminist revolution, these problems would mostly go away. Right now we are not living in that better world, and right now adoption makes enormous sense, especially but not exclusively as an individual solution to infertility. Taking in a baby that needs parents is surely more reasonable than risking one's life and health in low-success infertility treatments.

But we are left with the painful contradictions that adoption presents; creating a family in joy, helping others to create a family in joy, being humiliated in public agencies because of one's infertility, being humiliated in those same agencies because of one's fertility, giving a baby, losing a baby, adopting a baby, buying a baby—adoption is all of those things. Since it is the infertile, would-be adoptive parents who have the most power, they are the ones whose definition of adoption has the most power. For them, adoption is a solution to infertility, their creation of a family, a way of having children of their own. And that becomes the cultural understanding of adoption, as we focus on the welcoming arms and turn away from the empty arms.

Beyond the moral dilemma of relying on one problem, women who have to give up babies, to solve another problem, people who are infertile wanting babies there are practical problems. For a brief historical period, using one problem as the solution to the other problem seemed to work, partly because as a society we turned a deaf ear to the anguish of the birth mother, and partly because the birth mother also often felt this was her best choice. But pragmatically, two problems cannot be used as a solution to each other, because if the two are not kept "in synch" solving one problem comes to look like the creation of the, other problem.

And that is precisely what did happen. We have come a long way toward solving the dilemma of American women being forced to give up babies. We solved it with legalized abortion, making it possible for women with unwanted pregnancies to avoid creating a baby only to lose it. And we solved it by making it more acceptable for a woman to raise a baby by herself, without a husband.

But solving the one problem intensified the other. So now some people talk about how awful it is that young women raise their babies alone, when there are such deserving couples waiting. And some people talk about what a tragedy it is that women are having abortions when there are so many homes waiting for babies—or at least for white babies. Others step in to solve the problem: some by importing babies from other countries, relying on their problems as our solutions. And some solve it by deliberately creating empty-armed mothers, making a business of baby brokering and of "surrogacy," encouraging women to have babies for the sake of giving them up to solve other people's problems. If the problem of an unwanted pregnancy is no longer sufficient motivation to create willing birth mothers, then the problem of poverty can be turned into the motivation.

It could have gone the other way, of course. Picture what would have happened had we somehow managed to find solutions to the problem of infertility first, and were able to get almost any woman pregnant at will. Then we would have been left with the problem of "extra," unwanted babies. Perhaps we would then speak disparagingly of couples having children, especially those having large families, while other children go homeless, with no one to care for them.

The painful irony is that we do have that problem, too—we do have children, not so much babies as children, going homeless. And we haven't enough people who feel so strongly the need of a child to adopt that they are willing to take in, to take on, the troubled, distressed, needful child.

Orphans Real and Imaginary

Adoption is a triangle. The third side, the one I have not yet discussed, is the child. For an infertile woman or couple, adoption is a route to parenthood. For a birth mother, adoption is a way to solve an unwanted pregnancy, or to provide care for a child she cannot raise herself. For a child, adoption is survival. It is parents, a family, a place in the world. In Eileen Simpson's autobiographical account of her orphanhood, *Orphans Real and Imaginary,* she recounts how she and her sister lost their mother to TB shortly after Eileen's birth. Their father, faced with raising two very young daughters, shuffled them around in foster care, finally placing them, prophetically, in an orphanage. A few years later, he too died. She writes of her life in the orphanage, later in a "preventorium" to treat "pre-tubercular" children, and still later with battling relatives who apparently wanted the small legacy that went with them more than the children. In her book, Simpson places her own orphanhood in larger context. She discusses orphans in history and in literature, from Charles Dickens to Little Orphan Annie and more. She discusses "half" orphans, people who lost one parent (how horrified I was to think of myself, who lost a father in childhood, as any kind of orphan at all), and "psychological" orphans, people whose parents were physically present but psychologically absent. The category broadened, became meaningless. Is there anyone who has never felt orphaned—abandoned, unloved? We move from true orphanhood, the pathetic inhabitants of a Dickensian please-sir-may-I-have-some-more orphanage, to existential loneliness, the orphanhood of all modem people.

A basic theme of Simpson's book, expressed in her essay on orphanhood but more poignantly presented unstated in her autobiography, is the manipulation of children in the interests of adults, and the achingly sad ability, in the face of such manipulation, of children to continue to love.

The father moved the girls from one foster home to another whenever people spoke of splitting up the two sisters, but he also moved them when foster parents, "equally distressing to my father," hinted at adoption. He preferred the orphanage. Several times a year he came and whisked the girls away, straight to Best and Company, where they were transformed with new clothes and haircuts into the daughters he wanted, and photographed the way he liked them. But each year, by the time the photos were framed, the girls were back to being orphans, returned to the institution.

Their father was unwilling to make the sacrifice it would have taken either to keep his children with him or to give them up. Instead, he kept his apartment in Greenwich Village, his life of independence. And he kept his two children—as stored property. These are the things *I* saw as I read this book. These are not the things Eileen Simpson always saw. A loving daughter, she never questioned her father's abandonment.

I have been thinking about this book, about orphans, as I have been attending meetings on the new procreative technology. Infertility specialists announce with pleasure that they have broken the age barrier: with egg donations even old women can have babies. We know scientists have helped to complete the pregnancies of women who have died: the bodies of brain-dead women have been kept functioning to bring a fetus to term and then been unplugged after the birth. Doctors are helping to solve the infertility problems of older men: men in their fifties and over, often starting second families, make up a sizable segment of infertility patients. At a recent meeting I attended one specialist said he'd solved the infertility problem of a seventy-one-year-old man. Another topped it: he'd helped a seventy-eight-year-old become a father. But the first took the prize: he'd twice (twice!) removed live sperm from men after their death. They do it all the time with prize bulls, said the veterinary scientist at the meeting, describing the technique. "Just how we did it!" said the doctor who had just solved the problem of deaths let alone age, as a cause of infertility.

In her discussion of orphans in history and literature, Simpson talked about "posthumous" children, children born after their father's death. Now we have children born after their mother's death, children conceived after their father's death; now we can create orphans to order with the freezing of embryos.

But *why*? Why would a man want his sperm to live after him? Is this the route to immortality? Is virility, aliveness, so tied up with motile sperm that if those little tadpoles can still wriggle a man still lives? What can it mean to be a child created, brought forth into the world, just so a sperm could live?

What of Baby M and the other children of "surrogates"—children brought into the world not just because someone wants a child to rear and to love, but because a "genetic link" is needed. No orphan, Baby M—she suffers from too many, not too few, parental claims. But still her situation highlights the contradictions in our relations with children. Stern, her father, claims intent: he *planned* on that child. Whitehead, her mother, claims love: she had *not* planned on loving that child. Like countless women before her, however a pregnancy began, she fell in love with her baby. Relatively few of us had parents who so carefully planned us; most of us were lucky enough to have had parents who grew to love us.

Is intent a substitute for relationship, for love? Simpson shows us not. Her father's intentions, his bursts of attention, made her love him. But far more did she need ongoing care, the matter-of-fact love of parenting. She missed parents, seen from the outside as people who

> had the power to soften the discipline, slow the tempo, make exceptions. They bestowed affection on their children, offered them special tidbits at the table, selected their clothes with an eye to what suited them, took account of their preferences, and were indulgent about defects of character (especially, those that reflected-their own). Parents felt no need to disguise their preferences: they unashamedly preferred their own children.

Those are the needs of children: preference, specialness, daily love. And what are the needs of adults for children? Sometimes to love and be loved, so the needs of parents and of children match. Mostly it works out

But now we can separate out our genetic material from ourselves, from our lives, in space and in time. Now we can create children with whom we have no tie but the genetic. We can deliberately create abandoned, orphaned children. We can do it out of our own sense of orphanhood, as Mr. Stern, who had no "blood kin," had Baby M produced, so he would have a genetic relation. Certainly he intended to raise the child, to love her. But what of the old men who want a baby? What of the scientists rescuing sperm from dead men's testicles?

To overcome our adult orphanhood, our existential loneliness, we create orphans: the children of intention, not of love.

The orphanages are opening up again Simpson reminds us. Not filled with the indirect victims of TB, but of the newer diseases of poverty: drugs, crime, abandonment. Children still move from foster home to foster home, finally to the orphanages, the state unwilling to terminate parental rights and genetic claims, even after years of neglect and abandonment. So some orphans sit, abandoned property, while others are created—from the living or the dead—so that genes may live on.

Excerpt from **Adoption Nation**

A History of Meeting Needs

By Adam Pertman

Adoption in some manner, with or without the name or laws to formalize it, has been around for millennia. Every Passover, Jews around the world celebrate the ancient Hebrews' exodus from Egypt under the guidance of a young adoptee named Moses. It's a lucky thing for the institution of adoption that children rarely get as upset with their parents as Moses did in ancient Egypt (although the story is instructive in showing how intense adoptees' drive to find their biological roots can be). Typically, though, adopted people are more like another famous member of their ranks, Clark Kent, who adored his ma and pa here on Earth even as he maintained an emotional bond to his birth parents from Krypton.

Informally, of course, adoption has always existed. Aunts or grandparents, godparents, or even close friends would step in, and most often still do, when mothers and fathers abandon their children, become incapacitated, or die. Through much of recorded history, though, adoption by nonrelatives has been used more to meet the needs of adults than to help children. That's still often true today, but it used to be far more blatant. It is believed, for example, that in Rome, China, and other ancient civilizations, many infertile couples and parents who had only daughters formally adopted adult males to serve as heirs, to carry on family names, or to participate in religious ceremonies.

English common law, on which America's founders modeled our own legal system, made no reference to adoption at all; in fact, it wasn't until 1926 that England approved its first generalized adoption statute. Scholars believe that nation saw no need for organized adoption because inheritance was dependent solely on bloodlines; children without relatives to care for them were placed in almshouses, then made apprentices or indentured servants at a very young age. The colonists in this country initially followed those traditions, but adoption in the New World quickly evolved into new forms that reflected the unique nature of a society inventing itself.

For instance, the need for farm labor in the 1700s, especially on large plantations in the South, turned a practice called "informal transfer" of dependent children into a widespread phenomenon. The hardships of the Industrial Revolution, accompanied by a huge influx of immigrants, left so many children homeless in the early nineteenth century that public demand grew for improving their care. Charitable organizations, invariably led by and affiliated with religious groups, spearheaded this movement to end indentures and systematically place children in permanent homes with families.

At about the same time, adoptive parents began clamoring for laws to give their sons and daughters some of the same rights, such as inheritance, that were automatically granted to biological children. Meanwhile, as a result of rampant poverty and disease, the number of children without parents kept growing. P. C. English, a pediatrician who studied the history of unwanted children, wrote a chilling description of the scene in New York City during the middle of the nineteenth century: "The Lower East Side of Manhattan was the most crowded area in the world: The population

Adam Pertman, from *Adoption Nation: How the Adoption Revolution Is Transforming America*, pp. 19–34. Copyright © 2001 by Basic Books, a Member of The Perseus Books Group. Reprinted with permission.

density of 250,000/square mile was twice that of the most crowded areas of London. Waves of immigration, begun by the Irish following the potato famine of 1846, packed a mass of poorly fed humanity into tenements, with unclean water, inadequate sewage and no facilities for preparation and storage of food." Similar scenarios played out all over the country: Squalid, cramped conditions killed so many people that tens of thousands of children, and perhaps many more, were left to wander the streets.

Responding to all these gathering social forces, Massachusetts in 1851 enacted legislation that set out strict procedures for giving children new parents. It was the first U.S. adoption law, and it set several precedents. The most important was that it defined the needs of children as paramount—though this principle hasn't always prevailed in practice during the 160 years since.

The Massachusetts statute also marked the start of mandatory court approval for adoptions and presaged that the process would fall under the jurisdiction of the states rather than the federal government. For better and for worse, these were two portentous decisions that every other state legislature emulated by 1929, and that we all live with to this day. The resulting process has helped to prevent abuses and maintain local standards, but it has also flung open the door to frivolous decision making by individual judges and led to a jumble of state laws that have left adoption under-regulated, unconscionably expensive, and unnecessarily difficult, emotionally and logistically, for everyone concerned.

One of the most remarkable chapters in the American adoption story unfolded during the period when the Massachusetts legislature rook its groundbreaking legal action. In large cities everywhere, public and private "foundling homes" sprang up in response to the horrendous conditions in which armies of young children were living and dying. These well-intentioned refuges rapidly turned into disease-ridden warehouses where at least as much harm as good was accomplished.

A novel alternative to institutionalization was devised by the Reverend Charles Loring Brace in New York. He founded a benevolent association called the Children's Aid Society, branches of which still exist around the world, and he embarked on an ambitious program of relocating needy children into permanent homes. Reverend Brace believed the optimum circumstances for child rearing existed in rural areas, where the spaces were open, the people were honest, and the work was hard. His solution was the orphan train movement, as it came to be called, which continued into the early twentieth century. By the time it stopped running, an estimated two hundred thousand two- to fourteen- year-olds had been transported from eastern cities to farms in states as far west as Nebraska and Kansas.

News accounts of the time described how the Children's Aid Society announced the impending arrival of orphan trains in communities on its route, and how the children were put on display so that locals could choose the ones they wanted. Records indicate that few of these de facto adoptees were ever legally made members of the families that took them in, and some were evidently viewed as little more than cheap laborers. Nevertheless, most presumably wound up in homes that were more secure and loving than the ones they left behind—not a hard accomplishment, considering that so many of them had left nothing behind at all.

However noble the motives or favorable any outcomes from such efforts, the people who ran the orphan trains typically ignored the wishes of any biological parents who were still around, in a grim antecedent to the condescension experienced by birth mothers like Sheila Hansen. Simultaneously, the children themselves were dealt with less as individuals with rights, desires, and emotions than as possessions that could be taken at will and given away. That attitude still is evident in too many adults' behavior toward young people today and is perpetuated by current adoption law, which essentially treats the transfer of a child from one family to another as a property transaction.

The popular notion is that "everyone wins" in adoption because it allows birth mothers to resolve a problem, satisfies a deep desire for adoptive parents, and places children with families in which they can thrive. It's a wonderful ideal, but it was a myopic vision during the time of the orphan trains, and it remains so now. Adoption's glory is that it has fulfilled the dreams of millions over the years; but it has always been an emotionally wrenching and legally complicated process, because, by its nature, it must balance the rights and needs of vulnerable people. One of the stark realities of this little-understood institution is that the overwhelming majority of infant adoptions are initiated by women and men suffering from heartbreak and loss. For many of these participants, including some who reap benefits from the ensuing process, the wounds never completely heal.

Adoptive parents may love their children absolutely, but many nevertheless feel the ache of their infertility forever—and never stop wondering about the biological baby that never was. And birth parents part with the lives they have created, tiny beings who look like them, who gestated inside their mothers' wombs and, for nine months, were as much a part of them as their limbs. It's incomprehensible that there are people who believe that a woman, especially, can relinquish a child and then put the experience aside, forget about it, pretend she didn't part with a piece of herself. During the current period of fundamental change in adoption, perpetuating the myth that "everybody wins" can impede progress by trivializing or even ignoring the feelings of grief, insecurity, and identity confusion that are integral components of adoption, for adoptees as well as their two sets of parents.

Within the adoption world, such simplistic views can undermine relationships among adoptive relatives, between adoptive and birth families, and between professionals and their clients. They also can lead people inside and outside the extended family of adoption to unintentionally say and do things that inflict emotional pain on relatives, friends, and acquaintances who have ties to adoption. Children tend to get hurt the most, and the most often. Even in the midst of this revolution, we live in a nation in which "You're adopted!" is sometimes used as a taunt or an insult. "What kind of woman would give away her baby?" is still asked thoughtlessly, and "I'm sorry you couldn't have children of your own" is still meant as an empathetic remark.

Discovering a New World

One of the unequivocal benefits of the growing candor about and openness within adoption is that people feel increasingly comfortable confronting and trying to remedy their problems. As a result, just as civil-rights activists over the past few decades have sensitized Americans about their language and conduct toward ethnic and sexual minorities and women, adoption activists are finally helping people understand that adoptees and their various parents have hot buttons, too.

Naturally, some of these buttons differ within the many distinct types of adoption being practiced. Adoptees from foster care typically are older and have lived with their birth mothers, for example; their sensibilities and sensitivities therefore can differ markedly from those, say, of children adopted as infants from abroad or those adopted domestically at any age who don't share the skin color or cultural backgrounds of their adoptive parents. It would be unreasonable to expect everyone to understand such subtleties and complexities overnight, but it's easier for people to excuse the occasional slight if they feel they are generally treated with respect.

Few members of minority groups believe they have fully achieved equal status, while people outside those groups often have trouble fully grasping the gravity of the problem. (How many generations has it taken for people to "get" that racist and sexist jokes, even if they strike some listeners as funny, hurt people's feelings and perpetuate negative stereotypes?) Here are two examples to illustrate the point as it pertains to adoption:

As recently as the turn of the twenty-first century, newspapers around the country published a "Herman" cartoon—actually a reprint from years earlier, run that day because the cartoonist was on vacation—that showed a bratty-looking boy holding a pair of shears, which he's just used to cut down one end of a hammock. A hawk-nosed man lies on the ground between two trees, telling his son: "Tomorrow, I'm having you adopted."

Around the same time, the American Greetings company issued a Valentine's Day card with a cat on the front saying, "SIS, even if you were adopted, I'd still love you …" Inside, the thought continued: "not that you are, of course. At least I don't think so. But, come to think of it, you don't really look like Mom or Dad. Gee, maybe you should get a DNA test or something. Oh well, don't worry about it. We all love you, even if your real parents don't. Happy Valentine's Day!" (The revolution is having positive effects; today, American Greetings is putting out e-cards celebrating November as National Adoption Month, with the message "Of all the things a child needs … the most important thing is you")

Is it "political correctness" to label such attempts at humor as thoughtless and destructive? The people who wrote them didn't intend to hurt anyone, and perhaps they wouldn't if birth parents ceased feeling pain when they relinquished their children, but they don't. Or if adoptive parents were perfectly secure about their children's emotional development, but they aren't. Or if a seven-year-old boy, looking for a card for his sister on Valentine's Day, understood that his birth mother gave him a new home as an act of love and sacrifice. But he hasn't internalized that difficult concept, at least not yet, so the "joke" just inflames his sense of rejection and fuels his resentment at being different.

Because adoption occurred clandestinely for so long, most people have learned so little about it that even the smartest and best-intentioned among us accept erroneous stereotypes, draw unfair conclusions, and act without realizing that our actions can inadvertently inflict pain on a family member or a friend. This is not to say America has been a breeding ground for generations of emotionally damaged or dysfunctional residents because of adoption. Whatever issues the process may raise, it has benefited the vast majority of its participants and has enriched us as a nation. After all, everyone faces hurdles in life, and most of us figure out how to get around the ones we can't get over. (As Roseanne Roseannadanna used to say on Saturday Night Live, "It's always something.") For some of us it's adoption; for others it's racism or divorce or Uncle Charlie, who promised two years ago that he would move in "for only six weeks." Most important, unlike many other complexities of life, adoption is seldom an oppressive or minute-to-minute concern. And, in most cases and for most people, its upside is huge.

That's why tens of thousands of Americans each year adopt boys and girls with special needs from foster care—where there are minimal or no initial financial costs—and why tens of thousands of others are willing to deplete their savings, borrow from relatives, or even take out bank loans to pay the $20,000 to $40,000 it typically rakes to adopt a baby in this country or a child from abroad.

It's an outrageous sum of money that can have a negative impact in many ways. ... What's clear, nevertheless, is that neither cost nor any of the other myriad obstacles that line its road have prevented the process from becoming an increasingly prevalent means of creating a family.

"After we discovered our fertility problem, we resigned ourselves to not having children," said Susan Correia. Her husband, Russell, nodded his head in agreement as he put their smiling Chinese daughter into her baby seat. "We never thought we'd adopt, that's for sure," he explained. "We thought from the beginning that we didn't want to get onto that roller coaster." Even without doing much research, they knew the procedure could be bureaucratic and anxiety-producing. They'd heard the heart-wrenching stories about prospective parents who thought they had "their" babies, only to learn that the mothers had changed their minds. And they believed the costs might be prohibitive.

"We didn't have a whole lot of information, but there are so many potential pitfalls, and the fear of the unknown may be worst of all. It was our sense of things that it could turn out to be a nightmare," Susan recalled. Then, one day, a friend told her that infant girls in China were being abandoned and, she said, "It went straight through my heart." She decided to talk to her husband about the possibility of adoption.

Infertile couples seldom fully accept the notion that they'll never have children. Often they try sophisticated and expensive medical interventions; increasingly they turn to sperm or egg donors (a misnomer, since both the male and female "donors" are usually paid); sometimes they employ a surrogate mother. Invariably, they fantasize about somehow defying physiological reality and becoming pregnant.

At the time they were talking about forming their family, the Correias were both social workers who lived in a modest house in Portland, Maine. They didn't consider any of the costly modern methods available for appealing nature's ruling that they would not produce offspring. Still, after deciding that they wanted to adopt from China, they had to find a way to pay the adoption agency, to pay for the airline tickets to travel halfway around the world, to pay for the hotels and all the other expenses they would incur. They took out a home-equity loan.

Eighteen months and $18,000 later, the Correias came home with Hope—in every sense of the word. She was ten and a half months old and weighed just ten pounds when her new parents first took her into their arms. That was about two hours after they arrived at the well-kept, two-room brick building, a couple of hours' drive from Beijing, where forty-eight infant girls were unknowingly awaiting their turns to become someone's daughter again.

Susan and Russell stayed away from domestic adoption largely because they didn't want to be disappointed or hurt. But having children is always a gamble, whether the risk is miscarriage or a stillbirth, a frustrating bureaucracy, or a pregnant woman's change of mind about parenting her own baby. Adoptive mothers and fathers invariably have tales to tell, and sometimes they're unnerving. They end with a common conclusion, however (notwithstanding aberrational incidents such as the Tennessee woman who "returned" her adopted son to Russia in 2010): The parents would almost always go through it all again in a heartbeat to get the child they found at the end of their journey.

When the Correias arrived at the orphanage in Gao Ming, they saw a couple of attendants carrying a baby out the door. It was Hope. She was being rushed to the hospital, where she had spent much of the previous week being treated for bronchitis and pneumonia. "They told us she was very sick," Susan recalled. "I'm not religious, but I thought, God's not going to send us this far for something horrible to happen."

It didn't. The hospital prescribed antibiotics for Hope (whose English name is a translation of the name she had been given at the orphanage) and soon released her to the Correias. They took the child to a private clinic, where they paid a doctor to examine her again, and he pronounced her ready for travel. In another week, after all their final paperwork was completed and processed—China operates one of the most efficient adoption programs in the world—Russell and Susan took their daughter home to Portland.

For primarily cultural reasons, though finances also are a frequent factor, more than 90 percent of all the people who adopted infants outside of the public child-welfare system during the twentieth century were white, like the Correias. Blacks, Latinos, and Asians historically have cared for needy children within their extended families whenever possible, adopting them formally or informally but seldom taking in unrelated babies. This, too, is changing as the revolution unfolds. For instance, data from 2007 indicate that 19 percent of the parents adopting privately in the United States that year were African Americans, as were 8 percent of those adopting internationally.

For the most part, white adults who seek to adopt want infants of their own color, though this is changing, with steady increases in transracial adoptions from abroad and from foster care, along with the growth of intermarriage across color lines and a steady shift in social attitudes as the population of our country becomes increasingly diverse.

Ironically, some of the same factors that have coalesced to improve both adoption's image and its reality also have reduced the number of available white infants. The stigma attached to unwed mothers, for example, led large percentages of them to relinquish their babies through the middle of the twentieth century. Historically, white unmarried women have relinquished their infants for adoption far more often than women of color; researchers estimate that about 20 percent of babies born to never-married white women were relinquished for adoption by the early 1970s, and the percentage was probably significantly higher in the decades before that. The latest figures, based on the years 1996 to 2002, indicate that relinquishments for this group of mothers had fallen to 1.3 percent. The comparable percentages for births to all never-married women were 8.7 percent before 1973 and 1 percent in 1996-2002.

Whatever the absolute number, it's nowhere near large enough to satisfy the desires of infertile, late-parenting baby boomers and members of the generation that followed. The laws of supply and demand (along with their frequent companions, greed and graft) are largely responsible for the escalating costs of adoption; they are also among the key reasons so many Americans came to rely on other nations to complete their families.

A small number of international adoptions took place after the two world wars, when Americans took in orphaned children from Europe. But the practice didn't become systematic, and didn't start regularly crossing color lines, until Americans began adopting the mixed-race children whom GIs had fathered during the Korean War. South Korea remained the major source of young adoptees until the 1990s, when China opened its doors to the adoption mainly of little girls, who were viewed as less valuable than boys there. The Soviet Union's breakup further accelerated the pace of international adoptions, particularly since many of the children there were white Europeans. Russia became the biggest "sending" country for most of the 1990s, but from 2000 to 2009 (the last year for which statistics were available at this writing), Americans adopted far more children from China than from any other nation.

Turmoil in other nations, whether caused by a political decision such as China's one-child policy in 1979 or a natural disaster like the hurricane in Haiti in 2010, has contributed mightily to the adoption revolution in this country. That's true because it has placed children of color in previously all-white schoolyards in small towns from coast to coast, forcing teachers, fellow students, other parents, and members of the communities at large to deal with issues that have long been commonplace in larger, already diverse cities and towns. And it's true because of the media attention these adoptions have received, which has raised adoption's public profile, and—because so many of the kids look so different from their parents—the new families themselves have continued to thrust adoption into the open, simply because no one can pretend the caramel kid and his sunflower sister look very much like their freckled Irish mom or olive Italian dad.

Unlike its domestic counterpart (that is, the adoption of newborns), for which no single source of records is available, international adoption is precisely tracked, because the State Department requires the submission of legal documents for everyone who enters the United States. Just under 1,700 children came into this country for adoption in 1964, the first year for which the Immigration and Naturalization Service (INS) statistics office could provide me with data. Within twenty years, the number had climbed to almost 9,500. By 2004, it reached a historic high of 22,884— but, for a variety of reasons ... the trend line has been heading steadily downward ever since; by 2009 it had fallen to 12,753, and indications are that it hasn't hit bottom yet.

Nationalists in Russia and some other nations are critical of cross-border adoption, arguing that Americans are capitalizing on the misfortunes of other societies by taking their children, and then are depriving those children of their heritage by raising them in a foreign land. It's an argument with direct parallels to transracial domestic adoption; for instance, detractors maintain that African-American culture generally, and black children individually, lose out in adoptions by whites.

The confounding dilemma in the adoption world is that there are probably more than enough needy children in the United States to fill the homes of everyone considering adoption. There's a big obstacle in the doorway, though: These children are rarely perfectly healthy white babies. Instead, they're older boys and girls of every race, many with emotional and behavioral problems. There are perceptual obstructions, too: Some Americans believe they'd have to cut through exasperating bureaucracies to secure one of these children (and they're too often right). Many also think the older child they adopt from abroad will have fewer problems than the one they would get from foster care (and they're too often wrong).

The good news is that the revolution, fueled by greater knowledge and philosophical changes in the field, is shaking the public system to its core, with potentially huge consequences for adoption and for our nation. More than half a million children were mired in temporary living situations toward the end of the last century, draining the public's tax dollars with too little promise of growing up to be productive citizens. But today, state after state has revised its standards for the placement of children under its supervision. For decades, the defining principle in the child-welfare system had been "family reunification" at almost any cost, a wonderful ideal that entailed putting kids in foster homes while their mothers (and fathers, when they were around) received help to deal with their violence, alcoholism, drug addiction, or other problems. Unfortunately, far too often, the children were shuttled back and forth between foster and biological parents for years. They grew up amid instability and worse, so a large number developed emotional and behavioral problems that hurt them personally and made them less appealing prospects if and when they became eligible for adoption.

Studies underscore this point, which is intuitively evident anyway: The younger the child, the more likely he is to be adopted. They also indicate a direct correlation between the age of a child and the long-term stability of an adoption (the earlier, the better), and virtually every piece of current research agrees that stability and love during children's youngest years play critical, lifelong roles in their psychological development, their emotional well-being, and their ability to learn. Adoption policies and federal laws have led to shorter times in foster care for many of these children today, and greater numbers of them are being adopted more quickly. Far more progress is needed, however, if we're going to help the additional tens of thousands of boys and girls who need "timely permanency" each year, whether by being reunited with their birth relatives or by being adopted.

So there's no mystery about the goal: Inform prospective parents so they know they can adopt without spending tens of thousands of dollars by using the public system for little or no money instead. And reform the government bureaucracies that conduct adoptions so the process is less intimidating to enter and easier to navigate. Even if these changes were implemented, for a variety of reasons not everyone would pick this option—and it probably will never provide enough infants for all the people who want them and can afford to adopt them elsewhere. Many more people would use the public system, however, if the children were younger and less challenging, and if the procedures for adopting them weren't so wrapped in red tape.

It's quite a dream, but not a fantasy. Nationwide, in response to inducements ranging from budget crunches to altruism to court orders, the phrase "best interests of the child" is finally being interpreted as "timely permanency." So, after a specified period that can be as short as several months, state officials must now either determine that children will live with their birth families—which is usually the case, and should be—or take legal action to terminate parental rights and open the door for adoption.

This approach was accelerated by federal financial incentives enacted during the Clinton administration, and it has led to stunning increases in public-sector adoptions. From 1995 to 1998, as timely permanency became the primary objective, the annual number of these adoptions soared to more than 36,000 children nationwide—an increase of about 40 percent. And the numbers kept climbing into the new century, leveling off at just over 50,000 per year until 2008 (the last year tor which statistics were available), when they climbed to 55,000. "The system … was so inefficient that it was relatively easy to make changes that had a huge impact," says Jeff Katz, executive director of Listening to Parents, a nonprofit organization that advocates for improvements in the foster-care system.

If implemented well and sustained as a matter of policy, the changes in foster care could have a pervasive positive impact even beyond helping the millions of children and adults who will be directly affected. First, assuming the number of people turning to the public system continues to grow—as seems increasingly possible, especially given the abating availability of children from abroad—money could play a declining role in a greater percentage of adoptions. At the same time, the growing number of children adopted from the public system could gradually apply pressure on private agencies and lawyers to become more competitive.

Be prepared for horror stories, too. Revolutions produce victims, and in this one there inevitably will be birth parents who don't get sufficient opportunities to keep their children, adoptive parents who won't receive enough resources to deal effectively with their new families, adoptees who will be trouble and troubled. Bur the new approach to foster care is meant to make kids the number-one priority, and they should be the big winners in the long run, whatever the short-term difficulties.

Obviously, the overarching benefit for children is the chance to grow up in a secure, loving environment. They will also gain, however, if money becomes less of a factor in adoption. Children are concrete thinkers who have trouble grasping a conceptual distinction like the one between paying for services required to adopt a child, and buying the child. A five-year-old might not talk about it or even consciously consider the implications, but imagine the potential psychological effects of seeing a television program on which it's mentioned that the adoption of some child from her home nation "cost only $18,000." Or if she overhears someone, maybe her grandmother or her father's fishing buddy, asking, "How did you find the $25,000 to get your daughter?"—a question she might easily hear as "… to buy your daughter?"

The problems abound, yet more energized people are working harder to get things right in the adoption world than ever before. A world in flux can be a disconcerting place in which to live, yet adoption is helping to make America a more exciting, vital nation rather than a more unsettled one.

I remember the moment it dawned on me that we all might be in the midst of a phenomenon bigger than just a sociological blip caused by aging, infertile baby boomers seeking alternative ways of forming families. As West Coast bureau chief for *The Boston Globe,* I was covering the O. J. Simpson murder trial at the time. Dozens of us reporters sat shoulder to shoulder in a small pressroom on the twelfth floor of the Los Angeles courthouse. I was typing my daily story, on deadline, when the interruption came.

"This is awful," said Diana, a computer specialist and the only non-journalist in the room. She was standing right behind me, rustling a newspaper and pointing to a story in it. I turned around and asked what was wrong. Diana showed me the offending article. It was about the Baby Richard case, in which an Illinois man won custody of his biological son from the adoptive parents with whom the four-year-old boy had lived nearly all his life.

"Imagine how I feel," I replied. "I have an adopted son." (We hadn't adopted our daughter yet.)

"Really?" said the Chicago *Tribune* reporter sitting at my left elbow. "I've got two adopted kids."

The *Time* magazine correspondent to his left looked amazed. "I've got two adopted kids, too," he said.

Diana, wide-eyed with disbelief, whispered: "I'm adopted."

I was surrounded, and so are we all. Suddenly—or at least it feels sudden—adoption is being transformed from a quiet, lonely trip along America's back roads to a bustling journey on a coast-to-coast superhighway. The infrastructure has become so extensive that it has made all of us—not just adoptees, birth parents, and adoptive parents—into fellow travelers. We should do all we can to make this a smooth ride.

The Post-Nazi Era

By Masha Gessen

At a breakfast table at a Viennese hotel, I was telling my companions about this book.

"But you cannot test for race!" one of them objected, horrified. She was German.

True, I said, unless the person tested wants to interpret the test that way. And many do, because today's racial characteristics are still the most useful shorthand for the information genetic testing gives us about ourselves. The third person at the table, an Ashkenazi Jewish woman from the United States, pointed out that Ashkenazi Jews carry certain mutations for which genetic testing is available and useful.

The first woman cringed. "You are constructing biological identity out of anxiety!" she shouted. "Have you even read Foucault?"

We had read Foucault, but we both felt, at the risk of sounding old-fashioned, that the facts were too bad for Foucault. The German woman tried to withdraw from the conversation altogether, noting resignedly that she was a postmodernist.

"This is the post-Nazi era," the American Jewish woman quipped, eliciting a joyous laugh from me and a frightened one from our German colleague.

But here we were. The German woman felt she had no right to move into the post-Nazi era. The other woman and I, both being Jewish, could use the privilege of historical victimhood to make that decision for ourselves. There were two of us and only one of her, and we could laugh and tell her that this was the reason Israel would lead the world in the science and application of medical genetics.

We were in Vienna because each of us had at one point received a journalism fellowship from the Institut für die Wissenschaften vom Menschen—literally, "the institute for the study of man," located here in Vienna, where man had historically been studied to excess. This was the geographic heart of Europe and the home of the twentieth century: the city where Hitler spent his formative years; home of Sigmund Freud and birthplace of psychoanalysis; home of Theodor Herzl, the founder of Zionism; and, not coincidentally a site of one of that century's creepiest experiments in the application of genetics.

After breakfast I took the tram to an outlying neighborhood, where I searched the plain 1960s apartment buildings for the home of an old man who had lived to tell the tale. He had lived long enough, that is, and he had also made a life out of telling his story.

Masha Gessen, "The Post-Nazi Era," Blood Matters: From *Inherited Illness to Designer Babies*, pp. 57–68. Copyright © 2008 by Houghton Mifflin Harcourt Publishing Company. Reprinted with permission.

Johann Gross was short and portly, dressed in black trousers and a white undershirt, and he could not breathe. An oxygen tank nearly as big as the man himself sat puffing in the middle of his tiny apartment, and a white plastic cord stretching from it delivered oxygen directly to his nose. His mouth was occupied alternately by a foul, raw-smelling cigarette and a salad-green plastic inhaler. Wheezing constantly and halting occasionally, he told me his story. He had lived in the United States for four years some forty years earlier, and he could tell his well-honed story in English, so I came without an interpreter. It seemed, though, that Johann Gross could not understand anything I said. So his speech was a monologue.

When Johann Gross was eight years old, he had been living with a foster family for four or five years. He had no memory of his biological family: His mother had abandoned them when he was a year old, his father was a drunk, and little Johann lived in an orphanage before he was placed with his foster parents. As he remembered now, it was a good foster family: He was fed, schooled, and perhaps even loved there. But then Austria was annexed by Nazi Germany, and this meant that Johann Gross had to go home to a father he did not remember. His father was a very poor man: He was born missing an arm and had never really worked. State care for the children of the poor and the infirm contradicted some basic tenets of Nazi public health policies. Most important, using state funds to raise someone like Johann Gross meant engaging in what eugenicists called "counterselection": increasing the chances for survival, success, and procreation for the progeny of those less fit—and, in Gross's case, apparently genetically damaged.

"We had not much to eat. I slept in a little bed with my sister. I was hungry all the time." Johann Gross was inducted into Hitler-Jugend, which obligated him to spend his days going door-to-door with a tin cup, collecting funds for the Nazi cause. After about six months, eight-year-old Johann Gross ran away, tin cup in hand, back to his foster home. His foster mother called the child welfare service, which sent not a social worker but a Nazi Party officer, who expelled Johann from the children's organization on the spot and assigned him to an orphanage. After three or four escape attempts from the orphanage, the little boy was deemed "asocial" and placed in a psychiatric institution, on a children's ward called Spiegelgrund, or "mirror reason." The old man opened his book for me: He had published a memoir called *Spiegelgrund*. It was illustrated with his own drawings. He pointed at one of a wheelbarrow loaded with children's naked bodies, a mess of arms and legs with a little girl's body lying awkwardly on top. "I saw this," he said.

Most of the children at Spiegelgrund suffered from psychiatric conditions or mental retardation. From 1940 to 1945 they were studied, then starved or medicated to death and studied some more in the process. After they died, their brains were excised and placed in formaldehyde jars for further study.

Johann Gross watched the murders of the sick children from a short distance. He himself was considered problematic but not sick, so he was not killed. "I had a normal body. I think what saved my life was I was always very good in school," said this old man, who had had perhaps four years total of formal education. "They were not so quick to kill. When people were psychopathic, they were killed." Johann was not sufficiently disturbed to warrant a researcher's interest, so his brain was allowed to remain, functioning, in his body. He was, however, medicated systematically, excessively, and painfully after each of his ten escape attempts. "They gave me injections on my arms and legs," he remembered, visibly cringing sixty-five years later. "The injections on my arms—I would be on the toilet for twenty-four hours. The injections on my legs, I would be walking on the floor on my hands, I couldn't get up, and then it hurt for three weeks, and then I would run away again." While most of the children at Spiegelgrund received injections as part of a study, the treatment of Johann Gross may have been simple punishment: pure torture.

"The man from whom I got the most injections was a man with my name, this Heinrich Gross," Johann Gross told me. Heinrich Gross, a psychiatrist, administered what the Nazis called "euthanasia" to the disabled inmates of Spiegelgrund, and preserved their brains, which he kept studying after the war. He continued publishing on the Spiegelgrund brains into the 1970s.

Heinrich Gross was tried and convicted by a Viennese court in the late 1940s, and sentenced to two years in prison for his part in killing the children at Spiegelgrund. The Austrian Supreme Court threw out the verdict on a technicality, though, leaving Heinrich Gross free to embark on a second career as a neurological psychiatrist and court expert. In 1968 he became head of a research institute in Vienna. In 1976 he was called on to testify in the case of a man who had been interned at Spiegelgrund, like Johann Gross, as a "hardly reformable" youth. Heinrich Gross quoted from the man's Nazi file in court—and the man confronted his former doctor. The media exposed Heinrich Gross as a Nazi criminal, but it took another twenty years for the Viennese prosecutor to bring a criminal suit against him. The court ruled that Gross was demented and unfit to stand trial. "They didn't do him because they didn't want to do him," Johann Gross told me.

The brains of Spiegelgrund were finally buried in the year 2002.

I took a bus to the scenic outskirts of Vienna to see the hospital named for Otto Wagner, the Austrian Art Nouveau architect, another of the city's great twentieth-century figures. I entered and climbed up a very steep path in the middle of the vast grounds, punctuated with all manner of signs and arrows, including red plywood temporary-looking signs that pointed to something having to do with "NS Medizin." The warm autumn sun forced me to squint. The place seemed full of young people, some apparently medical students. Two teenage boys ran down the gravel path toward me, screaming, unable to stop.

I entered Building V, near the top of the hill, through a lovely sunporch. The room where the Spiegelgrund museum was located was Otto Wagner-stylish: all the whitest of white, sun-drenched, with double-height ceilings and a checkered tile floor. A wispy-haired young man, not much older than the teenagers I had just seen, sat at a little desk in the corner. As it turned out, he knew next to nothing about the exhibit he was overseeing: He was just performing his alternative civilian service to avoid being drafted into the army. This was a shoestring operation that had been recently-mounted by a group of enthusiasts, led by a city councilor who failed to get reelected.

A circular semienclosed wall formed a room within a room. Inside, photographs of children killed at Spiegelgrund were tacked to the wall, captioned with first names, surname initials, and ages, from two to seventeen. Most looked obviously mentally impaired. Some looked terrified. One, Friedel F., looked exactly like my daughter: long thin eyebrows, huge eyes, ears that stuck out, and a bad haircut. Friedel F., had been nine when she died.

Displays lined the rest of the room, aiming to educate the casual visitor about Spiegelgrund and Nazi medicine.

"In the late nineteenth century a new discipline developed in Great Britain somewhere between anthropology, medicine, and biology, for which its founder Francis Galton coined the term 'eugenics,'" explained a printout pinned to one of the stands, "While 'valuable' individuals were to be promoted ('positive eugenics'), carriers of an allegedly inferior genotype should be systematically excluded from reproduction ('negative eugenics'), which would lead to a genetic improvement of humankind. The idea met with public approval in many European countries and North America." The rest of the page listed Nazi eugenic efforts—forced sterilization, "euthanasia," and the fight against intermarriage—while attempting to walk the middle line between two traditional interpretations of the relationship between the science founded by Francis Galton and Nazi eugenic policies. One tradition interprets the National Socialists as enemies of science who perverted the spirit of eugenics. The other tradition, implicitly accepted by all who treat *eugenics* as a suspect term, has it that Hitler's Germany was a land where science prospered, and in this fertile environment Galton's ideas yielded the only fruit they possibly could: crime against humanity.

Some of the definitions of racial hygiene, a concept that predates Hitler's rise to power by several decades, sound conspicuously like possible definitions of contemporary medical genetics. One of the founders of the fields Hugo Ribbert, wrote that a goal of racial hygiene was "the prevention and conquest of diseases afflicting the entire human race, diseases from which each of the various races might suffer in similar, manner." His colleagues objected to the contamination of the value-free science of racial hygiene with "vulgar race propaganda." These concerns notwithstanding, racial hygiene, or eugenics, lent itself extraordinarily well to use by the Nazis, who claimed that "National Socialism [is] the political expression of our biological knowledge." At the same time, eugenics was perceived as the cutting edge of science not only in Germany but in the wealthy countries of Europe and, perhaps most of all, in the United States. In the period between the two world wars, Germany was far from unique in adopting laws based on eugenic ideas. In 1924 President Calvin Coolidge signed into law a bill that restricted the inflow of immigrants to the United States in accordance with then-dominant eugenic ideas. Coolidge himself had made his views known earlier. "America must be kept American," he had said. "Biological laws show ... that Nordics deteriorate when mixed with other races."

In Nazi Germany and annexed Austria, the practical application of eugenics proceeded in rapid stages. First, all forms of social deviance and difference, from Jewishness to Marxism and from homosexuality to criminality, were framed in biomedical terms. (Even the concentration camps and, some years later, the liquidations of the ghettos in Poland, were framed in terms of "quarantine.") Second, public health policies changed to accommodate this understanding. Medical care for "the weak" endangered the race because it interfered with natural selection by allowing the unfit to survive. Public health had to concern itself with the good of the race as a whole, not just the individual: This was the view of Alfred Ploetz, the man who coined the term *racial hygiene*.

The first of the racial-hygiene legislative acts was passed by the Nazi government in July 1933. It was called the Law for the Prevention of Genetically Diseased Offspring, which mandated the forcible sterilization of individuals whom a genetic health court found to suffer from any of a number of diseases then believed to be genetic, including numerous psychiatric conditions, hereditary epilepsy, Huntington's chorea, genetic blindness or deafness, and severe alcoholism. (By this time, similar sterilization laws were on the books in twenty-eight American states and one Canadian province.)

Unlike sterilization, Hitler's euthanasia operations were mandated not by public law but by the Führer's secret directives, illegal even in Nazi Germany. The body appointed to oversee the child-murder operation, which began in 1939, was called the Committee for the Scientific Treatment of Severe, Genetically Determined Illness. This was a cover name, but a telling one. The doctors who served on the committee, as well as those who carried out its directives, believed that the proper scientific treatment for severely disabled children was death—a mercy death, in their opinion, for their lives were not worth living. The committee did not issue orders; doctors simply received expanded powers, which included the right to commit murder, and acted in accordance with their beliefs. Four years later, the "euthanasia" program expanded to include healthy children of undesirable races, such as the Jews. The adult "euthanasia" program, initiated shortly after the child-murder campaign, claimed the lives of roughly four hundred thousand psychiatric patients.

After the annexation of Austria, Vienna became the second-largest city of the Third Reich. Its officials raced to catch up with the implementation of racial-hygiene policies. The ground was fertile enough: As elsewhere in Europe, eugenic ideas were popular. Vienna had a city office of marriage counseling, created to stem the tide of anti-Darwinian selection. Attendance, however, was voluntary, and apparently modest. The new regime acted quickly to streamline Vienna's health-care system, adding new offices and entire new fields, such as "hereditary and racial health care." Public health offices were charged with inventorying the city's population, consolidating records culled from psychiatric hospitals, the police, and the office of youth welfare, to create a list of the genetically suspect All those defined as inferior would be denied welfare benefits and health care. Public health officers were to pay particular attention to an individual's potential productivity. This was why Johann Gross, the son of a disabled man, lost his place at the orphanage but ultimately was allowed to live: He was right to tell me that it was his good school grades that saved him.

~

The easiest way to think of medicine under the Nazis is to believe that science was abused, and so, in some way or another were the doctors who applied it. The problem is, that does not seem to be true. "One could well argue that the Nazis were not, properly speaking, abusing the results of science but rather were merely putting into practice what doctors and scientists had themselves already initiated," writes Robert Proctor, a scholar of Nazi medicine. "Nazi racial science in this sense was not an abuse of eugenics but rather an attempt to bring to practical fruition trends already implicit in the structure of this branch of science."

The line of thinking launched by Francis Galton in the nineteenth century produced the desire to improve the human race, and particular races among humans. As knowledge accumulated, so did the drive to act on it, leading to the policies of National Socialism. That is why my German colleague cringed as I described my research. That is also why the very word *eugenics* sounds, if not exactly obscene, then at least accusatory. The problem with this view, though, is that it really does make it impossible to mount any credible defense of the contemporary science of medical genetics.

Where does one draw the line between Nazi eugenics and contemporary genetics? For one thing, many of the racial hygienists went on to second careers as human geneticists, drawing on the experience gained while serving the Nazi regime—just as Heinrich Gross continued his study of disabled children's brains even after he was no longer allowed to kill them for his research. The hardest place to try to mark a division between the Nazis and us is at the science itself. Many of the enduring obsessions of racial hygienists have either remained germane research topics for geneticists or have been revisited in the last few years. These include the studies of twins to estimate the genetic components of everything; the heritability of behavior, such as a propensity for violence, crime, or alcoholism; and Jewish intelligence. Even the once-ridiculed claim that Jews have a higher incidence of certain genetic diseases has now yet again been affirmed by scientists.

What makes matters even more complicated is that some of the Nazi public health measures live on: For example, the restructuring of the Viennese health-care system, designed to prioritize public health over individual care, is still in effect. Indeed, it is difficult to object to the basic argument advanced by Alfred Ploetz, who claimed that on a policy level public health trumps individual medical care. In 1936 Ploetz was nominated for the Nobel Peace Prize for his public health work.

Some researchers have focused on the economic arguments inherent in Nazi public health policies, which calculated the value—and care-worthiness—of human life according to the person's potential productivity. But economic arguments are extremely important in contemporary public health policy as well. Professional journals regularly publish articles arguing, for example, that widespread testing for certain conditions is economically viable because care for full-blown disease is very expensive. In the mainstream media, discussions on, say the cost and economic defensibility of life support for hopelessly brain-damaged patients are commonplace.

A term that used to sound so damning as to provide a potential demarcation line was "lives not worth living." But in recent years, American legal practice has virtually rehabilitated the concept by allowing so-called wrongful-birth lawsuits, in which plaintiffs argue that they or their offspring, were born as the result of medical errors or negligence—for example, because a disability was not diagnosed prenatally. The basic premise of such lawsuits is, certainly, that some lives are not worth living. The conditions at the heart of "wrongful-birth" suits—such as severe mental disability, for example—tend to be the same conditions that the Nazis believed rendered lives unworthy.

Of course, the easiest place to draw a line is at forced medical interventions. Nazi "euthanasia" was actually murder. Nazi sterilizations were involuntary. A basic tenet of contemporary medical genetics, to a degree even greater than in Western medicine in general, is that any tests or resulting care must be chosen by the patient voluntarily. But starting in the early twentieth century, a number of European countries and more than half of all American states enacted forcible sterilization laws. The language of the German law was, in fact, quite scrupulous: It allowed sterilization only in cases where genetically defective offspring was a likelihood and criminalized the sterilization of heterozygous carriers. It seems obvious now that forcible sterilization, no matter how finely defined, is indefensible. But the question remains: Were such laws the first step down a preordained slippery slope, which Germany simply slid down much faster than other countries would have, or was that catastrophic path unique to Germany?

I wandered the city of Vienna, thinking about this. As a historian, I was less than a dilettante. But I had chosen to write a book on a topic over which a giant historical shadow is cast. I had no other option now than to try to draw my own dividing lines.

Of the industrialized powers of the twentieth century that could lay claim to serious scientific achievement, the first one conspicuously to reject eugenics was the Soviet Union. Indeed, the Soviet Union banished genetics altogether. That did not serve to prevent the institution of racist policies, including wholesale deportations of entire ethnic groups—it was just that the Soviets, instead of claiming that members of the group were inherently inferior, ascribed to the groups behaviors, such as cooperating with the Nazis, and then laid collective blame. Nor did it prevent nationalism: Even several years after the collapse of the Soviet Union, in the early twenty-first century, more than half of all Russians owned up to supporting "Russia for the Russians." Indeed, the only thing the rejection of genetics succeeded in doing was holding back Russian medical science: Russia did produce a crop of ambitious young geneticists once the ban was lifted, but in the absence of any institutional support, most of them emigrated,

(In fact, about a hundred of them settled in Chicago, where they were doing most pioneering work on improving the human race. ...) It serves as a good reminder that even in the twentieth century the rifts and crimes of nationalism existed independently of the science of either genetics or eugenics, perhaps because they resulted from differences that are real. The advances in genetics have served to remind us of these divides, which American culture in various ways and with varying success has tried to obliterate, especially when it came to the Jews, subsuming them into the general Caucasian population and deeming them a religious rather than ethnic or racial group. This time genetics came with a warning label, like cigarettes.

Cigarettes, doctors will reluctantly tell you, are dangerous only when consumed in large doses: Very light smokers can have the pleasure without the risk of lung cancer. But only a very few people ... are inured to the temptations of cigarette addiction and can go on smoking five or fewer cigarettes a day for years. I was one of those smokers: two or three a day, for nineteen years. Genetic research, like most knowledge, can be like a drug: It leaves most of us wanting more. To separate the knowledge effectively from collective behavior, we must take it in small doses: apply it to individuals and not groups. Once it is used to generalize and create population-wide policies, the risks skyrocket.

My own task now was to apply my new genetic knowledge to myself.

All You Need Is Life

By Dominic Lawson

"How wrong it is to think of Down's children as something 'other,' a mere aberration of nature."

Congenital Defects Do Not Justify Abortion

Dominic Lawson, an editor of the London *Sunday Telegraph*, is the father of a daughter with Down's syndrome. In the following viewpoint, he maintains that aborting a fetus because of a deformity is reprehensible and is a form of eugenics. Lawson argues that a baby born with a mental or physical handicap will not necessarily be an unhappy person. All children have a right to life, he contends, whether or not they are handicapped.

As you read, consider the following questions:

1. What was Lawson's reaction to the consultant's diagnosis of his daughter's Down's syndrome?
2. Why is it increasingly improbable that children with Down's syndrome will be born, in Lawson's opinion?
3. Why did Lawson and his wife decide not to "have the tests" for Down's syndrome?

After only two and a half hours' labour Domenica emerged at lunchtime on Thursday 1 June 1995, with a shocked, empty stare on her face. She was also completely blue and inert. 'Slow coming round' was the midwife's later, written, observation. Only when the six-pound five-ounce form was finally bullied into breathing did I finally stop asking—in the useless way in which fathers drive busy midwives demented—'Will she be all right? Will she be all right?'

The Diagnosis

But even after my own abject panic was ended by hearing the first splutterings of a pair of tiny lungs, there remained in the room a faint but palpable tension. The duty pediatrician did not smile while she examined Domenica with

Dominic Lawson, "All You Need Is Life," *Spectator*, June 17, 1995, pp. 123–129. Copyright © 1995 by The Spectator. Reprinted with permission.

what looked, even to my untrained eyes, like professional concern. Then she wheeled the little baby out of the room, and asked me to follow both of them down the corridor, to the office of the senior consultant.

He went through a similar rigmarole of clinical examination, all the while asking a series of seemingly irrelevant questions: what was the condition of any other of my children? what sort of pregnancy had this been? Perfectly normal, I said, except that my wife had broken her leg in four places, half way through her confinement, and was still on crutches. The consultant seemed not to hear this last remark, and interrupted my off-pat explanation of how Rosa had sustained a quadruple spiral fracture of her right leg while trying to get into her car.

'Yes, well, we have a problem.'

'What?'

'I am certain that your daughter has Down's syndrome.'

This came as an enormous relief. Since our second daughter, Natalia, had emerged too premature even for the magic of modern medicine, at 22 weeks' gestation, I had been morbidly anxious throughout the succeeding pregnancy. The consultant's 'We have a problem' I instantly interpreted as 'This one won't make it, either'. His 'Your daughter has Down's syndrome' sounded more to me like 'But this one will live'.

The doctor then repeated his earlier clinical examination, this time giving me an idiot's guide to my daughter's ten-minute-old body. 'Here, you see her grip is very weak. She is very floppy. Her head has three fontanelles, instead of the normal two. And, here, her tongue is very large. If you look at her eyes, you'll notice these epicanthal folds, and a slightly Asiatic appearance. If you look at her ears, you might be able to see how they are folded over at the helix. You notice, here, that there are some extra folds of skin behind her neck. Now, if you look at her feet, here, and here, you'll see that there is an unusually large gap between the big and first toes. These, I'm afraid, are all phenotypes of Down's syndrome. Now, to be absolutely certain, we can take a blood sample, and do a chromosomal analysis. But that would be a formality in this case, and is not necessary for my diagnosis.'

Anger, Love, and Grief

Two emotions coursed through me as the consultant gave me a guided tour of the stigmata of Down's syndrome. The first was anger. While I understood that the doctor was only doing his professional duty—to explain as clearly and as quickly as possible the condition of his patient—I wanted to shout out, 'This is my daughter you are prodding, not some random strip of flesh.' The second emotion was love.

This surprised me. While I love my eldest daughter, Savannah, it took me many months to do so. During the earliest part of her life I found her endlessly fascinating, and a source of great pride, but I did not feel the pang of love. I gather that this is quite common among new fathers. Or, at least, that is what I told my wife. Yet now, after so little and so strange an introduction, I felt an intense, almost physically painful love for this third daughter.

It would be a sin of omission not to record that in the succeeding days I did not also feel a sense of grief. Grief at the thought that Domenica's life expectancy is not much more than half her elder sister's. Grief at the thought that she will almost certainly not experience the joy of having children herself. But this grief always coexisted with the feeling of elation which accompanies birth. It is a dizzying mix of emotions, this combination of sadness and elation, and I suspect it is appreciation of this that lies behind the anxiety with which some friends approach us. They want to sympathise and they want to congratulate, but how do they do both at the same time?

My wife has experienced a different form of grief, which, say all the textbooks, is absolutely characteristic of mothers in this predicament. They grieve for the loss of the child they thought they were carrying. Many mothers-to-be seem to have a very clear idea of the nature of the person who is squirming and kicking in their belly. That person does not have Down's syndrome, with all the attendant problems, both physical and mental. But this sense of two different people, the imaginary perfect child and the real handicapped one, is, of course, no more than a powerful illusion.

> ### Happy and Productive Lives
>
> Down's syndrome children are becoming extinct. Most are now aborted before they can be born.
>
> Ninety percent of Down's children are only mildly to moderately retarded. And while they are prone to a wide variety of physical ailments, nearly all are treatable. In fact, most Down's children, with love and care, can live happy, productive, surprisingly independent lives.
>
> Francis X. Maier, *Commonweal*, March 26, 1993.

Genetic in Origin

It is not even as though Down's syndrome is something which afflicts normal children in the womb, as a result of stress or illness, although that was what many doctors tended to believe until 1959, when a French professor named Jérôme Lejeune declared that the characteristic features of Down's syndrome were genetic in origin. He discovered that the Down's children had 47 chromosomes in every DNA molecule, instead of the normal 46, and that this extra genetic material, amounting to no more than about 50 to 100 genes in all, was the cause of all the differences which later come to light—the sort of differences which my daughter's pediatrician was so anxious to explain to me.

The DNA make-up of a person is settled almost at the moment of conception, when the female and male nuclei, which contain the chromosomes that will endow the offspring with his or her hereditary characteristics, fuse to form a single nucleus. The extra characteristics of the future Down's baby are caused during the first cellular subdivision of that nucleus, when 47 chromosomes are created rather than 46. This cellular self-multiplication is then repeated constantly for approximately 266 days, at the end of which you have a baby ready for delivery.

It is worth spelling this process out because it demonstrates first, that the Down's baby is as much a product of his or her parents' genes (and of their parents') as any other child, and second, that there is no sense in which the Down's baby could ever have been constructed in any other way, once conception had occurred. There is no possible alternative Domenica Lawson without Down's syndrome. That is her identity, her very essence, along with all the other genes she has inherited from us.

Her elder sister was formed by a different merging of the same parental genes, along more orthodox lines. …And the extraordinary similarities of these two girls, at least as babies, also illustrates how wrong it is to think of Down's children as something 'other', a mere aberration of nature. Despite all the peculiarities outlined by Domenica's pediatrician, she looks like a twin of her sister, as I am constantly reminded by the picture of Savannah aged two weeks which I carry in my wallet. They have a number of identical facial expressions. And, exactly as Savannah did, Domenica sleeps in an absurd parody of deep thought, with her right fore-finger resting on her top lip and her right thumb appearing to prop up her chin.

One visitor, a good friend who has the endearing habit of uttering exactly what is on her mind, exclaimed with relief upon seeing Domenica, 'Oh, I was so frightened about what she would look like. But she looks just like her sister.' I do not repeat all this out of parental pride—or not just out of parental pride—but to make the point, again, that the Down's children are not monsters formed at random. Of course Domenica's intellectual and physical progress will never be as rapid or fluent as her sister's, and it will doubtless cost both her and us enormous amounts of effort. But the point is, she will continue to develop, however slowly, along lines which will reveal her to be a true mixture of the genes which her parents married in order to perpetuate.

The Risks Involved

And yet. And yet a whole industry has been developed to make it increasingly improbable that children like Domenica Lawson will be allowed to live. In England, the National Health Service advises all mothers-to-be over 35 to undergo medical procedures which extract fluid from around the foetus, which is then subjected to chromosomal analysis. The NHS provides this service free because the probability of Down's syndrome—far and away the commonest form of

> ### Life Is Worth It
>
> My life of disability has not been easy or carefree. (Hershey is severely disabled from a rare neuromuscular condition.) But in measuring the quality of my life, other factors—education, friends, and meaningful work, for example—have been decisive. If I were asked for an opinion on whether to bring a child into the world, knowing she would have the same limitations and opportunities I have had, I would not hesitate to say, "Yes."
>
> Laura Hershey, *Ms.*, July/August 1994.

congenital mental handicap in the population—appears to grow rapidly when the mother's age increases beyond the mid-thirties.

But these procedures, either chorionic villus sampling or amniosentisis, have a significantly higher statistical risk of causing miscarriage than the 36-year-old mother has of carrying a Down's syndrome baby. The chances of that woman having a Down's baby, regardless of whether or not she has already had such a child in the past, is about one in 300. But even the less risky of the two procedures pressed on middle-aged women by the NHS, chorionic villus sampling, will, in about one case in a hundred, produce a spontaneous abortion.

According to Dr. Miriam Stoppard's *Pregnancy and Birth Book*—which is by no means hostile to these procedures—'very occasionally CVS may lead to rupture of the amniotic sac, infection and bleeding. Even so, the procedure only seems to increase the risk of miscarriage by 1 per cent.' Even so? Only 1 per cent? It is amazing that these facts are meant to reassure us. There is method in this madness, however. The NHS will provide, gratis, an abortion, if their tests show that the mother is expecting a Down's baby; an abortion even well after the normal legal limit of 24 weeks into the pregnancy, 'if there is a substantial risk that if the child were born it would suffer from such physical or mental abnormalities as to be seriously handicapped'.

This is nothing less than the state-sponsored annihilation of viable, sentient foetuses. In the People's Republic of China, the authorities wait until such children are born naturally, before starving them to death. In Hitler's Germany, even before the final solution to the Jewish 'problem', the Nazis were exterminating wholesale the mentally retarded. In this country the weeding-out process is done before birth, and only with, the parents' consent. I do not think, however, that this constitutes a triumph for democracy.

To the extent that this policy is more than half-baked eugenics, it is, to take the most charitable interpretation, based on the utilitarian idea that the child born with a physical or mental handicap will be an unhappy person, so unhappy that he or she would have been better off dead. One needs only to state this proposition to understand how presumptuous it is.

Not surprisingly I have, in the past week, been told by a number of well-meaning people that 'they'—meaning children with Down's syndrome—'are particularly happy people'. I have no idea if this is true, and I am inherently suspicious of such generalisations. But I see no reason why Domenica should be an unhappier person than her older sister, despite the extra chromosome which she has in her every cell.

Yet one or two acquaintances have still asked us, 'Didn't you have the tests?' My wife says she thinks it will be difficult to remain friends with such people. I think they are merely missing the point, although it is a very important point.

A Happy Life

Of all the letters which I have received since Domenica was born, perhaps the one which grasped this point best was from a fellow-atheist who wrote, after approving of our not 'having the tests': 'The reason "why [such a decision] is admirable, of course, is that the sanctity of life is not just some obscure abstract principle. A life is a life, and every life can be filled with all kinds of positive things and real happiness—as I am sure your daughter's will be.'

At the moment, however, the happier of our children is the elder. She hated being the only child. Indeed she would often wail, heart-rendingly, 'I am so only! I am so only!' She is not only any more.

Inconceivable

Prologue

By Carolyn and Sean Savage

We have three children. Or do we have four? A strange question, but the kind that parents who have lost a child ask themselves from time to time. That absent child is always with you, a loss you feel some days as yearning and other days in a gasp of pain. My husband Sean and I still grieve the son we lost, despite the unusual way he left us. Or rather, we still grieve him and the circumstances that forced us to give away a baby we thought of as our own. This was a child whom I nurtured and we both protected from the forces conspiring against his survival. Yet I understand that I may never hold him in my arms again and that the next time I see him, he will think of me as a stranger. Perhaps I will never be able to heal the ache that is the place he occupies in my heart. At the same time, I know that if Sean and I had this decision to make again, we'd do exactly the same for Logan.

For us, having children has been the biggest challenge in our sixteen years of marriage: twenty ovarian stimulation cycles, three in vitro fertilizations (IVFs), two frozen embryo transfers, and four miscarriages in the twelve years that we tried everything we could to expand our family. We knew that our struggle was coming to a close on the morning of February 6, 2009, when we entered the fertility clinic for one last try. I was nearly forty years old, and if this attempt at transferring our last embryos did not work, we were done. We would thank God for our three beautiful, healthy children and move forward. Two of my three pregnancies had been difficult, and one nearly lethal, but we were determined to fulfill our pledge to give every embryo a chance at life. Our beloved fertility doctor, who had helped us conceive our third child, Mary Kate, when other doctors had failed, would perform the transfer that morning. Little did we know that, because of a terrible mistake, I would receive another couple's embryos and eventually give birth to a baby we would not be allowed to raise.

All through the Christmas holidays of 2008 and into the New Year, I had been anxiously preparing for this day: taking estrogen pills, injecting lupron and progesterone, and enduring the bloating and grumpiness brought on by those drugs. Although I had started out thinking that I didn't want to go through all of it again, that I was tired of all the anxiety surrounding our infertility treatments and pregnancies, when Sean and I arrived at the clinic we were hoping for a second miracle. I had just slipped on my hospital gown when the fertility doctor entered the examining room. He was brusque and efficient, a man who clearly had many things on his mind as he described the condition of our thawed embryos.

"The five that survived all have developed to between nine and twelve cells. How many will you be transferring today? Remember, I don't do selective reductions."

Carolyn and Sean Savage, from *Inconceivable: A Medical Mistake, the Baby We Couldn't Keep, and Our Choice to Deliver the Ultimate Gift*, pp. 1–4, 7–12, 65–66, 89–94. Copyright © 2011 by HarperCollins Publishers. Reprinted with permission.

He meant that if he transferred all five and they survived, he would not eliminate any in utero to give me and the others a better chance. His policy on this was one of the reasons we chose him as our doctor. Besides, I wasn't sure any of these embryos were going to make it. Nine cells after four days in a Petri dish was not robust growth.

"Can you give us a moment?" I asked.

"I'll see you in the operating room. Let me know then."

"Sean, they should be eighty to a hundred cells by now. They are very, very behind. I think we should transfer three. I actually don't think any of them will take."

Sean knew how well I had educated myself about pregnancy, miscarriage, and the science behind IVF these last ten years.

"What happens to the other two embryos?"

"They'll watch them until tomorrow, and if they are still alive, they'll refreeze them. The ones we aren't transferring probably won't survive."

"Okay. Three it is," Sean said.

Before the nurse led me into the operating room, she had me check my wristband to confirm the information there. "Carolyn Savage." "Yes." "Social security number …" "Correct." "Birth date …" "Wait … actually, the day and month of my birthday are correct, but my birth year is wrong. It's 1969, not 1967."

This didn't seem like a serious error, so I didn't think anything of it. The nurse wrote a nine over the seven, fastened the bracelet to my wrist, and escorted us down the hall.

In the operating room, I lay down on the table and placed my feet in the stirrups. Sean came in a few minutes later, gowned in surgical attire.

"How many are we transferring?" the doctor asked me.

"Three," I said.

"We're doing three," he called back into the lab. A few minutes later, the embryologist entered the room holding a catheter.

"You are Carolyn Savage?"

"Yes."

He flipped my wrist over and confirmed my answer with a glance at my hospital wristband, then handed the catheter to my doctor. Sean held my hand tightly.

The nurse squirted ultrasound gel on my stomach and rubbed the wand over my abdomen. Up popped a vivid image of my uterus on the screen.

"There's the catheter entering the uterus through your cervix," the doctor narrated. "Now watch. Do you see that?"

I could see the catheter moving into my uterus, and although I couldn't see the embryos as he released them, I thought of them as light and graceful orbs. I pictured them nesting gently.

"Congratulations. You are now officially pregnant."

I looked at Sean and smiled. Now that our embryos were back where they were supposed to be, they might grow happily.

"That's it, guys. All finished. Good luck. I'll talk to you in ten days, after your pregnancy test," he said as he exited.

I lay still, standard procedure immediately following a transfer of embryos.

"How does it feel to be pregnant with triplets?" Sean said.

I laughed. "Don't look so worried! I know that however this turns out, we'll be able to handle it. Triplets? That would be scary, but we'd survive. Twins? No sweat. A singleton? Perfect! No pregnancy? We'll be okay with that too!"

"Mr. and Mrs. Savage?" A gowned man asked as he entered the room.

"Yes?"

"For your baby album!" he said as he handed me a picture. Sean and I marveled at this snapshot of our three embryos, labeled with my name, Sean's name, and our personal identifying information.

"Their first picture, you know? Congratulations," the man said to us.

Sean and I looked at the picture and beamed at each other.

The Call to Character

CAROLYN

I ROLLED over and glanced AT the clock. It was three o'clock in the afternoon, I felt like hell, and 1 was pretty sure I knew why. I had been pregnant often enough to recognize that I was experiencing those symptoms, but considering my history, I couldn't allow myself to feel certain. Not yet. I knew a virus was going around. The dizziness and nausea from the flu was about the same as what I felt with morning sickness. Soon enough I would get the results of the pregnancy test I'd had that morning. Why hadn't they called me yet? I thought for sure I would know by lunchtime.

That morning I'd rallied long enough to drag myself out of bed, throw on a bra and some sweats, and make a pathetic attempt at doing my hair before hauling myself to a lab for my pregnancy test. It was a chilly February morning in Sylvania, Ohio, and the cold air BOOSTED my spirit as I drove to the appointment at a lab, leaving our sons Drew, fourteen, and Ryan, twelve, to sleep in on their day off from school. Sean had taken our one-year-old, Mary Kate, to his mom's so I could rest. As I entered the laboratory to have my blood drawn, the happy thought that I was about to give her a sibling close to her in age brought a skip to my step at a time when normally I would have been dragging.

Home from the lab, I discovered the remnants of the feast of biscuits and pancakes the boys had made before they went to play with some neighborhood friends. The house was quiet when I drifted back to sleep in our bedroom, enjoying the familiar hormones of pregnancy coursing through my body, with the cell phone and the house phone resting on a nearby pillow.

When I woke at 3:30, there had been no call from my clinic. I felt eerily out of sorts and a little disturbed, as though someone were with me in the room, even though I knew I was alone in the house. Then I had a rush of energy, as if something important had just happened and I needed to attend to it. By the time the clock passed 3:45 and there had been no call, doubt started to creep in. What if I wasn't pregnant? I shivered and pulled the covers tighter around me. I wondered if my shakes were the flu. I rolled onto my left side and felt acid reflux. Why was that there? And I remembered … because I was pregnant. Again, I grinned as I nodded off to sleep.

When I woke again as the clock edged toward 4:00, I wondered if I should call the clinic. Surely they hadn't forgotten.

SEAN

IN FEBRUARY 2009, the atmosphere at the financial services company where I work was frenzied. I had been putting in long hours since the markets began collapsing the previous summer, trying to contain the panic virus that was spreading among investors, including some of my clients. Each time my phone rang, I heard my clients' fears; every time I glanced at the computer, the graphs showed global assets in a freefall. On February 16, Carolyn and I were hoping for some good news for a change: the results of her pregnancy test. Carolyn had been ill the night before and early that morning. Perhaps it wasn't the flu, but morning sickness. It was past 3:30, and a call from her was long overdue. My cell phone rang, and I answered it.

"Sean, do you have privacy?" It was our fertility doctor, his voice trembling. *This can't be good,* I thought as 1 rose to shut my office door.

"I have bad news, but it is not the type of bad news you would expect," he said. "Carolyn is pregnant with another couple's genetic child." My mouth fell open, but words escaped me. *How could that be true? How could that happen?* The hand that held the phone started shaking.

The day before, he said, his clinic's embryologist discovered the error and called him into the clinic, where the embryologist tearfully confessed that he had mistakenly pulled another couple's embryos from cryopreservation. Without knowing, the doctor had transferred them into Carolyn. Our doctor had decided to wait for the outcome of the pregnancy test before letting us know about the mistake. He said he did not have the words to express how sorry he was for the error.

I thought of the day of the transfer, of those embryos floating down to her womb, and then of Carolyn lying sick in bed this morning.

"Does the other family know?" I asked.

"Not yet. I wanted to see what you and Carolyn were going to do. I didn't know whether you would want to continue with this pregnancy. Actually, I thought I would reach Carolyn at this number," he said. "Can you give me her number?"

"No," I said. No way was I giving the doctor that number.

"I think you must consider carefully if you want to continue this pregnancy," the doctor said. "With Carolyn's health at stake and the emotional toll...."

"Call this number in an hour," I said.

After we hung up, I sat at my desk, unable to move. My mind bounced from one urgency to another, like a super ball trying to find a spot to settle. I had to relay this news in person. Carolyn had been my rock, my soul mate, for more than twenty years. We had always done the heavy lifting together; neither one of us shouldered big burdens alone. It was a partnership in every sense of the word. Thinking of how much this would hurt her made me sick to my stomach.

Stand up, grab your keys, and get home, I thought.

I had made the sixteen-minute drive home so often that I could do it in my sleep, which was good, because I wasn't focusing on the road. *This is a life-changer,* I kept thinking, but I couldn't process much beyond that. Mostly I was trying to decide what words to use when I told Carolyn.

As I pulled into the driveway the pounding of my heart shook my bones. I knew Carolyn was in the bedroom resting, and I thanked God that the boys were off at the neighbor's and our youngest was with my mom. I walked upstairs in the silent house, filled with trepidation.

The bedroom curtains were drawn, and the room was nearly dark. Carolyn looked weak and tired in the dim light. I approached her side of the bed, startling her.

"I have some really bad news," I said. She sat straight up in bed. "You are pregnant, but the doctor transferred another couple's embryos into you."

"What?"

"They made a horrendous mistake. Another couple's embryos are inside you. The doctor called to tell me."

"You are joking," she said.

I shook my head no.

She repeated loudly, "You are joking!"

I shook my head no again, and terror flitted over her face.

"You are joking!"

I moved to comfort her, but she flew out of bed. I stood back. She walked toward me with her finger pointed at my chest, as if she was going to make me take back what I just said. Then she stopped. I watched tears building in her eyes, while tears of my own ran slowly down my face. I was her husband, and I was not able to help her. No one could.

CAROLYN

SEAN'S FACE WAS ASHEN and his shoulders slumped, his body drained of his usual confidence. Deep down, I realized he wasn't kidding. As the seconds passed and I understood what he was saying, I lost control.

Sean reached to comfort me, but I didn't want to be touched. I ran toward our bathroom. He followed. I ran from the bathroom to the closet, back to the bathroom, to the bedroom door, and back to the bed, as if I needed to get away, but there was no escape. The problem was *inside* of my body. I realized I was gasping for air. I caught a glimpse of myself in our bedroom mirror. My skin was covered in red blotches, and my eyes were bloodshot and swollen. *Get a grip, Carolyn,* I thought to myself. Then I looked at Sean, who was standing in the corner of our bedroom, tears streaming down his face. I'd only seen him cry twice before: the day his dad died and the day Ryan was born, when I nearly died. Once again, he was crying tears of helplessness. He didn't know what to do for me.

I plopped down on the bed, grabbed my pillow, and hugged it to my chest. Staring at the wall, I tried to catch my breath. I couldn't look at Sean. I couldn't look anywhere.

After a few minutes of silence, Sean moved closer. He hesitated and spoke softly.

"You know, the doctor wants you to terminate."

"What? They want me to do what?"

"He said it would be best for you to terminate."

Our fertility doctor didn't believe in abortion. How could he go against his personal ethics?

I looked up at Sean, and our eyes locked. We both knew what the other was thinking. This was a human life, and we would protect it. It didn't matter that this child was in the wrong womb. That wasn't his or her fault. I put myself in the place of this child's mother. If I were her, I would be terrified that my child's life was going to be taken away because he or she was in the wrong place at the wrong time. What if my unborn child was in the wrong woman? Would that woman be merciful and allow my child to live?

I looked at Sean knowing this was one of those decisions we didn't need to discuss.

"We'd never do that," I said.

Sean nodded his head in agreement. And that was it. We would endure this pregnancy. I looked up at him, but his eyes had drifted to the portrait of our family on the beach that hangs over our bed. I closed my eyes. I wanted to shut it all out. When I opened them again, Sean was sobbing.

One Step Forward, Two Steps Back

Our lawyer sent this note to the genetic parents' lawyer on March 11, 2009.

Attached please find an ultrasound taken on this date. My clients would like your clients to know that as of March 11, 2009, the baby was measuring 7w1d and had a heart rate of 129 beats per minute indicating continued healthy development. Their next appointment and ultrasound is scheduled for Tuesday, March 24, 2009. If anything develops with the pregnancy before then, they will communicate that through my office.

At this early stage, my clients are nor comfortable agreeing to further communication. They will continue to provide updates regarding medical progress after appointments. They will also communicate any other developments that arise regarding the health and development of the pregnancy.

My clients do request that your clients understand how devastated they are by this situation. Their journey to expanding their family has consumed the past twelve years of their lives and has included a lot of loss and heartbreak along the way. They are still in shock regarding this situation and are fraught with anxiety regarding the long-lasting ramifications that this situation will have on their family and lives. They are simply trying to cope with their grief at this early stage.

They do understand how anxiety ridden your clients must be regarding the health of their unborn child. The only thing they can communicate to ease your clients' fears is that they will treat this unborn child as if it was their own. They have superb medical care and are following the advice of their physician.

Lastly, my clients have agreed /n receive a list of questions that your clients may have for them. Please forward the list to me as soon as your clients have it completed.

Respectfully Yours, Mary E. Smith

CAROLYN

I HAD NEVER FELT so stifled in my life. At a moment when I needed support more than anything, I wasn't allowed to share my burden with my friends and my family. The only people I could talk to about my heartbreak were Sean, the lawyers, and Kevin Anderson, thank goodness. All of them were in agreement that I should say nothing. I had never lived in such an interior world. At the same time, I'd never had so much to say.

Maybe, Maybe Not

March 24, 2009
At this time my clients are able to provide your clients with the following information.

- *They are approximating that they live no more than 100 miles from your clients.*
- *They do have living children that are in perfect health and have experienced normal development from birth.*

Attached, please find an ultrasound picture taken on Monday, March 23, 2009. The baby was measuring 9 weeks 1 day at the time of the ultrasound, which is indicative of healthy fetal development. The heartbeat at the time of the ultrasound was 180 beats per minute, which is very healthy as well. It should also be noted that the ultrasound picture shows the disappearance of the subchorionic hematoma that was visible in prior ultrasound pictures. This is also promising progress.

Their next prenatal appointment is scheduled for Tuesday, March 31, 2009. It is scheduled for late in the afternoon, so communication regarding the results of that appointment will not occur until Wednesday, April 1, 2009.

CAROLYN

ONCE THE PREGNANCY REACHED ten weeks, I felt more confident that this baby would live, and I started to worry all the time about our embryos. I had an unsettling feeling that they were already lost. If they weren't gone, I imagined they had been damaged in the mistake.

I didn't know whether any of what I imagined was true, but the vision I had seemed so plausible. I pictured the embryologist discovering his error and rushing to the cryopreservation tanks to find out if what he feared was true. I imagined him unscrewing the tank, like one would unscrew the top of a thermos. As liquid nitrogen wafted up, he would have searched frantically for my embryos.

When he found them, I pictured him removing the catheters where my embryos were stored, a procedure that is supposed to happen just before they are thawed. He would have lifted them out of the tank and stared at them for a while. I feared that he had thrown all protocol out the window at that point, laying the catheters on the counter while he double-checked my chart, hoping and praying he was reading it wrong. My embryos would have been thawing with every second that passed. I imagined that it took him a few minutes to gather himself and put my embryos back into the tank. By then, the damage would have been done.

I would force myself to turn away from the horror of that image and hope and pray that my embryos harbored one or two more children for our family. Not all of them were likely to be viable; nevertheless, I thought, *Surely God will reward us for saving this baby. Surely there is a baby for us at the end of this nightmare.* So I prayed for them. Just like I prayed for Drew, Ryan. Mary Kate, and the baby I was carrying. I prayed that God would protect my future children and deliver them safely to me ... sooner rather than later.

I also wanted to do something for us. For me. It felt like everything we had done since February 16 had gone toward helping this unborn child and the other family. I just wanted to have something to hope for, something to look forward to.

Long before we ever did IVF, Sean and I traveled to see a doctor in the Indianapolis area for a consultation. He had an excellent reputation and had helped friends of ours finally achieve their family after ten years of failures. He was the first doctor to recommend that we seriously consider IVF. Although we did our first IVF with our local doctor, the doctor in Indianapolis was the first one who popped into my mind as I tried to figure out what to do with our remaining embryos.

I called his practice and asked to speak to the head embryologist, who seemed very sympathetic to our situation. The plan we made was for me to pick up my embryos at the old clinic, which would place them in a portable cryopreservation tank about the site of a fire extinguisher, and then strap them into MK's car seat with bungee cords and drive them to meet with the new embryologist and doctor.

A few days after my birthday, the phone rang. I recognized the number as the Indianapolis doctor's office. I expected that it would be someone confirming all the plans for the big move. Instead, it was the embryologist. He sounded contrite as he asked me how I was doing. I sensed that something was wrong.

"After much discussion, we have decided we are unable to help you," he said.

"I'm sorry. What?"

"We are not going to be able to accept you as a patient here. So it won't be necessary for you to move your embryos here next week."

Panic washed over me.

"We don't know where else to turn," I blurted out. "We don't HAVE a relationship with any other fertility practices. I don't even know how to start a search for a new clinic under these circumstances!" I could feel the tears streaming down my face.

"I'm sorry. I feel really bad about this. If you want, I'll look into some other options for you," the embryologist said.

"No. No. We'll figure it out. I have to go. My boys are getting off of the bus. They can't see me crying."

I shook my head as I hung up the phone, frantically brushing away tears. His office probably didn't want to be associated with us, and I couldn't blame him for that. Who would? After all, I knew I was likely to become the poster child for the humdinger of all assisted reproduction disasters.

I began wondering what I was going to do. What if no one wanted to help us? What if no one wanted to be associated with our situation? I knew we had done nothing wrong, but it was just a matter of time before the media would be all over this story. No one wanted to be mistakenly seen as the clinic that did this to us.

To the Generic Couple's Lawyer

April 1, 2009

> *Attached please find the most recent ultrasound picture provided by my clients. It was taken yesterday, March 31, 2009. As depicted in the picture, the baby is measuring 10 weeks and 3 days. The heart rate was 184 beats per minute. These are both signs of continued healthy fetal development.*
>
> *My client's next prenatal appointment is scheduled for Wednesday, April 8, 2009. Results from that appointment will be forwarded that afternoon.*

SEAN

SOON AFTER LEARNING that we would have to find a new clinic for our embryos, we had our weekly appointment with Kevin. Carolyn explained that she felt as though our embryos had been disregarded by everyone but us. He asked, "Are you familiar with the concept of equanimity?"

Carolyn and I shook our heads.

"Equanimity is the idea that when things are going well, we are at peace. And when things are not going well, we are at peace. The ideal in a spiritual life is to be at peace with what is and always react steadily."

We must have looked dumbfounded.

"Have you heard the story 'Maybe, Maybe Not'?"

Again, we answered no. So he told it to us.

There was a farmer who used a great horse to help him on his farm. One day his horse ran away. His neighbors said to him, "Farmer, that is awful. You lost your horse." He replied, "Maybe, maybe not."

Within a few days the farmer was surprised to find that the horse had returned—-with three additional wild horses. The new horses could be quite useful on his farm. His neighbors marveled at his good fortune. "Farmer, you are so lucky. You now own several horses. You will work so much faster in your fields." The farmer replied, "Maybe, maybe not."

The next day the farmer's son tried to ride one of the wild horses but was bucked, resulting in a broken leg. The neighbors came to visit the farmer and said, "Farmer, this is tragic. Your son cannot walk." The farmer replied, "Maybe, maybe not."

Soon an army troop stormed the town, kidnapping all of the town's young men to press into service in their war. The troop was attacked, and all of the town's young men perished. The neighbors came to the farmer and said, "Farmer, you are so lucky. All of our sons have died, yet you still have yours because he was too injured to go with the soldiers." The farmer replied, "Maybe, maybe not."

This was an "aha" moment for both of us. I had never viewed the events of my life in this manner. Carolyn's eyes were lighting up as she processed the concept and the story. Was this the worst thing that had ever happened to us? I certainly thought so. Could we learn something from it? Hard to imagine, but… maybe, maybe not.

Genomics and Its Impact on Science and Society

The Human Genome Project and Beyond

By the U.S. Department of Energy Office of Science

A Primer

Cells are the fundamental working units of every living system. All the instructions needed to direct their activities are contained within the chemical DNA (deoxyribonucleic acid).

DNA from all organisms is made up of the same chemical and physical components. The DNA sequence is the particular side-by-side arrangement of bases along the DNA strand (e.g., ATTCCGGA). This order spells out the exact instructions required to create a particular organism with its own unique traits.

The genome is an organism's complete set of DNA. Genomes vary widely in size: The smallest known genome for a free-living organism (a bacterium) contains about 600,000 DNA base pairs, while human and mouse genomes have some 3 billion. Except for mature red blood cells, all human cells contain a complete genome.

DNA in each human cell is packaged into 46 chromosomes arranged into 23 pairs. Each chromosome is a physically separate molecule of DNA that ranges in length from about 50 million to 250 million base pairs. A few types of major chromosomal abnormalities, including missing or extra copies or gross breaks and rejoinings (translocations), can be detected by microscopic examination. Most changes in DNA, however, are more subtle and require a closer analysis of the DNA molecule to find perhaps single-base differences.

Each chromosome contains many genes, the basic physical and functional units of heredity. Genes are specific sequences of bases that encode instructions on how to make proteins. Genes comprise only about 2% of the human genome; the remainder consists of noncoding regions, whose functions may include providing chromosomal structural integrity and regulating where, when, and in what quantity proteins are made. The human genome is estimated to contain some 25,000 genes.

Although genes get a lot of attention, the proteins perform most life functions and even comprise the majority of cellular structures. Proteins are large, complex molecules made up of chains of small chemical compounds called amino acids. Chemical properties that distinguish the 20 different amino acids cause the protein chains to fold up into specific three-dimensional structures that define their particular functions in the cell.

The constellation of all proteins in a cell is called its proteome. Unlike the relatively unchanging genome, the dynamic proteome changes from minute to minute in response to tens of thousands of intra- and extracellular environmental signals. A protein's chemistry and behavior are determined by the gene sequence and by the number and identities of other proteins made in the same cell at the same time and with which it associates and reacts. Studies to explore protein structure and activities, known as proteomics, will be the focus of much research for decades to come and will help elucidate the molecular basis of health and disease.

U.S. Department of Energy Office of Science, "Genomics and Its Impact on Science and Society," *U.S. Department of Energy Office of Science*. Copyright in the Public Domain.

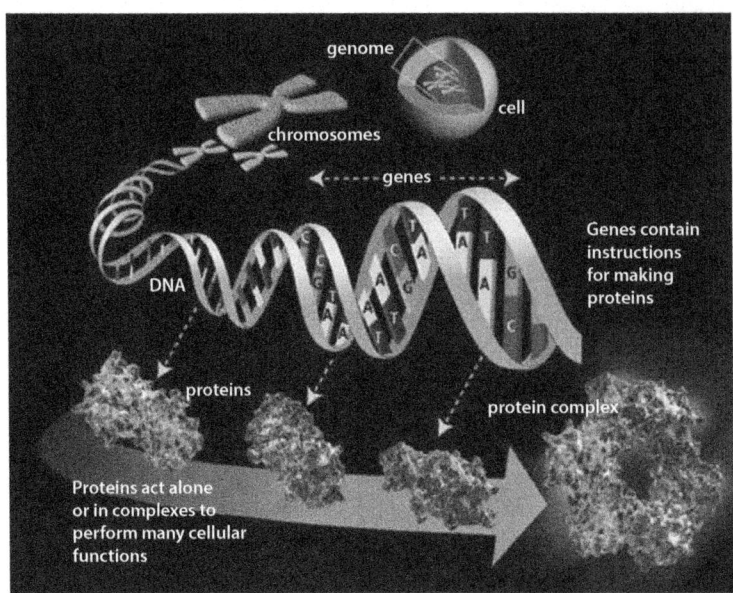

The Human Genome Project, 1990–2003

A Brief Overview

Though surprising to many, the Human Genome Project (HGP) traces its roots to an initiative in the U.S. Department of Energy (DOE). Since 1947, DOE and its predecessor agencies have been charged by Congress with developing new energy resources and technologies and pursuing a deeper understanding of potential health and environmental risks posed by their production and use. Such studies, for example, have provided the scientific basis for individual risk assessments of nuclear medicine technologies.

In 1986, DOE took a bold step in announcing the Human Genome Initiative, convinced that its missions would be well served by a reference human genome sequence. Shortly thereafter, DOE joined with the National Institutes of Health to develop a plan for a joint HGP that officially began in 1990. During the early years of the HGP, the Welcome Trust, a private charitable institution in the United Kingdom, joined the effort as a major partner. Important contributions also came from other collaborators around the world, including Japan, France, Germany, and China.

Ambitious Goals

The HGP's ultimate goal was to generate a high-quality reference DNA sequence for the human genome's 3 billion base pairs and to identify all human genes. Other important goals included sequencing the genomes of model organisms to interpret human DNA, enhancing computational resources to support future research and commercial applications, exploring gene function through mouse-human comparisons, studying human variation, and training future scientists in genomics.

The powerful analytical technology and data arising from the HGP present complex ethical and policy issues for individuals and society. These challenges include privacy, fairness in use and access of genomic information, reproductive and clinical issues, and commercialization (see p. 8). Programs that identify and address these implications have been an integral part of the HGP and have become a model for bioethics programs worldwide.

A Lasting Legacy

In June 2000, to much excitement and fanfare, scientists announced the completion of the first working draft of the entire human genome. First analyses of the details appeared in the February 2001 issues of the Journals *Nature* and *Science*. The high-quality reference sequence was completed in April 2003, marking the end of the Human Genome Project—2 years ahead of the original schedule. Coincidentally, it also was the 50th anniversary of Watson and Crick's publication of DNA structure that launched the era of molecular biology.

Available to researchers worldwide, the human genome reference sequence provides a magnificent and unprecedented biological resource that will serve throughout the century as a basis for research and discovery and, ultimately, myriad practical applications. The sequence already is having an impact on finding genes associated with human disease. Hundreds of other genome sequence projects—on microbes, plants, and animals—have been completed since the inception of the HGP, and these data now enable detailed comparisons among organisms, including humans.

Many more sequencing projects are under way or planned because of the research value of DNA sequence, the tremendous sequencing capacity now available, and continued improvements in technologies. Sequencing projects on the genomes of many microbes, as well as the chimpanzee, pig, sheep, and domestic cat are in progress.

Beyond sequencing, growing areas of research focus on identifying important elements in the DNA sequence responsible for regulating cellular functions and providing the basis of human variation. Perhaps the most daunting challenge is to begin to understand how all the "parts" of cells—genes, proteins, and many other molecules—work together to create complex living organisms. Future analyses of this treasury of data will provide a deeper and more comprehensive understanding of the molecular processes underlying life and will have an enduring and profound impact on how we view our own place in it.

Medicine and the New Genetics

Gene Testing, Pharmacogenomics, and Gene Therapy

DNA underlies almost every aspect of human health, both in function and dysfunction. Obtaining a detailed picture of how genes and other DNA sequences work together and interact with environmental factors ultimately will lead to the discovery of pathways involved in normal processes and in disease pathogenesis. Such knowledge will have a profound impact on the way disorders are diagnosed, treated, and prevented and will bring about revolutionary changes in clinical and public health practice. Some of these transformative developments are described below.

Gene Testing

DNA-based tests are among the first commercial medical applications of the new genetic discoveries. Gene tests can be used to diagnose and confirm disease, even in asymptomatic individuals; provide prognostic information about the course of disease; and, with varying degrees of accuracy, predict the risk of future disease in healthy individuals or their progeny.

Currently, several hundred genetic tests are in clinical use, with many more under development, and their numbers and varieties are expected to increase rapidly over the next decade. Most current tests detect mutations associated with rare genetic disorders that follow Mendelian inheritance patterns. These include myotonic and Duchenne muscular dystrophies, cystic fibrosis, neurofibromatosis type 1, sickle cell anemia, and Huntington's disease.

Recently, tests have been developed to detect mutations for a handful of more complex conditions such as breast, ovarian, and colon cancers. Although they have limitations, these tests sometimes are used to make risk estimates in presymptomatic individuals with a family history of the disorder. One potential benefit to these gene tests is that they could provide information to help physicians and patients manage the disease or condition more effectively. Regular colonoscopies for those having notations associated with colon cancer, for instance, could prevent thousands of deaths each year.

Some scientific limitations are that the tests may not detect every mutation associated with a particular condition (many are as yet undiscovered), and the ones they do detect may present different risks to various people and populations. Another important consideration in gene testing is the lack of effective treatments or preventive measures for many diseases and conditions now being diagnosed or predicted.

Revealing information about the risk of future disease can have significant emotional and psychological effects as well. Moreover, the absence of privacy and legal protections can lead to discrimination in employment and insurance or other misuse of personal genetic Information. Additionally, because genetic tests reveal information about individuals and their families, test results can affect family dynamics. Results also can pose risks for population groups if they lead to group stigmatization.

Other issues related to gene tests include their effective introduction into clinical practice, the regulation of laboratory quality assurance, the availability of testing for rare diseases, and the education of healthcare providers and patients about correct interpretation and attendant risks.

Families or individuals who have genetic disorders or are at risk for them often seek help from medical geneticists (an M.D. specialty) arid genetic counselors (graduate-degree training). These professionals can diagnose and explain disorders, review available options for testing and treatment, and provide emotional support. (For more information, see the URL for Medicine and the New Genetics)

Pharmacogenomics: Moving Away from "One-Size-Fits-All" Therapeutics

Within the next decade, researchers will begin to correlate DNA variants with individual responses to medical treatments, identify particular subgroups of patients, and develop drugs customized for those populations. The discipline that blends pharmacology with genomic capabilities is called pharmacogenomics.

More than 100,000 people die each year from adverse responses to meditations that may be beneficial to others. Another 22 million experience serious reactions, while others fail to respond at all. DNA variants in genes involved in drug metabolism, particularly the cytochrome P450 multigene family, are the focus of much current research in this area. Enzymes encoded by these genes are responsible for metabolizing most drugs used today, including many for treating psychiatric, neurological and cardiovascular diseases. Enzyme function affects patient responses to both the drug and the dose. Future advances will enable rapid testing to determine the patient's genotype and guide treatment with the most effective drugs, in addition to drastically reducing adverse reactions.

Genomic data and technologies also are expected to make drug development faster, cheaper, and more effective. Most drugs today are based on about 500 molecular targets, but genomic knowledge of genes involved in diseases, disease pathways, and drug-response sites will lead to the discovery of thousands of additional targets. New drugs, aimed at specific sites in the body and at particular biochemical events leading to disease, probably will cause fewer side effects than many current medicines. Ideally, genomic drugs could be given earlier in the disease process. As knowledge becomes available to select patients most likely to benefit from a potential drug, pharmacogenomics will speed the design of clinical trials to market the drugs sooner.

Gene Therapy, Enhancement

The potential for using genes themselves to treat disease or enhance particular traits has captured the imagination of the public and the biomedical community. This largely experimental field—gene transfer or gene therapy—holds potential for treating or even curing such genetic and acquired diseases as cancers and AIDS by using normal genes to supplement or replace defective genes or to bolster a normal function such as immunity.

Almost 1200 clinical gene-therapy trials were identified worldwide in 2006.[*] The majority (67%) take place in the United States, followed by Europe (29%). Although most trials focus on various types of cancer, studies also

---

[*] Source: Journal of Gene Medicine web site (www.wiley.co.uk/genetherapy/ clinical/), August 2006.

involve other multigenic and monogenic, infectious, and vascular diseases. Most current protocols are aimed at establishing the safety of gene-delivery procedures rather than effectiveness.

Gene transfer still faces many scientific obstacles before it can become a practical approach for treating disease. According to the American Society of Human Genetics' Statement on Gene Therapy, effective progress will be achieved only through continued rigorous research on the most fundamental mechanisms underlying gene delivery and gene expression in animals.

Other Anticipated Benefits of Genetic Research

Expanding Impacts of New Technologies, Resources

Rapid progress in genome science and a glimpse into its potential applications have spurred observers to predict that biology will be the foremost science of the 21st Century. Technology and resources generated by the Human Genome Project and other genomic research already are having major impacts across the life sciences. The biotechnology industry employed almost 200,000 people in 2003, and revenues for that year totaled more than $39.2 billion.[†] Future revenues are expected to reach trillions of dollars.

A list of some current and potential applications of genome research follows. More studies and public discussion are required for eventual validation and implementation of some of these uses.

Molecular Medicine

- Improve diagnosis of disease
- Detect genetic predispositions to disease
- Create drugs based on molecular information
- Use gene therapy and control systems as drugs
- Design "custom drugs" based on individual genetic profiles

Microbial Genomics

- Rapidly detect and treat pathogens (disease-causing microbes) in clinical practice
- Develop new energy sources (biofuels)
- Monitor environments to detect pollutants
- Protect citizenry from biological and chemical warfare
- Clean up toxic waste safely and efficiently

Risk Assessment

- Evaluate the health risks faced by individuals who may be exposed to radiation (including low levels in industrial areas) and to cancer-causing chemicals and toxins

Bioarchaeology, Anthropology, Evolution, and Human Migration

- Study evolution through germline mutations in lineages
- Study migration of different population groups based on maternal genetic inheritance
- Study mutations on the Y chromosome to trace lineage and migration of males
- Compare breakpoints in the evolution of mutations with population ages and historical events

---

† Source: Biotechnology Industry Organization web site (www.bio.org), August 2006.

DNA Identification

- Identify potential suspects whose DNA may match evidence left at crime scenes
- Exonerate persons wrongly accused of crimes
- Identify crime, catastrophe, and other victims
- Establish paternity and other family relationships
- Identify endangered and protected species as an aid to wildlife officials (e.g. to prosecute poachers)
- Detect bacteria and other organisms that may pollute air, water, soil, and food
- Watch organ donors with recipients in transplant programs
- Determine pedigree for seed or livestock breeds
- Authenticate consumables such as caviar and wine

Agriculture Livestock Breeding, and Bioprocessing

- Grow disease-, insect-, and drought-resistant crops
- Optimize crops for bioenergy production
- Breed healthier, more productive, disease-resistant farm animals
- Grow more nutritious produce
- Develop biopesticides
- Incorporate edible vaccines into food products
- Develop new environmental cleanup uses for plants like tobacco

Societal Concerns Arising from the New Genetics

Critical Policy and Ethical issues

From its inception, the Human Genome Project dedicated funds toward identifying and addressing the ethical, legal, and social issues surrounding the availability of the new data and capabilities. Examples of such issues follow.

- Privacy and confidentiality of genetic information. Who owns and controls genetic information? Is genetic privacy different from medical privacy?
- Fairness In the use of genetic information by insurers, employers, courts, schools, adoption agencies, and the military, among others. Who should have access to personal genetic information, and how will it be used?
- Psychological impact, stigmatization, and discrimination due to an individual's genetic makeup. How does personal genetic information affect self-identity and society's perceptions?
- Reproductive issues including adequate and informed consent and the use of genetic information in reproductive decision making. Do healthcare personnel properly counsel parents about risks and limitations? What larger societal issues are raised by new reproductive technologies?
- Clinical issues including the education of doctors and other health-service providers, people identified with genetic conditions, and the general public; and implementation of standards and quality-control measures. How should health professionals be prepared for the new genetics? How can the public be educated to make informed choices? How will genetic tests be evaluated and regulated for accuracy, reliability, and usefulness? (Currently, there is little regulation.) How does society balance current scientific limitations and social risk with long-term benefits?
- Fairness in access to advanced genomic technologies. Who will benefit? Will there be major worldwide inequities?

- Uncertainties associated with gene tests for susceptibilities and complex conditions (e.g., heart disease, diabetes, and Alzheimer's disease). Should testing be performed when no treatment is available or when interpretation is unsure? Should children be tested for susceptibility to adult-onset diseases?
- Conceptual and philosophical implications regarding human responsibility, free will vs. genetic determinism, and understanding of health and disease. Do our genes influence our behavior, and can we control it? What is considered acceptable diversity? Where is the line drawn between medical treatment and enhancement?
- Health and environmental issues concerning genetically modified (GM) foods and microbes. Are GM foods and other products safe for humans and the environment? How will these technologies affect developing nations' dependence on industrialized nations?
- Commercialization of products including property rights (patents, copyrights, and trade secrets) and accessibility of data and materials. Will patenting DNA sequences limit their accessibility and development into useful products?

Excerpts from **Motherhood, Rescheduled**

The New Frontier of Egg Freezing and the Women who Tried It

By Sarah Elizabeth Richards

Introduction

There was one time in my life when I was grateful for the biological clock. I was thirty-two years old and summoning the courage to leave a relationship. After nearly eight years of living with a man I deeply loved, I wasn't miserable. I just wasn't happy.

We had been doing the stuff the advice books say you're never supposed to do. We punished each other with silence, criticized each other's driving, made separate holiday plans, argued in public, and butted heads so fiercely about meals, budgets, sex, housework, exercise schedules, movie choices, and vacation destinations that it became easier to spend most of our free time apart.

We tried the standard fixes: we went to couples counseling, swapped lists of behaviors we were willing to change, and spoke in "I feel" statements. There were brief improvements, but the tension always returned, and I became increasingly certain that I did not want children with him. How could we agree on how to take care of another human being if we couldn't decide when to do laundry? I made sure never to miss my birth control pills.

I knew we had no future, but I also felt no urgency to overturn my life with a crushing, consuming breakup. There never seemed to be a good time, either. Who wanted to be alone during the holidays, the Fourth of July, the first day of fall? I would give it six more months, I told myself. Maybe we could read more books. Maybe we could try a new therapist. Maybe we could go on a long vacation. It wasn't *all* bad, I reminded myself.

Then that terrifying book came out. In the spring of 2002, Sylvia Ann Hewlett was detonating bombshells on nearly every talk show with *Creating a Life: Professional Women and the Quest for Children*. The message was clear: your fertility fades much sooner than you think; your eggs deteriorate dramatically after thirty-five and are pretty much fossils by your early forties. So listen up, all you clueless careerists! You've got to make having a family a priority. You'd better think twice about all your indulgent plans for advanced degrees, foreign postings, and after-work cocktails. Otherwise you're going to break your heart and the bank pursuing futile in vitro fertilization (IVF) treatments in an attempt to "snatch a child from the jaws of menopause." That's not to mention the increased risk of having a baby with Down syndrome if you manage to get pregnant.

I joined my generation in a collective gasp. "*Now?*" I whined to myself. I had just finished graduate school and was trying to launch my career as a freelance journalist. Plus, I still had to break up, grieve, find a new apartment, move out, lose ten pounds, acquire new relationship skills, and try to meet someone else. *Then* I had to get engaged, marry, and make a baby. That left very little contingency for rebounds, bad judgment, and trouble becoming pregnant.

Sarah Elizabeth Richards, "Introduction," *Motherhood Rescheduled: The New Frontier of Egg Freezing and the Women who Tried It*, pp. 3-8. Copyright © 2013 by Simon & Schuster, Inc. Reprinted with permission.

If everything went as planned, I could have my first baby at thirty-seven and maybe fit in a second by thirty-nine. "My God!" I exclaimed to my girlfriend over the phone. "I've already lost my third child!"

Before Hewlett's book, I had assumed that I would be a mother, just as I knew I would marry, buy a home, and at some point fit into those Oshkosh B'Gosh short overalls I bought two sizes too small in college. I sleepily went about my life and took comfort in the pleasant stupor that was *someday*. I had little sense there was an actual deadline and that it was looming. Life was challenging enough without God suddenly setting a timer.

Without knowing it, I had become a Clock Ticker, and my pleasant stupor was replaced by the loud hum of the clichéd biological clock, which began to torment me like a clunky old air conditioner. My friends started having babies, and I was suddenly behind. I overheard my parents making excuses for me to their friends: *She's busy with her job. She's a late bloomer. She's picky.* In the most discouraging sign, relatives stopped asking when I planned to get married and start a family, as if I had been relegated to being the Crazy Aunt at family gatherings.

There were statistics to prove you were not alone, and that you were a member of a swelling demographic of women who had delayed marriage and motherhood. Supposedly one in five women was waiting to start her family until after age thirty-five, a percentage that had increased nearly eight-fold since 1970. And for the first time in history, more children were born to women over thirty-five than to teenagers.

You saw enough older new mothers in your neighborhood to know the statistic was true, but secretly you still wondered if there was something wrong with you because life hadn't worked out for you the way it had for Everyone Else. You told yourself that there was nothing wrong with being the Last One Left. You were simply on a different path and would make good decisions for your future. But you still felt a little twinge of sadness every time you saw your single-line listing on a family reunion attendance list. Or shopped for boxed Christmas cards of New York City snow scenes because it seemed ridiculous to write a holiday letter about yourself. Or realized that you were one of a few friends from high school holiday get-togethers available to go out after 8 p.m.

I wish I could say that I trusted everything would work out and that I carried myself with a *Secret*-like confidence that made me wildly attractive. I didn't. I spent the majority of my thirties alternately freaking out and talking myself down. I paid thousands of dollars for therapy, drank too much wine, and harassed my busy friends and family with distraught phone calls. I often repeated their encouraging words in my head before I went to sleep: *I still have time. There are lots of good guys out there. I am in a better place now to choose a mate than I was in my twenties. I have learned a lot of relationship lessons. I still have time.* But only one thing gave me real comfort. If I actually did run out of time, I had a list of motherhood options taped to my desk lamp: donor eggs, foreign and domestic adoption, other couples' leftover IVF embryos, stepchildren. I knew the alternatives came with their own complications, but I thought they were ones I could live with. And if I had to live with them in the same house as my fabulous new husband, all the better.

So why did I still feel so awful? When the panic subsided, I was gripped with sorrow that I was losing my chance to have a biological child. Not an abstract baby but the baby I had dreamed about my entire life. Her name had changed over the years from Ashley to Chloe to Claire, and she wore various outfits and hairstyles. But in my imagination, she was always three years old, clomping around in my high heels, freezing apple juice in ice cube trays, and saying things that made me go gooey inside, such as "This is the best day ever, Mommy."

I wondered why it was so important that she shared my DNA. Was I curious to see if she had my high forehead or loved mustard and rainy mornings like I did? Was I intrigued by the idea of creating an extension of myself and the man I loved? Or did I crave seeing several generations of my family in one photo? All I knew was that the idea of never meeting Claire (or her younger brother, Henry) seemed utterly tragic.

I can't remember when I first heard about egg freezing, a procedure that promised to make the biological clock obsolete. The concept was extraordinary. Hormone shots made your body pump out eggs, which were surgically extracted and frozen. When you were ready to become a mother, the eggs could be thawed and fertilized in a lab with your future partner's sperm to make embryos. Just as in standard IVF, those embryos would be placed inside your uterus to grow into babies. The only difference is that you would be using your younger, hardier eggs in case your current eggs were no longer viable. And since it's possible for women to carry a baby well into middle age, you technically could become a mother whenever you wanted. Not that you would necessarily want to have a baby at, say, fifty or sixty, but the point was that you *could*.

When egg freezing first appeared in the cultural cosmos early in the past decade, my friends and I talked about it in a hyperbolic way, as when a seventh-grader frustrated with boys shouts, "Fine! I'll just become a nun!" We loved this handy metaphor to communicate our fears about becoming lonely spinsters. "Well, at this rate, I'll have to freeze my eggs," we might say in the same tone as "move to Alaska" (a state with a heavily skewed male-female ratio). We threw it around as cheap drama intended to be oddly reassuring because, after all, who would really have to resort to something so expensive and extreme?

It was only after I turned thirty-five—the point of no return—that I began to seriously consider what egg freezing could do for me. I fantasized about what it would be like to be free from the suffocating press of time that constantly reminded me that my entire future happiness depended on the decisions I made over the next few years. It meant I could escape the penalties for lacking the spine to leave a relationship I knew was not working. It meant redemption.

Egg freezing seemed too good to be true, in the same baffling way a diet pill promises to magically wipe out the caloric damage of waffle fries or Botox can make you look forever twenty-five. It felt unnatural and sort of unfair, as if I could buy the privilege to take the final exam later than the rest of the class or skip filing taxes. I wondered if I would approach dating differently if I was no longer in such a rush. Maybe I'd treasure these next few "free" years unencumbered by baby anxiety and write a bunch of books, train for a marathon, and solidify a marriage. That way, I'd be in an even better position to be a mom.

Would egg freezing clarify my life? Complicate it? Or leave me right where I started?

My girlfriends and I loved to linger over dinner and imagine what life would be like off the clock. We speculated that some of our married friends may have been more selective and would now enjoy better marriages if they hadn't feared being "put out to pasture." We lamented peers who had panicked prematurely and gotten stuck with reluctant fathers or left home alone as single moms. We wondered whether gun-shy friends would make more of an effort to date if they thought their ovarian age no longer mattered. We mused about what it would be like to have the same reproductive freedom as men, even to date and think like men. Or (gasp!) actually date *younger* men—a biologically attractive pairing, considering women live on average six years longer than men. Men would also have more choice of partners, since those who wanted children wouldn't have to seek out for their egg quality women who would never understand why they spent nights and weekends playing Dungeons & Dragons in high school.

In any case, surely men would appreciate a little less pressure from us. They also might be more willing to give relationships a serious try if they didn't fear they were wasting our last chance at motherhood.

However, the idea of stopping the clock also made us a little uneasy. You could never actually count on egg freezing, and any relief was overshadowed by the awareness that your remaining fertile years were still ticking away. So far, the success rates of egg freezing ranged wildly and were always accompanied by asterisks explaining that the technology was rapidly improving and that you could game the odds by freezing several rounds of eggs. Still, it was a bewildering equation. How were you supposed to be cautious and hopeful at the same time?

Even if egg freezing did work, the question remained: Would tinkering with such a finely tuned reproducing machine lead to harmful social and personal consequences? You would be an older mother and might endure a more difficult pregnancy. You might not see your children marry or know your grandchildren. Your own parents might not even meet their grandchildren. As my wise friend Janelle said, "Maybe you'd just drag out the whole thing. At forty-five, you'd still worry if you were ready to be a mom. Without the clock, there's no trigger to force you into action." She had a point. Deadlines serve a purpose in life.

But my friends and I could only speculate because, like most people who talked about egg freezing in 2005, we had not frozen our eggs or met anyone who had. As I considered the procedure, I wanted to meet other women who could tell me how egg freezing had affected their lives. Did it take off the pressure and help them relax more? Did they date differently? Marry later? Most important, did their frozen eggs help them have babies years later, when their natural fertility was gone? The journalist in me wanted to explore this medical breakthrough and changing social ideas about coupling, mating, and parenting. The Clock Ticker in me wanted to find a group of big sisters who could share how they navigated this difficult and confusing time.

Excerpts from **Medical Apartheid**

The Black Stork: The Eugenic Control of African American Reproduction

By Harriet Washington

We don't allow dogs to breed. We spay them. We neuter them. We try to keep them from having unwanted puppies, and yet these women are literally having litters of children...

-BARBARA HARRIS, FOUNDER OF CHILDREN REQUIRING A CARING KOMMUNITY (CRACK),
C. 1990

National Socialism is nothing but applied biology.

-RUDOLF HESS, BERLIN, 1934

She might easily have endured the life of quiet desperation dictated by her birth, then vanished without a ripple. The granddaughter of a slave, the daughter of sharecroppers, and younger sister to nineteen siblings, she was intelligent, hardworking, and loved to read, but she was also dark-skinned, uneducated, and a woman, a recipe for failure in rural Mississippi. The year was 1961, but it might as well have been 1861. She helped her family eke a hardscrabble existence on a plantation in Sunflower County by picking three hundred to four hundred pounds of cotton a day for one dollar a hundredweight. They spent their days exhausted, hungry, and shabbily garbed, but her family never earned enough to break the cycle of debt and remained trapped in the usurious latter-day slavery called sharecropping. But she was not angry: A deeply religious person, she focused her energies on helping others and eagerly awaited the day she would have her own family.

Her name was Fannie Lou Hamer.

One day in 1961, Hamer entered the hospital to have "a knot on my stomach"—probably a benign uterine fibroid tumor—removed. She then returned to her family's shack on the plantation to recuperate. But in the big house, ominous tidings circulated. The owner's wife, Vera Alicia Marlow, was a cousin of the surgeon who had treated Hamer. Marlow gossiped to the cook that Hamer had lost more than a tumor while unconscious—the surgeon had removed her uterus, rendering Hamer sterile. The cook repeated the news to others, including a woman who happened to be Hamer's cousin, and thus Hamer was one of the last people on the plantation to learn that she would never have a family of her own.

Harriet Washington, "The Black Stork," *Medical Apartheid*, pp. 189-192, 202-206. Copyright © 2006 by Random House LLC. Reprinted with permission.

"I went to the doctor who did that to me and I asked him, 'Why? Why had he done that to me?' He didn't have to say nothing—and he didn't. If he was going to give that sort of operation then he should have told me. I would have loved to have had children." But a lawsuit was out of the question, Hamer recalled. "At that time? Me? Getting a white lawyer against a white doctor? I would have been taking my hands and screwing tacks in my casket."

A rage seized her and she complained bitterly about her fate. But she also grew fascinated by political power as a means to redress injustice, and soon she did the unthinkable: She tried to register to vote. But she was rejected at the polling booth, and when she arrived home, the angry owner threw her off the plantation where she had lived for nineteen years.

It didn't matter, because Hamer was no longer a sharecropper. She was now an uncompromising political dynamo who would become one of the most powerful leaders and symbols of the southern civil rights movement. She always spoke of her "Mississippi appendectomy" as the galvanizing force that propelled her into a national leadership role, and she always spoke regretfully of the children she would never have.

She was a lifelong opponent of birth control.

Evolutionary Laggards

The twentieth century saw the dawn of the medical philosophy *eugenics*, derived from the Greek word *eugenes*, meaning "well-born." The word was coined by Francis Galton, a cousin of Charles Darwin. Between 1900 and 1910, geneticists discovered human traits that adhered to a Mendelian pattern of inheritance, one in which the breeding of two carrier parents resulted in a mathematically predictable mixture of well, ill, and carrier offspring. Several metabolic conditions were among these Mendelian discoveries, including sickle-cell anemia, red-green color blindness, and polydactyly (having more than the normal number of fingers or toes). The birth of an affected child from unaffected parents signaled that the parents were carriers.

Armed with this knowledge, Galton first formulated the desirability of using selective procreation to refine the human race while conquering social dysfunction. This goal was widely embraced on both scientific and popular levels by the 1930s, not only in the United States, but also abroad, and eugenic yardsticks were applied to not only populations but to individuals. Eugenicists proposed that society use medical information about disease and trait inheritance to end social ills by encouraging the birth of children with good, healthy, and beautiful traits. This was positive eugenics, but the movement also had a negative face: Eugenicists promulgated the weeding out of undesirable societal elements by discouraging or preventing the birth of children with "bad" genetic profiles. The term *well-born* has a double meaning of "born healthy" and "born wealthy," and this is fitting, because eugenic scientists and their disciples constantly confused the concepts of biological hereditary fitness with those of class and race. Highly educated persons of good social class were considered eugenically superior; the poor, the uneducated, criminals, recent immigrants, blacks, and the feebleminded were eugenic misfits. Eugenicists invoked the term *racial hygiene* as frequently as they did the word *eugenics*, and even a cursory glance at the charts, photographs, and diagrams used to popularize eugenic ideals reveals that the unfit were "swarthy" "black" and ugly by Anglo-Saxon standards, with flattened noses, wiry black hair, and prognathous profiles.

African Americans were roundly disparaged by eugenic theory as scientists continued to seek and find wide physiologic evidence of black inferiority. In a refinement of earlier scientific racism, eugenics was appropriated to label black women as sexually indiscriminate and as bad mothers who were constrained by biology to give birth to defective children. The demonization of black parents, particularly "mothers, as medically and behaviorally unfit has a long history, but twentieth-century eugenicists provided the necessary biological underpinnings to scientifically validate these beliefs. The sexual irrepressibility and the bad mothering were biologically located in the hereditary apparatus, they contended. Thus eugenics undergirded medicosocial movements that placed the sexual behavior and reproduction of blacks under strict scrutiny and disproportionately forced them into sterility, both temporary and permanent. Scientists also vigorously researched black fertility, compiling data on black birth rates and using women of color predominantly to test many reproductive technologies and strategies, from involuntary sterilization to Norplant to "the shot." ...

The "Mississippi Appendectomy"

The Pill may have been flawed and the IUD deadly, but these methods were at least quasi-voluntary and their effects were usually temporary. The most damaging threat to African American reproductive freedom has been invasive and permanent: compulsory surgical sterilization. When the infamous German eugenic sterilization initiative began in January 1934, seventeen U.S. states were already performing sterilizations routinely, and that year, between two thousand and four thousand Americans were sterilized. Indiana passed legislation requiring the sterilization of the mentally unfit in 1907. By 1911, six states had passed laws providing for compulsory sterilization of the "mentally unfit." In 1935, twenty-seven states had such laws for the feebleminded, those on welfare, or those with genetic defects. Forced sterilization was encouraged by the infamous 1927 *Buck v. Bell* decision, wherein Justice Oliver Wendell Holmes ordered the sterilization of the allegedly imbecilic poor white girl Carrie Buck, intoning, "Three generations of imbeciles are enough." By the 1930s, compulsory sterilization had become a global enterprise, and by 1941, sterilization had been forced upon 70,000 to 100,000 Americans, 9,931 of them in California alone.

African Americans have always been staggeringly overrepresented in the ranks of the sterilized. When the North Carolina Eugenic Commission sterilized 8,000 mentally retarded persons throughout the 1930s, 5,000 were black. By 1983, when blacks constituted only 12 percent of the population, 43 percent of the women sterilized in federally funded family planning programs were African Americans.

This has been achieved under the auspices of a government fed by the myth of the lazy, hyperfertile welfare mother. Say "welfare mother" and most people think of an unemployed black woman, yet most women on welfare are not black. A 1990 survey revealed that 78 percent of whites think blacks prefer welfare to employment. But most black women are employed full-time and hold at least one job, and women on welfare are likely to be employed part-time at low-wage jobs with few if any benefits. However, a black woman is more likely to receive AFDC (Aid to Dependent Children, the form of public assistance given to people with minor children) than is a white woman. Black women constitute 6 percent of the population but represent one-third of those on AFDC. And in some poor urban areas such as Baltimore, which is 86 percent black, the majority of people on welfare are also black.

Forced sterilization and welfare have been linked for nearly half a century. Mississippi state legislator David H. Glass instituted a bold experiment when he sought legal means to force sterilization upon welfare mothers in 1958. By 1960, his "act to discourage immorality of unmarried females by providing for sterilization of the unwed mothers" passed in the House by a vote of seventy-two to thirty-seven but died in the Senate as the black activist Student Nonviolent Coordinating Committee (SNCC) protested and distributed a pamphlet entitled "Genocide in Mississippi."

But most sterilizations of poor black women have been performed outside the law and in violation of medical mores. In June 1973, the abuse of two young sisters in Montgomery, Alabama, exposed the decades of stolen African American fertility. Twelve-year-old Mary Alice Relf and her sister Minnie, fourteen, lived on relief with their parents, who had left their meager living as field hands in an unsuccessful search for work in the city. A Montgomery Community Action Agency nurse took the girls to the hospital for a federally funded contraceptive shot and obtained the "X" of each illiterate parent on the consent form. But their parents later learned that the girls had been surgically sterilized, and they asked Atlanta's Southern Poverty Law Center for help. When SPLC filed a class-action lawsuit to end the use of federal funds for involuntary sterilization, its lawyers discovered that 100,000 to 150,000 women had been sterilized using federal funds and that half these women were black. Today, one-third of all adult Mississippi women and 57 percent of all Mississippi women sixty-five and older say they have undergone a hysterectomy.

Sometimes the physician removed the woman's uterus on some pretext after coercing or tricking her into assent for unnecessary sterilization. The women were also sterilized while unconscious, as Fannie Lou Hamer was. In the

South, rendering black women infertile without their knowledge during other surgery was so common that the procedure was called a "Mississippi appendectomy."

Involuntary hysterectomies were also commonly practiced in the North. A 1973 study by Bernard Rosenfeld of Los Angeles County Hospital discovered that "doctors … are cavalierly subjecting women, most of them poor and black, to surgical sterilization without explaining either the potential hazards or alternate methods of birth control. In most major teaching hospitals of New York it was the unwritten policy to do elective hysterectomies on poor black and Puerto Rican women with minimal indications to train residents." In 1972, medical students at Boston City Hospital (BCH) protested the policy of performing unnecessary hysterectomies on black women in order to allow residents to practice. The students also complained that experimental procedures, the coercion of patient signatures, and falsifying medical records were common practices among black patients. So did students at Columbia University. The chairman of the BCH OB-GYN program did not deny the charges, but blamed "one bad apple."

Across the nation, black women who trusted obstetricians to deliver their children were being surreptitiously sterilized, and this revelation poisoned relationships between them and their doctors. To accomplish the sterilizations, practitioners lied to patients, forged consent forms, or falsified medical records to reflect an "appendectomy" or "gallbladder removal," so it is now impossible to know the exact number of African American women who were sterilized without their knowledge. Nor is there any record of how many hysterectomies, if any, were medically justified. Some women, like Fannie Lou Hamer, were never told by their doctors that they had been sterilized, and others never found out. One of the few methodical surveys conducted revealed that at least 60 percent of the black women in Hamer's native Sunflower County (Mississippi) unwittingly suffered postpartum hysterectomies.

By 1980, sterilization had become the most common form of birth control, and it still is, edging out condom use by 1 percent. But African American women remain far more likely than whites to undergo a hysterectomy, although researchers have known for over a decade that they are at higher risk of the procedure's complications and are more likely to die from the surgery. According to the National Center for Health Statistics (NCHS), 41 percent of black women who use contraception were sterilized, compared with only 27 percent of white women.

Within a century, reproductive coercion had taken a 180-degree turn for black women. During slavery, black women had been forced to procreate, but now they were being forced into sterility. The consistent factor was white control.

Women were also forced into sterility by governmental welfare programs, upon which unskilled black women workers relied to supplement their meager wages. While a social worker in upstate New York during the 1980s, I learned from old case files that during the 1960s and 1970s, social workers conducted frequent late-night raids on the homes of aid recipients. If a man was discovered, the family's aid could be cut off unless the woman agreed to sterilization, guaranteeing there would be no additional children for the state to support.

Black women are still more likely than white women to be pressured or misled into sterilization, which tripled between 1970 and 1980, in part because hysterectomies are offered as the only curative option for ailments that can be treated more conservatively, such as fibroids and endometriosis.

By 1978, doctors also began administering the drug Depo-Provera— but only in research studies and almost exclusively to poor women of color. Depo-Provera is the Upjohn Company's brand name for medroxyprogesterone acetate, which is also called DMPA. In 1978, the drug had just been FDA-approved for use as a cancer therapy. In 1973, after the government discovered that beagles on which the drug had been tested developed breast cancer, it had refused to fund further testing of the drug as a contraceptive. Cancer medications carry significant risks, which are acceptable when one is fighting a deadly illness but not when a healthy woman is simply trying to avoid pregnancy. However, licensed physicians may administer legal medications for any use they deem appropriate, and American doctors found it appropriate to administer Depo-Provera as an experimental contraceptive to healthy Native American and black patients. In 1978, the FDA criticized an Emory University study of Depo-Provera as having needlessly imperiled the lives of 4,700 women, all black, and in 1992 an FDA board warned, "Never has a drug whose target population is entirely healthy people been shown to be so pervasively carcinogenic in animals as has Depo-Provera."

Section Four

Appendices

Appendix A

Points for Further Discussion

It is often helpful to consider some important points that not only connect the different readings, but may help you to think about where the course may lead from here.

Section One

1. What are the major distinctions between and among the three (time) periods in American Childbirth?
2. What is meant by the term "childbed fever?" How did Americans manage to understand the constancy of loss that accompanied childbirth and child rearing?
3. What is the perspective of the physician/author in "Maternity Care in Crisis"?
4. What have been some of the factors leading to divorce (and increased divorce rates) in the US?
5. What is meant by the term "agency" in discussing women in the reading "Determinants of Gender Equity"?
6. What are some of the advantages of a birth attended by a Nurse Midwife? Do you think it likely, given the inevitability to changes in health care (reform) that we may come to embrace a more natural approach to childbirth in the US?
7. What does the term "youth bulge" mean? (Reading on MENA) How do you expect the fertility (and population) rates in this region to change the economic and political landscape more broadly?
8. In general, what happened to the population [and fertility rates] in Iran during the 1980s and 1990s? Specifically, how did the political climate affect women's roles and overall population trends?

Section Two

1. What is meant by the term "Patriarchal Risk"?
2. What is meant by the term "son preference"? Why might women be complicit in maintain son preference?
3. What does the use of force and violence and control really mean about the differences in value between women and men?

4. What are the core social and economic differences between the groups surveyed in the research for *Motherhood and Morality*? How do they view the significance of Motherhood in their lives?
5. What are the key differences between the positions of the right to life and pro-choice? How might we might understand these positions more clearly if we consider the contexts of history and culture?
6. What really prompted Souad's brother-in-law to set her on fire? What did her birth order have to do with her prospects of getting "married off"?
7. What are the social conditions that allow for female infanticide?
8. What do you think should happen to physicians who participate in sex-selection abortions—where it is currently illegal for them to do so?

Section Three

1. What are some of the reasons to explain the increase in the use of "third party" (In vitro fertilization, surrogates, donated egg and sperm,) reproduction in the US?
2. In the cases of "childless" women, were there any common themes that united the women—for example, did the women in the study all regret (equally) not having children?
3. What did we learn, if anything as a culture, from the final outcome of the Baby M case (Mary Beth Whitehead's surrogacy case)?
4. What are some of the social consequences of sex selection?
5. What is really meant by the term "commodification" of pregnancy? (Is it possible to imagine making a commodity of pregnancy and childbirth?
6. What are the reasons that international adoption has become more common in the US?
7. Describe the significance of the social factors that led so many women to be "encouraged" to "surrender" their babies for adoption in the US according to *The Girls Who Went Away*.
8. What is meant by the term New Eugenics?
9. In what ways do men and women experience fertility declines differently? What is meant by the term "subfertile?"
10. Strongly recommended reading—Michael J. Sandel's, *The Case Against Perfection: Ethics in the Age of Genetic Engineering* (2007), is just a fantastic work examining our ideas about increasing expectations for our offspring and the real dilemmas this presents. (This is a "don't miss.")

Appendix B

Film Resources

The following feature films and documentaries work well with the course and the themes in the readings. This is by no means based on an exhaustive search, rather, these have been recommended [through the years] by graduate students, undergraduate students, colleagues and friends and family. I have indeed shown many of these in my classes, or talked about them and often, have suggested many of them to the students who want to know more …

Note: These are only listed in terms of section—no specific order or preference should be assumed.

Section 1: The Start of Reproduction
Pregnancy, Childbirth, Mating

The Miracle of Birth (1998, documentary, Nova)
Love Me (2014)
The Business of Being Born (2008, Ricki Lake and Abby Epstein)
More Business of Being Born (2011, Ricki Lake and Abby Epstein)
Monsoon Wedding (2001)
A Walk to Beautiful (2011, documentary, Ethiopian women, childbirth complications)
No Woman No Cry (2010, documentary)
Babies (2010)
Doula! The Ultimate Birth Companion (2010, Great Britain)
Laboring Under an Illusion: Mass Media v The Real Thing (2009)
Revolutionary Road (2008)

Section 2: Autonomy, Patriarchy, and Reproductive Control
Patriarchy, Consequences of Patriarchy, Abortion, Value of Children

Leila (1996, Iranian)
Two Women (1999, Iranian)
The Circle (2000, Iranian)
Children Underground (2001, documentary, Romania)
China's Lost Girls (2004, National Geographic)
Born Into Brothels (2004, documentary)
L'Enfant (2005, France)
Syrian Bride (2004)
20 Fingers (2004, Iran)
The Magdalene Sisters (2002)
Provoked (2006, India)
Jane: An Abortion Service (1998, documentary)
4 Months, 3 Weeks, 2 Days (2007, Romania)
After Tiller (2013)
Vera Drake (2014)
Saving Face (2012)

Section 4: What Are We Really Creating?
The Future and Reproductive Technology, Eugenics

Test-tube Babies (1998, Nova)
Paternal Instinct (2004, documentary)
Gattaca (1997)
Code 46 (2003)
Children of Men (2006)
My Sister's Keeper (2009)
Fixed to Fail: Buck v. Bell (2006, documentary)
Google Baby (2009)
Philomena (2013)
Somewhere Between (2011)

CPSIA information can be obtained
at www.ICGtesting.com
Printed in the USA
BVOW11s2322250716
456791BV00009B/32/P